Time Out

D0720738

Paris
Eating & Drinking

timeout.com

Published by Time Out Guides Ltd, a wholly owned subsidiary of Time Out Group Ltd.
Time Out and the Time Out logo are trademarks of Time Out Group Ltd.

© Time Out Group Ltd 2005
Previous editions 1996, 1997, 1999, 2000, 2002, 2003

10 9 8 7 6 5 4 3 2 1

This edition first published in Great Britain in 2005 by Ebury
Ebury is a division of The Random House Group Ltd,
20 Vauxhall Bridge Road, London SW1V 2SA

Random House Australia Pty Limited, 20 Alfred Street, Milsons Point, Sydney, New South Wales 2061, Australia
Random House New Zealand Limited, 18 Poland Road, Glenfield, Auckland 10, New Zealand
Random House South Africa (Pty) Limited, Endulini, 5A Jubilee Road, Parktown 2193, South Africa

Random House UK Limited Reg. No. 954009

Distributed in USA by Publishers Group West
1700 Fourth Street, Berkeley, California 94710

Distributed in Canada by Penguin Canada Ltd
10 Alcorn Avenue, Toronto, Ontario, Canada M4V 3B2

For further distribution details, see www.timeout.com

ISBN 1-904978-39-8

A CIP catalogue record for this book is available from the British Library

Colour reprographics by Icon, Crowne House, 56-58 Southwark Street, London SE1 1UN

Printed and bound in Germany by Appl. Papers used by Ebury Press are natural, recyclable products made from wood
grown in sustainable forests.

Time Out Guides Limited
Universal House
251 Tottenham Court Road
London W1T 7AB
Tel + 44 (0)20 7813 3000
Fax + 44 (0)20 7813 6001
Email guides@timeout.com
www.timeout.com

Written and researched by:
Marie-Noëlle Bauer, Whitney Barton, Gemma Betros, Maryanne Blacker, Anna Brooke, Peterjon Cresswell,
Alison Culliford, Natasha Edwards, Duncan Fairgrieve, Ethan Gilsdorf, Hannah Goldberg, Lisa Hilton,
Michelle Hoffman, Rosa Jackson, Mary Kelly, John Laurenson, Jennifer Joan Lee, Alexander Lobrano,
Sophie Lyne, Lyndal Manson, Nicola McDonald, Stephen Mudge, Lisa Pasold, Nick Petter, Joshua Phillips,
Isabel Pitman, Ariadne Plaitakis, Mathura Premaruban, Mark Rebindaine, Adam Reid, Louise Rogers Lalaurie,
Emily Rueb, Sharon Sutcliffe, Anna Watson.

Additional contributions by:
Karen Albrecht, Elizabeth Andrews, Kate van den Boogert, Ritu Chada, Paul Hines, Sarina Lewis, Martyn Nutland, Joe Ray,
Katherine Spenley.

Special thanks to Samuel Landry.

Area maps Philippe Landry.

Other maps JS Graphics (john@jsgraphics.co.uk).

Illustrations Jane Webster.

Photography Britta Jaschinski and Karl Blackwell, except: page 169 Thomas Skovsende; page 257 Flammarion-Mariage
Frères, Photo Francis Hammond. The following images were provided by the featured establishments/artist: pages 273, 287.

Contents

About the guide

How the Guide was produced

The contents of the Guide were entirely originated by journalists living in Paris – most of them long-term residents – and based on real experiences in restaurants, cafés and bars. Restaurants are tested anonymously, with Time Out paying the bill.

For this seventh edition, as well as adding new restaurants, cafés and bars we have discovered over the past year, we have also re-tested most of the establishments listed in the sixth edition.

Every review, as well as addresses, prices and opening details, has been double-checked for accuracy. But details can, of course, change (particularly for annual holidays) so it's a good idea to ring ahead.

How to use the listings

Restaurants are divided into sections denoting the type of establishment and style of food. Within each section, restaurants are listed in order of arrondissement, or area, then alphabetically. We also provide two indexes (*see p292*): one by arrondissement and type of restaurant, the other alphabetical.

Critics' picks

A star – ★ – after the restaurant's name indicates that it is a critics' favourite, one of the best in its category. Stars are awarded not only for great food (or drinks, in **Bars**), but also for a particularly fun atmosphere.

Telephones

Paris and Ile de France numbers begin with 01. From abroad, leave off the 0 at the start of the ten-digit number. The country code is 33.

Transport

The Métro or RER stop listed is the one nearest the restaurant. Two stops are listed if they are both very near the restaurant and on different Métro lines.

Opening hours

Times stated for restaurants apply to service hours, when you can order food, rather than opening and closing times. Those given for bars and cafés are opening and closing hours, with food service hours if relevant.

Credit cards & currency

The following abbreviations are used: AmEx: American Express; DC: Diners' Club; MC: Mastercard; V: Visa. A 15 minimum spend usually applies to credit card transactions. Most Paris restaurants will not accept payment by travellers' cheques.

Prices & prix fixe menus

Average means the average cost à la carte for a three-course meal without drinks. If no average price is listed, the only option is the prix fixe. In our listings, 'Prix fixe' indicates the price for the restaurant's set-price menu at lunch and dinner. If served only at lunch, the fixed-price menu is listed separately under 'Lunch menu'.

Within reviews, we make a distinction between set menus and the 'carte', which allows you to order items individually. Set menus, or prix fixes, are the most popular way of eating in Paris restaurants and often represent the best value. A 'formule' is a type of prix fixe, but often with a more limited choice of dishes and a two-course option.

Service & tipping

Prices on restaurant menus (and listed in this guide) must by law include a 12-15 per cent service charge. A small tip of one to five euros (or small change in a café) is a nice, though entirely optional, gesture.

Wheelchair access

In general, only new or renovated restaurants offer full wheelchair access, including disabled toilets. Where we

have listed 'Wheelchair access', the dining room is easily accessible and the owners have shown a willingness to help the disabled. It's worth ringing ahead to check if an establishment can cater for you.

Smoking

Restaurants are required by French law to have a non-smoking section. However, most either allocate one or two tables near the loo to non-smokers or ignore the law altogether. In our listings, 'Non-smoking room' means that the restaurant has a separate room for non-smokers. 'Non smoking' means that the entire restaurant is smoke-free.

Maps

Each restaurant, café and bar in this guide has a map reference which corresponds to the maps starting on page 320. We also provide detailed area maps for five neighbourhoods: the Marais, the Champs-Elysées, St-Germain-des-Prés, Oberkampf and Bastille. Restaurants, cafés and bars are located on these maps by name. The same grid is used for all the maps.

Savoir faire

Learn to saunter into Paris restaurants with a certain insouciance.

Restaurants are busiest at lunch between 1pm and 2pm. In the evening, the French rarely venture into a restaurant before 8.30pm, much later in trendier places. Popular restaurants sometimes have two sittings, around 8pm and 10pm. For a meal in the middle of the afternoon, try brasseries, cafés and tea rooms.

Aperitifs, wine, water & digestifs In the more expensive restaurants, wine waiters might make it hard for you to refuse Champagne or other aperitifs, which can add significantly to your bill. However, it can be fun to indulge in old-fashioned French aperitifs such as Lillet or Pineau des Charentes.

As well as standard 75cl bottles, wine comes in half-bottles (37.5cl) and carafes or pichets, usually 25cl (un quart), 46cl (un pot lyonnais) and 50cl (un demi-litre, or une fillette if served in a tall carafe).

You're entitled to ask for 'une carafe d'eau', which is tap water, though most waiters will try to sell you mineral water. Be warned that restaurants now commonly charge 4-5 for a litre bottle of mineral water (or sometimes even for a half-litre).

Digestifs offer the opportunity to discover potent drinks such as vintage Armagnac or a flaming prune eau-de-vie.

A matter of course French meals usually consist of three courses – entrée (starter), plat (main course) and dessert – although at more formal restaurants, there may be an additional amuse-bouche or amuse-gueule (appetiser or hors d'oeuvre), a fish course before the main course, cheese (before dessert), and petits fours served at the end with the coffee. This is invariably black (un expresso or un express) – if you ask for a café au lait after dinner, expect to receive a strange look.

Loafing Bread is served free with any café or restaurant meal and you're entitled to as much as you can eat – don't be afraid to ask for more, or to have it changed if it is stale.

Dress You are what you wear in Paris. Restaurant goers on the whole opt for the 'smart-casual' look, so while you won't need a tie, leave the bermuda shorts and tracksuits behind. Haute cuisine restaurants normally expect a jacket and tie in the evening.

Reservations It's always a good idea to book at popular restaurants. Famous haute cuisine establishments take bookings months ahead (they will ask you to call back to confirm the day before your meal) and the most currently fashionable bistros require booking up to a few weeks ahead. However, it's also worth trying at the last minute to see if there's room. Some hard-to-book tables are much more accessible at lunch.

Bar & café customs Drinks prices often vary in a café: they're cheapest at the bar, more at a table and even more sitting outside. There will often be a further increase (majoration), generally about 50 cents, after 10pm. If you want a table, sit down and wait for the waiter to arrive.

Paying When you want your bill, ask for it – waiters don't like to give the impression they're rushing you out. Bills are paid at the table.

A day in the life of an
haute cuisine chef

From testing truffles to inventing new dishes, head chef
Eric Fréchon has plenty on his plate, writes Alexander Lobrano.

It's only 7am in the immaculate kitchens of the Hôtel Bristol, but chef Eric Fréchon already has a finger in every pot. 'Morning is my favourite time – it's when the most important work is done. What this means is making all our stocks (fish, shellfish, veal, chicken, and beef), reductions and sauces from scratch,' says the amiable 41-year-old Norman, who began his career at 15 and became head chef at the Bristol eight years ago.

Wouldn't it be easier to make stock in large batches? 'Out of the question,' says

Eric. 'As soon as you refrigerate stock, it loses half of its flavour. And since stock is an ingredient in almost every sauce we make, it must be as fresh as possible.' So the simmering stock pot is revealed as the heart of French haute cuisine cooking.

As head chef, Eric is personally involved with every dish served for breakfast, lunch and dinner at the hotel's two-star Le Bristol restaurant, and also supervises the hotel's room service and banqueting. With a staff of over 30, Eric and his team feed between 300 and 400 people in a

day, and this to standards that have placed the restaurant at the pinnacle of French gastronomy. 'The other reason I like morning so much is that it's when I receive the day's produce, something I always find exciting.' Eric turns away to sample a reduction of gibier (game) – since it tastes 'rich, deep and wild' he approves the sauce, and then he takes a call from his butcher.

While he's on the phone, an older woman with rosy cheeks and a waxed-canvas jacket places her wicker hamper on the steel counter. A herb farmer from the Yvelines region west of Paris, she has been up since 5am, when she rose to clip the most fragile of the herbs she delivers daily to a coterie of chefs. Now Eric greets her with a warm pain aux raisins, and they go over his order – everything from classic thyme to herbs like lemongrass, which have only recently found a place in French cooking. Saying goodbye, she gives him a pinch on the

cheek. 'He's a remarkable cook,' she says. 'He invited me once, and my husband and I still talk about that meal.'

Next up is a pretty young woman whose vintage Hermès scarf is a clue to her lucrative calling. Opening a metal hamper, she releases a royal stink. Inside, something is wrapped in linen towels – truffles, of course. In season, Eric uses four to five kilograms of fresh truffles a week, which cost around 1,500 a kilo. Eric examines a few tubers for worm damage, and chooses several, which are weighed, wrapped again and tucked into a locked compartment inside a locked fridge with his caviar (he gets through 700 grams a week, which costs about 2,000).

'The real extravagance at the Bristol, though, is the fish,' says Eric. 'Supplies of the best quality fish have become frighteningly rare and staggeringly expensive.' Today, Eric's fishmonger delivers two three-foot-long sea bass that were line-caught off the Ile d'Yeu hours earlier, some striped mackerel and a huge flat turbot, to which Eric turns his attention after signing off a few more deliveries.

'We're sort of like a rugby team,' says Eric as he deftly works on the enormous fish, eventually to become fillets. 'I may be the captain, but the whole team works together.' In an era when many well-known chefs just swan through their kitchens for a cursory tasting, Eric is not only present six days a week, but happily taking on a tough chore usually fobbed off on a junior.

After a quick meeting with pastry chef Gilles Marchal and baker Jérôme Paysan (his bread, baked twice daily in a separate but on-the-premises bakery is so good, it's regularly delivered to the Thai royal family), Eric stops to chat with four Japanese journalists touring the kitchen with the Bristol's press officer. Then, after a quick bite with the staff around 11am – they dine on veal Marengo, rice, salad

Eric uses four to five kilograms of fresh truffles a week, which depending upon the market, cost around 1,500 a kilo.

and cheese – the lunch service starts, and the almost monastic calm of the morning becomes the fascinating ballet of a well-run kitchen in action.

During the lunch service, Eric is omnipresent, tasting everything and making constant tiny adjustments, a few more dots of sauce here, another whisker of chive added there. 'Every dish served here passes through my hands,' he says, working with an assistant to dress plates before they go out. On this winter day, a meeting of bankers in a private dining room is sampling a created-just-for-them dish of chicory (endive) rolled in thin slices of ham, gratinéed with parmesan and topped with slivered black truffles. Changing into a clean white chef's jacket, he sets off to see how the money men liked lunch. Returning a few minutes later, the thumbs up sign he makes to the crew is met with laughter.

After a quick foray into the main dining room – a French cabinet minister is entertaining foreigners, and decorum dictates the chef greet them – Eric has a coffee and then spends several hours in his office planning menus, going over orders, and meeting with the stylist and photographer of *Everything You Have to Taste at Least Once in Your Life*, a handsomely illustrated book for which Eric prepared recipes such as grouse roasted with juniper berries in goose fat and tips for cooking wasp larvae the way they do in Réunion (he's an inveterate traveller).

Finally, the chef has a few minutes to tinker with a new recipe. 'I've been experimenting to see how long I should smoke the baba (sponge pastries) that will garnish a new dish. I know I want some of the taste of pine smoke, but I'm not sure how much.' About 15 minutes later, several versions of the dish are served, including chicken bouillon garnished with a pine-smoked baba with melted beaufort cheese. With several tasters, Eric agrees that the smoke must be present but subtle, a result achieved by a minute or two in the smoker. 'I love creating new dishes, but it's important to respect the equilibrium of the palate,' says Eric.

Eric excuses himself to take a call from his wife, and returns in a clean chef's jacket. Having just eaten dinner, the kitchen staff are taking their places in preparation for the dinner service. It's 7pm, and during the 12 hours that have passed since he started, Eric couldn't have been off his feet for more than 45 minutes. Having taken the day's problems in his stride – he was unhappy with the quality of the lamb he'd received in the morning and a promising young saucier, or sauce chef, is leaving to go elsewhere – Eric mentions how much he's looking forward to the inauguration of the Bristol's second on-premises restaurant early in 2006. 'It will have a big rotisserie and it will be very produce-driven,' he says.

Even though he makes everything seem so easy, won't the responsibility of an additional restaurant be pushing his limits? 'Not at all,' he says, surprised by the idea. 'You do this job because it's your passion.'

Whirlwind wine tour

Sophie Lyne takes a spin round the regions, from Alsace to Bordeaux.

France offers a greater array of wine styles than any other country in the world. From the clean, aromatic, mineral rieslings of Alsace in the north-east to the powerful, chunky reds of the south-west, you'll find a wine to suit every mood, food and palate. However, the visiting wine buff needs a quick Tour de France to navigate complicated wine lists.

The big difference between a bottle from the New World and from France is that the grape variety that you know and love (chardonnay, merlot or sauvignon blanc for example) is seldom seen on a French wine label. The reason being that in France wine isn't just made from grapes – it's made from 'terroir'. This doesn't just mean the soil in which the vine is planted, it means all of the ways in which the place it comes from can influence the flavour of a wine.

So, let's climb aboard our velos and have a spin around the main wine producing regions, starting in the north-east with an aperitif. **Alsace** produces mainly white wine (the red is usually more like rosé) and is unique in France in describing the wines by grape variety. We have the clean but rather bland sylvaner, the classic lime- and mineral-infused rieslings, the spicy pinot gris (or tokay), the grapey muscat and the oily and exotic gewürztraminers.

Surprisingly close to Paris itself is **Champagne**, the undisputed king of sparkling wines. If you can afford it, step up to the mature complexity of a vintage, or 'millésime'.

Heading south into the heart of the country, the **Loire Valley** gives us clean, fresh, inexpensive muscadet, a traditional match for oysters. Also look for more serious flinty, steely sauvignon blancs of Sancerre and Pouilly-Fumé, sweet (yet rarely heavy) wines from Vouvray and Coteaux du Layon and some light reds from Chinon and Bourgeuil. More potent is the ruddy Saumur-Champigny.

The first chardonnay vineyards we hit south of Paris are those of Chablis, in **Burgundy**. Traditionally unoaked with good acidity these are the sharpest, most mineral expressions of chardonnay, a world away from the big, fat, buttery wines of Australia or California. Further south, Burgundy has hundreds of appellations but really only two wine styles – classic barrel-matured chardonnays and seductive, raspberry- and cherry-fruited pinot noir reds. St-Véran and Mâcon usually offer good deals,

the more famous Pouilly-Fuissé less so. Just south of here is **Beaujolais** – juicy, purple-coloured, lip-smacking, quaffing reds best drunk leaning against the zinc bar of a Parisian bistro. Look for the Villages appellations, such as Morgon and Brouilly.

Moving ever closer to the Mediterranean we hit the **Rhône Valley**. In the north there are some wonderful syrah-based reds with aromas of blackcurrants, plums and olives (Côte Rôtie and Hermitage are the great names) and around Avignon and Orange the sun-baked, powerful red Côtes du Rhônes of which Châteauneuf du Pape is the best. White Rhônes are usually thick and heavy, but the peachy and flowery viognier grape reaches its zenith in Condrieu.

Further south into **Provence**, we move into rosé country, where vast quantities are produced for popular summer drinking by locals and tourists. There is a small production of generous whites, from more obscure varieties such as rolle, ugni blanc and clairette. In Bandol, powerful tannic reds made from mourvèdre provide wonderful food wines.

The biggest revolutions are taking place in the **Languedoc-Roussillon**. An area originally known for the enormous quantities of very mediocre wine produced by cooperatives has been re-thinking, re-planting and challenging the old ways, with huge success. Sommeliers will be happy to recommend producers.

Moving north up the Atlantic coast we come to **Bordeaux**. The area is dominated by its reds: slow-maturing, classic cabernet sauvignons from the Médoc and the Graves and plumper, less structured merlot-based wines from St-Emilion and Pomerol. Look out for Fronsac, Côtes de Francs and Côtes de Castillon, which are far cheaper than their more illustrious neighbours. You won't find Pomerol's Château Pétrus at under €1,000 per bottle but less than a kilometre away lie the vineyards of Lalande de Pomerol, whose smooth and supple wines are still reasonably priced. Bordeaux is also home to magnificent sweet wines such as Barsac and Sauternes.

France also has hundreds of country wines, vins de pays and vins de table that can often surprise and delight at low prices. Remember, though, that the appellation gives an indication of the style of wine, but most important is the work of the individual winemaker.

A day in the life of a
bistro chef

With 16-hour days, a tiny kitchen and two sittings, the heat is always on for Christian Etchebest. Rosa Jackson tries to keep up.

At 8am burly chef Christian Etchebest looks far from bleary-eyed as he sips the first of the day's many coffees and inspects the produce delivery piled high on a wooden table in Le Troquet's rustic yet lovingly decorated dining room.

The boxes of carrots and oranges, aubergines, mushrooms, endives and tomatoes won't fit in the 11-square-metre kitchen, where two young cooks are already hard at work: unflappable Benoît cracks 100 or so eggs and measures litres of milk for the day's desserts, while Guy simmers stocks, trims meat and chops onions.

Since he bought Le Troquet from his uncle in 1998, Christian's days have followed much the same routine, one that begins at 8am and never finishes before midnight on weekdays, 1am on Fridays and Saturdays (the restaurant is closed on Sundays and Mondays). The hours came as no surprise – he had worked in restaurant kitchens for 14 years before opening his own bistro.

'I never wanted to become a cook,' he explains, 'but my mother forced me to go into this business at 15. It was only at the age of 20, when I worked in the kitchen of the Hôtel de Crillon with Christian Constant, Eric Fréchon and Yves Camdeborde, that I came to love it.'

By 9.30am the vegetables are under way for the day's side dishes – potatoes are cooking in their skins, celeriac is boiling for a purée to accompany the scallops in crab sauce, and aubergines are roasting. Benoît has already finished most of the desserts and is now baking piquillo cake, one of the many recipes from Christian's native Basque region. The chef completely rewrites the menu every three weeks, which keeps the cooks on their toes. But Benoît, who spent two years in the spacious but demanding kitchens of Le Grand Véfour before having his first bistro experience at Le Troquet, prefers it that way. 'At Le Grand Véfour the menu rarely changed, so you could get bored making the same dishes. We're never bored here,' he says.

Le Troquet's three-course menu might cost a reasonable 30, but a peek into Christian's small freezer shows that he takes no short cuts. It holds just a slab of bacon – chilled for easier slicing – and home-made ice-creams, which are frozen solid before being churned in a powerful machine just before serving. This is the kitchen's only high-tech gadget – Benoît even whips the egg whites for the soufflés by hand. The fish are delivered fresh from Brittany every day (Guy, a former fisherman from Saint-Malo, is the specialist) and the meat, along with the piquillo and Espelette peppers, comes direct from the Basque country.

At 10.25am Christian's wife Patricia (known by all as Pacy) walks in, having dropped one child off at school and left the other with a babysitter. Trained as a secretary, she has worked with Christian since he opened Le Troquet. Pacy spends at least an hour and a half each day on paperwork (which is notoriously complex for French business) and also waits tables, only at lunch since the birth of their second child. 'I'm not a trained professional so I greet people as I would guests to my own home,' she says.

In the kitchen, much red wine is being poured into giant saucepans for game stews and the daube provençale. At the same time, Guy is wiping down the counters and putting things away, restoring perfect order before the staff meal at 11.30am and the lunch rush. Then the babysitter arrives with the children and Christian drops everything to greet them with big hugs and kisses. 'My two stars are my children,' he says. 'All the rest means nothing to me.'

Every day Christian prepares lunch for four-and-a-half year old Antxou and his babysitter (15-month-old Peïo is still on purées). When I ask if they have the same meal as the staff, he looks horrified. 'No! Children are sacred.' Today Antxou is having stuffed pork with spiced chickpeas,

> Does anything ever go wrong, I wonder? 'The kitchen is so small that we smell it right away if something is burning.'

while the staff sit down to a delicious pork sautée made with the trimmings and the same chickpeas.

By noon the cooks and chef are back in the kitchen prepping their work stations for lunch and breaking the stems off a crateful of wild mushrooms. At 12.38pm the first plate leaves the kitchen – escargots in the style of Christian's grandmother, with lamb's lettuce, bacon, capers, pistachio vinaigrette and tiny croûtons. By 1pm the pace has picked up, with 20 people in the dining room. Head waiter Martin keeps a close eye on who has been served wine and is therefore ready for their food. Christian serves a glass of Champagne to a journalist at the bar while Guy and Benoît keep the kitchen running smoothly. Does anything ever go wrong, I wonder? 'The kitchen is so small that we smell it right away if something is burning,' says Christian. 'It does happen, but it's rare.'

By 2.30pm the cooks are cleaning the kitchen, but it's not time for a break yet –

Christian starts trimming and slicing veal for his axoa de veau, a regional dish involving bell peppers and Espelette chilli, while Guy and Benoît shell an enormous potful of sea snails. As they work, they engage in some verbal jousting. 'Every Basque dish has the same ingredients,' Guy taunts Christian. 'If you hate my region, why do you both take your holidays there?' the chef retorts.

'I appreciate working with Christian because he doesn't yell,' says Guy, who has worked in some of the city's best bistros. 'And he lets us tease him, which allows us to let off steam.' In two years at Le Troquet Guy has never missed a day, except when the restaurant closes at Christmas and in August. He now rents an apartment in the same building as the restaurant, which allows him to nap during his one- to two-hour break in the afternoon. 'But I need to work this much,' he says, 'otherwise I would do nothing.'

During his break, Christian picks up his elder son from school and spends time with his children before returning at 5.30pm to prepare for the evening service. I venture into the cellar, where the wine is stored along with the oils, Basque charcuterie and rows and rows of Banyuls vinegar, something of a secret weapon in Christian's cooking. Le Troquet can serve 80 people on a busy night, but as it's unusually quiet before Christmas, Christian retires to his office after the staff meal to do some paperwork.

I sit down in the dining room to grand-mère's escargots (that was some grand-mère), seared scallops in crab sauce, and a truly towering vanilla soufflé with cherry jam. 'So, do you have a secret?' I ask Benoît. 'No' he replies innocently, and then I catch him moulding a thick ring of butter around the top of the soufflé dish. 'That's just to be sure the soufflé rises properly', he says, as if it were obvious.

Even on a quiet night the kitchen heats up considerably, and by 10.30pm the cooks show signs of fatigue. Christian always pitches in when necessary, but leaves them to it at the end of the night.

'I work them hard but it's for their own good,' he says. 'I was 29 when I opened my restaurant. 'They'll be ready to open theirs by the time they are 27 or 28.'

A la carte

Where to go...

...to eat after midnight
L'Atmosphère, Bars & Pubs
Bon 2, Trendy
Chez Papa, Budget
A la Cloche d'Or, Bistros
Curieux Spaghetti Bar, Trendy
Georges, Trendy
Les Philosophes, Cafés
Le Tambour, Bars & Pubs
Taninna, North African
La Taverne de Nesle, Bars & Pubs
La Tour de Montlhéry (Chez Denise), Bistros
Viaduc Café, Cafés

See also p86, Brasseries

...to drink after 2am
Le Bréguet, Bars & Pubs
Les Chimères, Bars & Pubs
La Chope des Artistes, Cafés
Le Crocodile, Bars & Pubs
Favela Chic, Bars & Pubs
Flann O'Brien's, Bars & Pubs
Harry's Bar, Bars & Pubs
Impala Lounge, Bars & Pubs
Nirvana, Bars & Pubs
Le Purgatoire, Bars & Pubs
Le Tambour, Bars & Pubs
La Taverne de Nesle, Bars & Pubs
Tsé, Bars & Pubs
Viaduc Café, Cafés

...to eat al fresco
Apollo, Trendy
Café Marly, Cafés
Café Noir, Bistros
La Cagouille, Fish & Seafood
Le Châlet des Iles, Classics
Contre-Allée, Bistros
La Contrescarpe, Cafés
Il Cortile, Italian
L'Espadon, Haute Cuisine
La Fontaine de Mars, Bistros
Georges, Trendy
La Girondine, Bistros
Laurent, Haute Cuisine
Le Parc aux Cerfs, Bistros
Pavillon Montsouris, Classics
Pitchi Poï, Jewish
Point Bar, Bistros
Le Pré Catelan, Haute Cuisine
Restaurant du Palais-Royal, Contemporary

Rouge Tomate, Contemporary
La Terrasse du Parc, Contemporary
Le Zéphyr, Bistros

...for ancient walls
Allard, Bistros
L'Ami Louis, Classics
Anahi, The Americas
Chez Marianne, Jewish
L'Ecurie, Budget
Mon Vieil Ami, Bistros

...for the artworks
La Coupole, Brasseries
Guy Savoy, Haute Cuisine
Juvénile's, Wine Bars
Le Méditerranée, Fish & Seafood
Pétrelle, Contemporary
Le Stresa, Italian
Taillevent, Haute Cuisine
Wadja, Bistros
Willi's Wine Bar, Bistros
Ze Kitchen Galerie, Contemporary

...for unusual beers
Le Bouillon Racine, Bistros
La Fabrique, Bars & Pubs
Le Frog & Rosbif, Bars & Pubs
Le Général Lafayette, Bars & Pubs
Graindorge, Regional
La Gueuze, Bars & Pubs
Le Lèche-Vin, Bars & Pubs
La Taverne de Nesle, Bars & Pubs

...for a business lunch
Aki, Japanese
L'Astrance, Contemporary
Bath's, Regional
Benoît, Bistros
La Butte Chaillot, Bistros
Chez Georges, Bistros
Chez la Vieille, Bistros
D'Chez Eux, Regional
L'Estaminet Gaya, Fish & Seafood
Flora, Contemporary
Le Graindorge, Regional
Le Grand Colbert, Brasseries
Le Pamphlet, Bistros
Savy, Bistros

See also p75, Haute Cuisine.

...for a carnivorous feast
Au Boeuf Couronné, Brasseries
Le Bouclard, Bistros

Chez Omar, North African
Le Duc de Richelieu, Bistros
Georget, Bistros
La Maison de l'Aubrac, Brasseries
Le Nemrod, Cafés
L'Opportun, Bistros
Le Père Claude, Bistros
Au Petit Marguery, Bistros
Le Pied de Cochon, Brasseries
Le Plomb du Cantal, Cafés
Savy, Bistros
Sébillon, Bistros
La Tour de Montlhéry (Chez Denise), Bistros

...to celebrity spot
Alain Ducasse au Plaza Athénée,
  Haute Cuisine
Les Ambassadeurs, Haute Cuisine
L'Ami Louis, Bistros
Anahi, The Americas
L'Atelier de Joël Robuchon, Contemporary
Brasserie Lipp, Brasseries
Café de Flore, Cafés
Chez Arthur, Bistros
Le V, Haute Cuisine
L'Espadon, Haute Cuisine
404, North African
Market, Contemporary
Le Père Claude, Bistros
Le Square Trousseau, Bistros
Le Stresa, Italian
Le Voltaire, Bistros

See also p98, Trendy.

...for the cheese course
Astier, Bistros
Au Pressoir, Classics
Le Bistro de Gala, Bistros
Chez Michel, Bistros
Chez René, Bistros
Les Fernandises, Regional
Le Graindorge, Regional
Montparnasse 25, Contemporary
Point Bar, Bistros
Le Timbre, Bistros

See also p75, Haute Cuisine

...with children
Altitude 95, Bistros
Berthillon, Tea Rooms
Café Le Dôme, Cafés
La Coupole, Brasseries
Flam's, Budget
New Nioullaville, Far Eastern
Le Président, Far Eastern
Quai Ouest, Contemporary
Le Rostand, Cafés
Scoop, The Americas

Thoumieux, Bistros
Le Troquet, Bistros
Wadja, Bistros

...for cocktails
AbracadaBar, Bars & Pubs
Andy Wahloo, Bars & Pubs
Boteco, Bars & Pubs
Calle 24, Americas
Chez Richard, Bars & Pubs
China Club, Bars & Pubs
Le Crocodile, Bars & Pubs
Favela Chic, Trendy
F.B.I Paris, Bars & Pubs
Harry's Bar, Bars & Pubs
Hemingway Bar at the Ritz, Bars & Pubs
Impala Lounge, Bars & Pubs
The Lizard Lounge, Bars & Pubs
Le Plaza Athénée, Bars & Pubs
Le Rosebud, Bars & Pubs
Le Train Bleu, Brasseries
Zéro Zéro, Bars & Pubs

...for designer style
Aki, Japanese
Alain Ducasse au Plaza Athénée,
  Haute Cuisine
Alcazar, Brasseries
Andy Wahloo, Bars & Pubs
Antoine et Lili, La Cantine, Tea Rooms
Atelier Renault, Cafés
Café des Initiés, Cafés
Café Marly, Cafés
De La Ville Café, Bars & Pubs
Maison Blanche, Contemporary
Le Martel, Trendy
Pétrelle, Contemporary
Le Salon d'Hélène, Contemporary
La Table du Lancaster, Contemporary
Le Trésor, Bars & Pubs

See also p98, Trendy.

...for unusual desserts
Les Ambassadeurs, Haute Cuisine
Angl'Opéra, Contemporary
L'Epi Dupin, Bistros
Flora, Contemporary
Maison Blanche, Contemporary
L'Ourcine, Bistros
Petrossian, Contemporary
Pierre Gagnaire, Haute Cuisine
Spoon, Food & Wine, Trendy
Willi's Wine Bar, Bistros
Ze Kitchen Galerie, Contemporary

...on a diet
Alcazar, Brasseries
L'Avenue, Trendy
Blue Elephant, Far Eastern

Hôtel Costes, Trendy
Le Jardin des Pâtes, Budget
Khun Akorn, Far Eastern
The Kitchen, Budget
Rose Bakery, Cafés
Le Salon d'Hélène, Contemporary
Tanjia, Trendy

See also p196, Japanese; p153, Vegetarian.

...with your dog
Café Beaubourg, Cafés
Le Clown Bar, Wine Bars
La Galère des Rois, Bistros
Khun Akorn, Far Eastern
Pétrelle, Contemporary
Le Safran, Bistros
Le Suffren, Brasseries
La Table de la Fontaine, Bistros

...before/after a film
L'Avenue, Brasseries
Chez Lili et Marcel, Cafés
Cosi, Budget
La Coupole, Brasseries
Les Editeurs, Cafés
Korean Barbecue, Far Eastern
La Maison de l'Aubrac, Brasseries
Nils, Budget
Le Reflet, Cafés
Le Rendez-vous des Quais, Cafés
Le Wepler, Brasseries

...with a foodie
Allard, Bistros
L'Arpège, Haute Cuisine
L'Astrance, Contemporary
L'Atelier de Joël Robuchon, Contemporary
Le Chamarré, Contemporary
Au Gourmand, Contemporary
Hiramatsu, Haute Cuisine
Kinugawa, Japanese
Mon Viell Ami, Bistros
Pierre Gagnaire, Haute Cuisine
Le Pré Verre, Bistros
La Table du Lancaster, Contemporary
La Table de Joël Robuchon, Contemporary

...on a first date
L'Avenue, Trendy
Café Marly, Cafés
Chez Dom, Caribbean
China Club, Bars & Pubs
Le Clown Bar, Wine Bars
404, North African
Julien, Brasseries
Martel, Trendy
Le Reminet, Bistros
La Terrasse du Parc, Contemporary

...for game
Astier, Bistros
Auberge le Quincy, Bistros
La Biche au Bois, Bistros
Chez Casimir, Budget
Chez Michel, Bistros
Chez Toinette, Budget
Michel Rostang, Haute Cuisine
Au Petit Marguery, Bistros
Le Repaire de Cartouche, Bistros
La Traversière, Classics
Le Troquet, Bistros

...with grandma
Angelina, Tea Rooms
Chez Jenny, Regional
Le Dôme, Fish & Seafood
Josephine 'Chez Dumonet', Bistros
Ladurée, Tea Rooms
Lasserre, Classics
La Méditérranée, Fish & Seafood
Le Soufflé, Classics
Le Train Bleu, Brasseries
La Truffière, Classics

...with a group of friends
Alcazar, Brasseries
Ave Maria, Bars & Pubs
Blue Elephant, Far Eastern
Le Café du Commerce, Budget
Chez Gégène, Eating with Entertainment
Chez Michel, Bistros
Entoto, African & Indian Ocean
L'Escapade, Budget
Fajitas, The Americas
La Fresque, Budget
Mon Vieil Ami, Bistros
New Nioullaville, Far Eastern
Le Pacifique, Far Eastern
Les Petits Marseillais, Bistros

...for kitsch
Atlas, North African
La Charlotte en l'Ile, Tea Rooms
La Chine Masséna, Far Eastern
Le Dénicheur, Cafés
La Madonnina, Italian
Au Pied de Cochon, Brasseries
Stella, Budget

...for a late lunch
L'Atelier de Joël Robuchon, Contemporary
L'As du Fallafel, Jewish
Brasserie Zimmer, Brasseries
Café du Commerce, Budget
Café Marly, Cafés
Camille, Bistros
L'Entracte, Cafés
Georges, Trendy

La Grande Armée, Brasseries
Juvénile's, Wine Bars
Le Nemrod, Cafés
New Pondichery, Indian
Polichinelle Café, Cafés
Restaurant Pho, Far Eastern
Soufflot Café, Cafés
Le Tambour, Bars & Pubs

...for unusual loos
Abazu, Japanese
Le Bar Dix, Bars & Pubs
Le Cristal Room, Trendy
L'Etoile Manquante, Cafés
La Folie en Tête, Bars & Pubs
Le Lèche-Vin, Bars & Pubs
The Lizard Lounge, Bars & Pubs
Le Pantalon, Bars & Pubs
Pétrelle, Contemporary
Les Philosophes, Cafés
Tokyo Eat, Trendy
La Tour d'Argent, Haute Cuisine
Le Trésor, Bars & Pubs

...to eat organic
Bioart, Bistros
Les Cinq Saveurs d'Anada, Vegetarian
Phyto Bar, Bistros
Le Potager du Marais, Vegetarian
Rose Bakery, Cafés
Le Safran, Bistros

...for a romantic meal
L'Angle du Faubourg, Contemporary
L'Astrance, Contemporary
Le Châlet des Iles, Classics
Le V, Haute Cuisine
L'Enoteca, Wine Bars
L'Espadon, Haute Cuisine
Flora, Contemporary
Gallopin, Brasseries
Le Grand Véfour, Haute Cuisine
Lapérouse, Classics
Le Pamphlet, Bistros
Le Pavillon Montsouris, Classics
Le Pré Catelan, Haute Cuisine
Restaurant du Palais-Royal, Contemporary
Sardegna a Tavola, Italian
La Tour d'Argent, Haute Cuisine
Le Train Bleu, Brasseries

...to talk about the rugby
L'Ami Jean, Bistros
The Bowler, Pubs
Brasserie de l'Isle St-Louis, Brasseries
The Frog & Rosbif, Bars & Pubs
Kitty O'Shea's, Bars & Pubs
La Maison de l'Aubrac, Brasseries
Au Métro, Budget
La Régalade, Bistros

...for interesting salads
Apparemment Café, Cafés
Bistro du Peintre, Bistros
Blue Elephant, Far Eastern
Café Beaubourg, Cafés
Chez Papa, Budget
L'Entracte, Cafés
Le Grizzli, Bistros
Khun Akorn, Far Eastern
Le Nemrod, Cafés
Polichinelle Café, Cafés
Rose Bakery, Cafés

...for the soufflés
L'Atelier de Joël Robuchon, Contemporary
La Cigale-Récamier, Bistros
Flora, Contemporary
Pierre Gagnaire, Haute Cuisine
La Régalade, Bistros
Le Soufflé, Classics
Le Troquet, Bistros

...for rare spirits
L'Alsaco, Regional
La Cagouille, Fish & Seafood
Dominique, Other International
Les Fernandises, Regional
Mazurka, Other International
Pitchi Poï, Jewish
Au Trou Gascon, Classics

See also p75, Haute Cuisine.

...for a bistro feed on Sunday
Alexandre, Regional
L'Alivi, Regional
L'Ambassade d'Auvergne, Regional
L'Ami Louis, Bistros
L'Ardoise, Bistros
L'Assiette, Bistros
L'Auberge du Clou, Bistros
Benoît, Bistros
Le Bistrot d'à Côté Flaubert, Bistros
Le Bistrot des Vignes, Bistros
Bouillon Racine, Bistros
La Butte Chaillot, Bistros
Café Burq, Bistros
Café Noir, Bistros
Camille, Bistros
Chardenoux, Bistros
Aux Charpentiers, Bistros
Chez Janou, Bistros
Chez Maître Paul, Regional
Chez Paul, 11th, Bistros
Chez Paul, 13th, Bistros
Chez Ramulaud, Bistros
Le Dauphin, Bistros
L'Entracte, Bistros
La Fontaine de Mars, Bistros
Ma Bourgogne, Bistros

Le Mâchon d'Henri, Bistros
Mon Vieil Ami, Bistros
Le Parc aux Cerfs, Bistros
Le Père Claude, Bistros
Le Petit Marché, Bistros
Les Petits Marseillais, Bistros
Le Petit Pontoise, Bistros
Le Poulbot Gourmet, Bistros
Le Réconfort, Bistros
Le Reminet, Bistros
Rendez-Vous des Chauffeurs, Bistros
La Rôtisserie du Beaujolais, Bistros
Sébillon, Bistros
Thoumieux, Bistros
La Tour de Montlhéry, Bistros
Au 35, Bistros
Le Vieux Bistro, Bistros
Le Zéphyr, Bistros

...for a sunny café terrace
Café Beaubourg, Cafés
Café de Flore, Cafés
Café du Marché, Cafés
La Chope Daguerre, Cafés
La Contrescarpe, Cafés
Les Deux Magots, Cafés
La Palette, Cafés
Le Rendez-vous des Quais, Cafés
Le Rostand, Cafés
Le Soleil, Cafés
Tabac de la Sorbonne, Cafés
Vavin Café, Cafés

...for a timewarp
Allard, Bistros
Chardenoux, Bistros
Chartier, Budget
Chez Georges, Bistros
Chez René, Bistros
Aux Crus de Bourgogne, Bistros
La Fermette Marbeuf, Brasseries
Julien, Brasseries
Perraudin, Bistros
Le Petit Rétro, Bistros
Savy, Bistros
Le Train Bleu, Brasseries
Vagenende, Brasseries

...with a vegetarian friend
Alexandre, Regional
L'Arpège, Haute Cuisine
La Bastide Odéon, Regional
Chez Marianne, Jewish
Au Coco de Mer, African
La Connivence, Bistros
Kastoori, Indian
Macéo, Contemporary
Le Safran, Bistros
Le Souk, North African

Spoon, Food & Wine, Trendy
La Voie Lactée, Eastern Mediterranean
Willi's Wine Bar, Wine Bars

...for the view
Altitude 95, Bistros
Bar Panoramique, Bars & Pubs
Georges, Trendy
Le Jules Verne, Haute Cuisine
Maison Blanche, Contemporary
Le Rostand, Cafés
La Tour d'Argent, Classics
Ziryab, North African

...for weekend brunch
Alcazar, Trendy
Blue Bayou, The Americas
Breakfast in America, The Americas
Café Charbon, Bars & Pubs
Forêt Noire, Tea Rooms
The Lizard Lounge, Bars & Pubs
Pitchi Poï, Jewish
A Priori Thé, Tea Rooms
Quai Ouest, Contemporary
404, North African
Zebra Square, Brasseries

...for the wine list
Astier, Bistros
Le Bistrot du Sommelier, Classics
Chez Georges, Bistros
A la Grange Batelière, Bistros
Macéo, Contemporary
Le Passage des Carmagnoles, Bistros
Spoon, Food & Wine, Trendy
La Truffière, Classics
Wadja, Bistros
Willi's Wine Bar, Bistros
Yugaraj, Indian

*See also p261, Wine Bars;
p75 Haute Cuisine.*

...with a writer
Café de Flore, Cafés
Café des Lettres, Cafés
Le Couvent, Bars & Pubs
Les Editeurs, Cafés
Le Fumoir, Bars & Pubs
Le Perron, Italian

...on your own
L'As du Fallafel, Jewish
L'Atelier de Joël Robuchon, Contemporary
Le Bar à Huîtres, Fish & Seafood
La Contrescarpe, Cafés
Fish, Wine Bars
Isami, Japanese
Laï Laï Ken, Japanese
Mirama, Far Eastern

French Cuisine

Bistros

If anything shows how resistant Paris restaurants remain to dramatic change, it's the enduring popularity of the bistro. The fashion pack might dash from one 'concept' restaurant to the next, but even the most fickle folk keep a beloved neighbourhood address up their sleeve. This, in the end, is the essence of Parisian eating – the local cantine, as it is fondly known, where the owner greets you with a fond handshake and the food, no matter how wonderful, comes second to the feelgood factor. That said, the bistro genre is not stuck in a timewarp: with an increasing number of highly trained chefs opening their own restaurants, the standard has improved tremendously in the past few years, and there is no doubt that bistros offer the best-value meals in Paris. The original 'chef's bistros' – La Régalade and Chez Michel, to name just two – have now spawned their own offspring, run by even younger and just-as-ambitious chefs. These restaurants, such as L'Ourcine, L'Entredgeu and L'Ami Jean, show how hard this generation is willing to work to win a loyal clientele. At the other end of the spectrum are those bistros that thankfully never seem to change: Allard, Josephine 'Chez Dumonet', Benoît. Prices have gone up overall in bistros and real bargains are now rare (see pp136-152 **Budget**). However, lunch is often more affordable (as well as less hectic and smoky) and prix fixe menus appeal to tight budgets in the evening. Be warned that many bistros close entirely on weekends for a much-needed break after a week of 16-hour workdays.

1ST ARRONDISSEMENT

L'Absinthe

24 pl du Marché-St-Honoré, 1st (01.49.26.90.04/ www.michelrostang.com). M° Tuileries. **Open** 12.15-3pm, 7.45-10.30pm Mon-Fri; 7.45-10.30pm Sat. Closed one week in Aug. **Average** €32. **Prix fixe** €29, €35. **Credit** AmEx, MC, V. **Wheelchair access. Non-smoking room. Map** G4.

You can't help but wish that the dramatic glass structure of the Marché St-Honoré housed a food market rather than expensive furniture shops but, as if to compensate, it's surrounded by a growing number of bistros with terraces that take advantage of this traffic-free spot. One of the most popular is L'Absinthe, part of the Michel Rostang empire and run by his daughter Caroline. Several Rostang classics appear on the menu, such as pâté en croûte with chunks of foie gras and his moelleux chocolat-café for dessert, so we felt confident of a good meal as we ordered. Unfortunately, whoever was in charge of the kitchen lacked the great chef's magic touch. Scorpion fish soup, though advertised as 'mousseux' (foamy), turned out to be a thin orange broth topped with a thick layer of fat and scum. No better were the petits farcis d'étrilles, clam shells stuffed with a burnt crab filling. A scallop brochette with smoked paprika looked more like a starter portion than a main course, and pork ribs in a crustacean sauce were a disaster. Desserts of a yoghurt cake with candied kumquats and pear tarte Tatin with pecans were much better. Though the downstairs dining room with its brick walls and giant clock is pleasant, next time we'll try one of the competing bistros.

L'Ardoise ★

28 rue du Mont-Thabor, 1st (01.42.96.28.18). M° Concorde or Tuileries. **Open** noon-2pm, 6.30-11pm Tue-Sun. Closed 25 Dec-3 Jan, first week in May, Aug. **Prix fixe** €31. **Credit** MC, V. **Map** G5.

One of the flagship modern bistros in the capital, L'Ardoise has had the bright idea of opening on Sundays, making Sunday lunch a tempting prospect. By 1pm the rather anonymous room was packed with serious gourmets, both tourists and locals, anxious to explore the €31 blackboard menu featuring Pierre Jay's reliably delicious cooking. We chose six oysters with warm chipolatas and a pungent shallot dressing, an unusual combination from Bordeaux which works with unexpected force. The charming waitress warned that the hare pie with an escalope of foie gras nestling in its centre was 'gamey'. Instead we chose firm, shelled langoustines which were placed around a delicate mousseline of celery and coated in a luscious chervil sauce. Puddings included petits pots, one a rich chocolate cream and the other a mascarpone version, which made a winning duo. If the rum baba was a rather more mundane choice its preparation was irreproachable. Our raspberry-scented Chinon made a perfect complement, chosen from a wine list which is sensibly arranged by price. This popular bistro lives up to its widely broadcast reputation.

Chez La Vieille

1 rue Bailleul/37 rue de l'Arbre-Sec, 1st (01.42.60.15.78). Mº Louvre-Rivoli. **Open** noon-2pm Mon-Wed, Fri; noon-2pm, 7.30-9.30pm Thur. **Average** €45. **Lunch menu** €26. **Credit** AmEx, MC, V. **Map** J6.

The brief was simple: to have lunch Chez La Vieille and be sufficiently alert to confront a business meeting in the afternoon. We ate on the first floor, a plain, bright room in sharp contrast to the rustic charm of the ground floor, which was already bursting with well-rounded regulars. From the wondrous ad-lib selection of starters including a hot chou farci, we decided to try the home-made terrine de foie gras. The smiling waitress, from the all-female team headed by the Corsican patronne, quickly arrived with a whole terrine which we could gorge on at liberty; the liver was of outstanding quality, and decidedly moreish. The tripe lover between us pronounced his cast-iron casserole of the stuff the finest he had eaten in Paris. The foie de veau was equally impressive, coated in a pungent reduction of shallots and vinegar – only the tepid potato purée disappointed. With a classy half-bottle of Bordeaux, we emerged light of heart and fleet of foot. Opening hours are limited, booking is essential, and the prix fixe is a bargain.

Le Dauphin

167 rue St-Honoré, 1st (01.42.60.40.11). Mº Pyramides. **Open** noon-2.30pm, 7.30-10.30pm daily. **Average** €40. **Prix fixe** €37. **Credit** AmEx, DC, MC, V. **Wheelchair access. Non-smoking room. Map** H5.

Don't be put off by the uninspiring demeanour of this bistro – chefs Edgar Duhr and Didier Oudill trained with star chef Michel Guérard, before wowing the critics at the Café de Paris in Biarritz. Here they present a pared-down version of their exciting, south-western food, combining influences from the Basque country and the Landes. Diners are encouraged to share starters such as tuna confit, rustic terrines and goose rillettes, all served from Kilner jars and accompanied by toasted country bread. The grill menu offers various combinations of seafood, meat and vegetables. And for more conventional tastes there's a classical carte, with three courses for €37. From the latter, a tasty cep

L'Ardoise. See p24.

Chez Georges. *See p27.*

soup came with a plump foie gras ravioli in the centre, while anchovies and piquillo peppers marinated in olive oil were bursting with vibrancy. Well-roasted, if smallish coquilles St-Jacques topped a rich mixture of crushed potatoes and black olives, but the star dish was the meltingly tender pig's cheek, cooked for seven hours in aged Armagnac. Desserts are a really strong point – we shared a fabulous tartelette à l'orange, with crisp sablé pastry, a drizzle of sticky orange confit and a refreshing orange sorbet. The wine list is mostly regional French, with a few prestigious bottles thrown in for good measure.

Point Bar ★

40 pl du Marché-St-Honoré, 1st (01.42.61.76.28). M^o *Tuileries.* **Open** 11.30am-2pm, 7.45-11pm Tue-Sat. Closed first two weeks in Aug. **Average** €45. **Prix fixe** €20, €25. **Lunch menu** €15. **Credit** AmEx, DC, MC, V. **Map** G4.

The daughter of Tours chef Jean Bardet has a smart hit on her hands with this stylish new restaurant, which has quickly become popular with a curious mix of financial and fashion folk at noon, and neighbourhood trendies and tourists in the evening. In good weather, the tables set out on the pavement are much sought-after. Service is relaxed and smiling, and the decor is streamlined and airy. Though the kitchen is inspired by a variety of other cuisines to create an original approach, it's still solidly French in terms of technique and produce. Try the egg with achards (green mango pickles popular in Mauritius and India) to start and then go with one of the delicately flavoured main courses, perhaps the shrimp tempura with aubergine caviar or the sea bream lacquered with curry. Casserole-roasted chicken is delicious as well, and the wine list is particularly rich in Loire Valley bottles.

Le Safran

29 rue d'Argenteuil, 1st (01.42.61.25.30). M^o *Pyramides.* **Open** noon-2.30pm, 7-11pm Mon-Fri; 7-11pm Sat. **Average** €38. **Prix fixe** €24-€39. **Lunch menu** €14.50. **Credit** AmEx, DC, MC, V. **Wheelchair access. Non-smoking room. Map** G5.

Our Saturday night out at Caroll Sinclair's saffron-inspired bistro hovered between comedy and tragedy. We were shown into a snug corner of the rather cluttered room, which was rapidly filling up with a tourist-led clientele. Someone had been hard at work on administration, as files were strewn over the adjacent tables, and our own tablecloth remained spotty and unchanged. Nursing a tepid kir, we realised the charming waiter was all alone, and that the glamorous and talented Ms Sinclair had only one helper in the kitchen. The harassed waiter's fretful, barked requests for dishes became the burden of our evening. Our own order took over an hour for a first course of rather delicious scallops with a crustacean sauce, and pretty much the same for an excellent slice of rare tuna topped with foie gras, and an expensive (€29) plat du chef, a tender magret de canard with few if any of the promised morels. The same rather disorganised, but tasty selection of sautéed vegetables accompanied both dishes. We finished up our excellent Burgundy and abandoned ship before enjoying the crumble, chocolate fondant or crème brûlée. The cooking here is sound and worthwhile, using largely organic products, but the Saturday night gridlock needs to be fixed.

La Tour de Montlhéry (Chez Denise)

5 rue des Prouvaires, 1st (01.42.36.21.82). RER Châtelet-Les Halles. **Open** noon-3pm, 7.30pm-6am. Closed 14 July-15 Aug. **Average** €45. **Credit** MC, V. **Wheelchair access. Map** J5.

At the stroke of midnight, this place is packed, jovial and gruff. Think to reserve ahead at this venerable all-night den if you want to eat before 2am. Come hungry, too, for a feast of savoury traditional dishes, and thirsty for the house Brouilly, served by the litre. 'Water? Oh, we don't serve that here!' the waiter jokes to diners devouring simply towering rib steaks served with marrow and a heaping platter of fries, home-made and among the best in Paris. The Tour de Montlhéry dates back to when the Les Halles neighbourhood was still the city's wholesale market and this corner the meatpackers' district (a few wholesale butchers are still next door), and this accounts for the reverent place game, beef and offal have on the menu. Adventurous souls can try tripes au calvados, grilled andouillettes (chitterling sausages) or lamb's brain, or go for an interesting stewed venison, served with succulent celery root and home-made jam. There are a few fish dishes, too. Tourists mingle with regulars in the intimate red checked dining room. It's a friendly place and, like us, you could end up tasting a portion of the neighbour's roasted lamb or chatting by the barrels of wine stacked atop the bar.

Willi's Wine Bar ★

13 rue des Petits-Champs, 1st (01.42.61.05.09/ www.williswinebar.com). M° Pyramides. **Open** 12.30-2.30pm, 7-11pm Mon-Sat. Closed two weeks in Aug. **Average** €35. **Prix fixe** €25 (lunch), €32 (dinner). **Credit** MC, V. **Wheelchair access**. **Map** H5.

If you haven't yet discovered Willi's, you're missing something very, very good. The narrow passage alongside the long bar gives way to a small and elegant beamed room accented with crisp white linen; the effect is airy and spacious. From our table we watched François Yon's tiny, perfect kitchen through the service hatch, and whetted our appetite on the stray aromas. The cooking is ambitious, but never gratuitously so; the hardest thing you'll have to do is choose, but then there's no such thing as a mistake. Starters such as succulent quail breasts sizzled in a sophisticated version of barbecue sauce or a creamy 'cassolette' of cockles, Puy lentils and shredded leek set the tone. But the mains, at once classic and innovative, were more than we'd hoped for. An impossibly melt-in-your-mouth côtelette de biche, glazed in a translucent pepper sauce and paired with roasted pear, cranberries and sweet potato crisps, conquered first our eyes then our palate. Yon is a star meat chef who matches precision cooking and fine sauces with superb presentation. A thick fillet steak, humorously crowned with a tiny shallot Tatin, was likewise exquisitely tender and just-right rare; and a flaky chunk of roast cod, set in a dark, earthy sauce of chanterelle mushrooms and artichokes, was audaciously robust. Our favourite dessert was a real tongue teaser: unctuous mango compote with vanilla cream. Willi's wine list is appropriately long (Côtes du Rhône offerings loom especially large) and the bilingual staff are genuinely friendly, always happy to offer informed, enthusiastic advice. With post-euro inflation rampant, prices – especially at lunch (all the same courses for 7€ cheaper) – represent excellent value. For those on small budgets, a word of advice: Go on, splurge!

2ND ARRONDISSEMENT

Chez Georges

1 rue du Mail, 2nd (01.42.60.07.11). M° Bourse. **Open** noon-1.45pm, 7-9.45pm Mon-Sat. Closed three weeks in Aug. **Average** €45. **Credit** AmEx, MC, V. **Map** H5.

It would have been difficult, on that particular Parisian lunchtime, to have found diners entering a restaurant with such happy confidence, but one look at the exquisitely hand-written menu in the window of Chez Georges' wood-panelled exterior tells you it's the sort of place you can't go wrong. However, as the clock crept round to 2pm, the terrible thought started to dawn on us: this place is not what it's cracked up to be. Not that there aren't many things to adore about Chez Georges (the maternal, uniformed staff, for example, or the decor that's so old-fashioned it's almost Eastern European). But the cooking isn't worth the money. For those who know the food at the big, bargain bistro Chartier, it's kind of the same thing here but (more than) twice the price. Except for the starters. Our great earthenware terrine of tangy Baltic herring, left on the table just in case we felt like ten or 11 rather than the usual two or three, was a splendid starter with its huge bowl of thick cream. As was our egg in aspic, which looked tremendously 19th-century with its tarragon leaf and strip of ham caught in clear jelly as if frozen in ice. The egg was perfect: cooked but with a yolk ready to run across the plate at the prick of a fork. The mains, though, were mediocre. Our pavé de rumsteak was the size of a cannonball but not even vaguely à point (medium), once past the crispy outside. Veal kidney, too, seemed carelessly prepared – copious but hastily cut, in a tedious cream-and-mustard sauce Charlotte. After such huge mains, we decided to share a pudding, thinking fromage blanc with a chestnut cream would be something special here. It wasn't. If you want to eat like this you might as well stay at home. It is time for firm words in the kitchen.

Aux Crus de Bourgogne

3 rue Bachaumont, 2nd (01.42.33.48.24). M° Sentier or Les Halles. **Open** noon-3pm, 7.30-11pm Mon-Fri. **Average** €36. **Prix fixe** €20 (dinner only). **Credit** AmEx, MC, V. **Wheelchair access**. **Non-smoking room**. **Map** J5.

Daily specials, grills and lobster (served hot on Thursdays) are definitely the best bet at this time-warp 19th-century bistro on a tree-lined pedestrian street. Taking our cue from the growing crowd of well-heeled regulars, we paid homage to the Thursday lunchtime homard and found it fresh, firm and sweet, whether hot (with plain rice and a somewhat over-pungent, spicy bisque sauce) or cold as a starter with salad and mayonnaise. Wines dispensed by the glass were of superb quality, and excellent value at €4.50 (hardly anyone ordered the rather pricey bottles). A delicious white Burgundy went down well with an attractively presented first course of translucent Italian ham with rocket, diced

red peppers and thickly sliced parmesan, followed by a whole grilled sole served with three meltingly buttery boiled potatoes: utterly plain, but utterly right. Our neighbours' osso bucco with chunky, homespun sautéed potatoes and shredded spinach looked mightily appetising, as did the day's desserts – huge glazed strawberry halves on a crisp pastry base or brick-sized slabs of millefeuille with creamy filling – but there were none left once we were done grappling with the crustacean claws. We had to make do with an unsuccessful chocolate fondant (dry and impenetrable on the outside, the consistency of a well-known choc 'n' hazelnut spread within) and a deeply unextraordinary rum baba. This is an atmospheric, unpretentious but pricey address: starters average around €11, mains €16 and grilled lobster €24, so book (and eat) early to get your money's worth.

Le Gavroche

19 rue St-Marc, 2nd (01.42.96.89.70). M° Bourse or Richelieu-Drouot. **Open** 7am-3am Mon-Sat. Closed Aug. **Average** €30. **Lunch menu** €13. **Credit** MC, V. **Wheelchair access. Map** H4.

We've always been besotted with the joie de vivre of a place that happily serves up trencherman portions of wine, meat and frites – especially since this is one of the last corners of Paris where the frites come with the golden edges and irregular shapes that thrillingly indicate they were only recently hand-carved from a bona fide spud – which is why we're going to be a tad cranky about our most recent meal here. A jolly table of six from all compass points, we happily noshed through fatty, peppery terrine de campagne, marinated fresh anchovies, and heart-of-palm salad with wonderful fresh baguette, while quickly scarfing down a first bottle of Juliénas (this place is known for its Beaujolais). Then the main courses arrived, along with a suspicion that something had changed. Steaks were stone cold, a veal cutlet was leathery and steak tartare had an almost soapy lather. Too timid to inquire in front of the gendarme and his mistress at the adjacent table, we waited until they'd moved on to their nocturnal pleasures to ask about the kitchen: change of owners. But not change of kitchen staff, so apparently it was just a rummy night on the nerves behind the kitchen door. Or so we hope, especially since it was an unwelcome surprise to find that the Juliénas was ticketed at €22.50, in a place that's always been proud of pouring it on.

Le Mesturet

77 rue de Richelieu, 2nd (01.42.97.40.68). M° Bourse. **Open** noon-3pm, 7-10.15pm Mon-Fri. **Average** €25. **Prix fixe** €19, €25. **Credit** AmEx, DC, MC, V. **Wheelchair access. Map** H4.

Alain Fontaine, former co-owner of La Baracane and L'Oulette, has created an exemplary bistro in this old café space not far from the old Paris Stock Exchange and the former Bibliothèque Nationale. If the tile floors and wooden chairs are standard issue, cloth napkins, paper tablemats with groovy graphics, low lighting and flea market-find decorative objects instantly make the point that this is a real bistro serving freshly prepared food. Here, for very modest prices, you'll find cooking that sincerely seeks to highlight the best of French produce, with Fontaine taking particular pride in his ingredients he obtains from small producers in his native south-west. The menu is cleverly accented by a blackboard selection of dishes that change daily, making it even easier to become a regular at this thoroughly likeable place. Starters of free-range chicken terrine with vegetable chutney and an aubergine and cheese terrine with salad were excellent, as were mains of blanquette de veau and sea bream with vegetables. It's obvious there is a pro in the kitchen, in this case a young chef who previously worked at L'Oulette. Finish up with a creamy, runny rocamadour or maybe a fruit crumble. From an outstanding wine list, the Marcillac was a treat at €15.

3RD ARRONDISSEMENT

L'Ami Louis

32 rue du Vertbois, 3rd (01.48.87.77.48). M° Arts et Métiers. **Open** 12.15-2pm, 7.30-11pm Wed-Sun. Closed mid-July. **Average** €120. **Credit** AmEx, DC, MC, V. **Non-smoking room. Map** K4.

A strange place, this bistro that time forgot, where wealthy clients – bankers, artists and intellectuals, according to the owner, but mostly tourists on the basis of our visit – tuck into expensive dishes such as poulet-frites or côte de boeuf. Bill Clinton may have squeezed down the narrow staircase to use the gents, and the carefully preserved pre-war interior, resplendent with stovepipe and red gingham curtains, could have been the inspiration for 'Allo 'Allo, but the food is pricey for the quality. A large plate (enough for two) of decent, if too thickly cut ham from the Ardennes and a côte de boeuf (again for two) – nicely grilled on the outside, but grey, stringy and flavourless on the inside – notched up a whopping €117. Of course, there are some redeeming factors. The service is professional, unobtrusive and genuinely warm (perhaps with the exception of the proprietor, who seemed to be having an off day), and although the wine list features plenty of grand bottles at grand prices, producers are well chosen – we drank a juicy St-Joseph 2000 from Bernard Gripa at €52. If our experience is anything to go by, the food is unexceptional and you need an expense account.

Camille

24 rue des Francs-Bourgeois, 3rd (01.42.72.20.50). M° St-Paul. **Open** 8am-1am daily. Closed Christmas and New Year. **Average** €35. **Lunch menu** €18. **Credit** AmEx, DC, MC, V. **Wheelchair access. Non-smoking room. Map** L6.

Jazz faded into the background as Camille filled up with the right mix of real people and thankfully few of the Marais main drag fashionistas. The food at

Camille was just as welcome: expert classics executed with flair and delivered by aproned waiters who ruled the dining room with prompt efficiency (even stopping to check that we were enjoying our starters). Indeed, we were pleased with a buttery pumpkin velouté made with a magical stock, plus a melt-in-your-mouth warm herring salad with potatoes and carrots. Contentment continued with a cod fillet, olive oil and mash plate that looked and smelled almost too good to eat, and creamy lentils with a perfectly pink ham slice so tender it shredded under the fork. Desserts are mostly old-fashioned tarts; we bit into a mousse-like chocolate variation with a shortbread crust. The menu shifts from winter mode to summer, with a few plats du jour thrown in for good measure; otherwise, no flairs. Come to Camille for consistency and simple, fresh, flavourful dishes.

Chez Janou

2 rue Roger-Verlomme, 3rd (01.42.72.28.41).
M° Chemin Vert. **Open** noon-3pm, 8pm-midnight Mon-Fri; noon-4pm, 8pm-midnight Sat, Sun. **Average** €30. **Lunch menu** €13 (Mon-Fri). **No credit cards. Map** L6.

It's hard to be negative about a restaurant that's as popular as this long-running bistro with a winsome Provençal menu (there's even a potted olive tree by the door), a fabulous decor of 1,900 tiles and flea-market finds, and one of the edgiest crowds in Paris. So what's not to like? Well, the food. Not because it's bad, but because it's just OK. The other reality of a meal here is that, as attractive and friendly as the staff may be, their clear intention is to turn tables as quickly as possible, which might explain a recent meal that passed like gunfire after a long wait at the bar for a booked table. Spinach, tomato and chèvre salad was all right, while there was nary a trace of rosemary on the rosemary-roasted chèvre, which turned out to be a tiny disc of cheese in a casserole filled with the same chopped tomatoes sautéed in olive oil with herbes de Provence that turn up all over this menu. Our neighbour agreed that les petits farcis – that superb Niçois dish of baked, stuffed vegetables – were awful. They were so overcooked that the meat filling was like an obstinate golf ball. Pot au feu was a huge letdown, too – a small bowl of dried-out potatoes, meat and carrots with a big bone but no marrow. The Beaume de Venise red was fine and fairly priced, so we skipped dessert, preferring instead to soak up the fun atmosphere.

Georget (Robert et Louise)

64 rue Vieille-du-Temple, 3rd (01.42.78.55.89).
M° St-Paul. **Open** noon-2pm, 7.30-10pm Mon-Fri; 7.30-10pm Sat. Closed Aug. **Average** €31. **No credit cards. Map** L6.

The name game is complicated here: the family is called Georget, but the restaurant is also known as Robert et Louise. This anachronism is only the beginning of the charm offensive. As you enter the long, old-fashioned room, with its dusty artwork and distressed ceramics, your eye is immediately drawn to the blazing wood fire over which hunks of meat are being grilled. The scene could come from a Victor Hugo novel, a country bistro from a couple of centuries back in the heart of the trendy Marais. An elderly matriarch encourages an obese poodle to come to her side. Desolately peeling a carrot, she is helped by a group of relaxed young waiters and cooks. The starters, which included a tasty herring on some warm potatoes, are just an excuse for the main event, a Desperate Dan-sized portion of côte de boeuf, a woody crust cutting into perfectly rare beef, accompanied by some classic pommes de terre sautées and a freshly dressed salad. Other choices include various omelettes for the less carnivorous. Puddings, including a reasonable chocolate Charlotte, are as ordinary as the grill is exceptional. As we drained a light, scented bottle of Chiroubles, we noticed that as the flames were dying down in the hearth, cast-iron cauldrons were being placed on the embers; a beef stew as a plat du jour for that very evening. This is where Madame's carrot had been destined and we were tempted to watch over the pot with her until suppertime.

Le Hangar

12 impasse Berthaud, 3rd (01.42.74.55.44).
M° Rambuteau. **Open** noon-3pm, 6.30pm-midnight Tue-Sat. Closed Aug. **Average** €30. **No credit cards. Wheelchair access. Map** K5.

Unless you are visiting the doll museum, you are unlikely to find yourself in the impasse Berthaud, but it is worth making the effort to check out Le Hangar, a bistro near the Pompidou Centre with a pleasant traffic-free terrace and excellent cooking. The exposed stone walls and smartly set tables are immediately welcoming, and on a Friday lunchtime the light, long room was comfortably full with locals and a table of slightly baffled Americans. A bowl of tapenade and toast accompanied us as we chose from the fairly comprehensive carte. We picked some tasty and grease-free rillettes de lapereau (rabbit) alongside a perfectly balanced pumpkin and chestnut soup. Our main courses included a well-seasoned steak tartare, served with a crisp salad and some pommes dauphines, and a superb ris de veau on a bed of melting chicory. We were tempted by the puddings, particularly the chocolate soufflé and warm white wine tart with cinnamon, but resisted not through lack of appetite, but because the bistro refuses credit cards, and we were busy doing mental arithmetic. Fortunately a nice plate of complimentary home-made petits fours satisfied our sweet tooth. The charming owner pointed out that there is a cash machine nearby and they take cheques, but tourists rarely travel nowadays with a wad of notes. Not that the Hangar is expensive – the pichet of red wine was reasonable and perfectly drinkable, and our bill of around €70 was fair enough – but we are sure that even the strong local following would appreciate the ease of plastic.

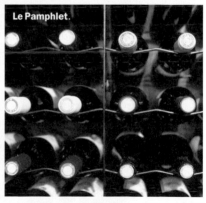

Le Pamphlet.

Le Pamphlet ★

38 rue Debelleyme, 3rd (01.42.72.39.24). M° Filles du Calvaire. **Open** 7.30-11pm Mon, Sat; noon-2.30pm, 7.30-11pm Tue-Fri. Closed 7-22 Aug. **Average** €30. **Prix fixe** €30, €45. **Credit** MC, V. **Non-smoking room**. **Map** L5.

Discreet chef Alain Carrère and larger-than-life front of house act Fred are clearly a successful team in this comfortable Marais restaurant, with its massive beams (apparently fake) and well-spaced tables that evoke an upmarket establishment in the provinces more than a boisterous Parisian bistro. Indeed, the refined offerings on the three-course €30 menu could easily pass muster in much grander establishments, changing every day to reflect market produce and accompanied by inventive appetisers: a creamy parsnip velouté and a remarkable combination of whole oysters in a light foie gras-infused sauce on a bed of finely chopped leeks. Our dishes beautifully reflected the season too: a starter of scallops with girolle mushrooms, potent red partridge in a wine sauce, and fillet of sea bass in a light foie gras sauce on a dense pumpkin purée. The menu has plenty to suit all tastes, including some south-western dishes from Carrère's Béarn, but he is particularly good with fish, which is delivered twice a week direct from St-Malo. We finished with an upside-down apple and quince tart with short, crisp pastry, while finishing off our Languedoc red, one of several potential discoveries on a short but interesting list.

Le Petit Marché

9 rue de Béarn, 3rd (01.42.72.06.67). M° Chemin Vert. **Open** noon-3pm, 7.30pm-midnight Mon-Fri; noon-4pm, 7.30pm-midnight Sat, Sun. **Average** €30. **Lunch menu** €13. **Credit** MC, V. **Wheelchair access. Map** L6.

Just a step away from the place des Vosges, the Petit Marché has become a hip Marais bistro, attracting a fashion-conscious, alternative local crowd. The woody interior is warm and welcoming, but on our last visit for Sunday lunch, we opted for a place on the heated terrace with an unprepossessing view of the gendarmerie opposite. The menu is short and modern with Asian touches. Raw tuna was flash-fried in sesame seeds and served with a Thai sauce, making an original, refreshing starter, while some crispy-coated deep-fried king prawns had a similar oriental lightness. The main course vegetarian risotto was rich in basil, coriander, cream and al dente green beans, which contrasted winningly with the unctuous rice. Pan-fried scallops with lime were accurately cooked to avoid any hint of rubberiness, and accompanied by a good purée and more beans. Desserts are more traditional, leading off with rice pudding, crumble and orange mousse. From the short wine list we chose a carafe of the house red (€9), which was unusually good. Service throughout was exceptionally friendly, and what with the long opening hours, fair prices and easygoing nature of the place, an ongoing success looks assured.

Les Petits Marseillais

72 rue Vieille-du-Temple, 3rd (01.42.78.91.59). M° Rambuteau. **Open** noon-2.30pm, 7.30pm-midnight daily. **Average** €33. **Lunch menu** €14. **Credit** AmEx, DC, MC, V. **Map** L6.

Arrive at this Marais hotspot after 9pm and you're guaranteed time on the horse: a funky old gymnastics prop that seats latecomers at the gleaming copper bar. But acrobats be warned, when you get to your table even elbow room is scarce. On a pulsing Friday night we were convivially sandwiched between two Anglophone parties, mixed gay and straight like the neighbourhood. The remarkably genial staff impressed us with their linguistic agility. Not only did they try to translate the entire menu into English for one table; they were unphased when another spelled out its choice of a tongue-twister wine letter by letter. And indeed the B.R.O.U.I.L.L.Y (a tangy Beaujolais red) is a good bet. Foodwise, though, we were less impressed, especially given the prices. A starter of lightly crisped calamari zapped with lemon, garlic and parsley was faultless. But mains lacked oomph. We both opted for fish and, as befits the kitchen of two long-time Marseille pals, the rare tuna (just a minute a side) and red mullet fillets were fresh and expertly prepared. Less successful were the accompanying sides: a dry, tasteless mash; a black olive 'jam' that lacked intensity; and a bland cup of tomato sauce (for dipping the tuna). The desserts were likewise uninspiring; we left our slice of over-rich chocolate-orange marquise unfinished. The draw here is undoubtedly location and the resolutely hip ambience; from overheard conversations we gathered that most diners were contented regulars.

Le Réconfort

37 rue de Poitou, 3rd (01.49.96.09.60). M° St-Sébastien Froissart. **Open** noon-2.30pm, 8-11pm Mon-Fri; 8-10.30pm Sat; noon-3pm (brunch), 8-10.30pm Sun. Closed one week in Aug. **Average** €30. **Lunch menu** €13, €17. **Credit** MC, V. **Wheelchair access. Non-smoking room. Map** L5.

Votive candles, menus glued into kitschy novels, plenty of red velvet – Le Réconfort may be a 'boutique' restaurant, but the at-home ambience is

wildly successful with quality food and decent prices to match (though the clubby groove music is a tad too in-your-face). Chef Guilhem livens up French standards without taking too many risks, as in starters of marinated mushrooms stuffed with chèvre alongside a beetroot and rocket salad, or the sardine and sesame seed rillettes served with artichokes. Both the chicken breast with lemon-cream sauce and parmesan polenta, and the breaded monkfish with sun-dried tomato 'red pesto' and olive-laced mashed potatoes tasted comfortingly familiar, but innovated just enough to be fresh. Indian touches appear throughout: a little cumin here, a sari-clad waitress there. Desserts included ginger ice-cream and a whipped-up pistachio tiramisu. Bucking the bistro trend of overcharging for alcohol, Le Réconfort's list of very reasonably priced wines, including several at €3 a glass, was a welcome relief.

Taxi Jaune

13 rue Chapon, 3rd (01.42.76.00.40). M° Arts et Métiers. **Open** noon-2.30pm, 8-10.30pm Mon-Fri (bar open 9am-1am). Closed last week in July and first week in Aug. **Average** €28. **Lunch menu** €13. **Credit** MC, V. **Map** K5.

In a corner of the Marais dominated by wholesale handbag-sellers, this delightfully grungy bistro allowed us to put aside all thoughts of glamour, thanks to its collection of taxi-related bric-a-brac and photographs set off against an attractive yellow-and-green colour scheme. The present owner explained to us that he had inherited the unusual name of this snug 1930s bistro, which is dominated by a comfortingly old-fashioned bar. On a steamy September lunchtime the little room was buzzing with a crowd of regulars who all seemed on teasing terms with the charming owner and his caring staff. Lunchtimes offer a bargain two-course deal for €13, and we tucked into a decent chicken liver terrine and a crunchy salad of green beans and mushrooms

topped with some cured ham. The main-course seafood lasagne was tasty and attractively presented, while puddings of carpaccio de mangues and a tarte aux mirabelles looked tempting. The carafe of house wine, a light Cahors, made an acceptable accompaniment to a meal which made us seriously consider flagging down a yellow taxi more often to explore the reasonably priced carte and the blackboard full of interesting wines.

4TH ARRONDISSEMENT

Baracane

38 rue des Tournelles, 4th (01.42.71.43.33/ www.l-oulette.com). M° Chemin Vert, St-Paul or Bastille. **Open** noon-2.30pm, 7pm-midnight Mon-Fri; 7pm-midnight Sat. **Average** €30. **Prix fixe** €22-€37. **Lunch menu** €10, €15. **Credit** MC, V. **Map** L6.

Baracane – the unassuming sister of the much grander L'Oulette (*see p107*) near Bercy – is a tiny neighbourhood bistro on the plain side of atmospheric, situated at the similarly plain and un-atmospheric top end of the rue des Tournelles, parallel to the place des Vosges. The reasonably priced menu assiduously avoids classic bistro standards, with sometimes highly acceptable results and the occasional howler. Blackboard specials on a quiet August lunchtime kicked off with a rich and satisfying cauliflower soup, while the pan-fried duckling breast was smothered in cream sauce and served with nothing but a small helping of dry couscous. A fine, crisp damson tart saved the day, and all for under €20. The à la carte 'menu du marché' offers any starter, main course and dessert for €27. Chilled watermelon soup with goat's-cheese-and-mint croutons sounded tempting, but was unpleasantly lumpy and served at room temperature (late August room temperature, that is), accompanied by soggy deep-fried filo parcels featuring not a lot of mint. Happily, the fish was a

Mon Vieil Ami.
See p35.

treat: a generous portion of firm, flavoursome rascasse (scorpion fish) with a crispy crust, green olive pesto sauce and melting scoops of potato, rough-mashed with lashings of butter and onions. A dessert of ice-cream with honey and rosemary was attractively drizzled with strongly flavoured, deep amber rosemary honey. Alas, the meal as a whole was marred on this occasion by the visibly impatient, short-tempered service. The wine list has a reputation for off-beat selections from the south-west, but we had clearly rolled in far too late (at 1.30pm) to be allowed to look through it at leisure, and plumped for house carafes (red and white, both excellent) instead. Baracane's laudable mission to serve innovative French food at rock-bottom prices might benefit from the occasional prod on the part of L'Oulette's noted chef, Marcel Baudis.

Benoît

20 rue St-Martin, 4th (01.42.72.25.76). M° Châtelet or Hôtel-de-Ville. **Open** noon-2pm, 8-10pm daily. Closed public holidays. **Average** €90. **Lunch menu** €38. **Credit** AmEx. **Map** J6.

Granted, the victory of getting a good table in a restaurant with a seating caste system is paltry and petty, but this didn't stop us from feeling a sense of satisfaction when we were whisked into the back of this monument to French bistro cooking and culture and seated in the intimate corral created by wood-panelling and etched glass panels. We ordered an aperitif and the young waiter returned with a bottle of lovely white Mâcon, opened it, served us, and left it in a wine cooler. Throughout the meal he was pure charm, particularly when dealing with a Swede who insisted on smoking a stinking stogie, but also in his careful explanation of the entire menu. Dense, rich, coarse terrine laced with chicken livers and served with celeriac rémoulade was superb, as was a delicate, almost-mousse-like mushroom terrine generously topped with fresh morels. Main courses of monkfish in red wine and veal shank à la provençale – a casserole of tender meat in a light and perfectly seasoned tomato sauce with rice – were excellent. Since portions are so generous, few opt for cheese, but when we ordered a nougat glacé to split, the waiter served big portions on two plates, a classy gesture. Benoît has a massive wine list with all sorts of gorgeous bottles, but the house-bottled wines are affordable, with a decent Fleurie going for €30. All told, it's great fun – especially when someone else is picking up the bill, which is a real stinker.

Le Dôme du Marais ★

53 bis rue des Francs-Bourgeois, 4th (01.42.74.54.17). M° Rambuteau. **Open** noon-2.30pm, 7.30-11pm Tue-Sat. Closed three weeks in Aug. **Average** €40. **Prix fixe** €29. **Lunch menu** €17, €23. **Credit** AmEx, MC, V. **Non-smoking room. Map** K6.

Lying somewhere between casual and formal, bistro and haute, Le Dôme du Marais seems perfectly at ease with its identity. The staff wouldn't turn a hair if you showed up in jeans, but should you feel the urge to mark the occasion with finery, the octagonal, domed dining room would provide a stunning backdrop. The building predates the French Revolution and once served as the auction room for state-owned pawnbrokers; today it has been done up (but thankfully not overdone) in burgundy and gilt, with tables dressed in sparkling white linen. Owner-chef Pierre Lecoutre loves to work with seasonal produce, and our early summer meal was a perfect example. Not wanting too heavy a meal, we shared a gratinée of mussels to start, which for €9 was a substantial dish of shelled moules de bouchot in a lightly curried cream sauce. One of us stuck with the fishy theme by ordering the filet de courbine – available for three weeks a year during the season of this white fish – in a cream sauce flavoured with spicy chorizo sausage, and fresh little broad beans that also have a brief season. Saddle of lamb with crushed coffee beans proved an unlikely success, the lamb rosy and meltingly soft, the coffee adding a distinctive but not overwhelming note. Froissé praliné chocolat and strawberry dacquoise lived up to their stunning good looks with flavour to match. At about €100 for two with a half-bottle of Champagne, this meal felt like great value.

Ma Bourgogne

19 pl des Vosges, 4th (01.42.78.44.64). M° St-Paul or Bastille. **Open** noon-1am daily. Closed Feb. **Average** €33. **Prix fixe** €32. **No credit cards. Non-smoking room. Map** L6.

On an early summer afternoon the terrace of Ma Bourgogne, under the arcades of place des Vosges, can hardly be bettered. The passing tourist trade dominates and our waiter was happy to provide a flourish of English to welcome us. We were less reassured when his mastery of the electronic ordering pad seemed rudimentary. Somehow the charm of ordering is lost when confronted with low muttering and much scrolling through the extensive menu. With such high-tech wizardry on display, it came as a body blow that the restaurant does not take credit cards. The food was acceptable if uninspiring; a plate of charcuterie was copious but lacked any star item, and the sarladaise salad was short on foie gras. The house speciality of steak tartare was well seasoned and excellent, but the accompanying frites squidged rather than crunched. Hot Lyonnais sausage would have been better without the rather insipid gravy. Hankering after a few more sips of our Brouilly (€22.50), we ordered cheese, which had to be chosen individually. The goat crottin was pleasant without being earth-moving, and much the same could be said for the bright pink Charlotte aux fruits rouges. Probably best to stick with a tartare and a bottle of wine and soak up the cosmopolitan atmosphere.

Mon Vieil Ami ★

69 rue St-Louis-en-l'Ile, 4th (01.40.46.01.35). M° Pont Marie. **Open** 8-10.15pm Tue; noon-2.15pm, 8-10.15pm Wed-Sun. **Average** €40. **Prix fixe** €38. **Lunch menu** €15. **Credit** AmEx, DC, MC, V. **Map** K7.

Antoine Westermann, chef of the acclaimed Buerehiesel in Strasbourg, is one of the most talented and modest chefs in France, which is why it was with high hopes that we set off for this handsome bistro on the Ile St-Louis, in which he's an investor and Antony Clémot, his former second, is chef. Happily the master's touch was apparent throughout a superb meal, and Clémot is a splendid chef in his own right. You don't have to work too hard on the Ile St-Louis to pull a crowd, as the many candle-lit places serving indifferent food prove, so it was a thrill to have such an excellent meal. A party of five, we were seated at the black-stained oak table d'hôtes in a sophisticated and relaxed space with oak floors, moss-green velvet curtains, ancient black-painted wooden beams overhead, exposed stone wall and frosted glass panels. On a wintery Sunday night, the menu offered a short but tempting assortment of things we yearned for. Starters of pâté en croûte – buttery pastry enclosing delicious terrine with a cap of beef aspic and a lobe of foie gras, a really sophisticated accomplishement – and mixed root vegetables in bouillon with foie gras were outstanding. Then a slow-braised shoulder of roebuck came with celery, quince, chestnuts and prunes, along with a pretty Alsatian faïence casserole, generously filled with white beans that had been stewed with garlic cloves, bay leaf and tomato and topped with tender squid. Both of these dishes were perfectly cooked and tremendously satisfying, as were roasted scallops with caramelised endives and a parsley coulis. Desserts continued the remarkable performance – sautéed apples with home-made vanilla ice-cream and pistachio cream, and a first-rate chocolate tart. Service was unfailingly attentive and friendly, and our only complaint is the pricey wine list with nothing less than €25. Still, with food this good this is one 'old friend' we're not letting out of our sight.

Le Vieux Bistro

14 rue du Cloître-Notre-Dame, 4th (01.43.54.18.95). Mº Cité or St-Michel. **Open** noon-2.30pm, 7.30-10.30pm daily. **Average** €35. **Prix fixe** €25. **Lunch menu** €27. **Credit** MC, V. **Map** J7.

With a corny name and a location just across the street from Notre-Dame, the odds would seem stacked against this long-running bistro serving even half-decent food. All of which makes it a great surprise to discover that the food here is often excellent, the dining room comfortable and well-run, and prices, given the quality, quite reasonable. Regulars quibble over which dining room is more desirable – the front one is more spacious, but the back room is cosy and its diners more likely to be French – but everyone agrees that the tiny terrace out front is a fine spot for a romantic meal in good weather, and also that the boeuf bourguignon is superb. Start with sliced pistachio-studded sausage and potatoes dressed in vinegar and oil or the sublime pâté de tête, chunks of head cheese in a dark amber-coloured beef aspic, and then sample the sole meunière, the bourguignon, a first-rate rib of beef for two, or maybe scallops sautéed in whisky. The house Bordeaux, a Château Layauga 1999 at a very reasonable €25, is excellent and goes down a treat with cheese, or choose from a short list of homely desserts including crème caramel.

5TH ARRONDISSEMENT

L'AOC ★

14 rue des Fossés-St-Bernard, 5th (01.43.54.22.52/ www.restoaoc.com). Mº Jussieu or Cardinal Lemoine. **Open** noon-2pm, 7.30-11pm Tue-Sat. **Average** €30. **Lunch menu** €10-€14. **Credit** AmEx, MC, V. **Wheelchair access. Non-smoking room. Map** K7.

Stepping in off the pavement on a wet night, we immediately met Jean-Philippe Latron and his charming wife Sophie, and the tone was set for the rest of the meal. Latron, overseeing a wonderful rôtisserie with a tumble of potatoes roasting at the bottom in the dripping, vaunted the roast pork with enthusiasm but no sense of obligation, and then Sophie slipped Nyons olives and sliced saucisson on to the table as nibbles while we perused the menu. The idea here is that everything is AOC, or Appellation d'Origine Contrôlée – a French certification for produce that meticulously respects the rules set down by a governmental body appointed to determine specifically authentic regional foodstuffs. And here it's not only a clever idea to serve up pedigreed produce but one that really works, since the food is simple, hearty and delicious. Marrow bones with Guérande sea salt were a treat, as was delicious terrine de foie gras de canard, and the pork roast and roast lamb were both tender, full of flavour and generously served. Further, this is a relaxed, happy dining room filled with a savvy clientele, making for a low-key atmosphere that is richly welcome in this age of soulless fashion restaurants. We finished up with a first-rate baba au rhum and a delightful crème brûlée redolent of AOC vanilla from Réunion. A nice wine list, comfortably spaced tables and low lighting contribute to a very pleasant – and informative – night out.

Le Buisson Ardent

25 rue Jussieu, 5th (01.43.54.93.02). Mº Jussieu. **Open** noon-2pm, 7.30-10.30pm Mon-Fri. Closed Aug, one week at Christmas. **Average** €30. **Prix fixe** €28. **Lunch menu** €15. **Credit** AmEx, DC, MC, V. **Map** K8.

This sepia-toned bistro, gathering place for Jussieu academics, has all the hallmarks of a traditional restaurant, from the 18th-century pastoral scenes painted on the walls to the sweetbreads with brown butter on the menu. Classic Gallic dishes, such as a meaty salad of quail, sausage, smoked duck breast and foie gras, are well executed here, but it is a more ambitious, modern sensibility that dominates the menu. Using French cuisine as its anchor, the kitchen successfully flirts with Mediterranean,

Le Petit Pontoise. See p38.

Asian and North African flavours. We enjoyed a delicate feta and leek ravioli with crayfish tails in a shellfish broth, as well as the pillowy polenta that accompanied tender lamb chops with a rosemary jus. Some over-zealous combinations, such as a duck breast roasted with tandoori spices and served over risotto, are less successful, but these seem more the exception than the rule. The restaurant even bakes its own yeasty bread, which reveals a lot about the effort it makes to please. The extensive wine list is laden with reasonably priced bottles, intelligently selected from all over France. Desserts continue to be a weak point here, though, lacking some of the finesse and attention paid to the rest of the menu. Still, this earnest bistro is a welcoming and rewarding stop after a walk in the neighbouring Jardin des Plantes.

Chez René

14 bd St-Germain, 5th (01.43.54.30.23).
M° Maubert-Mutualité. **Open** 12.15-2.15pm, 7.45-11pm Tue-Fri; 7.45-11pm Sat. **Average** €40. **Prix fixe** €30 (dinner only). **Lunch menu** €29. **Credit** MC, V. **Non-smoking room. Map** K7.
It's not for nothing that the woodwork at Chez René is Beaujolais wine-coloured, because wine impregnates everything here, from the kir aperitif to the legendary boeuf bourguignon and deep purple-dyed coq au vin. Opened in 1957 and still family-run, this is a picture-postcard bistro that exudes bonhomie and tradition – which the clientele, mainly portly, scholarly Latin Quarter types plus a few foreigners, lap up with gusto. We shared a plate of saucisson, then dug our forks into authentic, long-simmered coq au vin, and all our fingers into the massive bowl of garlicky frog's legs (a rarity nowadays) – wickedly scrumptious if a little greasy and a killer to any hopes of ever having a figure. Blackcurrant sorbet was a refreshing finale, as we finished up our Beaujolais Nouveau.

L'Equitable ★

1 rue des Fossés-St-Marcel, 5th (01.43.31.69.20).
M° Censier Daubenton or St-Marcel. **Open** noon-2.30pm, 7.30-10.30pm Tue-Sat. Closed three weeks in Aug. **Prix fixe** €28, €33, **Lunch menu** €20.50, €26. **Credit** MC, V. **Wheelchair access. Non-smoking room. Map** K9.
At Yves Mutin's bistro, first impressions are deceptive. With the stable-like entrance, auberge trimmings and starchy ambience, we braced ourselves for a stolid meal of country-style fare, but the setting belied an inventive cuisine making the €28 or €33 prix fixe menus stunning value for this part of town. The lower-priced option featured starters of crispy pig's trotters or duck terrine followed by mains of magret de canard and a knuckle of pork stew. From the more intricate, pricier menu, we chose a generous portion of marbled foie gras, guillotined by a wafer-thin slice of pain d'épice and deliciously set off with apple compote sprinkled with balsamic vinegar, as well as a superb dish of langoustines in a savoury lentil broth. The wide choice of mains included a tenderly cooked sea bass in a truly Gallic garlic and parsley sauce, and a winter dish of roasted calves' kidneys which was a little over-roasted, but well-matched with the salty pancetta and braised endives. To round off this feast, we enjoyed two impressive desserts of crème brûlée with pistachio and morello cherries, and a thick, caramelised chunk of pineapple in a rich rum sauce flambéed by the waiter.

Les Fontaines

9 rue Soufflot, 5th (01.43.26.42.80). RER Luxembourg. **Open** noon-3pm, 7-11pm Mon-Sat. Closed 1 May, 25 Dec, 1 Jan. **Average** €40. **Credit** DC, MC, V. **Map** J8.
Its heart-of-the-Latin-Quarter location is much of the charm of this long-running bistro – sitting at a pavement table you have the Panthéon to your right

Restaurant Wadja.
See p43.

quality cooking. Calves' brains were nicely done, though, and served with boiled potatoes, and sliced kidneys in cream sauce were cooked to a T and attractively presented in a small copper casserole. A veal escalope was ruined by a burnt coating of breadcrumbs and served with a tangle of cold spaghetti topped with melted cheese; steak tartare was oddly flavour- and texture-less; and red mullet was overcooked and served in a sauce with a choking amount of paprika. Desserts were disappointingly limited, including just vanilla ice-cream and pear sorbet, île flottante, crème caramel, and a small, pricey assortment of mixed berries. Better than average, but just barely. Recommended, however, for anyone who is keen on off-cuts and gizzards, since the menu brims with them.

Le Moulin à Vent

20 rue des Fossés-St-Bernard, 5th (01.43.54.99.37). Mº Jussieu. **Open** noon-2pm, 7.30-11pm Tue-Fri; 7.30-11pm Sat. Closed Aug, 24, 25 Dec. **Average** €50. **Lunch menu** €35. **Credit** MC, V. **Map** K8.
The amber-tinted walls here are the first sure sign that this long-running bistro decorated with polished copper pots and pans and sawn-off wine kegs will make good on the promise of a soul-satisfying bistro feed. And it does, from the moment you're settled on the sprung-bottom banquette before a snowy tablecloth and served bread by gentle, professional waiters, to the last sip of very good and fairly priced coffee (€1.75). If the place is packed with academics at noon, there's a decided whiff of vieille France here in the evening as well-heeled young couples who weekend at different compass points in la campagne meet friends for dinner and discuss the antiques in Figeac, the skiing in Méribel or the great new chef in St-Jean-de-Luz. Start with a big platter of garlicky frogs' legs that easily serves two, excellent saucisson de Lyon, escargots or a salad, and then head directly for some one of the best beef in Paris. Theirs is Salers from the Auvergne, and the chateaubriand, richly flavoured and wonderfully tender, is enough to make a carnivore coo. The regulars order it à l'échalote, with shallot sauce, but their béarnaise sauce is heavenly as well, as are the sautéed potatoes that come as a garnish, with butter-drenched haricots verts or champignons à la Provençale worth adding for a supplement. Desserts are not the strong suit of this menu – our baba au rhum had a curiously dry texture – so the best bet is probably to order some cheese to finish off your Beaujolais. The sublime Chiroubles is a better choice than the tannic house Bordeaux favoured by the aristos.

Le Petit Pontoise

9 rue de Pontoise, 5th (01.43.29.25.20). Mº Maubert-Mutualité. **Open** noon-2.30pm, 7.30-10.30pm daily. **Average** €40. **Credit** AmEx, DC, MC, V. **Wheelchair access. Map** K7.
This intimate neighbourhood bistro has become a firm favourite and even on Monday lunchtime we only just squeezed in. The menu of bistro dishes

and, in the evening, the light show of the Eiffel Tower to your left. Curiously, the locals – a mix of professorial and fashion types, plus a large number of trust-fund students – prefer the smoky interior dining room with its 1970s motorway restaurant decor. Though this isn't a place where you'll throw your head back in pleasure, huge portions, friendly service and decent wines (pleasant Bergerac for €18.30) compensate somewhat for the uneven cooking. The fact is that the food here has been better in the past. During a recent dinner, a table of six gave the kitchen a good workout and came away well-fed but underwhelmed. Marinated herring and sardine escabèche were just fine, as was the signature salad of chicory with a big dollop of mayonnaise and a slab of blue cheese, but as is the kitchen's wont, lavish servings stand in for better follows the fashionable tendency of mixing in a few modern elements to give the classics contemporary twists. A Thai-style assiette de pétoncles (small scallops) was a heap of shellfish mixed with lime, beansprouts and coriander, while a seasonal risotto de bolets et cèpes was rich and full of autumn warmth. By comparison our main courses were slightly disappointing: rognons de veau (veal kidneys) and joues de porc aux épices (spiced pig's cheeks) both had incorporated into the sauce the same mangetouts, carrots and new potatoes, giving the dishes an unwanted twin look. The kidney was pink but the sauce tasted universal, while the pork was tasty and melting but seemed over-caramelised. A crème brûlée was fine but the rather pretentiously named Amadeus turned out to be a decent version of our old friend moelleux au chocolat. Service was charming, the Provençal rosé well chosen, and the bill for under €85 seemed reasonable enough. Providing that not too many short cuts creep into the cooking this will remain a useful address.

Phyto Bar

47 bd St-Germain, 5th (01.44.07.36.99). M° Maubert-Mutualité. **Open** 11am-11pm Mon-Sat; 11am-7pm Sun. **Average** €25. **Lunch menu** €14.50, €15.50. **Credit** MC, V. **No smoking. Map** K7.

Next door to La Nature à Paris, a health food shop selling organic products and dietary supplements, the Phyto Bar is one of a small handful of organic restaurants in Paris. Somewhere between a bar and a café, it has a pleasant atmosphere and helpful, accommodating staff. Many of the healthy-looking intellectuals were sipping one of the organic juices such as carrot and ginger, or one of the health-giving infusions. We were, however, out for lunch, choosing as starters a rather uninteresting vegetable terrine, but an excellent soupe de potimarron (a chestnutty squash), which for once did not rely on cream or spices for its taste. The main courses included an assiette découverte and, as a concession to meat-eaters, an organic bavette. The assiette was attractively presented with a delicious seaweed tartare and well-flavoured rillettes de légumes, the centrepiece being an omelette with various seeds and grains, but despite a good texture it was judged too medicinal-tasting. As punishment for our carnivorous greed, the bio bavette was tough and lifeless, but accompanied by good baby vegetables and a slice of compact potato gratin, its real drawback being its excessive price of over €14. Puddings were excellent, a golden tarte Tatin with crème fraîche and a chocolate cake with a cinnamon-flavoured crème anglaise. The Bordeaux Clairet was a good choice from the list, but organic Left Bank living seems to come at a high price.

Le Pré Verre

8 rue Thénard, 5th (01.43.54.59.47). M° Maubert-Mutualité. **Open** 7.30-10.30pm Mon; noon-2pm, 7.30-10.30pm Tue-Sat. Closed first two weeks in Aug. **Prix fixe** €25 (dinner only). **Lunch menu** €13. **Credit** MC, V. **Non-smoking room. Map** J7.

Philippe Delacourcelle knows how to handle spices like few other French chefs, having lived in Asia for long enough to come to grips with ingredients such as cassia bark and tamarind. He also trained with the late Bernard Loiseau and learned the art of French pastry at Fauchon. Marinated salmon with ginger and poppyseed was probably the most conventional starter on the €25 menu, but remarkable for the quality of the salmon. In the potato and foie gras pressé, layers of potato looked exactly like layers of fat, which made this terrine sprinkled with coarse salt quite surprising to eat. For the main course, everyone was tempted by the salt cod with cassia bark and smoked potato purée. What this lacked in size it made up for in crunchy texture and rich, cinnamon-like flavour, and the super-smooth potato cooked in a smoker made a startling accompaniment. The meat options were satisfying too: duck fillet with tangy tamarind and slow-cooked fennel, and melting lamb knuckle with a vegetable compote flavoured with coriander seeds. Spices have a way of making desserts seem esoteric rather than decadent, but all of ours were a success – even the roasted figs with olives won us over. The purple-grey walls are lined with framed jazz album covers which echo the music, and on a post-rentrée weeknight the main floor and cellar were packed (try to eat on the main floor, with its view on to the street). Choose an unusual wine from a small producer – we had a Rasteau for €25 from Corinne Couturier in the Côtes du Rhône – and enjoy the buzz.

Le Reminet ★

3 rue des Grands-Degrés, 5th (01.44.07.04.24). M° Maubert-Mutualité or St-Michel. **Open** noon-2pm, 7.30-11pm Mon, Thur-Sun. Closed two weeks in Aug, two weeks in Feb. **Average** €34. **Prix fixe** €17 (Mon, Thur dinner only), €50. **Lunch menu** €13 (Mon, Thur, Fri). **Credit** MC, V. **Map** J7.

The Reminet has always been one of our favourite Left Bank bistros, helped by the fact that it has had the bright idea of opening on weekends and closing for a couple of days midweek. The bargain €13 lunch menu is only available on weekdays, and our Sunday lunch seemed more expensive than on previous occasions, but Hugues Gournay's cooking remains accurate and delicious. We began with some crisp fried filo parcels of black pudding, while our Italian guest unnervingly ordered nationalistic ravioli. Fortunately these passed with flying colours: whole gambas in light pliable dough, bathing in coconut milk. Main courses were equally fine: a perfectly timed fillet of beef with a shallot purée, and some tender scallops on firm, well-sauced tagliatelle. As it was Sunday we were tempted by the puddings, which included light coffee quenelles and Earl Grey mille-feuilles with mint sauce, which might sound like an English culinary joke but was in fact irresistible. Service in this intimate eight-table restaurant was charming and our bottle of €29 red Gigondas bore up well, but the promoted wine of the month at over €50 seemed a dangerous trap.

La Rôtisserie de Beaujolais

19 quai de la Tournelle, 5th (01.43.54.17.47).
Mº Jussieu. **Open** noon-2.15pm, 7.30-10.15pm
Tue-Sun. Closed four days at Christmas.
Average €35. **Credit** MC, V. **Wheelchair**
access. **Map** K7.

Little sibling to La Tour d'Argent (*see p78*) across
the street, La Rôtisserie de Beaujolais is another
ballgame altogether, but an entertaining one.
Wooden tables covered with red-checked cloths set
the unpretentious tone, and the menu of solid bistro
classics attracts a clientele that has lived through at
least one World War, sometimes two. A group of
five, we happily ate our way through the autumn
menu, which was peppered with game dishes.
Scrambled eggs with truffle lacked the punch one
might hope for, but made up for it with a nice,
creamy texture, while the compôte de lapereau, a
rillette-like spread, was generous enough to share.
The rest of the poor bunny presumably went into
one of the seasonal picks, lapereau with lemon,
whole garlic cloves and spoon-soft polenta – a
successful southern-influenced dish. Crisp-skinned
roasted pigeon came on a slightly soggy bed of
paillasson potatoes, but by now the Beaujolais for
which this bistro is named was working its magic
and we were willing to overlook small flaws.
Desserts are wonderfully classic, including a coffee-
flavoured parfait glacé and, for the devil in anyone,
the alcoholic cherry and chocolate concoction
dubbed 'le petit diable'.

La Table de Michel ★

13 quai de la Tournelle, 5th (01.44.07.17.57).
Mº Maubert-Mutualité or Cardinal Lemoine. **Open**
7-11pm Mon; noon-2.30pm, 7-10.30pm Tue-Sat.
Closed Aug. **Average** €45. **Prix fixe** €27. **Lunch**
menu €19. **Credit** AmEx, MC, V. **Non-smoking**
room. **Map** K7.

While the name might scream trad French, the food
politely informs Italian-French: buffalo mozzarella
and tomato salad as well as escargots, all prepared
with care and flair. The fixed price menu is
interesting enough (poached eggs in white truffle
cream with parmesan or a stand-out spaghetti with
squid ink, garlic and prawns in a deep-fried crêpe
basket) but the daily specials offer some real, albeit
more expensive gems: a starter of tiny pan-fried ratte
potatoes topped with copious slices of black truffle
and served with marinated artichokes, or a perfectly
cooked risotto with some chubby prawns. For a
tasty finale, try the brie stuffed with roquefort and
walnuts or a square of majestic tiramisu. The
genuinely friendly, efficient service so often missing
in action in busy Paris bistros is another reason to
race in here.

6TH ARRONDISSEMENT

Allard

41 rue St-André-des-Arts, 6th (01.43.26.48.23).
Mº Odéon or St-Michel. **Open** noon-2pm,
7-11.30pm Mon-Sat. Closed three weeks in Aug.

Average €50. **Prix fixe** €32. **Lunch menu**
€24. **Credit** AmEx, DC, MC, V. **Non-smoking**
room. **Map** H7.

If St-Germain seems to be turning into a suburb of
Milan with the proliferation of Italian restaurants,
it's reassuring to come across a truly excellent
example of a traditional bistro. With its vanilla-
coloured walls and a coat rack in the narrow hall
connecting the two small dining rooms (the front one
has more atmosphere), Allard has a delicious pre-
war feel, a first impression that is confirmed by the
kitchen itself (though not the rather steep prices). It
sends out glorious Gallic grub that's exactly what
everyone dreams of finding in Paris. Winter is the
perfect time of year for this place – start with sliced
Lyonnais sausage studded with pistachios and
served with potato salad in delicious vinaigrette, or
maybe a sauté of wild mushrooms, and then choose
between one of the three classics: roast shoulder of
lamb, roast Bresse chicken with sautéed ceps or
roast duck with olives. All three are superb, but be
forewarned that portions are truly enormous. If you
have any space left, finish up with the tarte fine de
pommes and go with one of the good, if slightly
pricey Bordeaux.

Au Bon Saint-Pourçain

10 bis rue Servandoni, 6th (01.43.54.93.63). *Mº St-*
Sulpice or Mabillon. **Open** noon-2pm, 7.30-10.30pm
Mon-Sat. Closed Aug. **Average** €35. **No credit**
cards. **Map** H7.

This corner bistro just behind St-Sulpice is
atmospheric and almost claustrophobically intimate.
The patron has a reputation for being a character
whom customers either love or fear. On our last
lunchtime visit the boss was absent and a charming
young waitress was in charge of the boat, but one
thing is sure: you are going to overhear your
neighbours in the tiny room which feels more like
the kitchen of a farm lost in the middle of the French
countryside than an urban bistro. Our fellow guests
included a couple of supremely elegant French
ladies-who-lunch discussing the properties of
various face creams and a funky home counties
family of English tourists. Our meal of comforting
old-fashioned bistro cuisine began with a generous
fromage de tête with a perky caper relish and a
compote de lapereau, a little cold but accompanied
by a well-dressed salad with walnuts. For our main
courses we chose a gorgeously gelatinous tête de
veau, sauce gribiche, and a well-cooked quality
entrecôte with a pot of potent marchand de vin
sauce. The steak was accompanied by a dried-up
gratin dauphinois, which was disappointing, but the
waitress sweetly replaced it with a pile of French
beans. Homely puddings complete a reassuringly
traditional meal, but don't order the horrid reheated
filter coffee – better to stick with the drinkable but
rough St-Pourçain red wine. Despite a reasonable
bill, remember that this is a technology-free zone: no
credit cards are accepted and the cash machine is
not next door.

French Cuisine

Bouillon Racine

3 rue Racine, 6th (01.44.32.15.60). M° Cluny-La Sorbonne. **Open** noon-2.30pm, 7-11pm daily. **Average** €35. **Prix fixe** €26. **Lunch menu** €15.50 (Mon-Fri). **Credit** AmEx, MC, V. **Wheelchair access. Map** J7.

Embellished with pale green iron columns and floral tiles, this art nouveau Latin Quarter bistro has been under new management since 2003. The result? A new chef at the helm, anachronistic (but moody) jazz music and a rejuvenated menu. Apparently word is getting out: on a Wednesday night, dining rooms on both levels were clogged and the plat du jour was already depleted by 8pm. The gruff maître d' seemed unprepared for the massive rush, but our frazzled waitress grinned and bore it, despite numerous Americans demanding extra attention. Remarkably, our first courses arrived without delay. The raw tuna marinated in coconut milk was an inventive take on a sashimi standard, while the glace d'étrilles surprised us: we expected chilled crab meat with a subtle fennel cream, but not set in a block of aspic, so be prepared. Mains were less of a shock: roast cochon de lait with potatoes and gravy, well-prepared but a gristly cut; and a sea bream fillet atop seaweed-flavoured risotto and tomato reduction sauce. The meal ended on a high note: a moist slab of baked apples and spice bread called pressé de pommes and a runny chocolate cake both fulfilled our half-baked dessert fantasies. An extensive selection of Belgian beers on tap remains, while wines are pricey. First and third Tuesdays of the month are jazz nights.

Les Bouquinistes

53 quai des Grands-Augustins, 6th (01.43.25.45.94/ www.lesbouquinistes.com). M° St-Michel. **Open** noon-2.30pm, 7-11pm Mon-Thur; noon-2.30pm, 7-11.30pm Fri; 7-11.30pm Sat. **Average** €50. **Lunch menu** €26-€50. **Credit** AmEx, DC, MC, V. **Map** J6.

This sleek modern outlet of the Guy Savoy group has an unbeatable position on the banks of the Seine, and very quickly the restaurant was packed with a tourist-led crowd eager to enjoy this bistro take on haute cuisine. We were disappointed not to be automatically presented with the 'retour du marché' lunch menu. After we plucked up courage and asked for it, the menu was politely brought to the table, but by then we had been left too long with the carte, and the limited €26 menu looked decidedly less appealing. It's strange how many top chefs come 'back from the market' with a rather uninteresting selection of ingredients for their lunch menus. Here the menu's tourte de pommes de terre (potato pie) seemed no match for the hare and foie gras tourte on the carte, which had caught our eye and was a comforting autumnal treat. A dish of huîtres tièdes (warm oysters) with fennel was frothed in the modern manner and served with some seaweed bread. Initially this seemed an exquisite dish, but it failed to sustain interest to the last spoonful. Our main courses were both up to standard with a

perfectly cooked thick slice of pan-fried foie gras accompanied by a sweet apple and celery compote, and a main course-sized portion of one of the starters, some musky wild mushrooms with light gnocchi. We dodged the good-looking puddings in favour of an economic 'café et l'addition'. The golden white Quincy was well-chosen as at all Guy Savoy restaurants, but the service cuts corners on numbers, and obtaining the bill in a full restaurant took too long, even with a Seine view.

Brasserie Fernand

13 rue Guisarde, 6th (01.43.54.61.47). M° Mabillon. **Open** noon-2.30pm, 7pm-midnight Mon-Sat. Closed three weeks in Aug, one week at Christmas. **Average** €30. **Credit** MC, V. **Map** H7.

Dan Brown enthusiasts can check out this cosy neighbourhood bistro near marché St-Germain and St-Sulpice (whose floor marker indicating the solstices and equinoxes is a clue in Brown's latterday Grail quest). The lack of midwinter sun in the long, narrow, windowless interior of Brasserie Fernand was no problem in early December, but may prove off-putting around the aforementioned equinoxes. The atmosphere is civilised, efficient but unfrenetic, with a well-heeled crowd of forty- to fifty-something regulars (all greeted by name) tucking into a mix of à la carte staples and specials based on thoughtfully deployed seasonal ingredients. First up was a salad of rocket, parmesan and mushrooms (a change from the other heavily wintry starters: black pudding and apple tart, beaufort cheese and artichoke gratin, pumpkin soup, etc). Generously proportioned but oddly bland, it demanded more

Chez L'Ami Jean.
See p46.

Savy. See p48.

carefully sourced ingredients. The massive, succulent entrecôtes with hunks of marrow bone were clearly popular, but a daily special of pigeon with kumquats and mushroom polenta sounded more adventurous, and lived up to its promise: tender pink-roasted meat, crisp skin and creamy polenta were perfectly offset by a well-textured bittersweet sauce (although the polenta required a tastier alternative to the ubiquitous champignons de Paris). Desserts (no less than 15) were rich and warming (moelleux de chocolat, tarte Tatin, banana gratin) with a few lighter, but less imaginative options (fromage banc with fruit coulis, sorbet). The mi-cuit au chocolat was less 'death by chocolate' than 'instant transportation to chocoholic paradise' via a ramekin containing a perfectly baked confection somewhere between soufflé, creamy mousse and meltingly warm fondant. This chocolate-lover had found her Holy Grail.

Aux Charpentiers

10 rue Mabillon, 6th (01.43.26.30.05). Mº Mabillon or St-Germain-des-Prés. **Open** noon-3pm, 7-11.30pm daily. Closed 25 Dec, 1 May. **Average** €32. **Prix fixe** €26 (dinner only). **Lunch menu** €19. **Credit** AmEx, DC, MC, V. **Map H7.**

It was 25 years since we had last eaten at Aux Charpentiers, when it was a cheap and cheerful student haunt overlooking the marché St-Germain. Now, with unchanged vintage decor, it has become a serious Parisian bistro, where simple hearty dishes are prepared with unusual care and served by a friendly team, which knows how to welcome tourists and regulars alike. We began our meal with a salad of crisply fried sweetbreads and a compote de lapereau – a highly seasoned rabbit terrine with an earthenware jar of crunchy gherkins on the side. We chose the plat du jour of stuffed cabbage (the ultimate comfort food) and a more elaborate duck with olives and port, which was well cooked but with just a touch of tourist blandness. Resisting the great-looking rum babas, we plumped for a slice of well-aged brie.

Looking around at the splendid zinc bar and happy St-Germain crowd, we vowed not to wait another 25 years before returning here, particularly as even à la carte prices remain surprisingly competitive.

Chez Marcel

7 rue Stanislas, 6th (01.45.48.29.94). Mº Notre-Dame-des-Champs. **Open** noon-2pm, 7-10pm Mon-Fri. Closed Aug. **Average** €35. **Lunch menu** €16. **Credit** MC, V. **Map G8.**

This tiny, turn-of-the-20th-century gem serves food in its own image – strong on tradition, taste and off-beat charm, savoured on our visit by an unhurried, regular lunchtime crowd. We half-expected a shot of absinthe to accompany the pungent old-style staples – pig's ear in jelly, beef brawn terrine and the rather fearsome house speciality, gras double (Lyonnais-style stewed tripe). Sounds offal? The fainthearted will appreciate artichoke leaves with vinaigrette, tarragon chicken fricassée or steaks 'n' sauce. A terrine of salt pork and lentils was sweetly seasoned with fresh dill and basil in creamy lemon dressing. Pink slices of duck magret were magically crisp on the outside, meltingly tender within, on a superb bitter orange sauce. Fish dishes are equally robust, including skate in roquefort sauce with tagliatelle-style courgettes. 'Seasonal cheese' (a generous slab of gorgonzola) and a frequently replenished basket of white and walnut bread were welcome touches. Torn between melt-in-the-mouth cherry or apple tarts (the latter with crumbly almond topping), we were served both, unprompted. The full-bodied wine of the week, a 2000 Moulin à Vent, held its own in such flavoursome company.

L'Epi Dupin

11 rue Dupin, 6th (01.42.22.64.56). Mº Sèvres-Babylone. **Open** 7-10.30pm Mon; noon-2.30pm, 7-10.30pm Tue-Fri. Closed Aug, one week in Feb. **Prix fixe** €31 (dinner only). **Lunch menu** €22. **Credit** MC, V. **Map G8.**

François Pasteau, owner-chef of this tiny spot in the much-monied 6th, has a mile-high reputation that,

French Cuisine

judging from the crowd waiting outside for a drizzly Monday night's packed second service, has gone global. His cooking is innovative with an emphasis on arresting flavours (like the coriander caramel sauce that swathed our remarkably sweet starter, an endive and goat's cheese Tatin, or the bold blend of sea bream and boudin noir that made a surprisingly light main) and eye-catching presentation. The sea bream came modishly layered in a pastry-less mille-feuille, while desserts such as the chocolate-orange cannelloni decorated with delicate balls of grapefruit sorbet looked almost too good to eat. Top-quality, fresh ingredients (plump duck breasts, melting beef cheeks, crisp salads) are, of course, de rigueur and the pots of rough sea salt and crusty home-made bread, punningly shaped like a wheat sheaf (épi de pain), simply confirm that Pasteau is happily, for the few who can squeeze into the cramped dining room, a man with a food mission. We had only one complaint: the waiters are obviously pressed and, in turn, insistently pressing; for all of its culinary excellence, this is resolutely not the spot for either quiet or relaxed dining. Booking is obligatory.

Josephine 'Chez Dumonet'

117 rue du Cherche-Midi, 6th (01.45.48.52.40).
M° Duroc. **Open** 12.30-2.30pm, 7.30-10.30pm Mon-Fri. **Average** €45. **Credit** AmEx, MC, V. **Map** F8.
This bastion of classic bistro cooking, where the use of luxury ingredients brings a splash of glamour, is guaranteed to please the faithful, well-heeled local clientele. The room with its nicotine-coloured walls and massive cast iron radiators looks comfortingly old-fashioned, while the formal staff reinforce the impression of serious Parisian eating. The good news is that all dishes are available as half portions, opening up the possibility of exploring some classy numbers without your credit card melting in the machine. As this was the truffle season, we were tempted by a salad of lamb's lettuce, warm potatoes and truffle shavings in its €31 half-portion version. This was a sexy dish, with the musky perfume of black truffles gloriously present. After a slab of excellent home-made terrine, we decided to try the often-abused tournedos Rossini. Here the fresh truffles and slice of foie gras on a tender fillet might have found favour with the great musician, whose incitement to an impatient chef to 'tournez le dos' if he did not want advice gave a name to this star dish. Delicious sautéed potatoes, rich in goose fat and a touch of garlic, accompanied both this and a top-quality andouillette. After finishing our bottle of Côtes du Rhône, we resisted the sumptuous-looking puddings and settled for some excellent petits fours, coffee and a pear digestif, served from an impressive bottle that had an eye-catching position on the traditional bar.

Le Mâchon d'Henri

8 rue Guisarde, 6th (01.43.29.08.70). M° Mabillon.
Open noon-2.30pm, 7-11.30pm daily. **Average** €24.
Credit MC, V. **Map** H7.

This bistro in the heart of St-Germain immediately put us in a good mood – firstly it was open for Sunday lunch, an increasingly rare phenomenon, and secondly we were given a plate of outstanding saucisson sec while we looked at the menu and enjoyed a chilled bottle of fruity Julienas (€20). In an area where tourist tat wins out over gastronomic excellence, this tiny bistro provides a reasonably priced selection of traditional rustic dishes. We began with a ramekin of escargots, doused in garlic butter and served with potatoes, and a Desperate Dan-style plate of marrow bones, accompanied by wholemeal toast and coarse salt. Main courses were equally authentic, with a generous, well-seasoned bowl of Caen-style tripe, and a superbly cooked magret de canard, served whole rather than fanned out on the plate in the modern fashion. The gratin dauphinois was wholesome rather than inspiring, but by then we were already on good terms with the charming waiter and the couple opposite, something which is inevitable in such intimate surroundings. Rather than attack a homely pudding we plumped for a serious vieille prune digestif, which was rightly recommended by a fellow diner.

Le Parc aux Cerfs

50 rue Vavin, 6th (01.43.54.87.83). M° Vavin or Notre-Dame-des-Champs. **Open** noon-2pm, 7.45-10.45pm daily. Closed Aug. **Prix fixe** €35 (dinner only). **Lunch menu** €29. **Credit** MC, V. **Non-smoking room.** **Map** G8.
Aside from a lamentable policy of linguistic segregation – lumping all the Anglophones into the bar area up front – this stylish Montparnasse bistro is a delight for its worldly crowd and excellent modern bistro cooking. In a neighbourhood that's known round the world for hackneyed myths of la vie de Bohème past, this place surprises by actually serving up a lot of atmosphere with just enough of that odd but appealing edge that's created by a lot of creative types gathered in one place. So, billeted up front with friends from Chester and Goult, we were a happy sixsome who ate our way through the menu with tremendous pleasure on a surprisingly busy weekday night. Starters of smoked salmon and chèvre terrine, tomme cheese and black cherry relish on salad, and foie gras were excellent, and a fricassée of free-range chicken with coriander and olives, a daily special, was the star of the main courses. Salers steak in port sauce came with a wonderful round pile of creamy potato gratin, and sea bream in a light sauce of preserved lemon and white wine was accompanied by couscous. Desserts such as apple crumble with salted caramel ice-cream were splendid, and it was a nice surprise to find such a lavish wine listt. Note that there's a charming interior courtyard for summer dining too.

Restaurant Wadja

10 rue de la Grande-Chaumière, 6th (01.46.33.02.02).
M° Vavin. **Open** 7.30-11pm Mon; noon-2.30pm, 7.30-11pm Tue-Sat. **Average** €35. **Prix fixe** €13.57.
Credit MC, V. **Map** G9.

Despite its Polish name, Wadja is the epitome of the French neighbourhood bistro. On our last lunchtime visit the place was not so much humming as vibrating to the animated chatter of the regulars. Gentle banter from the patronne and a charming if overstretched waiter add to the fun of the old-fashioned room, decorated with some unusually attractive artwork. The cooking follows the modern trend for 'improved' classic bistro dishes. Starters included a cassolette d'escargots in a rich wine and shallot sauce or some home-smoked salmon over a fish tartare, both of which were first-rate. A gigot de sept heures, which is one of the place's signature dishes, lived up to its reputation, with spoon-tender meat and a rich, well-reduced sauce. The plat du jour of a crispy rissole of pied de porc was creamy, but a little cloying after a while, saved by a well-dressed accompanying salad. We resisted yet another moelleux au chocolat, but the tarte aux mirabelles looked tempting and home-made. With a bottle of fruity Chiroubles the bill was reasonable and the cooking justified the chattering crowd's enthusiasm.

Aux Saveurs de Claude

12 rue Stanislas, 6th (01.45.44.41.74/www.aux saveursdeclaude.fr). M° Vavin. **Open** noon-2.30pm, 7.15-11.30pm Mon-Sat. Closed three weeks in Aug, ten days at Christmas and one week at Easter. **Average** €30. **Lunch menu** €15, €20. **Credit** AmEx, MC, V. **Non-smoking room. Map** G8.
Run by a charming and talented young couple who sincerely want you to have a good meal (and you will), this sweet mini-bistro in Montparnasse is worth wending your way to the neighbourhood for. With parquet floors, soft lighting, vanilla-painted wainscoting and mirrors, the intimate room is a relaxing and pleasant place to dine. Recent starters on the blackboard have included a fine fricassée of ceps and other wild mushrooms, and ravioles de Royans (tiny ravioli stuffed with cheese) with yellow chanterelles. Typical main courses are the entrecôte with bordelaise sauce and puréed potato, veal kidneys sautéed with wild mushrooms and chestnuts, and salmon with an unusual 'gâteau' of rice mixed with fromage blanc. As part of the attentive care you will receive here, staff also let you in on the dish, dessert or even coffee 'du moment'. Desserts include a first-rate tarte Tatin or an equally delicious chocolate tart. Book ahead.

Au 35

35 rue Jacob, 6th (01.42.60.23.24). M° St-Germain-des-Prés. **Open** noon-2.30pm, 7pm-midnight daily. **Average** €35. **Lunch menu** €18, €22 (Mon-Fri). **Credit** AmEx, MC, V. **Map** H6.
Despite a largely successful attempt to turn every bookshop in what was the heart of literary Paris into a clothing boutique for the impossibly rich, the publishers have survived, tucked away in their cobbled courtyards. This is one of the places they lunch, and a healthy hubbub of genteel conversation is usual. It's cosy without being pokey or cramped and on a cold winter's day there are few snugger

places to be than on the red banquettes of Au 35. We enjoyed a simple, traditional and carefully prepared meal whose high point was the snails. They were neither rank nor covered in garlicky, green slime (the usual snail traps), but were buttery and light on the stomach. The pot au feu was good too, though we would have liked to see more adventurous cattle parts (tail for example) in among the shin of beef. Our 50cl of Brouilly was OK but a bit expensive at €14 and the puddings, though there was nothing really wrong with them, took a walk on the dull side. All in all, though, Au 35 is a good choice for lunch on the Left Bank.

Le Timbre

3 rue Ste-Beuve, 6th (01.45.49.10.40). M° Vavin. **Open** noon-2pm, 7.30-11pm Mon-Fri; 7.30-11pm Sat. Closed three weeks in Aug. **Average** €30. **Lunch menu** €20. **Credit** MC, V. **Map** G8.
Chris Wright's restaurant, including the open kitchen, might be the size of the average student garret, but this native of Manchester aims high. His menu of three to four starters, main courses and desserts changes every week, and his suppliers include La Poissonerie du Dôme, one of the finest fish stands in Paris, and Le Comptoir Corrézien, which provides truffles and foie gras to the city's top chefs. Taking the cue from our neighbours, we chose the tartines de légumes – strips of lightly cooked courgette and carrot on toasts spread with tapenade (which could have been a bit more flavourful). Just as spring-like was a plate of green asparagus, elegantly cut in half lengthwise and served with dabs of anise-spiked sauce and balsamic vinegar, and a little crumbled parmesan cheese. Like these starters, main courses were pure in presentation and flavour – a thick slab of pork, pan-fried but not the least bit dry, came with petals of red onion that retained a light crunch, while juicy guinea fowl was served on a bed of tomato and pineapple 'chutney'. We continued with the outstanding mille-feuille du Timbre – a delicate square of puff pastry and vanilla cream assembled at the last minute. The ruby-red strawberry soup, served in a wide, shallow bowl, looked just as tempting. Should you opt for cheese, you will have a choice between 'le vrai' (British cheddar) or 'le faux' (goat's cheese from the Ardèche).

7TH ARRONDISSEMENT

L'Affriolé

17 rue Malar, 7th (01.44.18.31.33). M° La Tour-Maubourg or Invalides. **Open** noon-2.30pm, 7-10.30pm Mon-Fri. Closed Aug. **Prix fixe** €32 (dinner only). **Lunch menu** €23. **Credit** MC, V. **Map** D6.
While we lapped up Thierry Verola's light, modern, all-round delicious food, we left Affriolé feeling that a second visit was unlikely. The service – indifferent and at times downright disagreeable – left a bad taste in our mouths. Yes, the country bread is delicious, the complementary pork-olive tapenade a

Velly. *See p52.*

nice touch. Likewise the teeny pots of chocolate, vanilla and coffee cream, whole walnuts and chocolate-crusted marshmallows following dessert. But they were all dropped without a word or a flourish. Starters of caramelised chicken wings, and dark mushroom soup with a froth of white Tarbais beans were excellent, and we couldn't fault the rosy-centred duck in pastry on a bed of lentils or the tuna steak coated in tapenade and cooked perfectly pink. Dessert was right on track, too: coffee jelly, divinely rich praline and chocolate mousse layered in a glass, and a dainty apple turnover anointed with cream. If only the staff mirrored the polish and performance evident on the plates.

Altitude 95

1st level, Tour Eiffel, Champ de Mars, 7th (01.45.55.20.04, www.altitude-95eleor.com). M° Bir Hakeim. **Open** noon-2.30pm, 7-9.30pm daily. **Average** €50. **Lunch menu** €21, €28 (Mon-Sat). **Prix fixe** €50 (dinner and Sun lunch). **Credit** AmEx, DC, MC, V. **Wheelchair access. Map** C6.

There is a certain thrill in eating on the first floor of the Eiffel Tower, especially if one manages to exercise enough charm to gain a window seat. Mimicking the Jules Verne theme captured by the haute-cuisine establishment one floor up, Altitude 95 is supposed to resemble an airship, although with its quantity of nuts and bolts, and its rather sombre aspect, the decor is closer to *20,000 Leagues Under the Sea.* On the whole, the cuisine is not as uplifting as the view. The à la carte option is pricey and unadventurous; the two-course lunch menu is better value but offers very limited choice. The rabbit terrine starter interlaced with figs was enjoyable, despite the disconcerting jelly base covering the entire plate. The main course of pike-perch with Swiss chard was satisfying if a little bland, while the seared tuna was served on an unappetising purple bed of mashed kidney beans. Despite the rather average food, this is a novel lunch location, and a handy method for bypassing the tourists queuing to ascend the metallic monster the orthodox way.

Chez Michel. *See p52.*

Au Bon Accueil

14 rue Monttessuy, 7th (01.47.05.46.11). M° Alma-Marceau. **Open** noon-2.30pm, 7.30-10.30pm Mon-Fri. **Average** €45. **Prix fixe** €31 (dinner only). **Lunch menu** €27. **Credit** AmEx, MC, V. **Map** D6.

Ever since Jacques Lacipière opened this bistro in 1990 it has been one of the good deals of the 7th arrondissement, and local residents' loyalty is still well-merited. The pleasantly redone dining room, with big windows, well-designed lighting and a stone satyr beaming down from a pilaster, provides the setting for excellent updating of French classics. We started with a chaud-froid combination of raw marinated sardines sandwiched between tiny, new spring leeks and a frazzle of deep-fried onion and chervil, and a tomato stuffed with petits gris snails, which was tasty though the tomato was neither quite cooked nor quite raw. To follow, rosé veal kidneys were attractively presented pyramid-style on a bed of fresh spinach, while a rich braised beef cheek in deep red wine sauce, cleverly offset by the tart flavours of stewed rhubarb, showed how Lacipière injects tradition with a few surprising touches. A well-ripened assortment of cheeses from Marie-Anne Cantin, and a chewy macaroon with raspberries and vanilla ice-cream completed the €27 lunch menu, as we finished off an excellent 1998 Graves chosen from the good-value suggestions at the front of the wine list. A relaxed atmosphere and courteous, conscientious staff make this an address to cherish only a few metres from the Eiffel Tower.

Le Café Constant

139 rue St-Dominique, 7th (01.47.53.73.34). M° Ecole Militaire or RER Pont de l'Alma. **Open** noon-2.30pm, 7-10.30pm Tue-Sat. **Average** €27. **Credit** DC, MC, V. **Map** D6.

Curiously, it's at this winsomely simple and very brightly lit neighbourhood café that we've again discovered why we were once so impressed by chef Christian Constant, who worked at the exalted Crillon before setting up shop at Le Violon d'Ingres (*see p105*). Try as we might, we've always found Constant's Violon squeaky, while this café purrs with good times, good food and good value, as an appealingly diverse crowd of locals and Constant fans have quickly sussed out. The blackboard menu changes constantly, with starters costing €7, mains €11 and desserts €6, but it offers a good range of dishes that allow you to design a satisfying meal. If you're very hungry, start with the peppery pâté de campagne or maybe the oeufs en gelée au saumon (salmon-wrapped poached eggs in gelatin with salad), and follow with the steak, grilled steak tartare or calf's liver, all of which come with a generous choice of side dishes, such as pommes dauphinoises or green beans. Finish up with the peach melba, a real treat made with fresh peach. For a lighter feed, begin with the green bean salad or maybe the salade niçoise, and follow with pasta au pistou or salmon tartare. All of the food served here is spectacularly fresh and flavourful, portions are more than fair and the wine list is a true gift, with a lovely Cahors going for a mere €14. No booking, but if you come early or late, there's rarely a wait.

Chez L'Ami Jean

27 rue Malar, 7th (01.47.05.86.89). M° Invalides. **Open** noon-2pm, 7pm-midnight Tue-Sat. Closed Aug. **Average** €35. **Prix fixe** €28. **Credit** MC, V. **Map** D6.

Stéphane Jego was second-in-command to Yves Camdeborde at La Régalade (*see p64*) before taking over the long-established L'Ami Jean. In the tradition of young bistro chefs, Jego has barely touched the tavern-like decor – lots of dark wood, a dim light show – of this 'auberge'. He has also kept several classic Basque dishes on the menu, such as axoa, pronounced 'achoha' (a veal sauté with Espelette pepper), and piquillo peppers filled with brandade de morue (salt cod paste). But the menu isn't entirely predictable – we tried barely cooked scallops served in their shells and topped with sharp ewe's milk cheese, a surprising combination that worked, followed by red mullet cooked in olive oil and served with a North African-inspired couscous salad. Less virtuous was the duck confit and potatoes cooked in goose fat (not quite as fluffy and crisp as we had imagined). Lemon cream was something between a mousse and a milkshake, refreshing and frothy; while a winter fruit salad with cranberries failed to thrill either of us. That's the joy of market-inspired bistro cooking, though – chefs feel free to experiment, and some creations work better than others.

La Cigale Récamier

4 bis rue Récamier, 7th (01.45.48.87.87). M° Sèvres-Babylone. **Open** noon-2.30pm, 7.30-10.30pm Mon-Sat. **Average** €42. **Credit** MC, V. **Non-smoking room.** **Map** G7.

If you remember Le Récamier for its hearty Burgundian dishes, it will come as a shock to find that under the new owners it now specialises in soufflés – and egg yolk-less ones at that. No longer the haunt of jolly literati and politicos, it now provides fluffy sustenance to shoppers from the nearby Bon Marché and ladies-who-lunch. Visiting on a sunny spring day, we were delighted to sit on what must be one of the most pleasant terraces in Paris, thanks to its pedestrian cobblestone setting with a little garden hidden at the end of the impasse. Though it is possible to order something other than a soufflé, that seemed pointless here, so we chose a couple of the more unusual ones – tomato-mozzarella, and the day's special of melon with cured ham. We don't know what the chef's secret is: not only were they towering in height, but they kept their shape remarkably. Unfortunately, though, the first tasted bland and the second both artificial and sickeningly sweet. Things looked up with the chocolate version for dessert, but then it's hard to go wrong with chocolate. Come for the terrace, perhaps, but keep your culinary expectations in check.

Le Clos des Gourmets

16 av Rapp, 7th (01.45.51.75.61). M° Alma-Marceau or RER Pont de L'Alma. **Open** 12.15-2pm, 7.15-10.30pm Tue-Sat. **Average** €33. **Prix fixe** €33 (dinner only). **Lunch menu** €25, €29. **Credit** MC, V. **Map** D5.

As its name suggests, this small, elegant address three minutes from the Eiffel Tower takes its food very seriously. Pompous it's not, however. Arnaud and Christel Pitrois offer a genuinely warm welcome, happy to explain the ins and outs of a menu that's always inventive and, at €29 for a three-course lunch, excellent value. Roast mackerel, fresh market salad tossed in walnut oil, a lentil 'cappuccino', and hare terrine all sounded appetising as starters, but we opted for a superb cream of sweet chestnut soup, served with tiny chicken gnocchi and croûtons. Main courses lived up to the same

standard. Roast sea bass came on a bed of puréed potatoes and black truffles, set off by a delicate wild rocket sauce. Spring chicken came topped with pine nuts, mushrooms and crunchy roast potatoes, served in a rich jus. We deliberated long and hard over the mandarin soufflé, poached fennel and warm chocolate tart, before eventually opting for a sublime – and highly unusual – avocado mille-feuille in a tangy orange sauce. A couple of glasses of Sancerre from a good list rounded things off nicely. Be sure to book in advance.

La Fontaine de Mars

129 rue St-Dominique, 7th (01.47.05.46.44). M° Ecole-Militaire or RER Pont de l'Alma. **Open** noon-3pm, 7.30-11pm daily. **Average** €45. **Lunch menu** €23 (Mon-Sat). **Credit** AmEx, DC, MC, V. **Non-smoking room.** **Map** D6.

This place is so popular that people were already standing outside the door before it opened when we came for an early weekday dinner. And indeed with its red and white napkins, banquettes and tiled floor, the Fontaine de Mars speaks quintessential bistro. Yet there's something ersatz about it all. Too clean? Too air-conditioned? Too professional? Or just too easily mastered for an American clientele. A translated menu is available and waiters speak passable English, which clearly reassured the group of Americans of a certain age and their two accompanying priests who were sitting behind us. But don't let this put you off – the cooking is reliable if not wildly exciting, ranging from south-western stalwarts like duck confit to more modern fish dishes. Our pâté de cèpes with a small lamb's lettuce salad was tasty though rather more egg than cep, while oeuf en meurette was a little overpowering. A plat du jour of veal in a creamy sauce with beans, young peas and carrots was good bourgeois home cooking, while desserts speak tradition in îles flottantes and fruit tarts. Amuse yourself with the humorous prints on the walls and ads for old-fashioned aperitifs, including a poster for something called Fred Zizi (which goes down well with French schoolkids but was probably lost on the tourists).

Nabuchodonosor

6 av Bosquet, 7th (01.45.56.97.26/www. nabuchodonosor.net). M° Alma Marceau. **Open** noon-2.45pm, 7.30-11pm Mon-Fri; 7.30-11pm Sat. Closed 1-15 Aug. **Average** €35. **Prix fixe** €30 (dinner only). **Lunch menu** €20. **Credit** MC, V. **Wheelchair access.** **Map** D6.

Jovial boss Eric Rousseau was turning punters away at lunchtime at this chic bistro named after a 15-litre bottle of Champagne, and we were happy to have made a reservation. The lunch menu, which apparently does not include puddings, shows the chef's light, modish take on traditional bistro cooking, but one senses the real pleasure of the boss is his excellent collection of wines and Havana cigars. Our white Rully, which he recommended, was quite outstanding. Starters included an attractively presented shredded chicken salad, but the spongy and lifeless accras de morue came with an insufficiently punchy sauce. Main courses equally promised slightly more than they delivered: some delicate breaded medallions of pork with parmesan were mostly overcooked, but the fried ravioles made an interesting and moreish accompaniment. The gigot was a thick slice of quality lamb accompanied by garlicky green beans, but ordered pink it arrived as red as a Clapham omnibus. Puddings were a pizzeria-style tiramisu but also a sophisticated and refreshing cold nectarine soup. We noticed that many of the happy businessmen were tucking into the à la carte côte de boeuf which looked impressive, and despite some gastronomic imprecision on this occasion, the enthusiasm and good nature of the place leave an undeniably positive impression.

Le Petit Troquet

28 rue de l'Exposition, 7th (01.47.05.80.39). *M° Ecole-Militaire.* **Open** 7-10.30pm Mon, Sat; noon-2pm, 7-10.30pm Tue-Fri. Closed three weeks in Aug & one week in Jan. **Average** €32. **Prix fixe** €29 (dinner only). **Lunch menu** €19. **Credit** MC, V. **Non-smoking room. Map** D6.

A gentle whiff of old Paris survives in this street as the buildings, while handsome, have none of the grandeur of those found along the showy avenues in this pricey part of town. And this makes it a perfect setting for this almost-too-perfect bistro. Arriving, you step through heavy curtains into a small room where the walls are covered with enamelled advertising plaques the owners have found in flea markets all over France. The winsome ads recall a simpler time, and the kitchen tries to do the same with simple, nutritious home cooking that pleases the clientele of pennywise locals and guidebook-clutching North Americans. The two tribes might make for an odd mix if it weren't for the charming, bilingual attentions of the chef's wife, whose trilling voice and easy courtesy count for almost as much as what you find in your plate. The food is pretty good, though not really the bargain it once may have been. The basic idea is to fill you up with good bread and a rich starter – maybe carrot soup with bacon and croûtons, foie gras or a pleasant salad garnished with fried slices of Morteau sausage and bacon – so that the relatively modest portions of main courses aren't objectionable. And they're not. Venison medallions in a cranberry sauce, and beef fillet both came with mash and mixed veg, and both were likeable enough if not memorable. Puddings, on the other hand, were excellent, including a pear crumble with salted caramel ice-cream and a moelleux au chocolat. A sweet little place if you find yourself in the neighbourhood.

Thoumieux

79 rue St-Dominique, 7th (01.47.05.49.75/www. thoumieux.com). M° Invalides or La Tour-Maubourg. **Open** noon-2.30pm, 7-11pm Mon-Sat; noon-11pm Sun. **Average** €40. **Prix fixe** €33 (dinner only). **Lunch menu** €20 (Mon-Sat). **Credit** AmEx, MC, V. **Non-smoking room. Map** E6.

Thoumieux sprawls along the rue St-Dominique, undisturbed since 1923. Run by the same family since it opened, this big, popular bistro groans with tradition, from its stern, black-jacketed waiters to its red velvet banquettes. The menu presents every bistro standard you can think of: sole meunière, tripes, foie de veau, côte de boeuf, pied de porc and coq au vin are all correctly made with high-quality products. Don't be surprised, however, if the crust on your onion soup is a bit blackened. Even so, you won't feel compelled to complain to your weary waiter when he comes to collect your plate, as this detail seems unimportant. Move on, instead, to well-cooked beef from the Limousin region, or take on the enormous cassoulet, loaded with confit duck and the famed white beans from Tarbes. We paired ours with an outstanding Cahors, Prieuré de Cenac 2001, one of the less expensive choices on a pricey list. Indeed, prices have crept up here over the last several years, but it is nonetheless a pleasure to sit back and watch this juggernaut roll on.

Le Voltaire

27 quai Voltaire, 7th (01.42 .61.17.49). M° Rue du Bac. **Open** 12.30-2.30pm, 7.30-10.15pm Tue-Sat. Closed in Feb, May, Aug, Nov and one week at Christmas. **Average** €70. **Credit** MC, V. **Map** G6.

With its perfect riverside setting, the Voltaire might be just another tourist-led Parisian bistro, but past the velvet curtains, after maître d' Antoine has escorted you to one of the cosy tables, you realise that this is a genuinely chic spot whose regulars treat it like a private club – at lunch many of the ladies were greeted with a kiss on the hand. From a delicate nibble for an anorexic duchess to a serious feed to satisfy a ravenous rock star, Le Voltaire caters to everyone. Our guest kept us waiting, slightly too intimidated to enter after Jean-Paul Belmondo popped in for a spot of lunch. Full marks to the staff who took the presence of a screen legend in their stride, indulging his celebrity lap dog. A vast bowl of lamb's lettuce and beetroot salad was exemplary, while a golden feuilleté encased fresh and tangy goat's cheese. Lobster omelette was just the sort of luxury (€41) nursery food that Le Voltaire does so well; creamy and thick with firm morsels of shellfish. A tasty sauté de lapin was a real country treat and the plate of well-cooked fresh vegetables and crisp fries were exemplary. A bowl of intense chocolate mousse and a blackcurrant sorbet completed an expensive but exquisite lunch, accompanied by raspberry-scented, chilled Chinon (€29.50). Monsieur Belmondo seemed happy, too.

8TH ARRONDISSEMENT

Savy

23 rue Bayard, 8th (01.47.23.46.98). M° Franklin D Roosevelt. **Open** noon-2.30pm, 7.30-11pm Mon-Fri. Closed Aug. **Average** €40. **Prix fixe** €26.50 (dinner only). **Lunch menu** €19.50. **Credit** AmEx, MC, V. **Wheelchair access. Map** E4.

Le Bistrot Paul Bert. *See p54.*

Paris's answer to Simpson's on the Strand is a firm favourite with the media barons from neighbouring radio stations and newspaper groups. With its original art deco surroundings complete with pewter bar and mirrored booths reminiscent of the carriages in an old steam train, Savy is light years from the ultra-snob theme food emporiums of the Champs-Elysées. Famed for its thick-cut, juicy Aubrac de Laguiole rumpsteaks accompanied by home-made fries, the menu also offers the hearty, no-nonsense specialities of Aveyron including farçou, a formidable herb and vegetable dumpling-type affair with sausage and superb Cantal charcuterie. Wednesday brings home-made aligot: a groaning panful of melted laguiole cheese mixed with puréed potato and fresh cream. In fact, all the dishes are of the down-home-at-the-farm type, from the marinated herrings with oily potatoes, and slabs of foie gras and game terrine to platters of 'artisanal' charcuterie with huge dried Auvergne sausage, and raw ham cut off the bone. On a sleety, miserable autumn evening, we scuttled inside to enjoy the meat, under the reproachful gaze of the formidable wild boar head on the wall. The thick, juicy slice of rumpsteak with traditional béarnaise sauce didn't disappoint, neither did the extra tender fillet of beef complemented by a snappy pepper sauce. Fish eaters will appreciate the daily arrivals of fresh produce direct from Le Guilvinec. We savoured the last drops of our truffly, earthy cru bourgeois Château Puy la Rose with our cheese. We even managed to make room for a generous slice of rustic apple tart and an unctuous chocolate mousse.

Sébillon

66 rue Pierre-Charron, 8th (01.43.59.28.15/www. restaurantgerardjoulie.com). M° Franklin D Roosevelt. **Open** noon-3pm; 7pm-midnight daily.
Average €40. **Prix fixe** €34 (dinner only). **Lunch menu** €29.50. **Credit** AmEx, DC, MC, V. **Non-smoking room. Map** D4.

Perhaps the English hunting club decor with stained glass, faux bookshelves, leather and dark wood makes the dining room extra convivial. Perhaps because we dined on New Year's Day the waiters were particularly giddy, or perhaps they are that way all the time. All we know is they seemed to be having fun, posing for photos with one table, joking with another, sitting down for a spell with a third, and that spilled over to the entire room. And the food? Traditional fare, with a focus on seafood and all-you-can-eat Aveyron leg of lamb (sliced tableside). We went for a crab and tender leek Charlotte, fantastic with a slight vinegar flavour, and a surprisingly dense onion soup – more like a casserole but still dark and earthy, its soaked toast topped with crispy cheese. As for the lamb, it did not disappoint, nor did the ideal roasted half-chicken served with puréed potatoes. A half-carafe of red Mâcon washed it all down smashingly. With no room left for dessert after this meat-and-potatoes feast, we left rosy-cheeked and happy.

9TH ARRONDISSEMENT

L'Auberge du Clou

30 av Trudaine, 9th (01.48.78.22.48). M° Pigalle or Anvers. **Open** 7.30-10.30pm Mon; noon-2pm, 7.30-11.30pm Tue-Sat; noon-3pm, 7.30-10.30pm Sun.
Average €37. **Prix fixe** €18, €24. **Lunch menu** €15, €18.50. **Map** H2.

With its real log fire upstairs, beamed ceiling and sash windows, the Auberge du Clou resembles a comfortable private house and makes a lovely setting for a winter meal. The inventive cuisine injects a whirl of cosmopolitan ideas on to classic foundations, and while the two- or three-course weekly menu is superb value, it's à la carte where you'll find the most interesting dishes, including accomplished creations such as crunchy, warm oyster tempura with beansprouts; and sea bream sandwiched with daikin, wasabi and rocket, making a pretty study in green and white with flaky fish punctuated by bursts of spice. There are also more classic dishes, such as a delicious combination of artichokes and warm foie gras, and a generous serving of monkfish with girolles and a gratin of ratte potatoes. We finished with an original take on crème brûlée made with fromage blanc and passion fruit. The wine list is pleasantly global. We had a gently perfumed Argentinian white – or on Monday evenings (when upstairs is closed) you can bring your own.

Bistro de Gala

*45 rue du Fbg-Montmartre, 9th (01.40.22.90.50).
Mᵒ Le Peletier or Grands Boulevards.* **Open** noon-3pm, 7pm-midnight Mon-Fri; 7-11pm Sat. **Prix fixe** €26, €30 or €40. **Credit** AmEx, MC, V. **Map** J3.
Intrepid gourmets that we are, we fought off a first instinct to flee from this bistro, hemmed in on one side by a tourist-trap district full of crêpes and gyro and, on the other, by kosher bakeries full of sticky honey-filled desserts. But our wariness subsided as we eased our way through the meal, constantly surprised by the quality of the food and unobtrusive efficiency of the service. There's nothing radical about the fare, but the chef clearly aims to be true to each dish. The foie gras was cut in a thick slab, with a delicate but pleasing flavour. A tuna tartare was perhaps weakened by an overpowering vinaigrette, but an excellent langoustine risotto in lobster sauce more than compensated for it. The wines, though

L'Auberge le Quincy. *See p57.*

not sexy, are affordable and drinkable, including a lovely red Sancerre and others from the Loire valley. The only flashy things here are the smiles beaming down from film posters that decorate the walls – a holdover from the former owner, a film producer. The room, rimmed in velvet curtains and kindled in intimate light, is often filled with chatty foreigners excited by this bona fide find, a rarity in such a tourist-heavy area.

Casa Olympe

48 rue St-Georges, 9th (01.42.85.26.01). Mᵒ St-Georges. **Open** noon-2pm, 8-11pm Mon-Fri. Closed one week at Christmas, one week in May and three weeks in Aug. **Prix fixe** €37. **Credit** MC, V. **Map** H3.
Dominique Versini (otherwise known as Olympe) is one of the rare female chefs in Paris to have achieved a sort of celebrity status, thanks to the jet-set restaurant she once ran in the 15th arrondissement. In her current location, the mood is far more businesslike with Roman ochre-painted walls, a pretty Murano chandelier, rather horrid oil paintings and an almost entirely male, suit-wearing crowd at lunch. At first a little put off by the cramped seating arrangement in the tiny dining room, we mellowed out when the staff finally noticed us and brought a fillette (50cl) of Cahors. It was truffle season so, spotting a bowlful of the jet-black tubers, we ordered a potato salad laced with this earthy treasure (€1,600 a kilo) for a €15 supplement. The luxe continued with potimarron (squash) soup dressed up with chestnut and foie gras. A main course of veal sweetbreads was slightly disappointing, though, with the sweetbreads a little undercooked and the entire dish sprinkled with some unnecessary paprika (a dinner-party touch that cropped up in other dishes). Cocoa and fromage blanc sorbets were obviously home-made, though, and if it's a little expensive and formal for lunch, Casa Olympe would be a fine choice for dinner with someone you want to impress.

A la Cloche d'Or

3 rue Mansart, 9th (01.48.74.48.88). Mᵒ Blanche. **Open** noon-2pm, 7.30pm-1am Mon; noon-2pm, 7.30pm-1am Tue-Fri; 7.30pm-5am Sat. Closed Aug. **Average** €35. **Prix fixe** €26. **Lunch menu** €16. **Credit** MC, V. **Map** G2.
The golden bell has not only been tolling good times in Pigalle ever since it was opened by actress Jeanne Moreau's parents in 1928, but it's an endearingly campy Gallic retort to the theatre-district restaurant traditions of New York and London. The mock medieval decor here, including a big ersatz hearth with spit, may have you waiting for Catherine Deneuve as the character she played in that 1970s classic *Peau d'Ane*, but it's far more likely you'll share your meal with an edgy mix of off-duty go-go girls and boys, bouncers, club owners, foreign tourists, neighbourhood regulars and the occasional real-life actor or actress. The soundtrack that plays here is pure *Cage aux Folles*, while service is friendly, flirtatious and English-speaking. If the kitchen is

unlikely to leave you with lasting memories, the general quality of the trad French grub they send out is considerably better than what you find in the other late-night option – Paris brasseries – these days. The house terrine with onion jam was quite good, the steak tartare better than average, and the accompanying frites bliss. Less successful was a very bony slice of lamb roast with ratatouille, but the cheese tray was tempting and offered a good excuse to order a bit more of the eminently drinkable Cahors, one of the less expensive wines on the list. This winsomely eccentric quartier, which has blessedly survived the furious tides of fashion, is well worth discovering.

Georgette

29 rue St-Georges, 9th (01.42.80.39.13). M° Notre-Dame-de-Lorette. **Open** noon-2.45pm, 7.30-11pm Tue-Fri. Closed first three weeks in Aug. **Average** €30. **Credit** AmEx, MC, V. **Map** H3.

A mix of 1950s-vintage Formica tables (with matching bar) and ancient wooden beams provides the external charm, but what has won Georgette a loyal following since this bistro opened three years ago is the female chef's loving use of seasonal ingredients. Forget pallid supermarket tomatoes – here, in late summer, they were orange, yellow and green, layered in a multicoloured salad or whizzed in a flavour-packed gazpacho. Another winning starter was the rocket salad with buffalo mozzarella, saved from banality by top-notch ingredients. Rib-sticking meat dishes satisfy the local business crowd, while lighter options might include sea bream (slightly bony) with Provençal vegetables, a Charlotte of juicy lamb chunks and aubergine, and even an unsweetened prune and pear compote (though the creamy Fontainebleau fromage blanc with raspberry coulis takes some beating). We've found it's unwise to order fish on a Monday here (when the wholesale market is closed), but otherwise Georgette is one of those charmed bistros where it's hard to go wrong – even the bread is delicious.

A la Grange Batelière

16 rue de la Grange Batelière, 9th (01.47.70.85.15). M° Richelieu-Drouot. **Open** 12.15-2.15pm, 7.30-10pm Mon-Fri. Closed two weeks in Aug. **Prix fixe** €29. **Credit** AmEx, MC, V. **Map** H3.

The trad waiters at this charmingly old-fashioned room were having a busy time on a Monday lunchtime with hungry dealers and buyers from the nearby Drouot auction house. Check out the charming chest of mini-drawers for the napkins of regulars from past generations and take a look at the blackboards listing the three-course set menu. This €29 deal is not the best bargain in town, but on our last visit it was freshly cooked and reasonably accomplished. A dish of carefully fried langoustines on a brunoise de légumes was disappointing only in its quantity, for despite a €2 supplement the crustaceans looked undernourished and forlorn on the large plate, but the sauce was tasty. A smooth terrine de foies de volaille was more generously

served with a teaspoonful of onion confit. Our main course choices were a well-cooked suprême de pintade coated in a crème de morilles, and a magret de canard, sauce Apicius. Apicius seemed to have favoured cream and alcohol, but would surely have found ducks with bigger breasts for Roman legionnaires. The highlight of the meal was the first-rate puddings, a fondant au chocolat which oozed not just molten cocoa but a pungent green pistachio sauce, and a macaronade de fraises which featured a first rate macaroon accompanied by excellent crème pâtissière in which strawberries were nestling. With a sprinkling of pungent coulis this was a delightful summer treat. A bottle of raspberry-scented Chiroubles served us well and we will return if things have gone our way at the auctioneers.

Jean

8 rue St-Lazare, 9th (01.48.78.62.73). M° Notre-Dame-de-Lorette. **Open** noon-2.30pm, 7.30-10.30pm Mon-Fri. Closed Aug. **Average** €45. **Prix fixe** €58 (dinner only). **Lunch menu** €34. **Credit** AmEx, DC, MC, V. **Map** H3.

This quietly elegant vintage bistro is in sure hands when updating bourgeois cuisine, less so when attempting modern fusion which hasn't yet sussed out a reason – as in a taster we sampled from the forthcoming carte of earthy duck cappuccino, deep-fried bread sticks and a 'pickle' of crunchy beetroot, apple and onion. Were we meant to eat each element separately and in what order? Should we dip the sticks in the pickle, in which case it wasn't saucy enough, or the soup? What other than the current fad for serving three different things in three different ways was the reason for putting them together? Much better were the round presse of chicken under a mesclun salad and a lovely herby combination of chickpeas, courgettes, carrots and cauliflower in a chicken broth with whole fresh basil leaves. We liked the grey mullet fillet on steamed potatoes with steamed lettuce on top and a well-prepared, Italianate veal piccata, with a veal ragoût and a thin slice of veal under a pile of courgette and almond slivers. The weekly-changing lunch menu makes a relatively affordable option, but with only two choices you can come unstuck – our pineapple dessert with ice-cream was refreshing but the yellow slab of 'semoule façon grand-mère' was a school-dinnerish semolina. There are some well-priced wines on the list and highly professional service, so opt for the more classic-sounding dishes to appreciate how good the cooking can really be here.

La Table de la Fontaine

5 rue Henri-Monnier, 9th (01.45.26.26.30). M° St-Georges. **Open** noon-2.30pm, 7.30-11.30pm Mon-Fri (2 May-9 Oct); noon-2.30pm Mon-Fri, 7.30-11.30pm Sat (10 Oct-1 May). Closed two weeks in Aug. **Prix fixe** €30 (dinner only). **Lunch menu** €25. **Credit** MC, V. **Map** H2.

The fuchsia-and-poppy jacquard tablecloths and napkins, terracotta walls painted with a motif of gilded rope, and flirty blonde hostess are a perfect expression of the way in which the once mumsy 9th arrondissement has become a major fief of Parisian bobos, or bourgeois bohemians. It's most interesting at noon when it pulls a diverse local crowd. The blonde runs a disciplined dining room – two or three times during our meal we shifted the ashtray to the empty neighbouring tables since neither of us smoke, and each time she returned it to its proper place on our table. The eclectic contemporary French menu offers a rather clear snapshot of the impact of the Costes brothers' trendy neo-brasseries on neighbourhood restaurants in Paris. Happily, though, there's a decent cook in the kitchen, so that a decidedly déjà vu starter such as a tomato-and-aubergine millefeuille – roasted slices of aubergine layered with fresh tomato – brimmed with flavour; while ravioles de Royans, tiny cheese-filled ravioli, were perfectly cooked, lightly sauced in cream and garnished with diced tomato. A special of lamb curry was attractively served and a pleasant westernised rendition of this Chutney Mary-style classic, while beef carpaccio with parmesan shavings and a balsamic-dressed salad of peppery rocket was prepared with high-quality produce.

Velly

52 rue Lamartine, 9th (01.48.78.60.05). M° Notre-Dame-de-Lorette. **Open** noon-2pm, 7.30-10.45pm Mon-Fri. Closed three weeks in Aug. **Average** €40. **Prix fixe** €31 (dinner only). **Lunch menu** €23. **Credit** MC, V. **Map** H3.

The setting is modest – old tiled floors, an art deco bar, bare wood tables – but the atmosphere is the real thing, that of a timeless neighbourhood bistro. Though it has only been open for about three years, Velly has the well-oiled feeling of a restaurant that has found its groove: the two dining rooms fill with office workers at lunch, locals and a fair number of well-informed tourists in the evening. The blackboard menu changes according to what's available at the wholesale Rungis market, offering a limited but tempting selection of classic dishes with a modern pirouette. Our meal started with an avocado and crab 'mosaïque' that in a lesser bistro could have been an iffy choice, but here it was zingy and fresh, with actual chunks of toothsome crabmeat. Ravioles d'escargots put a light spin on snails, with paper-thin pasta and a delicate herb sauce that needed a bit of an extra kick (black pepper did the trick). Technically, the risotto with scallops and mousseron mushrooms was not a risotto at all – it was rice in a mushroom cream sauce, presented in a cute little white bowl – but the flavours worked perfectly together. Onglet de veau proved to be red, juicy and easier on the jaw than most entrecôtes. The real surprise, though, was the salsify fritters, an original take on this hard-to-prepare root vegetable. Things went a tiny bit downhill with dessert – an average crème brûlée, and a banane créole that didn't taste of the promised rum – but we lingered happily over the last drops of our wine from the Pays Roannais, a little-known bit of Burgundy.

10TH ARRONDISSEMENT

Chez Arthur

25 rue du Fbg-St-Martin, 10th (01.42.08.34.33). M° Strasbourg St-Denis. **Open** noon-2.30pm, 7-11.30pm Tue-Sat. Closed Aug. **Prix fixe** €27, €22. **Credit** AmEx, MC, V. **Map** K4.

For three generations Chez Arthur has served the late-night crowd that swarms in from the Faubourg's independent theatres, and its wood-lined interior filled with actors' portraits and starched white tablecloths has probably barely changed. The menu, on creamy parchment in copperplate, is easy to negotiate so as not to detract from the discussion in hand. Everything we ordered from the good-value prix fixe was just as it should be: a decent foie gras de canard served with hot toast; hot goat's cheese on a crisp, well-dressed salad; a fine steak with creamy potato gratin; and flaky, firm cod with a crisp skin and garlicky tapenade, accompanied by a carafe of house red. Desserts such as crème brûlée and two-chocolate fondant with crème anglaise are also good, and though we were the last to leave we were not in any way hurried out by the charming Michael, grandson of the original Arthur.

Chez Casimir

6 rue de Belzunce, 10th (01.48.78.28.80). M° Gare du Nord or Poissonnière. **Open** noon-2pm, 7-11pm Mon-Fri. Closed three weeks in Aug. **Average** €27. **Credit** AmEx, MC, V. **Map** K2.

It's a relief to escape the busy boulevards around Gare du Nord and find this bright little bistro perched on a corner of a silent church square. Convivial places such as Chez Casimir are rare in this neighbourhood, which goes a long way to explain why this offspring of the popular Chez Michel next door was packed with a mix of tourists and locals when we visited. The blackboard menu presents a brief selection of seasonal offerings that are slightly more sophisticated than standard bistro fare. A house-made pot of guinea hen rillettes was generous, though the rosemary was indiscernible. Another starter, slices of cured salmon on a bed of carrot and celeriac rémoulade, was pleasant, as were hearty mains of roasted duck leg with braised salsify and tender pork belly over sautéed Swiss chard. The short wine list offers a broad selection of bottles all under €40. The dessert menu consists of satisfying versions of classics such as pain perdu, served with caramelised bananas, and rice pudding enlivened by citrus marmalade. The service, though well-meaning, could afford to be more careful, as it contributes to the sense that there is a lack of attention to detail here. Still, should you find yourself in the no-man's land around the station, this is an excellent address.

Chez Michel

10 rue de Belzunce, 10th (01.44.53.06.20). M° Gare du Nord. **Open** 7pm-midnight Mon; noon-2pm, 7pm-midnight Tue-Fri. Closed two weeks in Aug. **Prix fixe** €30. **Credit** MC, V. **Wheelchair access. Map** K2.

French Cuisine

Thierry Breton is from Brittany and flies the flag high. His menu is stacked with hearty regional offerings and he sports the Breton flag on his chef's whites. Chez Michel, with its old-style red velvet banquettes and woody interior, is just behind the imposing St-Vincent-de-Paul church and a few minutes' walk from Gare du Nord, and while the area isn't particularly classy, the food is. Marinated salmon with purple potatoes served in a preserving jar, pickled-herring-style, was melt-in-the-mouth tender. So too fresh abalone, and the rabbit braised with rosemary and Swiss chard might just be the best bunny in town. Blackboard specials, which carry a €5-€15 supplement, follow the seasons. Game lovers are spoilt in the cooler months with wood pigeon, wild boar and venison, and there are usually some juicy fat, fresh scallops on offer too. Breton's Paris-Brest, choux pastry filled with hazelnut butter cream, is simply too good to miss. Staff can be excruciatingly slow and adept at not catching your eye but they are good-natured enough.

Aux Deux Canards

8 rue du Fbg-Poissonnière, 10th (01.47.70.03.23/ www.lesdeuxcanards.com). M° Bonne Nouvelle. **Open** 7-10.15pm Mon, Sat; noon-2.30pm, 7-10.15pm Tue-Fri. Closed 24 July-24 Aug. **Average** €38. **Credit** AmEx, DC, MC, V. **Map** J4.

At first you seem to be getting special treatment, hearing Gérard Faesch's cheery explanation of Aux Deux Canards' colourful history (a former clandestine HQ for a Résistance newspaper during the Nazi occupation) and the kitchen's ancient recipe for citrus rind sauces (you are implored to sniff the contents of jars which, bringing to mind specimens in a pathology lab, are in various states of decay). After about the sixth recital of his schtick this wears thin, but food comes to the rescue: a trustworthy menu of inventive takes on bistro cuisine, with lots of fruity touches. A pan-fried foie gras with bilberry compote proved surprisingly complementary. Tender couteaux (razor clams) in garlic butter and parsley brought to mind skinny snails. Two tuna fillets served with beurre blanc, puréed carrots, and courgette and potato gratins were grilled to perfection. Though we didn't order the duck à l'orange, the plate is magnificently adorned with a candle lighting up a hollowed-out orange. An archetypal crème brûlée arrives with a branding iron ('Look at the two ducks!' our waiter declared, pointing at the dessert's crispy emblem before backing away into a cloud of smoke). It's all quite enjoyable while being a bit over-the-top. You're allowed one cigarette with your aperitif and one with your coffee.

L'Hermitage

5 bd de Denain, 10th (01.48.78.77.09/www. restaurantlhermitage.com). M° Gare du Nord. **Open** 7-10.30pm Mon, Sat; noon-2.30pm, 7-10.30pm Tue-Fri. Closed two weeks in Aug. **Prix fixe** €26. **Credit** AmEx, DC, MC, V. **Non-smoking room. Map** K2.

Whether travelling for business or pleasure, the first and last reflex of many is the solace of a good Gallic meal. Leaving the woeful quality of what's served aboard the trains these days to one side, it's also much too easy to go wrong with restaurants in this busy part of town. Happily, however, this excellent restaurant is just a few steps from the front doors of the Gare du Nord, and with a stunningly good-value menu, a pretty dining room done up in cherry wood parquet, mahogany panelling, and a team of talented cooks in the kitchen. Note straight away, however, that this place is very popular with the throngs who live or work in the neighbourhood, so if you want to tuck into a feast here, you should book ahead. The menu changes regularly, but a sauté of ceps with garlic and parsley, wild mushroom terrine, and oysters on the half-shell were all first-rate starters, and real care had been taken in the preparation of delicious main courses such as sautéed scallops surrounding a mousseline of sweet potato, roast pheasant with apples and buttered cabbage, and veal medallions with tomato relish and tagliatelle dressed with basil oil and lemon juice. The admirable thread of our most recent meal was the obvious commitment to quality, whether in terms of the perfect rougets (red mullet), the cheese plate, the freshly baked bread, or the splendid wine list on which the Crozes Hermitages Caillot comes highly recommended. The two caveats to be offered here are that they are not particularly attentive to solitary diners – a shame in a part of town where so many solo types would like a good meal – and service can be very slow, important to bear in mind if you're catching a train.

11TH ARRONDISSEMENT

Astier

44 rue Jean-Pierre-Timbaud, 11th (01.43.57.16.35/ www.restaurant-astier.com). M° Parmentier. **Open** noon-2pm, 8-10.15pm Mon-Fri. Closed eight days at Easter, Aug and eight days at Christmas. **Prix fixe** €27. **Lunch menu** €22.50. **Credit** MC, V. **Map** M4.

Ensconced at a table in the upstairs dining room surrounded by English speakers from all over, we wondered if our accents had banished us from the significantly more atmospheric downstairs. Finally, our paranoia subsided when a throng of neighbourhood locals joined us either side. The popular and resolutely old-fashioned Astier is obviously as much loved for its shabby walls and overrun tables as its good-value four-course menu. The cooking is well balanced between traditional dishes and seasonal specials, from chunky home-made terrines and snails in garlic butter, to smart scallop carpaccio with parsley vinaigrette and tiny cheese-filled ravioli bathed in pumpkin cream. The mains show the same dexterity: juicy pieces of roast Challans duck with sage, and rascasse croustillante (scorpion fish with nutmeg-spiked spinach in filo pastry) teamed with couscous and a buttery lemon sauce. Desserts, though, were undistinguished:

medicinal-tasting cassis sorbet, and wilted poached pear with bitter almond ice-cream. Better to indulge yourself with cheese from the impressive array on the self-serve tray that's plonked on your table.

Le Bistrot Paul Bert

18 rue Paul-Bert, 11th (01.43.72.24.01).
Mº Faidherbe-Chaligny. **Open** noon-2pm, 7.30-11pm Tue-Sat. Closed three weeks in Aug. **Average** €18 (lunch), €32 (dinner). **Prix fixe** €28. **Lunch menu** €15. **Credit** MC, V. **Map** N7.
We have the good fortune of having this classic bistro just around the corner from our apartment. It's a popular haunt of local businessmen and artisans, with a well-worn interior filled with that unmistakable smell of garlic and red wine. The boss chooses superb bottles and his list is interesting with some affordable treats. The wine of the month was Cheverny and we enjoyed a couple of fragrant glasses during our last lunchtime visit, where the €15 menu is remarkable value. The food here is not of the sophisticated modern bistro type, but good old-fashioned, no-nonsense cuisine. Egg mayo was raised from the mundane by a particularly good potato salad, while a small dish of cheese-topped salt cod was pronounced excellent, even if we suspect you need Mediterranean genes to appreciate the pungency of salt cod. Mains included a substantial and perfectly cooked piece of salmon with hollandaise sauce served with pasta, and a tender chuck steak with a couple of spoonfuls of flavoursome beef reduction accompanied by melting potato wedges. The cinnamon-rich apple crumble with crème fraîche sustained the high standard of the place, where there is also a €28 menu featuring nobler products prepared with the same honest care.

Le C'Amelot

50 rue Amelot, 11th (01.43.55.54.04). Mº Chemin Vert. **Open** noon-2pm, 7-10.30pm Tue-Fri; 7-10.30pm Sat. **Prix fixe** €32 (dinner only). **Lunch menu** €17, €24. **Credit** AmEx, MC, V. **Wheelchair access**. **Non-smoking room. Map** M6.
Older readers may remember Chez Bubune, the very special restaurant that resided at 50 rue Amelot before this one. The svelte and charming daughter dealt with front-of-house, while the considerably less svelte and charming mother sweated it out among the copper casseroles. There was only one thing to eat, which was great for non-French speakers because you'd just come in, sit down and the food would arrive. This place has retained some of that tradition in that there is no choice: one starter, one fish course, one main. But, judging by our last trips, it's worth putting your faith in chef Didier Varnier. The Jerusalem artichoke, though one of the tastiest vegetables going, is best avoided on that crucial first date as it tends to lead to a condition that, while hugely enjoyable for under-fives, is embarrassing for others. But here (big relief as, lest we forget, this was the only thing on the menu) the chef managed to prepare his soup in such a way as to avoid percussive side-effects. Moving swiftly on, our potted monkfish with crispy fennel rémoulade was a marvel, the rich and intense sauce nicely complementing the elegant simplicity of the fish. The duck magret main with crispy cabbage was as good as the fish course. Again, impressive talent in the kitchen turned what is often a bit of a let-down into something tremendous. Our rice pudding had something of the grand-mère about it which, where French cooking is concerned, is usually as good as it gets. The decor is as useless as ever. The ambience is still rather staid. But this is a place worth the detour for the food. It also has a fine list of aperitifs and digestifs from French regions.

Chardenoux

1 rue Jules-Vallès, 11th (01.43.71.49.52).
Mº Charonne. **Open** noon-2.30pm, 7-10.30pm daily. **Average** €42. **Credit** AmEx, MC, V. **Map** N7.
A change of management at one of the capital's quaintest bistros was greeted with suspicion by die-hard traditionalists. Superficially the restaurant remains unchanged, but cleaner and smarter than in recent times, its romantic belle époque decor gleaming in the winter sunlight. The menu sticks to its classical repertoire, but the new chef has a more self-consciously modern approach. We began with a dozen well-selected snails, while a terrine de foie gras, enhanced by layers of onions and figs, was a total success. Fans of the restaurant's classic tête de veau may be alarmed at the chef's rehashing of the dish – gone was the head meat covered by a thick sauce gribiche; enter a bowl containing a savoury mix of meat, lentils and potatoes, accompanied by a small dish of over-pungent sauce. It must be admitted that the new version was tasty, but it was nonetheless a surprise in a restaurant that was previously a bastion of classicism. Kidney fricassée was slightly on the grey side of the requested pink, but moist and tender, accompanied by bacon and baby onions. We shared a rather sweet chocolate cake to finish off our excellent carafe of white Quincy. A question mark now hangs over the enduring quality of this landmark bistro.

Le Chateaubriand

129 av Parmentier, 11th (01.43.57.45.95).
Mº Goncourt. **Open** noon-2pm, 8-11pm Tue-Fri; 8-11pm Sat. Closed three weeks in Aug. **Average** €30. **Lunch menu** €12. **Credit** MC, V. **Map** M4.
This hip bistro is the sort of place that might cheer up an estate agent, trying to persuade you that this rather bleak corner of the 11th is heading for gentrification. It has been said that designer Christian Lacroix eats here, but on this occasion our neighbours included a gentleman sporting a red-and-black velvet beret, a fair number of finely combed male ponytails, some rastafarian dreadlocks and wardrobes full of designer togs. The room is cream and sparsely decorated, but feels bright and airy. Amid the blackboards offering a wide selection of wine, you can see remnants of an original shop

L'Ourcine. *See p61.*

decoration offering a glimpse of another age. The lunch menu for €12 is a bargain, but fairly low on choice, and with one main dish already finished we mixed and matched from the few lunchtime à la carte items. A classic egg mayo was lent distinction by a rocket salad, but smoked herrings on a cold potato salad were not a particularly happy adaptation of the classic soused herrings on warm potatoes. Pike-perch with Swiss chard was both delicious and copious, and some marinated mackerel was pronounced excellent. Grapefruit soup or crème caramel were the only pudding choices on offer, but the wine available by the carafe was an outstanding Cairanne, Côtes du Rhône. The omnipresent English owner obviously knows how to choose her wine, and runs the thriving bistro with all the energy of an over-zealous headmistress.

Chez Paul

13 rue de Charonne, 11th (01.47.00.34.57).
M° Bastille. **Open** noon-2.30pm, 7pm-12.30am daily.
Closed 24, 25 Dec. **Average** €30. **Credit** AmEx, DC,
MC, V. **Map** M7.
Always crowded (we had difficulty getting a table on a Monday evening), with its nicotine-stained ceiling and wobbly tables, this restaurant owes its success more to its authentically worn decor and location at the heart of the teeming Bastille than to its food. It took a long time for our waitress to take our order. This wasn't her fault – the menu is very long and we couldn't decide on what wine to choose. When it arrived, our bottle of Brouilly was so over-chilled as to hurt our teeth. This was perhaps a good thing, as it would have been difficult for any decent bottle to stand up to the meal that followed. The

inclusion of a poached pear did little to brighten our shared starter, a plate of perfectly cooked, but under-seasoned and insipid foie gras terrine. Of the mains, the only element that stood out was the satisfyingly bitter braised endives that accompanied veal belly stuffed with an unidentified filling. Dried-out veal kidney with a gratin dauphinois that had seen better days only brought back unhappy memories of the school canteen. Fortunately, the waiters were friendly and the girls on the neighbouring table were pretty and talkative, because the bill for two, with a shared starter and no dessert, came to a whopping €76.50.

Chez Ramulaud

269 rue du Fbg-St-Antoine, 11th (01.43.72.23.29). M° Faidherbe-Chaligny or Nation. **Open** noon-2.30pm, 8-11pm Mon-Thur, Sun; noon-2.30pm, 8-11.30pm Fri; 8-11.30pm Sat. Closed one week at Christmas. **Prix fixe** €28 (dinner only). **Lunch menu** €15, €28. **Credit** MC, V. **Map** N7.

At the far end of the Faubourg, in an area formerly immune to fashion, a few interesting modern bistros are cropping up. Leading the bunch is Ramulaud, a relaxed neighbourhood place with wooden tables and a subtle retro decor. Our lunchtime visit found the room humming with a local crowd, who appreciate the care of the cooking and the reasonable prices. The blackboard offerings initially looked rather tame, but simplicity and clear, uncluttered tastes are always a winner. We began our meal with an olive and mushroom clafoutis – all the charm of a quiche with none of the crust. The main courses included perfectly cooked red mullet on a bed of aromatic fennel and other vegetables, and a chicken breast with pommes allumettes. Fearing industrial fried chicken, we were thrilled to find a magical golden parcel of moist, tasty meat, which was truly memorable. Turning our backs on the tempting dessert list, we opted for the à la carte cheese trolley, which we were left in charge of long enough to indulge in a tasty tour of well-aged specimens, washed down by the drinkable house red. In the evenings the menu is slightly more sophisticated and on occasional Sundays there is a guinguette – a retro-style French dinner-dance, which according to the extremely charming staff is très sympa, like the bistro itself.

Les Jumeaux

73 rue Amelot, 11th (01.43.14.27.00). M° Chemin Vert. **Open** noon-2pm, 7.30-10.30pm Tue-Sat. Closed three weeks in Aug. **Prix fixe** €33 (dinner only). **Lunch menu** €27. **Credit** MC, V. **Map** M6.

We waited nearly an hour for a latecomer, but that didn't irk the kind, quiet hosts of Les Jumeaux, a low-key and rather prim dining room about midway between the Marais and Oberkampf. White linens, beige carpet and splashy artwork create a minimalist hotel lobby-like mood, though the well-dressed guests, in blazers and skirts, clashed with the casual waiters, one of whom wore jeans. Beginning with the fabulous crusty bread, the food

pleased us overall. Camembert and cumin stuffed into a flaky pastilla pastry was a winning combo, though the celeriac and cantal soup needed jazzing up. For the second course, the grilled scallops harmonised nicely with a yummy green pea purée and pink grapefruit sauce, but the cassoulet was the star: not your typical stewy glop, this version had a light tomato-based broth, white beans cooked à point, and big hunks of goose, sausage and pork. One hitch at the end, though: the waiter muddled up our dessert order; by the time we'd flagged him down to remedy it, the chef had already gone home for the night. So we had to settle for a crème brûlée and orange-chocolate moelleux. That apple-ginger compote sounded great – maybe next time?

Le Marsangy

73 av Parmentier, 11th (01.47.00.94.25). M° Parmentier. **Open** noon-2pm, 8-10.30pm Mon-Fri; 8-10.30pm Sat. Closed ten days at Christmas, two weeks in Aug and ten days in May. **Average** €26. **Prix fixe** €20. **Credit** MC, V. **Map** M5.

With its blackboard menu and ox blood-coloured interior, this popular place is the very definition of what a neighbourhood bistro should be: friendly, generous, fairly priced and reliably delicious. It's not unusual to run into high-voltage film, fashion and television types having a low-key night; otherwise, the crowd is a comfortable mix of liberal locals with arty aspirations if not professions. Though something about the atmosphere makes it feel like a bistro out of a Hollywood film, the menu is a grand slam of traditional treats such as terrine and a fricassée of rabbit with olives, or more inventive dishes such as a mille-feuille of avocado and crayfish. A breast of pintade (guinea hen) in tarragon cream sauce was succulent and full of flavour, while onglet de veau (veal flank steak) in shallot sauce was also good if rather chewy. A first-rate cheese tray proved irresistible with the rest of a pleasant bottle of Gramenon Côtes du Rhône, a great buy at €17, while desserts, including a nice soupe de fruits rouges (berries in their own juices), succeed with simplicity.

Le Passage des Carmagnoles

18 passage de la Bonne-Graine, 11th (01.47.00.73.30). M° Ledru-Rollin. **Open** noon-3pm, 7-11.30pm Mon-Sat. **Average** €25. **Credit** AmEx, DC, MC, V. **Wheelchair access. Map** N7.

The song of the Carmagnoles was a revolutionary song of the sans culottes, and this friendly beamed bistro with a crowd of regulars is in one of the last passages of the Bastille still dominated by furniture makers. The former emphasis on andouillette seems to have shifted slightly, with only a couple of dishes featuring the famous tripe sausage. The boss claimed to have the best Beaujolais nouveau in town, not a big boast but we enjoyed a glass with our first courses, which included a tasty croustade d'escargots, and a salade du verger – a wholesome mix of beans, tomatoes, cervelas sausage and gizzards. Main courses included a tender autumn civet of ostrich bathing in pinot noir, and we couldn't

French Cuisine

resist the fricassée of andouillette with white wine, mushrooms and bacon, both dishes accompanied by herby potatoes. The andouillette was of excellent quality and the wine of the month, an oaky Gaillac, was outstanding. Our appetites flagged before the traditional puddings or tempting cheese board, so we opted instead for a digestif, and a chat with the boss who proudly promoted his philosophical dinners. Sartre's quotation 'hell is other people' was to be up for discussion; the accompanying good food and wine could sway the argument.

Le Repaire de Cartouche

99 rue Amelot/8 bd des Filles du Calvaire, 11th (01.47.00.25.86). M° St-Sébastien-Froissart. **Open** noon-2pm, 7.30-11pm Tue-Sat. Closed Aug. **Average** €35. **Lunch menu** €13, €24. **Credit** MC, V. **Wheelchair access. Map** M5.

'Cartouche's Hideaway' honours Paris's answer to Dick Turpin, Robin Hood and Fagin rolled into one (literally, in fact – the menu describes his gruesome execution, just to whet your appetite). On an icy January night, the dark panelling, impeccable white napery and leaded windows provided a civilised retreat from the bleak boulevards north of the Bastille, and the food was exceptional. After flavoursome goose rillettes and rustic bread, we enjoyed a perfect timbale of firm, fresh whelks with tiny ratte potatoes in creamy herb dressing, and a generous portion of foie gras, pan-fried and served in a rich, meaty glaze. To follow, the pink-roasted Pyrenean suckling lamb with plump haricots blancs was exemplary. A slab of seasonal venison, with its accompanying pile of finely diced, thoughtfully herbed wild mushrooms, melted in the mouth. Desserts included a sorely tempting cranberry and chocolate-chip clafoutis (cooked to order, in advance) but we plumped instead for a mille-feuille of feather-light chestnut mousse between slivers of dark bitter chocolate, and a chocolate mousse pavé given plentiful zing by the addition of fresh ginger extract. The wine list is exhaustive and well-presented, but look no further than the special selections accompanying each week's new menu: a golden-delicious white Burgundy from Vézelay (served by the glass) went down well with the whelks and foie gras, followed by a smooth, good-value Vin de Pays de la Principauté d'Orange. Rodolphe Paquin is a chef of stature (in every sense, as seen on his frequent sorties into the dining room), and a tireless communicator of his enthusiasm for fine ingredients and inventive takes on traditional French fare.

Au Vieux Chêne

7 rue du Dahomey, 11th (01.43.71.67.69). M° Faidherbe-Chaligny. **Open** noon-2pm, 8-10.30pm Mon-Fri; 8-10.30pm Sat. Closed one week at Christmas. **Average** €35. **Prix fixe** €29 (dinner only). **Lunch menu** €13. **Credit** MC, V. **Non-smoking room. Map** N7.

Our hearts sank when one of our favourite neighbourhood bistros closed for redecoration and a change of team. We need not have worried about the Vieux Chêne, which like a Hollywood actress needed not so much a refit as a minor facelift. All the charm of the old bistro remains in a cleaner, brighter form, something that extends to the carte with a mixture of bistro standbys and a few modern touches in the shape of exotic fruits and vegetables. Of course it is no longer the bargain of bygone times, but its gastronomic fence has been set several notches higher. We began our meal with some crispy langoustine cigars on a bed of mango, and an aromatic poêlée de girolles, which was added to the printed menu by our cuddly, accommodating waitress. A main course entrecôte was a vast portion of high quality meat, perfectly cooked with some skilfully underplayed gratin dauphinois. Even better was roast pigeon served on Chinese cabbage, moist and tender fowl perfectly complemented by the slightly bitter vegetable. Puddings sustained the high standard with a moreish moelleux d'abricots, and a chocolate ganache layered between some crisp buttery shortbread with a silky praline ice-cream. The wine of the month was a well-chosen Côteaux du Languedoc for a reasonable €20.

12TH ARRONDISSEMENT

Auberge le Quincy

28 av Ledru-Rollin, 12th (01.16.38.16.76). M° Gare de Lyon. **Open** noon-2pm, 7.30-10pm Tue-Fri. Closed 10 Aug-10 Sept and one week at Christmas. **Average** €70. **No credit cards. Map** M8.

Anybody seeking a massive feast of trad French cooking will be in gastro-heaven here. Our host, Bobosse, proposed a cornucopian selection of starters, including fine foie gras, well-aged wafer-thin country ham, delicious warm caillettes (pork and chard patties) on a bed of mesclun salad, and a hunk of home-made terrine accompanied by a garlicky cabbage salad. The main courses kept up the quality with a creamy, succulent côte de veau aux morilles served in a copper pan, and scallops which were untrimmed, quickly fried and served on a bed of pasta. Not sophisticated cuisine, but perfectly timed and irresistibly fresh. Our appetites were waning now and we resisted a serious-looking chocolate mousse, plumping instead for glasses of vieille prune served from a traditional wooden watering can and flambéed at the table by Bobosse with well-rehearsed theatricality. The bill, which included a handsome quantity of Brouilly, was substantial but worth every penny. Remember that the cackling patronne does not have any truck with credit cards, so a totter to the cash machine is involved, which might just give you a thirst for that final nightcap.

Les Bombis Bistrot

22 rue de Chaligny, 12th (01.43.45.36.32). M° Reuilly-Diderot. **Open** noon-3pm, 8-11pm Mon-Fri; 8-11pm Sat. Closed one week in Aug. **Average** €35. **Prix fixe** €25 (dinner only). **Lunch menu** €12, €14. **Credit** MC, V. **Wheelchair access. Map** N8.

La Régalade. *See p64.*

Under the stewardship of Hassan Nithsain, this neighbourhood bistro was fêted for its elegant cuisine served up in a softly lit dining room replete with endearingly eccentric features, such as the whimsical frescoes of a flying pig dominating the ceiling. Having recently changed owner and chef, it has retained the warm atmosphere, with the grey-haired proprietor playing affable host, mixing aperitifs and barbed repartee at the bar with regulars. Another pleasant surprise was that the new regime has ushered in a more affordable €25 menu. The crucial characteristic, however, behind the success of this bistro – the elegance and precision of the cuisine – has, alas, seemingly slipped. While the rabbit terrine studded with prune morsels was a satisfying starter, the snail and tomato crumble was a distinct disappointment and awash in grease. The main-course offering of pike-perch fillet with an olive oil emulsion, served with a rainbow of vegetables, was a dull, flavourless dish. We were also rather underwhelmed by the saddle of lamb accompanied by overcooked vegetables and distinctly unfresh peas. Desserts cover familiar bistro territory and were executed without flaw or flair. Despite the disappointment, the Bombis Bistrot was, on the occasion we visited, packed with a satisfied-looking crowd of locals.

Comme Cochons ★

135 rue Charenton, 12th (01.43.42.43.36).
M° Reuilly-Diderot. **Open** noon-2.30pm, 8-11pm Tue-Sat. **Average** €32. **Lunch menu** €15. **Credit** MC, V. **Map** N8.

Pigs get a bad rap in Anglo-American culinary lore where they conjure images of indiscriminate gobbling, but for the French, more sensibly, they're a symbol of friendly mingling ('être amis comme cochons'). At this popular bistro in the growingly trendy 12th, friendly exchange is dominated by the audible yum yums ('miam miam' in French) of near-ecstatic diners spurred on by the dynamic and

quirky waiters, eccentric photos of whom adorn the walls. Saturday lunch, in particular, functions like a drop-in centre with groups genially expanding as yet another chair is haphazardly added to a packed table. Some starters are only seasonal: the magnificent fricassée de girolles (a mass of grilled yellow mushrooms on a bed of tart leaves) is autumn only. Likewise the wine-rich civet de biche (a melt-in-the mouth stew of baby venison) and duo de canard (a scrumptious pairing of confit thigh and slices of rosé breast served on a bed of surprisingly memorable saucy white beans) are predominantly winter courses. But, with inspiration the chef's speciality, it's no wonder that each season brings new fuel for kitchen fantasies. Dinners are more resolutely gourmet while the excellent value lunch-menu is mindful that you may have to go back to work. The good selection of wines is well-priced with lots of southern finds. On our last visit, we couldn't decide between the home-made tarte Tatin or perfectly runny moelleux au chocolate, so we greedily had both: and what's wrong with a bit of gobbling anyway?

La Connivence

1 rue de Cotte, 12th (01.46.28.46.17). M° Ledru-Rollin. **Open** noon-2.30pm, 8-11pm Mon-Sat. Closed two weeks in Aug. **Prix fixe** €23.50. **Lunch menu** €16.50. **Credit** MC, V. **Wheelchair access. Non-smoking room. Map** N8.

Southern French cooking with an unusual Madagascan spin works brilliantly in this ochre-painted bistro near the place d'Aligre market. Chef Pascal Kosmala presents a thoughtful menu with several wholly vegetarian options, a bonus for Paris, based on seasonal ingredients enlivened by an original use of spices. We began with a light vegetable feuilleté flavoured with anise and cumin, and the star dish, a delicate crab galette refreshingly combined with citrus and cinnamon flavours. The duckling cooked three ways – confit, sautéed magret

two is a Cro Magnon's red meat feast par excellence, and there are also a few daily specials, including tripes and pot au feu when we popped in. Aside from fresh anchovies with garlic and marinated herring, Neptune's best doesn't get a look-in. Finish your wine with a first-rate cheese tray, or head for the puddings, the finest of which is the baba au rhum.

Le Saint Amarante

4 rue Biscornet, 12th (01.43.43.00.08). M° Bastille. **Open** noon-3pm, 7-11pm Mon-Fri; 7-11pm Sat. Closed Aug and one week at Christmas. **Average** €40. **Prix fixe** €32 (dinner only). **Lunch menu** €28. **Credit** MC, V. **Non-smoking room**. **Map** M7.
This offbeat bistro has been through several chefs since Rodolphe Paquin first put it on the map (he's now cooking at Le Repaire de Cartouche), but under Benoît Chemineau it has found its groove all over again. The bizarre decor of wood panelling, 1950s-style floor tiles, and an attempt to be dressy with a few dissonant details – orchid sprays in silver-plated cups – notwithstanding, this is a relaxed place with aspirations. Glasses of white wine ordered as aperitifs came with warm, airy little cheese puffs, and the meal itself was preceded by an amuse-bouche of frothy carrot soup. A first course of cauliflower soup with tempura oysters was fine and flavourful, and we were both delighted with our marine mains: cod steak on a bed of brandade (salt-cod purée) served with chard and spinach in a jus of baby clams, and small sole with mixed vegetables and a rich sauce of cream, butter and wine. Desserts were impressive, too, including a very original dish of fresh dates stuffed with marinated pineapple and a splendid frozen Grand Marnier soufflé. The owner's wife, assisted by a friendly young waitress, offers the type of proud, solicitous service you'll often find in the best restaurant in a smaller French provincial city, with wines to match.

Le Square Trousseau ★

1 rue Antoine-Vollon, 12th (01.43.43.06.00). *M° Ledru-Rollin.* **Open** noon-2.30pm, 8-11.30pm Tue-Sat. Closed first three weeks in Aug, one week at Christmas and two weeks in Feb. **Average** €40. **Lunch menu** €20, €25. **Credit** MC, V. **Non-smoking room**. **Map** N7.
Set the dial on your time travel machine to the year 1900 and fire her up. What? Time traveller on the blink again? No matter. An hour in the gentle glow of Le Square Trousseau is as good as a visit back in time a hundred years or so. Located on a picturesque residential square, its ruddy, mustard-coloured walls, burgundy velvet café curtains, plain wooden furniture and jokey waiters rushing about in long aprons all contribute to a simple, welcoming and decidedly old-fashioned Parisian atmosphere. While many dishes are rooted firmly in traditional bistro fare (think steak tartare – lean, heavy on the Worcestershire and among the best we've tasted in the city – terrine de campagne, seven-hour braised lamb and andouillette), others receive more modern garnishes and sauces. A blackboard special of

and parmentier – was delicious, with none of the greasiness sometimes found in traditional duck dishes, and the second main course, pâté d'oie, was equally good. Presented beneath a dome of brioche, a rich stew of goose and vegetables was balanced by the vinegary sharpness of marinated veal. Both dishes were hearty without being cloying, leaving plenty of room for iced nougatine in a berry coulis and an intriguing parfait of white chocolate and coconut on a juniper biscuit. The wine list favours youngish, southern wines, including increasingly fashionable Madiran, priced between €14.50 and €31; we were pleased with a chilled Brouilly at €22.50. Although we had booked late, there were still a few tables of youngish, well-groomed locals lingering with a glass of wine and listening to gentle jazz.

Le Duc de Richelieu

5 rue Parrot, 12th (01.43.43.05.64). M° Gare de Lyon. **Open** noon-1am Mon-Sat. **Average** €25. **Lunch menu** €14.50. **Credit** MC, V. **Map** M8.
The bistro boom in eastern Paris continues with this excellent new place run by the former proprietor of Le Gavroche (learning of his departure also explains why our last meal at Le Gavroche was such a thorough disappointment). Steps from the Gare de Lyon in a quiet residential street, this new place is not only ideal for a bite if you're transiting the station, but well worth seeking out for a first-rate blackboard menu and nicely chosen and fairly priced wines. The €14.50 lunch menu is especially worth noting as a remarkable deal in a part of town that isn't brimming with gastronomic bargains. If the menu follows the market, it's generally a carnivore's grand slam with starters such as Burgundian-style ham in parsleyed aspic or rabbit terrine, and then one of the best onglets (flank steaks) in town, steak tartare, breaded pig's trotter, veal cutlet à la normande (cream sauce) or a fine pavé de rumsteak au poivre. The côte de boeuf for

creamy céleri rémoulade, delicate with the mineral note of celery root and the sweetness of grated apple, came garnished with supple slices of smoked haddock. In smoked salmon 'canneloni', the salmon itself served as the pasta, encasing a savoury filling of brandade and blanched leek, and a sweet sauce of honey and warm spices accented slices of pork tenderloin. All three dishes dovetailed nicely with our 2001 Domaine de la Vielle Julienne vieilles vignes Côtes du Rhône, priced at the lower end of a list ranging from €19 to €69. Admittedly, our meal suffered from several mishaps of timing and communication, but we came to forgive them when our sweet but clearly overwhelmed waiter quietly admitted that it was his first night on the job, and that we were just his second table.

Les Zygomates

7 rue de Capri, 12th (01.40.19.93.04). M° Daumesnil. **Open** noon-2pm, 7.30-10.45pm Tue-Sat. Closed Aug. **Prix fixe** €22, €28 (dinner only). **Lunch menu** €14. **Credit** MC, V. **Non-smoking room. Map** Q10. This part of the 12th arrondisement, near the sprawling Finance Ministry and the soulless Bercy sports stadium, is one of Paris's less hip districts. The clientele of Les Zygomates, a converted art nouveau butcher's shop, reflects the vaguely provincial feel of the neighbourhood – on a Saturday evening the crowd was middle-aged and uncosmopolitan, the food conservative. The flavours and textures of the ingredients that went into the prawn ravioli in satay sauce or of the mille-feuille of Jerusalem artichokes and foie gras were inoffensively indistinguishable from one another, and unfortunately were far less intriguing than their monikers. Of the mains, the monkfish in a satisfyingly shrimpy scampi coulis stood out, the fillet of baby duck in a ginger sauce being acceptable but unremarkable. For dessert, we chose a platter of bite-sized portions of different sweets, and it is here that Les Zygomates comes into its own. This was unpretentious fare, but the juxtaposition of consistencies, between the crunchy cap of the tiny crème brûlée, the gooeyness of the chocolate fondant and the purity of the flavours, be it the astringency of the citrus sorbet or the vanilla-charged dab of crème anglaise, showed what can be achieved with simple cooking and meant that for us Les Zygomates had justified its name (the zygomatics are the facial muscles humans use to smile).

13TH ARRONDISSEMENT

L'Aimant du Sud

40 bd Arago, 13th (01.47.07.33.57). M° Les Gobelins or Glacière. **Open** 12.30-3pm Mon-Fri; 7.30-10.30pm Tue-Sat. Closed three weeks in Aug, one week at Christmas. **Average** €22. **Prix fixe** €22 (dinner only). **Lunch menu** €13, €16. **Credit** MC, V. **Map** J10. The name suggests an affection for the sun, a sentiment this modest bistro expresses with its golden-hued interior hung with nude-themed oil paintings, bar and table tops panelled in wine-crates and informal vibe from the waiters, who work against a background of Motown and 1980s hits. Most of chef David Sponga's menu is entrecôte and confit de canard territory, so look carefully for some innovation among the predictable if well-executed standards. We enjoyed our salmon carpaccio, bathed in a lemon marinade, and the chèvre croustillant, its cinnamon and nutmeg spicing pleasantly startling. A crisp and juicy saddle of lamb stuffed with fresh rosemary sprigs, and the filet mignon de porc infused with ginger were equally on target. Desserts are the expected classics, so we tried an exotic-sounding pistachio-flavoured clementine gratin, unfortunately soupy and ordinary, and the chocolate terrine, which scored high on the choco-meter. The wine selection is decent, though it's hard to find a bottle for under €20. The terrace would be more pleasant if the boulevard Arago wasn't so noisy, but interior tables are well shielded from the traffic.

Anacréon

53 bd St-Marcel, 13th (01.43.31.71.18). M° Les Gobelins or St-Marcel. **Open** noon-2.30pm, 7.30-10.30pm Tue, Thur-Sat; 7.30-10.30pm Wed. Closed Aug. **Prix fixe** €32 (dinner only). **Lunch menu** €20. **Credit** AmEx, DC, MC, V. **Map** K9. This bistro takes its cuisine very seriously. From the moment you walk through the door, you find yourself attended to by three precise waiters, who carefully recite a list of daily specials almost as long as the menu itself. The prix fixe consists of classic dishes with an unusual flavour often thrown in to let us know that chef André Le Letty has done his homework. He plays to an appreciative local audience, who don't have many other neighbourhood places where they can get a cassolette d'escargots infused with liquorice. Begin with a rabbit and foie gras terrine or opt for the more unusual terrine of lamb and poultry livers, a combination that curiously seems to work. To follow, an ample cocotte of pigeon, rich with rosy lardons, was unadulterated French grandmother fare, while a snowy wedge of cod flavoured a bit too heavily with cumin and fennel presented a more modern alternative. The thorough wine list yielded a particularly enjoyable 2000 Château des Annereaux (Lalande de Pomerol) to accompany our meal. For dessert, we couldn't resist the very unusual nougat ice-cream with seaweed confit and pineapple. This flavour gamble did not pay off, being rather too briny for a dessert. Unfortunately, a renovation this year has left the previously drab dining room feeling rather plasticised and out of step with service that is elegant and attentive, from the amuse-bouche to the home-made sablés that come with the bill.

L'Avant-Goût

26 rue Bobillot, 13th (01.53.80.24.00). M° Place d'Italie. **Open** noon-2pm, 7.30-11pm Tue-Fri. Closed one week in Jan, one week in May, three weeks in Aug and one week in Sept. **Average** €31. **Prix fixe** €28, €40. **Lunch menu** €12.50. **Credit** MC, V.

Chef Christophe Beaufront and his wife run this restaurant like a sort of all-comers' party every night, but service is commendably professional and prompt. With a money-spinner on his hands, Beaufront might have been tempted to cut all sorts of corners – raise prices, lower quality, turn tables faster but he hasn't for the simple reason that he insists on enjoying what he's doing. Starters of tuna tartare with roasted vegetables, herby cold spinach soup garnished with poppyseed-coated croûtons, and a medley of spring vegetables in a light bouillon with a poached egg were all first-rate. Beaufront's signature dish is a pot-au-feu de cochon, and it was every bit as good as we remembered – a big, round casserole brimming with off-cuts of pork, fennel and sweet potato, served with gherkins, horseradish sauce and ginger chips. Coley with broccoli purée and a drizzle of black olive cream was tasty, though the fish was a tad overcooked. We finished up our delicious €21 Cairanne with an intriguing terrine of roquefort, butter and preserved pear, plus an unusual cocoa soup. Beaufront's takeaway address across the road would be reason enough to move to the area.

Bioart

1 quai Francois-Mauriac, 13th (01.45.85.66.88).
M° Quai-de-la Gare or Bibliothèque François
Mitterand. **Open** *brasserie* noon-11.30pm Mon-Sat;
restaurant noon-3pm, 7pm-midnight Mon-Sat.
Average €30. **Lunch menu** €10.80. **Credit** MC, V.
Wheelchair access. Map M10.

Though the French are coming rather late to the healthy eating show – most organic/health food places in the capital are still stuck in a decidedly dusty 1968 timewarp – this new table in the work-in-progress neighbourhood around the Bibliothèque François Mitterand is rather better than one might expect. For once healthy eating isn't misconstrued as some sort of culinary punishment, and the duplex setting itself has some style. Picture windows and parquet successfully reset the pendulum to 2004, and if the kitchen doesn't approach the superb mastery of organic cookery one finds in California or Australia, the menu more than makes good on a promise to nourish and pleasure simultaneously. There are all sort of salads and veggie preparations to start, but you can also order a better than average terrine of scallops with a sauce of its coral, or smoked salmon. Come the mains, those dreary grain-and-veg plates of yore are nowhere to be found. Rather, the menu offers a nice run of pastas, grain dishes, potatoes, fish, and organic meats. The grilled sea bass was pleasant, as was a fricassée of free-range chicken with Indian spices, and the best puddings were all fruit-based. Request a table with a view of the Seine when you book.

Chez Paul

22 rue de la Butte-aux-Cailles, 13th (01.45.89.22.11).
M° Place d'Italie or Corvisart. **Open** noon-3pm, 7.30-
11pm daily. Closed one week at Christmas. **Average**
€38. **Credit** MC, V. **Wheelchair access.**

On a quiet Sunday night, the villagey Butte aux Cailles still had a happy buzz, with a young crowd making its way from bar to bar. Against this backdrop, Chez Paul plays the quietly self-important, grown-up restaurant in relation to the many other livelier ones nearby. A bit of folklore – the sea salt in a little wooden basket, a proper pepper mill, flea-market carafes for water – is meant to link this place to its surroundings, and it would likely work were it not for the servers wearing uniforms and the rather-stiff-for-the-neighbourhood prices. The food itself is just fine. Starters included provocative rustic grub such as tablier de sapeur (fireman's apron, which is breaded tripe as eaten in Lyon), along with marrow bones, country terrine, oysters, and delicious ham braised in hay, sliced thin and served with salad dressed with mixed peppercorns and cumin seeds. Mains are classic with no deviating flourish whatsoever, including boudin noir, onglet (flank steak), prime rib, suckling pig, and sea bass fillet, all served with curiously boring potato purée. The quality of the meat here is very good, however, and aside from some rather dull desserts – a short list runs to cherry clafoutis and apple tart – and a similarly uninteresting wine list (the Beaumes de Venise rouge is probably the best bet), this place makes for a pleasant if surprisingly expensive meal.

L'Ourcine ★

92 rue Broca, 13th (01.47.07.13.65). M° Gobelins.
Open noon-2.30pm, 7-10pm Tue-Sat. **Lunch menu**
€19. **Prix fixe** €28 (dinner only). **Credit** MC, V.
Map J10.

This cream-and-red restaurant near Gobelins is a wonderful destination for anyone who really loves Basque and Béarnais cooking, since the kitchen sends out a roster of homely, delicious and impeccably prepared regional classics that move from the Bay of Biscay to the peaks of the Pyrenees. Start with pipérade (scrambled eggs with peppers and onions), succulent chorizo or maybe a very original plate of sliced beef tongue with piquillo peppers. Then try the sautéed baby squid with parsley, garlic and Espelette peppers; the piquillos stuffed with brandade (whipped salt cod); or cannelloni stuffed with a capilotade of lamb and aubergines. Service is friendly, and an appealing atmosphere is generated by a growing band of regulars who find gastronomic pleasure here. The wine list is quite short but offers several pleasant south-western bottles, with the Madiran being a better buy than the Irouleguey. Grandmotherly desserts include gâteau basque and ewe's milk cheese with black cherry preserves, but we savoured a super tart. Book ahead.

Au Petit Marguery ★

*9 bd du Port-Royal, 13th (01.43.31.58.59/www.
petitmarguery.fr). M° Gobelins.* **Open** noon-2.15pm,
7.30-10.15pm Tue-Sat. Closed Aug. **Prix fixe**
€33.60. **Lunch menu** €25.20. **Credit** AmEx, MC, V.
Non-smoking room. Map J9.

'We really should go back in the game season,' is a comment often made about the attractively old-world Petit Marguery, formerly run by the Cousin brothers, and so it was with something of a sense of triumph that we entered the restaurant to have lunch in the first week of October. The three-course prix fixe (€33.60, plus rather too many supplements) is a game-lover's fantasy and we plunged straight in with a grouse purée, and a pheasant and foie gras terrine. The purée was a real winner, a mousse-like paste with a rich game and juniper flavour. The terrine was well-made but there was disappointingly no perceptible taste of pheasant. Warming to our task we continued with that most classic of French game dishes, lièvre à la royale, a long-marinated wine-infused dish with a chocolate-brown sauce in which blood and foie gras play a part. This was a joyful autumn dish, as was the wonderfully moist partridge served plainly on liver-spread croûtons with its thick bacon barding. Our strong Crozes Hermitage red (€24) held up well to the game assault, and to finish our meal we indulged in soufflés au Grand Marnier, which although spectacular in appearance and making, lacked enough punch to crown our hunter's feast. The downside of the meal was the rather sullen service; perhaps our waiter hadn't bagged his bird.

Le Terroir

11 bd Arago, 13th (01.47.07.36.99). M° Gobelins. **Open** noon-2.15pm, 7.45-10.15pm Mon-Fri. Closed Aug and one week at Christmas. **Average** €35. **Credit** MC, V. **Map** J10.

Although we've been fans of this place for a long time, a certain ebbing generosity, reflected in ever higher prices on both menu and wine list, and a certain penny-pinching ambience in the dining room have started to seriously wither the pleasure we've always found in coming here. For starters, the service is often terse, especially towards foreigners, even going so far as to refer a complimentary nibble of radishes to the table of regulars next to ours and scowling when we requested same. The most serious problem, however, are the prices. Yes, the cooking, including carefully made bistro dishes like sautéed cod steak, roast lamb and good quality steaks, is very good, but doesn't really warrant such vertiginous tariffs. This is one of the rare restaurants in Paris that doesn't offer a lunch or dinner menu either, so if you come, you'll do so in search of a solid bistro feed with a solid bill at the end of it. If you decide to throw caution to the wind, don't miss the lentil terrine with foie gras, that great cod steak, and the chocolate mousse.

14TH ARRONDISSEMENT

L'Assiette

181 rue du Château, 14th (01.43.22.64.86). M° Mouton-Duvernet. **Open** noon-2.30pm, 8-10.30pm Wed-Sun. Closed Aug. **Average** €65. **Lunch menu** €35. **Credit** AmEx, MC, V. **Map** G10.

Eccentric, hands-on chef Lulu, still sporting her trademark beret, continues to pull celebrity crowds to her deluxe bistro. The stripped-wood floor and wipe-off laminated veneer tables make this an unusually relaxed and lively room for what is actually one of the capital's most expensive bistros. The exceptional freshness and quality of the products, coupled with the simple precision of the cooking, almost justify the price. Refreshingly free of frilly appetisers, our autumn meal began with a pheasant and foie gras terrine which retained a taste of game, and a mound of the plumpest imaginable cockles bathed in a frothy lemon butter. A simply roasted wild duck with a punchy jus was served with a preserved pear, which may have come from the tree that harboured our other dish of moist partridge. This was accompanied by gravy-infused cabbage, which had been cooked to melting point without sacrificing colour or texture. Lulu makes an apology on the menu for the nursery puddings such as crème caramel and marquise au chocolat, claiming disingenuously that these are the only ones she knows how to make. They looked the part but we opted for a pile of thinly shaved cheese from the Pyrenees, which brought the meal to a memorable close. The wine list features many regional choices, and our tannic red from the Roussillon region (€36) perfectly complemented the game. We will save up for a return visit to sample some fish, which looked tempting on our neighbour's assiette.

Contre-Allée

83 av Denfert-Rochereau, 14th (01.43.54.99.86/ www.contreallee.com). M° Denfert-Rochereau. **Open** noon-2pm, 7.30-10.30pm Tue-Sat. Closed one week at Christmas and three weeks in Aug. **Average** €42. **Credit** AmEx, MC, V. **Non-smoking room**. **Map** H10.

In a room at once cosy and contemporary with soft lighting, ochre walls and rough linen curtains, Contre Allée conveys a pleasant sense of quiet, modern style. In keeping with this mood, undulating lines of ground spices on the rims of our plates both surprised and engaged our senses. A particularly good starter, quenelles of mild chèvre on a cloud of velvety smooth eggplant purée were unified by deep green pistachio oil and brightened by pink peppercorns and pomegranate seeds. Foie gras was served with an apple mango chutney that intrigued us with sweet, tart and floral notes. Hachis parmentier, usually a modest shepherd's pie, contained chicken, foie gras and chanterelles in place of the usual beef. Speaking of beef, an imposing fillet was carefully cooked and festooned with sautéed chanterelles. We were less convinced, though, by sea bass served in a pool of shellfish broth alongside basmati rice that was over-anxiously flavoured with almond. The friendly, English-speaking waiter suggested a fruity, medium-bodied 2002 Chinon Juette-Jaulin Domaine de Briançon that bridged the wide expanse of our meal beautifully for a very reasonable €24.

French Cuisine

Natacha

17 bis rue Campagne-Première, 14th (01.43.20.79.27).
M° Raspail. **Open** noon-2.30pm, 8-11.30pm Tue-Sat.
Closed two weeks in Aug. **Average** €35. **Lunch menu** €19, €26. **Credit** AmEx, DC, MC, V. **Non-smoking room. Map** G9.

Though the hipsters, most notably Mick Jagger, who once made this Montparnasse bistro a legend have moved on, it maintains a quiet chic that pleases a polite but self-satisfied crowd of publishing, showbiz, media and political types, many of whom would secretly like to find themselves as fodder for the sort of people-press magazines you find at the hairdresser's. Rich and successful, perhaps, but not famous, even if their eyes dart hopefully around in the room. But this low-lit, high-ceilinged Pompeian red-painted room with cushioned banquettes still has a worldly charm whether you decide to play games with the regulars or not. The food is good, too, running to a roster of Gallic treats such as langoustine bisque, artichoke with poached egg or sautéed langoustines with salad in a delicious peppery dressing to start, followed by braised veal shank with vegetables, hachis parmentier (the French version of shepherd's pie) or fish. Don't bother with the côte de boeuf, which is disappointingly dainty, and be prepared for rather patronising if efficient service.

L'O à la Bouche

124 bd du Montparnasse, 14th (01.56.54.01.55).
M° Vavinn. **Open** noon-2.30pm, 7-11pm Tue-Sat.
Closed three weeks in Aug. **Average** €50. **Prix fixe** €29 (lunch only). **Lunch menu** €19. **Credit** AmEx, MC, V. **Non-smoking room. Map** G9.

Franck Paquier's Montparnasse bistro is evidently a thriving enterprise: on the Saturday evening we visited, it was wall-to-wall with well-heeled grey-haired diners, and a long queue of hopefuls waiting at the bar. Success has also driven the prices

upwards, with the good-value prix fixe menu now relegated to lunchtime; evening dining has become a rather expensive à la carte affair. Unfortunately, the quality of the cooking has inversely responded to the price hike. The blackboard dishes were enticingly described, and arrived at breakneck speed, but were all afflicted by a disappointing lack of flavour. The ricotta-stuffed ravioli were drowned in an insipid sauce, and well-cooked scallops were served with a bland risotto festooned by limp wild mushrooms. The pheasant served in a steaming cast-iron pot looked impressive but was disappointingly tough and again served in the ubiquitous watery sauce. An exception was the pan-fried foie gras, delicately cooked in mouth-melting fashion, but this time overwhelmed by an over-sweet sauce of sultanas and quince. Desserts were uplifting – the pastry chef's trademark buttery apple tart was flawless, as was an intriguing praline craquante with excellent banana and mango sorbets. Under the icy glare of the formidable hostess, service is indeed efficient, but we were left with the feeling that commercial efficiency had triumphed over gastronomy at this venerable address.

Les Petites Sorcières

12 rue Liancourt, 14th (01.43.21.95.68). M° Denfert-Rochereau. **Open** 8-10pm Mon, Sat; noon-2pm, 8-10pm Tue-Fri. Closed mid-July to mid-Aug. **Average** €35. **Lunch menu** €25. **Credit** AmEx, MC, V. **No smoking. Map** G10.

Homely is the atmosphere at this living room-like bistro, with copper pots and portraits of grand-mère on the walls, and just a few of the namesake witches dangling here and there – a theme thankfully not taken to extremes. We wished the service wasn't so batty, though. Apparently unauthorised to hand out menus, the poor greeter/bread-cutter/water carafe girl looked flustered trying to keep herself busy while we waited a full 15 minutes to see the carte.

Le Père Claude. *See p65.*

Le Petit Rétro. See p66.

The demure proprietress finally brought them over, only to rush us through the specials board and our orders. At least the more-than-satisfying food arrived quickly. We began with a vivid spring green minestrone soup with escargot and a cold smoked haddock, shallot, radish and green bean salad. The main dish portions were a little dainty for the price, though superb: a cod fillet with flageolet beans and a balsamic drizzle, and an exceptionally tender duck magret steak and roasted potatoes doused in a tangy honey Sichuan sauce. Two made-to-order crumbles – pineapple-raisin-rum with coconut ice-cream, and apple – were worthy finishers. Perhaps on another night the sorcerers will let some of that kitchen wizardry rub off on the waiters.

La Régalade

49 av Jean-Moulin, 14th (01.45.45.68.58). M° Alésia. **Open** 7-11pm Mon; noon-2.30pm, 7-11pm Tue-Fri. Closed Aug. **Prix fixe** €30. **Credit** MC, V.
Wildly popular under chef Yves Camdeborde, La Régalade is in competent new hands: Bruno Doucet belongs to a group of Camdeborde-inspired young chefs who are renewing the bistro genre. The country terrine that lands on your table once you have ordered is reassuringly the same as before, and Doucet has wisely left the lace curtains and provincial feel of the dining room untouched. We started with a soup of white Paimpol beans with chorizo, ladled out of a giant tureen in typically generous south-western French style. While the soup itself was creamy and richly flavoured, the thin slices of sausage seemed a little meek. Shelled escargots nestled in a little cassolette (earthenware dish) of lentils were a great idea and delicious, if very salty. Gigot d'agneau de Bellac turned out to be a plate layered with thin slices of rosy lamb – a pretty

presentation at first, but less so as the lamb cooled on the plate. Slices of poitrine de cochon (pork belly) lacked the promised croustillant and were even a bit dry, despite this being a fatty cut of meat. Both our dishes came with smooth potato purées served in cast-iron pots, one flavoured with mustard and the other with diced andouille (tripe sausage). Grapefruit salad with cassis sorbet was tangy and palate-cleansing, while the Grand Marnier soufflé (which had been a Camdeborde classic) could have used a splash more of the orange liqueur, but was otherwise suitably puffy and proud. Though it wasn't perfect, this meal was considerably more generous and tasty than most Paris bistros at this price.

15TH ARRONDISSEMENT

Bistro d'Hubert

41 bd Pasteur, 15th (01.47.34.15.50/www.bistro dhubert.com). M° Pasteur. **Open** 7.30-10.15pm Mon, Sat; 12.30-2pm, 7.30-10.15pm Tue-Fri. **Average** €55. **Prix fixe** €35. **Credit** AmEx, DC, MC, V. **Map** E9.
The decor of this friendly bistro, like its location near where the Métro comes hurtling out of the ground, is unassuming and gives little indication of the more adventurous traits of the cooking. After an appetiser of home-made duck pâté, we tucked into our starters – a beef carpaccio that had been livened up with powdered hazelnuts, and the fraîcheur de crabe, a crab meat salad sandwiched between wafer-thin biscuits and dressed with a pastis and star anise sauce. Often vegetables fade into the background of the food they are served with. Here, they don't just accompany the cooking, they underpin it. The tender wok-fried chicken was served with a pile of sautéed mushrooms, and the juicy and perfectly prepared slice of veal came with fried chayotte (or sayote)

squash, a delicately flavoured vegetable. Both dishes arrived at the table with their little bowl of fluffy mashed potato. We had originally planned on ending the dinner at this point, but when we came upon the dessert menu this idea was quickly abandoned and we brought our meal to a sticky and gooey close with the gâteau de caramel, a salted-caramel concoction served with apple mousse and elderflower syrup.

La Dînée

85 rue Leblanc, 15th (01.45.54.20.49). M° Balard. **Open** noon-2.30pm, 7.30-10.30pm Mon-Fri. **Prix fixe** €29, €32. **Credit** AmEx, DC, MC, V. **Non-smoking room. Map** A10.

This classy address is well worth the trip to the end of Métro line 8. The eclectic mix of regulars and out-of-towners filling the place on a midweek evening underlined the point. There's a hint of something Japanese about the low-key atmosphere – it's simple yet elegant with prints of fruit and vegetables on the ochre walls, bamboo placemats and attentive yet unobtrusive service. The prix fixe menus are an excellent way to sample Christophe Chabanel's inventive, often witty creations. From a tempting array of starters, we chose a light crab soufflé with mushrooms and raspberry coulis, and the sautéed prawns in a tangy pepper and tomato gazpacho, set off île flottante-style by a peak of frothy egg white and chives. Haddock lasagne was tempting as a main, but we opted for a superb plate of mixed lamb cuts with fresh mint and tabouleh, and a juicy suprême de pintade on a bed of chicory and mushrooms. The melting chocolate tart in a dark chocolate sauce was rich enough for the most decadent of palates; the flambéed banana in ginger coconut milk, accompanied by a delicate coconut-infused crème caramel, was a lighter alternative. The Sancerre 2001 balanced things out nicely.

L'Os à Moelle ★

3 rue Vasco-de-Gama, 15th (01.45.57.27.27). M° Lourmel. **Open** noon-2pm, 7-11.30pm Tue-Thur; noon-2pm, 7pm-midnight Fri, Sat. Closed three weeks in Aug and one week at Christmas. **Prix fixe** €38 (dinner only). **Lunch menu** €32. **Credit** MC, V. **Wheelchair access. Map** B9.

Lunch or dinner in this light and airy corner bistro with its lacy apple-patterned curtains is a treat and well-deserving of a detour deep into the less tourist-travelled 15th. Chef Thierry Faucher consistently produces food that is attractive, satisfying and good value for money, an increasing rarity nowadays in Paris. Starters of creamy cauliflower soup came embellished with fresh thyme and crispy croûtons, and lobster bisque adorned with cubes of Auvergne ham and fresh coriander were paragons of simplicity zinging with fresh flavour. Lobster made a reappearance in the mains as plump roasted pieces bound with couscous and studded with pungent chorizo. Roast pigeon was teamed with chestnuts and a fricassée of waxy potatoes – a perfect melding of wintry flavours. To finish off: slices of st-nectaire,

tomme and Corsican brebis with salad leaves drizzled with walnut dressing. The lunch menu offers several choices while dinner is a pre-set affair. The casual sister establishment La Cave de l'Os à Moelle, just opposite, serves robust food buffet-style, in a cellar-like setting.

Le Père Claude

51 av de la Motte-Picquet, 15th (01.47.34.03.05). M° La Motte-Picquet-Grenelle. **Open** noon-2.30pm, 7.30-10.30pm daily. **Average** €50. **Prix fixe** €30. **Credit** AmEx, MC, V. **Non-smoking room. Map** D7.

Recent renovations have made this bistro as neat and unfussy as the lobby of a modern luxury hotel – beige carpeting, Scandinavian-style furniture, and pleasant, professional waiters. But the sleekness belies the basic if well-executed bistro food, some of it roasted right behind the zinc-and-marquetry bar. A chèvre croustillant with salad was just the right combination of creamy and crisp, while the cold fish terrine cleverly came with garlicky tomato salsa. For mains, we couldn't resist that sizzling rotisserie meat, ordering a mixed grill of chicken, beef, pork and boudin, and a poulet rôti moelleux, both accompanied by silky mashed potatoes that added to the home-cooked, comfort-food feeling. For dessert, we enjoyed an apple clafoutis and an assortment of sorbets, including green apple worthy of an Italian gelato. Surprisingly, the light-filled, glassed-in terrace jutting on to the pavement is reserved for non-smokers, a real plus. On the afternoon we visited, the crowd was mostly middle-aged couples and business bods (we were the sole English speakers) and, seeing the photo near the entrance of a smiling Chirac with Gregory Peck, we wondered how often heads of state and Hollywooders really eat here. Just then Lionel Jospin and his entourage arrived for lunch, proving that even ousted party leaders appreciate a humble lunch in an executive setting.

Le Sept/Quinze

29 av Lowendal, 15th (01.43.06.23.06). M° Cambronne. **Open** noon-2.30pm, 8-11pm Mon-Fri; 8-11pm Sat. Closed two weeks in Aug. **Prix fixe** €26 (dinner only). **Lunch menu** €17, €23. **Credit** MC, V. **Map** D8.

There is a lot to like about this convivial Mediterranean bistro, stranded on a rather lonesome strip between the 7th and 15th arrondissements. Considering the quiet neighbourhood, we were surprised to find the place absolutely packed with a young, professional, mostly French crowd when we visited on a Saturday night. The mood inside was deafeningly festive. No one seemed to mind that their elbows brushed their neighbours' as they sliced into crispy brik pastry packages of beef topped with black olive tapenade. Gently priced, modern and sunny, this food is a refreshing change from heavier, standard bistro fare. A rewarding combination (a special the night we visited) was a shallow dish of warm Jerusalem artichokes in cream sauce, topped by a glistening heap of salty salmon roe and garnished with a cool wedge of lemon. Unfortunately, not all the dishes were so well-balanced. A rocket, apple and walnut salad with an oversweet vinaigrette was mounted on a tuile of Asiago cheese that was chewy where it should have been crispy, and tender little squid grilled a la plancha with oranges and almonds just tipped the flavour scale over into bitter. Still, this light and elegant fare hits more than it misses. The short wine list was augmented by specials that included, unusually, both a Californian red zinfandel and an Argentinian sauvignon. Their sweet, bold notes are just right for this cuisine, and their presence on the blackboard shows that someone here is paying attention. Judging by the crowd, it's paying off. The same team runs the very likeable Bistro d'en Face (24 rue du Docteur-Finlay, 15th, 01.45.77.14.59), which is popular with editors from the nearby Hachette publishing house.

Le Troquet ★

21 rue François-Bonvin, 15th (01.45.66.89.00). M° Sèvres-Lecourbe. **Open** noon-2pm, 7.30-11pm Tue-Sat. Closed three weeks in Aug and one week at Christmas. **Prix fixe** €30 (dinner only €38). **Lunch menu** €22, €26. **Credit** MC, V. **Non-smoking room. Map** D8.

The wicker pelote racket and the tablecloths with seven stripes indicate chef Christian Etchebest's allegiance to the Pays Basque. This is also reflected in some of the ingredients, such as chipirons, brebis cheese with cherry jam, and the Espelette pepper sprinkled on the plates. The €30 three-course blackboard menu is remarkable value, though a few of the day's specials, such as a seasonal sauté of ceps and girolles and the game dishes, cost extra. In fact the cooking is if anything even better than on our previous visit, and good-humoured, enthusiastic service and a cheerful Saturday night crowd all contribute to make this one of the most reliable bets in the capital. Chilled mushroom soup was a delicate treat, though our winning starter was the unlikely combination of chipirons (baby squid) and ris de veau with chicory and pine kernels, a deliciously inky mix of textures. We continued with a succulent saddle of lamb with white Tarbes beans and a refined ballotine of poulet – chicken breast rolled and stuffed with mushrooms – served with a mousseline purée. We finished sagely with pots de chocolat, and a chewy meringue with damsons with homemade ice-cream, while the Italians next to us enjoyed their impressively risen soufflés so much that one of them rang home to describe it to a friend.

16TH ARRONDISSEMENT

Le Bistrot des Vignes

1 rue Jean-Bologne, 16th (01.45.27.76.64). M° La Muette or Passy. **Open** noon-3pm, 7-11pm daily. Closed three weeks in Aug. **Prix fixe** €28 (dinner only). **Lunch menu** €25. **Credit** AmEx, DC, MC, V. **Wheelchair access. Map** A6.

Tucked away on a quiet corner in the 16th, just down from Passy Plaza shopping central, the Bistrot des Vignes pulls in a crowd of locals. Such is their loyalty that many even have their own table constantly set aside, just in case they drop by. Just try bagging a table, unannounced, for Sunday lunch. Impossible! A relaxed, friendly vibe prevails with butter-yellow walls garnished with black and white photos of vineyards and grape pickers, and tangy-coloured chairs (red, blue, green and yellow) adding a capricious country touch. Food follows the seasons, with starters running from salads (spinach leaf and fresh parmesan, red peppers marinated in pesto), to feathery red mullet 'doughnuts' with a sweet chilli dipping sauce or a marinated salmon and broccoli tart. Mains in the form of duck breast coated in honey, served sliced on triangles of toasted gingerbread, and John Dory fillets baked with spicy aubergine and peppers with a watercress sauce showed a chef adept at turning out likeable, nicely balanced food. The île flottante is a dessert delight.

La Butte Chaillot

110 bis av Kléber, 16th (01.47.27.88.88/www.butte chaillot.com). M° Trocadéro. **Open** noon-2.30pm, 7-11pm Mon-Fri, Sun; 7-11pm Sat. Closed three weeks in Aug. **Average** €45. **Prix fixe** €32. **Credit** AmEx, DC, MC, V. **Wheelchair access. Non-smoking room. Map** B5.

What a shame this restaurant has such dismal decor. Brown walls, leather chairs, glass light fixtures, bland prints, a flat-screen telly (that happily wasn't switched on) and a smattering of African vases make it look like the lobby of a chain hotel that hasn't been decorated since the '80s. Happily the food was better, as you would expect from a menu devised by one of Paris's top chefs, Guy Savoy. The set menu draws from the à la carte and offers reasonable value. A starter of nutty terrine de pintade in thin slices with a fruity chutney, frisée and a dribble of pistachio sauce looked and tasted great, while the creamy wild mushroom and foie gras soup was also delicious, though tepid. A crisp-skinned sea bass fillet on a round of sweet potato with an overly frothy lemongrass sauce was far tastier than it looked, and while the magret de canard was a little fatty, it was accompanied by a perfect mushroom risotto. The moelleux au chocolat, which went by the name of 'coulant' (runny), was average, and the saveurs de clementine et figues was a glass of refreshing sorbet, clementine pieces and clementine pulp but not much sign of the fig. Our charming Senegalese waiter did, however, make this a better experience than it might have been. If they cure the draught from the door, serve the food a bit hotter and call in the decorators it could be a good address.

Le Petit Rétro

5 rue Mesnil, 16th (01.44.05.06.05/www.petitretro. fr). M° Victor-Hugo. **Open** noon-2.30pm, 7-10.30pm Mon-Fri; 7-10.30pm Sat. Closed three weeks in Aug. **Average** €35. **Lunch menu** €19, €24. **Credit** AmEx, MC, V. **Non-smoking room. Map** B4.

A la Pomponette. *See p72.*

Just around the corner from the fountains of place Victor-Hugo this art nouveau-tiled bistro serves hearty dishes that would make a butcher proud. There's lots of lovely offal and the dishes of the day chalked on a blackboard looked particularly enticing. We chose the œufs pochés with foie gras, an indulgent combination of nannyish runny eggs and grown-up foie gras, while the regular menu yielded an impressive cassolette d'escargots with pleurottes. Like a magician at a children's party, the chef emerged from the kitchen to demonstrate how to cut the puffy crust of this dish and mash it in the wonderfully earthy snail- and mushroom-filled gravy. Utterly delicious. The croustillant de boudin was equally good: black pudding in a pastry crust with rich sauce, served with fried potatoes and apples, and the blackboard's canaillette grillée (duck andouillette) on a bed of potato purée was marred only by too much Dijon mustard in the sauce. Stuffed almost to the gills, we had to request a respite before the ice-cream filled profiteroles, lolling in their potent chocolate sauce, and a stickily good nougat glacé. Our only complaints are that the service is too swift for such lavish fare and that the waiter couldn't help much with our choice of wine. We struck out with a Beaumes de Venise, a bitter bottle that did not merit its €24 and rather marred our meal. The kir aperitifs, though, were perfect.

Le Scheffer

22 rue Scheffer, 16th (01.47.27.81.11).
M° Trocadéro. **Open** noon-2.30pm, 7.30-10.30pm Mon-Sat. Closed Sat in July & Aug. **Average** €29. **Credit** AmEx, MC, V. **Map** B5.
All locals and no English spoken here, which may explain the blasé reception we received upon entering this neighbourhood bistro on a dead street a few blocks from the Trocadéro district. Other diners in the pleasingly deep red, streamlined interior ranged from middle-aged ladies out for a

midday meal to business folk on their lunch breaks. We enjoyed our starters of plain green beans and a cold lentil and smoked magret salad, followed by a succulent confit de canard with sautéed potatoes and wild mushrooms, and rouget (red mullet) fillets in tomato cream sauce with rice. We both ordered the tarte du jour – fresh plums in season, which was so tart it made our eyes water (and the crust was tough and dull). The Monsieur who greeted us was affable enough, if bored, but Madame was about as cold as the plate of asparagus vinaigrette. No matter. Perhaps the only way classic, unpretentious and uninventive but reliable bistros such as Le Scheffer will stay authentic is to shun outsiders.

17TH ARRONDISSEMENT

L'Abadache

89 rue Lemercier, 17th (01.42.26.37.33) M° Brochant.
Open noon-2.15pm, 8-11pm Mon-Fri; 8-11pm Sat. Closed two weeks in Aug and one week at Christmas. **Prix fixe** €24. **Lunch menu** €14, €18. **Credit** MC, V. **Non-smoking room. Map** F1.
Since chef Yann Piton is a solid talent, the prices are gentle, the produce excellent and the service obliging, the trek to this sweet little bistro with an open kitchen and a tellingly hip crowd in the ever-trendier Batignolles neighbourhood north of the Place de Clichy is well worth it. Just be advised that the setting itself couldn't be much simpler – an over-lit dining room where the only real atmosphere is the bonhomie generated by a crowd that's contentedly and communally sharing a bargain, a clever secret (this place is still an insiders' address) and some very good food. Piton's blackboard menu is short and market-driven, but a recent meal offered a good illustration of his homely but inventive style. Starters of creamy watercress soup garnished with thin slices of stilton and lots of chervil, and a crispy 'brik' filled with sautéed deboned rabbit were

delicious, as were main courses of meltingly tender osso buco, and a thick pork chop (free-range from Brittany) with a sautée of baby vegetables. Our neighbours went for the Irish côte de boeuf for two, a sumptuous piece of meat served in red-wine sauce with hand-cut frites, and were happy indeed. The selection of French and English (stilton and cheddar) cheeses for €6 was a lovely way to finish the wine, and a shared pear financier with liquorice ice-cream provided perfect punctuation to a very pleasant meal. Oh, and if you're wondering about the Anglo touches on the menu, suffice to say that Piton's wife is a Brit. An excellent address if you're planning a bar tour of this lively part of town.

Le Bistrot d'à Côté Flaubert ★

10 rue Gustave-Flaubert, 17th (01.42.67.05.81/www. michelrostang.com). M° Ternes or Pereire. **Open** noon-2pm, 7.30-11pm daily. Closed one week in Aug. **Average** €50. **Lunch menu** €29 (Mon-Fri). **Credit** AmEx, DC, MC, V. **Map** D2.
Michel Rostang has his finger in so many pies now that you might not expect a visit to one of his offshoot bistros to be so special. But this meal proved possibly the most enjoyable we have had this year. Le Bistro d'à Côté Flaubert was the original baby bistro when it opened in 1987 and the food continues to please. Rostang's formula is so right – not dressing up bistro food with faux haute cuisine presentation, but elevating it with great ingredients and spot-on cooking. The dining room, a former belle époque épicerie, is fun and charming with its tongue-in-cheek decor of toby jugs and old Michelin guides and an elegant portrait of Rostang's grandmother on the burgundy-coloured walls. Waiters and waitresses slide between the tightly arranged tables in bright red ties. They seemed rather inexperienced, but were certainly good-humoured and enthusiastic. Most diners were talking loudly in English; they included a typically 17th mix of big hair and leopardskin, one old lady who kept her fur coat on throughout the meal, and bourgeois parents taking out their sullen children. A lobster salad was a fresh and appetising pyramid of mesclun, coriander, the most succulent lobster flesh and tiny ravioli; the wild duck and foie gras pâté en croute was deliciously moist with its taste-enhancing jelly, and the crusty bread is wonderful. The same could be said of the flavoursome tendrons de veau stuffed with mushrooms and the daily special of sea bass in a Thai-style sauce. Glazed cubed carrot and turnip and the lemongrass-spiced risotto that came with the fish were served in mini cast-iron casseroles that keep their heat. Like many diners, we suspect, we didn't realise until it came to looking at the desserts that you have to order the fondant au chocolat before the meal starts. But after a little bit of banter with the waitress this extra-bitter version of the moelleux arrived and melted like magma when we cut into it. The pain perdu with marmalade sorbet was equally good. And though it took consultations with three waiters to get a genuine wine recommendation, we were pleased with the excellent Saumur Champigny Vielles Vignes that we finally drank – and amused that, despite the Beaujolais Nouveau cards sitting on each table, one waitress expressly told us: 'Whatever you do, don't order it'.

Café d'Angel

16 rue Brey, 17th (01.47.54.03.33). M° Charles-de-Gaulle-Etoile or Ternes. **Open** noon-2pm, 7.30-10pm Mon-Fri. Closed two weeks at Christmas and three weeks in Aug. **Average** €38. **Prix fixe** €38. **Lunch menu** €19, €22. **Credit** MC, V. **Map** C3.
Since this easygoing spot with white tiles (it was once a butcher's shop), red walls and an open kitchen has long been lauded by French food writers, we came to dinner hungry and curious. Two hours later, nearly deaf and so impregnated with cigarette smoke that we hung our coats outside overnight, we were relieved to be in the street again. If we hadn't eaten badly, we came away in what is perhaps the saddest of all states after a restaurant meal – indifference. To be fair, the service was prompt and kind, the bread good, and the house wines were well chosen and priced – we went with the Gaillac at €16 – but, quite simply, the food here is overwrought. A starter of marinated salmon topped with a thatch of too-salty celeriac rémoulade and a few dessicated crayfish set the tone for a meal that was consistently too rich and and too complicated. The house foie gras was nicely made, but main courses of sea bream and guinea hen both came with sautéed potatoes and shallots and a similar coral sauce that seemed to have been cast as the all-purpose culinary thrill and frill for the evening. This neither-fish-nor-fowl motif extended to almost everything we ate here, aside from a very nice dessert of roasted almond tuile with vanilla ice-cream and spiced pears.

Chez Léon

32 rue Legendre, 17th (01.42.27.06.82). M° Villiers. **Open** noon-2pm, 7.30-10pm Mon-Fri. Closed Aug and one week at Christmas. **Prix fixe** €29. **Credit** AmEx, MC, V. **Map** E2.
From the outside this place looks rather impressive, intimidating even, with all its brass and starched napkins. Inside, you find yourself in a simple and unselfconsciously old-fashioned Parisian bistro full of pullover-wearing pillars of the local community. All very untrendy and rather pleasant, especially as, exceptionally enough in the age of the euro, prices have actually come down here since last year. You can now get a three-course supper with wine for €29, which is good value as the menu includes some of the middle-class heroes of French cuisine. The home-made ham in parsley aspic, for example, was an extraordinarily savoury (if slightly rich) starter. We drank a big Languedoc red with it. It needed something lighter – a Touraine, for example – but still, it was a happy reunion with this fine Burgundian classic. Andouillette with Dijon mustard sauce and an impeccable steak-frites were the sort of thing you think you must be able to do as well at home but can't. Puddings of banana tart

and croustillant aux pommes were similarly irreproachable. A good place to celebrate your 20th wedding anniversary.

Le Clou

132 rue Cardinet, 17th (01.42.27.36.78/www. restaurant-leclou.fr). M° Malesherbes. **Open** noon-2.30pm, 7.30-10.30pm Mon-Fri; 7.30-10.30pm Sat. Closed two weeks in Aug and one week at Christmas. **Average** €35. **Prix fixe** €30 (dinner only). **Lunch menu** €20. **Credit** AmEx, DC, MC, V. **Map** E1.

This red-fronted former brasserie is somewhat off the beaten track, but its combination of honest cooking, smiling service and terrific value makes it well worth seeking out. Though keeping costs down means that tables are crammed together, the decor is classier than you'd expect, with white tablecloths, decent glassware and an abundance of dried flowers. Chef and owner Christian Leclou eschews any gimmickry in favour of careful sourcing of ingredients, producing rustic dishes such as a chunky terrine de volaille, or a more refined croustillant d'escargots, made with petits gris and filo pastry. Fish features strongly on the daily changing menu, with, for example, a warm salad of coquilles St-Jacques and cod cheeks, or a huge fillet of pan-fried sea bass resting on chopped, roasted tomatoes. But the star (and one of the few permanent menu fixtures) must be the rosemary-scented, long-simmered, confit d'épaule d'agneau, meltingly tender and served with a smoky aubergine purée. Desserts maintain the high standard, with a home-made nougat glacé, studded with walnuts and candied angelica, and an excellent moelleux au chocolat. Wines are selected just as carefully as the food, making for some truly remarkable prices.

Restaurant L'Entredgeu ★

83 rue Laugier, 17th (01.40.54.97.24). M° Porte de Champerret. **Open** noon-2pm, 7.30-10.30pm Tue-Thur; noon-2pm, 7.30-11pm Fri, Sat. Closed three weeks in Aug, ten days at Christmas and one week in May. **Lunch menu** €22, €28 (Mon-Fri). **Credit** MC, V. **Map** C2.

After stints at the helm at Chez Michel and its off-spring Chez Casimir, chef Phillipe Tredgeu and his wife struck out on their own in 2003. Despite an awkward location and tongue-twisting name, this bistro has been packed since it opened with diners drawn by the inventive, impeccably executed cuisine delivered at reasonable prices. The blackboard menu changes daily, with a broader choice than the usual bistro ardoise, and all the ingredients deployed by Tredgeu have a crispy freshness. Starters vary from reworked classics such as the home-made, heavy-duty country paté to the original verrine de legumes, a delightfully presented dish of grilled vegetables with warm goat's cheese. On our visit, the waiter arrived theatrically with the crème de langoustine, a high-brow take on the bistro classic of fish soup, and we swooned over the gamey morsel of quail set off perfectly by the sweetness of the dried-fruit and bulghur wheat accompaniment. Matching the

excellence of the starters were the mains of duck breast and grilled foie gras served atop mashed potato and celeriac doused with a luscious gravy, and a seared wild white tuna on a bed of crispy fried vegetables. Desserts are similarly inventive, with the highlights being oven-roasted figs with real vanilla ice-cream on a delicate brandy snap, and a sweet brioche perdue with cardomom-infused poached apricots. Complaints have been voiced about the sardine-style seating and the rapid turnover of tables, but after such a good meal it would be churlish to quibble.

La Soupière

154 av de Wagram, 17th (01.42.27.00.73) M° Wagram. **Open** noon-2pm, 8-10.30pm Mon-Fri; 8-10.30pm Sat. **Average** €40. **Prix fixe** €28, €55. **Credit** AmEx, MC, V. **Map** D1.

This quiet and well-mannered little spot in the 17th drives mycologists mad with pleasure, since it's perhaps the only restaurant in Paris that specialises in mushrooms all year round. Autumn is, of course, the most glorious of all seasons for funghi freaks, as ceps, girolles, morels and other fleshy fodder of the forest floor start to appear in local markets and on menus. At the Soupière (soup tureen) they come in a variety of guises, including a sublime salad of finely sliced raw ceps with olive oil and sea salt as a starter, along with a lusciously earthy mushroom soup, followed by main courses such as brill with a sautée of mixed mushrooms or a splendid sautee of girolles in wine sauce with cinammon, the latter proving to be an uncommon and surprisingly pleasant preparation. The wine list is a bit dull and service can be rather leisurely, especially at noon, but the cooking, using first-rate produce, is impeccable.

Tête de Goinfre

16 rue Jacquemont, 17th (01.42.29.89.80). M° La Fourche. **Open** noon-2.30pm, 8-10.30pm Mon-Sat. **Average** €30. **Credit** MC, V. **Map** F1.

Sensitive about your weight, or emotionally attached to pigs? Be warned: the name translates as 'greedy guts', and the interior designers' motif was clearly 'porky'. Dinky pig ornaments abound, their cute factor jarring abrasively against the reality of the free platter of charcuterie you get while waiting for a seat in this popular bistro. Having kicked off with honourable, if not inspirational leeks in vinaigrette and mackerel rillettes, we homed in on a black pudding that had a sensuously crumbly texture; the 'C'-word ('congealed') was uttered approvingly. Things wobbled from the moment we realised that the poached salmon was in need of a holiday; the strawberries and the tart (of strawberry tart fame) seemed estranged; while the chocolate mousse headed straight for the roof of the mouth and clung there doggedly. So OK, we couldn't rave about the food. Maybe this was an off-day, because, as we've noted, it's busy enough. But we can recommend Tête de Goinfre for its atmosphere. It's fun, it's friendly, and the overall experience is delightful.

Le Poulbot Gourmet. See p72.

18TH ARRONDISSEMENT

Le Bouclard

1 rue Cavalotti, 18th (01.45.22.60.01/www.bouclard. com). M° Place de Clichy. **Open** 7-11.30pm Mon-Sat. **Average** €40. **Credit** AmEx, DC, MC, V. **Non-smoking room**. **Map** G1.

Hidden behind the place de Clichy, Le Bouclard, which in old Parisian slang means workplace, has a daunting mock rustic-meets-belle époque decoration, and its boast of cuisine grand-mère looks initially compromised, but the sight of the warm rolling presence of boss Michel Bonnemort reassured us that the food would be serious. A picture of his nicely rounded great-grandmother, whose recipes were the chef's culinary inspiration, looked down on us encouragingly as we ordered a gratin d'écrevisses

(crayfish) and a tourte de gibier. The compact gamey tourte came with a spicy redcurrant coulis, and the creamy gratin was equally successful. We chose the plat du jour, which was a sauté d'agneau aux girolles, with tender morsels of lamb nestling in an intensely flavoured wild mushroom sauce, accompanied by potatoes fried in goose fat and a splendid cheese-topped purée. We resisted the more ordinary-looking trad puddings in favour of another glass of the exceptional 1998 Côtes du Rhône. Big parties of fellow guests were all having a good time, lapping up the cuisine and very French atmosphere, complete with noisy hits of the '60s. Not somewhere to go for a quiet evening, but for a decent priced, authentic feed in garrulous company don't hesitate to sample Bonnemort's cooking.

Café Burq

6 rue Burq, 18th (01.42.52.81.27). M° Abbesses or Blanche. **Open** 8pm-midnight Mon-Sat. **Average** €23. **Credit** MC, V. **Map** H1.

Formerly Le Moulin à Vins, this compact two-level café with no decor to speak of beyond several lighting fixtures made from orange Plexiglas has been taken over by a new team – an architect and an actor. They've made it such a febrile success that the good-natured waiters always seem perilously close to letting the whole place slip completely out of control. Not ideal for a tranquil tête-à-tête, but very much a happy, happening pre-club launch pad with a group of friends, this place is all about a bawdy, smoky good time. Surprisingly, given such anarchic circumstances, the food is quite good and very reasonably priced, too. From the blackboard menu, go with starters such as baked camembert with salad or a delicious chicken breast salad in a ginger-and-soy sauce vinaigrette, and then opt for an onglet with red onion-and-balsamic sauce or maybe the lamb shoulder or roast salmon. All mains come with delicious mash. The wine list is intelligent, if veering towards rather high-octane bottles; the Beaumes de Venise clocked in at a hefty 14 per cent. Desserts are excellent, too – try the chocolate quenelles. A great snapshot of the new energy in Montmartre.

Chez Toinette ★

20 rue Germain-Pilon, 18th (01.42.54.44.36). M° Abbesses. **Open** 7.30-11pm Tue-Sat. Closed Aug. **Average** €25. **Credit** MC, V. **Map** H2.

This stalwart purveyor of bistro fare in a side street behind the Théâtre de Montmartre has steadily increased its prices in line with its burgeoning success. The blackboard menu is still, however, good value in an area notorious for tourist rip-offs. Squeezing into the seats at our table, we were immediately set at ease by the amiable waiter, who described each dish with pride, and then presented us with an appetiser of olives, ripe cherry tomatoes, and crisp radishes. From the starters, try the red-blooded wild-boar terrine, the pleasing chèvre chaud with a glorious creamy st marcellin on a bed of roquette and lettuce, or the soufflé-like asparagus quiche. This is something of a red meat emporium with a string of toothy carnivorous mains including mignon de porc, spring lamb and assorted steaks, with only the occasional fish dish. We opted for one of each, and the lamb seared in rosemary was a delicious lean morsel; the simple and elegant John Dory accompanied by an effective combination of fluffy mash and steamed vegetables. If the desserts mainly cover standard ground of crème brûlée and chocolate mousse, we rounded off a satisfying meal on a high note with the alcoholic option of Armagnac-steeped prunes.

Chez Grisette

14 rue Houdon, 18th (01.42.62.04.80). M° Abbesses or Pigalle. **Open** 7-11pm Mon-Fri. **Average** €25. **Prix fixe** €21, €27. **Credit** MC, V. **Map** H2.

In a steep Montmartre lane that's stuffed with really interesting young designer boutiques, this delightful wine bistro is just the sort of place you'll wish was on your local corner. The proprietress, a warm, knowledgeable and very friendly ex-school teacher, instantly makes everyone welcome in her fiefdom, and it's a comfortable and pleasant place to tipple and nibble to your heart's content. Packed in the evening with an intriguing crowd that runs from arty locals to tour-bus aunties, flutey-voiced bankers to cross-dressing prostitutes, this place is a treat for Saturday lunch, since it's quiet and sunny, and you get a good chance to have a chat with your hostess, a lady who travels all over France finding her own excellent wines. We chose an all syrah Cuilleron Remeage from vineyards abutting those that produce Côte Rôtie in the Rhône valley, and if it took a while to open up, it was delicious by the time we got to coffee. The food here is excellent, too, ranging from dense, earthy terrine de campagne served with green tomato jam from the proprietress's garden to a jacket potato with melted gaperon – a garlicky, peppery cheese from the Auvergne, followed by one of the blackboard specials, maybe a delicious pork shin on a bed of lentils or a plate of cold meats from Aurillac that included a ham as melting and flavourful as a good Jabugo. Desserts are moreish nursery treats such as baked apple in caramel sauce – otherwise finish up with some cheese, maybe bleu d'auvergne with another basket of some of the best baguette to be found anywhere in Paris. A real find, so book.

L'Entracte

44 rue d'Orsel, 18th (01.46.06.93.41). M° Abbesses or Anvers. **Open** noon-2pm, 7-10.30pm Wed-Sat; noon-2pm Sun. Closed one week at Easter, Aug and one week at Christmas. **Average** €35. **Credit** AmEx, MC, V. **Map** J2.

Many a famous French thespian has unwound after facing the footlights at this intimate theatre-themed bistro just across the street from the Théâtre Charles-Dullin, and the low lights, lavish floral arrangements and framed photographs create an atmosphere of understated glamour in a place that would feel like a private club were it not for chef-owner Gilles Chiriaux and his wife Sonia's warm attentions. Though it's located just at the foot of the funicular that takes tourists uphill to the Sacré-Coeur, few tourists find their way to this cosy spot where everything is freshly cooked in a shoebox of a kitchen. Chiriaux, an able chef and a bit of a character, dotes on his customers and he'll come into the dining room, a distance of just a few steps, to see why someone hasn't finished their plate – if they don't like it, he'll offer to make them something else. Known for making some of the best frites in Paris, he does everything from scratch, which is why this is a great place to sample such homely French classics as mackerel marinated in white wine or pâté de tête (head cheese), along with other simple pleasures like sautéed veal kidneys, hand-chopped steak tartare and a perfect rack of lamb. Don't miss the heavenly chocolate mousse either.

La Galère des Rois

8 rue Cavallotti 18th (01.42.93.34.58). M° Place de Clichy. **Open** noon-2.30pm, 7.30-11pm Mon-Fri; 7.30-11pm Sat. Closed Aug and one week at Christmas. **Average** €35. **Lunch menu** €12.50, €15. **Credit** MC, V. **Non-smoking room. Map** G1.

With its pine-panelled walls and '70s fitted carpet, this is a nearly fly-in-amber example of that once common genus, the neighbourhood bistro. Such bistros were never meant to induce a gourmet swoon, but rather to offer a fair feed for a fair price in a convivial setting, and once this has been sorted, La Galère does a great job in its class. The male welcome is rather barking but, without being asked, the waiter brought a bowl of water for our dog, and, cued by our accents, patiently explained the daily specials in English. Starters of warm breaded goat's cheese on salad, and green asparagus in mushroom juice with a poached egg were a notch better than average, and mains of braised lamb shank and steak were just fine, although the duck fat-laced pommes de terre sarladaises were jarring with lamb and beef. Enjoying a superb Cahors at a knock-down bargain price of €14 we almost gave dessert a miss, but the chocolate mousse was a treat when we gave in. A useful address, since there's a lot of nightlife nearby.

Aux Négociants

27 rue Lambert, 18th (01.46.06.15.11). M° Château-Rouge. **Open** noon-2.30pm Mon; noon-2.30pm, 8-10.30pm Tue-Fri. Closed Aug. **Average** €26. **Credit** AmEx, MC, V. **Map** J1.

Ah, now you know why you came to Paris! Little bistros like this, like the superb papeterie next door, are getting rarer by the year, but at the Négociants the ceiling just gets a little browner, the patron a little balder and the menu a little porkier as time goes by. This restaurant not only boasts a handsome, horseshoe-shaped bar, but people actually stand there, drink wine and read the newspaper while you're eating. How authentic is that? And the food is absolutely worthy of the place. We enjoyed a couple of faultless starters: pork rillettes, and herring fillets with onion, juniper berries and warm potatoes.

Although the cooking leans towards Lyon, the blackboard wine menu is quite ecumenical with what looked like considered and dependable choices from all around France. As we forked our way happily through the day's specials of stuffed cabbage and sabodet dauphinois (a big sausage with pistachio nuts), we sloshed down a bottle and a bit of light, fresh and gently priced Côte Roannaise (Loire Valley). It was getting towards siesta time as we ambled towards afters and there was nothing left but chocolate mousse. As disappointments go, this we could cope with.

Le Petit Caboulot

6 pl Jacques-Froment, 18th (01.46.27.19.00). M°
Guy-Môquet. **Open** 11am-3pm, 6pm-midnight Mon-Sat. **Average** €26. **Lunch menu** €10 (Mon-Fri).
Credit DC, MC, V. **Wheelchair access. Map** G1.
Though it looks like any old corner bistro from the outside, some effort has been put into the decor of this neighbourhood place behind the Cimetière de Montmartre. The owners saw the retro appeal of the zinc bar and cream paint interior complete with a glassed-in phone box, and have added a jolly collection of provincial enamel advertising plaques, making it look like a restaurant that's trying to be French in Clapham or Greenwich Village. It was good ingredients rather than presentation that impressed us in the food. The old Robochef (food processor) had clearly been put to use for the tricolor avocado and red pepper mousse with tomato salsa – three deliciously different flavours that danced on the tongue – while the ragoût of snails and ratte potatoes was pretty tasty, with maybe a touch of truffle oil. Mains – rather pricey at €13 for simple dishes – nevertheless provided good, wholesome fare. The succulent rosemary-roasted knuckle of lamb and garlicky farm-bred chicken came with flat pools of mashed potato that looked like they had been lingering in the warming drawer but tasted good. We both went for the tarte fine aux pommes, more like a flat, round tarte Tatin and delicious with its melting ice-cream. There's a good wine list by the bottle or glass and our robust Cahors was well worth its €20.

A la Pomponette

42 rue Lepic, 18th (01.46.06.08.36). M° Abbesses
or Blanche. **Open** noon-2.30pm, 7-11pm Mon-Thur; noon-2.30pm, 7pm-midnight Fri, Sat. Closed Aug.
Average €42. **Prix fixe** €32. **Lunch menu** €18.
Credit AmEx, DC, MC, V. **Wheelchair access.**
Map H1.
Few other restaurants in Paris evoke the bistro genus with such unselfconscious charm as this almost century-old (1909) table founded by Arthur Delacroix, a retired soldier (hence the military paraphernalia) and still run with tremendous professionalism by his great-grandchildren. Happily, there's nothing hokey about it either – it remains a much-loved and respected neighbourhood institution that doesn't go out of its way for the tourist trade, since it doesn't have to, but does

Café Noir. *See p74.*

delight in teaching les étrangers a thing or two about real bistro food. A mood of bonhomie greets you, and it only gets better when starters such as snails sizzling in garlic butter, rabbit in aspic, country terrine or marrow bones (a real rarity) come to the table. Then go with dishes such as braised veal with olives, boeuf mode (beef stewed with carrots, onions and bay leaf), chicken in cream with morel mushrooms or skate grenobloise. The menu changes regularly, but remains a loveable battery of pre-war classics. Desserts are a bit less interesting, although the cheese course is just fine, as is the floating island.

Le Poulbot Gourmet ★

39 rue Lamarck, 18th (01.46.06.86.00).
M° Lamarck-Caulaincourt. **Open** noon-2pm, 7.30-10pm Mon-Sat; noon-2pm Sun (closed Sun 1 June-30 Sept). Closed two weeks in mid-Aug. **Average** €35.
Lunch menu €18. **Credit** MC, V. **Map** H1.
From the cordial Gallic welcome to the pleasant but precise service and a kitchen that has thoroughly mastered a register of old-fashioned bourgeois cooking now so rare that it has become a fascinating delicacy, this proud, snug restaurant in a quiet residential corner of Montmartre is a blueprint for a certain type of very civilised, very adult French dining experience. With pretty 19th-century mouldings, snowy linens and a tidy, well-lit, well-run dining room, this place offers a beautifully prepared menu of festive eats, ranging from simple pleasures such as foie gras with a glass of Jurançon or a plate of good oysters, to more complex starters such as a tartelette of goat's cheese, viande des grisons (dried beef), endive and artichoke; here, the endive was splayed on the plate like petals, the meat was snipped into tiny pieces, and a plump artichoke heart was capped with a thick slice of warm, runny cheese. Another excellent starter with a similarly elaborate and unexpected construction involved house-smoked salmon, aubergine caviar and endive. It's a pleasure to experience the work of seasoned

chef Jean-Paul Langevin, who feels no need or desire to parade around the dining room. Instead, he lets main courses such as an impeccably cooked fillet of sea bass in a rich red wine sauce or pan-fried scallops placed on pools of garlicky green sauce carry his message of intelligent, politely provocative gastronomy, where good produce is dressed up but never overwhelmed by inventive sauces and garnishes. The caramelised apple and raisin tart is superb, as is the terrine of bitter chocolate with spice bread and cherries soaked in eau de vie. Avoid the thin, acidic Alsatian pinot noir and go with something stouter.

Rendez-vous des Chauffeurs

11 rue des Portes Blanches, 18th (01.42.64.04.17). M° Marcadet-Poissoniers. **Open** noon-2.30pm, 7.30-11pm daily. **Average** €24. **Prix fixe** €14 (until 8.30pm). **Credit** MC, V.

Much like the diner in America, the old-fashioned worker's budget lunch spot is an endangered breed in Paris, hurt by competition from chains and fast food outlets. Hip addresses have taken up some of the slack, but every now and then, in an unexpected corner of the city, vieux Paris reappears in the form of check tablecloths and meat-laden menus, with a patronne who has a smile for everyone and knows the names of most of her customers. Even if you're not a regular, you'll feel like you've been part of this tradition forever as you chow down on rillettes, steak or andouillette. The highlight of pretty well every dish on the menu is the fabulous fat French fries. The house wine included in the menu is a surprisingly decent option, but if you're ordering à la carte, check out the blackboard for wine selections, most of which hover at the affordable and beautifully drinkable €22 mark. Sit with your back to the wall so you can admire the art deco stylings of the bar, and don't hesitate to linger over your coffee with a newspaper: this establishment prides itself on efficiency, but gives no one reason to rush.

19TH ARRONDISSEMENT

La Cave Gourmande

10 rue du Général-Brunet, 19th (01.40.40.03.30). M° Botzaris. **Open** 12.15-2.30pm, 7.30-10.30pm Mon-Fri. Closed one week in Feb and three weeks in Aug. **Prix fixe** €32 (dinner only). **Lunch menu** €28. **Credit** MC, V. **Non-smoking room.**

Obscure Métro line fans rejoice. You now have an excuse to take the 3 bis AND the 7 bis en route to La Cave Gourmande, leaving others to wonder why anyone would trek so far to be ensconced in a dated dining room. American chef Mark Singer provides the answer in the food. Singer, whose prix fixe-only menu changes every six or seven weeks, keeps diners on their toes, daring them to imagine what 'suckling pig with pineapple and clove' tastes like then surprising them as every artfully presented dish arrives. Starters of frog meat in giant wonton-style wrappers swam in a pool of sweet garlic sauce. A main dish of cod served in a sauce made with green onion and pomelo illustrated Singer's knack for dishes rich in flavour minus the heaviness, thanks to a menu that favours olive oil over butter. Ditto for desserts of white peach gratin laced with rum and a dark chocolate sabayon with nougatine sprinkled like rock candy over the top, which left us feeling pleasantly full, but not bloated. For cheese-lovers, the €6 splurge for the cheese of the moment is well worth it.

Restaurant L'Hermès ★

23 rue Mélingue, 19th (01.42.39.94.70). M° Pyrénées. **Open** noon-2pm, 7.30-10.30pm Tue, Thur-Sat; 7.30-10.30pm Wed. Closed Aug, one week in Feb and one week at Easter. **Average** €33. **Prix fixe** €26. **Lunch menu** €13. **Credit** MC, V. **Non-smoking room. Map** D3.

Just north of the Pyrenees, literally and figuratively (it is hidden between the Buttes Chaumont and Pyrénées Métro) is this neighbourhood secret worth discovering. Yellow walls, Mediterranean checked tablecloths and oil paintings of vegetables make for a welcoming atmosphere, and the friendly staff are passionate about south-western cuisine. The prix fixe changes weekly and the à la carte fortnightly, so seasonal produce is much in evidence, such as the reinette apples and wild mushrooms of our early autumn visit. There is also a luxury plat on offer for gourmands – on that day a civet de lièvre à la royale (stuffed with foie gras) for the princely sum of €35, and a cassoulet. From the €26 prix fixe, all three daily specials proved good – a salad of marinated squid with a hint of aniseed came with unusual green lentil quenelles; the 'jolie gigue de lapereau' with prunes and a jus de grenache was delicious, and the strawberry cake was perfect with its kiwi coulis. From the carte, the starter of aumônière de langoustines au foie gras de canard et Noilly Prat was almost haute cuisine, tenderly wrapped in its brik parcel with fabulous flavours within. The main dish of Gascon porc à la paysanne (topped with grilled cheese) was rather mundane, though we liked the omelette aux fines herbes, pommes dauphines and carrot purée that accompanied it, and rejoiced in the choice of a honey- and cinnamon-drizzled croustillant de reines de reinette to finish. Wines are chosen with equal care – our half-bottle of Domaine Lerys fitou (€12) was robust and flavoursome, and the house aperitif of citrus-spiked wine is a real taste of the country. Be sure to book as there is a policy of one lot of diners per table per night.

20TH ARRONDISSEMENT

Bistro des Capucins

27 av Gambetta, 20th (01.46.36.74.75/www.le-bistro-des-capucins.com). M° Père-Lachaise or Gambetta. **Open** noon-2.45pm, 7.30-9.45pm Tue-Sat. Closed three weeks in Aug and one week at Christmas. **Average** €25. **Lunch menu** €20. **Credit** AmEx, MC, V. **Map** D5.

Halfway up the hill bordering the west side of Père Lachaise sits this plainly appointed bistro amid anonymous surroundings. But get past the red-and-white checked tablecloths, stained wood panelling and straight-faced waiter, and chef Gérard Fouché delivers brilliant bang-for-euro food that's a clever adaptation of French standards. He clearly likes to improvise, too: on our visit, a dish called 'fish of the moment depending on the chef's mood' was pike-perch, potatoes and curry sauce, hampered only by the overcooked fillet. But we found the seafood tartare in watercress sauce starter scrumptious, the silken chestnut velouté ladled over freshwater crayfish to die for, and the suprême of guinea fowl with morels elemental. Desserts can be plain, like three boules of fruity sorbet, or complex, such as the cannelé with spiked pear balls and prune ice-cream. Remarkably, the prices don't rise when the sun sets: starters are €6, main dishes €15 and desserts €4 both at lunch and dinner. There's even a steak-frites children's menu for €9.

Café Noir ★

15 rue St-Blaise, 20th (01.40.09.75.80). M° Porte de Bagnolet. **Open** 7pm-midnight daily. Closed 1 May, Christmas and New Year. **Average** €30. **Credit** MC, V. **Wheelchair access**.

The rue St-Blaise is one of the most attractive cobbled streets in this area and the Café Noir has a menu of surprising sophistication. The place is probably not aimed at the parents of the children playing around the delightful al fresco setting, but at what the French call bobos, bourgeois bohemians, who earn enough to treat themselves to foie gras of an evening, but enjoy announcing to well-heeled friends that they live in a loft in the far-flung 20th. They are certainly not slumming it at the Café Noir, where we enjoyed excellent starters of a mille-feuille of artichoke firmly stuffed with foie gras, and a light ricotta terrine laced with peppers. The main course special of turbot à la crème de cèpes was a good-sized piece of fish coated in a pungent cream, but surrounded by too many fiddly vegetable mounds. Puddings were rhubarb crumble and the irresistibly named 'damnation', which combines hot chocolate, chestnuts and crème fraîche with predictably sinful results. The owners are adorable and our bottle of chilled light red made a perfect complement to the chatter of designer families overlaid on occasion by the shouts of disaffected urban youth.

Le Zéphyr

1 rue du Jourdain, 20th (01.46.36.65.81/www. lezephyrcafe.com). M° Jourdain. **Open** noon-3pm, 7-11.30pm daily. Closed two weeks in Aug. **Average** €40. **Prix fixe** €20 (dinner only). **Lunch menu** €13 (Mon-Fri). **Credit** AmEx, DC, MC, V. **Map** P3.

Bohemian French yuppies who have set up home in the 20th arrondissement are not spoilt for choice when it comes to friendly sophisticated bistros, and the enduring success of Le Zéphyr looks assured. Even at 2pm on a Monday the attractive art deco dining room was comfortably full of fashionable-looking types, some sitting on the terrace enjoying a drink, others having a full meal. We opted for the plat du jour (€26), although there is also a limited choice lunch menu for €12.50, but nothing much was left on this occasion. Our main dish was a complex mixture of coquilles St-Jacques and ris de veau in a rich morel sauce alongside a mountain of baby vegetables, plus a filo parcel of wild mushrooms for good measure, all topped with inextinguishable, smouldering thyme. This daring combination came off well, but in the end the dish was muddled by its profusion of components, and our initial enthusiasm was eventually tempered by gastronomic exhaustion. The ensuing plateau de fromages was served on a wooden board with a good selection of well-chosen, ripe cheeses. A handsome slice of watermelon and a bunch of excellent grapes made pudding unnecessary. The Cairanne Côtes du Rhône had been well chosen, and providing the kitchen is on top form Le Zéphyr still offers a valuable exercise in stylish bistro life.

Haute Cuisine

Paris haute cuisine establishments are beginning to shed their atmosphere of hushed reverence for something more, dare we say, fun. For the first time since we started producing this guide, most of the reviews in this chapter suggest that the critic had a thoroughly enjoyable time, despite any flaws in the food or service. The enjoyment factor is something that had long been neglected in this style of restaurant, where everyone seemed to take themselves and the food just a bit too seriously. Now waiters are starting to crack jokes, diners are dressing more casually and some sommeliers will even ask the woman's opinion – in short, centuries of formality are at last giving way to a slightly more relaxed approach. Another reason to visit restaurants in this category is their good-value lunch menus, which – as more casual restaurants grow increasingly expensive – start to look like veritable bargains (if you can sidestep the aperitifs and choose the wine carefully). It's certainly worth going to one of these restaurants at least once in your life, and the more confident you act, the more respectful the waiters are likely to be. Keep in mind that you will need to confirm your reservation the day before or risk losing your table.

Le Carró des Feuillants

14 rue de Castiglione, 1st (01.42.86.82.82).
Mº Tuileries or Concorde. **Open** noon-2pm, 7.30-10pm Mon-Fri. Closed Aug. **Average** €130. **Prix fixe** €150. **Lunch menu** €65. **Credit** AmEx, DC, MC, V. **Map** G5.

Alain Dutournier has been perfecting his style at the subdued but elegant Carré des Feuillants for several decades and, following a major redecoration of the dining room, his cooking is now better than ever. Suddenly this long-running place has been very quietly lifted from the level of reliable culinary excellence it has long inhabited to a new, exalted plateau. It's kid gloves from the moment they open the front door, and such impeccably well-drilled and cordial service is a rare treat. The new decor is handsome, though a large metal-clad square pillar in the middle of the main dining room is a very masculine detail in a perhaps too-masculine room that's done up in tones of anthracite, with rather cold lighting and chilly modern art. This relentlessly serious setting is what probably emboldened the grouchy-looking finance minister of a Central American country to repeatedly take calls on his mobile phone, as his wife and daughter intently studied the small Zen-like flower arrangement. A first course of cep mushroom caps stuffed with warm pâté was an unctuous sensual contrast of earthy flavours and textures, while griddled squid with courgettes were spiked with Espelette pepper and garnished with a silky black leaf of squid's ink pasta and a gateau of tomato and aubergine, a brilliant contemporary riff on Basque country cooking. Ris de veau (veal sweetbreads), crisply pan-fried and served in a sort of sauce gribiche sharpened with oyster juice, was brilliant, while a thick slab of turbot was cooked to alabaster perfection and served with an inventive side of quinoa (the Peruvian grain that's all the rage in Paris at the moment), mixed with morel mushrooms. Desserts were magnificent as well – in a take on cherries jubilee, plump cherries were sautéed in flaming kirsch and served with tiny chocolate baba (sponge) pastries and a lemon verbena sauce. A good run of reasonably priced south-western French wines, notably the Jurançon and Madiran, white and red respectively, complement the food well and keep the bill down. All told, a magnificent meal that trounced any initial doubts about the vaguely sad, corporate decor.

L'Espadon

Hôtel Ritz, 15 pl Vendôme, 1st (01.43.16.30.80/
www.ritzparis.com). Mº Madeleine or Concorde.
Open noon-2.30pm, 7.30-10.30pm daily. **Average** €180. **Lunch menu** €68. **Credit** AmEx, DC, MC, V. **Wheelchair access. Map** G4.

In Michel Roth, head chef of L'Espadon, the Ritz is lucky to have a truly fine chef. It also has one of the best sommeliers in Paris – this man is a real charmer who not only happily recommends the best of the least expensive bottles on the list, but also listens very carefully. Our 1999 Blagny, a lesser-known red Burgundy, was a luscious and sensual treat that saw us through a tough-to-match menu that might have caused other wine waiters to despair. If there's any intrinsic problem with a meal here, it's the fact that the Ritz is, well, the Ritz, which raises possibly unreasonable expectations of transcendental perfection. On the other hand, a meal here costs a mint – the mediocre house Champagne set us back a stunning €24 a flute – and since the hotel peddles itself as the pinnacle, it's not unfair to expect the best. And now for the carping. Just before Christmas, the lack of decoration was a disappointment, the wall next to our table was oddly streaked and scraped, and the service was uneven. Our main waiter was tremulous charm incarnate, but his second was a real hack, which slashed a hole in the sails of our la-vie-en-rose fantasy. Happily, Roth's cooking kept us on course. A tourtière – shiitake mushrooms and foie gras sealed into a bell-shaped pastry with a cap of crunchy potato slices – in a textbook-perfect Périgueux sauce was sublime, as was foie gras au torchon. Main courses were stunning, too, including what may be the sexiest fish course in Paris – turbot, grilled or sautéed as you like, served with a choice of five sauces in silver sauce boats. Shopping for bliss, get the fish grilled and consume as much sauce Choron with it as you can. The fish comes with potato croquettes rolled in breadcrumbs and stuffed with duxelles (minced mushrooms). The other star, in season, is the roasted wild duck, which is beautifully carved tableside. The single cheese trolley looked ascetic in the context of this plush dining room, so we ordered a salted caramel mille-feuille with two forks, and – a ritzy gesture at last – it was served as two separate mille-feuilles and was stunning. All told, L'Espadon is a splendid place for a blow-out, but the service needs drilling and they should be more generous – a single mignardise with coffee seemed stingy.

Le Grand Véfour

17 rue de Beaujolais, 1st (01.42.96.56.27/www. relaischateaux.com). M° Palais-Royal. **Open** 12.30-1.30pm, 8-9.30pm Mon-Thur; 12.30-2pm Fri. Closed Aug. **Average** €200. **Prix fixe** €250 (dinner only). **Lunch menu** €75. **Credit** AmEx, DC, MC, V. **Non-smoking room. Map** H5.

At the Grand Véfour, splendid is how you feel and splendid is what you get. Opened in 1784 as the Café de Chartres, this is one of Paris's oldest and most historically powered restaurants. We were duly impressed at the thought that many of the greats of this world had feasted on this very spot, from Napoleon Bonaparte and his Josephine to the literary elite: André Malraux, Colette, Sartre, Simone de Beauvoir and Victor Hugo, who was a regular. We were seated at the table named after him, the best in the house because not only does it afford a view over the majestic gardens of the Palais Royal, it is also the perfect spot from which to admire the mirror-studded dining room with its magnificent painted ceiling and wall panels. Another appreciable aspect of this gourmet experience is that the thrill is unmarred by the bombastic pomposity that is all too often typical of similar establishments. Each and every member of staff is perfectly charming, particularly the knowledgeable sommeliers and the dashing premier maître d'hôtel, Christian David. If

luxury can be equated to attention to detail then here it comes with a capital L. From the beautifully presented amuse-bouches offered with a glass of pink Taittinger Champagne, through the selection of salted or unsalted butter to the range of luscious petits fours, all was a treat for the eye and the palate. We splashed out à la carte and were treated to a fantasia-style succession of delicacies beginning with miniature frog's legs artistically arranged within a circle of sage juices and a 'special' first course of creamed Breton sea urchins served in their spiny shells with a quail egg and topped with caviar. Another stunningly presented starter was flash-fried langoustines served with a tangy mango sauce nestling inside a curled shell, tiny girolles and a swirl of coriander juice for extra exoticism. We continued with turbot meunière in white truffle oil and fillet of sole with a Mediterranean-style compote of vegetables – both very slightly overcooked, we thought. Having decided to go the whole hog, we opted for desserts of tiramisu-style chestnut mousse with a flavoursome orange and pumpkin sorbet, and an adventurous but not quite so successful artichoke flan with sugar-preserved vegetables and a refreshing bitter almond sorbet. Increasingly reluctant to leave the beautiful cocoon, we extended the experience as long as possible with cups of Arabica accompanied by blackcurrant and mango fruit jellies and ambrosial rose- and lemon-flavoured chocolates. The sommelier then recommended a superb, complex and aromatic Armagnac from Domaine Boinguères. All good things come to an end, but this particular pleasure trip had a truly spectacular finale.

Le Meurice ★

Hôtel Meurice, 228 rue de Rivoli, 1st (01.44.58.10.10). M° Tuileries. **Open** 12.30-2pm, 7.30-10pm Mon-Fri; 7.30-10pm Sat. Closed Aug. **Average** €110. **Prix fixe** €70 (dinner only). **Lunch menu** €68. **Credit** AmEx, DC, MC, V. **Wheelchair access. Map** G5.

Yannick Alléno, chef here since 2003, has hit his stride and is doing some really stunning if understated contemporary French luxury cooking. Few chefs working in Paris today exercise such restraint when it comes to allowing really superb produce to star at the table, but Alléno has a magician's light touch, subtly, mysteriously teasing the flavour out of every leaf, frond, fin or fillet that passes through his domain. On an autumn evening, it was a huge treat to begin with slowly roasted ormer (or conch) fished off the Channel Islands and slow-roasted for 72 hours before being placed on a bed of white beans in a deeply reduced veal jus in the shell. Next up, one of the most elegant salads imaginable, a brilliant dish of delicately cooked scallops dressed in a very light apple caramel and garnished with fresh walnuts, lamb's lettuce, and a bavarois made with 'walnut water', and another of Alléno's signature dishes, crab meat dressed with citrus fruit and served with herb cream and caviar.

French Cuisine

Le Meurice. *See p76.*

Turbot was sealed inside clay before cooking and then sauced with celery cream and a coulis of flat parsley, while Bresse chicken stuffed with foie gras and served with truffled sarladaise potatoes (cooked in the fat of the fowl) was breathtakingly good. A fine cheese tray, including a stunningly good extra-aged comté, came from Quatrehommes in the rue de Sèvres, and the pastry chef wowed us with a gorgeous conconction of caramelised pastry leaves filled with egg whites beaten with citrus rind, plus somewhat superfluous pieces of candied fennel bulb and heavenly lemon sorbet. The service here carries on such a waltz that you might wish you were a merry widow, but the bemused complicity of the courtly but friendly waiters and sommeliers makes for a truly memorable meal.

L'Ambroisie

9 pl des Vosges, 4th (01.42.78.51.45). M° Bastille or St-Paul. **Open** noon-1.30pm, 8-9.30pm Tue-Sat. Closed two weeks in Feb, three weeks in Aug. **Average** €200. **Credit** AmEx, MC, V. **Wheelchair access. Non-smoking room. Map** L6.

Chef Bernard Pacaud, a master craftsman, never compromises on quality and always complies with the seasons. Autumn brings rosy-fleshed partridge escorted by meaty ceps and chestnuts, lightly crumbed turbot with superlative celeriac purée and braised fresh celery stalks, aromatic crayfish soup chock-full of sweet-tasting tails, embellished with young celery leaves. This is serene, sophisticated food, high on tradition; Pacaud sees no need to innovate purely for the sake of it. Thus his signature dish of pearl-pink langoustines with a light curry sauce balanced between almost transparent sesame seed discs, a dish gorged with flavour, is still on the menu and always in demand. His foie gras flavoured with 12 herbs and served with tiny pickled fruit and veg is a wonderful contrast of soft and crunchy, technically perfect. For dessert, tarte fine sablée, a foamy, feathery chocolate tart with vanilla ice-cream, and a choc-coated igloo of crunchy hazelnut ice-cream. Honestly, sweets just don't come any better. On previous visits we've groaned about the service – frosty, overly serious – but this time it was charming, with waiters ever-attentive but displaying wit and warmth in equal parts. The wine list is remarkable, but as you'd expect in this 17th-century townhouse-cum-palazzo, replete with Aubusson tapestries, ample marble and gilt and a 400-year-old stone floor from an abbey (worn wonky by many a monk's knee acrobatics quipped the waiter), the price tags are majestic too.

La Tour d'Argent

15-17 quai de la Tournelle, 5th (01.43.54.23.31/ www.tourdargent.com). Mº Pont Marie or Cardinal Lemoine. **Open** 7.30-9pm Tue; noon-1.30pm, 7.30-9pm Wed-Sun. **Average** €180. **Lunch menu** €70. **Credit** AmEx, DC, MC, V. **Wheelchair access**. **Non-smoking room**. **Map** K7.

'There is nothing more serious than pleasure' is the motto of La Tour d'Argent's octogenarian owner, Claude Terrail, who has never left the restaurant for more than five days. If the cuisine of the Tour refuses the pirouettes of other top chefs, this remains one of the best treats in the capital. The position on the banks of the Seine overlooking Notre-Dame with a lift ride to the top floor immediately sets you up for a special experience. The €70 lunch menu was not tucked away on some separate if-you-are-poor appendage, but took centre stage, allowing you to feast on the best quenelles de brochet you are ever likely to taste, followed by a classic caneton rôti à l'orange. The signature dish of pressed duck can be enjoyed for a €22 supplement, but even with the orange version you get a postcard with the number of your little feathered chap on it. Of the exemplary caring waiters, we were particularly grateful to the charming sommelier who guided us through the biblical wine list towards a velvety bottle of 1988 Volnay Premier Cru. Only the puddings of a pear and chocolate tart and a frozen gourmandise aux marrons are less complex than some more fiddly haute cuisine creations, but this is the way it has always been, and if the legendary Claude asks you

with practised enthusiasm 'comment allez-vous?', you can only reply with a dreamy 'très bien… trop bien'. Serious pleasure indeed.

Restaurant Hélène Darroze

4 rue d'Assas, 6th (01.42.22.00.11). Mº Sèvres-Babylone. **Open** 7.30-10.15pm Tue; 12.30-2.30pm, 7.30-10.15pm Wed-Sat. **Average** €120. **Prix fixe** €168. **Lunch menu** €68. **Credit** AmEx, DC, MC, V. **Wheelchair access**. **Map** G7.

With its hip decor in tones of orange and plum, Hélène Darroze's restaurant is one very serious establishment, with legions of knowledgeable waiters, well-spaced tables, glistening glasses and a trolley groaning with aged Armagnacs. Darroze hails from the south-west so, of course, there are some regional classics on her menu, but in her creative hand everything old seems new again. Foie gras appears in various guises including a luscious terrine layered with chunks of farm-raised chicken and black truffles. Duck liver mousse comes with a sugared crème brûlée coating, topped with apple sorbet. And while a spring vegetable salad might sound ho-hum, her version with gem-coloured peas in their shells, tiny fennel, onions, carrots and artichokes draped with ruby red Bellota ham and shaved parmesan was alive with flavour. Out came milk-fed lamb encased in an anchovy and manchego cheese crust, deftly cooked scallops, squid and clams resting on a bed of al dente pasta, and line-caught sole, deboned tableside and served with a shellfish sauce flecked with tiny scallops (pétoncles). Inventive pairings and classy flavours that confirm the Ducasse-trained Darroze's sure touch. Desserts were just as impressive: wild Andalusian strawberries with a Toron nougat parfait, and witty and delicious pineapple Victoria – tiny pieces of fruit in a froth of vanilla, piña colada, lemon and curry. And to finish, a trolley laden with macaroons, chocolate truffles and stacks of other sugary morsels.

L'Ambroisie. *See p77.*

L'Arpège

84 rue de Varenne, 7th (01.45.51.47.33/www.alain-passard.com). M° Varenne. **Open** 12.30-2.30pm, 8-10.30pm Mon-Fri. **Average** €250. **Credit** AmEx, DC, MC, V. **Map** F6.

Assuming you can swallow a brazenly high bill – we're talking €42 for a starter of potatoes here – and forsake the normal full-dress drill of an haute cuisine meal, odds are good that you'll have a spectacular time at chef Alain Passard's Left Bank table. Infinitely confident and decidedly ballsy, Passard at times seems to have thrown the baby out with the bath water in an attempt to plane down and simplify the haute cuisine experience. For example, the new chrome-armed chairs in the already minimalist dining room look like something you would have found in the private lunch room of the East German Communist party, and the only decorative element in the room aside from Lalique glass inserts in the panelling are bound bunches of trimmed twigs on each table. But then something edible comes to the table, superb sourdough bread with bright yellow Breton butter so good you want to eat it by the spoonful. Next, the signature amuse-bouche of an egg shell filled with a raw yolk, cream and smoky maple syrup, a superb combination, and then the brilliant first courses. Tiny potatoes are smoked in oat straw and served with a horseradish mousseline, the sweet taste of the potatoes is amplified and framed by the sharp horseradish and the smoke enobles the dish, giving it perfect balance. In contrast, delicate vegetable-stuffed ravioli in lobster bouillon were elegant and quietly sexy, but nowhere near as satisfying, especially at €58. A main course of free-range chicken sautéed at a low temperature over a long period of time and garnished with a roasted shallot, an onion, potato mousseline and pan juices was the apotheosis of comfort food, while plump scallops from Granville in Normandy wore bay leaf collars and sat on tiny beds of baby leeks. What made this dish eloquent were the unexpected texture added by the nob of muscle that had once fastened the scallop inside its shell – most kitchens would have trimmed it away – and the two brilliant condiments, a smoky tomato relish and a slightly bitter yellow Thai curry. Desserts are similarly elegant and edgy, including the famous tomato roasted with 12 flavours, a Christmas pudding spectrum of tastes that includes whole almonds and raisins, and a brilliant avocado soufflé with pistachios and a stoned yellow plum inserted into its folds. Service is impeccable, and the atmosphere surprisingly low key – the chef himself appeared several times in Converse All-Stars, before settling down with a Japanese couple to discuss a possible restaurant in Tokyo, and many of the male diners were tieless. The one terrible drawback to a meal here, however, is the wine list, which is so expensive as to repel anyone who's neither a millionaire nor on an expense account. Good as it was, our Jolivet Sancerre at €102 was hardly worthy of such brilliant cooking, and it's decidedly unfriendly that no half-bottles or wines by the glass are available.

Le Jules Verne

Second Level, Eiffel Tower, Champ de Mars, 7th (01.45.55.61.44) M° Bir-Hakeim or RER Champ de Mars. **Open** 12.15-1.30pm, 7.15-9.30pm daily. **Average** €160. **Prix fixe** €120. **Lunch menu** €53 (Mon-Fri). **Credit** AmEx, DC, MC, V. **Map** C6.

From the unbeatable view and attentive service right down to the compartmentalised china, a meal at the Jules Verne, 125 metres up on the second level of the Eiffel Tower, offers an experience not unlike a first-class airline flight. Like the first-class cabin, the decor is handsome enough, if a little stale; a modernist symphony in grey and black. As on most flights, lunchtime diners here covered the gamut from grey flannel to plaid flannel, and the food, though respectable and fancy, felt a bit soulless. Our starters, an aspic of crabmeat garnished with céleri rémoulade (addled with a surfeit of white pepper) and slices of a dark, gamey venison and foie gras terrine with quenelles of apple-quince compote and onion jam, all afloat in a pool of gossamer apple-quince gelée, were technically impressive, though not stirring. Saddle of rabbit was a mixed bag, with a perfectly textured, luminescent reduction sauce accenting desperately overcooked meat, and stewed veal shank suffered from a common pitfall of that cut – it was tender to the point of being mushy. The meal took a sharp upswing with dessert, a deeply flavoured chocolate mousse accompanying an imaginative terrine of pain d'épices and chocolate ganache. Even though we didn't swoon over most the food, the combined forces of elegant service, spectacular location and dazzling view made lunch at this institution into a singular, and very satisfying (if expensive), experience. Do count on lunch, though – when we called in November to make a dinner reservation, the first opening was in late March.

Alain Ducasse au Plaza Athénée

Hôtel Plaza Athénée, 25 av Montaigne, 8th (01.53.67.65.00/www.alain-ducasse.com). Mº Alma-Marceau. **Open** 8-10.30pm Mon-Wed; 12.30-2pm, 8-10.30pm Thur, Fri. Closed last two weeks in Dec, mid-July to mid-Aug. **Average** €320. **Prix fixe** €190, €300. **Credit** AmEx, DC, MC, V. **Wheelchair access. Map** D5.

The sheer glamour factor would be enough to recommend this restaurant, Alain Ducasse's most lofty Paris undertaking (though he is only rarely in the kitchen). The high-ceilinged, grey-painted dining room might feel a little odd, its chandeliers veiled as if to mute their luxuriousness, but we relished taking in the buzzing scene from our corner table. Because of the dining room's layout the many waiters are a conspicuous presence, but they are also personable with none of the stiffness sometimes encountered in this style of restaurant. Christophe Moret, the former Spoon, Food & Wine chef, has taken over after Jean-François Piège's departure for Les Ambassadeurs, and we couldn't help feel that there was something Spoon-like about the food on the night we visited. We opted for the €190 menu, which allowed us each to try three half-portions from the 'Plaisirs de table' part of the carte – the dishes without truffles or caviar. The meal started beautifully with an amuse-bouche of a single langoustine in a lemon cream with a touch of Iranian caviar. A raw-cooked salad of autumn fruits and vegetables proved an odd mish-mash, however, surrounded by a red, Chinese-style sweet and sour sauce. We lapped up a crayfish velouté with a poultry-liver royale (flan), but found the turbot in a stock of shellfish and 'bouquet' prawn sauce strangely characterless, while Breton lobster came in a rather overwhelming sauce made of apple, quince and spiced wine. Then a good half-hour went by before we were served a delicious breast of pigeon and royale-style hare in a sauce so strong that the small portion became difficult to finish. Cheese was predictably delicious, as was the rum baba comme à Monte-Carlo with a choice of the finest rums for dousing. A grapefruit and quince tart was interestingly bitter rather than hedonistic. We turned down the sommelier's initial suggestion of a Riesling for a €100 bottle of 1999 Chambolle-Musigny that was the kind of nectar we prefer. It may be a few more months before Moret grows into one of the most prestigious chef's jobs in Paris.

Les Ambassadeurs

Hôtel de Crillon, 10 pl de la Concorde, 8th (01.44.71.16.17/www.crillon.com). Mº Concorde. **Open** noon-2pm, 7.30-10pm Tue-Sat; Sun brunch noon-3pm. Closed three weeks in Aug. **Average** €185. **Lunch menu** €70. **Credit** AmEx, DC, MC, V. **Map** F5.

To mark the arrival of former Ducasse chef Jean-Francois Piège, who arrived from the Plaza Athénée in 2004, the hotel updated the decor of its prized, showcase restaurant, choosing softer tones and subtle colours to enhance the light-flooded space already blazing with magnificent Baccarat chandeliers. Yet despite the new, young chef and the contemporary touches, the dining experience to be had in this former 18th-century ballroom, opulently gilded and furnished with seven types of marble and sky-high mirrors, is rooted in classicism. Befitting the luxurious surroundings, the menu is predictably expensive, and, well, just a little predictable: caviar, foie gras, lobster, duck and venison, among other upper-crust classics. At a recent lunch, we went for the €70 prix fixe, which could be construed as a bargain if you think that à la carte, a mere starter might cost even more. The menu began with an excellent tile of unctuous duck foie gras, crusted with a caramelised apple crackle and served with apple juice jelly. Perfectly executed, it was a delight. A main course of turbot from Brittany, served with oven-roasted chestnuts and a fennel emulsion, was also expertly prepared, although the subtlety of the flavours verged on blandness, not unlike the other choice of starter – a lightly breaded scallop steamed in cabbage. Faithful to the autumn season, another main course of 'semi-wild' duck was served with a pumpkin purée – both as a side dish, and as a garnish on the rare slivers of duck. While it would seem churlish to criticise the obvious expertise that went into the dish, it was, again, hardly memorable – more like a refined version of a hunter's meal. Desserts, on the other hand, were brilliant with flavour and creativity. A mint and chocolate chaud-froid was splendid, and uncannily reminiscent of the classic after-dinner mint that inspired it. The vacherin ice-cream meringue cake, singing with raspberry, rose and lychee notes and crowned with a delicate, icing sugar trellis, was art on the plate and palate. Mignardises were equally enchanting, particularly the melt-in-the-mouth macaroons. Service was courteous and professional, even incongruously friendly for such a formal ambience. And while €70 may seem reasonable enough for a three-course lunch, don't be fooled – you could end up spending twice as much on the wine, where the least expensive investment is a €40 half-bottle, on the Champagne aperitifs temptingly wheeled about the room, or even on the coffee. Then again, isn't that the price to pay for dining like royalty?

Le Bristol ★

Hôtel Bristol, 112 rue du Fbg-St-Honoré, 8th (01.53.43.43.00/www.lebristolparis.com). Mº Miromesnil. **Open** noon-2.30pm, 7-10.30pm daily. **Average** €100. **Prix fixe** €130. **Lunch menu** €70. **Credit** AmEx, DC, MC, V. **Wheelchair access. Map** E4.

The Bristol is one of the most romantic of Parisian palaces. In a city that sometimes lacks green credentials, the hotel's central garden is a jewel. The summer dining room, which sometimes spills out on to a terrace, feels gloriously airy and, as we waited for our violinist virtuoso guest, we had plenty of time to appreciate the atmosphere and the delicious amuse-bouches. Like all luxury venues the world over, chic has been replaced by platinum credit cards, and as our fellow guests set up tripods to photograph their pumped-up poulet en vessie, the primitive and the sophisticated mingled uncomfortably. Star chef Eric Fréchon (*see p10* **A day in the life of an haute cuisine chef**) is a name that the sleek maître d'hôtel slipped frequently into his description of the dishes, and of course we nodded knowingly. The lunch menu for €70, while nobody's idea of a bargain, is surprisingly reasonable for this quality of cooking. Three little eggs sitting in a serried rank were filled with a delicious cep and egg mixture, and accompanied by a crispy mushroom toast. The raw langoustine bathed and cooked in piping hot seafood bouillon at the table was just the sort of dish at which top chefs and professional service excel. None of us could resist the ris de veau, écrevisses and ceps, a dish of stunning simplicity, perfectly timed, with firm mushrooms, melting sweetbreads and plump crustaceans. The violinist plucked a flambéed dish of mirabelles and ice-cream from the menu while wily clients tucked into the splendid cheese board. Fortunately for the non-platinum credit card holders our musician requested rosé, which neatly avoided wine list extravagance. If only he hadn't ordered that Champagne rosé as an aperitif.

Le V

Hôtel Four Seasons George V, 31 av George V, 8th (01.49.52.70.00/www.fourseasons.com). Mº George V. **Open** noon-2.30pm, 6.30-11pm daily. **Average** €250. **Prix fixe** €120, €230. **Lunch menu** €75. **Credit** AmEx, DC, MC, V. **Wheelchair access. Map** D4.
Everything you've heard about the wonders of Le Cinq and chef Philippe Legendre is true, judging by our autumnal meal here. Like the staidly beautiful surroundings – grey walls, gilt flourishes and soaring flower arrangements – the food is lush but never overworked. Lobster, sevruga caviar, truffles, foie gras, milky veal and turbot are handled with exacting respect and imagination. The mâitre d' confided that some diners return habitually for Legendre's leeks stuffed with black Périgord truffles; beneath the silky poached leeks and copious truffles, hidden by the sieved plate, lurks the finale, a clear, addictive broth. Velvety foie gras comes paired with tiny columns of earthy truffle and fruity jam. Roasted pigeon is teamed simply with steamed green cabbage and rich pan juices, veal shares a plate with a squirt of capers and parmesan and tiny braised winter vegetables – all made heady in this chef's hands. Dessert, while delightful, was less superlative – roasted pineapple with mango, paw-paw and a ten-flavour exotic sorbet – but the suggested dessert wine, South Africa's Klein Constantia, was a transcendent indulgence at €30 a shot. Service was seamless, masterfully poised between attentive and imperceptible. Worth a credit card blow-out any day.

Les Elysées du Vernet

Hôtel Vernet, 25 rue Vernet, 8th (01.44.31.98.98/ www.hotelvernet.com). Mº George V. **Open** 7.30-10pm Mon; 12.30-2pm, 7.30-10pm Tue-Fri. Closed 26 July-26 Aug, 25 Dec-1 Jan, public holidays. **Average**

€120. **Prix fixe** €130 (dinner only). **Lunch menu** €60, €68. **Credit** AmEx, DC, MC, V. **Wheelchair access. Map** D4.
There is a whiff of ageing dowager about this dining room – it just seems that bit out of step with time and fashion, though new carpeting, chairs and abstract paintings added in late 2004 have brought it a touch of modernity. Chef Eric Briffard is creative but, if our meal was any indication, he needs to cut the fuss factor. Sweet sole fillets were rendered weighty under beads of pear, and a hefty dollop of ginger confit, along with diced ceps and nuts, and then there were the extras: fried calamari with the aperitif, shot glasses of spider crab with creamed lettuce and walnuts, and frothy brebis in between courses, plus dessert fruit pastes made from celery, beetroot and pumpkin (ugh!) and scores of other assorted, and ultimately untouched, sweet treats. Granted, this kind of overkill may be what people of a certain age – and there were a lot of them – expect from a ritzy hotel restaurant with a glass domed ceiling by Gustave Eiffel and a starry reputation. Tuna belly paired with marinated vegetables worked well, as did venison with barberry and wild mushrooms, while a biscuity tart of thinly sliced ceps with a layer of aubergine caviar was a bit unremarkable at €42. Desserts — chocolate and raspberry soufflé-like tart with green tea sorbet, and thyme-lemon sponge with lemon balm sauce and mascarpone ice-cream – were a triumph, though. Waiters flapped and flurried but failed to bring our wine until halfway through the starters, and then it wasn't chilled. Petty? Maybe. Acceptable? No.

Laurent

41 av Gabriel, 8th (01.42.25.00.39/www.le-laurent. com). Mº Champs-Elysées-Clemenceau. **Open** 12.30-2pm, 7.30-10.30pm Mon-Fri; 7.30-10.30pm Sat. Closed public holidays. **Average** €150. **Prix fixe** €150. **Lunch menu** €70. **Credit** AmEx, DC, MC, V. **Non-smoking room. Wheelchair access. Map** F4.
This Napoleon III pavillion in the gardens behind the Champs-Elysées used to belong to the maverick businessman Jimmy Goldsmith and it tends to attract people a little like him. On our last visit, the ex-boss of Vivendi-Universal Jean-Marie Messier was among the captains of industry lighting up cigars the size of chair legs as the clock moved round to 2pm. Laurent is as discreet, refined and relaxed as a gentlemen's club. The lunch menu starts to look like a pretty good deal when you scan down the à la carte prices. For €70 you can have a single dish such as the roasted and spiced rack of lamb, bulghur, coriander-lemon and baby artichokes – or, if you go for the lunch menu, the same main plus a starter, a pudding and drive-by from the mahogany cheese trolley. Our first lunch menu starter, a plate of slivers of root vegetable with aromatic oils and spices, was a dazzling demonstration of the skills of the young Robuchon-school chef Alain Péguret. Péguret is good at glazes and the colours and sheens of this dish made it worth ordering just to be able to look at it. Our other starter, a blanquette of frog's legs

Laurent.
See p81.

a truffle ceremony (big wooden box, respectful sniffs, white gloves and a goodly grate of magic mushroom) performed for moneyed regulars, or the seductive elegance of the spacious Second Empire salon (handbags get their own upholstered stools), that makes eating here a truly divine experience. It's the celestial quality of the cooking. Smoked eel perched on a lie-de-vin-glazed canapé of toast; peppery hare terrine with a side of gold-leafed meat jelly; delicate strips of red mullet floating in a vivifying sauce of its own very fishy liver; melting breasts of herb-encrusted poule faisane, wrapped around an impossibly unctuous, just-cooked liver and paired with juice-quenched roasted roots and a single sprout farci. Desserts likewise had us in raptures (try the chocolate mille-feuille: paper-thin slivers of crunchy chocolate layered with sweet mascarpone cream and an oomphy scoop of bitter coffee sorbet). As far as heavens go, lunch at Ledoyen has a reassuringly democratic spirit: the set menu is a mere €73 and excellent wine comes miraculously by the glass (€15 a shot). And, if you can splurge a bit more, invest €22 in the potent allure of the heaving cheese trolley.

Lucas Carton

9 pl de la Madeleine, 8th (01.42.65.22.90/www. lucascarton.com). Mº Madeleine. **Open** 8-10.30pm Mon, Sat; noon-2.30pm, 8-10.30pm Tue-Fri. Closed last week in Feb, Aug. **Average** €200. **Prix fixe** €300. **Lunch menu** €76. **Credit** AmEx, DC, MC, V. **Non-smoking room. Map** F4.

Sitting in the beautiful art nouveau interior by Majorelle with its booths and mirrors is a more informal experience than many of Paris's haute-cuisine establishments, and the €76 lunch menu is a veritable bargain, but its cooking is right up in the top league as 65-year-old Alain Senderens continues to hone classic ingredients with subtle use of spices, often inspired by travel or by books he has read. The warm foie gras, wrapped and lightly steamed in crisp leaves of green Savoy cabbage – a Senderens trademark – left to be seasoned with just a pinch of sea salt or Sichaun pepper, was a marvel of simplicity and purity, and shows just how cleverly he can blend innovation and grand tradition. Our main courses were a tender saddle of milk-fed lamb, deboned in a neat roll, and intense, succulent slices of marinated and roast wild duck, accompanied by aubergines, confit tomatoes and little red peppers stuffed with duck liver. We followed with a crisp mille-feuille sandwiched with Tahiti vanilla cream and a Sichaun pepper dacquoise with chewy meringue, delicate ginger ice-cream and candied quince. But in fact what is listed on the menu is only a fraction of the meal, interspersed by all the complimentary extras that are sometimes the most exciting part, from the slivers of foie gras with pistachios, and the delicate pétoncle (small scallop) ravioli in an appley butter froth with raw cep matchsticks as the debut to the trio of desserts (cardamom-flavoured tiramisu, pistachio cream and

and coco beans with a whipped nutmeg jus, was again impressive to look at but didn't manage to overcome the fact that, while there's nothing especially horrible about frog's legs, there's nothing especially great about them either. The old 'it tastes like chicken' line was as relevant as ever here. We mis-chose again for one of our mains. The 'freshly salted' cod was – surprise – really salty. Neither were we too enthusiastic about its heavy layer of herbs. Our pan-fried scallops with buckwheat mousse were much better. For pudding, our beautifully glazed chocolate dessert of almond paste and bitter chocolate with cocoa and cardamom sorbet was splendid, and our freshly made fruit sorbets were the best we'd ever tasted. Best sampled in summer when the tables are set up in the lovely garden.

Ledoyen ★

1 av Dutuit, 8th (01.53.05.10.01). Mº Champs-Elysées-Clemenceau. **Open** 8-9.30pm Mon; 12.30-2pm, 8-9pm Tue-Fri. Closed Aug, 24-26 Dec. **Average** €180. **Prix fixe** €168. **Lunch menu** €73. **Credit** AmEx, DC, MC, V. **Wheelchair access. Map** F5.

Lunch at Ledoyen, with the autumn foliage glistening gold outside the opulent, window-wrapped dining room, is paradise incarnate. Christian Le Squer is a culinary deity with a provocative sense of humour: who else would pair a liquid peanut butter tart with a slice of foie gras, both doll-sized, for their opening flourish or serve tiny lemon-mousse marshmallows and candy apples – minute tongue teasers of bright red candy filled with apple sorbet and surmounted by a sphere of green-topped Granny Smith? As pre-dessert mignardises? It's not the chance to witness mini pears in red wine) that came after the 'real' dessert. Senderens is also passionate about matching wine and food – the wine list is a weighty volume of illustrious vintages (though there are also some decent, less expensive lunchtime suggestions), while the à la carte menu is accompanied by suggestions for a different wine by the glass to go with each dish.

Pierre Gagnaire

6 rue Balzac, 8th (01.58.36.12.50/www.pierre-gagnaire.com). M° Charles de Gaulle-Etoile or George V. **Open** noon-2pm, 7.30-10pm Mon-Fri; 7.30-10pm Sun. Closed one week in Feb, last two weeks in July. **Average** €150. **Prix fixe** €195. **Lunch menu** €90. **Credit** AmEx, DC, MC, V. **Wheelchair access. Map** D3.

Pierre Gagnaire's cool grey and polished wood dining room felt a little deserted on our lunch visit, with no more than four tables occupied. Could it be that his culinary acrobatics combined with stiff prices are starting to put off even the very rich (who, we have noticed, appreciate value for money as much as anyone)? Most starters now cost more than €100, which seems to be the price of culinary experimentation (Gagnaire is something of a scientist, often working with 'molecular gastronomy' specialist Hervé This). One of us ordered the €90 lunch menu to compare it with the à la carte offerings, and it was far from the same experience. The menu's starter and main course – caramelised onion with salsify and diced carrot, then venison flavoured with juniper and served with parsnip cream – were both conventionally presented on single plates, while each à la carte dish involved four or five plates. Even the shared amuse-bouches filled the table: an egg 'raviole' (interesting technically but jarring to the palate), crisp-like waffled potatoes with chilli, ricotta with green apple, fish in a cauliflower 'jelly', and glazed monkfish. La langoustine, at €122, came in four variations – raw, skewered, grilled and in a creamy sauce – for a grand total of five langoustines. The most spectacular of our dishes was the seafood main course, which included an enormous, 25-year-old oyster grilled tableside in goose fat (in the end, it tasted much like a cooked oyster) and John Dory with a delicious spice mix, along with scallop and sea urchin concoctions. The best thing about the lunch menu is that it brings you four desserts (half 'le grand dessert'), which the waiter kindly replicated for the à la carte meal. These clementine, raspberry and vanilla, chocolate and passion fruit puddings offered the kind of indulgence you crave at this type of restaurant. Coffee is shockingly priced at €8.50, but if you care you shouldn't be here. Remarkably, though, if you don't finish your wine (we managed to polish off our Anjou) staff will let you take it home – what could be more chic than a Pierre Gagnaire doggy bag?

Stella Maris

4 rue Arsène-Houssaye, 8th (01.42.89.16.22). M° Charles de Gaulle-Etoile. **Open** noon-2.15pm, 7.30-10.30pm Mon-Fri; 7.30-10.30pm Sat. Closed two

weeks in Aug, 25 Dec. **Average** €50. **Prix fixe** €79, €115. **Lunch menu** €39. **Credit** AmEx, DC, MC, V. **Wheelchair access. Non-smoking room. Map** D3.

This jewel box of a restaurant offers the perfect showcase for Japanese chef Tateru Yoshino's refined interpretation of French haute cuisine. Beautifully designed and recently redecorated, everything from the two-storey, art deco glass façade, to the pristine black parquet floor, to the dozens of delicate lamps that hang like pendulums from the high ceiling is impeccable. Prices have gone down since the revamp, suggesting that Yoshino hopes to appeal to a broader clientele. His extensive menu is divided into traditional dishes, such as a textbook tourte of wild duck, pheasant and foie gras, as well as more experimental ones, such as thinly sliced conch in gelée, enlivened by a delicate horseradish cream. We opted for the chef's tasting menu, a selection of seven dishes drawn equally from both categories. From the moment that the sommelier suggested an entirely inappropriate 2002 Pouilly-Fuissé, however, the meal began to unravel. The first two courses, more amuse-bouches, a thin onion tart and a rather bland mille-feuille of tuna and eggplant, arrived before we had even been served our wine. When the wine did come, it was far too cold. Plate after plate was put before us without an explanation, only heightening our impression that the staff were seriously under-trained. The food itself, though beautifully presented and generally very good, was a bit uneven. The conch gelée tasted murky and the chef's signature seafood couscous seemed unbalanced, the spiced couscous overpowering a delicate assortment of fish and shellfish. The tourte de gibier we had selected as our meat course was excellent, but our enjoyment of it was lessened by another gaffe regarding the glass of red wine we had ordered to accompany it. The cheese course, a beetroot gelée with roquefort cream, was forgotten altogether and then delivered after the pre-dessert sorbet, while our desserts were left to melt at the hostess stand. Unbelievably, even the bill had been miscalculated, a final reminder that attention is just not being paid to detail in this dining room.

Taillevent ★

15 rue Lamennais, 8th (01.44.95.15.01/www. taillevent.com). M° Charles de Gaulle-Etoile or George V. **Open** noon-2pm, 7.30-10pm Mon-Fri. Closed Aug. **Average** €180. **Prix fixe** €130, €180. **Lunch menu** €70. **Credit** AmEx, DC, MC, V. **Wheelchair access. Map** D3.

Like La Tour d'Argent, Taillevent owes much of its ongoing success to the personality of its owner, Jean-Claude Vrinat. Change (including a recent refurbishment) always seems to occur seamlessly here, yet Vrinat is not afraid to hire young chefs with *caractère*. One of his most brilliant recent decisions was to put Alain Solivérès in charge of the kitchen, which on the day we visited was turning out truly flawless food. We were led through the spacious and rather subdued front room to the livelier, almost brasserie-like second room, where we were seated conspiratorially side-by-side. Prices here are not as shocking as in some restaurants at this level – with a bottle of wine at €64, some mineral water and two coffees, our bill came to €300 à la carte. However, we found out only after this meal, upon consulting the website, that a €70 lunch menu is available – a shame that none of the staff mentioned it. One of our starters, the rémoulade de coquilles Saint-Jacques, had been introduced only the previous day, and the gallant, good-humoured waiters were eager to see our reaction. It was quite a technical feat, with slices of raw, marinated scallop wrapped in a tube shape around a finely diced apple filling, all of it encircled by a mayonnaise-like rémoulade sauce. An earthier, and lip-smackingly good dish was the chef's trademark épeautre – known in English as spelt – cooked 'like a risotto' with bone marrow, black truffle, whipped cream and parmesan cheese, and topped with sautéed frog's legs. Whole pan-fried red mullet was again typical of Solivérès' southern-influenced cooking: the fish had been completely deboned and stuffed with a delicate spider crab filling. We couldn't resist the chef's recreation of a medieval dish by Guillaume Tirel, the chef known as Taillevent in the 14th century: the caillette de porcelet aux épices et raisins de Malaga, a spicy round sausage alongside two beautifully juicy little pork chops, all perched atop a mound of caramelised cabbage and Puy lentils. To follow, ravioli au chocolat araguani was perhaps the most surprising and wonderful dessert we had tasted this year: pillowy pockets of soft chocolate pasta that explode in the mouth, releasing liquid bitter chocolate. The young sommelier's suggestion of a white 1998 Hautes Côtes de Nuits from Domaine A Gros was part of what made this meal so pleasurable.

Hiramatsu ★

52 rue de Longchamp, 16th (01.56.81.08.80).
M° Trocadéro or Boissière. **Open** 12.30-1.30pm,
7.30-9.30pm Mon-Fri. Closed three weeks in Feb/Mar,
three weeks in Aug. **Average** €150. **Prix fixe**
€130, €180. **Lunch menu** €70. **Credit** AmEx, DC,
MC, V. **Non-smoking room. Map** K7.

From the moment you arrive at Hiramatsu's new quarters, which occupy the premises of the former Faugeron restaurant, you know you're in for a first-class experience. Glide through the three doors leading into the restaurant, opened successively by doormen who have magically anticipated your arrival, and enter a hushed, well-appointed dining room accentuated with the finest luxuries: vases and water glasses by Baccarat, Champagne flutes by Riedel, cutlery by Christofle, porcelain from Limoges. The heavy, leather-bound tome of a wine list is, of course, de rigueur. In contrast to the tiny dining room of Hiramatsu's former Ile St-Louis address, this one breathes light and space, a much needed commodity when you consider the sizeable team of sommeliers and waiters skilfully performing their roles with orchestrated moves and balletic

grace. As for the cuisine, let's just say that it soars well beyond the expectations created by the sumptuous surroundings. The menu découverte, indeed a voyage of discovery with its novel tastes and textures, was a culinary tour de force: every one of the ten courses delighted the eye and astounded the palate. Just an amuse-bouche of spiced crab with apple mousse was stunning in its clarity of flavours and aesthetic simplicity: the ambrosial spoonful was served on top of a shiny red apple presented like a Magritte painting. The play on colour, texture and flavour would be a leitmotif for the rest of the meal – each dish that followed was refined, light and imaginative, such as a starter of barely-cooked Breton lobster in jelly, green pea and chestnut purée, and vanilla coulis. Flavours that shouldn't go together? Take another bite. A main course of smoked Challans duck, dusted with pain d'épices and served with an intense violet-flavoured sauce, was another revelation. The choice of desserts concluded the experience with a bang – go for the caramelised homespun cotton candy on poire william jelly with Champagne: a very grown-up concoction that brings out the awestruck child in all of us.

Jamin

32 rue de Longchamp, 16th (01.45.53.00.07).
M° Trocadéro or Boissière. **Open** 12.30-2pm, 7.45-
9.45pm Mon-Fri. Closed one week in Feb, Aug.
Average €110. **Prix fixe** €95, €130. **Lunch
menu** €50. **Credit** AmEx, DC, MC, V. **Wheelchair
access. Map** C5.

Benoît Guichard, former second to the iconic Joël Robuchon, is a gifted chef and a surefire sauce whizz. His menu du marché, a no-choice bargain comprising starter, fish, meat and dessert, testifies to his prowess with pairings: creamy fennel soup awash with tiny clams; snowy white lieu (pollack) dabbed with vibrant pink coral, rabbit steeped in red wine with button mushrooms and bacon chunks. A la carte, oyster mushrooms, mussels, oysters, langoustines and minute cubes of foie gras floating in a glossy mushroom broth was a sublime melding of earth and sea, dense and light all at once, and simply grilled John Dory on a mound of creamy, comforting leeks ringed with jammy red wine and shallots was a lean winter delight. No disappointments from the state-of-the-tart dessert trolley either, a slice of grapefruit flan paired with zingy grapefruit sorbet, and pineapple and pistachio tart crowned with meringue. Serious suits, a lunchtime fixture, audibly sighed at first bite. Some might lament the decor – pale green walls, pink striped banquettes and potted palms – but look beyond to your plate; that's where the real appeal lies.

Le Pré Catelan

rte de Suresnes, Bois de Boulogne, 16th
(01.44.14.41.14/www.lenotre.fr). M° Porte Maillot,
then 244 bus. **Open** noon-1.45pm; 7.30-9.30pm Tue-
Sat (year-round); noon-1.45pm Sun (May-Oct). Closed
last week in Oct, three weeks in Feb. **Average** €150.
Prix fixe €120, €160. **Lunch menu** €60. **Credit**
AmEx, DC, MC, V. **Wheelchair access.**

This grand French restaurant in the Bois de Boulogne is known as an ideal spot for a leisurely Sunday lunch during the summer, but it does wonders for the soul any time of the year. On a brisk day in November, we ducked out of our offices for lunch, longing for a mid-week break from the city grind. A short taxi ride later, we were seated beside a roaring fireplace in this welcoming belle époque mansion, perusing the business lunch menu and nibbling complimentary scallops served on the half-shell. Frédéric Anton's cooking is simple yet inventive. For starters, we chose the lightly fried langoustine with a caviar-laced sauce and drizzle of avocado cream, and the slice of silky foie gras encrusted with coriander and fennel seeds. Our main courses included the ultra-fresh cod simply cooked with onions and confit tomatoes, and a house speciality – tender pigeon breast cooked in bouillon and served on a bed of broccoli-flecked couscous with bite-size merguez made from the leg meat. The outstanding cheese trolley is one of the best in Paris, with an extensive selection delivered fresh daily from the famed Alléosse cheese shop. For dessert, don't miss the tower of mille-feuille. Service is remarkably efficient, cheerful and accommodating. The impressive selection of wines includes an assortment of half bottles priced at a palatable €14.

Guy Savoy

18 rue Troyon, 17th (01.43.80.40.61/www. guysavoy.com). M° Charles de Gaulle-Etoile. **Open** noon-2pm, 7-10.30pm Tue-Fri; 7-10.30pm Sat. Closed mid-July to mid-Aug. **Average** €190. **Prix fixe** €210, €285. **Credit** AmEx, DC, MC, V. **Wheelchair access**. **Map** C3.

Be prepared to blow your salary and opt for one of the dégustation menus that allow you to try a selection of both Guy Savoy's seasonal inspirations and his personal classics. Thankfully, the sober Jean-Michel Wilmotte-designed dining rooms create a calm setting for the flurry of activity – a whirlwind of staff wielding trays, pushing trolleys and spooning sauces – though slightly brighter lighting would flatter the food more. Some of the greatest pleasures come from some of the simplest-sounding ideas, brilliantly carried out, such as the tiny potato stuffed with a mushroom in a buttery froth that began the menu d'automne. We continued with a land-sea combination of mousseron mushrooms and mussels, then a pyramid of raw duck foie gras with huge shards of black truffle around a pile of leeks, bathed in truffle juice – the perforated dish subsequently lifted up to reveal the second, more robust aroma of leeks bathed in duck stock. Red mullet with barely cooked spinach and a mini-aubergine followed, though it was the wafer-thin circle of buttery potato to accompany it that was a crowning moment. Another was the artichoke soup with more black truffle (a Savoy classic). Only then the meat course: gamey pigeon served so rare (or raw), that they took it back and cooked it a little more, on pumpkin dribbled with cress purée, and a spoonful of truffled

mash (a gift from the 'truffle menu'). Everything comes with appropriate different breads, made by Maison Kayser in the 5th, wielded by an enthusiastic young waiter who coaxed us into sampling the colossal cheese trolley, too, before another trolley intervened, laden with marshmallows, sorbets and chocolate mouse, as a prelude to the clementine in various guises – warm and spicy, jellied, caramelised and frozen in a sorbet. With the coffee and plate of tiny madeleines, we thought we had finished. Not so. An Earl Grey sorbet was so good that just when we thought we really could not eat any more… we did.

Michel Rostang

20 rue Rennequin, 17th (01.47.63.40.77/www. michelrostang.com). M° Ternes or Pereire. **Open** 7.30-10.30pm Mon, Sat; 12.30-2.30pm, 7.30-10.30pm Tue-Fri. Closed two weeks in Aug. **Average** €120. **Prix fixe** €170. **Lunch menu** €70. **Credit** AmEx, DC, MC, V. **Non-smoking room**. **Map** D2.

The cosseting dining room of Michel Rostang's flagship restaurant in the 17th arrondissement feels discreetly luxurious and just the place to invite a star of the Paris Opera. Hopefully the obsequious maître d'hôtel was duly impressed. Happily seated we studied the €70 lunch menu over a glass of Champagne and some nibbles. One starter was no longer available, news of which should have reached front of house before it was ordered. We plumped for the starter of the day, pan-fried foie gras, accompanied by ceps, grapes, pine nuts and spinach – a classy little number, which neatly side-stepped rich overkill with its sweet and sour dressing. Our rognons de veau were cooked in a peppery papillotte, but it was disappointing that the operatic opening of the parcels was done out of sight of our celebrity guest. The kidneys emerged perfectly cooked, but then coated at the table in a rich meat reduction, judged as being a tad heavy by the leading lady, especially as the accompanying dish of baby noodles bathing in cream and ceps was a meal in itself. To end our meal, soufflés au caramel came cutely puffed to the table, where a hole was inserted and some caramel sauce poured in. A squeak of glee from the diva as her soufflé magically grew in size, but just the vague feeling that this dessert is better with stronger flavours than caramel. An excellent and reasonably priced Bordeaux stood up well to the meal, which promised slightly more than it delivered.

Guy Savoy.

Brasseries

To see Parisians at their most Parisian, there is no better setting than a brasserie. Elderly lone diners slurping oysters; three generations tucking into a giant platter of choucroute; couples having breakfast at noon; dashing waiters dressed in black and white; groups of foreigners. They all look perfectly at home against a backdrop of art nouveau extravagance or updated brasserie style. Whatever might be said about the Flo group and the Frères Blanc, who have taken over many historic brasseries (the food has grown more uniform, the settings every so slightly Disney-ish), their restorations have often been more successful than privately undertaken ones. Still, some of the best brasseries, such as Brasserie Lipp, the newly renovated Stella or Le Boeuf Couronné, remain independent. What Flo is to vintage brasseries, the Costes brothers are to the modern take on this genre, and their Grande Armée is becoming a classic (*see pp214-232* **Cafés** and *pp98-103* **Trendy** for more Costes addresses).

Café Zimmer

1 pl du Châtelet, 1st (01.42.36.74.03). M° Châtelet. **Open** 9am-1am daily. **Food served** 11am-12.30am. **Average** €32. **Prix fixe** €18.90. **Credit** AmEx, MC, V. **Wheelchair access**. **Non-smoking room**. **Map** J6.

Perhaps it's the location – place du Châtelet resembles a giant roundabout – but Café Zimmer doesn't quite have the same trendy cachet of other bars and eateries in the Costes brothers' empire (Café Beaubourg, Georges, Hôtel Costes, etc). When we arrived at 8pm it was full of fashion people, tourists and theatregoers and our harassed waiter assigned us a table in a draughty corner near a window. Twenty minutes went by before the aperitif-drinking crowd was replaced by calmer diners and our waiter chilled out, gave us menus, served us drinks and allowed us to move to a better table. Apart from a soggy cherry strudel, the food was fine. A shared starter of mille-feuille of crisp spice bread, prawns and a guacamole-like concoction was simply prepared and got gobbled up quickly. The main course choucroute – one seafood, the other accompanied by sausages, bacon and salted pork – were perfectly accompanied by half a bottle of very drinkable gewürztraminer. Do not be put off by the trendy accoutrements – chintz, leopard skin, French baroque – and the piped electronic lounge music. This remains a brasserie where one can eat decently, without fuss and without breaking the bank.

Chez Flottes

2 rue Cambon, 1st (01.42.60.80.89). M° Concorde. **Open** 7am-12.30am daily. **Average** €30. **Prix fixe** €21, €26. **Credit** AmEx, DC, MC, V. **Wheelchair access**. **Non-smoking room**. **Map** G5.

This shrewdly conceived restaurant opened several years ago in response to a lack of restaurants in an area awash with hotels. So Flottes hung out its shingle knowing that it would be a roaring success, which it is, at least in terms of the impressive volume of faces fed in any 12-hour period. At noon, office workers and boutique sales people mix it up with tourists, and in the evening the tourists take over, with big tables of sleepy looking sightseers hailing from Hamburg and Houston, Madrid and Manchester, Tokyo and Turin. If the locals come for a quick feed with modest expectations, they won't be disappointed. Service is rushed and English-speaking, and the decor is an odd hybrid of olde worlde (faux stone walls) and Costes hip (slick lighting fixtures). Similarly, the menu wants to be all things to all punters, which is probably why there is a pasta heading alongside onion soup, chicory and blue cheese salad, steaks galore, lamb chops and, for a dose of character, Auvergnat dishes such as sausage with aligot (whipped potato and cheese curd with garlic). To be fair, the food is just a shade better than average. It's a shame, however, that this rather soulless cooking ends up being carried off to far corners of the globe as 'typical French food'.

Au Pied de Cochon

6 rue Coquillière, 1st (01.40.13.77.00/www.piedde cochon.com). M° Les Halles or Châtelet. **Open** 24 hours daily. **Average** €40. **Credit** AmEx, DC, MC, V. **Wheelchair access**. **Non-smoking room**. **Map** J5.

Open 24 hours a day, this brasserie is a reminder of the time when Les Halles was a wholesale market, and barrow boys would sit down to a bowl of onion soup in the early hours of the morning. Nowadays it is an ornate, pig-orientated tourist favourite, but its smart professional approach to catering does not disgrace its history. We began our meal with some delicious Provençal-style baked mussels and cabbage stuffed with the signature dish of pigs' trotters. It was slightly spoilt by a muddy brown sauce, but the wholemeal baguette was deliciously crisp and proved eminently suitable for mopping up. Resisting the choice of more porcine trotters, ears and tails, we chose the rognons de veau flambés au Cognac as a main course; fine kidneys perfectly cooked, but the bland sauce lacked bite and the accompanying potato wedges with mushrooms were unrefined and disappointing. Our St-Amour Beaujolais was excellent and we were tempted by some crêpes flambées, but we settled for some discreet people-watching over coffee instead. Next time we decided it might be better to order a dish of oysters and a simple steak or perhaps a breaded piglet trotter.

Gallopin ★

40 rue Notre-Dame-des-Victoires, 2nd (01.42.36.45.38/www.brasseriegallopin.com). M° Bourse. **Open** noon-midnight Mon-Sat. **Average** €30. **Prix fixe** €19.50-€33.50. **Credit** AmEx, DC, MC, V. **Wheelchair access. Non-smoking room. Map** J4.

You can't find much more classic brasserie style than at Gallopin, with its vintage mahogany panelling, brass coat hooks, tiled floor and white table linen. But Gallopin does it on an intimate scale, creating a perfect, discreet backdrop for the financial chat of its Bourse-side clientele. The polite, professional waiters didn't flinch at our lack of suits and our accompanying dog, and if most of the customers come here to talk figures, they also come for the food. While you will find steaks and tartares, the real treat here is the expertly prepared fish. We began with excellent fines de claires oysters and a plate of smoked salmon, then a roast fillet of sandre (pike-perch) on a Mediterranean-style base of aubergines, tomatoes and fresh basil, and a sumptuous whole roast sea bream, marred only by sadly undercooked potatoes. Desserts come in equally classic vein, including rum baba, fruit tarts and a creamy tiramisu. A bit of old Paris to be prized, and – increasingly rare today – one of those brasseries where you can still find a meal at all times of day.

Le Grand Colbert

2-4 rue Vivienne, 2nd (01.42.86.87.88). M° Bourse. **Open** noon-1am daily. **Average** €29. **Lunch menu** €18. **Prix fixe** €27. **Credit** AmEx, DC, MC, V. **Wheelchair access. Map** H4.

This slightly over-the-top brasserie with banquettes, high ceilings and potted palms was filling up fast on a Monday evening, which must mean they are getting something right. Our initial impression was compromised by the horridly tepid sangria, which was enthusiastically suggested as a house aperitif. The menu looks like a kindergarten project, written in childish multicoloured lettering, probably aimed at giving a light-hearted feel to the whole experience, which endeavours to mix formality and tourist fun. To begin, one of us chose the langoustines, which were the special of the day. They were overcooked with a pasty texture, and needed lashings of good mayonnaise to cheer them up. The other enjoyed battling with dishes of bulots, pronouncing the sea snails fresh and delicious. Main courses included a tasty slice of foie de veau with a raspberry glaze, a good quality andouillette, and a well-seasoned steak tartare, all accompanied by above-average frites. The inevitable moelleux au chocolat was ordinary,

Gallopin's classic style creates the perfect backdrop for its Bourse-side clientele.

but the baba, served with its own little jug of rum, brought smiles – as did the bill, which despite a manly quantity of fruity Chiroubles was reasonable, making this a good place for a fun evening with a group of friends.

Le Vaudeville ★

29 rue Vivienne, 2nd (01.40.20.04.62/www. vaudevilleparis.com). Mº Bourse. **Open** 7-11.30am (breakfast), noon-3pm, 7pm-1am daily. **Average** €40. **Prix fixe** €23.50, €33.50. **Credit** AmEx, DC, MC, V. **Map** H4.

Yes, it's another Flo conquest (at last count, the chain had gobbled up nine brasseries in Paris), but Le Vaudeville has maintained its old-fashioned vibe, mainly through the stunning art deco interior and faultless service. The 1920s detailing – engraved glass, ironwork, warm-toned marble and inlaid wood – was designed by the Solvet brothers, whose only other remaining masterworks are La Coupole (*see p94*) and La Closerie des Lilas (*see p90*). We sat at one of the long tables against the wall and marvelled at the waiters in their impeccable outfits, constantly busy on our late Friday night visit seasoning dishes, delicately boning fish fillets on the sideboard or cheerily mixing up each steak tartare to order. The food, too, harkens back to days of yore – no nouveau anything. We first sampled a plain but satisfying cheese and cream ravioli dish and a well-executed salad with chèvre encrusted in toasted hazelnuts. Fine fish, such as a trio of charred salmon, red mullet and cod, or the chunky slab of grilled cod with truffle-infused mashed potatoes, made succulent main courses. Le Vaudeville's no-frills food is refreshingly confident about what it is and what it is not.

Bofinger

5-7 rue de la Bastille, 4th (01.42.72.87.82/www. bofingerparis.com). Mº Bastille. **Open** noon-3pm, 6.30pm-1am Mon-Fri; noon-1am Sat, Sun. **Average** €42. **Prix fixe** €32.90. **Lunch menu** €22.50 (Mon-Fri). **Credit** AmEx, DC, MC, V. **Non-smoking room. Map** M7.

Inside the antique revolving door Bofinger is all timewarp belle époque decor, white-aproned waiters and quiet, civilised talk, albeit a tad compromised by the trappings of chain-dom. Like other revered Paris eateries of yesteryear, it belongs to the Flo group – witness the table paraphernalia and a menu that can smack of over-zealous portion control somewhere up the food chain. There are many kinds of choucroute to complement a reliable line-up of brasserie basics (oysters, seafood, grills). Our starters clearly pointed the way to go: six plump, garlicky snails were a fail-safe alternative to a peculiar goat's cheese mille-feuille – sparse filo pastry leaves sandwiched around a flavourless, piped cheesy concoction served with preserved strips of pepper. Next up, beef tartare with anchovies was good enough, but prepared away from the table and disappointingly bland. A choucroute de la mer (pickled cabbage with smoked haddock,

langoustines and other fishy bits) was thin on fish and big on cabbage: the kraut was decidedly sauer, with little of the hoped-for flavour of juniperberries and riesling. Wines were uniformly excellent: working our way through the special offers (all white, all served by the glass) we enjoyed an aperitif of honeyed vendanges tardives followed by a rich, herby 2000 Hermitage – just the right side of dry, and perfect with the choucroute. Our waiter also produced a fine Bordeaux for the tartare. Staple desserts (fondant au chocolat) were better than a mildly innovative berry gazpacho. A word of praise for the kids' menu, which comes complete with a gastronomic colouring book and crayons and a fruit cocktail served in a sugar-frosted glass. Tender veal steak with cream and ceps (no less) was wolfed down in wide-eyed silence, and the îles flottantes were some of the best we've seen.

Brasserie de l'Isle St Louis

55 quai de Bourbon, 4th (01.43.54.02.59). Mº Pont Marie. **Open** noon-1am Mon, Tue, Fri-Sun; 6pm-1am Thur. Closed Aug and 23, 24, 25 Dec. **Average** €35. **Credit** DC, MC, V. **Map** K7.

The Ile St-Louis is one of the most visited sights in Paris, but island life does not include many down-to-earth restaurants. Happily this old-fashioned brasserie soldiers on while exotic juice bars and fancy tea shops come and go. The terrace has one of the best summer views in Paris, and was packed with tourists on a sunny September lunchtime. We decided to sit in the dining room, whose shabby chic charm reminded us of our student days. Stuffed game and nicotine-stained walls make for a convivial Parisian experience, and our slightly gruff waiter had obviously served a good many choucroutes and tartares in his life. We began with a well-dressed frisée aux lardons and a slab of fairly ordinary terrine, followed by a greasy slice of foie de veau, prepared à l'anglaise with a rasher of bacon, and a more successful pan of warming tripe. Nothing was gastronomically exciting, and a tad more sophistication in the kitchen would transform this delightful place into something more exceptional. We dodged the very ordinary looking puddings and instead enjoyed a lesson on how to make a steak tartare from our waiter, who at one point almost raised a smile.

Le Balzar

49 rue des Ecoles, 5th (01.43.54.13.67/www. groupflo.fr). Mº Cluny-La Sorbonne. **Open** noon-11.45pm daily. **Average** €30. **Prix fixe** €23 (from 10.30pm). **Credit** AmEx, DC, MC, V. **Map** J7.

On our last visit to Le Balzar we were happy to see two senior French film critics, engaged in animated conversation, tucked away in a corner of the legendary Left Bank brasserie. Intellectuals have obviously not entirely abandoned this atmospheric mirrored haunt, despite it being part of the Flo group, a fact brought home by the tacky wine promotion leaflets placed on the table. We hit one of those days when nothing seemed on track in the kitchen. Oeuf en meurette came in a pleasantly flavoured sauce, rich in wine and bacon bits, but the poached egg was slightly overcooked, which spoils the runny fun of the dish. This was followed by a reasonable steak tartare with too coarsely chopped pieces of onion, but good frites. Skate wing in golden butter had been overcooked and become tough and listless, accompanied by leathery sautéed potatoes. When we pointed this out to the waiter, he was charm itself, and brought another vastly superior fish, but blamed the poor potatoes on the general state of European agriculture. A glass of free Bordeaux with the still-excellent rum baba almost made amends for what was, despite the authentic 1930s feel, a disappointingly routine meal – and, at getting on for €100, hardly a bargain.

Restaurant Marty

20 av des Gobelins, 5th (01.43.31.39.51/www. marty-restaurant.com). M° Les Gobelins. **Open** noon-midnight daily. **Average** €50. **Prix fixe** €36. **Credit** DC, MC, V. **Non-smoking room.** **Map** K10.

While most Parisian brasseries sport belle époque gilded and mirrored luxury, Marty is pure art deco. Sumptuous curves, leopard-print wooden chairs, and period chandeliers and murals adorn the spacious split level dining areas. Were it not for the food and efficient staff (one monsieur wears a classic handlebar moustache) you might think this was a Prohibition-era jazz club. We found the starter of crabmeat and avocado purée rich and thoroughly rewarding with the tangy sourdough rolls. Likewise, an Asian-inspired starter of cold root veg and mangetout stuffed into a blossom-shaped crispy crêpe. Mains of salmon and cod brochette with corn cake, and a mixed grill of tuna, sea bream and salmon were competently prepared, if a little over-salted. But a fresh fruit-topped rice pudding, creamy and big enough to share, was thoroughly beyond reproach. All in all, the €36 prix fixe is a steal, the covered terrace provides a fine refuge from foul weather, and the downstairs room would host a memorable reception. Afterwards, take a stroll up nearby rue Mouffetard to walk off this classy brasserie experience.

Alcazar

62 rue Mazarine, 6th (01.53.10.19.99/www. alcazar.fr). M° Odéon. **Open** noon-3pm, 7pm-12.30am daily; *bar* 7pm-2am. **Average** €50. **Prix fixe** €38. **Lunch menu** €17, €24, €27. **Credit** AmEx, DC, MC, V. **Wheelchair access.** **Non-smoking room. Map** H7.

Though you may have the feeling that you might as well be in London as in Paris – compounded by English diners not even attempting to speak French to the waiters – Conran's Parisian gastrodrome with its glassed-in kitchen running along one side has a certain clean-cut appeal. Sunday lunch is a popular choice, and you can have a free shiatsu massage as part of the package. We had arrived intending to have brunch but the concept of wolfing down

yoghurt and muffins followed by a rich menu main course such as chicken stuffed with foie gras didn't appeal. There are eggs, but then it seemed silly to spend €27 on such simple fare when the equally priced lunch menu includes three courses and a glass of wine. Of our starters, the tataki de saumon was a rewarding choice: generous slices of super-fresh raw salmon accompanied by pickled ginger, wasabi and soy sauce. The mille-feuille de thon on the other hand would have been better described as a 'muddle' of raw tuna, avocado, mango and coriander attempting, unsuccessfully, to resemble ceviche. The Sir Tel trademark fish and chips was wonderful – nothing like your local chippy, but firm, meaty cod in a crisp batter with fat, hand-cut fries and watercress salad. Vinegar (Sarson's, we do believe) is amusingly served in a small pot. The farm chicken with foie gras and shiitake mushrooms was generous (served in a bowl), but that's about all it had going for it as the mushrooms and foie gras made it rather slimy. The cuisse de canard, which our very grown-up five-year-old had as part of his brunch, is better, but the zingy orange juice sent him into a coughing fit and made our eyes water when we tried it. It's worth knowing, too, that aside from the fish and chips, vegetables aren't served with the mains. We added a side order of creamy, chive-sprinkled mash, but it didn't come till after we had finished the chicken and duck. But hey, there is a saving grace – the puddings are good. Both the moelleux au chocolat (included in the brunch) and roast figs in a coulis with ice-cream were entirely satisfying. The glass of red with the menu was far superior to what you'd get in Soho too.

L'Arbuci

25 rue de Buci, 6th (01.44.32.16.00/www. arbuci.com). M° Odéon or Mabillon. **Open** 9.30am-12.30am daily. *Jazz club* Thur-Sat midnight-5am. **Average** €45. **Prix fixe** €30. **Lunch menu** €20. **Credit** AmEx, DC, MC, V. **Non-smoking room. Map** H7.

The banquettes are mauve, the interior chic though unsurprising, the service crisp and the atmosphere just this side of straight. To borrow from the restaurant's own PR-speak, an interior overhaul has led L'Arbuci to 'play the trendy card', resulting in a menu that reads like a cross between classic French and eclectic fusion – a rather risky approach for a brasserie. Still, L'Arbuci keeps it in hand, stopping far short of El Bulli-esque weirdness with dishes such as roasted duck fillet in cocoa sauce, and sweet grilled scallops drizzled in caramelised orange sauce alongside a quartet of endives wrapped in ham. For those seeking something less contrived, a classic starter of haricots verts followed by the all-you-can-eat rotisserie formula should fit the bill. As for the salty ambrosia of the eat-till-replete oyster menu, we stopped at 30 with more still on offer. Thankfully service has improved since our last visit: the team of black-clad waiters could not be faulted, catering to the lunch crowd with bilingual charm.

Brasserie Lipp ★

151 bd St-Germain, 6th (01.45.48.53.91/www. brasserielipp.com). Mº St-Germain-des-Prés. **Open** noon-1am daily. Closed 24, 25 Dec. **Average** €40. **Credit** AmEx, DC, MC, V. **Map** H7.

When somewhere as old and stylish as the Lipp – fuelling Paris politicos and Left Bank intellects in art nouveau grandeur for more than a century – lets plebby newcomers sit at the coveted ground floor tables, you know that something revolutionary is afoot. But the democratic urge was short-lived. We were tucked comfortably into the back room where we ogled not presidential hopefuls but an army of starched, black-tied waiters (all surely contemporaries of the eponymous Léonard) as they strove, amid the swirl of gargantuan, tender côtes de boeuf, surreally pink platters of piggy choucroute, and some of the zingiest steak tartare we've ever eaten, to tame the barbarian invasion. But when our neighbours asked to have their raspberry-hued Gevrey-Chambertin put on ice, the staff simply and heroically refused. Competition may have made Lipp relax some of its time-honoured snooty standards, but there has been no accompanying compromise of culinary rigour. After succulent, meaty mains – all spot-on, bloody or blue as required – we opted for a barrage of classic desserts: chilly profiteroles swimming in thick chocolate, a slab of beautifully caramelised tarte Tatin and the famous wedge-like mille-feuille courtesy of Dalloyau (for something different try the praliné '2,000 feuilles' imported from fashionable pâtissier Pierre Hermé). As the heavy, revolving door whirled us back on to the street, we felt the ghost of Mitterrand, still a Lipp regular no doubt, wish us good night.

La Closerie des Lilas

171 bd du Montparnasse, 6th (01.40.51.34.50). Mº Port-Royal. **Open** noon-1am daily. **Average** €40. **Credit** AmEx, DC, MC, V. **Map** H9.

Once, at the end of a long evening at the Closerie bar, we found to our horror that we didn't have enough money to pay the bill. The barman took what we had with a big smile and a magnanimous 'Don't worry about it'. Elegance abounds at this Montparnasse institution that has, at one time or another, counted Ingres and Chateaubriand, Trotsky and Lenin, Apollinaire, Picasso and (bien sûr) Hemingway among its regulars. On our last visit we spotted one of the leaders of the Parti Socialiste and a legend of French rock. The restaurant has recently recovered a good, fine-eating reputation, but we (and the French rock legend as well, apparently) prefer the simpler and cheaper brasserie, because there you can sit closer to the piano and the dark, velvety atmosphere of the bar. We ate well from an unpretentious menu which is strong on seafood (tremendous oysters and a fine clam soup). Our mains of poached pike dumplings and a fish panaché, though nothing outstanding, were carefully cooked and nicely presented. Chocolate profiteroles were, as always when done right, that

sublime meeting of crisp and creamy, hot and cold. Staff were efficient, discreet and friendly – obviously forgetting that we owed them money.

Vagenende

142 bd St-Germain, 6th (01.43.26.68.18/www. vagenende.com). Mº Odéon. **Open** noon-1am daily. Closed Aug. **Average** €32. **Prix fixe** €23. **Credit** AmEx, DC, MC, V. **Wheelchair access. Non-smoking room. Map** H7.

Thanks to the intervention of André Malraux, Minister of Culture in De Gaulle's government in the 1960s, plans to build a supermarket on this site were shelved. Instead, Vagenende's belle époque interior – elaborate carvings, sparkling mirrors, painted glass and faience – was preserved for the nation, being listed as a historical monument in 1983. With its red velvet banquettes and white-clothed tables, no place could be more typically French. Discreet waiters in traditional uniform glide across the room, while diners of all ages tuck into classic brasserie dishes (it's amazing the fun children can have with a plate of seafood). The food, though, is the last reason to come. Tasty onion soup with a thick layer of melted cheese, a slightly dry chicken liver terrine with Armagnac and cornichons, a chicken suprême with rice, mushrooms and tarragon sauce, or boeuf bourguignon with fresh pasta neither thrill nor particularly disappoint. However, portions are generous, the bread is good and wine (particularly the Saumur Champigny) is reasonable. Oh, and Jane Birkin is reputedly a regular.

L'Avenue

41 av Montaigne, 8th (01.40.70.14.91). Mº Franklin D Roosevelt or Alma Marceau. **Open** 8am-1am Mon-Sat, 9am-1am Sun. Closed 31 Dec. **Average** €65. **Credit** AmEx, DC, MC, V. **Non-smoking room. Map** D4.

Of all the Costes brothers' restaurants, this is the one that probably works best in terms of what any Paris restaurant should do – serve good food with service that shows an understanding of the quartier. So here it's a real 'bingo', since the svelte young waitresses are fetching and chilly – a mirror image of the avenue Montaigne, one of the world's most famous fashion precincts. Oddly, they seat the French-speakers in the dark, smoky main dining room and banish foreigners to the terrace tables, which is where anyone would really want to be. So, settled at your too-small table, ease into the lounge music beat over a glass of decent chardonnay, and browse a menu that lets you lead off with a glass of fresh carrot juice; or, more temptingly, macaroni with morel mushrooms, smoked salmon, an excellent salad of baby artichokes, rocket and parmesan; or another contemporary Parisian classic – green beans and mushrooms in a balsamic vinaigrette. Main courses of tuna steak with balsamic reduction – a pleasantly sticky syrup of the famous Italian vinegar – and a first-rate chateaubriand with hollandaise sauce were offered with green beans, spinach, chips, mash or salad, another nice touch. Desserts aren't a forte here, and there are just two cheeses from fromager Marie-Anne Cantin – st-nectaire or rocamadour – but coffee is good and comes with a tiny bar of delicious Fouquet's chocolate.

Le Boeuf sur le Toit

34 rue du Colisée, 8th (01.53.93.65.55/www. boeufsurletoit.com). M° St-Philippe du Roule or Franklin D Roosevelt. **Open** noon-3pm, 7pm-1am daily. **Average** €45. **Prix fixe** €33.50. **Credit** AmEx, DC, MC, V. **Non-smoking room. Map** E4.
With soaring ceilings, mirrored walls, dark wood trim and art deco detailing, Boeuf sur le Toit feels both inviting and invigorating. At dinner we saw elderly regulars; suited, cigar-smoking captains of industry (there is, however, a non-smoking room); guidebook-toting, T-shirt clad tourists; and French families. They all come for crowd-pleasing brasserie classics such as steak tartare, foie gras, and grand platters of oysters and shellfish that seemingly fly through the room on waiters' shoulders. Don't miss the oysters – ours were cold, succulent and briney-sweet, with dark rye bread, salted butter and a tangy shallot-laced mignonette sauce. A 2002 Gustave Lorentz riesling (a half-bottle of which was included in the prix fixe) made a lovely accompaniment. The rest of our meal was seasoned conservatively. Warm leeks vinaigrette with serrano ham, though visually appetising, required a dash of salt and a little more vinegar. Steak au poivre was thick and carefully cooked, but peppery in name only, and we finished a plate of filet de rascasse (scorpion fish) thinking 'butter' not 'fish'. Perhaps it was an off-night, but the service was more showy than efficient. We were seated amid the smokers despite having reserved a non-smoking table, we had to ask twice for water and the bill, our waiter mis-identified a cheese on the menu and the bill at the next table was incorrect too.

Brasserie Lorraine

2-4 pl des Ternes, 8th (01.56.21.22.00). M° Ternes. **Open** noon-12.30am daily. **Average** €60. **Credit** AmEx, DC, MC, V. **Wheelchair access. Non-smoking room. Map** D3.
With a spacious terraced location that offers a front-row take on the street life in one of the better-heeled bourgeois neighbourhoods of Paris, this long-running brasserie reopened in September 2004 after a top-to-bottom makeover that proves the rule that all restaurateurs should wait at least a year when they feel the urge to redecorate. Why? Invariably the old look is teetering on the brink of acquiring an honest vintage charm – in this case, the Lorraine's 1947 decor had a wonderful aura of Cocteau, new-look Dior and post-war Paris – at the same time that an ambitious young marketing type decides that everything must go. And here everything did, to be replaced by a sort of Busby Berkeley take on a Paris brasserie with raspberry fabric, crystal chandeliers, too much blond wood panelling, and bits and pieces of art deco mosaic work, with the whole shebang being curiously overlit to boot. The look is confused Hôtel Costes wannabe, and so is the service, from a

Shellfish rule at **Brasserie Lorraine.**

hostile voiturier to the inevitable wish-I-was-a-model hostess, and waiters whose performance ranges from frosty to bored and bumbling, and often both. The heroes of the story are the oyster shuckers in wellies out front, since it's the freshness of the oysters and shellfish platters they prepare that puts this place in the running. Otherwise, the menu is a strange mixture of fashion eats – salmon with noodles and wok-fried vegetables, etc – and better-than-average brasserie standards such as choucroute garnie. Not all of the classics work: steak tartare was a sorry, soggy, flavourless affair served stone cold with wilted frites. Ditto desserts, which are dull. The house wines by the carafe are decent, though, and this place is at its best for weekend lunch or Sunday dinner, when a ladies-in-pashminas and gents-wearing-blazers-with-jeans crowd prevails.

Fermette Marbeuf 1900

5 rue Marbeuf, 8th (01.53.23.08.00/www. fermettemarbeuf.com). M° Alma-Marceau or Franklin D Roosevelt. **Open** noon-3pm, 7-11.30pm daily. **Average** €50. **Prix fixe** €30. **Credit** AmEx, DC, MC, V. **Wheelchair access. Non-smoking room. Map** D4.
First of all, avoid the non-smoking room. The main reason for coming here is the smoking-allowed conservatory where, in 1978, a worker uncovered an art nouveau masterwork designed in 1898 by the architect Hurtré and the painter Wielharski. It was

fully restored in 1982 and declared a historic monument. There is still something of the hidden treasure about this dining room which has no windows on the outside world but is surrounded by glass, no plants but is full of greenery. We sipped our Martinis and perused the lunch menu with a little trepidation. Our previous meal at the Fermette had been disappointing. There's the occasional rustic flourish to the menu – 'home-made' pâté and foie gras or a basket of nuts with the cheese – but following the advice of the waiter, we went for a green salad with scallops and Dublin bay prawns in an orange and vanilla sauce. Although the wine we ordered with it (a superbly full-bodied but elegant white Côtes du Rhône from Saint-Perray) was tremendous, the orange zest sauce was a bit overpowering. Our best main was the tournedos Rossini. For those unfamiliar with this particular French extravagance, this is a slice of toast with a tender cut of beef, fresh foie gras and a slice of black truffle (which here proved rather odourless). We also enjoyed the retro pommes dauphines, potatoes mixed with choux pastry and fried until they rise to the size of croquet balls. The crêpes with Grand Marnier are famous here but we had cheese instead, including a particularly good livarot. Not a bad feast on a cold winter's day in a romantic setting a stone's throw from the Champs-Elysées.

Fouquet's

99 av des Champs-Elysées, 8th (01.47.23.70.60/ www.lucienbarriere.com). M° George V. **Open** 8am-2am daily (last orders 11.30pm). **Average** €80. **Prix fixe** €78. **Credit** AmEx, DC, MC, V. **Wheelchair access. Non-smoking room.** **Map** D4.
Chef Jean-Yves Leuranguer, formerly of the Martinez in Cannes, has made dining at Fouquet's a real, if expensive, delight. We adored our five-course menu dégustation. A starter scallop salad with fresh mango and sautéed leeks – all light and modern – was followed by a rich and rustic risotto of wild mushrooms and warm foie gras. This was definitely the high point of our dinner but the turbot with squid sauce, tomatoes, courgette flowers and aubergines was good too, with strong Mediterranean colours and flavours. With the Chablis going slightly to our heads, the desserts (yes, plural) went by in a flurry of sorbets, chocolate, praline and petits fours. The service was impeccable, even after we asked to be moved away from a table of noisy trade union leaders. As for the decor of the place, although the textured, red wallpaper is rather more reminiscent of a British city pub than a Parisian café, the overall effect is pleasantly old-style, creating a kind of 1950s French charm.

Garnier

111 rue St-Lazare, 8th (01.43.87.50.40). M° St-Lazare. **Open** noon-3pm, 6-11pm Mon, Sun; noon-3pm, 6-11.30pm Tue-Sat. Closed Aug. **Average** €60. **Credit** AmEx, DC, MC, V. **Non-smoking room.** **Map** G3.

Maybe it's the proximity of the station, all the offices or the department stores but there is something impersonal and characterless about the St-Lazare district that is well represented at this unimpressive brasserie. The decor has been tarted up so many times you feel they should gut the building and start again, while the staff should take a prolonged break in a monastic retreat so they can return with a renewed love of humanity. The sparse and ageing clientele hand over their money for reliable though unexceptional food in an atmosphere of dozy peace and quiet. There are lots of seafood options (even a snug little oyster bar at the entrance), so this is where we started. The mussels and clams were especially plump and good, but a small worm in one of the oyster shells didn't do much to stoke our appetites. If you want a warmer, spicier starter there's the sautéed calamari with parsley and Espelette pepper. We were disappointed by the sole meunière which managed to remain watery and dull despite being accompanied by lemon confit and a rather good, highly buttery purée of small ratte potatoes. The salt cod brandade was more interesting with some lively caramelised red onions. We managed to get through a couple of bottles of Languedoc white, which wasn't badly priced at €21. A fine pear tart and tedious stewed apple with dried fruit completed a forgettable evening's dining.

La Maison de l'Aubrac

37 rue Marbeuf, 8th (01.43.59.05.14/www.maison-aubrac.fr). M° Franklin D Roosevelt. **Open** 24 hours daily. **Average** €34. **Credit** AmEx, MC, V. **Non-smoking room.** **Map** D4.
On a Thursday night, just off the chic Champs-Elysées, we found ourselves hemmed in by scrums of big, beefy men tucking into plates of saucisse aligot (pork sausages with a mix of mashed potatoes, garlic and cheese), giant ribs of beef and juicy steaks. This rustic little Auvergnat corner, complete with wooden booths, paper placemats and glossy photos of man and beast (in particular), is a beacon for rugby lovers. We weighed in with a slab of fine foie gras then, deciding against the 'three meats platter' (tartare, sirloin steak and boeuf pressé), we went for slices of leg of lamb from the Lozère region (tender if a tad overcooked), roasted and served with green beans and crisply fried potato slices, and a perfectly grilled entrecôte. The excellent wine list is pricey with good choices from the Rhône and Languedoc-Roussillon. Service is friendly and efficient and the place, like a rugby line-out, is always jumping.

Charlot, Roi des Coquillages

81 bd de Clichy, 9th (01.53.20.48.00/www.lesfreres blanc.com). M° Place de Clichy. **Open** noon-3pm, 7pm-midnight Mon-Wed, Sun; noon-3pm, 7pm-1am Thur-Sat. **Average** €65. **Prix fixe** €35. **Lunch menu** €25, €30. **Credit** AmEx, DC, MC, V. **Non-smoking room.** **Map** G2.
Aside from its endearing, campy glamour – apricot velvet banquettes and peculiar laminated lithographs of shellfish – the main reason that this

Terminus Nord.

long-running fish-house is so popular is its flawless catch-of-the-day menu. A curious but buzzy mix of tourists, night people, arty locals, executive couples and good-humoured folks in from the provinces patronise this place and, given such an eclectic clientele, staff are to be commended for their outstanding professional service. Depending on the season, the seafood platters are what the regulars opt for, and even in the middle of summer – off-season for many shellfish – the prawns, sea urchins and lobster are impeccable. Otherwise, start with the excellent fish soup, followed by a classic such as grilled sea bass or superb aïoli (boiled salt cod with vegetables and lashings of garlic mayonnaise), and finish off with crêpe suzette or the delicious tarte Tatin with cinnamon.

Julien

16 rue du Fbg-St-Denis, 10th (01.17.70.12.06/www. julienparis.com). M° Strasbourg-St-Denis. **Open** noon-3pm, 7pm-1am daily. **Average** €26. **Prix fixe** €23.50, €33.50. **Credit** AmEx, DC, MC, V. **Wheelchair access**. Map K4.

Behind two doors and a red velvet curtain off the seedy Faubourg-St-Denis is a world of potted palms, stained glass peacocks and art nouveau maidens. The maître d' clapped his hands and a waiter bustled to ready the table for a lone male diner who might have been Flo group chairman Jean-Paul Bucher himself, such was the flurry. Busy in the evenings, Julien is a peaceful refuge for Sunday lunch, a rarity in this city. There are no surprises on the menu but the food is dependable. To see how à la carte might compare with the prix fixe, we went for the set menu,

which included half a bottle of a decent house white and the 'ardoise du jour'. The menu's starter of passable foie gras was rather meagre, while the girolle mushrooms cooked à la bourguignonne with garlic, breadcrumbs and parsley arrived with ceremony sizzling in their copper dish but were distinctly flavourless. The mains were excellent. The prix fixe's suprême de flétan (halibut) was crispy on the outside and firm on the inside, nestling among red and yellow peppers with pistou. Sea bass was brought whole to the table for inspection then taken away and de-boned, topped and tailed. When we expressed disappointment that we couldn't eat the cheeks, the waiter smiled and brought back the head on a saucer. With this delectable fish came a side dish of buttery fennel that was its perfect accompaniment. Desserts were just as good – a dark chocolate tart topped with firm chocolate mousse and served with crème anglaise, and a divine charlotte aux framboises, moist with fresh and juicy fruit in a raspberry sauce. The chocolate truffles that come with coffee are fabulous.

Terminus Nord

23 rue de Dunkerque, 10th (01.42.85.05.15/ www.terminusnord.com). M° Gare du Nord. **Open** 11am-1am daily. **Average** €25. **Prix fixe** €33.50. **Lunch menu** €23.50. **Credit** AmEx, DC, MC, V. **Non-smoking room**. Map K2.

This Flo brasserie's clientele of local seafood addicts has been supplemented in the last few years by famished Anglophone travellers emerging from the Eurostar terminal across the road. Among the standard brasserie fare of seafood platters, steaks and choucroute is an improbable house speciality of bouillabaisse, a quintessential southern dish consisting of monkfish, eel and sea bass served up in a rich broth – and all for €21. We opted for lighter dishes. Both our soups were excellent, the satisfying French onion soup topped with just the right amount of melted cheese, and a veritable vat of excellent fish soup accompanied by crispy croûtons and a spicy rouille. Mains of buttery salmon on a bed of starkly contrasting red cabbage, and the suckling pig did not excite extreme emotions either way, though the dainty dessert of a trio of pear, apple and apricot tarte Tatins was a feast. The fin-de-siècle decor, the hubbub of the dining room, the good humour of the dozen white-uniformed waiters and the good-value menus make this an ideal location for a final dose of authentic French brasserie ambience before departing for Albion.

Le Train Bleu

Gare de Lyon, pl Louis-Armand, 12th (01.43.43.09.06/www.le-train-bleu.com). M° Gare de Lyon. **Open** 11.30am-3pm, 7-11pm daily. **Average** €50. **Prix fixe** €43. **Credit** AmEx, DC, MC, V. **Wheelchair access. Map** M8.

This has to be the most glamorous station buffet in the world, complete with 19th-century frescoes to welcome travellers on the famous train bleu, which used to link Paris with Ventimiglia. On our last visit we took a prima donna who was appearing at the Palais Garnier and the operatic setting seemed perfect. The cooking is classic but a cut above the average brasserie, and we began with a saucisson de Lyon served on warm ratte potatoes, which set us up nicely for main courses, including a long-cooked, crisply breaded pied de porc; a tartare to which a slug of Cognac gave an added punch; and the most sophisticated dish, a plump and juicy veal chop served with creamy wild mushroom lasagne. The evening ended on a high note with a scrumptious vacherin, a chocolate sortilège – an upright cone of mousse-filled dark chocolate accompanied by pistachio ice-cream – and a rum baba, with a whole bottle of rum temptingly left on the table for extra dousing. Service throughout was particularly efficient and charming. The only caveat is the expensive wine list from which we chose a perfumed red Beaune, the suggestion of the month but hardly a bargain at €48 a bottle.

La Coupole ★

102 bd du Montparnasse, 14th (01.43.20.14.20/ www.coupoleparis.com). M° Vavin. **Open** 8.30am-1am Mon-Thur; 8.30am-1.30am Fri, Sat. **Average** €40. **Prix fixe** €33. **Credit** AmEx, DC, MC, V. **Non-smoking room. Map** G9.

Atmosphere, atmosphere. It's easy to criticise La Coupole – that it's now part of the Flo group, that Montparnasse has changed – but when it comes down to a celebration, you really can't go wrong here. Though Montparnasse is far from its avant-garde past when this restaurant opened in 1927 as a 'bar américain' with its cocktails and its basement

'dancing', La Coupole still somehow transforms the boulevard into something of its glamour of old. The people-watching remains superb, inside and out, while the long ranks of linen-covered tables, the highly professional waiters, the 32 art deco columns painted by different artists of the epoch, the mosaic floor and the sheer scale still make coming here an event. What's more, it continues to be a favourite with Parisians of all ages, as well as out-of-towners and tourists. The good-value set menu offers steaks, foie gras, fish and autumn game stews as well as wine. But the real treat here is the shellfish, displayed along a massive counter, whether you choose to make your own selection of claires, spéciales or belons or opt for one of the platters, brimming with crabs, oysters, prawns, periwinkles and clams. On our last visit we skipped the queue for the main dining room and slid into the window section for a late-night, post-opera feast of oysters, crisp white wine and ice-cream sundaes – a real treat.

Café du Commerce

51 rue du Commerce, 15th (01.45.75.03.27/www. lecafedecommerce.com). M° Emile Zola. **Open** noon-midnight daily. **Average** €35. **Prix fixe** €26.50 (dinner only). **Lunch menu** €12. **Children's menu** €7. **Credit** AmEx, DC, MC, V. **Wheelchair access. Non-smoking room. Map** C8.

The long-democratic Café du Commerce has upped its prices since a change of ownership, moving it out of budget territory. If we say that the decor is more memorable than the food, we should explain that this three-level art deco former workman's café has a tree growing through the middle of it and balconies lined with flower boxes that burst with colour. Much as this made us want to like the cooking, it was too hit and miss to merit a thumbs-up, the low point being a rubbery tête de veau. Our waiter was friendly, but loath to recommend wine and we ended up disappointed with a €20 Chinon. The food had bright spots: a green bean and parmesan starter came topped with the surprisingly successful combination of smoked duck breast slices and sun-dried tomatoes. Seared salmon over earthy lentils proved perfectly fine too. At the other end of the meal, chocolate cake and tarte Tatin were both done with a masterly mother's touch and we noticed a rum baba served with a bottle of rum, allowing you to choose your saturation level. A stiff bill, however, left a slightly bitter taste in our mouths.

Le Suffren

84 av de Suffren, 15th (01.45.66.97.86). M° La Motte-Picquet Grenelle. **Open** 7am-2am daily. **Average** €22. **Credit** AmEx, MC, V. **Wheelchair access. Non-smoking room. Map** D7.

The problems of entertaining a B-list celebrity can never be overestimated. Too hip and you look as if you are trying too hard, too chic and they will turn up in jeans and T-shirt, while a humble bistro is hardly grand enough to support their tenuous grasp on stardom. Brasseries like Le Suffren are an ideal compromise. We remembered it from a time when its maritime decor had a certain retro charm, and although the fashionable new look is reasonably successful, culinary authenticity seems in danger. We enjoyed a glass of chilled white Menetou-Salon before ordering starters of gratin de coquille St-Jacques, and a celeb-friendly diet-conscious seafood platter. King prawns, served on a square plate, were tough and the accompanying saffron rice overcooked and free of any spice taste. Steak tartare was enlivened by some parmesan shavings, but we agreed that the best element of the meal was the excellent frites. A marbré of chocolate and chestnuts was spoilt by some rather indifferent crème anglaise, and ice-cream with chocolate sauce was hardly earth-moving. The lunch was pleasant enough, but we have a lingering pang for the old Suffren with its more comforting atmosphere. The vast summer terrace is still undeniably pleasant.

Brasserie de la Poste

54 rue de Longchamp, 16th (01.47.55.01.31).
M° Trocadéro. **Open** noon-2pm, 7-10pm Mon-Fri; 7-10pm Sat. Closed three weeks in Aug. **Average** €26. **Prix fixe** €16, €26. **Lunch menu** €15. **Credit** AmEx, DC, MC, V. **Map** C5.

Discreet – as in subdued jazz, low 1930s-style lighting, smooth leather upholstery and impeccable service – is what this brasserie-cum-bistro is all about. It's a neighbourhood affair, drawing diners from the chic apartments and comfortable hotels that fill this posh patch of Paris. And on a weekend night, when the hipper chefs are out of town and the hotspots are just too happening, it's perfect for safe, satisfying food and a quiet tête-à-tête. Starters such as foie gras maison (elegantly served with a little spoon of fleur de sel, the Rolls-Royce of salt), and a surprisingly refreshing helping of potted rabbit, whetted our appetites without knocking our socks off. We opted for traditional mains – a chunky beef tartare shot through with a light chilli zing, and a thick, juicy steak paired with roasted potatoes and an unctuous pot of rich wine sauce – and we polished off every last bite before subjecting the chef to the all-important tarte Tatin test. It was spot-on, amber right through with a melt-in-the-mouth crust. When our neighbour's cheese plate arrived, runny brie and enticing roquefort in good sized chunks, we greedily eyeballed it but managed to resist. There is nothing glamorous or glitzy here – it's named after the big post office across the street, so what do you expect? – but just a few steps away is a great view of the Eiffel Tower, all 20,000 of its lights sparkling magically on the hour.

La Gare

19 chaussée de la Muette, 16th (01.42.15.15.31/ www.restaurantlagare.com). M° La Muette. **Open** noon-3pm, 7.30-10.30pm Mon, Sat; noon-3pm, 7-11.30pm Tue-Fri, Sun. Closed 25 Dec. **Average** €35. **Lunch menu** €15. **Prix fixe** €27, €32. **Credit** AmEx, MC, V. **Wheelchair access**. **Non-smoking room**. **Map** A6.

This was once a train station on the Petite Ceinture, the railway circling Paris built by Napoleon III. The ticket office is now the bar and the platforms downstairs have become a colossal dining area. After pushing the train theme hard, however, it seems the restaurant is now taking itself more seriously. The menu, while still dominated by the rôtisserie specialities, has been refined. We were seduced by the pince de tourteau (crab claw) with an avocado mousseline, and the black truffle risotto. Stuck awkwardly in the middle of the rice was a grilled wafer of comté: unexpected and delicious. The no-nonsense mains were excellent: the gigot d'agneau, accompanied with a jus so concentrated that it is served in a shot glass, was very tender and cooked exactly as we had requested. The portions seemed undersized until the giant bucket of accompanying purée was dropped off – salty but divine. La Gare is in the heart of the posh 16th – if you ask for water, they will assume you want it from a bottle – but prices are varied and reasonable. Evenings are generally calm, but lunch is often packed with locals with coiffed pooches in tow and an international crowd from the OECD, just around the corner.

La Grande Armée

3 av de la Grande-Armée, 16th (01.45.00.24.77). M° Charles de Gaulle-Etoile. **Open** 7am-2am daily. **Average** €35. **Credit** AmEx, DC, MC, V. **Non-smoking room. Map** C3.

A brasserie dedicated to the Napoleonic Grande Armée might not seem the obvious place for a Brit to turn to for lunch, but decoration is by trendsetting interior designer Jacques Garcia, who jointly owns the place with the Costes brothers. Jingoism is therefore limited to a few hussar prints and cut-outs; otherwise the room is pure Garcia with lots of deep red contrasting elegantly with powder blue, while each seat is covered with a velvet stole, like a discarded papal vestment. Designed to please successful young professionals for whom their parent's choice of restaurant would be too stuffy, but for whom straying far from the 16th would be unthinkable, the menu confirms this 'cool' formula, with expensive caviar listed amongst the starters and a would-be relaxed cheeseburger among the main courses. We chose a parmesan soufflé as a starter – a baby ramekin, nicely puffed and served with a well-dressed salad – plus a more interesting sea bass carpaccio with lime, strewn with coriander. Steak tartare was well seasoned and accompanied by outstanding thin frites, but it looked humble next to the parmentier de canard, which was luxuriously crowned with two slices of fried foie gras. Finishing our fruity Brouilly we resisted the puddings, which include the delicious pom pom pomme, a mixture of apple crumble, pie and ice-cream. Our waitress proclaimed with suitable belle époque insinuation: 'So, you are not a greedy boy.' We were as conquered as Napoleon's all-powerful army and didn't even mention Waterloo.

Le Stella ★

133 av Victor Hugo, 16th (01.56.90.56.00).
M° Victor Hugo. **Open** 11.30am-3.30pm, 7pm-1am
Mon-Fri; 11.30am-1am Sat, Sun. **Average** €40.
Credit AmEx, MC, V. **Wheelchair access.**
Map B4.

Deep in the velvet-lined precincts of the well-mannered, discreetly vieille France part of the 16th arrondissement, this long-running brasserie deserves kudos for an elegant updating that hasn't diminished its charm. This is a tweedy sort of place, since the Parisian bourgeoisie loves to affect a sort of off-to-the-hunt look, even if the plaids are Chanel for the ladies and cashmere for the gents. If you get the local codes, fine; if not, you won't be condescended to – there is real hospitality from the moment you step through the front door. The waiters are prompt and professional for a change, and miraculously enough – it's not a given in Parisian brasseries – the simple food is quite good. Start with oysters or maybe some prawns in their shells with a good lashing of home-made mayonnaise, and then eat well from a classic register that runs to dishes such as an impeccably prepared sole meunière or steak with béarnaise sauce and frites. The baba au rhum is the signature grown-up Parisian pudding, and the wines by the carafe – a flinty muscadet and a supple Bordeaux – were good and fairly priced. Ideal for a relaxed meal that offers a nuanced portrait of Parisian life.

Zébra Square

3 pl Clément Ader, 16th (01.44.14.91.91/www.
zebrasquare.com). M° Passy/RER Kennedy-Radio
France. **Open** noon-3pm, 7.30-11.30pm daily.
Average €35. **Lunch menu** €22. **Brunch** €24,
€28. **Credit** AmEx, DC, MC, V. **Wheelchair**
access. **Map** A7.

Zébra Square is next door to the centre of French radio and television, which is, despite its nickname 'Le Grand Camembert', a culinary blackspot. So when this stylish and modern restaurant opened up a few years ago, Parisian TV and radio folk tossed their hats in the air with glee. Lunch is what it's all about with a very good-value prix fixe: €22 including a glass of wine with a €6 supplement for pudding. We picked the well-chosen and well-priced house Touraine as our aperitif and kept them coming by the glass for the fishier parts of our lunch: marinated salmon with a window-box of dill and our plat du jour sea bream with orange butter sauce. Risotto was surprisingly fab, as was the steak tartare with well-cut chips. For pud we shared a mille-feuille, which came with a small earthenware pot of caramel sauce that you can pour over your dessert or knock back in one depending on how you've been brought up. Not really a tourist address, but there are many worse places you could end up after a visit to the Eiffel Tower.

Le Wepler ★

14 pl de Clichy, 18th (01.45.22.53.24/www.wepler.
com). M° Place de Clichy. **Open** noon-1am daily.
Average €42. **Prix fixe** €18, €25. **Credit** AmEx,
DC, MC, V. **Non-smoking room. Map** G2.

This big brasserie overlooking the busy place de Clichy is hugely popular, which makes for some of the most intriguing people-watching in Paris. The prix fixe menus are also very good value, and as long as you studiously avoid anything that requires careful cooking, odds are you'll come away satisfied by this place. The banc à huîtres out front does a roaring trade – everyone around us was indulging

Le Wepler.

in extravagant crushed ice-filled aluminium trays topped with artful, appetising arrangements of oysters, crab, mussels, whelks, clams, lobster, violets (a powerfully briny Mediterranean crustacean) and sea urchins. The choice of oysters is as admirable as their freshness is impeccable. So compelling, in fact, is the seafood here that a lady at a nearby table stoically received her husband's request for a divorce, wept for a minute or two until he left, and then resumed, completely consuming the fruits de mer that had been meant to be eaten à deux. C'est la vie, non? Otherwise, steaks are decent, though they could do better with the frites, and some of the fish dishes are good, including cod roasted in olive oil and served with an eggy courgette flan. Give the blanquette de veau a miss, however. Wines are pricey, but the cheapest Côtes du Rhône is good, as is almost everything served by the carafe. Finish up with the passable profiteroles and be sure to book, since this place, one of the last independently owned brasseries in Paris, is always packed.

Au Boeuf Couronné ★

188 av Jean-Jaurès, 19th (01.42.39.54.54/www.au-boeuf-couronne.com). M° Porte de Pantin. **Open** noon-3pm, 7pm-midnight daily. **Average** €45. **Prix fixe** €32. **Credit** AmEx, DC, MC, V. **Wheelchair access.**

The crowned king of meaty brasseries pulls in an old-school crowd that would be at home in a Claude Chabrol film: wealthy businessmen, ladies of a certain age (these two had a whole bottle of whisky on their table as they sat conspiratorially side by side), an aristocratic-looking man with his daughter. What are they doing in the working-class 19th arrondissement? These dedicated carnivores are in the know because the Boeuf Couronné is the last

vestige of the old meat district that all but disappeared when La Villette became the science and music complex it is today (keep your autograph book handy as performers from the latter often eat here). Everything is authentic about this brasserie, from the oak dresser with its baguette compartment to the prettily uniformed waitresses and the menu, which features such bygone specialities as tête de veau vieille France and os à la moelle. Like most of the diners, we went for the latter as a starter and it was gargantuan: three marrowbones whose squelchy contents were certainly enhanced by the sel de Guérande and black pepper served on the side. The snails were prime specimens too: large, garlicky and meaty. Give yourself a good three or four hours here because the steaks are beyond belief. The 340g Irish entrecôte was pure heaven, served with pommes soufflées (like little Yorkshire puddings, though we couldn't taste the stated truffle oil) and thankfully some refreshing watercress, while the chunks of tête de veau were incredibly fresh with their ravigote sauce (a vinaigrette of onions, capers, shallots and parsley). A half-bottle of 1999 Château rose du pont Médoc is a good choice if you are going for wine in moderation. Then we stumbled on the pudding zenith of our Paris eating days: a soufflé glacé flavoured with Grand Marnier, with a crème brûlée top and biscuit crust, surrounded by raspberry coulis and accompanied by a 'verre Nicole', a tiny glass of the orange liqueur. It's a shame, however, that cigar smokers aren't encouraged to retire to the dedicated fumoir as the pungent stink from the biggest cohibas ever rolled on naked thighs may well spoil your meal.

Café la Jatte

60 bd Vital Bouhot, Ile de la Jatte, 92200 Neuilly-sur-Seine (01.47.45.04.20/www.cafelajatte.com). M° Pont de Levallois. **Open** noon-2.30pm, 7.30-11pm daily. **Average** €40. **Credit** AmEx, DC, MC, V. **Wheelchair access.**

When Paris gets too much, it's worth a trek out to this tiny island to shake off the city blues. Painter Seurat obviously thought so – thus his famous canvas *Un Dimanche Après-midi à l'Ile de la Grande Jatte.* The Café is housed in a vast red-brick building that once served as Napoleon's riding school, but nowadays a giant faux dinosaur skeleton spreads its wings across the dining room ceiling. It's a winner with the kids, as are the nearby park and tree-lined riverbank. Less captivating was the food on a recent visit: a starter of tiny spinach leaves with generous slices of chicken drizzled with a curry sauce looked pretty but tasted like nothing at all. The home-made duck foie gras with nut bread was much better. Grilled swordfish, slapped on a plate with a soggy baked aubergine and braised fennel, was decidedly average; chicken pan-fried with pickled ginger, lemongrass and carrots was just as unimpressive. And the staff, bar one very obliging waiter, seemed bored beyond measure. But the sun was shining so things could have been worse.

Trendy

Fashion seems a more enduring phenomenon in Paris than in London, at least where food is concerned. Some of the restaurants in this chapter have been considered 'the place to be' for close to a decade, yet they manage to disguise their wrinkles and still guarantee an entertaining night out. Among the classics are Hôtel Costes, Spoon, Food & Wine and Thiou, while newcomers such as the Curieux Spaghetti Bar and Le Murano suggest that the Marais is the new capital of cool. Don't expect miracles from the food, but do keep in mind that these calorie-conscious destinations can be welcome when you can't face another three-course feast. You will, however, pay for the privilege of eating light.

Hôtel Costes

239 rue St-Honoré, 1st (01.42.44.50.25). Mº Concorde or Tuileries. **Open** 7am-1am daily. **Average** €70. **Credit** AmEx, DC, MC, V. **Wheelchair access.** **Non-smoking room.** **Map** G5.

By rights the of-a-certain-age Hôtel Costes should by now be ensconced in a corner with a bottle of Tio Pepe, muttering to itself about its glory days as the hottest place to push food around your plate. But while its trendy contemporaries have let themselves go and are all awaiting hip replacements, the Costes, with its permanent coterie of bright young things, a little discreet lifting and a calculated air of disdain, hasn't changed a bit. Same giggle-inducing prices, same stupid or stupidly named food ('an undressed lettuce heart and two weeping tigers, please'), same snooty but breathtakingly beautiful staff and, astoundingly, the same buzz. Nooks and crannies are strategically placed to accommodate the rich and the reclusive, but if your accessories (shoes, date, AmEx Centurion) are up to it then push for a visible table and enjoy your Champagne, your Marlboro Medium, the conversation at the next table and, of course, the attention.

Bon 2

2 rue du Quatre-Septembre, 2nd (01.44.55.51.55/ www.bon.fr). Mº Bourse. **Open** noon-3pm, 8pm-2am Mon-Fri; 8pm-2am Sat. **Average** €40. **Credit** AmEx, MC, V. **Map** H4.

Designed for traders who can't get enough of their jobs and journalists looking for something beyond the conventional brasserie, Philippe Starck's Bon 2 has become a hit in the Bourse area. 'Lounge' touches come from leather chairs, dark wooden tables, crystal chandeliers and modern Venetian mirrors. But the room is businesslike, too, with an electronic ticker tape posting quotations such as 'Punctuality is a waste of time' over the bar, and plasma screens in the most unexpected places. Unfortunately, the creativity seems to stop with the décor. For starters, the tuna avocado spring roll with yoghurt sauce was bland for an Asian-inspired dish,

and the aubergine confit with tuna, though well-spiced, quickly became monotonous. Main courses were better, including a well-cooked duck breast with cloves and cinnamon accompanied by sweet potato purée, and a sea bream fillet with surprising purple rice. For dessert, the fresh pineapple marinated in kiwi juice with coconut ice-cream was served too cold from the fridge, while chocolate fondant made little impression. The wine list was varied, ranging from €20 to €80, but in contrast to the street scene outside service was on the slow side. **Other locations**: Bon, 25 rue de la Pompe, 16th (01.40.72.70.00).

Le Murano ★

13 bd du Temple, 3rd (01.42.71.20.00/www. muranoresort.com). Mº Filles du Calvaire. **Open** 12.30-2.30pm, 8-11pm daily. **Average** €60. **Credit** AmEx, DC, MC, V. **Wheelchair access.** **Non-smoking room.** **Map** L5.

Le Murano, the restaurant in the pompously named new Murano Urban Resort hotel, has created a fashion-restaurant feeding frenzy not seen in Paris since the Hôtel Costes opened some ten years ago. And the real surprise is the quality of the contemporary French cooking by a team of young chefs. Cranberry velvet upholstered chairs and banquettes punctuate an all-white space, and a DJ spins bouncy lounge music. The menu, which changes regularly, runs from calorie-conscious dishes such as quinoa salad to more sophisticated choices such as roast sea bass with sweet Cévennes onions and three-pepper mousse. After a sharp reprimand from the hostess for stepping inside the closed front doors of the restaurant – what else were we supposed to do? – the evening went swimmingly, as we delected over such a purely *Ab Fab* crowd that it often seemed a parody of itself. Herb risotto with sesame-coated prawns was delicious, as was a generous sautée de girolles. Mains were excellent, too, including a smoked salmon steak with potato waffles and an interesting cranberry crème fraîche garnish, and veal steak with heart of lettuce. We decided to live large and pay €7 for a side of 'hay-cooked potatoes', which turned out to be a good but stingily served mash in a potato-shaped vessel of hardened hay. Reine claude plums in a salted caramel sauce were a superb dessert and, aside from the high-altitude service and a miserably overpriced wine list, the Murano offers a fun night out.

Curieux Spaghetti Bar

14 rue St-Merri, 4th (01.42.72.75.97). M° Hôtel de Ville or Rambuteau. **Open** 8am-2am daily. Closed 25 Dec. **Average** €20. **Lunch menu** €11. **Credit** MC, V. **Wheelchair access. Map** K6.

Curious, perhaps, but very clever, this new restaurant with a strategic location between Les Halles and Le Marais is pulling hungry young hordes, including a pre-clubbing crowd, with its amusing decor, easy prices and tasty high-carb menu. The walls are papered with Michelin maps of Italy, crystal chandeliers illuminate the crowd at the long red bar, and waiters with low-riding jeans swivel around the room serving a mostly but not exclusively male crowd who dig their show. A nice mix of lounge and house music puts everyone in a good-time groove, and the cheap house wines – the slightly acidic Bardolino costs just €16 a bottle – and generously served spaghetti do the rest. The namesake pasta comes in two portion sizes: assiette (plate) or marmite (casserole), and for an idea of how generously served the latter is, the menu also coyly notes that you can request a 'spaghetti bag' to take home your leftovers. If you're ravenous, start with bruschetta such as mortadella with capers or the pleasant mozzarella with pesto sauce, and then bag your spag as a classic with marinara sauce and deliciously garlicky meatballs. For something lighter, try the popular grilled chicken breast strips with lemon herb sauce. If you're feeling sloppy or are wearing a white shirt, you can wear a paper bib with a pre-stained tomato splotch, or tuck same into your pocket as the boy with the pierced eyebrow at the table next to us did after announcing that he was going to save it to wear at the beach next summer.

Georges

Centre Pompidou, 6th floor, rue Rambuteau, 4th (01.44.78.47.99). M° Rambuteau. **Open** 11am-2am Mon, Wed-Sun. **Average** €50. **Credit** AmEx, DC, MC, V. **Wheelchair access. Map** K5.

This Costes restaurant does not only concentrate on eating well. Instead, the dining room perched atop the Centre Pompidou is run like some sort of sociological chess board whose power game revolves around a single question: who gets the view? It all comes down to the shoes, it seems – turning up in your favourite Clark's or even a pair of hip, rustic Campers will get you banished to the dreaded, brightly lit tables near the toilets. Among the many other things that might get up your nose here is the fact that such a fabulous space, which is part of a state-owned museum, should have been dedicated to a commercially run enterprise. Oh, and the food. On our visit we found a range of inoffensive, fuss-free

and pricey dishes which did not excite our palates. Think lobster spring rolls, potato and (tasteless) truffle soup, aller-retour (a hamburger with green salad), a few Asian-themed fish and poultry dishes, and the inevitable moelleux au chocolat for dessert. It's a shame there's no bar here since the view is sublime, but you can come for a mid-afternoon drink.

Le Bélier

13 rue des Beaux-Arts, 6th (01.44.41.99.01/www. l-hotel.com). M° St-Germain-des-Prés. **Open** 12.30-2.15pm, 7.30-10.15pm Tue-Sat. Closed Aug, two weeks at Christmas. **Average** €50. **Lunch menu** €25.50. **Credit** AmEx, DC, MC, V. **Map** H6.

In the lush Jacques Garcia decor of L'Hôtel, which preserves just a phantom whiff of the premises' former incarnation as the flop-house where Oscar Wilde so famously expired, this intimate restaurant is a clubby hit with surprisingly excellent food. The lavishly upholstered Napoleon III room with several love seats and strategic sightlines is populated by neighbourhood editors and art and antiques dealers at noon, and stylish well-heeled locals in the evening, plus the occasional star staying in the hotel. Expect well-executed, high-quality French comfort food, with the odd cosmopolitan touch – Iberian ham with fresh tomato-rubbed bread or gazpacho, references to the young chef's Catalan origins. A starter of prawns with artichokes was excellent, as was foie gras with a layer of fig purée, and lacquered lamb shank was delicate, while a perfectly cooked steak on white beans was delicious. Cheese comes from Barthélémy, and desserts such as melted chocolate cake with fromage blanc ice-cream and a trio of lemon treats – mousse, sorbet and tart – echoed Wilde's famous, 'I can resist everything but temptation'.

Thiou

49 quai d'Orsay, 7th (01.45.51.58.58). M° Invalides. **Open** noon-2.30pm, 8-10.30pm Mon-Fri; 8-10.30pm Sat. Closed Aug. **Average** €35. **Lunch menu** €23. **Credit** AmEx, MC, V. **Wheelchair access. Map** E5.

Owner-chef Thiou subscribes to a simple mantra: super-fresh, high-quality ingredients prepared with care and flair. And it's proved a big hit. Thiou's previous stint at the restaurant of Les Bains Douches ensures that fashion puppies (and hounds) decorate this place, along with stylish young and old money. Start with juicy, peanutty chicken satay; a prawn soup heavy with lemongrass; or cold grilled aubergine topped with prawns and drizzled with a fish sauce vinaigrette (sounds awful, tastes great). Follow with impressive main courses such as kae phad prik wan – tender cubes of lamb sautéed with red and green pepper and served with fried rice – or grilled John Dory fillets with spinach, beansprouts and soy sauce. Desserts are mainly fruit-based; mini bananas with syrup and vanilla ice-cream makes a good finisher. The wine list is reasonably priced, the service is attentive, and the setting is elegant and cosy. A nearby annexe specialises in fish. **Other locations**: Le Petit Thiou, 3 rue Surcouf (01.40.62.96.70).

Le Buddha Bar

*8 rue Boissy d'Anglas, 8th (01.53.05.90.00/www.
buddha-bar.com). Mº Concorde.* **Open** noon-3pm,
7pm-2am Mon-Fri; 7pm-midnight Sat, Sun. Closed
first two weeks in Aug. **Average** €60. **Credit**
AmEx, MC, V. **Wheelchair access. Map** F4.

Meditate before you get here, as the Zen-ometer in
this trendster temple of Asian hype, nowadays
worshipped by businessmen and try-hard pilgrims
from around the world, is so stressed it is pointing
at 'nervous breakdown'. The staff army of
infamously spiky ice-queens greets you with a
militaristic walkie-talkie sparring match, before
marching you down the sweeping staircase and
ignoring you for most of the night. Get Dutch
courage at the balcony bar. Meanwhile, the giant
gold Buddha lords over the glamour, keeping his
cool despite the thumping fusion soundtrack. You
come for the spectacle, and it is unfailingly
magnificent. The food is also surprisingly good.
Starters included an intriguing mix of deep-fried
frogs' legs and squid or fresh, pulpy sushi of
yellowtail and salmon. Our main course of lacquered
duck blended well with a chunky pear and apple
confit, and 'maki' sole came in light, crisp slices with
black bean sauce and Chinese cabbage. The taste
pinnacle was dessert: an exotic fruit salad, bobbing
with aniseed and basil-flecked stawberry sorbet; and
a crême brûlée trio of chocolate, vanilla and coconut.
Definitely worth being treated like scum.

Man Ray

*34 rue Marbeuf, 8th (01.56.88.36.36/www.manray.
fr). Mº Franklin D Roosevelt.* **Open** 7pm-midnight
daily. *Bar* 6pm-2am daily. Closed 24 Dec. **Average**
€50. **Prix fixe** €27, €39. **Credit** AmEx MC, V.
Wheelchair access. Map D4.

Sliding down the snaking staircases of this
perennially hip restaurant, one cannot help but feel
fabulous. The cavernous space has the feel of a 21st-
century opium den, glowing with red lights and
pumping with house music. A mezzanine bar
horseshoes around the whole operation, providing
an ideal lookout over the beautiful people below –
which, let's be honest, is what everyone is here to do.
One should not be surprised, therefore, that the food
here is an afterthought. The menu offers some very
respectable, if pricey sushi and sashimi platters, as
well as a selection of caviars for the big rollers. The
'seasonal menu' presented alongside, however, dips
into the mediocre. We were presented with
unremarkable and diminutive portions of sea
scallops with caramelised endives, and steak with
'real' béarnaise that, to all appearances, had been
meted out into its little glass cup hours before
arriving at our table. Having arrived towards the tail
end of dinner service, we watched as the battalion
of black-clad, earpiece-bedecked servers was
replaced by an even speedier white-clad battalion,
who would guide Man Ray – no longer restaurant,
but nightclub – through to the dawn. And this,
really, is what Man Ray does best.

Market

*15 av Matignon, 8th (01.56.43.40.90/www.jean
georges.com). Mº Champs-Elysées-Clemenceau or
Franklin D Roosevelt.* **Open** noon-3pm, 7-10.30pm
Mon-Fri; noon-6pm, 7-10.30pm Sat, Sun. **Average** €60.
Lunch menu €32. **Credit** AmEx, MC, V. **Map** E4.

Is Market past its sell-by date? The dining room, all
in sleek grey tones by Christian Liaigre, is still full
of city slickers at lunchtime, but are we beginning
to see through the emperor's new clothes? The
celebrated raw tuna and wasabi pizza – a Jean-
Georges Vongerichten signature – sums up the
problem with his conceptual fusion cuisine: raw
tuna, slightly cooked by the warm base, which had
gone horribly soggy, and a layer of green wasabi.
There were more east-west meetings in the main
courses: steak (not rare as requested) with 'teak
sauce' resembled the plum sauce that comes with
Chinese duck, but also had an interesting bitter
green sorrel coulis; rather fatty magret came with
diced daikon radish and Chinese greens. Desserts,
from the macadamia crunch which resembled
nothing more than a cereal bar with a white
blancmange on top, to the exotic fruit salad in
passion fruit juice set off by an intriguing white
pepper ice-cream, went from the silly to the sublime.
Interesting, confusing, but quite simply not delicious.

Rue Balzac

*3-5 rue Balzac, 8th (01.53.89.90.91). Mº Charles
de Gaulle or George V.* **Open** 12.15-2.15pm, 8.30-
10.30pm Mon-Fri; 7.15-11.30pm Sat, Sun. Closed
Aug. **Average** €70. **Credit** AmEx, DC, MC, V.
Wheelchair access. Map D3.

Rue Balzac is Johnny Hallyday's baby (after his wife
Laeticia, that is). And, despite his dyed rocker roots,
it's all soothing burgundy and beige with pastel
geometric paintings and cute lamps. The menu is
designed by consultant chef Michel Rostang, who
runs his own haute cuisine restaurant and bistros in
Paris. Starters such as Laeticia's crispy, tempura-like
prawns with seaweed tartare, spicy tomato sauce and
mustard cream; a generous serving of delicious
minced lobster; and a sweet shelled lobster claw were
choice. Blanquette de veau and souris d'agneau lost
out to a neat little package of scallop 'tournedos', six
on a fat disc of mashed potato wrapped in a leek
ribbon, and a sad grilled sea bass with artichokes –
overcooked fish with two tiny charred artichoke
leaves and a hill of raw beansprouts. For dessert, we
had a chilly, barely edible gingerbread with diced
baked apple. Like Johnny, this Rue runs hot and cold.

Senso

*Hôtel Trémoille, 16 rue de la Trémoille, 8th
(01.56.52.14.14/www.hotel-tremoille.com) Mº
Alma-Marceau or Franklin D Roosevelt.* **Open**
noon-2.30pm, 7-10.45pm daily. *Bar* noon-11pm
daily. **Average** €50. **Lunch menu** €29, €36.
Credit AmEx, DC, MC, V. **Wheelchair access.
Map** D4.

Armies of pleasant and efficient waiters drift about
in dark grey suits, and the sombre but smart slate-

coloured dining room is decorated by a modern Murano-style ceiling light and a single amaryllis. As if on the set for a contemporary opera, everyone in the restaurant the lunchtime we visited was dressed in black, white and grey, except for one red jumper which matched the amaryllis. The lunch menu is not bad value, with a fixed-price two- or three-course meal including mineral water and coffee, and the chef is much better than at the Alcazar. Previous reports of stingy portions proved no longer to be true, with a 'panaché' of vegetables including heaps of mozzarella di bufala mixed with pan-fried carrot, asparagus, artichoke, fennel, leek, radish, rhubarb and pear, dribbled with balsamic vinegar. The 'riquette' salad (a southern French word for rocket) was copious too, with a nice lemony dressing, though there wasn't much parmesan and briny artichoke hearts might as well not have been there. Both our fish mains were good – a strong-tasting sea bream swishly presented as if wrapped round a skewer of dried fennel sticks, with a single mangetout sitting akimbo on a small pile of broccoli and fennel, and juicy chunks of sesame-coated tuna on a bed of beansprouts and courgette, with a delicious soy-based sauce. Don't bother with the pudding option: a mille-feuille was too light on the cream, and a tarte aux figues (the dessert of the day) was disappointingly tasteless. Our light red Saumur and superb Petit Chablis, at €7 a glass each, were fine defenders of the drink less, drink better maxim.

Spoon, Food & Wine

14 rue de Marignan, 8th (01.40.76.34.44/www. spoon.tm.fr). M° Franklin D Roosevelt. **Open** noon-2pm, 7-11pm Mon-Fri. Closed 14 July, last week in July, first three weeks in Aug and two weeks at Christmas. **Average** €80. **Prix fixe** €85, €120. **Credit** AmEx, DC, MC, V. **Wheelchair access. Map** E4.
Alain Ducasse is the great chef behind the concept of Spoon, billed as a restaurant and deluxe take-away. Within the Philippe Starck-inspired minimalist decoration, the menu zaps through world cuisine. Tables are equipped with scribbling pads and racks of foreign magazines are designed to be read by a new generation of gastro travellers. Despite the adorable staff, less hip clients might be more puzzled than excited by the menu with its lists of condiments and accompaniments to be mixed and matched to 'create the unthinkable'. Even if dishes are generally listed beside their most appropriate bedfellows, we were pleased to avoid all choice by ordering the new Spoonsum lunch menu, which offers two starters, a couple of main courses, and three puddings for €45 with only the puddings in common to our two meals. Starters and main courses were dominated by Chinese and Japanese dishes, and setting aside all the hype and pretension, it was the quality of the cooking and condiments which shone through. Starters included fabulous steamed seafood ravioli with a wasabi and oyster dip, delicate steamed cod, and various marinated raw fish dishes. Winners among the main courses were the

massaged Australian Wagyu beef, seared tuna and some fabulous wok-fried vegetables. Puddings of world-beating cheesecake, chewing gum ice-cream, and the best café liégeois you are ever likely to enjoy were accompanied by a plate of perfect cookies. The list of world wines is expensive but our homespun Burgundy (€32) played a role in this accomplished piece of flashy modern cookery.

Le Stresa

7 rue Chambiges, 8th (01.47.23.51.62). M° Alma-Marceau. **Open** 12.15-2.15pm, 7.30-10.30pm Mon-Fri. Closed Aug, 20 Dec-4 Jan. **Average** €100. **Credit** AmEx, DC, MC, V. **Map** D5.
The bizarre funk of white truffles, cigarette smoke and strong perfume on unwashed skin adds real olfactory drama to this snug dining room. Aside from some excellent old-fashioned Italian cooking, one of the other main reasons to frequent Stresa is to be reminded of the fact that plastic surgery only very rarely succeeds. The red velvet banquettes here are populated by pert and pricey silicone, long tell-tale earlobes and strategically placed Alice bands. In a dining room where everyone watches everyone else with chronometric precision, the game is to secure the extra attentions of the two brothers who run the place. And their game is to dole out their attentions with a pharmaceutical precision that keys off everyone else in the room as to how important a given table might be. Oh, and the food? Beef carpaccio with rocket and parmesan shavings came in a light lemony dressing, while artichokes alla Romana were a bore – overcooked and not as wholly edible as they should be in Rome. Spaghetti alla Belmondo – tomato sauce in an admirably perfect emulsion, bits of mozzarella, tiny black Niçois olives and a nosegay of fresh basil – was excellent, and so it should be for €30. Equally good was saltimbocca – tender veal scallops topped with fried ham and garnished with excellent fresh spinach. At €45, the Pio Cesare Barbera d'Alba was a good buy, too, though very few people actually look at the wine list, ordering red or white house wine without asking the price or what it is. Similarly, the white truffle at €10 a gram – how, one wonders, do they calculate how much has been served? Suffice to say that it's all rather like putting your money in the collection plate at church – you just hope and assume that it will be spent in a useful and honest way. Just about as close to San Marco and an *Ab Fab* scene as you'll find anywhere in Paris.

Tanjia

23 rue de Ponthieu, 8th (01.42.25.95.00). M° Franklin D Roosevelt. **Open** noon-2.30pm, 8-11.30pm Mon-Fri; 8-11.30pm Sat, Sun. **Average** €60. **Lunch menu** €22. **Credit** AmEx, MC, V. **Map** E4.
Themed restaurants by trendmongers usually have the lifespan of a gnat, but the still-accelerating popularity of Morocco, and especially Marrakech, as a jet-set playground explain why this place is still heaving with trendies despite a recent change of ownership. The crowd continues to be studded with

just enough famous faces to keep the name of this place in bold-face in the columns of the Paris people press, and the food, while expensive, is better than you find at most fashion restaurants in Paris. That said, don't come in the hope of an anthropological experience of Moroccan cooking, but rather a giddy, campy night out. Still, the kitchen knows what it's doing and the staff are sweet. We liked our mixed hors d'oeuvres for two, which included aubergine purée, carrots cooked with honey and cumin, tomato marmalade, briouate (meat-filled pastries) and other Moorish treats, and then went for the lamb tagine seasoned with 25 spices – the most apparent of which were cumin, clove, cinnamon and anise – and a delicious chicken tagine with preserved lemons and caramelised onion. The Moroccan wines are expensive, and since the only vineyard that's reliably good is President, give them a miss unless you're avid for authenticity and order one of the less expensive Bordeaux. Go late if you're hoping to wish upon a star, and avoid the pariah status that comes with being seated on the balcony.

Le Martel ★

3 rue Martel, 10th (01.47.70.67.56). M° Château d'Eau. **Open** 11am-3pm, 6pm-1am Mon-Fri; 6pm-1am Sat. **Average** €30. **Lunch menu** €16, €17. **Credit** MC, V. **Wheelchair access. Non-smoking room. Map** K3.

The 10th arrondissement, dominated by two railway stations, has always found it difficult to establish any strongly defined fashion personality, but a visit to Le Martel suggests things may be changing. The room with its dark tables and cream walls looks great, and the welcome on a Friday evening was unusually warm to our decidedly unstylish figures. The restaurant quickly filled with young men dressed in black and moody-looking yuppie couples. What draws the crowds is the interesting menu, which combines the best of North Africa and France. We decided to try both aspects of these parallel cuisines, beginning with a light chicken pastilla, which was less challenging than the thicker and spicier pigeon version and made a good starter, as did a crisp brick au thon et à l'oeuf. It almost felt as if we had changed restaurants as we moved on to our French main courses. A sesame-coated rare pavé of tuna was a first-rate version of this popular contemporary dish, accompanied by some excellent home-made frites and a spinach salad, for which the leaves were too mature for salad to be a viable option. The ris de veau were simply grilled with a little salt, tender and pure, served with a plate of sauté potatoes – not as good as the frites, which we ended up sharing. On another occasion we will plunge into a couscous royale or one of the handsome-looking tagines. Puddings follow a similar contrast with sticky oriental pastries face-to-face with plainer traditional French puds. We stayed with North Africa for our powerful Boulaouane red, and were pleased with our bill of under €100 for two for this international feast.

Apollo

3 pl Denfert-Rochereau, 14th (01.45.38.76.77). M° Denfert-Rochereau. **Open** noon-3pm, 8pm-midnight daily. **Average** €40. **Lunch menu** €18. **Credit** AmEx, DC, MC, V. **Wheelchair access. Non-smoking room. Map** H10.

Parisian RER stations may not be synonymous with suave dining but the brains behind Quai Ouest have transformed Denfert-Rochereau's cavernous railwaymen's offices into a bold and brash new restaurant. With starfish suspended from the high ceilings, and a backdrop of Damien Hirst-inspired encased monochrome junk, the Apollo caters well to its clientele of local trendies. Ubiquitous porthole convex mirrors promote mid-dinner preening, and stark '70s shiny white banquettes are perfect for showing off the latest Gucci purchase. The menu covers a familiar range of fashionistas' comfort food – Caesar salad, shepherd's pie, the ever-present club sandwiches (who actually orders these?) – as well as venturing into more daring territory with caramelised braised endives in a rich balsamic sauce, and the less-successful 'neige' of Puy lentils, literally sunk by a dishwater-style insipid soup. With a '70s soundtrack and stylish surroundings, there is ambience aplenty at the Apollo, even if culinary aspirations are resolutely earthbound.

Quinze ★

8 rue Nicolas-Charlet, 15th (01.42.19.08.59). M° Pasteur. **Open** noon-2.30pm, 7.30-10.30pm Mon-Thur; 7.30-11.30pm Fri, Sat. Closed ten days in Aug. **Average** €32. **Lunch menu** €26. **Credit** AmEx, MC, V. **Wheelchair acess. Non-smoking room. Map** E9.

Thierry Burlot's modern bistro continues to succeed in drawing in crowds with an enticing menu of artistically prepared food served in stylish and upbeat surroundings. Produced with fresh ingredients, the offerings vary from earthy truffle-laden dishes to lighter fish and seafood numbers, including the quite exquisite langoustines grilled with vanilla, served as a starter or main course. Our meal started with the excellent lightly poached egg topped with shards of truffles and framed by fresh leeks, contrasting with the less successful starter of an insipid mélange of ice-cold tomato gazpacho and chopped raw mackerel. From the mains, the oven-cooked sea bass came in a delightful herb and mushroom sauce, and the homely looking risotto transpired to be a creamy, savoury delight, topped with the ever-present truffles. Original desserts included a refreshing fromage blanc ice-cream, as well as intricate chocolate dishes and home-made caramel ice-cream (with old-style salted-butter caramel). Service was undertaken by an efficient, if rather charmless coterie of black-clad Parisian twentysomethings, but we ended our meal satisfied.

Le Cristal Room ★

8 pl des Etats-Unis, 16th (01.40.22.11.10). M° Iéna. **Open** noon-2pm, 8-10pm Mon-Sat. **Average** €80. **Credit** AmEx, MC, V. **Wheelchair access. Map** C4.

French Cuisine

Overlooking a tranquil square in the swanky 16th arrondissement, a sumptuous historic townhouse has become the glittering headquarters, boutique and showroom of Baccarat, the venerable French crystal company. There's also an intimate restaurant, Le Cristal Room, with a stunning decor by Philippe Starck and a light luxury snack menu by chef Thierry Burlot of Quinze. What makes this salon such a giggle is Starck's pastiche of grandeur – he left the wall spaces where tapestries or paintings had been hanging empty, exposing the brick walls behind to create brilliant contrast to the ox-blood red marble mouldings and huge Baccarat chandeliers overhead. The expensive menu is definitely conceived to please puckish rich types, but you can still eat well here if you have a real appetite. Start with chestnut soup with white truffles or scallops with caviar, and then go with risotto with white truffles or spaghetti with cherry tomatoes, or maybe something a little meatier such as hare à la royale with quince or lobster spit-roasted with vanilla bean. Desserts are excellent, including cocoa soufflé or a tarte Tatin of quince and pears, but the wine list is stiffly marked up. Don't miss the most spectacular bathrooms in Paris, and when you book specify that you want a table in the main room.

Tokyo Eat

Palais de Tokyo, 13 av du Président-Wilson, 16th (01.47.20.00.29). M° Alma-Marceau or Iéna. **Open** noon-3pm, 7.30-11.30pm Tue-Sat; noon-5.30pm, 7.30-10.30pm Sun. Closed 24, 25 Dec, 1 Jan. **Average** €40. **Lunch menu** €26. **Credit** AmEx, MC, V. **Wheelchair access. Map** D5.

An open kitchen, fabulous hanging spaceship-like lamps in white or pink, chairs decorated by André, Kolkoz and other artists, and a menu with lots of fashionable 'carpaccios' and world flavours (tuna with satay sauce, tandoori chicken brochette), perfectly suit the ambience of the voluminous, distressed-chic Palais de Tokyo art space. At times the cosmopolitan mish-mash goes a bit crazy. There was a little too much spicy red oil on the artichoke 'carpaccio' accompanied by a fresh goat's cheese, and the perfectly decent chunk of flaky cod on a tomato coulis was accompanied by positively nasty chickpea 'chips' (which looked disconcertingly like fish fingers), but stick to the simpler dishes or the day's special – a decent roast chicken with purée, the beef carpaccio with parmesan and rocket – and this is fun artworld eat. Sociable round tables in assorted sizes make this a good place to come with friends by night or with kids for weekend lunch. The house Bordeaux is perfectly decent and the loos are some of the wackiest in town (once you have worked out how the doors work). During good weather in summer, the restaurant migrates on to the terrace.

Sora Lena ★

18 rue Bayen, 17th (01.45.74.73.73). M° Ternes. **Open** noon-2pm, 8-11pm Mon-Thur; 8-11.30pm Fri, Sat. **Average** €50. **Lunch menu** €20. **Credit** AmEx, DC, MC, V. **Map** C2.

At last! A trendy restaurant with not only really good food, but great service, a charming setting and a groovy '70s disco soundtrack that animates the room without drowning out conversation. Run by a pair of Italian brothers, this is an ideal date restaurant, especially if you ask for a table at the very back of the room – the cool place to sit – when you book. The mocha-coloured decor is relaxing, but several Vietnamese paper lighting fixtures and Japanese lanterns add some modish dash, and service is by men in black with a nice sense of humour. It's the kitchen, though, that really surprises with the quality of its produce and the delicacy of the cooking. Start with a plate of superb Corsican charcuterie, a salad of artichokes, beets and parmesan, or maybe the tempura-like mix of squid and vegetables, and then try memorable main courses such as the delicious veal scallopine in lemon sauce with home-made mash or spinach, the similarly light and perfectly prepared veal cutlet alla Milanese, or maybe a pasta or the excellent risotto with gorgonzola and pear. Simple desserts of panna cotta and tiramisu were delicious, too, and there's a very good selection of Italian wines at affordable prices, including a memorably good Sicilian red.

Quai Ouest

1200 quai Marcel Dassault, 92210 St-Cloud (01.46.02.35.54). M° Porte de St-Cloud (then 175 bus). **Open** noon-3pm, 8pm-midnight Mon-Sat; noon-4pm, 8pm-midnight Sun. **Average** €40. **Lunch menu** €18 (Mon-Fri). **Credit** AmEx, DC, MC, V.

This airy warehouse-like restaurant with plate glass windows looking across the river to the Bois de Boulogne is reminiscent of Hammersmith and its River Café. With 400 covers, it attracts an almost full house for Sunday brunch, which does make it noisy, but there is a child-free room at the side if your hangover can't take it. After three years of searching, we finally found our brunch nirvana here: no slimmers' salads or elaborate pastries, just large glasses of orange juice (not freshly made, we suspect, but with juicy bits at least), fresh-from-the-oven muffins, scrambled eggs, bacon, fat potato wedges, a succulent beefburger (without bun, and with a roast chicken leg alternative) and creamy coleslaw, followed by authentic griddled pancakes and maple syrup, and a huge pot of coffee. We added a large glass of decent Bordeaux to remind ourselves that we were in France, even though the blatant ogling of another man's girlfriend by a bored dad with two small children on the next table amusingly served the same purpose. With face painting and balloon sculpting (don't kids ever get tired of this?), Quai Ouest keeps the little tykes amused, though if you don't have children make sure you are seated well away from the mayhem. The only thing to mar our meal was the repeated blasts of ear-searing music for the delivery of birthday cakes – we don't want to be party poopers, but TURN THE VOLUME DOWN... please.

Classics

Nouvelle cuisine came and went unnoticed by these restaurants, which excel at the bedrocks of French cooking: meaty terrines, spoon-tender stews, towering soufflés and crêpes flambéed at the table. They range from sedate dining rooms to spectacular historical settings – Maxim's and Lapérouse remain dazzling sights, even if the food plays second fiddle. The best of the bunch know how to change ever so subtly with the times, with gently updated dishes and affordable set menus that don't leave you feeling overstuffed.

Le Poquelin ★

17 rue Molière, 1st (01.42.96.22.19). M° Palais Royal. **Open** 7-10pm Mon, Sat; noon-2pm, 7-10pm Tue-Fri. Closed three weeks in Aug. **Average** €50. **Prix fixe** €30. **Lunch menu** €25. **Credit** AmEx, DC, MC, V. **Wheelchair access. Map** H5.

Next to the Comédie Francaise and named after its 17th-century master (Poquelin is Molière's real name), this elegant little spot takes its classical inheritance seriously. The decor is a cross between chocolate-box pretty and old-world salon; the gilded portrait of the man himself, elaborately wigged, sets the tone. But he is quickly forgotten amid the elegant stripes, grand mirrors, big bouquets and a host of other theatrical touches. From the moment we pushed back the heavy curtains flanking the door, Maggy and Michel Guillaumin, the multilingual co-owners who run their small court in a thoroughly hands-on fashion, attentively assured that the evening, from the first bite of unctuous pork belly (much less rustic than it sounds) through to the last lick of crème anglaise, delicately supporting an 'oeuf à la neige' (floating island) sprinkled with crunched up pink dragées, ran as smoothly as possible. Most diners are sedate, monied and looking for a classic and seamless night out. The menu mixes refined standards (such as thin slices of rare duck breast, melting meat with just-crisp skin, paired with a small chunk of rich duck confit) with some more daring flavours: the confit was mildly spiced and the whole rested on a bed of caramelised endives lightly zapped with an orange sauce. More adventurous still was our easy favourite: a pan-fried slice of dab (a cousin of sole) enlivened with basil tapenade and set on a bed of ginger-leeks and Puy lentils. À la carte options, including the tempting foie gras we shamelessly ogled at the next table, are pricier; the three-course prix fixe has plenty of choice and is a better bet. House wine is good value at €16 a bottle.

Le Soufflé

36 rue du Mont-Thabor, 1st (01.42.60.27.19). M° Concorde. **Open** noon-2.30pm, 7.30-10pm daily. Closed public holidays, two weeks in Feb, three weeks in Aug. **Average** €45. **Prix fixe** €29, €35. **Credit** AmEx, MC, V. **Non-smoking room. Wheelchair access. Map** G5.

The puffed-up little soufflé, wearing what looks like a wonky chef's hat and coloured, in turns, bright green (spinach or pistachio), zany pink (raspberry), dark chocolate brown or the perfect golden yellow of a classic cheese, is at once comic and sophisticated. When we first perused the menu, we laughed at what seemed like eggy overkill, the €29 all-soufflé menu; but after seeing a towering apple-Calvados version float by, only to be doused in a generous slosh of the apple liqueur (the bottle is left on the table for more sloshing as required), we decided to take the plunge. A fluffy spinach soufflé, with just the right balance of airy creaminess, was our favourite as a starter. For mains, alongside the traditional savoury options (such as cheese, shrimp, roquefort, morel mushroom), we tried an inventive escalope of salmon topped with its own unctuous mini salmon soufflé that was, despite another soufflé yet to come, irresistible. By the time we were tucking into dessert – chocolate with a dark chocolate sauce plus the apple-Calvados that had tempted us – we were swapping soufflé tips (ours only recently formed) with our 92-year-old neighbour, an impeccably dressed regular who advised us on seasonal specials. Many diners, especially at lunch, opt for a cheaper and lighter option – just two soufflés, a savoury and a sweet – and there are also excellent alternatives (like tender roast lamb with a gratin dauphinois) for the not-yet-converted. But when a soufflé is this good, why have anything else?

La Truffière

4 rue Blainville, 5th (01.46.33.29.82/www.latruffiere. com). M° Place Monge or Cardinal-Lemoine. **Open** noon-2pm, 7-10.30pm Tue-Sun. **Average** €90. **Prix fixe** €55, €72. **Lunch menu** €19 (Tue-Sat). **Credit** AmEx, MC, V. **Wheelchair access. Non-smoking room. Map** J8.

Having been the subject of many a truffle rip-off, we were a little wary of a restaurant devoted to the elusive tuber. What you can count on at La Truffière is an elaborate dining experience. The service is old-fashioned and doting (with sans-prices menus for the ladies); the beamed dining room and stone cellar atmospheric (despite the jarring pop music); and the chef has more than a few tricks up his sleeve. We were met with hot, organic rolls and a tiny celery and truffle oil velouté, while the youthful sommelier presented an overwhelming two-kilo wine tome. When we balked, he steered us without flinching towards a dark and fruity half bottle of Cahors Château de Coutale (€10). Then another treat: red pepper and mackerel mousse in a shot glass. We shared the petit menu dégustation's cloud-light blue cheese mousse on paper-thin tangy beef carpaccio before the more impressive of the mains: brill fillet poached in vanilla milk with truffle shavings. We couldn't detect the truffles in our duck parmentier, which tasted more like grandma's shepherd's pie. But the cheese plate was outstanding, including a lovely vache soaked in walnut liqueur. Dessert arrived in three courses: a mini prune-jasmine cream-peppercorn parfait, then a perfect sampler of fruit- and chocolate-based puddings, and finally a tray of petits fours we were invited to nibble by the foyer's gas fire (a clever way to make room for the 10pm sitting). Wine tasting lunches are held one Saturday every month.

Lapérouse

51 quai des Grands-Augustins, 6th (01.43.26.68.04). Mº St-Michel **Open** *12.30-2.30pm, 7.30-10.30pm Tue-Fri; 7.30-10.30pm Sat. Closed Aug.* **Average** *€100.*

Lunch menu €30. **Credit** AmEx, DC, MC, V. **Non-smoking room. Wheelchair access. Map** J6.

A contender for one of the most romantic spots in Paris, Lapérouse used to be a clandestine rendezvous for French politicians and their mistresses. Nowadays, though, the tiny private dining rooms upstairs no longer lock from the inside. Chef Alain Hacquard does a modern take on classic French cooking: the beef fillet is smoked for a more complex flavour; a tender saddle of rabbit is cooked in a clay crust, flavoured with lavender and rosemary and served with ravioli of onions; fleshy langoustines, sandwiched between thin sesame discs, come with minutely diced ratatouille with a hint of Sichuan pepper. Soufflé Lapérouse, with a hot wild raspberry sauce, is a delight. The only snag is the price, especially the wine (a half bottle of Pouilly-Fuissé costs close to €40). You can opt for the lunch menu but it's devoid of choice and, frankly, the seductive Seine-side dining room is best savoured at night.

Le Violon d'Ingres ★

135 rue St-Dominique, 7th (01.45.55.15.05/www.le violondingres.com). Mº Ecole-Militaire or RER Pont de l'Alma. **Open** *noon-2.30pm, 7-10.30pm Tue-Sat.* **Average** *€90.* **Prix fixe** €80. **Lunch menu** €50. **Credit** AmEx, MC, V. **Wheelchair access. Map** D6.

Chef Christian Constant greeted us at the door when we came for lunch. He stopped by our table to make sure everything was going well, and bid us a

Superb wines and serene surroundings at **L'Angle du Faubourg**. *See p106.*

Le Soufflé – from cheese to apple. *See p104.*

solicitous farewell when we staggered out after a generous and beautifully executed lunch. Even when Constant was not physically surveying the elegant dining room, his attention could be felt in every detail of this highly personal restaurant. Constant spent eight years running the vast kitchens at the Hôtel Crillon, training a generation of very successful young chefs, before leaving to open a place of his own. The restaurant's name is actually an homage to a painter from the chef's native Montauban, whose paintings are delicately rendered in toile, then set in thick black frames along the walls. The decor, more chic and modern than one often finds in fine Paris restaurants, sets off Constant's classic plates in much the same way. Our lunch menu, an unctuous polenta perfumed with black truffle, plump scallops bathing in butter and a refined parfait of bitter coffee, mascarpone and chestnut cream, provided us with more than we had expected in terms of both quantity and quality. The standard menu does not veer off on experimental paths, but it does what it does very, very well. Some have complained that the chef has lost his spirit for innovation. And while it is true that Constant is not reinventing the wheel, we come for another, rarer experience. Seated at a table here, we can watch while one of Paris's great chefs indulges in a personal pleasure, just as the famous Ingres took time out from his painting to privately play his beloved violin.

L'Angle du Faubourg

195 rue du Fbg-St-Honoré, 8th (01.40.74.20.20/ www.taillevent.com). M° Ternes, George V or Charles de Gaulle Etoile. **Open** noon-2.30pm, 7-10.30pm Mon-Fri. Closed 26 July-26 Aug. **Average** €70. **Prix fixe** €60 (dinner only). **Lunch menu** €55. **Credit** AmEx, DC, MC, V. **Map** D3.

Although baby sister to the lofty haute cuisine restaurant Taillevent, L'Angle du Faubourg is at home on an altogether different range. Despite its upmarket roots and roomy confines, there's nary an air or grace in sight. De-boned pigeon in a wine-soaked sauce, and braised lamb with glossy carrots soothe the palate. Ruby-red beetroot soup shot through with balsamic vinegar and topped with a dollop of green apple sorbet, and butter-tender tuna coated in sesame seeds and delicate spices sate more contemporary tastes. A main of shredded hare bathed in a foie gras sauce – a giant brown mound – wasn't among the chef's best, though: it begged for some vivid veggie respite. With walls the colour of ploughed fields and pale green china evoking the hues of the vineyard, it's no surprise that wine looms large in this restaurant's dogma. The female sommelier guided us to wines by the glass flawlessly matched to each dish, finishing with an ambrosial Alsatian pinot noir to complement the fiendishly rich chocolate pud Reine de Saba (Queen of Sheba), which took fashionably bitter to its extreme.

Le Bistrot du Sommelier

97 bd Haussmann 8th (01.42.65.24.85/www. bistrotdusommelier.com). M° St-Augustin. **Open** noon-2.30pm, 7.30-10.30pm Mon-Fri. Closed 25 Dec-1 Jan, three weeks in Aug. **Average** €70. **Prix fixe** €60, €75 (dinner only). **Lunch menu** €39-€54. **Credit** AmEx, MC, V. **Non-smoking room**. **Map** F3.

How does personal service from one of the world's best sommeliers grab you? This is precisely what you'll get at title-holder Philippe Faure-Brac's mecca for wine lovers where the list naturally includes not only France's most prestigious crus and vintages, but a marvellous selection of insiders' wines from Corsica (Philippe's wife hails from the Ile de Beauté) and the Rhône (he was born there). Despite the eye-popping bottle list and the interesting à la carte dishes from excellent chef Jean-André Lallican, we think the best idea is to go for one of the blind discovery options. Our five-course, €75 'menu tentation', presented as a 'voyage through classicism and originality', lived up to its description. Dinky, comté-stuffed ravioles de Royan with a parsley and tomato dressing went down a treat with a glass of Montravel. Next came an alliance of textures via the slab of sea bass in a tart vinaigrette with a wonderful wine from the quality-conscious Corsican Canarelli. A Pomerol reflected the earthy taste of the wild mushrooms which accompanied the chicken stuffed with goat's cheese. However, the best match of the evening came courtesy of the cheese course: a warm ste-maure goat's cheese on fig bread with a sprinkling of olive purée that was the perfect partner for the truffly, spicy flavour of a Jurançon Clos Lapeyre. All in all this was a marvellous, value-for-money experience.

Lasserre

17 av Franklin Roosevelt, 8th (01.43.59.53.43/ www.lasserre.com). M° Franklin D. Roosevelt. **Open** 12.30-2pm, 7.30-10pm Tue-Sat. Closed Aug. **Average** €140. **Prix fixe** €165 (dinner only). **Lunch menu** €110. **Credit** AmEx, DC, MC, V. **Wheelchair access. Map** E4.

Lasserre remains a bastion of traditional Parisian chic, where jacket and tie are compulsory. The dining room is reached by a padded lift controlled by uniformed staff, and the first impression takes you back to a 1950s dream of upmarket living. Quaintly old-fashioned chandeliers and bourgeois comfort frame the famous opening roof, which even in relatively inclement weather will perform its magical open-sky effect to please the child in all but the most hard-hearted diner. After some amuse-bouches of delicate foie gras toasts and a tasty parcel of fish we were impressed by our first courses. Seared foie gras accompanied by preserved fruits managed to be firm and free of any excess fat, while a timbale of black truffle and foie gras macaroni was intensely flavoured. Our main courses included one of the house specialities, pigeon André Malraux, which was exceptionally moist, plump and tender, accompanied by melting spears of salsify. Some pungent slivers of black truffle and a side dish of perfect pommes de terre soufflées crowned fork-tender fillet steak into which slivers of foie gras had been artfully introduced. It was hard to resist the pudding of the day, sensational crêpes suzette, prepared at the table with all the swish professionalism that can only be found at this sort of French establishment. We could have lived without the tinkling pianist's repertoire of muzak, but the rather unglamorous expense-account crowd seemed to be lapping it up.

Maxim's

3 rue Royale, 8th (01.42.65.27.94/www.maxims-de-paris.com). M° Concorde. **Open** 12.30-2pm, 7.30-10pm Tue-Fri; 7.30-10.30pm Sat. Closed 1 May, 1 Jan, 25 Dec. **Average** €90 (lunch), €200 (dinner). **Credit** AmEx, DC, MC, V. **Wheelchair access. Map** F4.

'I'm going to Maxim's...' sings Danilo in Léhar's operetta *The Merry Widow*, and as a Parisian landmark the restaurant is almost as famous as the Eiffel Tower. So, armed with a pretty young Parisian débutante, where better to go for a stylish lunch? The extravagant swirling belle époque decor lives up to its reputation, and the slight hint of shabbiness only adds to the charm – though we were suprised to find the dining room sparsely populated. Word had it that the cooking was no longer great, but despite the lack of modern fripperies such as appetising nibbles, a groaning plate of green asparagus with sauce mousseline impressed us, even if the terrine of duck with truffles and foie gras was only adequate. Our comforting main course was

a plump Challans duck for two, perfectly roasted with accompanying baby turnips and salsify. The puddings were a classic mille-feuille and a more elaborate construction of violet-scented wild strawberries with a rhubarb sorbet, which was pronounced as delicious by the débutante. The naughty '90s of Maxim's are long past, but the staff were wonderfully old-school, and the bottle of Maxim's own Mercurey surprisingly delicious. A time-warp experience, which if your budget can bear it, still has a unique dusty magic.

Le Céladon

Hôtel Westminster, 13 rue de la Paix, 9th (01.47.03.40.42). M° Opéra. **Open** 12.30-2pm, 7.30-10pm daily. **Average** €90. **Prix fixe** €66 (dinner only). **Lunch menu** €48 (Sat, Sun only). **Credit** AmEx, DC, MC, V. **Wheelchair access. Map** G4.

The Hôtel Westminster's illustrious neighbour, Cartier, may be a draw for the Elizabeth Taylors of this world, but its pastel-decorated restaurant, Le Céladon, draws a more eclectic, low-key clientele. On a recent evening visit, we were placed at one of the well-spaced tables in the liveliest section next to the bar, where our neighbours were a big family complete with five-year-old, a whispering American courting couple and three strait-laced vieille France seniors. We began with a glass of Laurent Perrier rosé, which made a worthy partner for the daintily presented selection of amuse-bouches. From a tantalising selection of starters, we chose delicious crab with caramelised spring onions encased in fried courgette flowers and flanked by a frothy shellfish sauce, and the scampi, which had received a too-liberal sprinkling of lemongrass but was accompanied by a thoroughly delicious gelée of étrilles (tiny crabs). For mains, the John Dory had an original 'snail-butter' sauce and the sole was served with a garnish of ratatouille-style tomatoes and courgettes which proved an incongruous match for this cold-water fish. Desserts were excellent, particularly the delicate Williamine soufflé and the state-of-the-art, shiny palet de chocolat. The hotel's Austrian manager ensures that the excellent wine list features this country's top bottles, while sommelier Richard Rahard has unearthed some of the Rhône's rarest whites.

L'Oulette

15 pl Lachambeaudie, 12th (01.40.02.02.12/www. l-oulette.com). M° Cour St-Emilion. **Open** noon-2.15pm, 8-10.15pm Mon-Fri. **Average** €55. **Prix fixe** €46, €80. **Lunch menu** €25-€46. **Credit** AmEx, DC, MC, V. **Wheelchair access. Map** P10.

The advent of the brightly lit trattorias and minimalist, hangar-like eating halls of Bercy village has been both a bane and a blessing according to chef Marcel Baudis. On the one hand, it has breathed new life into an area of Paris that was slipping gently into oblivion just a few years back; on the down side (for Baudis), the 'competition' is a darned sight cheaper and more convenient to the Métro. So is it worth making the extra effort to eat at L'Oulette? Yes, for the charming service; precision-cooked, seasonal dishes; and certainly the marvellous wine list which, besides the classics from Burgundy and Bordeaux, also has an admirable selection from Baudis' native south-west and the Rhône Valley. The choice of half-bottles, vintage Armagnacs and the cigar cellar are impressive too. However, we thought the toy-town food portions were way overpriced. Our starter of wild mushroom 'gâteau' turned up as a small, rather ordinary egg flan sporting a few bits of mushroom and a light alfalfa and walnut salad for €14 apiece. As for the 'lièvre à la royale avec foie gras' at €30, we had been drooling over visions of a steaming casserole with hunks of hare in rich, thick sauce. But our dreams came to an abrupt end at the sight of the small, but admittedly tasty, round of meat. Short but sweet, the dish was nevertheless a superb match for the complex flavours of our 1995 Bandol Domaine Terrebrune. We rounded off with a sticky prune and apple croustade and a vanilla ice-cream presented inside an eggshell complete with gingerbread 'soldiers'. Our advice would be to go for the €46 menu for a minimum of two people, a much better bet than à la carte as it includes wine and coffee.

Au Pressoir

257 av Daumesnil, 12th (01.43.44.38.21). M° Michel Bizot. **Open** noon-2.30pm, 7.30-10.30pm Mon-Fri. Closed Aug, 25-31 Dec. **Average** €110. **Prix fixe** €76. **Credit** AmEx, MC, V. **Map** Q9.

Once inside the wood-lined, clubby interior of Henri Séguin's temple to serious eating, we were quickly led to a table by the smiling patronne. Lunchtime saw an exclusively male clientele popping out of their business suits in all directions, sporting complexions which keep cardiologists in work. We knew we were in for some serious food; even the appetiser of cold lobster soup was sublime. The starters included a special of the day, foie gras terrine with the contrasting texture of artichokes; we also tried a salad of warm roseval potatoes topped with foie gras. Both portions were generous and the preparation of the liver exceptionally fine. The sommelier suggested an excellent Bordeaux from the cheaper end of the list. The tournedos aux cèpes surpassed all expectations; not only was the meat spoon-tender but it seemed to be permeated by the rich mushroom sauce. An escalope de foie gras chaud was a perfect version accompanied by some nicely tart quartered apples. We had greedily watched the cheese trolley from the beginning of the meal and found ourselves with groaning platefuls. A dessert of wild strawberries magically held in thrall by spun sugar, accompanied by home-made vanilla ice-cream, was unmissable. Our eye had also been caught by a silver chalice of soupe au chocolat, which turned out to be possibly the richest pudding we have ever tasted; later the dish and its accompanying sponge cakes had to be almost pulled away from us.

Le Traversière

40 rue Traversière, 12th (01.43.44.02.10). M° Gare de Lyon or Ledru-Rollin. **Open** noon-2.30pm, 7-10.30pm Mon-Sat; noon-2.30pm Sun. **Prix fixe** €28, €38.50. **Credit** AmEx, MC, V. **Wheelchair access. Map** M7.

The spacious dining room and warm welcome feel reassuringly provincial at this popular bistro, which specialises in game and fish, near the marché d'Aligre. As we were at the climax of the season, we were slightly disappointed to read that the best of the game goodies, in this case wood pigeon and wild duck, both came with a €5 supplement on the more expensive of the two menus, priced at €28 and €38. Feeling financially chastened, we plumped for the cheaper of the two options, which did at least feature a comforting civet de sanglier (wild boar) as a plat du jour. An appetiser of cream of ceps was rich and flavoursome, even if it didn't provide much contrast with the warming crème de lentilles au foie gras starter, while a filo parcel of boudin noir on a pungent tomato coulis is a culinary idea that has had its day. The civet itself came in just the right unctuous chocolatey sauce, accompanied by some chestnuts and potato purée, but the meat itself was fairly dry and fibrous. Decent puddings of moelleux au chocolat and a white chocolate mousse coated in dark chocolate sauce continued the brown theme of our meal, which was accompanied by a very competitively priced Mercurey. Another time we may throw penury to the wind and hunt down the delights of the flying game birds.

Le Pavillon Montsouris

20 rue Gazan, 14th (01.43.13.29.00/www.pavillon-montsouris.fr). M° Glacière/RER Cité Universitaire. **Open** noon-2.30pm, 7.30-10.30pm daily. Closed two weeks in Feb. **Prix fixe** €49. **Credit** AmEx, MC, V. **Non-smoking room.**

We made the mistake of revisiting the Pavillon by night, which deprived us of the romantic view over the lake in pretty Montsouris park. The restaurant had been closed for many months for a complete overhaul and the present neo-classical decor creates a formal yet relaxed atmosphere thanks mainly to the cosy open fire near the entrance and the sometimes stiff, sometimes friendly service. We couldn't help feeling an inexplicable pang of nostalgia for the provincial charm of the flowery pink, chintzy decor of old. However, the restaurant still attracts a faithful following of hand-holding couples and vociferous family groups. Delicious amuse-bouches and the crunchy home-made bread kept us occupied as we perused the wine menu, interestingly presented via the bottle labels instead of the usual interminable listings. Both of us enjoyed our respective starters of a creamy haricot bean soup topped with crunchy bacon bits and a plump prawn, and two fat slices of decent foie gras, served too cold and sporting a superfluous blob of Chantilly. One main of lightly fried plaice laced with girolle mushrooms and a caramelised sauce proved faultless, but the pike-perch and its overcooked aubergine had been spiked with so much clove and cinnamon that we could hardly taste the fish. Our desserts looked as though they'd jumped straight from a posh 'look but don't touch' recipe book. A 'farandole' of multi-flavoured ice-creams and sorbets beautifully presented on a large green glass plate kept us hovering with the spoon deciding which one to dig into first and our chocolate cravings were staved for weeks with the pistachio-spiked and dark chocolate mousses and moist cake with a tart raspberry sauce.

Le Chalet des Iles

Carrefour des Cascades, lu inférieur du Bois de Boulogne, 16th (01.42.88.04.69/www.lechaletdesiles. net). M° La Muette or RER Henri Martin. **Open** noon-2.30pm, 8-10pm Tue-Fri; noon-3.30pm, 8-10.30pm Sat; noon-3.30pm Sun. **Average** €50. **Lunch menu** €23, €30 (Mon-Fri). **Children's menu** €10, €16. **Credit** AmEx, MC, V. **Wheelchair access.**

Even the most blasé Parisians can't help but revel in the idyllic island setting of Le Chalet des Iles. After a short, soothing boat ride across the Bois de Boulogne's Lac Intérieur, Le Chalet rewards with a light and airy room, elegant, ever-so-slightly formal French country decor (in soft greens, yellows and rusts actually found in nature… unlike the large arrangements of artificial flowers), solicitous service and menus in English, on request. By and large, we were also rewarded by lunch, starting with an unusual rendition of classic oeufs en cocotte with earthy girolle (chanterelle) mushrooms and sweet chestnuts, a salad of firm green lentils with toothsome quail confit in a solid-citizen vinaigrette, and a velvet-textured crème de lentilles with parmesan (and a noticeable surfeit of salt). For main courses we dodged tourist-friendly offerings of macaroni and cheese gratin and sauté de poulet 'shop suey au wok' in favour of a winey risotto with six beautifully seared, sweet scallops; daurade (sea bream) with a mirin-laced Asian glaze; and a thick chunk of seared, well-cooked cod in brown butter accompanied by rich and chunky mashed potatoes. The desserts we sampled – brioche perdue (a variation on French toast); a trio of small, lightly flavoured chocolate, coconut and pistachio panna cotte; and profiteroles with a small pitcher of warm bittersweet chocolate sauce for pour-it-yourself fun – were rendered with somewhat less skill. Better to simply order yourself a digestif and savour a few extra moments in this unexpected slice of Parisian countryside before the boat returns you to the bustling city.

La Grande Cascade ★

allée de Longchamp, Bois de Boulogne, 16th (01.45.27.33.51/www.lagrandecascade.fr). M° Porte Maillot, then taxi or 244 bus. **Open** 12.30-2.30pm, 7.30-10.30pm daily. Closed two weeks in Dec and Feb. **Average** €150. **Prix fixe** €70, €165. **Lunch menu** €59. **Credit** AmEx, DC, MC, V. **Wheelchair access.**

La Grande Cascade has long been a favourite with stately folk; it was built as a hunting lodge for Napoleon III in the 1800s, then transformed into a restaurant for the Great Exhibition of 1900. These days the luxurious dining room, with crystal chandeliers, glorious frescoes and metres of plush fabric, is a popular haunt for corporate titans and acutely wealthy Français of all ages, often accompanied by a yapping dog. Chef Richard Mebkhout's inventive cooking pays homage to French traditions, a vestige no doubt of his time with the iconic Paul Bocuse. A savoury biscuit pastry slathered with vegetables (fennel, carrots, snow peas, onions, etc) was a lip-smacking bite of spring; and a main of fleshy langoustines threaded on to stems of rosemary resting on creamy saffron risotto and studded with calamari, olives and sweet red peppers was another big flavourful success. Two cheese trolleys housed an irresistible array, from oozing chèvres to heavily veined blues and giant well-matured wheels. Desserts, less exciting but utterly agreeable, included pain perdu topped with pear roasted in vanilla and marzipan-flavoured ice-cream. The umbrella-strewn terrace is a marvellous summer lunch address.

La Braisière ★

54 rue Cardinet, 17th (01.47.63.40.37). M° Malesherbes. **Open** noon-2.30pm, 7.30-10.30pm Mon-Fri; 7.30-10.30pm Sat. Closed Aug. **Average** €45. **Lunch menu** €30. **Credit** AmEx, DC, MC, V. **Wheelchair access. Map** E2.

A few doors down from the house where Claude Debussy wrote *Pelléas et Mélisande*, this rather staid patrician restaurant is very in tune with the image of the 17th arrondissement – elegant, buttoned-up and understated. On a recent lunchtime visit the warm, cosseting room was full of local couples and knowing businessmen. The saucisson and crispy biscuits immediately alerted us to the fact that someone serious was in charge of the kitchen, confirmed by two pots of meaty and highly seasoned rillettes d'oie as a pre-starter to the €30 menu. Before our first courses arrived, chef Jacques Fausset passed through the restaurant shaking hands, a nice personal touch which set us up perfectly for a rich and delicious gâteau de pommes de terre au foie gras bathing in some girolle-perfumed cream, and a venaison de Colbert au foie gras – a duck terrine enriched with chunks of liver. By now we were settling down to this life of bourgeois comfort and our pleasure was confirmed by the tender pink rognons de veau served on a circle of crushed potatoes with a layer of spinach, which we enjoyed with one of the white wines of the month, a rich and vibrant St-Joseph. To finish this fine meal we opted for cheese, a plate of perfectly ripe st-nectaire accompainied by two glasses of fruity Bordeaux. If Fausset had been around in Debussy's time, the composer might not have found the will to leave the table and finish his masterpiece.

Contemporary

Even in the most innovative restaurants, very few Paris chefs aim to shock (an exception might be Giles Choukroun of Angl'Opéra). Instead, they are content to update French classics with a dash of imagination and a soupçon of spice. Chefs such as Pascal Barbot at L'Astrance and William Ledeuil at Ze Kitchen Galerie subtly draw on Asian ingredients, while other restaurants – such as Au Gourmand, Flora and Joël Robuchon's two addresses – borrow from all over the Mediterranean. Flawless French technique always comes to the fore – these are among the most dedicated and highly trained chefs in the city. The restaurants in this chapter are the best places to start if you want to see where French cooking is going.

Macéo

15 rue des Petits-Champs, 1st (01.42.97.53.85/www. maceorestaurant.com). M° Bourse or Pyramides.
Open noon-2.30pm 7.30-11pm Mon-Fri; 7.30-11pm Sat. **Average** €45. **Prix fixe** €35 (dinner only).
Lunch menu €27, €30, €35. **Credit** MC, V. **Map** H5.
The name Macéo is a tribute to saxophonist Maceo Parker at this elegant establishment with its 'library' overlooking the Palais Royal. Second Empire pressed ceilings are brought into the 21st century with some rather stylish lighting and – wait for it – a separate vegetarian menu. The influence of English owner Marc Williamson, of the nearby Willi's Wine Bar, is in force here as vegetarians are invited to share the 'gustative adventure' that restores vegetarian cuisine to its 'rightful' place. The El Bulli effect was also evident, firstly in the shot glass of creamy endive soup that arrived after we ordered, and, less fortuitously, in the ring of salty foam that encircled a bland vegetarian lentil risotto. Happily the chef was more comfortable with meat and seafood, with starters of smoked haddock and scallops, and mains of trout and veal perfect. The wine was also excellent, largely due to the fact that Macéo's sommeliers are charged with a mission to reveal the unknowns of the French wine industry: our initial choice pronounced 'trop médiatique', we were directed to a delicious Taille aux Loups. Desserts are inventive, although, like the vegetarian mains, they don't always bring out the flavours of the ingredients as well as they might. The leather chairs in the bar are perfect for an after-work drink.

Restaurant du Palais-Royal ★

110 galerie Valois, 1st (01.40.20.00.27). M° Palais Royal or Bourse. **Open** *May-Sept* 12.15-2.15pm, 7.15-10pm Mon-Sat. *Oct-Apr* 12.15-2.15pm, 7.15-11.30pm Mon-Fri. Closed 18 Dec-18 Jan. **Average** €60. **Credit** AmEx, DC, MC, V. **Non-smoking room**. **Wheelchair access**. **Map** H5.
There can be few more magical places to dine in Paris than on the terrace of this restaurant late on a warm summer evening after the rest of this public

garden has been shut off to the hoi polloi. The Palais-Royal is a perfect example of the French 'rationaliste' approach to gardens, full of the crunch of gravel and trees in lines. But even in the red and quietly trendy dining room there is something very special about dining under these splendid arcades alongside the elegant commissars of arts and letters who work at the Ministry of Culture a few doors down. Prices have jumped since our last visit and there is no 'prix fixe' to soften the blow, but the food is very good. We shared one of three wonderful-sounding risottos as a starter. Ours, called Black, Black and Lobster, sounded like the sort of thing the guys in flowery ties at the next table should be buying for the Pompidou Centre. It was tremendous. The rice was still firm in a wash of squid's ink where we found lumps of garlic and parmesan. On top, tender but fleshy pink lobster, sun-dried tomato, a slice of courgette, a couple of beans and a pea. Exquisite. Our mains were, inevitably, more restrained but

Rouge Tomate. *See p111.*

good nevertheless – a roasted sea bass with 'melted' leeks, and a hare stew which managed to be both heartily countrified and refined. We'd ordered two 50cl jugs of wine: a light and pleasant Bourgogne aligoté and a Bordeaux. We were particularly enthusiastic about the latter even after we noticed, on the bill, that they'd actually given us a Chilean cabernet sauvignon instead. The waiter practically forced us into having a baba au rhum for pudding, which turned out to be fabulous. We especially liked the little, clear bottle of alcohol they brought with it just in case we thought the baba hadn't been sufficiently doused.

Rouge Tomate

34 pl du Marché-St-Honoré, 1st (01.42.61.16.09). Mº Tuileries or Pyramides. **Open** 11.30am-2.30pm, 6.30-11pm daily. **Average** €25. **Prix fixe** €16.50, €21.50. **Credit** AmEx, MC, V. **Non-smoking room**. **Map** G4.

A little trend seems to be blossoming in Paris: restaurants where a single product gets star billing. Here, the kitchen works with as wide a variety of tomatoes – fresh and preserved – as possible, including Zebra tomatoes (striped), Bielorussian tomatoes (also known as beefsteak tomatoes) and Roma tomatoes from Morocco. Sometimes they're the main attraction, while in other dishes they play a supporting role. What's interesting is to see how important the tomato is in so many different cultures, since dishes here come from Mexico, Italy, Morocco, Spain, the United States, and several other countries. The challenge is to obtain decent fresh tomatoes out of European season, and here they succeed surprisingly well. The menu changes regularly, but a starter of prawns with a green tomato salsa verde was pleasant, while penne with crayfish, beefsteak tomatoes, ginger and coriander was curiously underseasoned. Much better was the tomato relish that accompanied the grilled John

Dory, and several of the tomato-based desserts – it is a fruit, after all, and responds well to being treated like one – including a curious preparation of vanilla tapioca with black tomatoes (vastly tastier than it sounds here).

Angl'Opéra

39 av de l'Opéra, 2nd (01.42.61.86.25/www. anglopera.com). Mº Opéra. **Open** noon-2.30pm, 7.30-11.30pm Mon-Fri. **Average** €38. **Lunch menu** €17. **Credit** AmEx, MC, V. **Map** H4.

Giles Choukroun, who has a reputation as one of the more daring young chefs in the capital, is behind this hotel restaurant. Upmarket office types keep it busy at noon, but what happens at night? After hours, it turns out, this is a relaxed and very charming place for a meal in a stylish dining room with excellent service. Because it's written in the random style of Dadaist poetry, the short menu requires some considerable explanation, which seems to have violently antagonised many French food critics. 'Hot bouillon, herbs, ginger, soft-boiled egg…and foie gras' turned out to be tiny cubes of raw foie gras garnished with fresh mint, tarragon and lemon verbena, which you douse with hot bouillon and eat with spoonfuls of scrambled egg with 'apéro-peanuts' (peanuts surrounded with a crunchy shell). Salmon with lemon risotto, a shot glass of hot coconut milk and mussel juice; Chinese soup spoons of oysters on fresh peanuts in a herby dressing; and steamed skate in a sauce of poppy seeds, fennel and citrus fruit were all superb. Deep-fried camembert wedges with a salad of celery root and apple in a soy dressing were lovely, but the best conclusion to a meal here, from a menu that changes often, were the poached lychees in a soup of Schweppes, lemon verbena, and green and Mexican papaya. The wine list is wonderful, too, including a surprisingly good petit syrah from Mexico for a bargain €20. Angl'Opéra is a real treat.

Café Moderne

40 rue Notre Dame des Victoires, 2nd
(01.53.40.84.10). M° Bourse. **Open** noon-2.30pm,
7.30-10.30pm Mon-Fri; 7.30-11pm Sat. **Average** €30.
Prix fixe €26, €30. **Credit** MC, V. **Map** J4.

This newcomer to the Bourse area was positively
buzzing on our Monday lunch, creating an
immediately welcoming impression with its butter-
yellow walls, plush red banquettes and
contemporary art. Just what this neighbourhood
needed – or so we thought until our meal began. The
restaurant recently changed chefs, and Sébastien
Altazin, who is now in charge of the kitchen, has a
penchant for Mediterranean flavours. However, his
good ideas were badly executed – we had the feeling
that the kitchen had spun out of control, perhaps a
result of an unexpected rush that day. We chose the
€26 two-course menu – not cheap, we coudn't help
but think. The day's starter, lasagne d'escargots,
turned out to be a small, rather dried-out square of
tomatoey pasta in which escargots replaced the
traditional beef. Not awful, not memorable. After an
endless wait, our main courses arrived having
apparently been reheated and then forgotten until
they had cooled off. Dried-out, lukewarm shredded
oxtail came with cold potatoes, as did an original-
sounding but heavy tempura of partridge (our
neighbours' tempura looked better, so we might
have just been unlucky). Two of our dishes came
with €2 supplements, bringing the total price of our
rather parsimonious meal with a glass of wine each
to more than €70. As we scrabbled for our coats,
which had been heaped in a pile at the entrance, we
could only imagine that we had caught Café
Moderne on an off-day – but, at this price, it's hard
to forgive them.

Atelier Maître Albert

1 rue Maître Albert, 5th (01.56.81.30.01).
M° Maubert-Mutualité. **Open** noon-2.30pm, 6.30-
11.30pm Mon-Wed; 6.30pm-1am Thur-Sat; 6.30-
11.30pm Sun. **Average** €50. **Lunch menu** €23,
€28. **Credit** AmEx, DC, MC, V. **Wheelchair**
access. **Map** J7.

With a slick new decor by Jean-Michel Wilmotte,
who redesigned chef Guy Savoy's main restaurant,
this recent Guy Savoy annexe on a sweet little street
in the Latin Quarter looks as though it could become
a pretty good restaurant, even if the basic concept
was essentially launched by Jacques Cagna a good
decade ago. The indigo-painted and grey marble-
floored dining room with open kitchen and
rôtisseries on view is attractive but very noisy –
book a table in the quieter bar area if you want to be
able to chat over dinner without shouting.
Otherwise, the very short menu lets you get at a
Savoy classic or two to start, including oysters in
sea water gelée – good but tasting strongly of
powdered pepper – or more inventive dishes such
as a ballotin of chicken, foie gras and celery root in
a chicken liver sauce. This was actually a nice dish
except for the fact that it came on an austere and

ungarnished white plate; a bit of salad would have
been welcome. Next up, a rôtisseried faux-filet and
a chunk of tuna, served with tiny iron casseroles of
pommes dauphinoises and (much tastier)
cauliflower in béchamel sauce. Once this place
works out its major kinks – the awful noise, the
ungarnished plates, the too-brief menu – odds are
good that it will be perfect for a simple, tasty feed
with friends. Pleasant service and a good wine list.

Au Gourmand ★

22 rue de Vaugirard, 6th (01.43.26.26.45/www.au
gourmand.fr) M° Odéon or RER Luxembourg. **Open**
12.30-2.30pm, 7-10pm Mon-Fri. Closed two weeks in
Aug. **Average** €40. **Prix fixe** €35 (dinner only).
Lunch menu €25, €30. **Credit** MC, V. **Map** H7.

At a time when the culinary landscape in Paris has
been accused, yet again, of having become stolid –
by a miscellaneous pack of home-grown and foreign
critics – a flurry of new restaurants demonstrate the
quiet but invincible muscle of French gastronomy,
the marriage of breathtaking technique and a
superbly disciplined ability to invent new dishes.
Young chef Christophe Courgeau, who trained at
Arpège and the Crillon, has the good sense to offer
a limited but appealing choice of three starters, two
mains and five desserts daily, which lets him follow
the market as he sees fit. If not all of his ideas work
– a chilled melon soup with olive oil-and-basil sorbet
didn't make much sense – when they do, they are
remarkable, as in a carpaccio of veal with croquettes
of tapenade and feta cheese: bliss. Running the
simple but hip dining room is Courgeau's associate,
Hervé de Libouton, a former wine writer who
assures the prevailing excellence of the wine list. It's
a hit, so book.

Salon d'Hélène

4 rue d'Assas, 6th (01.42.22.00.11). M° Sèvres-
Babylone. **Open** 7.30-10.15pm Tue; 12.30-2.15pm,
7.30-10.15pm Wed-Sat. Closed two weeks in Aug.
Average €60. **Prix fixe** €30, €39. **Credit** AmEx,
MC, V. **Wheelchair access**. **No smoking**. **Map** G7.

For those days when you don't want all the bells and
whistles of a full gastronomic experience, media
darling Hélène Darroze runs the more casual Salon
downstairs, its banquettes lined with big cushions
perfect for sinking into (but slightly awkward when
it comes to eating). As much as we came prepared
to enjoy ourselves, everything about our lunch was
slightly wrong. After being ignored for a few
minutes at the entrance, we were seated side-by-side
and then ignored for another 15 minutes as we
watched the cooks working calmly in the open
kitchen. Finally, a waiter arrived with three kinds of
bread. 'This one is with piment d'Esmolette,' he said.
'Don't you mean Espelette?' we asked, as Darroze is
from south-west France where this chilli pepper is
cultivated. Blank stare. If he was clumsy in an
endearing way, later knocking our bottle of water
off the table, the more experienced waitress was
simply chilly. Ordering three dishes each from the
tapas menu, we had an uneven and unsatisfying

meal that did include two tasty dishes: the daube de cèpes à la mode landaise (a mushroom stew served in a dinky cast-iron pot with two grissini wrapped in excellent cured ham), and a similar little pasta casserole with duck foie gras and wild mushrooms. Two other dishes, though, were out-and-out flops: doughy gambas 'tempura' with poppy seeds, and a bizarrely cold chestnut 'Chantilly' that had separated in its glass. Desserts were delicious, however, including layers of chocolate cream and passion fruit jelly. One last detail jarred – wines are served in narrow Champagne flutes, and the €16 glass of white Bordeaux the sommelier chose for us (without announcing the price) left us cold.

Ze Kitchen Galerie

4 rue des Grands-Augustins, 6th (01.44.32.00.32).
M° St-Michel. **Open** noon-2pm, 7-11pm Mon-Fri;
7-11pm Sat. **Average** €50. **Lunch menu** €21-€33.
Credit AmEx, DC, MC, V. **Wheelchair access.**
Map H6.
The modern bistro of William Ledeuil, who was formerly chef at Guy Savoy's Les Bookinistes around the corner, works on a simple principle: a starter choice of soup, pasta or raw fish, and main courses – many of them fish – all speed-grilled on an iron plaque 'a la plancha'. The real element that distinguishes his style is the beautifully presented alliance of eastern and western techniques, high-quality French produce and Asian vegetables and flavourings. Ledeuil is especially influenced by visits to Thailand, and sources many of his products in the 13th arrondissement Chinese supermarkets. Our entrée du jour was a clever and colourful sandwich of raw tuna – thinly sliced grilled tuna and green asparagus with a purple beetroot coulis – while marinated raw sea bass came with a slightly overpowering mango and orange condiment and tiny baby leeks. Then on to the plancha stage. Perfectly timed sea bream a la plancha was surrounded by a citrus and ginger sauce, and accompanied by both crispy tempura and grilled vegetables. Even a more terroir-style dish of grilled lamb from the Lozère came with spinach and fingers of polenta speckled with Thai basil. Desserts were a similarly eclectic succession of ideas: a mandarin filled with mandarin sorbet and served with banana ice-cream and a tumbler of coffee milkshake, and a rich 'cappuccino' of chocolate mousse with coffee cardamom froth and crunchy pain d'épices wafers. At times we felt Ledeuil was overdoing the citrus elements, but in general the assorted techniques are used with reason and precision for some thought-provoking results.

L'Atelier de Joël Robuchon

5 rue de Montalembert, 7th (01.42.22.56.56). M° Rue
du Bac. **Open** 11.30am-3.30pm, 6.30pm-midnight
daily. **Average** €60. **Prix fixe** €98. **Credit** MC, V.
Wheelchair access. No smoking. Map G6.
If you don't want to queue at star chef Joël Robuchon's 40-seat restaurant, book either the 11.30am or 6.30pm sitting (the only hours at which

they accept reservations). The wait at peak times, however, is almost worth it for the amusing spectacle of cashmere-draped Left Bank lawyers and intellectuals, along with international foodies, being unceremoniously turned away. Once you're seated at one of the two bars in the black and red-lacquer dining room, the theatre continues. There are no tables and chairs (only counters and stools), Spanish hams hang from the ceiling, food is served on Bernardaud porcelain, Japanese pottery or slabs of lava from Fujiyama, and the cooks are on display. You can have a traditional three-course meal here, but sitting at the counter that didn't seem to make much sense. We chose six 'small plates' from a tempting list of about 15 dishes. Among the highlights were a fondant de légumes acidulé à l'avocat – an intense tomato jelly, as buttery on the tongue as whipped cream, topped with a smooth avocado purée – marinated salmon with horseradish, and a small but delicious dish of clams stuffed with subtle new garlic and herbs. After these, we had only one desire: to make this meal last even longer. So we ordered a main dish to share, the cannelloni de volaille de Bresse au foie gras – roasted Bresse chicken stuffed with foie gras and served with wild mushrooms, a straightforward but magnificent combination. For dessert, the passionfruit soufflé was stabbed before our eyes to introduce a scoop of ice-cream – fluffy, hot and melting, it made a dramatic end to a meal that left us feeling surprisingly sprightly, despite the bottle of Viognier we shared.

Le Chamarré ★

13 bd de la Tour-Maubourg, 7th (01.47.05.50.18).
M° Invalides. **Open** noon-2.30pm, 7.30-10.30pm
Mon-Fri; 7.30-10.30pm Sat. **Average** €100. **Prix**
fixe €85-€160 (dinner only). **Lunch menu** €28,
€40. **Credit** AmEx, DC, MC, V. **Wheelchair**
access. Map E6.
In a relaxed dining room furnished with banquettes scattered with tiny chocolate and orange velvet cushions and low-lit by coloured glass lights, Jérome Bodereau and Antoine Heerah serve a menu where the mainstay of each dish is European (Scottish grouse, Breton lobster, cochon de lait), overlaid with nuances of Mauritian cuisine that concentrate on the fruity rather than the spicy register. Tiny blobs of chutneys and dribbles of molasses are presented on the plate as on a painter's palette. The 'carte blanche' menu has the extra frisson of surprise – you don't know what you are going to get until it arrives in front of you. The procession of plates began with two variations on octopus: one side smoked, the other macerated in ginger, accompanied by mango, guava and tomato chutneys. Vegetables 'from here and elsewhere', including chestnut, nestled in a subtle sorrel-flavoured foam set off by Mauritian pesto (spicier than the Italian version). King prawns dressed in crispy jackets of angel hair were ideal for dipping in the various condiments; the lobster, caught off Brittany, was roasted with a seasoning

of crevettes and coloquinte, and served with a risotto of lentils, roe and bouillabaisse jus. The main dish, cochon de lait, with a wonderfully crispy skin that recalled that there is a Chinese as well as Indian influence on Mauritian cooking, was accompanied by a little cake of belly and trotters, and simply served in its cooking juices. Then not one but two desserts: an orange, which had been preserved with its bitter skin then fried with crispy sugar cane, accompanied by a divine pêche de vignes sorbet; and an unusual savarin. This meal was like a memorable piece of theatre, ably animated by the maître d' and waiters who deliver their descriptions of each dish with aplomb, smiles and humour, and accompany guests right outside the door.

La Cuisine

14 bd de la Tour-Maubourg, 7th (01.44.18.36.32). M° La Tour Maubourg. **Open** noon-2pm, 7.30-10pm Mon-Fri; 7.30-10pm Sat, Sun. Closed Aug. **Average** €55. **Prix fixe** €42. **Lunch menu** €29. **Credit** AmEx, DC, MC, V. **Wheelchair access.** **Map** E5.

It may not be immediately apparent, but this studiously well-mannered contemporary French restaurant in the most solidly bourgeois precincts of the 7th arrondissement can actually be a relaxing destination. The taupe, black and ivory decor, low lighting and carefully set tables communicate the truth that this is a very adult restaurant. The service, however, surprises by being not only attentive but smiling, even sort of friendly, and the cooking of a young chef from the Vosges region of France is sensual, imaginative and generous. The terrine of foie gras served with warm toast was impeccable, while an autumnal sautée of wild mushrooms was judiciously seasoned with very finely chopped shallot and a little flat parsley, both perfectly executed classical preparations. The star starter, though, was the scallop carpaccio with lemon vinaigrette and finely chopped oysters, a delicious contrast of textures and tastes. Main courses provided further evidence of a well-run kitchen brimming with talent, since noisettes de biche (venison medallions) were almost disarmingly tender in a rich sauce made from a reduction of its own gizzards with autumn fruit, while a saddle of rabbit stuffed with veal sweetbreads was the sort of outstanding dish you expect at haute cuisine altitudes of dining. Desserts were pleasant, if understated, including luscious cannelloni filled with chocolate mousse, and a cheese plate was a generously served assortment of perfectly ripened seasonal specimens, correctly running from chèvre to bleu and accessorised by a pleasant tangle of herbs and salad leaves. Bravo, too, for an impressive selection of wines by the glass, which is especially welcome in light of the pricey wine list. An absolutely perfect address for business or ceremonial occasions, this place works just as well as a spur-of-the-moment treat when you're hankering for a fine feed in a civilised setting.

Restaurant Petrossian

18 bd de la Tour-Maubourg, 7th (01.44.11.32.32/ www.petrossian.fr). M° Invalides. **Open** 12.15-2.30pm, 7.30-10.30pm Tue-Sat. Closed three weeks in Aug. **Average** €70. **Prix fixe** €48-€107 (dinner only). **Lunch menu** €38. **Credit** AmEx, DC, MC, V. **Non-smoking room. Map** E6.

Petrossian is famous for its glossy, premium Russian caviar and smoked fish, but the dove-grey dining room above the boutique dishes up much more exciting contemporary fare. Pastry virtuoso Philippe Conticini, who inaugurated an elegantly upmarket savoury and sweet menu, has departed but his predilection for playing with tastes and textures is evident in the cooking of Sébastien Faré. Langoustines coated in coconut, lightly fried and served on a disc of tomato chutney burnished with parmesan were paired with angelic chocolate buttons filled with a Curaçao 'vinaigrette', while a main of scallops came on a crusty biscuit of inky black rice adorned with jewel-coloured miniature spring vegetables. Desserts are just as stylish. Le kyscielli featured a curl of avocado and coconut mousse, a square of sweet fried pastry with apple confit, and dainty layers of fruit coulis and tea-flavoured jelly. The €48 prix fixe (the average price of a main), however, pales in comparison. A good address if you're feeling worldly and grown-up.

Chez Catherine

3 rue Berryer, 8th (01.40.76.01.40) M° Ternes or St-Philippe-du-Roule. **Open** noon-2pm, 8-10.15pm Tue-Sat. Closed one week in May, three weeks in Aug. **Average** €50. **Lunch menu** €45. **Credit** AmEx, DC, MC, V. **Wheelchair access. Non-smoking room. Map** D3.

Looking for a place to show off that new Chanel jacket or darling Yves Saint Laurent pullover? Here, the expensively dressed can feel at their ease as they take their clients out to expense-account lunches (the crumpled rest might feel a little squirmy on the orange benches). The food is what you might call genteel Mediterranean – a refined and careful preparation of rugged, colourful ingredients such as sardines and scorpion fish, grilled peppers and olives all daintily laid out on designer crockery. Nice enough but you can't help thinking they're missing the point. Choosing from the set lunch menu, we started with some tangy marinated sardines on a bed of peppers and a rather timid-tasting fish mousse with gribiche sauce (that's the one with vinegar, capers, gherkins and egg). Our best main was a filet of scorpion fish with fennel purée and black olive jus, which was good but not that good. The other main, rather incongruous on this menu, was a duck confit that seemed to have escaped from a neighbouring bistro. Our sommelier, though unable to suggest anything even remotely inexpensive, did at least find us something nice for our €48: a crisp and elegant Savennières. And we puddinged quite well on crème brûlée and something called apple Genoa bread in a bath of crème anglaise. Not bad, not great, not cheap.

Salon d'Hélène.
See p112.

Flora ★

36 av George V, 8th (01.40.70.10.49). M° George V.
Open noon 2.30pm, 7-11pm Mon-Fri; 7-11pm Sat.
Closed three weeks in Aug. **Average** €55. **Prix
fixe** €34. **Lunch menu** €26. **Credit** AmEx, MC, V.
Map D4.

Flora Mikula, one of the most talented female chefs
in France, is a whizz when it comes to dishing up
classy, creative food. Starters of pan-fried
langoustines, asparagus and truffle quenelles in a
silky asparagus soup, tempura of scallops and
calamari kebab-style, and snails with gnocchi and
pesto piled high into marrow bones exemplify her
confident cooking and clever layering of flavours.
And it doesn't stop there: sole comes bathed in black
truffle butter, milk-fed lamb is infused with thyme,
earthy wild mushrooms enrich a pink fillet of
roasted Charolais beef. Situated in Paris's Golden
Triangle (the area bordered by the Champs-Elysées,
avenue Marceau and avenue Montaigne), the
restaurant is stylish to the max: dove-grey and ivory
walls, cut-glass mirrors and hip glass panels
curtained with silver beads acting as dividers.
Service is sunny and professional, a lot like the chef,
who wandered past in her black Mao suit pausing
to say hello. The cheese trolley is a delight, so too
the amuse-bouches and sugary mignardises.

Maison Blanche

*15 av Montaigne, 8th (01.47.23.55.99/www.maison-
blanche.fr). M° Alma-Marceau.* **Open** noon-1.45pm,
8-10.45pm Mon-Fri; 8-9.30pm Sat; 8-10.45pm Sun.
Average €100. **Lunch menu** €45. **Credit** AmEx,
MC, V. **Wheelchair access. Map** D5.

For Thanksgiving we treated ourselves to lunch at
the Maison Blanche as a witty nod towards our
American cousins. The Pourcel brothers from
Montpellier were seemingly oblivious of the holiday,
or was that creamy pumpkin and chestnut appetiser

a coded acknowledgement? The sleek rooftop
restaurant with its spectacular view over Paris was
packed with a business clientele for lunch, but the
set menu was only presented on request,
encouraging all to order from the sophisticated carte.
Little cheese gougères augured well for our starters
of lobster tail salad with violet potatoes, and a
winning dish of crayfish and veal sweetbreads with
a pot of frothy cappuccino de cèpes. There is rather
too much frothing and moussing in the Pourcel
world, and asceticism seems to replace strong
flavours. A main course of partridge was paintably
displayed, but the promised sauce poivrade was thin
on the plate and the accompanying chestnuts and
quinces were dry. Sole fillets interleaved with slivers
of foie gras, and jambon de boeuf accompanied by
a rich purée of chestnuts was luxury comfort food,
but lacked culinary punch. Puddings included
delicious raspberry- and chocolate-filled nems in
their own glasses of mascarpone cream, as well as
les trois compositions de chocolat – three contrasting
dishes of white, milk and dark chocolate, served hot,
cold and frozen, the classic dark chocolate cake
being the most successful. A would-be refreshing
lime sorbet was too cleansing and we pounced on
the last petits fours. We enjoyed a nice white wine
from the Languedoc region, and the service was
impeccable, but our bill of well over €100 per person
ranks with the most expensive in Paris, and, despite
the feel-good factor, you can eat better elsewhere.

Pomze

*109 bd Haussman, 8th (01.42.65.65.83/www.pomze.
com). M° Miromesnil.* **Open** 8am-11pm Mon-Fri;
9.30am-11pm Sat. **Average** €38. **Prix fixe** €32.
Credit AmEx, MC, V. **Wheelchair access. Non-
smoking room. Map** F3.

The crucial point to make when discussing this
original and really excellent new restaurant is that
its core concept – the apple, in cooking and as a

beverage – is not at all the sort of silly gimmick you might fear. Instead, this handsome three-level place (there's a shop on the ground floor, a tea salon in the basement and a restaurant on the first floor) takes its theme quite seriously without losing the good humour evoked by the product itself. Upstairs, black-and-white photographs of apple orchards adorn the walls of a good-looking ivory-painted dining room, and service is crisp and friendly. Though they have a respectable wine list, the fun here is discovering cider in all of its infinitely nuanced variety, so start with a glass of Cidre des Vergers de Chouquet and let the waiter guide you through the menu, which changes seasonally. Superb starters ran to a croquemis of ste-maure cheese with Temptation apples and a lovely Calvados-seasoned terrine of rabbit with baby vegetables. Main courses were similarly original and delicious, especially duck breast grilled in red Thai curry with a cinammon-apple chutney – fascinating mixture of flavours, perfectly cooked meat. A grilled veal chop served with an apple purée and celery root scented with turmeric was pleasant, too, and the ciders selected to accompany each course were a revelation. Desserts are first-rate, including brioche perdue with a compote of nine apples and apple tart with freshly made salted butter-caramel ice-cream.

Publicis Drugstore

133 av des Champs Elysées, 8th (01.44.43.77.64/ www.publicisdrugstore.com). M° Etoile or George V. **Open** 8am-1am Mon-Fri; 10am-1am Sat, Sun. **Average** €40. **Lunch menu** €29. **Credit** AmEx, DC, MC, V. **Wheelchair access. Map** C3.

The '70s-vintage landmark Drugstore, just on the brink of becoming a *Wallpaper**-style design classic, was judged an embarrassment that had to be brought up to date. Michele Saare got the job, with middling results. If the façade is bad Vegas, with twinkling fibre optics, the restaurant space is overall a success. Curiously, the least appealing part of the room is the VIP corral dubbed 'Marcel' and located behind the bustling main dining room. This space, also troubled by cold fibre optical lighting, feels rather like an airport restaurant, while the main space, the 'Brasserie', has a groovy funk that immediately works. Whether you chose Marcel or the Brasserie, you'd better be prepared to spend a pretty penny. The days of the omelette have been ushered out in favour of on-the-run nibbles that might appeal to shoppers at the new Cartier across the avenue or the imminent Louis Vuitton mega-boutique just down the road. In the brasserie, think macaroni with ham and truffles (a sign that Alain Ducasse had a say in the menu), spit-roasted duck with spelt risotto, and baba au rhum. Marcel, behind the curving glass partition, is rather more ambitious with grilled foie gras in a balsamic reduction, veal chop with sautéed salsify and chocolate tart. Neither menu has a sandwich or a proper salad, a sure signal that the Champs-Elysées is no longer for punters in trainers but globo shoppers with AmEx black cards.

La Table du Lancaster ★

Hôtel Lancaster, 7 rue de Berri, 8th (01.40.76.40.18/ www.hotel-lancaster.fr). M° George V. **Open** 12.30-2.30pm, 7.30-10pm Mon-Fri; 7.30-10pm Sat, Sun. Closed mid July-mid Aug. **Average** €100. **Credit** AmEx, DC, MC, V. **Wheelchair access. Non-smoking room. Map** D4.

Previously reserved for hotel guests only, the elegant, intimate little dining room of the elegant, intimate little Hôtel Lancaster is now open to the hoi-polloi willing to dig up the €70-plus required for a meal here. Is it worth it? Well, yes. The chef, Michel Troisgros, has created a fascinating, if not always perfect menu that's divided up among six subheads – tomatoes, citrus, condiments and spices, wine and vinegar, vegetables and herbs, and dairy produce, each of which offers several starters and several main courses. With some good advice from the waiters, you'll eat very well indeed, as Troisgros is set on intelligent global inspiration – as opposed to 'fusion' cooking – and also knows that the fashionable fauna likely to alight here will want vivid but light cooking. He succeeds in a big way with dishes such as a scallop tartare with sea urchin roe to start. Main courses are similarly racy and satisfying, including a really brilliant dish of perfect cooked cod, smeared with Japanese mustard and set down on a bed of Japan's best rice before being doused with cod bouillon. Desserts are great fun, too – oeuf à la neige with maple syrup was a meringue with a well of syrup and a sublime maple-syrup Charlotte, the sweetness cut by a squeeze of kafir lime for anyone who chose. The wine list is a bit front-loaded to Bordeaux, although there are some lovely New World wines. Service, while still rather green, is friendly, attractive and eager to please.

Pétrelle

34 rue Pétrelle, 9th (01.42.82 11.02). M° Anvers. **Open** 8-10pm Tue-Sat. **Average** €50. **Prix fixe** €25. **Wheelchair access. Credit** MC, V. **Map** J2.

Jean-Luc André is as inspired a decorator as he is a cook, and the quirky charm of his dining room has made it popular with fashion designers and film stars. A faded series of turn-of-the-century tableaux is his latest flea-market find, while summer holidays were spent revamping the loos. Behind all this style is some serious substance – André seeks out the very best ingredients from local producers such as market gardener Joël Thiébault, who grows 1,400 varieties of vegetables. As André now runs the épicerie and stylish café Les Vivres next door, Pétrelle is open in the evenings only – but the €25 set menu, formerly only available at lunch, is now offered at dinner. This no-choice three-course meal is stunning value (on our last visit, marinated sardines with tomato relish, rosemary-scented rabbit with roasted vegetables, deep purple poached figs). It's tempting, however, to splash out on the more extravagant à la carte dishes such as the tournedos Rossini, a classic dish of steak, foie gras and truffle, or one of many game concoctions in winter.

Montparnasse 25

Le Méridien Montparnasse, 19 rue du Commandant René Mouchotte, 14th (01.44.36.44.25). M° Gaîeté. **Open** 12.15-2.30pm, 7.30-10.30pm Mon-Fri. Closed Aug, two weeks at Christmas. **Average** €100. **Prix fixe** €105 (dinner only). **Lunch menu** €49. **Credit** AmEx, DC, MC, V. **Wheelchair access. Non-smoking room. Map** F9.

This excellent restaurant with chef Christian Moine at the helm deserves better than being buried deep inside the Méridien Montparnasse, a chain hotel. The restaurant itself isn't unattractive, though, with artful lighting, a mostly black decor and an art deco theme. First courses of foie gras interleaved with dried fruit and drizzled with gooseberry coulis; sea bass carpaccio with celery rémoulade, mini artichoke hearts stuffed with brousse (a fresh Corsican cheese); and rocket salad with tomato oil showed off a chef with culinary nerve. Sole, perfectly de-boned and gently swabbed with a paste of pistou sauce and breadcrumbs, was sublime (although the side of minestrone was puzzling); pigeon was exquisite, perfectly cooked and garnished with tiny peas in lomo-spiked cream. Desserts may well be lovely, but Moine's excellent cooking aside, the great lure here is the cheese course, orchestrated by maître fromager Gérard Poulard. He brought his groaning trolley tableside and set to work with his knives, serving up exquisite lozenges of the cheeses that he so carefully culls from farmyards all over France.

Astrance ★

4 rue Beethoven, 16th (01.40.50.84.40). M° Passy. **Open** 12.30-1.45pm, 8.15-9.45pm Tue-Fri. Closed Aug. **Average** €100. **Prix fixe** €150. **Lunch menu** €70, €115. **Credit** AmEx, DC, MC, V. **Map** B6,

La Table du Lancaster. *See p116.*

When Pascal Barbot opened Astrance, he was praised for creating a new style of Parisian restaurant – refined, yet casual and affordable. Three years later, this small, slate-grey dining room feels exactly like an haute cuisine restaurant, with seemingly as many staff as there are customers and prices comparable to Taillevent's. We hesitated over the three-course lunch menu at €70 before settling on the more extravagant menu automne for €115 – most of those around us chose the menu Astrance at €150, giving free rein to the chef. We resisted the aperitif trolley being wheeled around and then had to wait 40 minutes, sustained by mineral water and a brioche amuse-bouche with dill butter, before our first courses arrived. From then on it was smooth sailing through the six courses. A celeriac velouté layered in a shot glass with lime yoghurt and juniper cream piqued our appetites, before foie gras interspersed with thin slices of white mushrooms, its delicate flavours lifted by a lemon condiment. Next up, the sweetness of a slice of (ever so slightly chewy) lobster was played off by the bitterness of candied grapefruit peel, a grapefruit and rosemary sorbet, and raw baby spinach leaves. Textures came to the fore in a dish of warm salmon served with chips of dried chestnut, tiny chanterelle mushrooms and mushroom vinegar. The meat course, crisp-skinned pigeon with bilberry chutney and quince confit, offered a beautiful contrast of tart, sweet and earthy. After a light, snowy-white sorbet of chilli pepper and lemongrass, we amazingly still had an appetite for dessert – a sign that Barbot keeps fats to a minimum. A thin, meringue-like coconut case contained a light, milky ice-cream, served with carefully selected exotic fruits – more of the fruits came with coffee and little madeleines flavoured with chestnut honey. Beautiful as this food was, it didn't send us into ecstasies – rather, the experience was quietly pleasurable, the only flaw being the reasonably priced wines by the glass that weren't elegant enough to stand up to the food.

Le Passiflore ★

33 rue de Longchamp, 16th (01.47.04.96.81/www. restaurantlepassiflore.com). M° Trocadéro or Iéna. **Open** noon-2.30pm, 7.30-10.30pm Mon-Fri; 8-10.30pm Sat. **Prix fixe** (dinner only) €38, €54. **Lunch menu** €35. **Average** €80. **Credit** AmEx, MC, V. **Map** C5.

Roland Durand's 30-year career has included the haute-bourgeoise heights of the Pré Catelan and the more prosaic challenge of bashing out 23,000 lunches at a sitting during the '98 World Cup, but it's his passionate exploration of Asian cuisine which informs the brilliance of his first solo venture. After our first sip of a sweet, spicy beetroot gazpacho, we abandoned the prix fixe and ate practically the whole menu, highlights of which included a fresh foie gras sautéed with pineapple and violets; a deep, fragrant wild boar and tamarind curry; and a ravioli of foie gras in a frothy truffle broth of pagan decadence. The masterpieces are the sorbets – some more familiar flavours like basil, bitter chocolate and lychee, others teasing with unfamiliar herbs such as cumin-like Vietnamese moom, all combining astonishing aromas in their creamy coldness. The wine list is as serious as the menu is whimsical, with a connoisseur's selection of Bordeaux as well as regional curiosities from Corsica and Savoie. The crowd is not 'les pipol' (celebrities) but the food is some of the most original, ambitious and exciting in Paris, with none of the pomposity of better-known gastro-shrines.

La Table de Joël Robuchon

16 av Bugeaud, 16th (01.56.28.16.16). M° Victor Hugo. **Open** *noon-2.30pm, 7-10.30pm daily.* **Average** €80. **Prix fixe** €150. **Credit** MC, V. **Wheelchair access**. **No smoking. Map** B4.

Though everyone understands the necessity of making and honouring reservations, the woman in charge of same at JR's new sitdown deluxe table is so harsh about the whole thing that it immediately dulls any anticipation: 'If you don't call back and confirm, your table will automatically be cancelled.' After this inauspicious prelude, things got off to a jagged start with the realisation that the flowers on the tables here are plastic blooms. Service seemed harried to the extent of being a distraction, and the crowd was wearing everything from Hermes to T-shirts and jeans. Evidently, the retired superchef has decided casual is the way to go. But wait. Just when all seemed lost, the food arrived. And it was truly dazzling. Gazpacho and foie gras were the ultimate definitions of themselves; main courses of a juicy veal chop glazed with lemon marmalade and served with baby vegetables, and sea bass were spectacular in all respects – gorgeous produce perfectly cooked with great imagination. A shared dessert of poached rhubarb with speculoos biscuit and Kriek (Belgian Abbey beer) ice-cream was brilliant, too, and under the circumstances of such a high-altitude restaurant, our Domaine Richaud Côtes du Rhône was a fair buy at €39. We'll never like the harsh gilt trip of this moody dining room, but we'll surely be back for more of brilliant young chef Frédéric Simonin's awesome cooking (he's the one who's actually in the kitchen). Bravo, too, for the 20 different wines served by the glass. Now about those flowers…

La Terrasse du Parc

Le Parc-Sofitel, 59 av Raymond-Poincaré, 16th (01.44.05.66.10). M° Trocadéro or Bossière. **Open** noon-2.30pm, 7.30-10.30pm Tue-Fri; 7.30-10pm Sat. Closed two weeks in Dec. **Average** €60. **Prix fixe** €90, €130. **Lunch menu** €45, €70. **Credit** AmEx, DC, V. **Wheelchair access. Map** B5.

Open only in summer, this terrace restaurant has one of the prettiest and quietest outdoor settings in Paris, occupying a courtyard lavishly planted with trees and flowers. It has a decidedly St-Tropez tint since it's been given a once-over by Patrick Jouin, Ducasse's favourite decorator – dusty rose canvas, cobalt-blue glasses, orange faïence and other touches create a holiday atmosphere. The menu, conceived by Alain Ducasse and chef Alain Soulard, is a stylish

roster of seasonal eating, including an inventive Caesar salad of steamed prawns, giant capers, parmesan and cos lettuce; white gazpacho (made with almonds and vegetables and topped with pesto and roast langoustines); tuna steak with green tea noodles; and almond milk ice-cream with apricot sorbet. Wine prices are a bit stiff, but it's a fun place.

Caïus

6 rue de l'Armaillé, 17th (01.42.27.19.20). M° Argentine. **Open** noon-2.30pm, 7.30-10.30pm Mon-Fri; 7.30-10.30pm Sat. **Average** €40. **Credit** AmEx, MC, V. **Map** C3.

In the ungainly caramel-coloured, wood-panelled setting of a former Jacques Cagna rôtisserie, this much talked-about new restaurant with a mannerist menu is a pleasant but puzzling place. Chef Jean-Marc Notelet is an able cook who likes to play with exotic spices, as seen in dishes such as his starter salad of grated white cabbage with tiny, sweet banana or lamb tagine accented with tamarind paste and ornamented with various dried fruits and nuts. Tasty food, but the one-off exotic note isn't really enough to make for an interesting meal. To be fair, dishes such as John Dory in a spiced bouillon or Tarbes beans with pork belly are alluring and satisfying, as are desserts such as coffee-spiked crème brûlée, but the kitchen's raciness doesn't completely work in an uptight dining room full of bankers. Further complicating things are a ferociously expensive wine list and service that's apparently been coached to isolate anyone who isn't wearing a tie into a charmless, draughty corner by the bar (we asked for another table but were told that they were all booked, a silly fib revealed as such).

Le Mandalay

35 rue Carnot, Levallois-Perret (01.45.57.68.69). M° Louise-Michel. **Open** noon-2.30pm, 7.30-10.30pm Tue-Sat. Closed Aug. **Average** €40. **Prix fixe** €30. **Credit** AmEx, MC, V. **Wheelchair access.**

One of the hottest restaurants in the Paris area is somewhat improbably tucked away in a quiet street in suburban Levallois-Perret. As word of mouth has spread, this place has filled up with gastronomically expectant young couples waiting to be impressed. Most of the time they don't go away disappointed, since the international menu that visits all points of the compass – from Brittany to India, and occasionally Japan, with stops in Africa and the Indian Ocean – provides a curious but appetising and creatively coherent meal. Start with crispy fried crab- and mango-stuffed spring rolls, the shellfish ravioli 'blanquette'-style in coconut milk, and green curry or seaweed salad with wasabi. Then sample a delicious steak cooked with coffee, duck in satay sauce or bream in chop suey-style vegetables. Though many of the dishes served here are original, the fusion they represent is so total as to bring the style very near to Creole cooking as found in the Indian Ocean. Friendly, efficient service and a good wine list, including several nice South African bottles, round out the pleasure of a meal here.

Regional

You might not notice it at first, but most of the finest bistros in Paris have some regional slant, be it Basque (a region that has produced an inordinate number of gifted chefs, such as Stéphane Jego of L'Ami Jean and Christian Etchebest of Le Troquet) or Breton, as at Chez Michel. Some restaurants fly the regional flag higher than others, though, and those that serve as ambassadors for a particular area are listed in this chapter. A meal in one of these restaurants will whizz you across the French countryside faster than the TGV.

ALSACE

Alsace's schizo-identity (it was alternately French and German four times between 1870 and 1945) is abundantly apparent in its cuisine: a German hardiness coupled with a French elegance. Local ingredients star alongside items introduced by Jewish immigrants – such as certain spices, foie gras and chocolate. Alsace's signature dish is choucroute (sauerkraut) – spiced, salt-pickled cabbage traditionally topped with sausage, ham and pork. Both beer and local wine are poured into the culinary equation in dishes such as beer-braised ham hock, wine-soaked truite au riesling and the meaty (and potatoey) bäckaofa. The region is also renowned for its charcuterie, freshwater fish, munster cheese, and fragrant white wines such as riesling, silvaner and gewürztraminer. Brasseries (see p86) originated in Alsace so you can be sure of finding (Alsatian) things that make you go 'woof' there, while renowned Strasbourg chef Antoine Westermann has opened the bistro Mon Vieil Ami (see p35) with his protégé Antony Clémot on the Ile St-Louis.

Chez Jenny

39 bd du Temple, 3rd (01.44.54.39.00/www.chez-jenny.com). M° République. **Open** noon-midnight Mon-Thur, Sun; noon-1am Fri, Sat. Closed 15 June-18 Aug. **Average** €24. **Prix fixe** €25, €28. **Credit** AmEx, DC, MC, V. **Wheelchair access**. **Non-smoking room**. **Map** L5.
Having booked our table we could happily bypass the queue of waiting punters to enjoy an extended family Sunday lunch in this popular Alsatian brasserie. These events are always fraught with problems. Will Granny enjoy the place? Will everyone decide what to eat before the staff gives up on us? As it was, our charming waitress was patience itself and allowed us time to enjoy an aperitif maison, the royal griotte – kir with attitude. Dressed in vaguely Alsatian costume, in keeping with the superb marquetry by Charles Spindler, she quickly guided our bewildered table towards platters of mixed Brittany oysters, whose briny freshness impressed all. This was followed by a massive choucroute Jenny for most of the table. Tension rose as Granny tucked in – choucroute, as she had remarked several times, was one of her most successful and revered specialities. But as she suspiciously forked some of the preserved cabbage into her mouth, a beatific smile came over her face, bringing sighs of relief all around. 'Not bad,' was what she actually said, but no praise could be higher for Jenny's signature dish, laden with sausages and pork produce of all sorts. A couple of bottles of top-quality Altenberg riesling put us in the mood for puddings. Crème brûlée seemed to have been prepared too long ahead of time, but the blueberry tart was a real Alsatian treat and Granny's café liegeois was finished with a speed that only pensioners can manage.

AUVERGNE & LIMOUSIN

France's mountainous central region is famous not only for its folklore but also its foodlore: hale and hearty cooking that's perfect when winter winds are howling. Cured hams and sausages, sturdy soups and stews feature along with prime Salers and Limousin beef, aligot (a creamy mix of mashed potatoes, garlic and tomme cheese served in long strands straight from the pan) and lentils. Auvergnat chefs have stacks of 'insider knowledge' - skilfully stuffing cabbage with pork, veal with sausage meat, and ravioli with local cantal cheese. Other local cheeses include bleu d'auvergne, st-nectaire and fourme d'ambert, which team well with St-Pourçain, a fruity red wine. As Auvergnats own many Paris cafés, regional produce often features on café menus as well as in bistros such as Chez Savy and Au Bon St-Pourçain (see pp24-74 **Bistros**).

L'Ambassade d'Auvergne ★

22 rue du Grenier St-Lazare, 3rd (01.42.72.31.22/ www.ambassade-auvergne.com). M° Rambuteau. **Open** noon-2pm, 7.30-10.30pm daily. Closed Sun mid July-mid Aug. **Average** €35. **Prix fixe** €27. **Credit** AmEx, MC, V. **Non-smoking room**. **Map** K5.
The Auvergne, a mysterious volcanic region of central France, is perhaps best known for one ingredient: lentils. A bit ho-hum, perhaps, or so you might think until you've tasted the Puy lentils tossed

with bacon and shallots and smothered in goose fat at L'Ambassade d'Auvergne, a country inn on the fringes of the Marais. The waiters charmingly refer to this dish as a salad, and you can think of it this way as you help yourself again and again from the big earthenware bowl that will be left on your white linen-draped table. The light eater of our twosome unearthed a salad (green leaves this time) with melting cabécou cheese and turbot with braised fennel from the otherwise hearty menu, while the guiltless gourmand tucked into the lentils, followed by côtelettes de canard (duck breast with the bone still attached) and sautéed oyster mushrooms. Often bland, these mushrooms were imbued here with meat jus to become wonderfully savoury; however, too much salt overpowered the dish. An iced parfait made with marc de prune, a regional eau-de-vie, provided the perfect ending to a reasonably priced meal (around €35 per person) made all the more enjoyable by the quirky maître d'. A word about the wines: there is a reason why the Auvergne is a little-known wine region, so you might be better off with something from elsewhere.

Bath's

9 rue de la Trémoille, 8th (01.40.70.01.09/www. baths.fr). M° Alma-Marceau. **Open** noon-2.30pm, 7-10.30pm Mon-Fri. Closed Aug. **Average** €60. **Prix fixe** €70. **Lunch menu** €30. **Credit** AmEx, DC, MC, V. **Wheelchair access**. **Non-smoking room. Map** D4.

Jean-Yves Bath was a bright star of the Clermont-Ferrand restaurant scene and Auvergne is never far from his culinary thoughts, but this is a serious, sophisticated restaurant where country dishes are reinterpreted with a light, modern touch. The dining room, where abstract art meets country house hotel, is not the happiest piece of interior design, but the welcome is genuinely warm. The lentil soup with pan-fried morsels of foie gras and slices of pungent black truffle was the sort of heady broth that nobody's granny ever served, while the ravioli stuffed with cantal cheese in a meat reduction were as light and melting as Chinese dim sum. Main courses were equally inventive, with a crispy and gelatinous pig's trotter Tatin and a quality fillet of Salers beef accompanied by virtuoso 'chips' of breaded cheese. It is unlikely that you will come across finer puddings in the capital; biscotin à la vanille with wild strawberries and a dollop of basil ice-cream was sublime (the biscotin being a hot puff pastry parcel oozing fragrant warm vanilla custard). We were equally enchanted with an Irish coffee-flavoured pavé glacé accompanied by whisky jelly. With a bottle of unusual chardonnay from the Auvergne (€27), we found the hefty bill competitive for the standard of cooking.

BRITTANY

Brittany's best-known staple is the ubiquitous crêpe and its buckwheat cousin, the galette, which serve as both main course and dessert, usually washed down with cider. Coastal Brittany also produces an abundance of top fish and shellfish – look out for conger eel, Cancale oysters, mussels and Breton lobster (*see also pp130-135*, **Fish & Seafood**). Also highly regarded are artichokes, sea salt crystals from the Guérande peninsula, pork products such as andouille (tripe sausage), and salt-marsh lamb from Belle-Ile and Mont St-Michel. Paris has plenty of crêperies to choose from – seek out the ones where the crêpes are made to order (and not reheated) and the cider is served in earthenware tumblers called bolées.

Crêperie Bretonne Fleurie

67 rue de Charonne, 11th (01.43.55.62.29). M° Ledru-Rollin or Charonne. **Open** noon-3pm, 7pm-midnight Mon-Fri; 7pm-midnight Sat. **Average** €11. **Credit** MC, V. **Map** M7.

Was it a stick-on beard? No, everything about this restaurant is authentic, including the crêpe chef's pointy chin thatch, wiggly pipe and striped sailor shirt. It has been amazingly quiet on our lunch visits, giving us plenty of space at the long, dark-wood benches with hinged lids to conceal hidden treasures. The menu at Bretonne Fleurie is reassuringly straightforward: to fill your savoury, freshly cooked buckwheat galette, you can choose a ham, cheese and egg combination (all three is a complète), andouille (tripe sausage) or the more inventive camembert with walnuts. The complète comes beautifully presented in a perfect square, topped off with a gleaming egg yolk, while the camembert variation stops short of overpowering. Old-fashioned manners prevailed: the sashaying waitress served the ladies first while the gents politely contemplated the Celtic flags, Breton Tintin book, black-and-white photos and puzzling tribal mask. Dessert crêpes were perhaps a little too crisp around the edges, but the oozy pear-and-chocolate and banana-and-chocolate fillings made up for it. Dry cider would have been the logical accompaniment, but we couldn't resist the Breton Breizh cola in its nifty glass bottle.

BURGUNDY

Burgundy's long history, wealth and world-famous wines have given rise to one of France's most refined and renowned regional cuisines. Even if many of the foods traditionally associated with the region, including snails (dubbed the oysters of Burgundy), frog's legs and mustard, are now imported and locally prepared, there is some produce, such as tangy époisses cheese, that remains distinctly local. Much of the cooking originated as farm food: jambon persillé (chunks of ham in a parsleyed aspic jelly), and oeufs en meurette (poached eggs in a red wine sauce with onions, mushrooms and bacon), as well as real classics such as coq au vin and boeuf bourguignon. Dijon is also famous for its pain d'épices, a spice bread recipe dating from the Middle Ages, and kir, the aperitif of blackcurrant liqueur and dry aligoté wine.

Crêperie Bretonne Fleurie. *See p120.*

Au Bourguignon du Marais

52 rue François-Miron, 4th (01.48.87.15.40). M° Pont Marie or St-Paul. **Open** 7.30-11pm Mon-Fri. Closed public holidays. **Average** €35. **Credit** AmEx, DC, MC, V. **Map** K6.

The long, wicker-furnished room feels very cosmopolitan and, with two tables of American tourists, it was only the arrival of a plateful of gougères, puffy cheese choux pastry, that reminded us which region is being explored at this popular Marais address. The menu is simple and appealing, prepared in a tiny galley kitchen at the back of the restaurant. From the starters, which include the classic Burgundy snails, oeufs en meurette, and jambon persillé, we chose the latter: a good version of the jellied ham speciality, served with lots of salad and some mango compote. Real fans of this starter might have wished for more parsley and jelly to avoid a rather too stolid texture. The main courses are generally simple with a good-quality andouillette and some garlicky sauté potatoes, but the blackboard special, a fricassée de langoustines with a galette de pied de porc, promised rather more than the kitchen could deliver, the galette being a hard unappealing version of British pork scratchings, and the langoustines lacking that freshly caught zing, but maybe we had strayed too far from the flinty hills of Burgundy. Things got back on track with a plate of ripe époisses, Napoleon's favourite cheese, accompanied by a Burgundy pinot noir. Both wine and cheese showed that products are carefully bought here, and on a future visit we will explore the short but expensive wine list and stay with the simpler items on the charmingly served carte.

Tante Jeanne

116 bd Péreire, 17th (01.43.80.88.68). M° Péreire. **Open** noon-2.30pm, 7-10.30pm Mon-Fri. Closed Aug and bank holidays. **Average** €65. **Prix fixe** €40 (dinner only). **Lunch menu** €34. **Credit** AmEx, DC, MC, V. **Wheelchair access.**

Something is missing at this elegant Burgundian address. And it's not just Bernard Loiseau, the chef who took his life in 2003, who continues to smile at diners from the cover of his cookbook in the dining room's display case. The service remains polished and attentive, the room itself still rustles with refinement, but it feels as if the soul of this restaurant has been lost. The food is at its best proficient, and at its worst lacklustre and unbalanced. A subtle artichoke ravioli was overpowered by a hazelnut-infused milk that was, at once, too nutty and too milky. Batons of marinated leek coated with a heavy garlic-cream dressing propped up three tired prawns. Veal cooked in salted butter and served with caramelised salsify was artfully presented and well-cooked, but it lacked the sparkling flavour that one expects from a restaurant with a doorman. The formidable wine list included a compelling selection of fine Burgundian wines, but the sommelier did not seem equal to the task, suggesting an Irancy from the Yonne region that, for all its smoky complexity,

was too pungent for the menu we had ordered. This restaurant has all the right elements. It just needs to be rejuvenated by a new identity and a new energy.
Branches: Tante Marguerite, 5 rue de Bourgogne, 7th (01.45.51.79.42); Tante Louise, 41 rue Boissy-d'Anglas, 8th (01.42.65.06.85).

CORSICA

As distinctive as the Corsicans themselves, the robust food of this rocky island features aromatic herbs, soft white brocciu cheese (the Corsican version of ricotta, made with goat's milk in summer and ewe's milk in winter), cured meats, chestnuts, kid, lamb and wild boar (in season). The cooking reflects the island's two habitats, wild mountain and rugged coast, with a limited number of fish and shellfish dishes. As a result of the Genoese rule, there are Italian-inspired preparations, such as aubergine gratin or brocciu and tomato salad. Chestnut flour (courtesy of the chestnut forests) is used as a substitute for wheat flour in an earthy-looking polenta. Wine growing dates back to Phoenician times, producing zesty reds, whites and rosés.

L'Alivi

27 rue du Roi-de-Sicile, 4th (01.48.87.90.20/www.restaurant-alivi.com). M° Hôtel de Ville. **Open** noon-2.30pm, 7-11pm daily. **Average** €30. **Prix fixe** €20 (dinner only). **Lunch menu** €15. **Credit** AmEx, MC, V. **Map** K6.

This popular spot hidden in the narrow streets of the Marais gives Corsican cuisine a touch of elegance. The big windows of the airy main room with its thick overhead beams, pale stone walls and tiled floors look on to a tiny and olive-treed street-side terrace. The upmarket crowd of serious food lovers is spaced far enough apart so that the risk of nose-bopping – when you gesticulate enthusiastically over the tangy selection of mountain cheeses, for instance – is minimised. The €20 two-course menu offers good value (a tarte aux herbes came packed with fresh flavour and we followed it with a smooth aubergine gratin stuffed with melting sheep's cheese) but it tends not to include the dishes for which Corsica is famous. It's worth splurging a little to sample innovative interpretations of classic ingredients (such as chestnut-laced duck pâté or sizzled tuna with chickpea flour galettes), as well as top-notch standards (plates of refined charcuterie or wild boar civet, one of the seasonal specials, and, of course, the selection of truly superior cheeses). There are lots of excellent AOC wines, all Corsican of course, and the local Colomba beer – bursting with chestnut and maquis herbs – is well worth a guzzle. As long as Corsica's separatist ambitions are thwarted, it offers one of the best regional cuisines France has to offer.

Le Cosi

9 rue Cujas, 5th (01.43.29.20.20). M° Cluny-La Sorbonne or RER Luxembourg. **Open** noon-2.30pm, 7.45-11pm Mon-Sat. Closed Aug. **Average** €45. **Lunch menu** €15, €20. **Credit** MC, V. **Non-smoking room. Map** J8.

French Cuisine

Russet-coloured, Latin Quarter Cosi soon makes you want to head for the Ile de Beauté, with its tempting bottles of olive oil, photos and a bookshelf of coffee table guides to the island, but it does its regionalism without overkill, meaning that you don't feel you have to be Corsican to come here. The food reflects both mountain peasant food and Mediterranean vegetable and fish preparations, varying from rustic – and sometimes rather heavy – to sophisticated. A sustaining soupe au figatelli, made with white beans and slices of figatelli, the pungent, near-black, smoked liver sausage that is the most distinctive of all Corsican charcuterie, and a lighter, warm herby tomato tart were typical of these contrasts. Main courses showed a similar range with medallions of monkfish, Italianate rigatoni pasta with aubergines (Corsica was long under Genoese rule) and a copious tianu stew of white beans, tomatoes and pork served in a terracotta dish, a sort of Corsican cassoulet. Follow advice on the unfamiliar wines – we had an excellent red Clos Reginu E Prove from near Calvi.

Vivario ★

6 rue Cochin, 5th (01.43.25.08.19). M° Maubert-Mutualité. **Open** 7.30pm-midnight Mon-Sat. **Average** €22. **Credit** AmEx, MC, V. **Map** K7.
Entering this tiny beamed and stone-walled nook, a quiet street in from the Seine, you're immediately struck by its understated warmth and the friendly neighbourliness of its tightly packed tables. With many diners confirmed regulars, there is a pleasantly no-nonsense attitude to service and space: just settle in, like everyone else, for a relaxed evening of good food. There's nothing better than a plate of fine charcuterie to set the Corsican mood and Vivario imports only the best of the island's smoked, dried and home-cured meats. Pair it with some juicy tomatoes with brocciu (if you're in the mood for sharing) to add some veg to your otherwise meaty night. The evening we visited they had already run out of the popular stuffed cabri (kid) so we settled for a magnificent roasted chicken, encrusted in flavour-packed herbs (thyme and rosemary were predominant) and coarse sea salt with a side of crisped, roughly cut potatoes. Other tasty choices included a generous cocotte de veau and chunks of tender stewed lamb. We fantasised about dessert only to discover that by the time we'd quaffed the last of our strong red Fiumicicoli (a good bet at €23.50 a bottle) the kitchen was closed and our meal abruptly ended. No one rushed us out, though, so we soaked up a bit more conviviality with our coffee before heading into the brisk night.

Paris Main d'Or

133 rue du Fbg-St-Antoine, 11th (01.44.68.04.68). M° Ledru-Rollin. **Open** noon-3pm, 8-11pm Mon-Sat. Closed one week at Christmas. **Average** €25. **Lunch menu** €11. **Credit** MC, V. **Non-smoking room**. **Map** M7.
The Paris Main d'Or, named after a diminutive adjacent street not a gold-fingered gangster, is a jam-packed temple to everything that's good about

Corsican cuisine: fabulous charcuterie, gamey roast meats, robust fish and lots of brocciu, a soft white cheese that features liberally in both starters and mains. We arrived just after 10pm, but still had to wait half an hour for a table; just enough time, in other words, to digest the full allure of the menu. We opted (after a copious plate of tasty saucisson and cured ham and a richly fishy suppa di pesci) for intense and meaty mains: a daube de boeuf, melting in a sauce of sturdy Corsican red and served without pretension in a brim-full stoneware pot, plus an incomparable version of the island's justly famous cabri, three generous slices of juicy yet crisply roasted kid paired with a hearty portion of roast potatoes. Vegetarians are likewise well served by the brocciu-stuffed courgettes. For dessert, try the local version of alcoholic tiramisu. Despite the uninspired decor and recent expansion, the place exudes an overwhelming Mediterranean charm and, even at the end of a long night, an engaging, southern-accented hospitality. After a few glasses of local wine (another of Corsica's enviable exports) you'll feel right at home – if home, that is, ever tasted this good.

LYON

Lyon, the traditional gateway dividing north and south, earned its reputation as a gastronomic capital during the second half of the 19th century with the development of the bouchon, a small bistro that served simple home cooking at any time of day. While few genuine bouchons remain, Lyon's culinary emissaries in Paris continue to serve up the kind of hearty, homely fare common in Lyonnais homes. Go armed with an insatiable appetite: typical dishes include warm potato salad with sausage slices, tripe in various forms (andouillette à la lyonnaise or tablier de sapeur), gratin dauphinois (potatoes cooked with cream) and poulet de Bresse.

Aux Lyonnais ★

32 rue St-Marc, 2nd (01.42.96.65.04). M° Bourse or Richelieu-Drouot. **Open** noon-2pm, 7.30-11pm Tue-Fri. Closed Aug, one week at Christmas. **Average** €40. **Prix fixe** €28. **Credit** AmEx, MC, V. **Map** H4.
When France's most successful chef Alain Ducasse took over this place with Thierry de la Brosse of L'Ami Louis, they had the humility and good taste to leave the unique Majorelle interior with splendid belle époque tiles intact. In it, they have created one of the best bistros in Paris. The young staff are keen, friendly and professional (look out for the sommelier's backroom-chic, brown leather apron) and the food is outstanding. The surprisingly light sabodet sausage with leeks and gribiche sauce, and the luscious sucking pig confit with foie gras are star starters. But the most uplifting for us this time was a small orange 'cocotte' of autumn vegetables. Vegetables don't often get to be things like 'intense' and 'comforting', but they were here. Next we had to have the quenelle (pike-perch dumplings) with crayfish, basically because of the name: 'Lucien

Tendret's recipe of 1892'. It was subtle and light, giving the lie to Lyon's reputation for hefty cooking. Black pudding with mashed potatoes, served, like the veggies, in a solid piece of kitchenware, was everything you could expect from this French staple. For pudding, we went for a waffle with orange flower water and quince marmalade, which was pretty good but not as amazing as the soufflé with Cointreau. Pure delight. As for the wine, leather apron or no leather apron, we turned down the sommelier's first suggestions which were all around the €60 mark. Our €30 Fleurie Beaujolais was fine. Something for €23 might have been better still.

Moissonnier

28 rue des Fossés-St-Bernard, 5th (01.43.29.87.65). M° *Cardinal Lemoine.* **Open** noon-2pm, 7.30-10pm Tue-Sat. Closed 24, 25 Dec. **Average** €35. **Lunch menu** €23 (Tue-Fri). **Credit** MC, V. **Map** K8.
Moissonnier, with its red leather banquettes and bright interior, has for many years stylishly upheld the cooking of Lyon. At lunchtime a mixture of

informed tourists and seriously greedy academics from the Jussieu university campus were sitting down to enjoy a gastronomic experience that leaves any afternoon activity seriously compromised. Begin your exploration of this region's cooking with the saladiers lyonnais. Twelve bowls will be wheeled towards you, but put aside any idea that salads are a low-calorie option, for this feast includes not only mushrooms, lentils and celeriac, but also tripe, pied de porc and various sausages, not to mention some meaty, well-seasoned rillettes and winning soused herrings. By this time your appetite should be well and truly open for a tablier de sapeur, a rare dish that is to tripe what wiener schnitzel is to veal, only here served with a rich sauce gribiche; or you could try the puffy expanse of quenelles de brochet floating in a torrid pool of seafood sauce. Bypassing Lyon you could also enjoy a simple grilled fish or steak, accompanied by the richest of potato gratins, weeping cream and garlic. By now, even buoyed by a carafe of light Coteaux du Lyonnais, your body should reject the idea of a

Aux Lyonnais. *See p123.*

traditional but carefully prepared pudding in favour of a long walk in the nearby Jardin des Plantes. Alternatively you could diet tomorrow, as the charming patronne suggested.

L'Opportun ★

64 bd Edgar Quinet, 14th (01.43.20.26.29).
Mº Edgar Quinet. **Open** 10am-midnight Mon-Sat.
Average €35. **Credit** AmEx, DC, MC, V. **Non-smoking room. Map** G9.

Corpulent owner-chef Serge Alzérat is passionate about Beaujolais, dubbing his convivial cream and yellow restaurant a centre of 'beaujolaistherapy' and a place for 'the prevention of thirst'. He's also an advocate for good, honest Lyonnais food. Thus his menu is littered with the likes of sabodet (thick pork sausage) with a purée of split peas, duck skin salad, tête de veau (a favourite of President Chirac whose photo graces the walls) and meat, lots of it. There's a lightweight 250g veal or beef onglet or, if you need a heftier protein fix, there's a 400g version, both served with mounds of savoury cabbage dotted with

bacon and crusty, baked potatoes. Starters are just as generous: a salad of dandelion leaves with roasted tomatoes, bacon chunks and a runny poached egg, and rounds of lightly toasted chèvre, accompanied by thick slices of ham and apple. Fromage fans should skip dessert and try the st-marcellin by Roanne's master cheesemaker Hervé Mons.

Chez Fred

190 bis bd Péreire, 17th (01.45.74.20.48). Mº Pereire or Porte Maillot. **Open** noon-2.30pm, 7.30-11pm Mon-Sat. Closed Christmas and New Year. **Average** €40. **Prix fixe** €28. **Credit** MC, V. **Map** C2.

Chez Fred has an unprepossessing ring to it in English, but this bouchon lyonnais near the Porte Maillot is well worth a visit. The room smells inviting with a table of hors d'oeuvres, cheese and puddings to greet you on entering. There is a warm, informal atmosphere to match, with marble-topped tables and lively attentive service, obviously much appreciated by a regular business crowd at lunchtime. After some tasty saucisson, we began our meal with a classic jambon persillé, which was moist and vibrant, with fresh parsley strewn on top for extra herby effect. The home-made terrine was also a real winner, moist and rich with just the right fat content. For one of our main courses we went for the plat du jour, a petit salé aux lentilles, with a generous helping of different joints of ham on a tender yet still shapely bed of lentils. The menu lists a number of lyonnais specialities and we couldn't resist the quenelle de brochet, a giant pike-perch dumpling gently absorbing a lake of lobster sauce. It's not a light dish, but here it was unusually flavoursome and comforting. Hitting our gastronomic stride we waddled for home with a melting slice of freshly baked fig tart, and a selection of perfectly matured cheese to finish up our fruity bottle of Beaujolais.

NORMANDY

Dairy produce and apples are the hallmarks of Normandy fare. While the famed creamy sauces of the region are frequently flavoured with refreshing local cider or Calvados (a potent apple brandy), the cheeses, including cow's milk cheeses camembert, livarot, neufchâtel and pont l'évêque, stand firmly alone. Despite the fields of cows – the dairy godmothers – pork is the favoured meat, and fruits, particularly apples and pears, act as a pleasantly sharp foil to the richness. Seafood also features in moules marinières, marmite dieppoise (fish stew) and sole normande.

Les Fernandises

19 rue de la Fontaine-au-Roi, 11th (01.48.06.16.96). M° République. **Open** noon-2.30pm, 7.30-11pm Tue-Sat. Closed one week in May, Aug. **Average** €30. **Prix fixe** €22 (dinner only). **Credit** MC, V. **Map** M4. Perfect camemberts are rare, but at Fernand Asseline's convivial bistro the selection of Normandy's finest – oozing, unctuous and ripened in-house – is virtually unbeatable. A large wooden platter was left at our table and no one grumbled when we carved a healthy slice of each of the eight varieties. Those doused in Calvados and lie de vin (wine sediment) were superb, the 'noix' (walnut) satisfyingly earthy, and the 'nature' a must for the purist, but the best surprise was 'foin' (delicately coated in hay). Pre-cheese treats included poultry-laden starters – a warm lentil salad laced with strips of tender duck and chicken livers – a nicely crisped duck breast paired with gratin dauphinois, and a tasty roast pigeon. For dessert there are scrumptious cider crêpes and a tarte aux pommes flambées that's well worth ordering for the spectacle of the two-minute flame dance. The wine list is reasonably priced and there is a good selection of Calvados.

NORTH

The hardy cooking of Picardy and Flanders is closely linked to that of neighbouring Belgium. Wine makes way for beer both at the table and in dishes such as carbonnade, a stew usually made with beef.

The classic Belgian moules-frites (mussels with chips) pops up in northern French cities such as Lille along with another import, waterzooï, a stew of chicken or fish and vegetables. A favourite side dish is braised chicory, known as chicon. Also on offer are the pungent northern cheeses such as maroilles, deep-orange mimolette (known as 'hollande' in the north) and, for the truly brave, sharp and salty vieux lille. Sweets include spice breads and speculoos, crunchy spice biscuits served with coffee.

Graindorge

15 rue de l'Arc de Triomphe, 17th (01.47.54.00.28). M° Charles de Gaulle-Etoile. **Open** noon-2pm, 7-11pm Mon-Fri; 7-11pm Sat. Closed Aug. **Average** €30. **Lunch menu** €28. **Credit** AmEx, MC, V. **Wheelchair access. Non-smoking room. Map** C3. The cuisine of the north is probably one of the least known in France, yet chef Bernard Broux makes it well worth discovering in his comfortable, art deco-inspired restaurant. Broux is from Lille and he treats the area's Franco-Flemish ancestry with quality produce and a light touch. We started with a cep pâté, resembling an airy egg and mushroom mousse in a deep-green parsley emulsion, and a pink terrine of Challans duck around a lozenge of foie gras. Main courses took an elegant spin on Flemish classics. Our guinea fowl braised in Gueuze beer was served in two ways: an aumônière of shredded breast meat with pine kernels in a bundle of filo pastry and a roast leg with an appetising mound of fresh broad beans. The waterzooï de la mer, a bowl laden with prawns, two types of fish, julienned carrots, leeks and boiled potatoes in a soup-like pink sauce, was a marine version of the Flemish meal in a dish. Desserts include apple crumble, a chocolate fondant with speculoos, and café liégeois, as well as a selection of northern cheeses. Our fellow lunchtime diners consisted mainly of a chatty business crew, but this is the sort of place where they greet you with equanimity whether you are in a suit or not.

PROVENCE & SOUTH

Mediterranean cuisine's rapid rise to fame has contributed to a variety of misconceptions about southern French cooking. While it's true that olive oil is almost always used in preference to butter, and that garlic, tomatoes, courgettes and aubergines appear in many recipes, the cuisine is varied and often more delicate than is popularly thought. Fish, vegetables and pasta figure in the cooking of the Riviera and Provence. Signature dishes include bouillabaisse (a once humble fishermen's soup, made from the lowliest part of the catch, which has become emblematic of Marseille); les petits farcis (baby vegetables stuffed with meat, vegetables and breadcrumbs); and aïoli, a garlic mayonnaise served with boiled cod and vegetables. From Montpellier to the Spanish border, the Italian influence yields to Catalan dishes, reflecting the fact that Perpignan to the Pyrenees was once part of this Spanish province.

La Bastide Odéon ★

7 rue Corneille, 6th (01.43.26.03.65/www.
bastide-odeon.com). Mᵒ Odéon. **Open** 12.30-
2pm, 7.30-10.30pm Tue-Sat. Closed Aug, 24, 25
Dec, 1 Jan. **Average** €38. **Prix fixe** €36.60.
Credit AmEx, MC, V. **Wheelchair access**.
Map H7.

It's not just its position tucked neatly beside the
Odéon theatre and seconds from the Jardins du
Luxembourg that draws well-dressed Parisians and
international visitors to the Bastide Odéon. It has
also discreetly become one of the most consistently
reliable addresses in the area, with its pleasant
service and modern spin on terroir. Although the
name and yellow- and russet-coloured decor suggest
Provence, chef Gilles Ajuelos' cooking is full of
southern inspiration rather than southern cliché. He
spreads his net right along the Mediterranean
seaboard (ingredients include feta, dates and
polenta) and beyond – the Bastide Odéon is one of
the rare places in France where you can eat British
Hereford beef – as he mixes stalwarts like pieds
et paquets with some more unusual combinations,
and ever-present herbs. Iberico ham with grilled
poivrons and artichokes, and a mille-feuille of
tomato and ricotta were pleasant starters before a
successfully tangy grey mullet with wild capers,
lemon, olives and tomato in a veal jus reduction, and
our long-time favourite of roast farm chicken with
whole cloves of preserved garlic and new potatoes
– simple but delicious. The attractively presented
desserts were good too: a mille-feuille with bourbon
vanilla and a saffron-tinted poached pear with
fromage blanc ice-cream.

Pataquès

40-42 bd de Bercy, 12th (01.43.07.37.75). Mᵒ Bercy.
Open 12.30-2pm, 7.30-10.30pm Tue-Sat. Closed three
weeks in Aug, Christmas and New Year. **Average**
€28. **Prix fixe** €21.50, €22. **Lunch menu** €12.80,
€13.50. **Credit** AmEx, DC, MC, V. **Non-smoking
room**. **Map** N9.

With its sun-inspired yellow and orange walls,
Pataquès does a good job of imitating the breeziness
of the south, abetted by its Provence-meets-Italy
menu: aubergine parmigiana, salmon ravioli, pistou
soup and salt cod lasagne. A starter of fresh sardines
stuffed with raisins and caramelised onions,
wrapped in pastry and deep-fried, served with green
salad, was a good choice but the grilled langoustine
tails were meagre, underdone, swamped by a pesto
sauce and hidden beneath a hill of salad leaves. Not
worth the price supplement. A swordfish main came
crumbed and fried (and served again with green
salad) and we couldn't help wondering why fry
when grilling seems a more sympathetic end for this
fleshy fish? No complaints about the rosy-pink
honeyed duckling with beans, though. To finish off,
patiences d'Aix (a biscuity house version of the
almond-flavoured calissons d'Aix) served with
creamy nougat ice-cream and sweet raspberry sauce
was summer on a plate.

SAVOIE & FRANCHE-COMTE

If Savoie is best known for its superb cheeses,
including beaufort, reblochon, tomme de Savoie and
the rare bleu de gex, there is much more to the
region's menu than the fondue and raclette that have
become its claim to culinary fame. Fishermen land
crayfish and omble chevalier (the delicate, much-
prized char lakefish). Crozettes, tiny squares of
buckwheat pasta, are eaten buttered with grated
cheese. Fine quality charcuterie includes viande des
Grisons (air-dried beef) and smoked sausage. Gratin
dauphinois and ravioles de Royans, tiny cheese-
stuffed ravioli from the Vercors, denote the adjacent
Dauphiné, while Mondeuse, a hearty red, is the best-
known Savoyard wine. The Franche-Comté's rich
pastures yield a variety of excellent cheeses. Smoked
Morteau and Montbéliard sausages are served with
warm potato salad, and excellent wines are produced
around Arbois, including the sherry-like vin jaune.

Alexandre

24 rue de la Parcheminerie, 5th (01.43.26.49.66).
Mᵒ St-Michel or Cluny La Sorbonne. **Open** 6-
11.30pm daily. Closed 25 Dec. **Average** €15.
Credit MC, V. **Map** J7.

The namesake of this cosy Savoyard restaurant is
Alexandre le Bienheureux, title character of the 1968
Yves Robert film. Rather than toil away on his farm,
Alexandre prefers to spend his days napping while
his industrious dog does his chores for him. His
lackadaisical lifestyle proves contagious in the
village, as it does in this restaurant, where one is
happy to consign oneself to a lumpy red velvet
banquette, listen to pop music on the radio, and
wield a long, skinny fork over one of the three
Savoyard specialities on the menu. The only hard
part about a dinner here is agreeing whether to order
fondue bourguignonne, pierrade or fondue
savoyarde, as each table shares one cooking pot. The
first yields 300g of raw beef to be cooked on skewers
in hot oil. The second results in the same, plus
onions, mushrooms, peppers and tomatoes to be
seared on a stone slab sprinkled with rosemary. The
third presents a bubbling pot of traditional cheese
fondue to be mopped up with cubes of bread. All
three are accompanied by a mixed salad and arrive
with a generous platter of rosemary-scented, golden
potatoes which, like the meat, will be replenished
upon request. There is nothing left but to raise a
plastic squeeze bottle of sauce and enjoy. No
bookings are accepted.

Chez Maître Paul

12 rue Monsieur-le-Prince, 6th (01.43.54.74.59).
Mᵒ Odéon. **Open** 12.15-2.15pm, 7.15-10.30pm daily.
Closed three days at Christmas and Sun, Mon in
July and Aug. **Average** €40. **Prix fixe** €29, €35.
Credit AmEx, DC, MC, V. **Map** H7.

The sweet maître d'hôtel of Chez Maître Paul creates
a feeling of well-being, as do waiters whose attention
to detail includes kindly removing the charred bits
from your mountain of cassoulet. Though the

La Maison de la Lozère.

walnut, comté and lettuce salad was ample, better ways to start were the warm dandelion and bacon salad, fried Jura sausage with potatoes, or a salmon and potato plate with a scrumptious corn galette (sadly, only one). A table of Americans could not resist taking matters into their own hands when it came to tackling the poulette fermière à la crème gratinée, a luscious hunk of chicken smothered in mushroom cheese sauce. Grilled scallops with minced cabbage and its tangy jus was a happy meeting of land and sea. For dessert, we took on a poached pear with eggy sabayon, pineapple sorbet, regional macvin liqueur and toasted almonds.

SOUTH-WEST

Combining Périgord (Dordogne), Bordeaux, Gascony and the Basque country, this part of France is known for its filling yet refined fare. Foie gras, the liver of fattened duck or goose, is a speciality of Gascony and the Dordogne. It is eaten in various guises; often very lightly cooked (mi-cuit) and served cold as a terrine (a foie gras 'pâté' is lower-quality, mixed with pork), or lightly pan-fried so that the inside still quivers. Duck also features heavily: magret is the breast, and confit de canard is duck preserved in its own fat. Another famed dish is cassoulet, a rib-sticking stew of white beans, duck or goose confit, lamb and sausage. Look out, too, for lamb from the Pyrenees. Bordeaux's contributions, unsurprisingly, often contain wine: à la bordelaise implies a red wine sauce. Ceps and pricey truffles from the Périgord are also prized. Basque cuisine is often quite spicy thanks to the addition of Espelette peppers. Try pipérade (scrambled eggs with

peppers, onions and ham), stuffed squid, tuna, delicate, raw-cured jambon de Bayonne, and the ewe's-milk iraty cheese of the Pyrenees.

La Maison de la Lozère ★

4 rue Hautefeuille, 6th (01.43.54.26.64/www.lozere-a-paris.com). M° St-Michel. **Open** noon-2pm, 7.15-10pm Tue-Sat. Closed five weeks in July and Aug. **Average** €23. **Prix fixe** €21, €25.50. **Lunch menu** €14.50, €16. **Credit** MC, V. **Map** J7.
The sparsely populated Lozère, a region of craggy stone houses, rough heather and tough goats on the southern slopes of the Massif Central, hides culinary secrets that its little Paris embassy (there's a regional cultural centre just next door) is bursting to reveal. Cheese aficionados, in particular, need look no further. Our roquefort salad starter was a cavernous bowl of crisp leaves weighed down with moist, crumbly slices of unadulterated blue heaven; a ripe, tangy zap to wake up our taste buds and a bold advertisement of things to come. After succulent mains of garlic-roasted lamb (be sure to eat the melting cloves that clutter the plate) and a lean pork fillet topped with tasty, not too rich black pudding and caramelised apples (we'll be back for more), we settled for an unmatchable dessert of more cheese. The day's selection of gently aged goat and ewe (smoothly fresh to nutty, hard crottins), a cantal and another chunk of blue, six in all, were come-hitherishly laid out on a heaving board that was left at our table long enough to encourage the full taste test; ditto the big loaf of country bread. Be sure to keep some of the robust Cévennes (the good value house red) to ensure that the cheeses achieve maximum flavour. Like the Lozère, this is an

understated, welcoming spot guaranteed to surprise the picky palate while satisfying even the most prodigious appetite. Be prepared to leave addicted.

La Table d'Aude

8 rue de Vaugirard, 6th (01.43.26.36.36). M° Odéon or RER Luxembourg. **Open** noon-2pm Mon; noon-2pm, 7-10pm Tue-Fri; 7-10pm Sat. Closed Aug. **Average** €35. **Prix fixe** €20-€40. **Lunch menu** €8-€26. **Credit** MC, V. **Map** H7.

The rich, decadent classics of south-western cuisine – confit and cassoulet – are what Bernard Patou's Aude outpost is all about. All you need to do is choose between duck and goose and before you can say Castelnaudary – the Languedoc-Roussillon town synonymous with cassoulet perfection – a piping pot of luscious, saucy beans and garlicky sausage topped with a confit thigh (chatty Bernard will advise the goose) will be yours for the eating. Die-hard fans with capacious appetites – perhaps the lunchtime custom lured from the nearby Senate – will find the prospect of a double portion, boldly advertised on the à la carte menu, at once outrageous and irresistible. If you settle for one of the prix fixe options (detailed with all their complex variations on a multi-lingual menu that is, at first glance, impenetrable) then you'll have starters such as occitane salad – rosemaried turkey livers and goose gizzards (a bit too tough for our liking) on a bed of mixed leaves – and sturdy desserts to contend with, as well as aperitifs and wine. Our favourite pud was a towering feuilleté-topped apple pie doused in a fiery, regional marc. Everything is best washed down with a robust Corbières. There is nothing refined about the Aude's table and outside of the cassoulet and confit the food is nothing special; likewise the ambience oddly lacks warmth, but when it comes to beany-fowl indulgence you won't be disappointed.

D'Chez Eux

2 av de Lowendal, 7th (01.47.05.52.55/www.chezeux. com). M° Ecole-Militaire. **Open** noon-2.30pm, 7.30-10.30pm Mon-Sat. Closed three weeks in Aug. **Average** €60. **Lunch menu** €33, €36. **Credit** AmEx, DC, MC, V. **Wheelchair access**. **Non-smoking room**. **Map** E7.

A warm welcome from the owner and long-serving staff are a prelude to a complimentary kir and a hunk of excellent saucisson. The cosseting, interlinked rooms feel comfortingly provincial and the menu is an essay in a certain type of traditional French cuisine. Begin with either the salad trolley, which includes plump fresh anchovies, delicious long-cooked pearl onions plus other delicacies, or the equally tempting range of charcuterie. Our mains included a guinea fowl grand-mère, served in a copper pan and carved at the table on its comfortable bed of potatoes, bacon and mushrooms. If the bird itself was slightly dry, the intensely flavoured jus compensated for this. An enormous slab of calf's liver was coated in a melting mixture of shallots and sharp vinegar. The meat itself was slightly less pink

than ordered, the sort of imprecision which is the downside to this rustic, country approach to big eating, but warming to the experience we tucked into the dessert trolley with gusto: a winning chocolate mousse, creamy vanilla ice-cream and an impressive collection of stewed fruits.

Au Trou Gascon ★

40 rue Taine, 12th (01.43.44.34.26). M° Daumesnil. **Open** noon-2pm, 7.30-10pm Mon-Fri. Closed Aug, 25 Dec-5 Jan. **Average** €65. **Lunch menu** €40. **Credit** AmEx, DC, MC, V. **Wheelchair access**. **Map** P9.

The grey lacquered chairs and modern artworks are sleek and contemporary – although glorious ceiling mouldings add an old world touch – and the cooking is a very classy take on the food of Gascony. But you'd expect nothing less from founder Alain Dutournier, who also runs the high-class Carré des Feuillants. All that is good about the south-west is celebrated, including foie gras, lamb, duck, ham and Madiran wines. Succulent Chalosse chicken came crammed with slices of pungent black truffle balanced by a delicate celeriac purée, while a steaming plate of cassoulet uniting lamb, pork sausage, duck and those peerless Tarbais beans was light years away from the heavy stew that so often bears the name. Starters, including a tart topped with peppery sour cream and scallop carpaccio, and just-cooked Scottish salmon confirmed that chef Jean-François Godiard is expert at highlighting natural flavours. Don't miss the baba landais with sticky vieux garçon liqueur sauce; it's a feathery-light sensation. All this, plus first-rate service and an encyclopaedic wine list means that an excursion into the less tourist-travelled 12th is definitely warranted.

L'Auberge Etchegorry

41 rue de Croulebarbe, 13th (01.44.08.83.51). M° Place d'Italie or Les Gobelins. **Open** noon-2.30pm, 7.30-10.30pm Tue-Sat. Closed 11-25 Aug. **Average** €40. **Prix fixe** €25-€37.60. **Credit** AmEx, MC, V. **Non-smoking room**.

This area was once a rural Paris suburb, and the Auberge a watering hole for literary city slickers like Victor Hugo, Jean de Béranger and Chateaubriand, who'd come here to cut loose and sing a few songs. A century later, the tavern is dwarfed by apartment blocks. Still, owners Maïté and Henri Laborde (who also run the adjacent Le Vert Galant hotel) successfully create a Basque-countrified ambience, from wreaths of garlic and piquillo peppers hanging from the beams to the three dark-red floral curtained dining rooms, plus a quiet outdoor street-side seating area. Look out for succulent confit de canard, tender roast duck breast (both with fantastic pan-fried potatoes and apples), beef fillet with morels, and foie gras, but also lesser-known fare such as the salade Etchegorry, a mixed plate of salmon, liver, bacon and melon, or pipérade, a scrambled egg, tomato, onion and smoked ham mixture. Various chocolate desserts can end the night on a rich note, or try the flaky apple tart with Armagnac ice-cream.

Fish & Seafood

Brasseries (*see pp86-97*) have traditionally sated Parisian longings for a feast of oysters or a gargantuan shellfish platter. For rather more intricate fish and seafood dishes, however, smaller restaurants reel in the diners, from classics such as La Méditérranée and Le Dôme (or its good-value bistros) to Christian Constant's tiny Les Fables de la Fontaine. In most of these restaurants, minimalism wins out over buttery sauces, highlighting the freshness of the catch. The best will always inform you whether the fish is farmed or wild and where it comes from.

L'Estaminet Gaya

17 rue Duphot, 1st (01.42.60.43.03). M° Madeleine or Concorde. **Open** noon-2.30pm, 7-10.30pm Mon-Fri. Closed three weeks in Aug. **Average** €45. **Prix fixe** €32. **Credit** AmEx, MC, V. **Map** G4.

With a handsome decor of vintage yellow, ivory and blue *azuelos* (hand-painted Portuguese tiles), this centrally located seafood house with notably cordial service is a fine bet if you're hankering after a quality maritime feed with an astute creative touch. A good indication of the intelligent modern approach here is the fact that seven different white wines are served by the glass and a large portion of bigorneaux (winkles) arrives as soon as you're seated. Good bread and delicious salted butter pleasantly framed superb first courses – a generous mound of prawns in chive-flecked vinaigrette on a bed of spaghetti squash, and a creamy shellfish gratin (mussels, cockles, baby clams) with gnocchi. Main courses were similarly impressive. A thick tuna steak bound in bacon came on a bed of freshly made ratatouille, while goujonnettes (grilled strips) of sole on rigatoni with oyster mushrooms turned out to be two perfectly de-boned whole fillets rather than the usual dubious little fish fingers. A bowl of raspberries with a big dollop of crème fraîche provided the perfect ending to a very good meal.

Iode

48 rue d'Argout, 2nd (01.42.36.46.45). M° Sentier. **Open** noon-3pm, 6-10.30pm Mon-Fri; 6-11.30pm Sat. Closed 10 days in Aug. **Average** €30. **Lunch menu** €15. **Credit** AmEx, MC, V. **Map** J5.

With an excellent catch-of-the-day blackboard menu offered at very gentle prices, an attractive setting in a hip neighbourhood and an engaging young serving team, this place not far from Les Halles is an ongoing hit. Book one of the terrace tables for a perfect summery feed – recent dishes have run to plump langoustines on a bed of rocket with sautéed slices of andouille, and tuna steak with saffron rice and tomato and rocket salad, both ideal eating on a warm night. Wry, bilingual owner Steve Harcelin has teamed up with husband-and-wife chefs Arnaud and Sandrine Cren, and this trio has succeeded in updating the stuffy and overpriced fish house idiom in Paris. Aside from great quality fish, what makes their approach so appealingly modern is the almost total absence of traditional sauces – instead, beurre noisette, balsamic vinegar, lemon juice and olive oil, in various combinations, stand in for anything heavier, and this allows all the goodness of the fish to come through. The wine list runs too heavily to the Loire Valley, and aside from good crêpes suzette, desserts are not memorable. But these are harmless snags in an otherwise silky performance. Book well in advance.

Le Bistrot Côté Mer

16 bd St-Germain, 5th (01.43.54.59.10/www. bistrocotemer.com). M° Maubert-Mutualité. **Open** noon-2.15pm, 7.30-10.15pm daily. Closed three weeks in Aug. **Average** €40. **Lunch menu** €17, €22. **Credit** AmEx, MC, V. **Map** K7.

'Would you like a seat inside or an ocean view?' the cheerful waiter asked the party next to us. Bistrot Côté Mer may be a block inland from the Seine, but its blue-and-yellow entrance does remind you of a beach cabin, while the interior stone walls could be seaside St-Malo (wave-shaped plates add to the nautical decor). A creamy mushroom amuse-bouche arrived with the menus, which were written on a ceramic platter we were afraid to drop. Skipping standards such as oysters and tuna, we were drawn to ravioli stuffed with scallops, tarama and a trace of ginger; and the crab and lobster nems with a papaya and passion fruit salsa – the former succulent, the latter disappointing given the rather puny portion and unannounced pork overpowering the microscopic seafood bits. Fortunately, the main courses won back our full admiration: sea bass, chard and artichokes in a tangy broth steamed inside an iron pot, and yellow pollack whose crispy skin was nicely accompanied by a green pea sauce, sautéed mustard greens and a winter vegetable mash. Desserts are tasty but also way overpriced (an €11 teacup of tiramisu). Still, given the labour which goes into their preparation, the Grand Marnier crêpes flambéed to caramelised indulgence seemed worth it.

L'Huître et Demie

*80 rue Mouffetard, 5th (01.43.37.98.21). M° Place
Monge.* **Open** noon-2.15pm, 7.30-10.15pm daily.
Average €46. **Prix fixe** €28. **Lunch menu** €11.
Credit AmEx, DC, MC, V. **Non-smoking room.**
Map J8.

We sometimes think that this reasonably priced fish
restaurant on the now disappointingly tacky rue
Mouffetard might be past its sell-by date. The
welcome is warm but the plastic-coated menu makes
you fear the worst, and the coiled mayonnaise
accompanying our langoustines was of a worrying
consistency with no recognisable taste. The quality
of the shellfish, however, was no worse than in a
more expensive brasserie, and some lime-marinated
salmon was excellent and, like the langoustines,
generously served. Main courses included crispy sea
bass in a creamy seafood sauce accompanied by a
fennel bulb that was more than a match for the
traditional fish knife. A neatly tied gigotin de lotte
(monkfish) with lobster butter was overcooked, but
ultimately rich and satisfying. A respectable plate
of cheese, and a flambéed omelette norvégienne
(baked Alaska) from the rather dull list of chocolate
mousse/dame blanche-style puddings completed our
meal, washed down with a drinkable carafe of rosé.
This old-fashioned tourist-driven restaurant still just
about manages to deliver a fish feast that will not
break the bank.

La Méditérranée

*2 pl de l'Odéon, 6th (01.43.26.02.30/www.la-
mediterranee.com). M° Odéon.* **Open** noon-2.30pm,
7.30-11pm daily. Closed 24, 25 Dec. **Average** €45.
Lunch menu €25, €29 (Mon-Fri). **Credit** AmEx,
MC, V. **Non-smoking room.** **Map** H7.

Facing the Théâtre de l'Odéon, this is a pearl of a
restaurant, with murals by Vertès and Bérard in the
dining room and doodlings by Cocteau – a former
customer, along with the likes of Jackie Kennedy and
Picasso – on the plates. It would be easy for a place
like this to rely on its setting to attract customers.
Fortunately, the publishers and aristocrats who lurk
in this area are a discriminating lot, and when
standards slipped a few years ago they jumped ship.
Now the restaurant is making a real effort in the
kitchen, sending out fresh-tasting, well-presented
plates and even offering affordable set menus on
weekdays at lunch. A menu might start with tomato-
goat's cheese tart with avocado salad and continue
with an intriguing dish of scorpion fish roasted with
Morteau sausage and served with raw spinach and
white beans. Ordering from the carte, we couldn't
resist the bouillabaisse, which turned out to be a
rather tame, if tasty, version of the Marseillais
classic, featuring three fish fillets. Sea bass served
with potatoes mashed with olives was a satisfying
choice. Desserts, such as an orange soup flavoured
with Moroccan spices and served with cinnamon ice-
cream, are just as tempting as the fish dishes, so
make sure you save some room. Service was both
friendly and unobtrusive.

Le Divellec

*107 rue de l'Université/Esplanade des Invalides,
7th (01.45.51.91.96). M° Invalides.* **Open** noon-2pm,
7.30-9.30pm Mon-Fri. Closed 25 Dec-1 Jan, 1 May,
Aug. **Average** €120. **Lunch menu** €50, €65.
Credit AmEx, DC, MC, V. **Wheelchair access.**
Non-smoking room. **Map** E5.

In dining terms, Le Divellec stakes out the high
ground that lies somewhere between classic and fine
dining. That means old-school black-suited waiters
laying down complimentary appetisers of tiny grey
prawns, fresh marinated anchovies and oysters with
a tomato gratin, an exhaustive and expensive wine
list (at €37 our sauvignon was a cheapie) and ample
tables of 7th arrondissement seniors. It's all a tad
crusty and very, very pricey, but there's no
mistaking the quality of the produce: meaty Cancale
oysters, fennel-laced salmon tartare, plump scallops
served with a potato pancake, tangy beetroot leaves
and mini vegetables, and thick cod steak in a meaty
wine sauce. Several of the fish, too, are wild rather
than farmed. A giant dessert trolley bulging with
creamy gâteau St-Honoré, chocolate mousse, rum
babas, poached pears and chocolate sauce, fresh
raspberries, apple tart and oeufs à la neige does the
rounds but you've got to be quick – most old dears
demand at least three portions.

Les Fables de la Fontaine ★

*131 rue St-Dominique, 7th (01.44.18.37.55)
M° Ecole Militaire.* **Open** noon-2pm, 8-10.30pm
Tue-Sat. **Average** €36. **Credit** DC, MC, V. **Map** D6.

With this popular seafood house, chef Christian
Constant extends his gastronomic occupation of the
rue St Dominique, where he already has the popular
Café Constant and the pricey Le Violon d'Ingres.
Blue-and-green tiled walls and a big refrigerated
counter immediately announce the maritime
vocation of this tiny 20-seater, and the blackboard
offers a really excellent catch-of-the-day menu at
extremely fair prices. Though Constant swans by at
the end of the service, it's his nephew Olivier Rossi
who runs the kitchen, and Rossi sends out fresh,
appealing, generously served dishes such as starters
of a salad of dressed crabmeat with avocado and
grapefruit, stuffed sardines, and daily specials such
as calamars façon pibale (squid cooked to resemble
the elvers that are a Basque country delicacy).
Typical of the main courses are scallops roasted in
their shells in salted butter, salmon fillet in a robe of
light fish mousse, or a big bowl of mussels. An
assortment of oysters is also available, and the house
bread comes from Poujauran. Desserts run to
pleasant old-fashioned treats such as tarte Tatin,
Paris-Brest and a splendid mille-feuille à la vanille,
and the wine list is short but generous and served
by the glass, carafe or bottle. The €20 muscadet is
uncommonly good. The only snag in the net here is
that you're jammed in elbow to elbow and that there
are two sittings, but it's this turnover that keeps
prices low and if you book the second sitting you
can linger longer.

Marius et Janette

4 av George V, 8th (01.47.23.41.88). M° Alma-Marceau. **Open** noon-2.15pm , 7.30-11pm daily. **Average** €70. **Prix fixe** €60. **Credit** AmEx, DC, MC, V. **Map** D5.

With rather camp portholes and knotty pine marine decor by Slavik, the famous Parisian restaurant designer, this seafooder had become one of those timeless places that no one ever thought about until the arrival of new chef Bernard Pinaud. Working with a superb catch of the day, Pinaud is sending out food that's pulling crowds again, including a superb gazpacho with crabmeat, delicate langoustine-stuffed ravioli, a first-rate aïoli – boiled salt cod with potatoes, carrots, leeks and signature garlic mayonnaise – and John Dory with carrot butter. This excellent cooking and the buzz in the room created by the presence of actor Jean-Paul Belmondo would have made for a truly glamorous, big-splurge night on the town, were it not for the assiduously unpleasant service, which seemed to be directed at English-speaking foreigners. Might we have some potatoes with the aïoli (which is usually served with boiled potatoes)? Dramatic sigh, and a plate of potato purée produced ten minutes later. This rough ride notwithstanding, we'd be back in a heartbeat for the fish, especially if we were in French company and they were paying.

Restaurant Cap Vernet

82 av Marceau, 8th (01.47.20.20.40). M° Charles de Gaulle-Etoile. **Open** noon-2.30pm, 7-11pm Mon-Fri; 7-11pm Sat. Closed 24, 25, 31 Dec and 1 May. **Average** €40. **Prix fixe** €45. **Credit** AmEx, DC, MC, V. **Non-smoking room**. **Map** D4.

We popped in for a late evening meal to this former Guy Savoy outlet, which enjoys a fine reputation for shellfish and modern fish cookery. The interior is bright with the nautical wood and metal effectively imitating a luxury yacht. The short carte has an impressive range of speciality oysters, but from the bank of seafood we chose some langoustines, which were firm and especially fresh. Plump crab ravioli were impressively refined, bathing in a subtle shellfish jus, which had been frothed in the modern manner. A pavé of Scottish salmon was seared on the outside with a rare interior, as requested, accompanied by a pungent ginger butter and some basmati rice, while steamed half-salted cod featured melting flakes of fish sitting astride some potatoes roughly crushed in olive oil, the whole dish scattered with a few slivers of olives. A Picpoul de Pinet was an unusual and reasonably priced white wine from the Languedoc to accompany the seafood. The pudding list looked tempting, including an original pain d'épices with a compote of dried fruits and a scoop of vanilla ice-cream, the perfect ending to a light, highly professional meal. The service remains curious; the front of house is the real thing, but the charming young waitresses lack the professional training one expects for what is a fairly expensive

experience. A starter was forgotten, a change of wine brought no change of glass, a touch of swearing when a cork resisted. Small points, but we would have been embarrassed if this had been a more formal occasion.

Le Bar à Huîtres

112 bd du Montparnasse, 14th (01.43.20.71.01). M° Vavin. **Open** noon-12.30am Mon-Thur, Sun; noon-1.30am Fri, Sat. **Average** €30. **Prix fixe** €23-€36. **Credit** AmEx, DC, MC, V. **Non-smoking room**. **Map** G9.

A relatively new addition to the Montparnasse brasserie strip, Le Bar à Huîtres serves the same style of food as its illustrious neighbours the Dôme and La Coupole, but in more relaxed surroundings. The Jacques Garcia decor consists of lots of wood and regimented clam shells, creating something of an urbane Breton sea shack, and it's great fun to sit up at the circular bar which has an atmosphere of bonhomie. The place seems to have attracted a loyal clientele too, with the party before us being warmly welcomed with 'the usual table?' and the early crowd, strong on Japanese tourists, being gradually replaced by black-clad St-Germain types, gauche young couples and the sort of faces you see on late-night book programmes. The waiter manning the oyster bar was not over-keen to guide us through the menu but confidently claimed anyone could eat oysters providing they were fresh. Our novice oyster-eater duly ploughed through six enormous spéciales claires, a crab and a sea urchin, an

interesting experience with its strongly briny innards. Both the fish mains we had chosen – sea bream fillet with pan-fried foie gras and monkfish with chestnuts – took a meaty approach, being accompanied by plentiful chanterelles, rich gravy and, in the case of the sea bream, crisp brussels sprouts. Both were successful, though rather heavy after the seafood platter, and we were glad of our half-bottle of chilled Sancerre (€14.50). Desserts are wonderful, the fruit-flavoured sorbets authentic and the lemon-vodka version delicately frothed with the spirit rather than drowned in it.

Other locations: 33 bd Beaumarchais, 3rd (01.48.87.98.92); 33 rue St-Jacques, 5th (01.44.07.27.37).

Bistrot du Dôme

1 rue Delambre, 14th (01.43.35.32.00). Mº Vavin. **Open** 12.15-2.30pm, 7.30-11pm daily. Closed Sun and Mon in Aug. **Average** €36. **Credit** AmEx, MC, V. **Wheelchair access**. **Non-smoking room**. **Map** G9.

The Dôme brasserie spun off two bistros a dozen years ago, one in Montparnasse and the other near the Bastille. This is the better of the two. The mood is serious but relaxed – staff, dressed in black and white, are thoroughly professional yet will even take pity on budget diners by filling wines by the glass practically to the brim. Each fish was prepared conservatively but expertly, and infused with flavour. The grilled skewers of little squid were tender, while the rusty-coloured fish soup reminded

us of other classic versions. Tiny soles meunières, drenched in flour and pan-fried in butter, and the monkfish in garlic cream were both respectably good. There's nothing particularly innovative happening in the kitchen, but that doesn't mean that you can't love it for its impeccable seafood standards and reasonable prices.

Other locations: 2 rue de la Bastille, 4th (01.48.04.88.44).

La Cagouille

10-12 pl Constantin Brancusi, 14th (01.43.22.09.01/ www.lacagouille.fr). Mº Gaîté. **Open** noon-2.30pm, 7.30-10.30pm daily. **Average** €40. **Prix fixe** €23, €38. **Credit** AmEx, MC, V. **Wheelchair access**. **Map** F9.

The modern marine decor might be a little on the cold side, especially in the depths of winter, but the simple seafood is reason enough to venture into this decidedly drab part of the 14th. Plus it's open all year round. Start with some fleshy Marennes-Oléron oysters and crispy deep-fried calamari sprinkled with garlic and onions before moving on to an expertly cooked sole served with steamed potatoes and onion confit or a char-grilled whole sea bass (bar). A bream fillet floating in a calamari- and shellfish-laced broth, however, left us wanting, mainly because the waiter's description implied a rich, creamy sauce, not a watery dieter's delight. Disappointingly, the prix fixe menu is limited to just a few dishes, none of which are really the pick of the bunch.

Restaurant Cap Vernet.
See p132.

Le Dôme ★

108 bd du Montparnasse, 14th (01.43.35.25.81). M° Vavin. **Open** noon-3pm, 7pm-12.30am daily. Closed Sun and Mon in Aug. **Average** €70. **Credit** AmEx, DC, MC, V. **Map** G9.

At a time when many Parisian brasseries seem to be on their uppers, this venerable old boat of a place continues to abide not only by its own myths but those of a livelier and more glittering Montparnasse. A mix of artists, editors, politicos, tourists and celebrating locals swan by for superb platters of shellfish, including some of the best oysters in the city, and other fabled marine pleasures such as an immaculate sole meunière, prepared with gorgeous fish caught off the Ile d'Yeu off the Vendée coastline, or salt cod aïoli made with cod they salt themselves. The bouillabaisse is also very good, although this dish just never tastes quite as good overlooking a ribbon of tarmac as it does facing the Med. This is a fine place to experience the best of classical French fish cookery – revolving around simple sauces such as hollandaise, garlic mayonnaise, melted butter, beurre blanc and olive oil – as the ingredients and preparation are first-rate. Finish up with some of the fine Auvergnat cheeses that the Bras family bring to the capital from the land of their ancestors, and don't hesitate to order from the lower echelons of the wine list, since it offers good value at all price points. Pricey but worth it.

L'Uitr ★

1 pl Falguière, 15th (01.47.34.12.24). M° Falguière. **Open** noon-2.30pm, 7-10.30pm daily. **Average** €30. **Prix fixe** €15, €19. **Non-smoking room**. **Credit** MC, V. **Map** F8.

Tucked away behind the botched urban renewal of the neighbourhood surrounding the Gare Montparnasse, this swell little sea shack is a great spot for anyone who can't get down to the shore for oysters, fish and other shellfish. As the name would indicate, oysters star on the blackboard catch of the day menu here, and they offer an admirable selection of varied sizes and provenances identified according to the individual producer. Yvon Madec's plump, briny Breton spéciales went down a treat with a bottle of muscadet, and a side of prawns came with delicious fresh mayonnaise. Even the bread and butter are good here, and the relaxed service at bare wood tables set with Basque linens evokes relaxed holiday dining a long way from city streets. If most of the many regulars come to feast on oysters at very reasonable prices, main courses are appealing too, including a very generous bowl of coques (cockles) lashed with lemony butter sauce and accompanied by a side of parslied potatoes, tuna steak or sardines. The wine list is brief but well compiled, including a good all-purpose muscadet for €13 and a luscious Irancy (a light Burgundian red) for €22. Finish up with cheese or the chocolate mousse.

Le Ballon des Ternes

Ballon & Coquillages

71 bd Gouvion-St-Cyr, 17th (01.45.74.17.98).
M° Porte Maillot. **Open** daily noon-3pm, 7pm-
midnight. **Average** €30. **Non-smoking. Credit**
AmEx, MC, V. **Map** B2.

Almost no larger than an oyster itself, this charming
little raw bar is a really great addition to the
neighbourhood around the Porte Maillot and Palais
des Congrès. Not only is it open daily till midnight,
but the round mosaic-topped counter is a haven of
conviviality in decidedly corporate precincts. Take
one of the red leather-covered stools and design your
own feast. The oysters – Gillardeau, spéciales de
Normandie, Utah Beach, and plates de Bretagne,
among others – are sold by threes and your first
order should comprise a minimum of nine.
Otherwise, garnish your tray with bigorneaux (sea
snails), red prawns, grey shrimp, langoustines
(rather pricey), clams, cockles and mussels, or opt
for one of their suggested platters, including a
tempting oyster sampler with four different types of
oyster. If you're still hungry afterwards, you can
order a plate of tarama served with hot toast,
smoked salmon, smoked eel and herring, or a
Scandinavian plate of smoked salmon, herring and
tarama. Save a little space, though, as you don't want
to miss out on the delicious home-made crème
caramel, served in a big blonde wedge. From a
curious and rather expensive wine list with almost
twice as many reds as whites, an excellent pick is
the Château Theullet Bergerac, a dry white that goes
well with shellfish.

L'Huîtrier

16 rue Saussier-Leroy, 17th (01.40.54.83.44).
M° Ternes. **Open** noon-2.30pm, 7-11pm Tue-Sun.
Closed July, Aug; Sun in May, June and Sept.
Average €45. **Credit** AmEx, MC, V. **Map** C2.

An understated nautical theme graces this all-
seafood restaurant. You manoeuvre through the
cramped dining room to aluminium chairs that look
like they were pinched from a 1920s luxury liner.
The obvious choice here is the oysters from the
Marennes-Oléron region, which are available in
multiple combinations and types. But if you're not
up for tucking into the raw ones, try the oversized
oysters lightly baked in a shallot and cream sauce,
voluptuous and positively naughty as they slither
down. The prepared fish and crustacean dishes
are also ocean-fresh, such as the platter of skinny,
deep-fried smelt (winter only), which you eat in
forkfuls like frites and dip into aïoli. The breaded
and pan-fried squid or gambas fricassée in garlic
and oil are also fine choices, though the selection
changes continually.

Taira

10 rue des Acacias, 17th (01.47.66.74.14).
M° Argentine. **Open** noon-2.15pm, 7.30-10pm
Mon-Fri; 7.30-10pm Sat. Closed two weeks in Aug.
Average €60. **Prix fixe** €30, €34, €64. **Credit**
AmEx, DC, MC, V. **Map** C3.

To qualify Kurihara Taira's establishment as a fishy
restaurant is a rather bad pun but an altogether apt
description. First of all, the smell that greets you
leaves no doubt as to what is on the menu and the
staff offer the sort of welcome that makes you
wonder whether you have inadvertently trespassed
on to private property. The surly hostess went about
her duties with all the enthusiasm of an exiled
Japanese empress reduced to waitressing. Her bouts
of temporary deafness each time we had the temerity
to ask for something almost had us believe we were
actually rather lucky to be served at all. But our
starters proved worth the 20-minute wait. The
lightly steamed baby squid were bathed in a
refreshingly light, warm basil, tomato and olive oil
dressing, while a plate of red tuna strips marinated
in ginger and fragrant argan oil enthroned on
feather-fine strips of white radish and carrot was
perfectly delicious. Unfortunately, the positive
side of the meal ended there. One main course of
steamed cod was undistinguished and insipid; the
other – steaks of bonite, a kind of very oily tuna –
tasted and smelled decidedly off. It did not appear
on the bill. The atmosphere being as grey as the
decor, with the waitress mumbling to herself in the
background, we opted to skip dessert and coffee.
The Japanese couple sitting at the table opposite
were treated to a smile and we got a scowl as
we walked out hurriedly into Paris's polluted but
unfishy air.

Ballon & Coquillages.

Budget

It's becoming increasingly difficult to eat cheaply and well in Paris. A coffee alone in an unremarkable café can easily set you back €2, and half-bottles of mineral water routinely go for €5 – before the advent of the euro and its accompanying inflation, the equivalent of €7 could have bought you a three-course lunch. Now, you should count on spending a minimum of €11 on the simplest hot meal, and that's if you avoid drinks (though happily, in this city, wine is often cheaper than mineral water). The number of budget joints with authentic Parisian atmosphere is diminishing as many have gone upmarket, changing the light fixtures and doubling their prices. Fortunately, however, some of the best continue to resist any kind of change.

The restaurants listed here are often jovial places, thanks to their youthful clientele. Don't hope for the best meal of your life, but do expect trad French grub and plenty of quaffable wine (order tap water by the carafe to keep costs down). In this chapter we have concentrated on restaurants where you can have an evening meal for €20 or less (and occasionally a bit more), but remember that many pricier bistros become accessible at lunch, when reservations are easier to come by (see pp24-74 **Bistros**). Many cafés also serve decent food prepared with fresh ingredients (see pp214-232 **Cafés**), though they are not necessarily cheap. Ethnic food can be a bargain alternative. For affordable Chinese, Vietnamese and Thai food, head to Belleville or the 13th arrondissement (see pp174-185 **Far Eastern**). North African couscous restaurants (see pp203-206) are another filling option.

1ST ARRONDISSEMENT

Chez Stella

3 rue Thérèse, 1st (01.42.96.22.15). M° Bourse or Pyramides. **Open** noon-2pm, 7.30-10pm Mon-Fri. **Prix fixe** €9.60-€11. **Credit** MC, V. **Map** H5.
'Weekends are sacred,' we heard the charming hostess Stella tell one of the many customers she greets with a bisou on each cheek. 'In 32 years we haven't changed anything and we're not about to start now.' On weekdays only, then, you can experience one of the last of a dying breed in Paris: a neighbourhood cheapie where the short menu never changes and everything tastes delicious. French country meets Asian kitsch in the tiny wood-panelled, yellow-painted dining room – Stella and her chef husband are from Vietnam, though you'd never know it from the simple bistro classics that come out of the kitchen. The €10.40 menu brings you two courses but for just 60 cents more you can add a third. We started with oeuf mayonnaise on a bed of fresh-tasting salade russe and the best hareng pommes à l'huile we've tasted in a long time, before mains of nicely charred steak in a herby green pepper sauce (for a €2.30 supplement) with decent frites, and the plat du jour – a thick slice of grilled ham with more frites (every dish comes with green beans, boiled potatoes, rice or frites). Whichever

dessert you choose, it will come bathed in crème anglaise (unless you tell Stella to hold the custard). Her frosted chocolate cake provides welcome respite from moelleux mania, and the clafoutis was a slice of apple heaven. Best of all, neither dessert went anywhere near a microwave. Maternal Stella wants to see the plates licked clean, but fortunately the portions are manageable.

Flam's

62 rue des Lombards, 1st (01.42.21.10.30/ www.flams.fr). M° Châtelet. **Open** noon-3pm, 7pm-midnight Mon-Fri; 12.30pm-midnight Sat, Sun. **Average** €15. **Prix fixe** €11.90, €16.90. **Lunch menu** €8.90. **Credit** AmEx, MC, V. **Map** K6.
Restore your street cred with your kids by taking them to this teeming student haunt with its thumping Euro-pap soundtrack. Green wooden tables are lit by halogen lamps and yellow sponge-painted walls are covered with Bud posters and modern paintings. Downstairs is a huge cellar with high red-brick arches and long tables ideal for parties. This is also the perfect place for insatiable appetites as the 'à volonté' menu really is genuine: as many flammenküche as you can stomach with a starter or dessert for only €11.90. The flammenküche is an Alsatian cross between a thin pizza and a crispy pancake, with a pliable base

covered in fromage blanc and sprinkled with different combinations of onion, mushroom, bacon and grated cheese. Alternatively try the lighter vegetarian version: tomato, runner beans, cabbage and carrots drizzled with olive oil. They come on big wooden pallets; you fold them over and eat with your fingers, and wash them down with beer or Picon bière, bitter-orange shandy. The starters and desserts are uninteresting – lazy salads and basic ice-creams – but the atmosphere is fun and you won't leave hungry.

La Fresque

100 rue Rambuteau, 1st (01.42.33.17.56). M° Les Halles. **Open** noon-3pm, 7pm-midnight daily. **Average** €18. **Prix fixe** €12.50. **Credit** MC, V. **Map** K5.

This bistro a step away from the Centre Pompidou remains one of the great-value eateries in the area. Named after a distinctly '70s mural in the otherwise trad café interior, it dates from the days when Les Halles was still a market and has a terrace walled in by plants to protect you from the madding crowd. We really couldn't fault the €12.50 menu, which includes 25cl of drinkable wine. Starters of a small salade sud-ouest comprised ungreasy gésiers confits (gizzards) on a bed of coco de Paimpol white beans, while the assiette Florence was a delicious concoction of spinach in hollandaise-style sauce with lardons and a perfectly poached egg. The lieu jaune au basilic was a tasty Mediterranean dish of pollack in Provençal sauce accompanied by stewed leeks and puréed carrots, and the cuisse de canard aux agrumes had a bitter orange glaze that made it far superior to the normal confit de canard. Puddings are a joy – a super little gratin aux figues, and the extremely alcoholic baba limoncello Chantilly (not for those who intend doing anything with their afternoon). On going inside to pay, we discovered the staff laughing uproariously with a group of customers, making us almost wish we'd chosen to eat in, though the strong smell of disinfectant from the post-lunch wipedown was a tad off-putting.

2ND ARRONDISSEMENT

The Kitchen

153 rue Montmartre, 2nd (01.42.33.33.97/www. thekitchen.fr). M° Grands Boulevards or Bourse. **Open** noon-3pm, 7-10.30pm Mon-Fri; 7-11pm Sat; noon-3.30pm Sun. **Average** €20. **Credit** DC, MC, V. **Map** J4.

Airy, clean, crisp, playful – the vast kitchen in which you're invited to pull up a seat is familiar, probably because it embodies the ideal set for your fantasy cooking show. Opened by a pair of Irishmen, The Kitchen excels in putting creative twists on old standards, such as a spinach soup with coconut or a salmon fillet rolled in gingerbread crumbs and served with a tangy mustard sauce. The daily menu, in addition to a short list of starters and main courses, offers four fresh soups and two-course

Le Trumilou. *See p140.*

The Kitchen.
See p137.

Soupes

French Cuisine

meals for €16.50; a quiche-soup duo costs €11.50 at lunch. Brunch, with an accent on fresh produce and herbs, is also popular. But it is the whimsy of the details that won over a duo of sceptical eaters frowning upon the distinctly non-French feel of the place – the little kitchen-style tables with the silverware inside; the smoke-free ground floor; the board games and cookbooks; earnest Anglophone staff delicately pouring tea; and simple, bright foods which taste of each individual veggie. After one too many dingy Parisian bistros, it is no small gift to relax in a wooden-and-white decor reminiscent of Habitat, and to absorb its Anglo-inflected sensibility.

Le Mimosa
44 rue d'Argout, 2nd (01.40.28.15.75). M° Sentier. **Open** noon-3.30pm Mon-Fri. **Prix fixe** €12, €14. **Average** €14. **Credit** MC, V. **Map** J5.

Around the corner from Les Halles, the yellow-bright Mimosa is a lucky find. With two- and three-course menus (€12 and €14 respectively) that change daily, it's a testament to the durability of Paris lunch culture: no fast food please and yes, we'll be back tomorrow. From noon to 2pm, when the narrow dining room is at its busiest, Thierry Soulat (doyenne of the tiny kitchen) and his welcoming partner Xavier Trauet sate the appetites of local office workers with tasty standards such as thick rump steak doused in herby butter, a fillet of perch zapped with basil and tomato or chicken breast with a tangy mustard crust. All mains come with a choice of two sides: scrumptious sautéed potatoes (a must), braised celery, spinach, al dente green beans and so on. The Soulat secret is simple ingredients with strong, fresh flavours. The tomato-mozzarella starter (usually a terrible bore) came vine-ripened, with real buffalo cheese and a healthy drizzle of dazzling green pesto; likewise the Bayonne ham was fine and fat-free. Desserts run from homey classics (apple compote, œufs à la neige, a pot of coffee cream) to regional curiosities (like the Auvergnat flognarde aux pommes), and wines are cheerful and not too pricey. In the summer, be sure to sit at one of the pavement tables and enjoy being a local for an hour or two.

3RD ARRONDISSEMENT
Fontaines d'Elysabeth
1 rue Ste-Elisabeth, 3rd (01.42.74.36.41). M° Temple or République. **Open** noon-3pm, 8-11pm Mon-Fri; 8-11pm Sat. Closed Aug. **Average** €15. **Prix fixe** €15. **Lunch menu** €12. **No credit cards. Map** L5.

Once through the curtained door of this backstreet restaurant, you'll quickly forget the urban bustle of the surrounding area. In its place, a homely bric-a-brac decor and welcoming staff invite you to settle in and peruse the simple handwritten menus that are passed around. The kitchen specialises in French provincial favourites that warm stomachs and satisfy tastebuds. To start, Lyonnais sausage served on a bed of waxy new potatoes was tender and well-

spiced, while a blue cheese salad helped us work up an appetite for the mammoth mains that followed. A sturdy cassoulet was, as it should be, a delicious stew of sausages and meat in a creamy white bean sauce. More impressive still was the Provençal roast lamb – the tender meat enriched by the tomato, garlic and sweet peppers of the dish. Against all odds we even managed to squeeze in a slice of the home-made apple tart and ice-cream. The owners were in no rush to clear us out once we had finished, so we lingered to enjoy the relaxed atmosphere.

4TH ARRONDISSEMENT
Café de la Poste ★
13 rue Castex, 4th (01.42.72.95.35). M° Bastille. **Open** noon-2pm, 7pm-2am Mon-Fri; 7pm-2am Sat. Closed Aug. **Average** €25. **Credit** MC, V. **Map** L7.

This small, friendly restaurant is just the type of place that originally created the myth that you can't get a bad meal in Paris. Why? Because good, simple, affordable food is cooked and served with care and pride in a pleasant, original setting. Bare wood tables, a bar and walls covered in a sort of Dadaist mosaic of cracked tiles and shards of mirror create a homely setting that evokes the vanished Paris of photographers such as Edouard Boubat. Start with the salad of melted goat's cheese served on thin slices of pear with triangles of toasted country bread and a bit of salad with a lovely mustard vinaigrette, or the delicious foie gras, home-made and generously served in two slices. Next go with the daily special – lasagne, perhaps – or a not unpleasantly chewy rump steak in tangy roquefort sauce with excellent chips. These golden, twice-fried potato slices are absolutely delicious. Though the fruit tarts are a word-of-mouth favourite, we missed the last slice of a pretty fabulous-looking tarte Tatin when we came for a late lunch and settled with little remorse for a textbook-perfect chocolate mousse with two langues de chat biscuits instead. A friendly crowd and attentive but unintrusive service – no mean trick in a space this small – make this a lovely place to come à deux or even on your own. Highly recommended.

La Canaille
4 rue Crillon, 4th (01.42.78.09.71). M° Quai de la Rapée or Sully Morland. **Open** 11.45am-2.15pm, 7.30-11.30pm Mon-Fri; 7.30-11.30pm Sat. Closed three weeks in Aug. **Average** €20. **Prix fixe** €20 (dinner only). **Lunch menu** €15. **Credit** MC, V. **Map** L7.

The purple, mural-covered walls, life-size statue of a blue cherub with golden wings and a protruding belly, and neon strip lighting told us this was no classic French bistro: an impression confirmed when the waitress carelessly tossed our menus on the table along with a pad of paper on which to write our orders. The reasonably priced menu, though a bit hard to navigate at first, was a pleasant surprise with its variety of modern French and world cuisine. We started off with a lovely smoked salmon tart drizzled with basil oil, and a small platter of Corsican charcuterie and parmesan shavings accompanied by a duo of roasted apples and pears. The roasted half duck with a syrupy white raisin sauce was oddly paired with a side of sweet potato gratin; the result was overwhelmingly sweet. A perfectly cooked steak with a spicy Sichuan pepper sauce, however, was a welcome respite, served with herb-smashed potatoes. Desserts were a gorgeous pastry-encased roasted pear with raspberry coulis, and an overcooked fondant au chocolat: not one ooze of chocolate escaped. We asked the waitress for another and after many loud sighs and rolled eyes, she brought us out another fondant just as dry. An odd place, but La Canaille does have its loyal fans.

Le Coupe Gorge

2 rue de la Coutellerie, 4th (01.48.04.79.24).
Mº Hôtel de Ville or Châtelet. **Open** noon-2pm,
7.30pm-midnight Mon-Fri. **Prix fixe** €16 (dinner
only). **Lunch menu** €10, €12. **Non-smoking
room. Credit** MC, V. **Map** K6.
On a cool, drizzly winter's night, the prospect of warmth, light and full bellies was inviting. When we arrived, the lone waiter and chef were chatting at the aged wooden bar over an aperitif. We were the first people in the dining room, but despite this the atmosphere was pleasant: dark wooden floors, cosy red velvet banquettes and eclectic modern paintings were illuminated by small candles and soft lighting. Filtered through old green bottles, the muted lights add a whimsical touch to an otherwise standard bistro setting. The bargain €15 three-course dinner menu offers a wide variety of traditional French bistro fare, which the waiter was happy to explain. We started the meal with a wonderfully light 'millefeuille' of bright red tomato and herb-infused fromage frais drizzled with basil-flavoured oil, and a hearty potage of seasonal vegetables. Main courses were average: both the herb-crusted lamb chops and the beef tournedos were a bit overdone, served with the same bland, cream-laden potato gratin. Things looked up with dessert – a rather exotic banana crème brûlée received rave reviews from all, as did the standard moelleux au chocolat (served with vanilla ice-cream and a dollop of whipped cream). By the time we finished our meal hours later, we realised that the dining room was now nearly filled with groups of boisterous French young people, filling the air with laughter and a haze of smoke. They've definitely got the right idea – come late, eat well and spend little.

Le Temps des Cerises

31 rue de la Cerisaie, 4th (01.42.72.08.63). Mº Sully
Morland or Bastille. **Open** 7.30am-8pm Mon-Fri.
Food served 11.30am-2.30pm. Closed Aug.
Average €18.50. **Lunch menu** €13.50. **No credit
cards. Map** L7.
An old-fashioned corner bistro on the edge of the Marais with a €13 menu is an increasingly rare treat. Le temps des Cerises fulfils many a Francophile dream. A curvy zinc bar, old-fashioned wrought iron

bistro tables and a sweet, caring patronne, aided by a leggy waitress who has her favourites, all give the place an essential Parisian buzz. The cuisine is tasty and simple without any pretence of gastronomic sophistication. We began our meal with two wafers of innocuous terrine de sanglier (wild boar), nicely served with some cornichons and salad, which we followed with a well-beaten bavette coated in a blue cheese sauce and served with some homey sauté potaotes. To finish, a crumble of apples, quinces and nuts was solid but comforting, while a selection of three cheeses cut at the bar accompanied the last of our fruity bottle of Coteaux de Quercy (a region to which the carte pays homage) with just the right traditional feel. As we left, regulars were embracing the staff and tables of tourists were congratulating themselves on having found the real thing. The only minus points are the refusal of all credit cards and lunchtime-only service.

Le Trumilou

84 quai de l'Hôtel de Ville, 4th (01.42.77.63.98).
Mº Pont Marie or Hôtel de Ville. **Open** noon-3pm,
7-11pm daily. Closed two weeks in Aug and one
week at Christmas. **Average** €25. **Prix fixe** €17.50,
€19 (Sunday only). **Credit** MC, V. **Wheelchair
access. Map** K6.
Ducking into this oddly named bistro from the windswept quai behind the Hôtel de Ville, we were greeted by the expansive owner Alain Charven, Champagne glass in one hand, Gauloise in the other – a slightly louche image that captured the atmosphere here. The food is dependable and copious, and by sticking to the traditional and eschewing adventurous dishes, you'll be treated to well-executed French classics such as magret de canard, hearty stews and generous steaks. From the starters, the cucumber salad was fresh but uninspiring, while the tarte au boudin noir turned out to be a more uplifting combination of slow-cooked apple segments with small slices of black pudding. The pot-au-feu, served in a steaming metal casserole, was clearly designed to provide natural protection from Parisian winters. Desserts, however, were below-par, and the apple tart grand-mère was anything but grandmotherly. Not ideal for a tête-à-tête, with its cloud of smoke and alcohol fumes, punctuated by raucous laughter from the owner as well as the diners, the Trumilou is nonetheless deservedly popular.

5TH ARRONDISSEMENT

Au Bon Coin

21 rue de la Collégiale, 5th (01.43.31.55.57/
www.restoauboncoin.com). Mº Gobelins. **Open** noon-
2pm, 7.30-11pm Mon-Sat. **Average** €20. **Prix fixe**
€13, €18. **Credit** MC, V. **Wheelchair access.**
It's easy to fall into a tourist trap along rue Mouffetard, so this old-fashioned bistro – far enough away from the Mouff' that you wouldn't find it by accident – is worth keeping up your sleeve. The

L'Auberge du Champ de Mars. *See p143.*

parallel cuisines in operation here, the menu and carte of tried and trusted bistro favourites and a complete list of North African couscous and tagines. As this was lunchtime and we had ambitious plans for the afternoon, we decided to choose a single main dish from the carte. The fillet steak with a little pot of creamy roquefort sauce was as tender as butter, sealed and browned over a high heat, accompanied by some good mash. Our other choice of tagine de poulet was a real winner, the conical earthenware dish arriving to reveal mounds of vegetables and chicken bursting with flavour. No messing about here with clever combinations of ingredients – all tagines come with the same winning combination of vegetables, preserved lemons, fruit and nuts. Our neighbour offered us a glass of his Sancerre, rather better than our humble Mâcon villages, and we entered into an unlikely but lively conversation about the pros and cons of château living. Les Grands Degrés remains a reliable budget home for the temporarily impoverished.

L'Ecurie

2 rue Laplace, 5th (01.46.33.68.49). M° Maubert-Mutualité. **Open** noon-3pm, 7pm-midnight Mon, Wed-Sat; 7pm-midnight Tue, Sun. **Average** €20. **Prix fixe** €15. **Lunch menu** €11.50. **No credit cards. Map** J8.

'This really is a charming little place,' we thought as we ducked in to enter the tiny ground floor dining room, most of which is taken up by two zinc bars and an open kitchen where meat is cooked on a wood fire. The stuff that's written on the menu about Minie being a descendant of the original stablewoman is a load of old cobblers, according to her amiable husband who chatted to us at the end of the meal, but the place is decked out in saddles and horsey regalia and if you descend to the subterranean dining rooms lit by lights made out of old bottles, or use the Turkish loo, it feels truly medieval. Shame then that the lunch prix fixe was disappointing. The starter salads of walnut and roquefort were OK, though it beats us how you grate roquefort. It was the mains that left us non-plussed. The rosemary-sprinkled lamb was tender but there was hardly any meat on the cheap cut, and the bavette was tough and burnt on the outside, a fact they seemed to have tried to hide by swamping it in sauce. The chips had that frozen packet feel. Chocolate mousse and crème caramel in ramekins saved the meal somewhat and the half-bottles of wine are decent – we enjoyed our €10 Bordeaux. We would consider returning to try the à la carte, which, with mains from €13-€18, one would hope is better.

L'Escapade

10 rue de la Montagne-Ste-Geneviève, 5th (01.46.33.23.85). M° Maubert-Mutualité. **Open** 6pm-12.30am daily. **Prix fixe** €17. **Credit** AmEx, MC, V. **Wheelchair access. Map** J7.

Anyone who thinks they miss being a student should go to this restaurant. It recreates an authentic element of higher education – the awful food.

three-course €18 prix fixe might not be the world's greatest bargain, but in light of euro inflation it looks not bad at all. The dining room is so classic as to be a cliché, its wooden tables covered by red-check tablecloths, the rather brusque hostess presiding behind the bar. Though there were plenty of empty tables in the dining room, she sat two men next to us at a table for four (not coincidentally we thought, as we were two women). They proceeded to chain-smoke throughout the meal while blatantly eavesdropping on our conversation – almost par for the course in this type of restaurant, but annoying nonetheless. Meanwhile, a table of at least a dozen American academics were savouring the French experience, ordering from the predictable menu of classics (oeuf mayonnaise, onion soup, a plate of crudités heavy on the grated cabbage and carrots). The sole meunière was surprisingly good, tender fish with plenty of butter and nicely cooked waxy potatoes. Order an île flottante as you fan away your neighbour's smoke and you'll feel that, for better or worse, some things in Paris never change.

Les Degrés de Notre-Dame ★

10 rue des Grands-Degrés, 5th (01.55.42.88.88). M° Maubert-Mutualité. **Open** 7am-midnight Mon-Sat. **Average** €25. **Lunch menu** €12. **Prix fixe** €23, €25 (dinner only). **Credit** MC, V. **Non-smoking room. Map** J7.

A lunchtime menu for €12 just opposite Notre Dame is what this hotel-restaurant promises and delivers in its characterful old room, filled with pictures and memories. We went back after the place had been shut a few weeks for a refit, and the charming owner was busy assuring her regulars that improvements were all backstage and that nobody would dream of touching the old-world decoration. There are two

Anyone who is still a student, however, will be laughing. The deal is €17 for an all-you-can-eat starter buffet, pick of the mains and puddings. And, more importantly, wine is included and on tap – you drink as much as you can handle. Sadly, the deadly caterer's fridge chill had bitten into the crudités, pasta salads and couscous salad on offer at the buffet, taking away most of the taste. The converted cellar dining room could have done with a radiator or two, as well. Clearly coping with the terrible hardship better than we were, our neighbours – a coachload of physics scholars – were going back for second, perhaps even third helpings and bucketloads of wine. Fried chicken and faux-filet both came with giant portions of chips, but the lacklustre tastes cut us off from the will to be greedy. Apple tart, presented with a dollop of spray cream, was the overall highlight.

Le Jardin des Pâtes

4 rue Lacépède, 5th (01.43.31.50.71). M° Jussieu or Place Monge. **Open** noon-2.30pm, 7-11pm daily. Closed two weeks at Christmas. **Average** €15. **Credit** MC, V. **Non-smoking room. Map** K8.
There is something immediately welcoming about the 20-year-old 'pasta garden', with its combination of stone and whitewashed walls, hanging plants, wooden tables, banquettes and folding chairs. The overall impression is one of cleanliness and professionalism, which extends to the good-looking and efficient staff. 'No freezer, no microwave' a sign

outside proudly announces, and indeed the food is freshly made, from the fluffy pile of crudités – far more appetising than the standard veggie plate – to the organic fresh pastas made with barley, buckwheat, rice or wheat flours. Tempted by the rice noodles with tofu, ginger and vegetables (this is a good address for vegetarians), we settled on the barley pasta with salmon, seaweed, leeks and cream – a little underseasoned and heavy on the sauce, but this is Paris, not Rome, and with a little help from the salt shaker it became a satisfying dish. Fizzy pear juice in a chunky glass completed a virtuous meal – we'll definitely be back to try the other pastas and enjoy the pavement terrace in summer.
Other locations: 33 bd Arago, 13th (01.45.35.93.67).

Perraudin

157 rue St-Jacques, 5th (01.46.33.15.75). M° Cluny-La Sorbonne/RER Luxembourg. **Open** noon-2.30pm, 7-10pm Mon-Fri. Closed Aug. **Average** €20. **Prix fixe** €18 (lunch), €28 (dinner). **Credit** DC, MC, V. **Non-smoking room. Map** J6.
This ever-popular Latin Quarter eaterie has the quintessential Parisian bistro look, except that here it is circa 1910. Its shabby dark red interior, red-checked tablecloths and frayed posters on dulled mirrors don't look immediately inviting. Nonetheless, at lunch, local bohemians and academics crowd into Perraudin for no-nonsense, hearty bistro food. From the starters, the snails were excellent and thankfully avoided the common bistro vice of over-butteriness.

Good-looking food and great desserts at polished and flirty **Juan et Juanita**. *See p145.*

We were also pleased with the Flemish tarte au maroilles, a tasty cheese and onion quiche. We resisted the waiter's exhortations to try the tête de veau, opting for the more sedate boeuf bourguignon, an acceptable rendition of the Burgundy classic, and the gigot d'agneau, parsimonious slices of lamb bolstered by an overflowing earthenware dish of gratin dauphinois – all washed down with a decent 1999 Bordeaux. Desserts covered familiar territory of heavy-duty profiteroles or dense chocolate mousse, but the more unusual tarte au sucre, another Flemish speciality, was enjoyable, though a little weighty at this stage of a copious meal. Perraudin does retain its eccentricities (closed on weekends), but the food is solid and unpretentious, the service efficient, and we were charmed by Mr Rameau, the owner, boasting with pride of his wife's bistro recipes.

6TH ARRONDISSEMENT

Le Petit Saint-Benoît

4 rue St-Benoît, 6th (01.42.60.27.92). M° St-Germain-des-Prés. **Open** noon-2.30pm, 7-10.30pm Mon-Sat. Closed Aug. **Average** €20. **No credit cards. Map** H6.

Could it be, hidden behind a veil of blue smoke and red-checked tablecloth, Marguerite Duras? Er, no – just a photo of her hanging out here 40 years ago. The robust Côtes du Rhône wine served with lunch may have clouded our vision, but this resolute throwback to an earlier generation of bistros is definitely haunted by the old ghosts of St-Germain-des-Prés intellectuals. In a moneyed district taken over by fashion, it's authentically crotchety in all the ways you love to complain about – snappy maternal waitresses who scrawl your order on the paper tablecloth; walls yellowed by the puff of tobacco clouds; no reservations, no credit cards and no modern toilet. Most of the food has likewise made few concessions to modernity. This is welcome in a stewed rabbit in foie gras sauce, less so in desserts, especially the house speciality 'Benoît aux pommes' – a clafoutis heavy enough to serve as light weaponry. The basic starters are what you might imagine for €3, but the beef and petit salé – salt pork with lentils – are reliable standards. The no-fuss vibe is what draws its regular crowd, mostly middle-aged, past the rotating door and into the rabbit's den of a room; and that is what you'll remember long after the budget meal has faded from the memory.

Le Polidor

41 rue Monsieur-le-Prince, 6th (01.43.26.95.34). M° Odéon. **Open** noon-2.30pm, 7pm-12.30am Mon-Sat; noon-2.30pm, 7-11pm Sun. **Average** €20. **Prix fixe** €19-€28. **Lunch menu** €12. **No credit cards. Map** H7.

To be honest, a shared sense of resignation descended on our jolly trio when we entered one of the longest-running budget addresses in Paris, founded in 1845. It's one of the rare bona fide bistros to have survived in St-Germain, a part of the city

that seems more inclined to pasta and salad these days than the slow-simmered carnivorous dishes that are the heart of any real Gallic menu. On a cold night, the foggy windows were a promise of conviviality, the room was packed, and the big zinc bar run by a big blonde hostess, scrubbed sideboard, nicotine-stained walls and worn tile floors created an appetising funk of pre-war Paris. Then we locked horns with the big blonde as we attempted to squeeze in to a wobbly table in a far corner of the main dining room. 'What do you think you're doing?!' she bellowed, almost a perfect caricature of the nasty shop clerks and foul-tempered concierges who were once deemed to be a classic element of the Parisian landscape. Shrugging off her temper, we studied the menu, ordered and continued our conversation. Then the wine came, a red from the Béarn at €12, and we had our first surprise – it was good, even surprisingly good at this price. A basket of bread arrived and it was delicious, as were first courses of oeufs mayonnaise, crudités (fresh vegetables with a creamy vinaigrette) and even a terrine de brochet (pike-perch). Was it possible that we were going to have a good meal at a budget restaurant? Caution still reigned, since in Paris today bargains are few. Then a delicious guinea hen braised with cabbage and bacon, and a very respectable steak-frites arrived and a quiet wonderment overtook us. OK, the fruit tarts were disappointing, but a cheese plate was well chosen, the crème caramel was good, and so was the coffee. Snarly service aside, we'll definitely be back.

7TH ARRONDISSEMENT

L'Auberge du Champ de Mars

18 rue de l'Exposition, 7th (01.45.51.78.08). M° Ecole-Militaire. **Open** 6.30-11pm Mon, Sat; noon-3pm, 6.30-10pm Tue-Fri. Closed Aug. **Average** €12. **Prix fixe** €17. **Credit** MC, V. **Non-smoking. Map** D6.

Down this quiet backstreet in the 7th arrondissement, a step off the rue Cler market, other neighbouring restaurants definitely have more charm than the Auberge but none can match its prices. Decent if unexciting fare is the speciality of the house, which seems to live off English-language interlopers who stop in for a €17 complete meal. Classics like beef filet and pan-roasted veal liver are happily hearty, following a list of lackadaisical starters – a salad which makes much ado over a few roasted pine nuts or a lobster terrine redolent of fish. Scallops cooked in papillote were tasty, but we found the bed of fettucine downright mushy and the red peppers and carrots cooked into indistinction. The one-room restaurant seems a bit homey, an effect accentuated by a host of bushy fake flowers at the bar and French pop music piped in straight from the 1970s. The main pleasures here are found in warming the belly on a cold day with a cooked meal which won't traumatise a travel budget, and then settling into the plush burgundy banquette to digest.

Chez Germaine

30 rue Pierre-Leroux, 7th (01.42.73.28.34).
M° Duroc or Vaneau. **Open** noon-2.30pm, 7-10pm
Mon-Sat. Closed Aug. **Average** €20. **Prix fixe**
€13.50. **Lunch menu** €9. **No credit cards. Non-
smoking. Map** F8.
There are no toilets at Chez Germaine. There is no
smoking. They do not take credit cards. These are
the rules. If you try to break them, you will have to
answer to a stern older woman wearing a gaudy
apron that announces 'Je conserve'. What seems to
have been conserved here is an ambience that cannot
have changed much since the restaurant opened in
1952. Enclosed behind the lace-curtained front
window, we had the distinct impression of being at
our grandmother's house. Judging from a steady file
of single male diners who dutifully take their seats,
we are not the only ones who feel this way. The food
here may be school canteen-ish, but one does not
come to Chez Germaine for a culinary revelation.
One comes for simple food honestly prepared and
served in an atmosphere that is increasingly hard to
find. Starters consist mainly of an exhaustive list of
basic salads and crudités. Mains are filling, meaty
dishes such as pot au feu or a hefty boudin noir
served with a heap of greasy frites. Desserts, arrayed
in Tupperware containers, include fruit salad, apple
compote, chestnut cream, and other concoctions that
can be dished into a little aluminium cup for you. If
you're feeling flush, you can indulge in a thick slice
of crème caramel. Just don't forget to say 'please' and
'thank you'.

8TH ARRONDISSEMENT

A Toutes Vapeurs

7 rue d'Isly, 8th (01.44.90.95.75). M° St-Lazare.
Open 7-11pm Mon-Sat. **Average** €10. **Credit**
AmEx, MC, V. **Map** G3.
A healthy new concept from the owners of Café Very
in the Tuileries, the idea here is that fast doesn't have
to mean bread (sandwiches), other starches (pizza,
pasta, potatoes) or fried (burgers, chicken, etc.).
Instead, you chose a wooden, not plastic, basket or
two, which is then anointed with a choice of different
seasoned oils or sauces, quick-steamed and brought
to you at your table in an attractive and relaxing
dining room where gentle lighting and good jazz or
world music replace the usual cursed fluorescence
and pop-radio associated with an expedient meal. If
it's long been Asian cuisines that have best used
steam as a cooking method, this place makes
ingenious use of European ingredients: the basket
of spinach, white mushrooms, morels, marinated
artichokes and fresh herbs gives off a delicious
liquid that blends beautifully with its vinaigrette.
Ditto a combination of free-range chicken,
mangetout, green beans, cherry tomatoes and red
peppers in a light satay sauce. Even the steamed
desserts are a treat, including apples, sultanas,
walnuts and cinnamon. Nice wines by the glass and
friendly service make this place a great budget bet.

9TH ARRONDISSEMENT

Chartier

7 rue du Fbg-Montmartre, 9th (01.47.70.86.29).
M° Grands Boulevards. **Open** 11.30am-3pm, 6-10pm
daily. **Average** €16. **Credit** DC, MC, V. **Non-
smoking room. Map** J4.
We had not been to Chartier for a while, and it was
good to see the vast 19th-century soup kitchen with
its mirrored interior, complete with napkin drawers
for the regulars, retaining its quintessential Parisian
buzz. We began with some plump escargots and a
salty rollmop herring accompanied by a very cold
potato salad. Main courses were a mixed bag: a do-
it-yourself steak tartare was fine and served with
crunchy frites, but the lapin sauce à la moutarde
was disappointing, with a cloyingly sweet mustard
sauce and some woefully overcooked pasta. A
complaint to the waiter brought a visit from an
accusatory manager. First he claimed that perhaps
we didn't know what rabbit tasted like, followed by
a comment that it was the moutarde à l'ancienne that
gave the sauce its 'special' taste. In the end our
unflappable old-school waiter changed the dish for
an excellent andouillette and some more of the crispy
fries. Some well-chosen cantal and brie accompanied
the last of our bottle of Bordeaux and restored our
spirits. The place used to be famous as an incredible
bargain, which is no longer the case, but it remains
competitively priced.

La Nouvelle Galatée

*3 rue Victor Massé, 9th (01.48.78.55.60). M° St-
Georges or Pigalle.* **Open** noon-10.30pm Mon-Fri.
Prix fixe €18.50, €21.50. **Lunch menu** €12.20.
Credit AmEx, MC, V. **Map** H2.
La Nouvelle Galatée's bargain traditional fare with
a few subtle twists attracts a happy throng of locals
and tourists. We were quick to join them, ravenously
tucking into starters of chicken liver and Armagnac
pâté, and smoked herrings with warm potatoes. To
follow, salmon cooked with fennel was enjoyable
without being spectacular. However, magret de
canard in a mulberry sauce was excellent – the sweet
fruitiness combined deliciously with the tender duck
meat, while tart acidity kept the richness in check.
When we'd finished, the friendly staff were happy
to let us enjoy our wine and make room for dessert.
And a good thing it was too: a mound of profiteroles
came smothered in thick dark chocolate sauce, and
crème brûlée spiced with cardamom was another
nice surprise that almost had us licking the plate
clean. On top of the good food, the room itself is
worth a visit – the walls are lined with mirrors from
a 1930s cruise ship – and the patron Charles seems
keen to be on first-name terms with every guest.

10TH ARRONDISSEMENT

Chez Papa

*206 rue Lafayette, 10th (01.42.09.53.87). M° Louis-
Blanc.* **Open** 11.30am-1am daily. **Average** €20.
Lunch menu €9.15. **Credit** AmEx, MC, V. **Map** L2.

French Cuisine

It's called salade Boyarde, it costs €6.40 and it's probably the best meal deal in Paris. A deep (really deep) earthenware bowl comes filled (really filled) with warm sautéed potatoes, chunks of crisp lettuce and tomatoes, crumbly cantal and tangy blue cheese, all topped with a generous slice of cured ham. For 80 cents more, and if your appetite is up to it, Papa will add two fried eggs to make it a Boyarde complète. Even more substantial versions of this hearty salad are on offer – laden with chicken livers, bacon, goat's cheese on toast, or a hunk of confit de canard – and the most it'll set you back is €11.20. By the look of the lively crowd at lunch and dinner, the Boyarde is a neighbourhood institution. Other bargains include the four-egg omelettes (all around €5) and the daily lunch special: the last time we went it was a thick tournedos with a coffee for €8; there's also a long list of by-the-glass wines from €1.70. For dessert, you'll find it hard to choose between the warm, caramelised croustade de pommes à l'Armagnac or the hot chocolate and pear tart.
Other locations: 29 rue de l'Arcade, 8th (01.42.65.43.68); 6 rue Gassendi, 14th (01.43.22.41.19); 101 rue de la Croix Nivert, 15th (01.48.28.31.88).

Rôtisserie Ste-Marthe
4 rue Ste-Marthe, 10th (01.40.03.08.30).
M° Belleville or Colonel Fabien. **Open** noon-2pm, 8-11.30pm daily. **Average** €12. **Prix fixe** €11 (dinner only). **Lunch menu** €8. **No credit cards. Map** M3.
There's more to ethical eating than animal welfare, bio-produce and fair-trade economics. In a down-market but buzzing spot in north-east Paris – filled with wobbly chairs, vinyl tablecloths and lots of babas (hippies) and bobos (bourgeois bohemians) – the 'social good' value of your euro will shoot sky high with every bite. Run by the Association Rôtisserie Ste-Marthe (who use the space for a community restaurant at lunch), the tiny kitchen is manned – or rather womanned – nightly by a different neighbourhood organisation that cooks to raise money for humanitarian projects. Given Belleville's ethnic mix, you'll be treated to traditional menus from Brazil to Morocco in aid of anything from an educational charity to a crèche. When we last visited, three diminutive Ecuadorian ladies were in charge of our dinner. Their labour of love – steaming plates of Quito's famous creamy potato, pork and avocado soup, spicy empanadas and salad, and thick slices of banana cake with coconut ice-cream – and its feel-good profits were in aid of a family of Ecuadorians seeking to open a canteen near Quito. There's nothing gourmet here (with wine at €1 a glass you won't notice), but if you want every bite to go further than your stomach, the rôtisserie, oozing warmth and spirit, is irresistible.

11TH ARRONDISSEMENT

Bar à Soupes
33 rue de Charonne, 11th (01.43.57.53.79/www.le barasoupes.com). M° Ledru-Rollin or Bastille. **Open** noon-3pm, 6.30-11pm Mon-Sat. Closed last week in July and first week in Aug. **Average** €12. **Lunch menu** €9. **Credit** MC, V. **Non-smoking room. Map** M7.
Weary of those mugs of semi-reconstituted anthrax with kryptonite croutons that pass for soup? Get ye down to the sunshine-coloured Bar à Soupes, where you can swill around such pukka potions as cream of garlic, carrot with pineapple and ginger, or cream of sorrel (to name but three choices from a constantly changing selection), all served up by staff with relentlessly chirpy attitudes. The broths are made fresh each day ('with fresh ingredients and love' coos the PR) and have a heavily vegetarian slant, but there's always at least one meat option that's far from being a mere gesture towards carnivores. If you decide to eat in, you get supplies of several kinds of excellent bread and the €9 formule includes a plate of cheese, charcuterie or dessert plus a glass of wine or coffee. You can, of course, opt for take-away and quaff deep while making the most of window-shopping and über groover-spotting opportunities in the neighbourhood.
Other locations: 5 rue Hérold, 1st (01.45.08.49.84).

Juan et Juanita ★
82 rue Jean-Pierre Timbaud, 11th (01.43.57.60.15). M° Couronnes. **Open** 8pm-2am daily. **Average** €25. **Prix fixe** €17. **Credit** AmEx, MC, V. **Map** N4.
In a neighbourhood full of dusty restaurants and bars, Juan et Juanita has cleared the cobwebs with its fresh-faced clientele and refined, elegantly presented cuisine. Carine Francart's seven-year-old gem is constantly reinventing itself – it started with a Californian menu, but is now decidedly French and consistently good. With dripping candelabras on every table and one in the ladies', the look is polished and flirty – and that goes for the staff too. We began with mesclun salads with toasted hazelnuts, one with a crispy st-marcellin brik. These starters, served with a wink, were followed by the special of the night, buttery rabbit with thyme, and a leg of lamb with mint, a house speciality so tender it needed no convincing off the bone. Desserts filing out of the kitchen looked too good to pass up so we indulged in a lime sorbet with vodka, and vanilla ice-cream with a red fruit coulis. The fairly ambitious wine list is strong on Graves and Gaillacs. Bring a date and go for the €17 menu, but ditch the dainty salad to save room for one of an entire blackboard of desserts that will surely make eyes at you from across the room.

Le Petit Keller
13 bis rue Keller, 11th (01.47.00.12.97). M° Bastille or Voltaire. **Open** noon-2.15pm, 7.30-10.30pm Tue-Sat. Closed Aug. **Prix fixe** €16 (dinner only). **Lunch menu** €9. **Credit** MC, V. **Wheelchair access. Map** M7.
Tucked away from the hip Bastille bars and the hype surrounding the neighbouring Pause Café, this quaint little bistro is a hidden gem. The bright red-and-white checked floor and funky geometric shapes suspended above the bar set the mood for a relaxed,

fun evening. Filled with a friendly mix of gay and straight artistic types, this place infuses its sense of style not only into the decor, but into the food as well. At a very reasonable €15, the prix fixe menu changes daily and presents well-prepared French standards with a creative twist. Excellent starters such as delicately spiced country terrine with sweet onion relish, and fava bean salad tossed in olive oil with toasted cumin and coriander, got our meal off to a beautiful start. The mains were equally delicious, the favourite being the brochette of grilled duck and figs. A perfect marriage of sweet and savoury, the succulent combination of grilled (rare) duck and figs, paired simply with a crispy gratin dauphinois, lifted our palates to unexpected culinary heights. Praiseworthy as well was the boudin noir with baked apples and grilled potatoes. With plenty of fresh bread and a carafe of well-priced Côtes du Rhône, we were happy diners indeed. Apple crumble and a pear tart with gingerbread were both average in light of the preceding courses. At this price, though, who's complaining?

La Ravigote

41 rue de Montreuil, 11th (01.43.72.96.22). M° Faidherbe-Chaligny. **Open** noon-2pm, 7-10.30pm daily. **Prix fixe** €18 (dinner only). **Lunch menu** €13. **Credit** MC, V. **Wheelchair access. Map** P7.

The rue de Montreuil still has vestiges of its furniture-making past, which has been lost in so much of this quartier. Popular with the neighbourhood's artisans and assorted ebony specialists, the Ravigote is one of our favourite local places. The narrow room with its views of old Paris could be a film set from the 1940s, and you half expect Jean Gabin to wander in with a Gauloise hanging from his mouth, dressed in his blue overalls. The welcome is warm and the often-harassed chef potters around, chatting with typical Parisian truculence. The food is unremarkable but reliable and generously served for €12.50 at lunch and €17 in the evening. On a recent visit the pâté was fine; we followed this with the restaurant's signature dish of tête de veau, sauce Ravigote, a gelatinous feast which always hits the spot. On the adjoining table a French group out on a hen night was devouring a steaming chicken tagine with obvious relish. A bottle of the wine of the month, a fruity Mâcon, nicely accompanied the meal through to the gâteau de semoule, served with a comfortingly large quantity of crème anglaise. For a budget meal you can't go far wrong at the Ravigote.

12TH ARRONDISSEMENT

A la Biche au Bois ★

45 av Ledru Rollin, 12th (01.43.43.34.38). M° Gare de Lyon. **Open** noon-2.30pm, 7-11pm Mon-Fri. Closed first three weeks in Aug. **Average** €23. **Prix fixe** €22.50. **Credit** AmEx, DC, MC, V. **Wheelchair access. Map** M8.

No doubt about it, La Biche is definitely a contender for the title of most popular, best bargain bistro in Paris. Anywhere else, we might be complaining about being jammed in so tightly, but however crowded it gets here, it doesn't seem to matter because everyone always seems so happy with the food and the convivial atmosphere. Unusually, fellow diners even say hello as you squeeze into your seat. It's impossible not to be enthusiastic about the more than generous portions offered with the €22.50 prix fixe menu, one of the very few in town to include a selection of game in season. The night we visited, there was even Scottish grouse, incredible when you consider that only the top restaurants offer it as a main course, at three times the price. We began with a massive salade niçoise, replete with fat chunks of tuna, Christmas-red tomatoes and plenty of olives, and a hearty slab of game terrine with the requisite jar of gherkins, both of which were virtually a meal in themselves. Mains included tasty portions of wild duck in blackcurrant sauce, traditional partridge with cabbage, and a filling wild venison stew which, like the coq au vin and the boeuf bourguignon, was served in the Biche's signature cast-iron casserole dishes. All came in gargantuan portions. Lingering too long over your choice of the many perfectly ripe cheeses incurs the risk of getting served automatically with half a dozen of them, doled out by the friendly waiters ever eager to ensure no one waddles home still hungry. If you can still do dessert, go for one of the home-made tarts laden with seasonal fruits or, for something lighter, one of the sorbets liberally drenched in vodka, Calvados or liqueur according to flavour. As for the wine list, it too has a reputation as one of the best-value selections in town, particularly the Rhône section. Book in advance, but expect to wait anyway – it's a small price to pay for a blissful experience.

L'Encrier

55 rue Traversière, 12th (01 44 68 08 16). M° Bastille or Gare de Lyon. **Open** noon-2pm, 7.30-11pm Mon-Fri; 7.30-11pm Sat. Closed Aug. **Average** €20. **Prix fixe** €16, €20 (dinner only). **Lunch menu** €12. **Credit** DC, MC, V. **Wheelchair access. Map** M8.

Through the door and past the velvet curtain, you find yourself face-to-face with the kitchen of L'Encrier, which was in full swing on a weekday evening with a crowd of locals, many of whom seemed to know the charming boss personally. Value is tremendous here, with a €12 lunch menu and a choice of €16 or €20 menus in the evening, as well as a few à la carte choices. We began with some fried rabbit kidneys on a bed of salad dressed with raspberry vinegar, an original and wholly successful combination. A spiced home-made terrine was more banal, but main course goose magret with honey was a welcome change form the usual duck version and served, like the andouillette we also ordered, with crunchy, thinly sliced sautéed potatoes. Our bottle of fruity Chinon was a classy red at a rather steep €24, but worth every cent. To finish our meal we shared a chocolate cake which had a nice spongy texture but was a little low on cocoa punch; the popular profiteroles looked better. The attractive space and friendly service attract a hip Bastille crowd.

Le Pays de Vannes

34 bis rue de Wattignies, 12th (01.43.07.87.42).
M° Michel Bizot. **Open** 6.30am-8pm Mon-Sat.
Food served 11.45am-3pm Mon-Sat. Closed Aug.
Average €15. **Lunch menu** €10. **Credit** MC, V.
Non-smoking room. Wheelchair access.
Map Q10.

Just the kind of neighbourhood restaurant you would like to find on your doorstep, the Pays de Vannes delivers much more than its café-like exterior promises. At lunch we found a jovial crowd of office workers tucking into hearty fare. The only tables left empty were a few inches from the loo doors, so we were entertained throughout with a constant stream of visitors. This did not seem to bother anyone else at the other two tables near us and everyone got on with recounting the latest gossip while downing fair quantities of the so-so house wine. The crab cocktail was just the thing for a light lunch and featured a shower of shredded real crab, not the usual surimi, on a bed of crisp, freshly torn lettuce. The snowy-white flesh of our main course – melt-in-the-mouth sole meunière – came, at our request, with chunky golden chips instead of the usual boiled or steamed spuds. We finished off this Breton-inspired meal with home-made far breton, a flan chock-a-block with plump, moist prunes, light-years from the often-proffered, dried-up version.

13TH ARRONDISSEMENT

Chez Gladines

30 rue des Cinq-Diamants, 13th (01.45.80.70.10). M°
Place d'Italie. **Open** noon-3pm, 7pm-midnight Mon,
Tue, Sun; noon-3pm, 7pm-1am Wed-Fri; noon-4pm;
7pm-1am Sat. Closed three weeks in Aug, 24, 25, 31
Dec and 1 Jan. **Average** €17. **Lunch menu** €10
(Mon-Fri). **No credit cards. Wheelchair access.**

The mood had just tipped from festive to raucous when we arrived at this no-frills Basque address on a Friday night. Packed in family-style, happy students were plunging into swimming pool-sized bowls of salad loaded with ham, fried potatoes and every other hearty topping imaginable. Chez Gladines occupies a corner in the heart of the Butte aux Cailles, a warren of narrow streets that forms a vibrant young neighbourhood behind the Place d'Italie. The simple and satisfying dishes it churns out keep its revellers well-nourished, and its efficient selection of inexpensive wines from southern France to northern Spain keeps them well-watered. We fell in step with the majority and ordered the salade Cinq Diamants, enough for a family of four, and a poulet basquaise, a more reasonably proportioned plate of chicken in a spicy tomato sauce. We shared a bread basket with our neighbours and gulped down a couple of chilly glasses of Irouleguy, a Basque red. Service was friendly and efficient, though we longed

L'Alchimie. *See p148.*

to pitch in and help our harried waitress. Standing at the narrow bar here, it almost feels like you're in San Sebastian, stopping to fill up with friends before continuing on into a busy night.

Le Temps des Cerises

18 rue de la Butte-aux-Cailles, 13th (01.45.89.69.48).
M° Corvisart or Place d'Italie. **Open** 11.45am-2pm,
7.30-11.30pm Mon-Fri; 7.30pm-midnight Sat.
Average €25. **Prix fixe** €13.50, €22 (dinner only).
Lunch menu €10. **Credit** AmEx, MC, V.
Wheelchair access. Non-smoking room.

'For God's sake turn your mobiles off!' This delightful message pinned to the door was our first greeting. The second was 'Salut, tu vas bien?' from a waiter dressed in full-length denim dungarees. Fashion and formality are resolutely absent from this workers' co-operative restaurant – and no matter how hurried you are, the waiters won't be. It's worth spending time over a meal here, however, settled at one of the long tables (a great leveller), in the charming, old-fashioned dining room. A starter of légumes tièdes was, well, a plate of warm vegetables cut into no-nonsense wedges. Amid the spuds and carrots, swedes and sweet potatoes did their best to liven things up a bit. You'll soon realise that the food is not going to be dazzling. A carafe of the incredibly cheap and surprisingly drinkable house red is probably a wise move. A chunky meat salad and ho-hum salmon with the same veg as the starter made us envy our neighbour's guarantee of satisfaction – he had simply ordered creamy cheese and a basket of bread. Pudding was our last hope, dashed by the plastic-tasting Charlotte au chocolat. Plenty of bonhomie, but not really bonne bouffe.

14TH ARRONDISSEMENT

Au Rendez-Vous des Camionneurs

34 rue des Plantes, 14th (01.45.40.43.36). M° Alésia.
Open noon-3pm, 6.30-10.30pm Mon-Sat. **Average**
€24. **Prix fixe** €13.50. **Credit** MC, V

This tiny restaurant is low on frills and high on conviviality. Surrounded by football posters and pendants, the ten small tables quickly fill with locals on a nightly basis. One instantly becomes part of the neighbourhood club as conversations are swapped across white paper-covered tables topped with crocks of Dijon mustard. We were seated by the patroness-cum-mother Monique; after taking our coats, she went over the blackboard specials of the evening, and offered us complimentary glasses of champagne. Her husband Claude, decked out in his white chef's coat, walked around the dining room greeting guests like old friends. The menu is as simple and straightforward as the setting, with the limited prix fixe menu a steal at €13.50. We skipped the grated carrot starter after spying the crousti de tomates; the thick slice of toasted bread topped with grilled tomato, onion, cheese and oregano reminded us of the French bread pizzas of childhood. The gigot de sept heures, lamb cooked for seven hours, was so tender it arrived as a pile of shredded meat with accompanying white beans. Sauté de boeuf looked unprepossessing with its side of plain pasta, but enhanced by a nice dollop from the mustard crock, the beef was actually quite tasty. Tarte aux pommes was bland and quite burnt, but the Mont Blanc – chestnut purée under a cloud of whipped cream – was pure bliss.

15TH ARRONDISSEMENT

L'Alchimie

34 rue Letellier, 15th (01.45.75.55.95) M° La-Motte-Picquet-Grenelle. **Open** noon-2.30pm, 7.30-10.30pm
Tue-Fri; 7.30-11pm Sat. Closed 10 days at Christmas.
Average €25. **Prix fixe** €20. **Credit** MC, V.
Map C8.

Formerly the popular La Folletterie, this promising bistro is having a few problems adjusting to its new identity. While the current prix fixe is exceptionally good value, L'Alchimie's imaginative presentation of classic French dishes is let down by a tatty interior. Bare walls and dead tulips rarely create an atmosphere. A similar sense of awkwardness showed in some of the dishes; we began with one of the daily specials, an excellent langoustine risotto with a €5 supplement, and a feuilleté of snails, buttery and fresh but literally dampened by an unnecessary wad of soggy spinach. To follow, a faux-filet of Charolais beef with a simple salad and sautéed potatoes was perfectly competent without being memorable, but the sea bream in a sauce of lightly curried mussels was a lovely combination of firm fish and mild, warming spices. The accompanying carrot purée didn't work, though, a

misjudgement which continued with the pudding, a respectable tarte aux pommes spoiled by poor-quality ice-cream. We were delighted with our choice of a smooth and fruity Languedoc-Roussillon at €18, and the wine list, though sparse, is thoughtful, offering a choice of unusual French regional wines in the €15-€22 range. At present, L'Alchimie isn't quite worth crossing town for, but if you're in the area, cooking of this standard at these prices makes it well worth a visit. Since the service was extremely friendly and professional, a few tweaks to the menu and an investment in some fresh flowers might well make it a magical destination.

Chez Charles-Victor

*19 rue Duranton, 15th (01.45.58.43.17). M°
Boucicault.* **Open** noon-2.30pm, 7.30-10.30pm Mon-Fri;
7.30-10.30pm Sat. **Average** €30. **Prix fixe** €19.90.
Credit MC, V. **Wheelchair access**. **Map** B9.

The Gaudet brothers have moved on since the last edition, but this corner bistro is looking bright and cheery under new ownership. The young local crowd obviously appreciates the competitively priced menu at €19.90. Bright yellow walls frame a blackboard menu that has a vaguely south-western feel – gésiers, magrets and confits to the fore. Foie gras was a quality slice for a tiny €2 supplement, while the home-made terrine was meaty and livery, and a goat's cheese filo parcel on salad up to standard. Main courses were pleasant, with a well-cooked magret de canard in a syrupy sauce, a handsome Argentinean entrecôte, and some tender veal kidneys in a mustard sauce. Only the quenelles de brochet were heavy and uninspired, but this dish needs culinary mastery to which the restaurant no longer seems to aspire. Puddings were simple affairs: an unspectacular dame blanche (vanilla ice-cream with chocolate sauce), excellent crème brûlée, over-chilled cheese. With charming service from the young owners, it was good to see this place attracting a lively crowd.

La Licorne

10 rue Nelaton, 15th (01.45.77.47.43). M° Bir-Hakeim. **Open** 7.30am-8pm Mon-Fri. **Average**
€20. **Prix fixe** €13.50, €15.50. **Lunch menu** €10.
Credit MC, V. **Wheelchair access**. **Non-smoking room**. **Map** B7.

Opposite the Ministry of the Interior and near the Eiffel Tower, this single-horned corner café almost becomes a ministerial canteen at lunch. We were happy to join the flow of pen-pushers, who obviously keep the standard of cooking higher than your average neighbourhood café. The bright, impeccably clean room is entirely given over to dining, and the welcome couldn't have been warmer. A starter of warm potato salad and marinated herring was a good version of the classic dish, and the main courses of a rare pavé de rumsteak au poivre with chunky home-made fries, and a giant campagnarde salad topped with a runny poached egg were both tasty and well prepared. The menus at €13.50 for two courses and €15.50 for three

Eating on the run

If a passer-by has ever stopped to wish you 'bon appétit' as you walk down the street munching on a croissant and you've thought how lovely the French can be, think again. There are some countries in the world where eating in the street is simply not done. Japan is one, France is another, and the 'bon appétit' that eating in the street is sure to elicit is not meant to aid you in the digestion of your sandwich, but is a sign of puzzlement, if not disapproval.

So, what are the alternatives? The obvious answer is to go for the quickly scoff-able from street vendors. Crêpes and gaufres (waffles) are almost acceptable and have the double advantage of being fairly easy to eat (avoid the crème Chantilly) and reasonably French. If you simply have to go inside, look for bakeries with seating or sandwich bars, or take the student option and go for a Grec or Turc. Following is an area-by-area guide to eating on the run with dignity:

Latin Quarter

Try the Grecs in the pedestrian streets (rue de la Harpe, rue St-Séverin) near the St-Michel Métro and RER station. Though the kebabs and sandwiches are predictable, the more elaborate plats du jour can come as a pleasant surprise. Up rue St-Jacques the Chinese noodle house, Mirama (*see pp174-177* **Far Eastern**) has been popular for decades. Along its upper end, rue Mouffetard is awash with kebab houses and crêperies, perfect sustenance for a night in the neighbourhood's Anglo bars.

Montparnasse

This area is a crêpe-lover's mecca. Rue du Montparnasse is the place for sit-down crêpes, while there are many crêpe stands to choose from around the cinemas of the boulevard du Montparnasse. One of the best is Alberto (79 bd du Montparnasse, 6th, 01.45.44.12.38), with its nifty rectangular crêpe contraption and chatty cook. Unfortunately the area is rather bereft of leafy squares, though there is a tiny one next to the church near rue Vavin.

Les Halles

There is no shortage of kebabs here either, but the Scandinavian sandwich shop Nils (36 rue Montorgueil, 1st, 01.55.34.39.49 and 10 rue de Buci, 6th, 01.46.34.82.82) offers an appetising alternative with its pleasant Ikea-style dining room and 15-minute meal philosophy. Along the pedestrian market street rue Montorgueil, you might slurp a plate of oysters at a café or assemble a picnic to eat on the Pont des Arts (a more atmospheric destination than the louche park at Les Halles).

Louvre-Palais Royal-Opéra

At lunch on a sunny day, the Palais-Royal gardens fill with office workers who have bypassed the three-course lunch in favour of a jambon-beurre sandwich or, better yet, hot pasta to go from nearby Mille Pâtes (5 rue des Petits-Champs, 1st, 01.42.96.03.04). The rue Ste-Anne is lined with affordable Japanese noodle houses (*see pp196-200* **Japanese**) and Asian supermarkets selling take-away sushi. Just off avenue de l'Opéra, La Ferme Opéra (55-57 rue St-Roch, 1st, 01.46.33.35.36) is not the only self-serve restaurant in Paris, but it's one of the best with its ultra-fresh produce from the Ile de France region.

Le Marais

The options are many in this area, starting with freshly fried falafel along rue des Rosiers (*see pp201-202* **Jewish**). Near pretty place des Vosges, the Italian épicerie Frascati (14 rue de Turenne, 4th, 01.42.77.27.42) assembles probably the best panini in town; across the street, Pasta Linea serves sublime pastas sauced with ceps, artichokes or truffle cream at its tiny counters or to take away.

courses represent government fiscal policy at its most thrifty. Small wonder there is a rather glamorous signed picture of the home secretary on the bar, from which we enjoyed a couple of glasses of bone-dry Muscadet. Tourists were not much in evidence on our visit and to have the opportunity to peek in at French bureaucratic life is alone worth the small price of a meal here.

Au Métro
18 bd Pasteur, 15th (01.47.34.21.24). M° Pasteur. **Open** noon-3pm, 6pm-1am Mon-Sat. Closed Aug. **Average** €20. **Prix fixe** €15, €23. **Credit** MC, V. **Map** E9.

This little bar/bistro proudly wears its south-west colours on its sleeve, from the hearty cassoulet to the rugby photos. With red paper tablecloths and no-frills decor, Au Métro is about good value in very simple surroundings: bring your own atmosphere. After-work drinkers gather around the bar quaffing cheap beer and going over the last Stade de France match while a dozen tables accommodate diners – just us on this occasion. Our salads were large and fresh, the magret de canard was juicy and the accompanying roast potatoes were a garlicky delight. The frites that accompanied the roast chicken had been undercooked in an oil that we suspected needed changing, but the bird itself was tender and, like everything else, huge. Basic desserts such as apple tarts and chocolate mousse are kept in the same display fridge as the Basque pâtés but this did not seem to affect their taste, for better or worse. The heavy portions are in sharp contrast with the featherweight bill.

16TH ARRONDISSEMENT
Restaurant GR5
19 rue Gustave Courbet, 16th (01.47.27.09.84). M° Trocadéro. **Open** noon-2.30pm, 7-10pm Mon-Sat. **Average** €25. **Prix fixe** €16.50, €21 (dinner only). **Lunch menu** €14. **Credit** AmEx, MC, V. **Map** B4.

Named after the famous hiking trail winding through the Jura to the Alps, this little refuge among the area's chic boutiques serves hearty cheese and potato-based Alpine cuisine. Red-and-white checked tablecloths and wood-panelled walls hung with dried flowers, cowbells and ski posters made convincing surroundings. The queyrassienne (€35 for two people) is an addictive take on traditional fondue: this bubbling pot of three cheeses contains chunks of smoky bacon and sweet onion confit, accompanied by bread cubes and potatoes. Absolutely divine. Tartiflette (potato, cheese and bacon gratin) with walnut salad is an equally rib-sticking option for €17. A €21 prix fixe menu offers traditional French fare, but no fondue. The wine of choice is the delicate Crépy – a crisp regional white wine that makes the perfect partner for the hearty cuisine. Though happily stuffed with cheese and potatoes, we couldn't resist ending our meal with

chocolate fondue. The tiny pot of chocolate was served with mixed fruit, marshmallows and ladyfingers. Good, but not quite worth €13. Fortified for the walk home, we headed into the chilly night air, straining our ears for the crunch of snow.

17TH ARRONDISSEMENT
Au Bon Coin
16 rue Jacquemont, 17th (01.458.60.28.72). M° La Fourche. **Open** noon-2.30pm Mon, Tue; noon-2.30pm, 8-10.30pm Wed-Fri. Closed two weeks in Aug. **Average** €15. **Credit** MC, V. **Wheelchair access**. **Map** F1.

When the people who run the Tête de Goinfre and Cave du Cochon restaurants up the street took over this run-down corner café, local aesthetes winced. Here, after all, was a perfect example of a now-rare breed of Parisian café, complete with vintage floor tiles and a Formica bar. But the Cochon people didn't fill the Bon Coin with little plastic pigs (as they have their other joints). They made it usable for the hordes of design students from across the street and other young locals, while the very cheap prices mean the old regulars still pop in for a beer (€1.80) or a glass of Sauvignon (€1). If you feel like indulging in something stiffer – whisky, vermouth or a shot of rum – in most Parisian cafés you'd be in for a financial kick to the solar plexus. Not here. The lunches (plus dinner as the weekend approaches) are simple and cheap, sometimes good (mussels with cream, sautéed veal and 'mousseline' mashed potatoes) and rarely less than OK. This is a lively place to come with friends.

18TH ARRONDISSEMENT
La Renaissance
112 rue Championnet, 18th (01.46.06.01.76). M° Jules Joffrin or Porte de Clignancourt. **Open** 9.30am-midnight Mon-Fri; noon-3.30pm Sat. **Food served** noon-3.30pm, 7-10.30pm. Closed one week at Christmas. **Average** €20. **Credit** MC, V.

La Renaissance is buried deep in a residential neighbourhood, so before making the trip we called to make sure it was open for lunch, only to be rudely hung up on by a hurried waiter. We began the journey grumpy, but were pleasantly surprised by the good bistro fare served with a twist and traditional atmosphere. With no prix fixe, we skipped the expensive, meal-like starters and went straight for the main – a steak au poivre in a tasty, if crème fraîche-heavy pepper sauce served with small, fresh fried potatoes instead of the standard frites. Our neighbours dipped into a nice-looking poulet rôti served on a full cutting board with vegetables and a steaming baked potato. Portions are generous, but with a 25cl carafe of Bordeaux our bill was already more than it should be, so we skipped the uninteresting desserts. This place is not worth going out of your way for, but it's a good bet in the neighbourhood.

Le Rendez-Vous des Chauffeurs

11 rue des Portes Blanches, 18th (01.42.64.04.17).
M° Marcadet-Poissonniers. **Open** noon-2.30pm, 7.30-
11pm daily. **Average** €25. **Prix fixe** €10, €14 (until
8.30pm). **Credit** MC, V.
Little here has changed over the past 80-odd years,
and once you take your seat at one of the long tables
you'll understand why no one is complaining. The
inexpensive three-course prix fixe gives you a fair
selection of dishes and even includes a pitcher of
house wine, which goes so well with the traditional
fare that we ended up ordering a second. We started
with a simple fisherman's salad, the mayonnaise of
the potatoes a good foil for the firm white fish, along
with a plate of saucisson sec. The waiter duly
unhooked the sausage from its traditional hanging
place behind the bar and sliced it up before us. Try
to order a main dish with frites, as they're made
fresh with wide potato slices. If you're feeling
particularly hungry, order one of the substantial à
la carte dishes, such as the lamb. Be sure to
accompany your meal with the well-priced bottle of
the month (€15), which sits enticingly on every table.

Les Trois Frères ★

*14 rue Léon, 18th (01.42.64.91.73). M° Château-
Rouge.* **Open** noon-3pm, 7.30-11.30pm daily. Closed
Aug. **Average** €25. **Lunch menu** €7, €12. **Credit**
MC, V. **Wheelchair access. Map** K1.
The Chez Omar of the Goutte d'Or, this great-value,
friendly little place is one of Paris's best-kept secrets.

Three brothers and their father have been dishing
up great grills and couscous to an eclectic local
crowd at this family affair for over two decades. The
small dining room is a little worn around the edges
but spotlessly clean and charming with its old-
fashioned fresco encircling the room and white linen
tablecloths. Choose two courses from a daily €7 or
€12 menu. The €7 menu includes an honest range
of choices with mains such as saucisse de Toulouse
with purée, or hachis Parmentier. The more
'expensive' option is the way to go, with choices
ranging from deep-fried bream with steamed
potatoes or beans to a really first-rate Limousin
faux-filet, followed by a mean chocolate mousse.
Wander off the menu for whole fried trout (€7) or
try the excellent couscous, ranging from a generous
three lamb chop version to quail. Everything here is
incredibly fresh and the portions are substantial.
The wine list is a little, shall we say, overlooked, but
with nothing over €10, including some quaffable
Bordeaux, who can complain? This place synthesises
a whole quartier's unpretentious fun. A concert
space recently opened out the back, which can only
complement the night-time possibilities offered by
their long-established neighbours, the Olympic Café.

Au Virage Lepic

*61 rue Lepic, 18th (01.42.52.46.79). M° Abbesses or
Blanche.* **Open** Mon, Wed-Sun 7-11.30pm. Closed one
week in Aug and one week at Christmas. **Prix fixe**
€19. **Credit** MC, V. **Map** H1.

A la Bière.
See p152.

A snug hideaway safely distanced from the tourist mayhem of Sacré-Coeur, this restaurant is exactly what the neighbourhood's history demands. The walls are covered with music-hall posters and old film star stills, and the red-checked tablecloths and traditional zinc bar provide the backdrop for a very satisfying two-course menu. We started with the feuilleté, a warm pastry filled with potatoes, cheese and bacon, and the onion soup, scalding hot with delicious slightly burnt cheese. Though all the mains looked tasty, we went with the magret de canard – crisp, perfectly cooked and dressed with fried potatoes – and the equally good roast chicken. Desserts, riz au lait and parfait au chocolat, coupled with an inexpensive bill, sent us out of the door smiling. Though the owner does his best to squeeze people in, showing up without a reservation will leave you stranded and envious.

19TH ARRONDISSEMENT

A la Bière ★

104 av Simon Bolivar, 19th (01.42.39.83.25).
Mº Colonel Fabien. **Open** 7am-7pm daily. **Average**
€13. **Prix fixe** €11.80. **Credit** MC, V. **Wheelchair**
access. Map M3.

When you've passed a place on every night of the week and it's always full you know they must be doing something right. A la Bière is one of those nondescript corner brasseries with noisy pop music and lots of smoke, but what they do is an amazing value €11.80 menu full of good-quality bistro favourites with a smile. Our starters of thinly sliced pork 'muzzle' with a nice French dressing on the salad and a home-made rabbit terrine exceeded our expectations. Could the mains live up to this fine start? Indeed they did. The entrecôte was charcoal grilled no less, and served with hand-cut chips, while the juicy Lyonnais sausages came with pommes de terre huilées that were simply delicious, drenched in olive oil, garlic and parsley. There must be a catch somewhere, we thought, expecting meagre helpings of tarte Tatin to follow, but no, they were copious, moist and, well, just as a tarte Tatin should be. The staff know their wine and never hurry the diners, and there was some jolly banter going on at the bar. This is one of the few bargains left in Paris – let's hope it stays that way.

20TH ARRONDISSEMENT

La Boulangerie

15 rue des Panoyaux, 20th (01.43.58.45.45/www.
restaurantboulangerie.com). Mº Ménilmontant. **Open**
noon-2.30pm, 7.30-11pm Mon-Thur; noon-2.30pm,
7.30pm-midnight Fri; 7.30pm-midnight Sat. Closed
two weeks in Aug. **Average** €25. **Prix fixe** €18.50.
Lunch menu €10.50, €11. **Credit** MC, V. **Map** P4.

Housed in an old bakery that has been boldly renovated to bread-themed glory we doubt the original ever had (check out the fabulous blue mosaic floors embellished with delicate wheat sheaves), Mohammed Mehanni's Boulangerie is a local institution. Paired with the buzzing place across the street (Lou Pascalou is owned by Mehanni's dad), it's a testament to the promise of immigrant success in a neighbourhood better known for tagines than terrines (ours of tasty, chunky poultry came spiked with Armagnac and port). Unfortunately, though, the food didn't live up to expectations. Starters (like the terrine) and desserts (a delicate banana Tatin with dark chocolate sauce and a chocolate mousse with chunks of coffee meringue) were uniformly good, but mains missed the mark. We spotted a tasty-looking cod brandade wrapped in brik pastry after we'd ordered the uninspired daily special – an almost sauce-less coq au vin – and a boney duck fricassée. There is an innovative twist to much of the cooking – the duck was flavoured with dates and star-anise – and lots of things, especially plate rims, come dusted with cinnamon. Service was pressed, with only one waitress juggling a busy Monday night, and there was no bread basket to sate our hunger while we waited. Nonetheless, the atmosphere was pleasant and the longish wine list helped pass the time.

L'Echappée

38 rue Boyer, 20th (01.47.97.44.58). Mº Ménilmontant
or Gambetta. **Open** noon-2.30pm, 8-11pm Tue-Sat.
Average €24. **Prix fixe** €16. **Credit** MC, V. **Map** P4.

Jean, of the old Chez Jean, has retired to the 5th ('so he can't be too badly off,' say the new owners), taking with him his garrulous wife and large collection of artworks. In their place, white walls, a trompe l'oeil of bookcases, tea lights and, on this Saturday night, Riton the barrel organ player complete with a book of French chanson words so you can sing along in a kind of Piaf-era karaoke. It's all very well-meaning and the two young men who run it are extremely pleasant, but we ended up feeling sad that the 20th is becoming a pastiche of its former self. The whiteboard menu covers bistro classics with some more international fare such as the Russian-style chicken croquettes and Senegalese maffe, which, though the chef appeared to be African, was not the large steaming plate of lemony curry infused for hours that you would get at a genuine Senegalese restaurant, though the fried plantain was tasty. The starters exhibited panache – a very fresh mille-feuille of avocado cut with crème fraîche and chives and dribbled with olive oil and balsamic vinegar, and creamy snails on a bed of leeks, served with delicious bread. Our other main, though, was similarly small in proportions and the black pudding with a round of apple and mashed potato was a little bit dry. Puddings of faisselle (fromage blanc) in a raspberry coulis and a frothy sabayon with red fruit were pleasant enough. It's the resolutely middle-class clientele that is blandest of all, many of them piling out of the Maroquinerie arts centre. However, this type of restaurant does provide a good address for visiting friends as it has a vegetarian option, a non-smoking area and nothing too scary on the menu.

Vegetarian

Announce that you're a vegetarian in an ordinary Paris restaurant and the waiter will most likely refuse to comprehend. One common, and entirely un ironic, retort we've heard is, 'You must be ill. There are good hospitals here'. Understandably, then, vegetarians are grateful for the existence of meatless restaurants in Paris, even if many of these remain stuck in a hippie timewarp with obscure links to spiritual leaders, too many grated raw vegetables and occasionally a strict no-alcohol policy. A healthy dose of hedonism wouldn't do any of these places any harm, but many of them are endearing nonetheless. Once you've exhausted their takes on seitan and tofu, be reassured that it is possible for a vegetarian to eat well in many Paris restaurants if armed with the right vocabulary (*see p155* **Going green**).

Foody's Brunch Café ★

26 rue Montorgueil, 1st (01.40.13.02.53).
M° Châtelet or Les Halles. **Open** 11.30am-5pm Mon-Sat. Closed one week in Feb and first two weeks in Aug. **Average** €9. **Prix fixe** €8, €9.50, €12.50. **Credit** MC, V. **Wheelchair access. Map** J5.

When the smell of kebabs gets to you and the idea of steak-frites seems too carnivorous, then stop off for a quick lunch at Foody's Brunch Café in a pedestrian street near Les Halles. The terrace makes a great place to people-watch in an exhaust fume-free zone, and opposite is a wholefood organic store to add to the feeling of well-being. The idea is simple; you choose your bowl, either small or large, and pile on as much of the fresh salads on display as possible. Even in the early afternoon, the salads were still fresh and well topped-up, with some excellent basil-flavoured pasta and a good couscous number, to which we added numerous vegetables to make up an impressively large platter, served with a hunk of crisp baguette. This all came to under €7, which has to be one of the city's best veg bargains. The wood-panelled interior resembles a Swiss chalet and those expecting style need to look elsewhere; bowls and cutlery are in ecologically unsound plastic. If you want a more substantial meal you can order one of the excellent soups and end your meal with a homey cake, accompanied by a vegetable juice or smoothie.

La Victoire Suprême du Coeur

41 rue des Bourdonnais, 1st (01.40.41.93.95).
M° Châtelet. **Open** 11.45am-2.30pm, 7-10pm Mon-Sat. Closed two weeks in April and Aug. **Average** €25. **Prix fixe** €15.90-€17.90. **Wheelchair access. Non-smoking. Credit** MC, V. **Map** J6.

Run by supporters of Indo-American guru Sri Chinmoy (whose photographs and paintings festoon the walls), this new-age restaurant offers plenty of choice for vegans. The pale blue dining room is entirely non-smoking, a blissful change from most Parisian restaurants. No alcohol is served, but

there's an excellent range of fruit juices, lassis, chai and other teas. Our starters were excellent: a flavourful mushroom terrine with onion chutney, and pakoras which, though more like lightly fried onion rings than any Indian dish, were fresh and comforting. The day's main course special was filling, a vegetable plate with a hearty serving of the delicious South American grain quinoa. Seitan steak resembled tough veal, drowning in a sauce that looked and tasted suspiciously like tinned soup. Our chakras were restored by dessert, a wonderful chocolate tart in custard sauce that helped us to look kindly upon the universe. The front counter also does take-away, useful if you're wandering through the fast-food wilderness of Les Halles.

Le Potager du Marais

22 rue Rambuteau, 3rd (01.42.74.24.66). M°
Rambuteau. **Open** noon-10.30pm Mon-Fri; 1-10.30pm Sat, Sun. **Average** €20. **Prix fixe** €15. **Lunch menu** €12. **Credit** MC, V. **Non-smoking. Map** K5.

At capacity, this place could pack a potential 33 leaf-eaters into a space that's as long and narrow as a railroad car; hope it doesn't happen, since the one-man kitchen and single friendly waiter couldn't possibly cope. As it was, on a quiet weekday night, we giggled almost alone over the idea of vegetarian choucroute garnie – the cabbage ornamented with various veg versions of the traditional pork – and wondered why it is that vegetarian cooking in Paris remains decidedly stuck in a hippie rut. The problem here is that the menu is conceived around the absence of meat and fish rather than celebrating it. Vegetarian pâté had a dark pea-green colour and a mushy texture that made it hard to appreciate its deep, rich flavour, while goat's cheese drizzled with honey and roasted on toast was pleasant but in no way original. Main courses varied from oily deep-fried breaded mushrooms with tartare sauce, salad and over-cooked rice to a miserably soggy sauté of vegetables and tofu. The only really memorable thing about this meal was the superb bread – chewy, pungent sourdough – and the kindly waiter. Desserts were no surprise — fromage blanc with fruit coulis or honey, fruit crumble, etc – and the brief wine list failed to offer any of the brilliant organic wines being made in France. Could do better.

Galerie 88

88 quai de l'Hôtel de Ville, 4th (01.42.72.17.58). Mº Hôtel de Ville or Pont Marie. **Open** noon-midnight daily. **Average** €15. **No credit cards. Wheelchair access. Map** K6.

Tucked away off the chaotic quai is this cosy little Moroccan-styled haven dishing up hearty servings of mostly meatless soup, salads, pasta and tapas (though cured ham and fish do crop up occasionally, so ask). The setting is rustic: weathered red banquettes and ochre-coloured walls in front, with exposed stone and wood beams in the back. Silk throws and gold and silver teapots add a touch of the exotic, while blues music and tattered hand-written menus suggest there is not a hint of pretension to this student hangout. Our generous salads arrived in colourful Peruvian earthenware dishes, accompanied by a small basket of rye bread and corn chips. The Mexican salad consisted mostly of tasty guacamole, while the assiette 88 was a display of their most popular tapas: lemony tabouleh, black olive tapenade, a rather bland aubergine caviar, chopped tomatoes and cucumber, and the guacamole. Second course was a shared bowl of earthy split-pea soup, subtly spiced with smoky undertones of cumin and coriander. Desserts didn't look especially appealing, but a pot of Moroccan mint tea made a perfect conclusion to this laid-back meal.

Piccolo Teatro

6 rue des Ecouffes, 4th (01.42.72.17.79). Mº St-Paul or Hôtel de Ville. **Open** noon-3pm, 7-11.30pm daily. **Average** €22. **Prix fixe** €15.10, €21.50. **Lunch menu** €9.10-€14.70. **Credit** AmEx, DC, MC, V. **Map** K6.

Unlike many veggie restaurants in Paris, this cosy Marais stalwart has a properly romantic atmosphere. The focus of the menu is gratin: you choose one of a variety of vegetable combinations to have covered in cheese and baked. We started with two soups – miso and the day's special, cream of celery, but both were bland. The first had little miso flavour, and the cream and cornstarch base overwhelmed the delicate taste of the celery. We consoled ourselves with an excellent Belgian beer. Our generous gratins came promptly and all was going well until we hit the middle of the courgette-buckwheat gratin. A green jelly-like substance oozed out from under the cheese; we scraped it on to the edge of the plate, where it congealed as we watched. The waitress insisted that the recipe contained only courgette, buckwheat and mint, which seemed unlikely. Our pleasant desserts of chocolate mousse and cake-like plum crumble only partially soothed our anxious stomachs.

Les 5 Saveurs d'Anada

72 rue du Cardinal-Lemoine, 5th (01.43.29.58.54/ www.anada5saveurs.com). Mº Cardinal-Lemoine. **Open** noon-2.30pm, 7-10.30pm Tue-Sun. Closed one week in Jan. **Average** €15. **Prix fixe** €12.90, €13.90. **Credit** MC, V. **Non-smoking. Map** K8.

Formerly Les Quatre et Une Saveurs, this wood-beamed restaurant near the top of rue Mouffetard has changed owners and name, but not its earnest approach to macrobiotic, '100 per cent organic' cooking. Like almost every other vegetarian restaurant in Paris, it takes itself just that little bit too seriously. Then again, it's hard to be hedonistic when you eschew meat, eggs, cheese, butter or sugar (the macrobiotic diet), and it can do anyone good to have a virtuous, cleansing meal. Recovering from a rich French feast the previous night, we were happy to tuck into our assiette garnie and assiette complète, the difference being that the complète adds seaweed and lentils to the mix. One had cod as its main ingredient and the other nutty-tasting seitan, served with a topping of preserved ginger. Our failure to get through the piles of raw grated carrot and beetroot, pickled cabbage, grains and colourful steamed vegetables earned us a bit of a scolding from the owner, and indeed the fresh vegetables deserved more respect. Making a tart without any of the naughtier ingredients – butter, sugar, eggs – creates a challenge, but pear tart with almonds in a pool of dairy-free custard proved surprisingly tender-crusted and tasty. It certainly appealed to us more than a bowl of agar-agar, one of the other choices. To drink, try one of the freshly made juices or a pot of tea prepared with unusual care.

Le Grenier de Notre-Dame ★

18 rue de la Bûcherie, 5th (01.43.29.98.29/ www.legrenierdenotredame.com). Mº St-Michel or Maubert-Mutualité. **Open** noon-2.30pm, 6.30-11.30pm daily. **Average** €30. **Prix fixe** €15, €17. **Credit** MC, V. **Map** J7.

Le Grenier's riot of exterior green picks out the restaurant in its hideaway near the Seine, while an extravagant array of vegetables painted on the outside tables hints at the equally comprehensive range on the menu. The welcome from manager Laurent Boiseau is warm as you settle among an international clientele in the intimacy of a playroom-bright decor. Inventive and imaginative are words to describe the fare which features, typically, long-time Grenier favourite meatless cassoulet, vegetarian lasagne and lentil moussaka, complemented by plenty of salad vegetables and an exceptional country bread with sesame seeds. The three-course dinner menu (€14.50) has less zap than à la carte, but for veggie reassurance 80 per cent of the ingredients and all the wines are organic, and the components of the 13 exotic non-alcoholic cocktails are processed as you listen. Special effects are a choice of 22 teas and a lightweight afternoon menu. The only downer was the dodgy FM-radio background music.

Going green

Nothing demonstrates the insularity of French restaurants more than their continued refusal to provide meat-free options. While chefs the world over treat vegetables (and vegetarians) with respect, most French chefs have yet to catch on; even those who declare themselves passionate about produce sadly fail to connect this with non-meat eaters. Vegetarians are usually left to poach the side dishes of their companions, while their assiette de légumes consists of a few vegetables boiled tasteless and a pile of rice.

Paris abounds in sweet little veggie cafés with soothing, organic-sounding names and food lacking in flavour or culinary flair. One crop of veggie places firmly entrenched in hippiedom does a fine line in meat-substitute products, out-of-date Brit favourites (think nut roast) and ingredients that should never be combined (olives and sultanas anyone?). Those few restaurants that do try and cater for vegetarians (usually foreign-

owned or self-consciously trendy) still haven't got it either. One such place serves as its veggie options a large plate of plain grated beetroot followed by a tagine that substitutes pepper for flavour.

But meat-free eating in your average Parisian establishment is still possible and with some care you can avoid the horror that is the jellied egg, paprika-covered melon and goat's cheese salad. Ordering two starters will raise at least an eyebrow and often an objection, but declare your vegetarian status and it will usually pass, as will a request for a side of chips or potatoes. You can also order a salad without meat or an assiette de légumes, but specify what you do and don't like: couscous, a tinned peach half, overcooked carrots and a pile of lettuce is one recent chef's imagining of what a vegetarian might like to eat. Some restaurants work the assiette into the formule, others will charge outrageously: welcome to the vegetarian tax. At a restaurant that doesn't normally cater to vegetarians, it can be well worth calling ahead to plan your meal.

Happily things are improving. Unsurprisingly, it's the big-name places such as **Terminus Nord** (*see p93*) and **Café de la Paix** (*see p225*) that have grasped that vegetarian food can and should mean good food that doesn't have meat in it. Provençal bistro **La Bastide Odéon** (*see p127*) offers tempting vegetarian options, and haute cuisine chef Alain Passard gives vegetables pride of place at **L'Arpège** (*see p79*). Italian, Indian and Lebanese restaurants remain viable options, though it's always a little frustrating for visitors to have to forgo French food altogether. Until the others catch up, the only solution is to be demanding. Enough requests and chefs might eventually get the message that vegetarians like food too. *Gemma Betros*

Le Grenier de Notre-Dame.
See p154.

Guenmaï

6 rue Cardinale, 6th (01.43.26.03.24). M° St-Germain-des-Prés or Mabillon. **Open** 11.45am-3.30pm Mon-Sat. Closed Aug. **Average** €20. **Credit** MC, V. **Non-smoking room. Map H7.**
Half-restaurant, half-health food shop, Guenmaï attracts a mainly local crowd with its Asian-influenced food. Although the restaurant serves only lunch, most dishes are also available for take-away and the shop stays open until 8.30pm. The green and white dining room is clean if slightly faded; tables jostle for position among racks of produce spilling over from the shop next door. The slight squeeze results in a friendly atmosphere whether you're with friends or on your own. The food is simple and healthy: on a cold winter's day two steaming pots of vegetable and miso soup were just right. The two lunch specials on our visit were a light tofu and vegetable soufflé, and delicately battered scorpion fish on a wooden skewer (the menu contains no dairy or wheat ingredients but usually has some fish). Each dish came surrounded by a colourful mix that included seaweed, leeks, beansprouts and rice. The fruit tarts looked a little dry, so we chose instead to linger over another glass of carrot and apple juice.

Aquarius ★

40 rue de Gergovie, 14th (01.45.41.36.88). M° Pernety or Plaisance. **Open** noon-2.15pm, 7-10.30pm Mon-Sat. Closed last two weeks in Aug and 10 days at Christmas. **Average** €15. **Prix fixe** €15 (dinner only). **Lunch menu** €11. **Credit** AmEx, DC, MC, V. **Wheelchair access. Non-smoking. Map F10.**
Aquarius has won a loyal following of families and fashionable diners alike with its imaginative, homely cuisine and warm-as-toast setting. We felt we were stepping into someone's front room, the atmosphere complemented by an ornamental 'bubbler' and enough art deco window glass to lend class. Mozzarella with a salad of tomato, carrot and sweet beetroot, plus perfectly seasoned creamed vegetable soup, feature on the €15 three-course

evening menu. Mushroom loaf, uplifted by a mushroom sauce, or cannelloni stuffed with spinach and ricotta and served with courgettes and lentils, are typical main courses. Helpings are astonishing value. Strikingly prompt service retains charm and efficiency. Wine is pricey in the organic regions of the list but a carafe of house merlot (€6.86) should satisfy most people. We went for the excellent, no-frills apple crumble instead of cocoa-rich chocolate ice-cream or the naughty gâteau. A la carte 'exotica' include three seaweeds in puff pastry or aubergine caviar. Booking is advisable.

Au Grain de Folie

24 rue de la Vieuville, 18th (01.42.58.15.57). M° Abbesses. **Open** noon-11pm Mon-Sat; 12.30-2.30pm, 7.30-10.30pm Sun. **Average** €15. **Prix fixe** €10, €12, €15.50 (12.30-1.30pm, 7.30-8.30pm). **No credit cards. Map H1.**
Seating just 14, Le Grain may not be the smallest restaurant in Paris, but there can't be too many other places where adult strangers can get this intimate without breaking the law. The menu, like the floor space, is limited but cleverly organised. For starters, the avocat au roquefort was nicely seasoned, the salad leaves crisp and fresh. The potage de légumes is a warming mini-meal, the vegetables changing with the season. If you want to sample the tzatzikis, houmous and guacamole, try sharing the €20 starter selection. Main courses are dominated by salads. Otherwise you can choose between vegetable tart, vegetable pâté or toasted goat's cheese. Everything comes with a generous dollop of lentils, plenty of bulghur wheat, and lashings of crudités. The food is produced to order in a kitchen the size of a Japanese phone booth, but the ingredients are treated with respect and served with almost Zen imperturbability. For dessert, don't miss the apple crumble with whole hazelnuts. Oh, and if you do need to visit the loo, don't close the outer door before you've opened the inner one. It's hard to remain dignified while reversing across somebody else's crottin de chèvre, especially with your knickers around your knees.

International

African & Indian Ocean

Instead of joining the traffic jams on the Périphérique, consider escaping city life with a leisurely paced meal at one of the city's many African restaurants (for **North African** restaurants, *see pp203-206*). A West African meal typically begins with a potent rum cocktail (or ginger juice), before hearty stews such as maffé or the Senegalese national dish, thieb'oudjen (a spicy fish stew). Seychelles cooking borrows from India, while you'll find a strong Portuguese influence in Cape Verdian restaurants. Ethiopian food is something else altogether – a convivial style of eating that must be experienced.

International

Au Coco de Mer

34 bd St-Marcel, 5th (01.47.07.06.64). M° St-Marcel or Les Gobelins. **Open** 7.30pm-midnight Mon; noon-2.30pm, 7.30pm-midnight Tue-Sat. **Average** €35. **Prix fixe** €20, €30. **Credit** AmEx, MC, V. **Wheelchair access. Map** K9.

There aren't many Parisian restaurants that send you home with joy in your stomach and sand in your shoes. This small enclave of the Seychelles does both. Dried banana leaves, the huge, hanging sea coconut pods and pine furniture all conspire to convince you that a stroll along the beach after the meal would be entirely possible. The nearest you'll get is with luxuriously soft sand that lines the wooden beach cabin room looking out on to the street. Rum cocktails set our tastebuds tingling as we studied the Indian-influenced offerings. Tuna tartare with grated ginger, fresh chives and lime juice was light, fresh and invigorating, while a swordfish carpaccio was rather heavily smoked. Filet de bourgeois (a Caribbean fish) was fleshy and meaty, but was rather overwhelmed by tomato sauce and curried cauliflower. Better was the octopus in a coconut milk curry, tantalisingly gentle on the spices. A St-André de Figuière rosé went down smoothly – and our coconut cake in caramel sauce made a stroll, beach or no beach, very necessary.

Chez Dom ★

34 rue de Sambre-et-Meuse, 10th (01.42.01.59.80). M° Colonel Fabien. **Open** noon-2.30pm, 7.30pm-midnight Tue-Fri; 7.30pm-midnight Sat, Sun. **Average** €25. **Credit** MC, V. **Wheelchair access. Map** M3.

The sisters are still doing it for themselves at this happy little joint run by Dominique Sy. With parents from Senegal and Martinique, she pulls in home-cooking secrets from both continents. The scent of soul food hits you as you enter through the kitchen, where food is sizzling behind an array of fruits macerating in rum. Everyone gets a planter's punch on the house to get things going as they scan the blackboard menu. We loved our starters of aloco (juicy, deep-fried plantain) accompanied by refreshing sauce chien (chopped tomato, onion, garlic, parsley and chives) and avocado salad. The curried pork with coconut is delicious, but then so are all the curries – from mild, lemony yassa to fiery goat colombo spiced with aromatic pepper. The pièce de résistance was definitely the grilled fish – a huge chunk of capitaine, crisply grilled and served with rice, aloco and sauce chien. Sexy chocolate lives up to its name but proved mere foreplay when compared to the gratin de mangue – a must. The wines can be a bit ropey – better to stick to rum or ginger juice.

Le Dogon

30 rue René Boulanger, 10th (01.42.41.95.85). M° République. **Open** noon-3pm, 7pm-midnight Mon-Sat. **Average** €22. **Lunch menu** €8.90. **Credit** MC, V. **Wheelchair access. Map** L4.

The ground floor isn't much – an empty bar – but the second floor feels like a West African hideaway with its rattan ceilings, snake and leopard skins, and singer strumming his kora. A bissap (hibiscus flower juice) or zingy ginger juice, spiked or not, is a fine way to start as you mull over the diverse menu which mixes and matches dishes from Mali, Senegal, the Congo and the Ivory Coast. We settled on a moist prawn mousse (with a heartbreaking flourish of ketchup and mayonnaise) and the assiette Dogon, an unusual plate of okra, black-eyed peas, raw cabbage and beansprouts. Our neighbours were native – digging into their mains with their hands – while we used forks and spoons for our foutou, a mussel and prawn stew with atieke, a mashed root vegetable. The spicy chicken (poulet spécial piment Dogon), with a fresh, tomato-based hot sauce, was exceptionally juicy. We were licking our spoons after ice-cream and the mystère Congolais, whose secret is revealed only to patrons of Le Dogon.

Ile de Gorée ★

70 rue Jean-Pierre Timbaud, 11th (01.43.38.97.69). M° Parmentier. **Open** 7pm-midnight Mon-Sat. **Average** €24. **Credit** MC, V. **Wheelchair access. Map** M4.

It's a 15-minute ferry ride from the coast of Senegal to Gorée Island, a once-pivotal centre of the West African slave trade; some choose to swim across in the writhing crystal-blue water. All we had to do was step off the pavement to tuck into its soulful cuisine and generous hospitality. Mango and peach punches and live kora music set the mood before simple but well-prepared boudin créole (black pudding with cinnamon) and aloco (sautéed plantains) with sweet tomato relish. Mains were hearty and honest: the dem farci (stuffed mullet) in brown sauce is the traditional dish of St-Louis, the former capital of Senegal. Thiou poisson (whole fish) with tomatoes, bell peppers, carrots, potatoes and basmati rice had been richly marinated with a sauce that tingled with flavour. Redemption Song wailed as we left, and as the cooks waved goodbye we vowed to catch the next raft back to this enchanted isle.

Restaurant Ethiopia

91 rue du Chemin-Vert, 11th (01.49.29.99.68).
M° Voltaire or Père Lachaise. **Open** 11am-3pm, 7pm-midnight daily. **Average** €15. **Prix fixe** €16-€30 (minimum two people). **Lunch menu** €7.50, €8. **Credit** AmEx, MC, V. **Wheelchair access.** **Map** N5.

Laid-back is an understatement at this homely little restaurant. Completely different to the other African cuisines available in Paris, the Ethiopian speciality is a big tray lined with injera bread and dotted with picnic offerings ranging from fiery chicken in a treacly sauce to boiled egg and various vegetable and pulse purées – spinach, chickpea, lentils to name but a few. The idea is to take a bit of the spongy, sourdough pancake and use it like a paper towel to scoop up morsels of baby food and stuff them in your mouth. It's all great fun but works out expensive for a couple (the price goes down according to the number of people in the group). Red wine proved a heavy accompaniment – herbal tea is a better choice.

Restaurant Grandplace

82 av Parmentier, 11th (01.43.57.27.21).
M° Parmentier. **Open** 6pm-2am Mon-Sat. **Average** €30. **Prix fixe** €35. **Credit** MC, V. **Wheelchair access.** **Map** M5.

Through its plate glass windows we had noticed a lively crowd till late in the candlelit Grandplace and were intrigued by its 'Afro-Indian' cuisine. All our imaginings about trans-continental fusion food were dashed, however, when we realised it was simply two separate menus containing the usual African and Indian specialities. Never mind. This is a trendy spot attracting a high-rolling African clientele. Behind a wall of plants six men were smoking the fattest cigars we had ever seen, while on the table next to us someone was pitching a film script. Eye candy is provided by a lifesize statue of an Indian goddess, a totem pole and stupendously good-looking staff, who are also extremely courteous. Choosing from the African menu, we were disappointed by our starters – a salade Grandplace of sliced red pepper, tuna and lettuce that could have been from anywhere, and inexpertly reheated accras. Our advice is to go straight for the main courses. Thieb'oudjen, the national dish of Senegal, is a delicious stew made from fresh and dried fish

cooked with groundnut oil; soupou kandia, in a similarly spicy sauce, contained smoked fish and gambas. This was real soul food, served in its own casserole with dinosaur-sized fish bones. For pudding the 'bimbo' – a tutti-frutti flavoured sorbet – proved a more satisfactory choice than the banana fritters. All was redeemed by complementary liqueurs and kora-player Moussa Kanoute.

Waly Fay

6 rue Godefroy Cavaignac, 11th (01.40.24.17.79).
M° Charonne or Voltaire. **Open** 8pm-midnight Mon-Sat. Closed one week in Aug. **Average** €19. **Credit** MC, V. **Wheelchair access.** **Map** N7.

Restaurants with interior design concepts that work are rare in Paris, and we were struck on entering Waly Fay by just how well the distressed interior had been managed. Artfully lit by candles, the mixture of exposed walls and perfectly laid tables created an atmosphere that was immediately welcoming, helped no doubt by a ti-ponch and a tingling ginger and rum cocktail. The cuisine lived up to the chic atmosphere: a shredded cabbage bayou salad with prawns, grapefruit and a touch of blue cheese was perfectly balanced with a pungent dressing, while the gratin de crabe was a savoury, highly seasoned celebration of the shellfish. The

Frenchman in our party played safe with his main course, ordering char-grilled brochettes of tender juicy lamb, chicken and beef served with good rice and a bowl of spiky pepper-based sauce. More adventurous was Senegalese speciality thieb'oudjen, an unidentified fish in a spicy tomato and vegetable sauce, more delicious than it sounds and prepared with real sophistication. We drank a well-chosen, strong organic Vacqueras red for €25, which stood up to the spices, and accompanied us right through to an exquisite corossol (an exotic fruit) sorbet and ginger ice-cream, both served with raisins doused in old rum. Service was outstandingly friendly.

Chez Céleste

18 rue de Cotte, 12th (01.43.44.15.30/www. chezceleste.fr.st). M° Ledru Rollin. **Open** 6pm-2am Mon; 10am-3pm, 6pm-2am Tue-Sat. Closed Aug. **Average** €18. **Lunch menu** €10. **Credit** AmEx, MC, V. **Map** N7.
Two steps from the teeming Place d'Aligre market just east of Bastille, Chez Céleste is a hole-in-the-wall Cape Verdian resto-cum-night spot. Reflecting the island nation's polyglot residents, the menu draws on Portuguese and West African cuisines. We tried the salade bacalhau (a ceviche-like marinated mix of salt cod, red peppers and oil), and the petite assiette sampler of nutmeggy black pudding and lightly fried accras (salt cod fritters). For mains, we had a delicious, sticky pile of barely blackened gambas in a creole sauce and fall-off-the-bone tender chicken colombo. Little Portuguese-inspired custard tarts were scrumptious though tough-crusted; slightly soupy coconut flan was the ultimate cold-weather comfort food. Live music from Thursday to Saturday might bring a mellow guitar duo crooning romantic Brazilian songs or more raucous rhythms. On packed weekend nights, the music will distract from the wait between courses, even as the fabulous smells floating from the kitchen drive you crazy.

Entoto ★

143-145 rue Léon-Maurice-Nordmann, 13th (01.45.87.08.51). M° Glacière. **Open** 7.30-11.30pm Tue-Sat. Closed two weeks in Aug. **Average** €25. **Credit** MC, V. **Wheelchair access. Non-smoking room. Map** J10.
If Africa has one unmissable cuisine, it's got to be Ethiopian. And Entoto is about as good as it gets. Novice and initiated alike need look no further than the beyayenetou entoto: a platter of seven different specialities, two meat and five lentil/vegetable; there's a vegetarian version as well. The whole lot is served up on a giant disc of injera, an airy, slightly sour pancake made of 'tef' (a sort of millet) that traditionally substitutes for cutlery. Little baskets of it, freshly cooked, are kept full and it's much better than a fork. We had zingy ground beef, tender chunks of lamb stewed in a thick hot-sour sauce, unctuous split peas and pink lentils, melting spinach, a delicately spiced bulghur wheat, plus pumpkin 'berbère'. Berber-style refers to the sophisticated mix of herbs and spices (pink pepper,

garlic, ginger, rue, basil, thyme, cinnamon and cloves) that gives so much Ethiopian food its distinctive taste; even spice-phobes will be seduced by its delicacy. If you still have room (try to!), finish off with a dark slice of reine de Saba chocolate cake, as alluring as the queen herself.

Le Mono

40 rue Véron, 18th (01.46.06.99.20). M° Blanche or Abbesses. **Open** 7-11.30pm Mon, Tue, Thur-Sun. Closed Aug. **Average** €20. **Credit** AmEx, MC, V. **Map** H1.
On a rainy winter night, a meal at Le Mono was an instant ticket to West Africa, specifically Togo, which is the home country of the family that runs this engaging little restaurant in Montmartre. Start with one of the potent punches, maybe mango or coconut, with such an inhibition-killing dose of rum that you'll start swaying to the tropical beat before you've finished half your glass. Among the best starters are prawn fritters served with a rosy tartare sauce and a fiery dish of bonnet chilli pepper. Next try the djenkoume, wonderful grilled chicken with a rich home-made tomato sauce and a big jiggly cake of steamed semolina, or other dishes you've probably never run into before including akouboudessi, mackerel and okra stewed in tomato sauce and garnished with a big dab of manioc paste; or akpavi (African carp) cooked with rice, tomatoes and onions. A wonderfully diverse crowd of African diplomats, students, venturesome tourists, local artists, and even the occasional dancer from the striptease clubs around Pigalle makes a point of coming on the weekend for the suckling-pig maffé, maffé being a peanut-based sauce. Dishes here are filling and few order any dessert aside from, you guessed it, another rum punch.

Rio dos Camarãos

55 rue Marceau, 93100 Montreuil-sous-bois (01.42.87.34.84/www.riodos.com). M° Robespierre. **Open** noon-2.30pm Mon; noon-2.30pm, 7.30-11.30pm Tue-Fri; 7.30-11.30pm Sat. Closed Aug. **Average** €30. **Lunch menu** €12, €13. **Credit** AmEx, MC, V.
Unlike most African restaurants, Rio dos Camarãos doesn't focus on a single country. Its pan-African, multi-talented kitchen prepares an extensive menu from Senegal, the Ivory Coast and Cameroon, plus lesser-known destinations such as Benin and the Congo. Starters come under the category 'waiting for the bush taxi', while set lunch menus have tongue-in-cheek names such as 'sans papiers' (illegal immigrants) and 'Paris-Dakar' (featuring European food). Dishes range from staples such as yassa and n'dole, to a version of a peanut-based maffé kandja with prawns, beef, cod, carrots and okra. Try the two house favourites: attiéké, a braised whole capitaine fish with a spicy tomato-pepper sauce; and the Rio dos Camarãos, a gourd seed gumbo with cod and prawns. A warm cinnamon and banana Tatin makes a fine finisher. Expect a short hike from the Métro into the Montreuil hinterland, unless you can find a bush taxi.

International

The Americas

There is no such thing as modern American cooking in Paris – what you'll find instead is nostalgic fodder for the homesick, from a re-created roadside diner to reassuringly predictable theme restaurants. New kid on the block **Scoop** makes its American-style ice-creams on the premises. With a few exceptions, Latin American cooking loses much of its fire when transplanted to Paris. What these restaurants lack in chilli varieties, however, they make up for in atmosphere.

NORTH AMERICA

Joe Allen Restaurant

30 rue Pierre Lescot, 1st (01.42.36.70.13/ www.joeallenparis.com). M° Etienne-Marcel. **Open** noon-midnight daily. Closed first two weeks in Aug. **Average** €22.50. **Lunch menu** €12.90. **Credit** AmEx, MC, V. **Wheelchair access.** Map J5.

Joe Allen, with its tavern-like exposed brick walls and oak floors, benefits from the meeting of American steakhouse cuisine and fiddly French ingredients. Scurrying waiters in starched whites and ties diligently filled water glasses and bread baskets, and the manager seemed to know many of the clients by name. Nostalgic for a good California cab, we reached for the Robert Mondavi import, which kept pace nicely with the starters of warm walnut-crusted goat's cheese over tangy frisée and steamed mussels in a buttery white wine and sweet onion bath. The simplicity of high-quality ingredients made the mains stand out: the seared salmon and accompanying grilled vegetables were dressed only in char-grilled lattice-marks, and the chicken breast stuffed with herbed goat's cheese over spinach came with thick sweet potato 'fries'. A rare find in Paris, carrot cake was served with cream cheese frosting and apple crumble would have done Mom proud.

Scoop ★

154 rue St-Honoré, 1st (01.42.60.31.84/www.scoop cafe.com). M° Palais Royal. **Open** 11am-7pm Mon-Sat; noon-7pm Sun. **Average** €15. **Prix fixe** €10-€14. **Credit** MC, V. **Non-smoking room.** Map J5.

What started as a joke between two friends is now an avant-garde ice-cream parlour. Charming American Anne Lederer missed her native mid-western ice-cream and was searching for something different from the traditional French bistro. So, along with a friend, she decided to create an upmarket diner that dishes out home-made ice-cream. From the minute we walked in, we became instant fans. The minimalist interior is incredibly cosy: the walls are adorned with stunning photos of rooftop views of Paris and the deep wine-red sofas swallow you up as you slurp on your smoothie. As the ice-cream is made on the premises, the offerings change regularly. From the tantalising menu of the moment,

we chose the tortue, a banana milkshake, and the apple ice-cream. The tortue (a scoop of vanilla topped with a generous helping of chocolate sauce and slightly roasted pecans) puts the ordinary sundae to shame, the apple-flavoured ice-cream tasted far more intense than it sounds, and the milkshake was satisfyingly filling. This elegant spot also serves healthy lunches to wash away any guilt induced by overindulgence, as well as a mean looking burger and brunch on Sundays. Located just around the corner from the Louvre and moments away from the swanky rue du Fbg-St-Honore, Scoop is the perfect place to hide from the summer madness.

Breakfast in America

17 rue des Ecoles, 5th (01.43.54.50.28/www. breakfast-in-america.com). M° Cardinal Lemoine or Jussieu. **Open** 8.30am-10.30pm daily. **Average** €10. **Prix fixe** €9.50. **Credit** MC, V. Map J7.

With red vinyl-upholstered benches, lots of grey Formica and a smattering of Americana, this winsome spot in the Latin Quarter is friendly, relaxed and eminently likeable. If you're pining for a real Yankee breakfast, which is what prompted expatriate owner Craig Carlson to action, this is the place to come. Breakfast here runs from 8.30am-3pm, and it's just like New York Greek coffee shop grub, maybe even several shades better. For €6.95 you get two eggs, two pancakes and bacon – sadly, though, hash browns have disappeared from the menu and coffee refills are no longer automatic. A variety of omelettes include a 'Connecticut' (ham and cheese) in honour of Carlson's home state. Tasty though breakfast may be, the lunch menu can be disappointing – the burgers lacked the handmade feel we were craving.

PDG

20 rue de Ponthieu, 8th (01.42.56.19.10). M° Franklin D Roosevelt. **Open** 7.45am-2.30pm, 7-11pm daily. **Average** €25. **Lunch menu** €20.50. **Credit** MC, V. Map E4.

A reference to the high-powered executives who lurk in this area, PDG (which means CEO) is also short for petit-déjeuner, déjeuner-dîner, goûter (the goûter, or snack, idea must have been dropped as the restaurant now closes in the afternoon). Small and crowded, with diner-red banquettes and bistro-style wooden tables, it takes a tasteful French approach to Americana with just a few movie posters, cheerful hanging lights and a bar for solo diners. We never thought the day would come when we'd feel happy to pay €15 for a burger, but here the bun is prepared by a 'meilleur ouvrier de France' baker, the meat is thick and juicy and the mustard is French's (as opposed to French). There are ten to choose from, including the extravagant jumbo bacon cheese for €19 – a double burger with double bacon and authentically fake cheddar – and the Mexican, served with guacamole on the side. Depending on which burger you choose (there are chicken and vegetarian versions), it might come with fries, sautéed grenaille potatoes or pan-fried spinach for the health-conscious. We also tried a huge pastrami club sandwich – a rather Parisian interpretation with thickly sliced meat, but satisfying nonetheless. The desserts are a let-down after this, so sip a coffee and enjoy the sight of CEOs negotiating a burger with red napkins tucked into their collars.

Planet Hollywood

76-78 av des Champs-Elysées, 8th (01.53.83.78.27/ www.planethollywood.com). M° Franklin D Roosevelt or George V. **Open** noon-1am daily. **Average** €25. **Lunch menu** €12 (Mon-Fri only). **Credit** AmEx, DC, MC, V. **Wheelchair access.** **Map** D4.

We were welcomed to poor-man's Hollywood by Sly Stallone (petrified), gloves propped out in an Ivan Drago square-off. Unlike the other diners taking part in birthday sing-alongs and hen parties, apparently oblivious to the Jaws replica looming overhead, we found conversation near-impossible in the sensory-overload surroundings. This was compounded by dawdling service from lax and inexperienced staff. The decidedly American menu is stroked by ze French touch (boeuf bourguignon is on offer). We started with Texas toast with chicken nuggets blanketed with BBQ sauce 'n' cheese and surprisingly tender blackened shrimp that pulled nods and raised eyebrows, as did the mountain of sizzling fajitas, which did Tex-Mex justice. The whopper BBQ bacon cheeseburger was truly Hollywood – more style than substance. Similarly, the double chocolate brownie sundae proved too flashy for its own good. Do take in the display of clothes worn by the California Governator next to the loo.

Hard Rock Café

14 bd Montmartre, 9th (01.53.24.60.00/www.hard rockcafe.com). M° Grands Boulevards. **Open** noon-1am daily. **Average** €20. **Children's menu** €6. **Credit** AmEx, DC, MC, V. **Wheelchair access.** **Map** H4.

If your mission in Paris is to find a restaurant with free refills, a decent burger and a black T-shirt souvenir to parade around school after your Paris vacation, then the HRC won't disappoint. No matter what kind of sordid paraphernalia is tacked to the walls (such as Eminem's spanking trainers), the food is reassuringly familiar. One glance at our neighbour's insurmountable helping of nachos sent us running for a modest helping of 'heavy metal' chicken wings. The bacon cheeseburger didn't let us down and where else in Paris but here does a 'classic' salad come piled high with tortilla chips? While a French group crowded around their brownie sundae for a photo op, we tucked unphotogenically into ours. Exactly what we expected – which is the point, we suppose.

Blue Bayou ★

111-113 rue St-Maur, 11th (01.43.55.87.21/ www.bluebayou-bluebillard.com). M° Parmentier or St-Maur. **Open** *restaurant* 7.30-11pm, *bar* 11am-2am daily. **Average** €25. **Prix fixe** €15 (dinner only). **Credit** AmEx, MC, V. **Wheelchair access.** **Map** M5.

Two-step up from the ground-floor billiards room and enter a cabin made up of 13 tons of lumber shipped from the sawmills of the Mississippi, imported Tabasco, a three-and-a-half metre-long embalmed alligator, a whole lotta bluegrass tunes and shipped-up attitude: we'd entered Louisiana back country, and when the wet naps arrived we knew we were in for something good, ooo eeee! The crayfish terrine starter was quickly sidelined when we began wrestling with the whole-shell blackened prawns to get their juicy meat into the rémoulade before they walked off the plate. Jambalaya, with chunks of spiced sausage, chicken and dirty rice, needed a good kick of Cayenne but was tasty nonetheless, while the gumbo was chock-full of seafood and Cajun goodness. We needed a hammock, but received grade-A pecan pie and New York cheesecake instead. Special nights featuring Cajun dance and an open crawfish bar burn down the house. Just don't ask for Coca-Cola – this is not an 'American' restaurant.

Indiana Café

14 pl de la Bastille, 11th (01.44.75.79.80/www. indiana-cafe.com). M° Bastille. **Open** 11.30am-1am Mon-Thur, Sun; 11.30am-3am Fri, Sat. **Average** €24. **Credit** DC, MC, V. **Map** L4.

Finding ourselves on the Place de la Bastille for a late lunch, the idea of an all-American burger and a Margarita or two seemed like fun. Staff in the mock-Western dining room were exceptionally charming and our full Monty of a burger with cheese, bacon and a fried egg was perfectly cooked with good-quality beef. The bun had an authentic damp cardboard quality, and the accompanying fries were reasonably crisp. A selection of Tex-Mex specialities, including guacamole, fried mozzarella sticks, chicken enchilada and a beef taco, was bland, but by now we were distracted by outside events, which seemed spicier than these Tex-Mex offerings. The terrace tables were brought in and metal grilles brought down to protect the premises from a growing demonstration outside. It was only on reading the slogans that we realised it was an anti-

Head for a Mojito or two at **Calle 24** – a slice of Havana in the Marais. *See p165.*

globalisation protest. The thought crossed our minds as we tucked into our delicious Ben and Jerry ice-cream sundaes and gooey brownies that maybe a Tex-Mex outlet was not the best place to make a stand against world capitalism, a thought obviously shared with the riot police who were busy encircling the restaurant. Eating a juicy hamburger had inadvertently become a controversial political act. **Other locations**: 7 bd des Capucines, 2nd (01.42.68.02.22); 130 bd St-Germain, 6th (01.46.34.66.31); 72 bd du Montparnasse, 14th (01.43.35.36.28).

LATIN AMERICA

Anahi
49 rue Volta, 3rd (01.48.87.88.24). M° Arts et Métiers. **Open** 8pm-midnight daily. Closed 25 Dec, 1 Jan, weekend of 15 Aug. **Average** €40. **Credit** MC, V. **Map** K4.
A rickety old building on a narrow and poorly lit street in the nether regions of the Marais houses Paris's trendiest Argentinian restaurant. That's if customers like Johnny Depp, Quentin Tarantino and

Thierry Mugler are any sign of style. It's the slabs of grilled beef fresh (well, vacuum-packed) from the pampas that pull them in, and the cheery welcome from Carmina and Pilat, the sisters who started Anahi in this old charcuterie 20 years ago. Surrounded by the original white tiled walls, stylish black and white photos of the sisters and an art deco ceiling painted by Albert Camus' brother, tuck into torta pascualina, a sweetish spinach tart with onions, or try the stand-out ceviche made with sea bass. Mains of skewered chicken breast marinated in lemon and served with apple and pineapple salsa and sweet potato purée, and cururù de camarào (grilled gambas with peanuts and okra) are satisfying and attractive, but the bif angosto – a tender, juicy fillet served with a simple green salad – is the star. Try to sneak in a flan, immersed in sweet caramel sauce, and wash it down with a choice Chilean red. *Delicioso*.

A la Mexicaine

68 rue Quincampoix, 3rd (01.48.87.99.34). *M° Rambuteau or Les Halles*. **Open** noon-3pm, 7-11pm daily. **Average** €30. **Prix fixe** (dinner only) €25, €43. **Lunch menu** €12 (Mon-Fri); €25, €43 (Sat, Sun). **Children's menu** €12. **Credit** MC, V. **Wheelchair access**. **Map** K5.

Walking into A la Mexicaine transported us to the little villages of the state of Michoacán, where long narrow dining halls are flanked by colourfully painted walls, hanging pottery and the obligatory shrine to La Virgen Guadalupe. Despite le señor, his wife and three hijas running the restaurant, the service was sometimes slow and always scattered, yet this too was comforting and authentic. The menu, written in French and nahuatl, the language of the Aztecs, offers detailed descriptions and translations. We started with delicious Margaritas, although we longed to have them served in the thick glasses from Guadalajara with the blue trim instead of tumblers. We satisfied our initial *antojito* (craving) with an assortment of appetisers. The flauta, a long corn tortilla filled with chicken then deep-fried, was topped with a green salsa bursting with roasted tomatillos, cilantro and fresh jalapeños. Sopecitos, little boats made from maize, overflowed with spicy chorizo, cooled by hearty guacamole. Two of our favourite aguas frescas quenched our thirst: jamaica (hibiscus flower) and horchata (rice milk), a taste worth acquiring. The deliciousness of the starters left us expecting great things from the main courses, mole negro de Oaxaca and enchiladas rojas. Mole means sauce and this mole negro, served in a crock covered with a maize gratinée, lacked the richness and sauciness of a true mole. The enchiladas were simply unexciting. Lesson learned: never order the dishes that your great-grandmother used to make, especially 9,000km from Mexico.

Calle 24

13 rue Beautreillis, 4th (01.42.72.38.34). *M° Bastille*. **Open** noon-2.30pm, 7.30-11.30pm Mon-Fri; 7.30-11.30pm Sat. **Average** €30. **Prix fixe** €21. **Lunch menu** €12.50. **Credit** MC, V.

This tiny Cuban bar-cum-eaterie booms out on a quiet Marais street as the place to be, at least for the noisy thirty- and fortysomethings who pack it nightly and make booking essential. Old Cuban adverts paper the ceiling, so as you crane your neck take care not to topple off the bar stool. Like everyone else you'll be guzzling Hemingway's favourite – mint-packed Mojitos – as you wait for a table. Main courses, such as the marinated, grilled chicken or cod-stuffed squid in an inky sauce, are decent and filling; with a choice of three side dishes that include rice, beans, fried plantain and a manioc gratin, you're guaranteed not to leave hungry and the €21 menu won't break the bank. Cuban food, as those who have tramped the streets of Havana know well, is resolutely non-gourmet, and Calle 24 is no exception. Go instead for atmosphere, cocktails, the large selection of appetite-quenching tapas – such as cod and sweet potato fritters, pork and bean pâté, and lime-zapped ceviche (chunks of raw perch) – and the wide smile of Mechy, the Cuban ex-pat and one-time dancer who reigns over it all.

Anuhuacalli

30 rue des Bernadins, 5th (01.43.26.10.20). *M° Maubert-Mutualité*. **Open** 7-11pm Mon-Sat; noon-2pm, 7-11pm Sun. **Average** €30. **Credit** AmEx, V. **Map** K7.

Opinions are divided as to which is the best Mexican restaurant in Paris, this one or the more vivacious A la Mexicaine (*see above*) just across the river. Anuhuacalli is definitely more subdued in its approach – the decor is elegant and low-key, with no sombreros or fake cacti – and more bourgeois in its clientele. Both prove that Mexican food is a far cry from rigid taco shells, runny beans and bullet-hard beef crowned with sour cream and guacamole. Start things off with a salad of cactus paddles, tomatoes and coriander or the summery, citrusy ceviche de pescado (it's firm because the acidity of the lime juice 'cooks' the fish) and bypass the dowdy prawn cocktail. Follow with a tender fillet of beef Moctezuma with cuitlacoche, a highly prized Mexican fungus that grows on the ears of maize; marinated pork cooked in banana leaves; or murky turkey – turkey cooked in a seriously brown sauce seasoned with chocolate, chillies, cinnamon, cloves, nuts and more than a dozen other surprises. Finish off with slices of mango and a dollop of mango sorbet, lemon or pineapple sorbets, or quince paste with sharp cheese.

Botequim

1 rue Berthollet, 5th (01.43.37.98.46). *M° Censier Daubenton*. **Open** noon-2.30pm, 8-11.30pm Mon-Sat; 8-11.30pm Sun. **Average** €30. **Credit** AmEx, MC, V. Brazilian food, like Brazil itself, is cosmopolitan and tropical with more than a hint of the European: think sturdy Portuguese with a coconut-banana twist and you won't be far off. The family-run Botequim (local bistro in Rio slang) looks, from the outside, less laid-back than it is; inside it's warm and convivial, and once we had tucked into a steaming pot of fejoada

Mi Cayito

What better than candle light and a rocking chair to discover the multiple flavours of cuban cuisine with a modern twist ? Our dishes, such as fricassee of shrimps and sweet potato, beef fillet flavoured with cumin and lime as well as other savoury and sweet dishes and a Sunday brunch menu give you a real taste of Cuba. Mi Cayito is about atmosphere and style and the welcoming smile of Reinaldo.

OPEN DAILY 7pm-2am

Tél : 01 42 21 98 86
CUBAN RESTAURANT IN THE MONTORGUEIL AREA
10, rue Marie Stuart 75002 PARIS – www.mi-cayito.com

AVERAGE À LA CARTE €25 – SUNDAY BRUNCH €15-€24

we found it hard to leave. Thick chunks of pork stewed in black beans and served with rice and a tangy mix of sliced orange and sautéed greens, this is an excellent rendition of the national dish. Lighter options (it's all relative) include a coconut and coriander prawn stew (the prawns are jumbo and juicy) and the house bacalhau (flakes of salt cod cooked up with onions, garlic and potato); the cod was a little dry but that was soon remedied with a few scoops of the prawn sauce. If you splurged on starters – such as the tasty panaché (a mixed plate of cod fritters), tiny shrimp tart or crab and red pepper stuffed in a clam shell – then you probably won't have space for dessert. But if you like sweets do save room for the pink and yellow torta de banana: an intensely rich, home-made egg and banana concoction that is simply incomparable. Wines include Portuguese vinho verdes (young and fizzy) but it's the cocktails, such as the limey Caipirinha, that have real appeal.

El Palenque

5 rue de la Montagne-Ste-Geneviève, 5th (01.43.54.08.99). Mº Maubert-Mutualité. **Open** 12.30-2.30pm, 7.30-11pm Mon-Sat. **Average** €30. **No credit cards. Map** J8.
El Palenque is an unpretentious eaterie for the unconditional carnivore. For starters try the grilled chorizo criollo, a mild cousin of the Spanish spiced sausage, simply served on a wooden platter with chunks of bread. After that, the options are all seriously high in protein. The parillada completa is a two-person challenge, a mountain of meat involving black pudding, sweetbreads, sausages, kidneys and ribs. Less stout hearts will find the steaks demanding in their own way, the standard cuts of Argentinian beef looming larger than their European equivalents. Our faux-filet was enormous, tender and perfectly cooked. Green salad and thick corn pancakes (torrejas choclo) are an unbeatable accompaniment. We washed it all down with a bottle of Trapiche pinot noir, light in colour but robustly fruity. The dessert list features quince and sweet potato in various guises, as well as a crème caramel doused in condensed milk. The milico membrill – sweet potato jelly with a slice of brie – was a surprising success. Dinner is served at 8pm and 10pm. Don't be late, as there's generally a queue of hopefuls waiting to pounce – carnivores all.

Fajitas

15 rue Dauphine, 6th (01.46.34.44.69/www.fajitas-paris.com). Mº Odéon or Pont Neuf. **Open** noon-11pm (non-stop service) Tue-Sun. Closed Aug. **Average** €25. **Prix fixe** €18.50. **Lunch menu** €10. **Credit** AmEx, MC, V. **Map** H6.
Bright red chilli peppers – some dried, some bottled and the rest hanging in great garlands on the wall – give this popular Tex-Mex eaterie, run by a Mexican/American couple, a colourful splash of authenticity. The heat, however, is almost all hot air. The sizzling platter of Miguel's signature fajitas, juicy strips of lightly spiced beef (or chicken) served

up with scoops of chunky guacamole and refried beans, is an easy favourite. But the soupy chilli con carne and sturdy enchiladas, faultlessly fresh and big enough to satisfy even cowboy appetites, cried out for fire; the bowl of saucy salsa that soon arrived was no help at all. Our ceviche starter, chunks of bland white fish (theoretically marinated in lime) and topped with coriander and tomato, was plain disappointing; the sizeable plate of nachos is a better bet. In keeping with the predominance of Tex, desserts include brownies and pecan pie as well as inventive, sweet chimichangas. The reassuringly tacky Margaritas are frozen and at night there's no shortage of tequila. An easy-going, friendly spot, Fajitas won't blast your tastebuds but it's a warm, filling and well-priced option after a cold winter's walk along the quays. And, if you'd rather whip up tacos at home, Fajitas also conveniently stocks Tex-Mex supplies and does take-away.

Arriba Mexico

32 av de la République, 11th (01.49.29.95.40). Mº Parmentier or République. **Open** noon-2pm, 7-11pm Mon-Fri; 7-11.30pm Sat, Sun. **Average** €25. **Prix fixe** €23-€30. **Lunch menu** €9. **Credit** MC, V. **Non-smoking room. Map** M5.
Arriba Mexico makes no show of offering genuine Mexican food, but you can hardly expect more at

Blue Bayou.
See p162.

these fiesta-provoking prices. The only touch of local colour here is the joyful profusion of kitsch: plastic parrots, 'Aztec' hanging plates, huge murals of old, corn-grinding Indians and rainbow-bright serapes at each and every window. A massive plate of tortilla chips dripped with orange cheddar squares, its flavour coming courtesy of the bowl of jalapeños we had asked for as an extra. Our other first course of prawn cocktail was quite attractively presented, featuring a reasonable amount of firm shellfish nestling in a spicy tomato sauce crowned by hefty chunks of avocado and an inordinate amount of freshly cut lettuce. Having been forewarned about the copious portions, we had decided to share the chicken tostada. This arrived with yet another mountain of lettuce, underneath which snuggled enough tangy sauce-laden chicken to serve three people. Unfortunately, the whole thing lay on the soggiest flour tortilla we have ever seen. Despite the hiccups, the overall impression is of an entertaining theme restaurant that doesn't take itself too seriously. If you know nothing about Mexican food and are just out to have a good time, you won't be disappointed.

El Paladar

26 bis rue de la Fontaine au Roi, 11th (01.43.57.42.70). M° République or Goncourt. **Open** 7.30pm-2am daily. **Average** €25. **Lunch menu** €10. **Credit** MC, V. **Map** M4.

Grafitti-covered pink and aqua walls and wooden tables set the tone at this pleasantly understated, four-year-old Cuban outpost. The outgoing staff were happy to explain the regularly changing menu of Cuban food from the fried and stewed schools of cooking. Yuca con mojo (sautéed manioc with onions and garlic) proved oily but delicious, and tostones (batter-fried plantains) were surprisingly light and crispy. Main dishes include pork, chicken, fish and the arroz a la cubana, an impressive load of tomatoes, eggs and rice. We sampled pavo saltiado (stewed turkey and potatoes seasoned with bay leaves), and pollo pio-pio (chicken fried in citrus). The pescado guisado fish struck the only false note with its oddly muddy sauce of tomatoes, garlic, onions, potatoes and peppers. Overall the dishes had plenty of substance and character. The flan maison, a stupendous sugar-soaked coconut custard, ended the meal on a high note.

El Bodegon de Pancho

8 rue Guy-Môquet, 17th (01.53.31.00.73). M° Brochant. **Open** noon-midnight Mon-Sat. Closed one week at Christmas, one week in Aug. **Average** €20. **Prix fixe** €12. **Credit** MC, V.

Pancho's little bar, a kind of hole-in-the-wall eaterie, is for Colombians, carnivores and those with a taste for the surreal. You don't have to love Botero's rotund women (check out the prints on the wall), but you might leave looking like one. Little bottles of sweet and fizzy pink soda – described by our motherly host as a Colombian fruit drink – labelled apple on the bottle and tasting like strawberry

Frutella, set the mood. Unless you're having the hearty two-course set menu, which includes an excellent, sturdy soup (a meal in itself) and the daily special, skip the starters; you can't afford to take the edge off your appetite. The justly popular bandeja paisa, a peasanty and very porky speciality, is magnificent in its proportions and will defy all but the hungriest: a large oval plate comes heaped with thick strips of crisply roasted pork, a scoop of spiced ground pork, a chunky chorizo sausage plus rice, black beans, a plantain fritter and a small, hard semolina biscuit. Just in case that's not enough, the whole thing is topped with a fried egg. You won't have room for dessert, but that shouldn't stop you from digging into the rich, tasty rice pudding or the more refined guava paste served with slices of tangy Andean cheese. The makeshift stools, plastic tablecloths and adverts for long-distance phone cards are a constant reminder that Pancho is a home away from home for the neighbourhood's Colombian community. If you're lucky, and speak a little Spanish, you might just get invited to play a round of sapo (a local game with metal discs and a frog's mouth) to work up your appetite.

Ay Caramba! ★

59 rue Mouzaïa, 19th (01.42.41.76.30/www. restaurant-aycaramba.com). M° Botzaris or Pré St-Gervais. **Open** 7.30-11.30pm Tue-Thur; noon-2.30pm, 7.30pm-2am Fri-Sun. Closed Christmas, New Year and 1-15 Aug. **Average** €35. **Credit** AmEx, DC, MC, V.

Despite its out-of-the-way location, Ay Caramba! is a roaring success. As you enter the coral-style bar you might think the place is empty, but just around the corner is the restaurant area which, on the night we visited, was packed with large groups of people, including quite a few South American families. Friday is mariachi night and on the small stage a group of five men with moustaches were serenading the crowd, including repeated maracas-accompanied versions of *Happy Birthday*. With all this hubbub you might expect the food to take second place, but having shouted our orders at the smiling waitress who was wearing a '24-hour fiesta' T-shirt, we were amazed at the deliciousness of our cactus salad and campechana – a kind of glorified prawn cocktail with ceviche and avocado. A lot of the main courses come on a huge wooden plancha; even those that are served on a plate such as our tampiquena (steak with cheese, taco, rice and salads) and carambola (chilli, taco, rice and salads) were substantial. The tampiquena in particular, with its pot of melted cheese to dollop on top, was very satisfying. Desserts are rather grown-up, suffused with alcohol but without the expected forest of cocktail umbrellas. Both the banana ice-cream with coffee liqueur and the tequila sorbet hit the spot. By this time the waitresses were clearing the tables for dancing. Swaying, we made our way out of the coral to be caught poncho-less on a bitterly cold night in northern Paris.

Caribbean

France presents the vibrant, colourful, multi-cultural islands known as Les Antilles to the world as her proper offspring, while the islanders themselves surf their cultural complexity – French, Creole, Caribbean – through great music, wry humour, wonderful literature and excellent cooking. In many ways, Antillais cooking is the ultimate fusion food, since French, African, Indian, Spanish, English and other culinary cultures have contributed to the islands' repertoire. However, this cuisine is under-represented in Paris considering the sizeable community of some 200,000 people from the French Caribbean – it may be that the grey climate is not suited to this sunny, slow-paced style of cooking.

Antillais cooking – the ultimate fusion food.

La Créole

122 bd du Montparnasse, 14th (01.43.20.62.12).
M° Vavin. **Open** noon-2pm, 7.30-11pm Tue-Sat.
Average €35. **Prix fixe** €22.50. **Credit** AmEx,
DC, MC, V. **Map** G9.
La Créole feels exactly like a typical Martiniquais 'habitation', a sugar cane plantation owner's residence. Hardly surprising when you learn that the owner, Charlie, is the president of the French Rum Academy. Vibrant bouquets of tropical flowers, sunny-natured waitresses clad in colourful, lacy damas, and white wicker furniture can lull even the most stressed-out wannabe holidaymaker into believing he's abroad. Once we'd slipped into 'wish-

you-were-here' mode thanks to the complimentary crunchy accras and particularly the warming effects of our luscious but pungent ti'ponch, we were ready to launch into our first course. In our spicy stuffed crabs, the flesh-to-breadcrumb ratio was tipped towards the latter but the tangy 'chiktai' salad of salty, toasted cod was lip smackingly good and the christophine gratin creamy yet light. The main courses were the star attraction, however, and the diva of them all was the magnificent ouassou: lobster-sized crayfish in a gloriously spicy red sauce that made finger licking imperative. A well-executed classic pork colombo sported plenty of meat and a psychedelic touch of bell peppers. The thick-cut char-grilled tuna steak proved lighter than it first seemed thanks to the oddly named 'sauce chien', a refreshing lime and garlic vinaigrette. The chocolate, coconut and orange desserts provided a satisfying finale but a thick white blancmange brought back less-than-fond memories of school canteens.

Le Flamboyant

11 rue Boyer-Barret, 14th (01.45.41.00.22).
M° Pernéty. **Open** 8-10.30pm Tue; noon-2pm,
8-10.30pm Wed-Sat; noon-2pm Sun. **Average** €30.
Credit MC, V. **Map** F10.
Though it's named after a feathery tropical tree with flamboyant flowers that's found in Martinique and Guadeloupe, you wouldn't know that this quiet place with a classic bistro façade and lace panels in the windows was antillais, or French West Indian, until you went in and opened the menu. Order some crunchy golden accras (salt cod fritters) to nibble while enjoying a ti'ponch (rum with sugar syrup and a squirt of lime), and then go for authentic, carefully cooked main courses such as shark curry, colombo de cabri (goat with colombo, a spice mixture that's a signature of French Creole cooking from Mauritius to Saint Martin) or spicy boudin noir (black pudding). The fresh fruit salad is a refreshing way to end a meal, invoking as it does the hope of a tropical holiday. A little expensive, but this doesn't prevent it from being very popular with Paris's prosperous Caribbean community.

Eastern Mediterranean

Thankfully there is more to Middle Eastern cuisine in Paris than the cheap and cheerful Greeks that line the Latin Quarter's pedestrian streets. Long-established **Mavrommatis** is renowned for its refined Greek fare, while the best Lebanese and Iranian restaurants serve the immigrant communities of the 15th, way off the beaten tourist track but not so far from the Eiffel Tower.

International

Les Délices d'Aphrodite

4 rue de Candolle, 5th (01.43.31.40.39/www. mavrommatis.fr). Mº Censier Daubenton. **Open** noon-2.15pm, 7-11pm Mon-Sat. **Average** €30. **Prix fixe** €17.20, €20.80. **Lunch menu** €6.90, €10.90. **Credit** AmEx, MC, V. **Map** J9.

Aphrodite's delicacies are dispensed by the little sister of Mavrommatis, a hallowed temple run by Cyprus's answer to the Roux brothers and serving 'the finest contemporary Hellenic cuisine in Paris, Europe, even the world'. Eager to sample the food of the gods, we weren't disappointed – here is authentic, carefully flavoured Greek country cooking, served in a rather soulless blue-and-white bistro with unobtrusive bazoukis tinkling in the background and a pleasing pair of olive trees in giant pots on the terrace. Mega pikilia was an assortment of cold and hot starters including crisp, herby vegetable fritters, exemplary taramasalata, smoked aubergine 'caviar' and kalamarakia me maratho (squid with fennel, fresh thyme, olive oil and aged vinegar). Spanakopitta (light, crispy sesame-glazed filo pastry with spinach, two kinds of ewe's cheese, leeks and dill) fulfilled all the precision and attention to detail of its menu description, and came with an equally tasty salad of bitter frisée and radicchio scattered with finely diced tomatoes and toasted pine nuts. The afelia, served on a huge square plate, featured four generous pork ribs artistically arranged north, south, east and west of a mound of perfectly textured cracked wheat with tantalising herb and floral notes, all on a rich, slightly syrupy sauce of red wine with coriander and cinnamon. From a well-chosen range of Greek wines we enjoyed a Cretan rosé and a bottle of Marathon beer. Alas, the coffee was about as Greek as grand-mère's.

Mavrommatis ★

5 rue du Marché des Patriarches, 5th (01.43.31.17.17/ www.mavrommatis.fr). Mº Censier Daubenton. **Open** noon-2.15pm, 7-11pm Tue-Sun. Closed Aug. **Average** €37. **Lunch menu** €28.50. **Credit** AmEx, MC, V. **Wheelchair access. Map** J9.

Light years away from the pseudo-Greek tourist traps of the nearby Latin Quarter, the Mavrommatis brothers' refined Cypriot cuisine has made us regulars for the last 15 years. Our latest visit was a mission to convert a chef friend who had sniffily informed us that no 'foreign' food could hold a candle to French gastronomy. But, however hard he tried, no amount of nit-picking could justifiably fault this excellent restaurant's ever-seductive food or its tasteful, understated decor. We kicked off with a warm salad of savoury octopus and rocket with a tangy lemon-and-olive oil dressing, and a generous plateful of grilled halloumi cheese flanked by a minty tomato sauce and toasted olive bread. Even our friend's hefty dose of Gallic scepticism buckled before crunchy, state-of-the-art vine leaf parcels packed with minced lamb and spinach. For mains we stuck with our favourites – quail in vine leaves marinated in a divinely fragrant honey and thyme sauce, served with a bulghur wheat and pistachio salad; and the tender, juicy '1821 Resistance-style' lamb – while our friend sampled the pot-roasted rabbit wafting out its scents of cinnamon and shallots. In the face of our sincere enthusiasm for good Greek wine, co-owner Evagoras fetched a berry-rich, liquorice treasure from his own stock. As usual, the service was friendly, efficient but relaxed. Our only gripe is that prices are sneaking skywards, but for the moment the quality, convivial atmosphere and sheer pleasure factor are enough to keep us, and our new convert, coming back for more.

La Voie Lactée

34 rue du Cardinal-Lemoine, 5th (01.46.34.02.35). Mº Cardinal-Lemoine. **Open** noon-2.30pm, 7-11pm Mon-Sat. Closed Aug. **Average** €20. **Prix fixe** €19.50 (dinner only). **Lunch menu** €11.50, €13.50. **Credit** MC, V. **Wheelchair access. Map** K8.

Formerly something of a '60s relic, the 'milky way' has redecorated in a smart style that reflects its exacting standards with dark green taffeta curtains, rectangular red lamps and 19th-century prints of Turkish monuments. It attracts a local clientele of middle-aged business types and quiet couples – no dancing on the tables but a good choice for a pleasant and reasonably priced meal out. Starters of mildly spiced sausage cooked in a papillotte with green peppers and herbs, and roast courgettes wrapped around a mild goat's cheese were wonderfully fresh. We continued with a perfectly char-grilled, lightly spiced beef brochette accompanied by rice and salad, and the surprise of the evening – sautée of veal on a bed of aubergine purée, the smoky tones of the purée contrasting with the tender veal and a harissa-flavoured sauce. The cinnamon-topped custard muhallivi tasted home-made, but the chef's angel hair pastry erred on the side of caution with its honey sauce and could have been crisper. Try some Turkish wine – the waiter recommended the enjoyable Pamukkale. Service was rather slow but extremely polite.

Al-Diwan
30 av George V, 8th (01.47.23.45.45). M° George V or Alma-Marceau. **Open** noon-1am daily. **Average** €40. **Credit** AmEx, DC, MC, V. **Non-smoking room. Map** D4.
After the lovely terrace, the interior of Al-Diwan comes as a let-down, although on a sweltering night the air-conditioning almost made up for the hospital cafeteria-like decor. As we washed down spicy, house-cured olives with an all-too-drinkable Lebanese red (Chateau Ksara), we decided against meze for two (ten starters for €58) in favour of bastorma (thinly sliced cured beef) and the plat du jour for the meat-eater, and three starters for the vegetarian. The plat du jour – grilled beef cooked with potatoes and tomatoes – had all the flavour of home cooking, as did the delicious makdous (pickled aubergine stuffed with walnuts and spices). Less successful were the briney vine leaves, the chanklishe (feta-like goat's cheese whipped with fresh tomatoes and herbs) which needed some more tomato to counter the saltiness, and the rather drab accompanying salads. Desserts were frankly disappointing: the baklava was so dried out it was falling to pieces, while other sweetmeats tasted as though they had been sitting around for a while. With food this simple and prices this steep, ingredients need to be fresh and top-quality. Better to stick to the sister take-away two doors down where the snooty service is absent and the constant turnover means that the food is always fresh.

Kibele
12 rue de l'Echiquier, 10th (01.48.24.57.74). M° Bonne Nouvelle or Strasbourg St-Denis. **Open** noon-3pm, 7-11.30pm Mon-Sat. Closed Aug. **Average** €15. **Prix fixe** €11.80, €14.90 (dinner only). **Lunch menu** €8.80. **Credit** AmEx, MC, V. **Wheelchair access. Map** K4.
On a Saturday night, Kibele was filled with families and students enthusiastically mopping up meze platters and, between bites, clapping and singing along with a trio of Turkish musicians. Following half their lead, we went for the meze too: creamy houmous, stuffed vine leaves, feather-light deep-fried calamari, baba ganoush (aubergine dip) and a basket of puffy Turkish bread to wipe the plates clean. Kibele specialises in Turkish and Greek food so that means lots of grills, lamb and yoghurt. Grilled octopus, although not exuberant portion-wise, was tender and the chicken kebabs full of barbecued flavour. For something meatier, try eli nazek (garlicky yoghurt, lamb and aubergine) or

sarapli kuzo (lamb and peppers fried in red wine). Desserts range from honey-drenched baklava to cinnamon-flavoured rice pudding. From Tuesday to Saturday the cellar bar hosts world music concerts.

Kazaphani ★
122 av Parmentier, 11th (01.48.07.20.19). M° Parmentier or Goncourt. **Open** noon-3pm, 7.30pm-midnight Tue Fri, Sun; 7.30pm-midnight Sat. Closed last two weeks in Aug. **Average** €30. **Prix fixe** €27, €32. **Lunch menu** €16. **Credit** AmEx, MC, V. **Wheelchair access. Map** M5.
The welcome at Kasaphani was so extraordinarily relaxed that we felt as though we had walked into someone's home. But, like everything at this family-run Cypriot, it warms up slowly and is all the better for it. We opted for the meze menu with three courses for €32. Though we were only two, the dishes just kept on coming, and what we gained in choice we did not lose in quality. Especially of note were the octopus in olive oil, lemon and garlic, wonderfully lemony mushrooms, a tasty paste of broad beans and a taramasalata so pale and creamy it was worlds away from the lurid pink concoction that so often insults the name. Next came plates of huge aniseed-flavoured gambas, calamari and deep-fried whitebait. We were almost defeated by the meat course but this was also of excellent quality, particularly the crisp meatballs and stuffed pork. Hatzimichalis or Nemea are good choices for red wines, though we went for the classic Kourtaki retsina. By the time we got on to délice d'Aphrodite (yoghurt, walnuts and honey) and fruit salad with coconut and sorbet, Pavlos was sitting at our table, offering us one of his alcohol-spiked coffees, talking about rembetiko (soulful Greek music) and how he remembered Lawrence Durrell from his childhood. Not just a restaurant, Kasaphani gives nostalgia its true meaning in Greek – longing for home.

Zagros
21 rue de la Folie-Méricourt, 11th (01.48.07.09.56). M° Richard-Lenoir or St-Ambroise. **Open** noon-2.30pm, 7pm-midnight Mon-Fri; 7pm-midnight Sat. **Average** €23. **Prix fixe** (dinner only) €18, €24. **Lunch menu** €11.50. **Credit** AmEx, MC, V. **Map** M5.
When we arrived at Zagros the owner was already enjoying an ouzo and meze with friends on one of the terrace tables. This set the scene for a relaxed meal at this off-Oberkampf address that serves as the meeting place for an arty Kurdish community: paintings on the walls are for sale and a saz (a stringed instrument) is stashed behind the till in case musical inspiration strikes. The menu roams all over the area covered by the Kurdish diaspora. Wines are Kurdish Greek as well as French, and our Cretan red from big-time producer Kourtaki proved rich and fruity - spot-on for this type of food. The starter of mixed cold meze was very satisfactory, but the hot oven-cooked aubergine with feta was melt-in-your mouth good, proving that the Kurdish 'village' dishes are the way to go here. Ditto for the hasti –

International

knuckle of lamb boiled then re-cooked in a tomato-flavoured sauce and topped with a slice of grilled aubergine and pepper – and kavouras, which involves lamb preserved in salt for months on end in Kurdish villages (or so we were told). Shame the accompanying grated carrot and lettuce were uninspired, though the bulghur wheat was good. We finished with fromage blanc, one with fresh diced fruit and the other with honey and walnuts, and moved inside for an 'Ottoman' coffee and brandies on the house. As we finally left, the evening was just kicking off for the Kurds, with Mahmut on the saz and a bottle of Metaxa on the table – not bad for a Monday night, lads.

Cheminée Royale

22 bis rue de l'Ingénieur-Robert-Keller, 15th (01.45.79.44.22). M° Charles Michels. **Open** noon-3pm, 7.30pm-midnight daily. **Average** €35. **Lunch menu** €13 (Mon-Fri). **Credit** AmEx, MC, V. **Map** B8.
Do you have a hankering for fesenjan (poultry in pomegranate and walnut sauce), gormeh sabzi (meat stew packed with fresh herbs) or khoresht-e bademjan (beef with aubergine and split peas)? Do you read Farsi? A magnet for Iranian émigrés, the Cheminée Royale has two menus and mysteriously these classics of Persian cooking have been left off the French one. For the uninitiated, the hearty meat brochettes served with out-of-this-world fluffy Iranian rice (try chicken marinated in yoghurt and lemon, the lamb Caucasian or a koubideh – spiced, minced beef on a skewer) will satisfy even the most meat-weary palates. But when we saw plates of our favourite stews whip by, we got curious. With characteristic Iranian hospitality, the waiter offered us a taste – actually, more like a generous bowl – of each: we'll certainly be back for more. Since we'd also tucked into a selection of starters such as mast moussir (thick yoghurt with wild garlic) and Caucasian salad (a misnomer for a delicious aubergine, onion and kidney bean soup), and polished off a jug of dough (a tangy mint and yoghurt drink), we didn't feel we had room for anything more than a cup of sweet black tea (you put the sugar cube in your mouth, not in the cup). Our ever-generous waiter thought otherwise and presented us with bite-sized Iranian pastries.

Mazeh

65 rue des Entrepreneurs, 15th (01.45.75.33.89/ www.mazeh.com). M° Charles Michels or Commerce. **Open** noon-10pm Tue-Sat; noon-9pm Sun. Closed Aug. **Average** €20. **Prix fixe** €16, €20. **Credit** MC, V. **Non-smoking restaurant. Map** B8.
If your acquaintance with the most refined of Middle Eastern cuisines – Iranian – comes from living in London, you may at first be disappointed by Mazeh. Where are the tinkling fountains, the mosaic-tiled bread oven, the pictures of the Shah and the melancholy music? Mazeh is the centre of a catering business and, though some effort has now been put into the decor, it's still utilitarian. Never mind, it's the food that attracts knowing locals and Iranian

families. The parchment-like lavach bread was not as piping hot as it should be, but starter dips of luxuriant yoghurt with cucumber and mint, and warm aubergine purée with its distinctive smoky flavour made up for it. Main courses are all variations on the kebab, served with the lightest buttery, saffron-flavoured rice. Char-grilled skewers of minced or cubed lamb or coquelet (cockerel) draw flavours from exotic marinades, such as tarragon and green pepper, basil and white wine, or tandoori. We stuck with the traditional lemon and saffron, which was delicious. Our wine was an acceptable house red, but for authenticity try the zingy yoghurt drink 'dough' or – if it's in season (during winter) – fresh pomegranate juice.

Restaurant Al Wady ★

153-155 rue de Lourmel, 15th (01.45.58.57.18).
Mº Lourmel. **Open** noon-3pm, 7pm-midnight daily.
Closed 1 Jan. **Average** €25. **Prix fixe** (dinner only)
€19. **Lunch menu** €11, €14. **Credit** AmEx, MC, V.
Map B9.

Al Wady is not the type of place we'd take a visiting
friend keen for a picture-postcard Parisian dining
experience. Unless, that is, said acquaintance had a
hankering for a Lebanese feast to rival the best in
the Middle East. The heroically long menu makes
for an agony of indecision so we settled on the meze
platter. At €38 for two it's a great way to sample
house specialities such as garlicky houmous, moist
tabouleh and smoky baba ganoush. And that's just
for starters. Pastries cooked golden brown hide the
perfect bite of delicately spiced lamb, while
succulent chicken pieces in a caramelised orange
glaze will appeal to those with a sweet palate.
Feeling particularly carnivorous, we bypassed sure-
to-please salads in favour of the mixed grill: a meat-
lovers' selection of lamb and chicken charred to
perfection and presented alongside a cooling salad
of yoghurt tossed with lemon, cucumber and tomato.
The yardstick for true greatness in Lebanese
kitchens is measured by the falafel – neither too
grainy nor too moist, Al Wady's are orbs of herbed
wonder. The coffee is strong and honeyed pastries
can be bought in boxes to take away.

International

Kibele. *See p171.*

Far Eastern

Great Asian food doesn't jump out at you in Paris – you have to look for it with a certain amount of devotion. Yes, there are Asian 'traiteurs' on nearly every corner, but many of these serve mass-produced food belonging to no particular Asian country. Fortunately, there are real treasures to be found in Chinatown (along avenue d'Ivry and avenue de Choisy in the 13th), in multicultural Belleville, and scattered throughout the city – this year's discoveries range from irresistible dim sum at Le Pacifique in Belleville to sophisticated Thai food at Silk & Spice, near Les Halles.

CAMBODIAN

La Mousson
9 rue Thérèse, 1st (01.42.60.59.46). Mᵒ Pyramides. **Open** noon-2.30pm, 7-10.30pm Mon-Sat. **Average** €25. **Prix fixe** €17.20, €21.90. **Lunch menu** €13, €17.30. **Credit** MC, V. **Map** H5.

Just steps from the cluster of Japanese restaurants on the rue Ste-Anne is this oasis of Cambodian hospitality. Furnished with items that could have come right out of Phnom Penh's colourful street markets – from the mass-manufactured mural of Angkor Wat to the woven cotton scarves that serve as tablecloths and the stackable plastic chairs – La Mousson still feels welcoming and comfortable, particularly if you begin the meal with the house cocktail, a fragrant concoction of rice wine and lychee juice. The food is equally simple and pleasant. Cold spring rolls, thick with lettuce, mint, vermicelli, shrimp and shredded chicken, satiated any pre-dinner hunger pangs. Caramelised filet mignon was decent, if somewhat overcooked. Amok, a classic Cambodian dish of tender fish fillets steamed in coconut milk within a banana leaf, was much better – soft and exotically perfumed. The best dish, however, was the excellent minced pork with lemongrass, a pungent mix of pork, coconut milk, shrimp paste and shrimp. Wrap a spoonful in a piece of crisp romaine lettuce and astonish your palate. Wash it all down with the very affordable wine, and your wallet will be pleasantly surprised too.

Le Cambodge
10 av Richerand, 10th (01.44.84.37.70). Mᵒ Goncourt or République. **Open** noon-2.30pm, 8-11.30pm Mon-Sat. Closed 1 Aug-15 Sept, 24 Dec-1 Jan. **Average** €18. **Credit** MC, V. **Wheelchair access**. **Map** L4.

This small restaurant doesn't take reservations, so it's best to go early. At opening time, it filled immediately and those who had lost the race for seats were asked to wait at the neighbouring bar. We were given pen and paper with our menus to write down our own orders and were served promptly. We started with a large prawn spring roll, tasty but cut into slices and difficult to handle – especially as the tiny, unsteady tables are set so close together that it's difficult to avoid poking your neighbour with your chopsticks. We followed with bò bùn, a fresh and nourishing bowl of beansprouts, thin rice noodles, stir-fried beef and onions, mint, coriander and grated peanuts in a clear sweet sauce. We also tried ban hoy, their 'Angkorian picnic', a variation on bò bùn. The same ingredients (minus the sweet sauce) are served on a plate, with stir-fried prawns, beansprouts and salad on the side. The house specialty, natin, is a fabulous Cambodian curry – quality pork or prawns in a delicious, rich and creamy peanut sauce with coriander, served with rice or prawn crackers. We finished off with a soothing, typically Asian dessert of hot tapioca, bananas and coconut cream. Modest surroundings allow the owners to keep the prices low.

La Coloniale ★
161 rue de Picpus, 12th (01.43.43.69.10). Mᵒ Porte Dorée. **Open** noon-2pm, 7.30-10.30pm Mon-Sat. Closed Aug. **Average** €25. **Lunch menu** €12, €15. **Credit** MC, V. **Wheelchair access**. **Non-smoking room**. **Map** Q9.

Chef Thaknol Moeur hails from Cambodia, while his French wife Dominique (who also speaks Khmer) flits about the dining room singing along to 1920s jazz tunes that match the pleasing, Asian-themed bric-a-brac scattered about. We're neighbourhood regulars, drawn again and again by the very reasonable prices and the kitchen's exemplary skill with fresh basil, coriander and hot peppers in its tangy soups and creamy curries that are leagues above the average corner Asian traiteur's pre-fab cuisine. Begin with a ginger chicken soupe de l'Indo, an orange-bright, coconut-based curry, or the chicken beignets – baguette slices fused to breast meat and deep-fried. Then dive into the succulent chicken satay, the loc-lak (beef fried rice) or the seafood noodles sauté – a mix of mussels, squid, scallops and prawns seared in black pepper. The amok is a memorable little soufflé-like steamed salmon, coconut and lemongrass concoction served in a ramekin. Most dishes arrive with superb dipping sauces and cute pickle garnishes carved into sea creature shapes. For dessert, try the bohbor kthi – jackfruit in squishy tapioca topped with toasted sesame seeds. Ask for one of the tiny non-smoking room's two tables for extra privacy.

CHINESE

Chez Vong ★

10 rue de la Grande Truanderie, 1st (01.40.26.09.36). M° Etienne Marcel. **Open** noon-2.30pm, 7pm-midnight Mon-Sat. **Average** €50. **Lunch menu** €23. **Credit** AmEx, DC, MC, V. **Non-smoking room. Map** J5.
The staff at this soothingly intimate Chinese restaurant obviously take pride in the excellent cooking here, which covers the great dishes of Canton, Shanghai, Beijing and Sichuan. From the warm greeting at the door to the knowledgeable and trilingual service (Cantonese, Mandarin and French), each phase of the dining experience is thoughtfully orchestrated to showcase the delicious possibilities of China's diverse cuisine. Tables, draped in pink cloth, are widely spaced; low lighting and green ceramic bamboo partitions heighten the sense of intimacy. The atmosphere is such a far cry from the clamour and brusqueness of typical Chinese restaurants, we wondered how authentic the food could be. Any doubts were quickly extinguished from the first arrival of the beautifully presented dishes, which are immediately placed on heated stands at the table. Expertly cooked spicy shrimp glistened in a smooth, robust sauce of onions and ginger. Silky ma po tofu melted in the mouth, its

spicy and peppery flavours melding with the fine pork mince in synergistic succulence. Very tender pepper beef, served with fresh baby corn, mushroom and carrots, came in a crisp, savoury 'bird's nest', an acknowledgement that garnishes should be not only edible but palatable. Ravioli of prawn, bamboo shoots and coriander were divinely delicate, the thin wrapper barely containing the textured ingredients. This perfect meal came at a price, but it was worth every cent.

Mirama

17 rue St-Jacques, 5th (01.43.54.71.77). M° Cluny-La Sorbonne or St-Michel. **Open** noon-10.45pm daily. **Average** €20. **Credit** MC, V. **Non-smoking room. Map** J7.
Serving surprisingly good food at fair value in an area otherwise packed with tourist traps, this tidy little Cantonese is a delightful place to refuel next time you're in St-Michel. Eyeing the lacquered ducks and glazed pork ribs hanging in the open kitchen at the entrance, we chose a table in the front room – a non-smoking area – where we had a clear view of the chef. Start with one of the many soups on offer, such as the noodle soup with chunks of tender braised beef and fresh green onion in a rich beef broth. We devoured a plate piled with sliced roasted duck and pork on rice that easily fed two. We also enjoyed the sweet and sour chicken, replete with pieces of pineapple and green pepper. A side dish of broccoli in oyster sauce was cooked perfectly crisp-tender, but the sauce lacked zing. Portions here are generous and there is a wide selection of classic dishes with (thankfully) no attempt to introduce non-traditional ingredients for the sake of being inventive. Service is pleasant and efficient.

New Nioullaville

32-34 rue de l'Orillon, 11th (01.40.21.96.18). M° Belleville. **Open** 11.45am-3pm, 7pm-1am daily. **Average** €20. **Lunch menu** €6.50-€13.50 (Mon-Wed). **Credit** AmEx, MC, V. **Wheelchair access. Map** M4.
The immense dining room, convivial atmosphere, wide selection of dishes from China and Thailand and gentle prices make this one of our favourite places to celebrate with a large group of friends – at the start of Chinese New Year, performers dressed as colourful dragons danced up and down the restaurant's aisles beneath a ceiling hung with bright red lanterns. Arrive hungry and hail down one of the dim sum carts circling the room. We particularly liked the steamed shrimp dumplings, shrimp balls and fried pork dumplings. For main courses, it's hard to go wrong with the Sichuan/Cantonese specialities. The Genghis Khan beef – tender strips of steak sautéed with ginger, onion, fresh basil and lemongrass – was outstanding. Prawns lightly fried with salt and pepper were plump and fresh. Chop suey was a delicious mixture of more than six vegetables, and cold Tsingtao beer from China hit the spot. Unfortunately, service can be erratic, with some dishes arriving long after

others on busy nights. For dessert, there is a large selection of Chinese cakes, plus Western-style ice-creams. There is free underground parking with direct entrance to the restaurant.

Le Président

120-124 rue du Fbg-du-Temple, 11th (01.47.00.17.18). M° Belleville. **Open** noon-2.30pm, 6pm-2am daily. **Average** €22. **Prix fixe** €121 (for 6 people). **Lunch menu** €9-€12.50 (Mon-Fri). **Credit** DC, MC, V. **Wheelchair access. Non-smoking room. Map** M4.

It's quite a trek through the lobby (porcelain, dried bits of shark, photos of visiting celebs – well, Serge Gainsbourg and Mitterrand – a 1989 award for Asian cuisine, etc) and up the imposing staircase. But, if the place looks a bit tired, the food is fresh and bright, and there's a roaring trade in Big Fat Asian Weddings (always a good sign) – hence the Imelda Marcos pavilion and sofa in the middle of the dining room, perfect for those happy snaps. At Sunday lunch, we joined cheerful (Western) family parties pondering their orders over hot, fresh dim sum from the steam trolley. The kids devoured chicken noodles and ice-cream, grimaced at the lobster tank and took turns on the sofa, while we tackled platters of tender pork with huge smoky-tasting mushrooms, stir-fried squid and chicken with cashews, all colourfully garnished with broccoli, crunchy water chestnuts and neat little stars of carrot. Then came creamy, steamed coconut dumplings on bitter chocolate sauce. We didn't try (but will) the Peking duck, Thai dishes and chef's specials, including lobster with garlic, and stir-fried chicken with mango in a shredded potato basket. We were even treated to a ravishing Chinese bride and much popping of corks. 'Whaddaya know,' said our eight-year-old, 'dinner and a show!'

Wok

23 rue des Taillandiers, 11th (01.55.28.88.77). M° Bastille or Ledru-Rollin. **Open** 7-11pm Mon-Thur, Sun; 7-11.30pm Fri, Sat. **Average** €20. **Prix fixe** €15.50, €19. **Credit** MC, V. **Wheelchair access. Map** M7.

Wok is the epitome of Bastille youth culture. The long central pine refectory table and the decor's Zen-like minimalism is coupled with loud rock music and a food concept that ensures great value and freshness. The idea is to take your bowl, already half-filled with noodles or rice, to a buffet of uncooked vegetables, meat and fish, which you pile on, preferably taking into account what might taste good together. You then present your bowl to the chef, who asks what spices and aromatics you are interested in, then with a sizzle and a crack your selection is tossed into the white-hot wok and returned to you in minutes as an authentic Chinese stir-fry. We were pleased with our efforts of combining squid and Chinese mushrooms with rice noodles, and the food benefits from the short time lapse between wok and mouth. The wine list is short and uninteresting, but our Provençal rosé was a pleasant enough accompaniment. The starters, in this case some ordinary vegetarian nems and heavy vegetable tempura, were poor, and the sweet nems with chocolate sauce seemed too hybrid an idea to come off, but for an excellent stir-fry in a hot ambience you need look no further.

Tricotin

15 av de Choisy, 13th (01.45.84.74.44). M° Porte de Choisy. **Open** 9am-11pm daily. **Average** €20. **Credit** MC, V. **Wheelchair access. Non-smoking room.**

Tricotin flanks a gloomy passage off the southern end of avenue de Choisy, aka Main Street Chinatown, complete with skyscrapers, exotic supermarkets and Cantonese calligraphy on the McDonald's next door. To the left, a small starched-linen dining room dispenses Thai, Malay and Cambodian cuisine, while the huge, bright canteen to the right is the place for dim sum, giant noodle soups, salads and Chinese standards. After a disappointing visit last year, we were delighted to find the latter right back on track: the kitchen bustling with a ship-shape crew of white-clad chefs, the tables packed with a multi-generational mix of locals and visitors from uptown. Perfect crispy nems with garden-fresh green salad and mint sprigs were followed by stacked baskets containing some of the finest steamed tit-bits we've had: perfectly textured rice ravioli concealing flavoursome jewel-bright greens and shrimp, and a huge sticky rice dumpling dotted with tender morsels of pork, neatly wrapped in a giant lotus leaf. Chicken noodles, glazed duck and crispy steamed Thai broccoli were all exemplary, as was a platter of pleasingly large, firm scallop slices with mushrooms and cashews. Less familiar exotica include the drinks – sweet red beans mashed in soya milk, fresh coconut juice with slivers of translucent flesh, mix-it-yourself chocolate syrup with hot condensed milk – and the house dessert, ban dout, a thick, jelly-like substance served with sweet 'n' salty soya milk, caramel and sesame seeds. But, with steamed baskets averaging €5 for three sizeable morsels, and mains at around €6.50, you can afford to experiment.

Le Pacifique ★

15 rue de Belleville, 20th (01.43.06.22.55). M° Belleville. **Open** noon-2pm, 7-10pm Tue-Sun. Closed three days at Christmas, three weeks in Aug. **Average** €30. **Credit** MC, V. **Wheelchair access. Non-smoking room. Map** N3.

We were expecting all the elements of a typical Sunday dim sum lunch: crowds, queues and surly service. Instead, we were swiftly welcomed into a fairly sedate restaurant partially divided into two rooms. The front – with floor-to-ceiling windows – looked out on to the hubbub of the busy street. No trolleys of food being pushed by gruff old ladies here. The comprehensive selection of dim sum is ordered off the menu and delivered to the table in quick succession, or even all at the same time. From the fluffy steamed pork buns to the plump prawn

International

dumplings and fragrant sticky rice steamed in lotus leaf, every dish that arrived was reassuringly authentic. It might not be the finest dim sum you can get in Paris, but it is certainly good enough. Given the variety of dishes on offer, as well as the restaurant's accessibility – a few steps from the Belleville Métro – this is probably the best bet for a headache- and hassle-free experience. The availability of high chairs for kids and choice of interesting teas are further incentives.

Salon de Thé Wenzhou
24 rue de Belleville, 20th (01.46.36.56.33). Mº Belleville. **Open** 10.20am-9.30pm Mon-Wed, Fri-Sun. **Average** €11. **No credit cards. Map** N3.
The most recent wave of Chinese immigration to France has been from the lesser-known Wenzhou province; the regional cuisine is hard to find in Paris, but this popular tearoom provides familiar dishes to the Wenzhou residents of Belleville. The front counter does a constant brisk business in pork buns, less doughy and with more herbs than the Cantonese equivalent – an ideal cheap snack as you're walking up this hill. If you're in the mood for lunch, grab a seat and order the fabulous triangle-dumpling soup (minced bamboo, carrots, herbs and pork, in substantial dumplings, float in a broth loaded with bok choy). The noodle dishes aren't particularly noteworthy, so if you're still hungry after the soup, order a round of small grilled herb ravioli (which, despite their name, contain pork). For dessert, don't miss the wonderful red bean buns rolled in sesame seeds, just sweet enough to finish your meal.

Sinostar
27-29 av de Fontainebleau, 94270 Le Kremlin-Bicêtre (01.49.60.88.88). Mº Porte d'Italie. **Open** noon-2.30pm, 7pm-1am Tue-Fri, Sun; 7pm-1am Sat. Closed two weeks in Aug. **Average** €18. **Prix fixe** €21.50. **Lunch menu** €12. **Credit** MC, V. **Wheelchair access. Non-smoking room.**
Billed as 'the largest Chinese restaurant in Europe', Sinostar is deceptively small and unimpressive on the inside, with multiple private rooms ringing the plainly decorated central salon and small stage. The chef hails from Macau, a casino island off the coast of Hong Kong, which may explain the lacklustre, for-the-masses, not-quite-Cantonese cuisine. We enjoyed the crispy stuffed taro root appetiser, and the steamed dim sum pork and carrot dumplings weren't bad, but the mains were dull: the Singapore vermicelli was flavourless, the whole poached sea bass undercooked and the sickly-sweet sesame chicken (drenched in orange preserves) nearly inedible. Gloppy soups, like the overpriced shark fin (€12 a cup), were equally mediocre. All in all, we'd expected a grander setting and more inventive food with fresher herbs and ingredients. On weekends, a lounge cover band plays nearly note-for-note versions of American, Chinese and French pop classics. After plenty of cheap cocktails and Tsingtao beers (both €4) you may find yourself sufficiently lubricated to strut your stuff on the dancefloor.

INDOCHINESE

Au Coin des Gourmets
5 rue Dante, 5th (01.43.26.12.92). Mº Cluny-La Sorbonne. **Open** 7-10.30pm Mon; noon-2.30pm, 7-10.30pm Tue-Sat; noon-2.30pm, 7-10pm Sun. **Average** €25. **Lunch menu** €11.50 (except on public holidays). **Credit** MC, V. **Wheelchair access. Non-smoking room. Map** J7.
Service is all smiles at this family-run Indochinese restaurant in the Latin Quarter. The cramped, brightly lit interior, decorated with posters and old adverts from Vietnam, Thailand and France, is packed with customers sitting shoulder to shoulder, but having too good a time to care. The ten tables in the main dining room – concealed from the street behind a lace curtain – are covered in crisp, white damask and pristine napkins: cleanliness still counts within the yellowing walls. Unfortunately, while the food is definitely palatable, it is neither generous nor skilfully prepared. Perhaps the cooks were stretched by the ambitiously long menu. A delicious dressing of lime juice, mint, red pepper, onions and shallots failed to override the chewy toughness of the main attraction in the cuttlefish salad. Mini Cambodian brochettes, subtly flavoured with lemongrass, were hardly more tender. The house speciality – fillets of white fish layered with cabbage and satay sauce and baked in banana leaf – smelled exotic but tasted rather bland. On a more positive note, a side order of coconut-flavoured glutinous rice steamed in bamboo was very good, as was the rather paltry wedge of hot coconut flan we chose for dessert. Still, with good-quality house wines priced at €5 per half-litre, served by infectiously happy staff, it is no surprise this charming eaterie remains a neighbourhood favourite.

Thanh-Lan
33 rue Lamartine, 9th (01.48.78.58.88). Mº Notre-Dame-de-Lorette. **Open** 11.30am-3pm, 7-11pm Mon-Sat. **Average** €20. **Prix fixe** €11-€25. **Lunch menu** €11. **Credit** AmEx, MC, V. **Map** H3.
There is a limited menu, a limited number of seats and limited ventilation at this new 'Asian grill' restaurant, where you cook your own meats and seafood on a built-in electric grill at your table. Don't let that dissuade you, because this tiny eaterie, crammed with big tables and rattan chairs, is generous where it counts: in the warm, personal service and the healthy portions of fresh food offered at charitably low prices. Best bet at lunch or dinner is to go for one of the set menus, which includes a starter of salad or deliciously satisfying nems, as well as a savoury, albeit watery and chicken-less tom khai kai, or Thai coconut soup. For the main course, choose from a variety of marinated raw meats and seafood – including tender, thin slices of beef entrecôte and tenderloin, chicken and fattened duck breast, as well as whole shrimps and scallops, garnished with a small mound of sliced mushrooms and onions. The meats are accompanied by two dips – a tangy soy-based sauce and aïoli – and a bowl of

rice. As the table is set with only one pair of chopsticks, do insist on a second pair for handling the raw meat. And do wear the kind of clothes you would normally cook in, because when you walk out you will smell like a short-order cook.

Kambodgia

15 rue de Bassano, 16th (01.47.23.08.19).
Mº George V or Charles de Gaulle-Etoile. **Open** noon-1.30pm, 7.30-10.30pm Mon-Sat. Closed Aug. **Average** €50. **Lunch menu** €18, €23. **Credit** AmEx, MC, V. **Non-smoking room. Map** D4.
We rang the bell and pushed the door to descend into the teak-clad basement of this elegant Asian restaurant near the Champs-Elysées. Settling into our wicker chairs, surrounded by a largely business clientele, we had an immediate impression of well-being. The menu is disappointingly low on Cambodian specialities and reads very much like that of an average Vietnamese restaurant. Our prawn tempura with almonds was tasty but slightly greasy, which misses the point of this feather-light dish. There were also only three prawns and a large number of vegetables, including an inedible thick slice of onion, scattered with ineffectual almond flakes. The dim sum were equally ordinary, saved by a spinach-wrapped roll with an interesting lemongrass-led stuffing. One of the only specifically Cambodian dishes, a cary de poulet, was well-flavoured and had something in common with a Thai curry, served with some good boiled rice. But magret de canard aux épices was under-spiced and over-fatty. Service was swift and professional, but when paying over €100 for two it is unacceptable to be asked to use the same cutlery for starter and main course, particularly as we were moving from fish to meat. Peripherals such as the excellent château Barberyrolle rosé and the first-rate coffee were fine, but sensing a growing bill we bypassed pudding, which featured mousse au chocolat, plus various sorbets and mango- or coconut-based confections.

INDONESIAN

Djakarta Bali

9 rue Vauvilliers, 1st (01.45.08.83.11/www. djakartabali.com). Mº Louvre-Rivoli. **Open** 7pm-midnight Tue-Sun. Closed 15-20 Aug. **Average** €40. **Prix fixe** €18-€43. **Credit** MC, V. **Wheelchair access. Non-smoking room. Map** J5.
If you have a nut allergy, stay far, far away. Virtually every dish served here is smothered in peanut sauce. Unimaginative, you might think, but the warm surroundings, friendly service and good food will help you forgive the repetition. The menu offers several types of rijsttafel, the Dutch-inspired smorgasbord of steamed rice served with an indefinite succession of small side dishes. The most comprehensive set was the rijsttafel Bali, which included about eight generously portioned courses and a handful of smaller sides and condiments. The feast kicked off with a clear and tangy chicken soup

perfumed with Indonesian herbs. Highlights that followed included deep-fried spring rolls, fried chicken liver and beef brochettes – all dipped, coated or marinated in an intense, dark peanut sauce. Despite the homogenous flavouring, each dish was uniquely delicious. A la carte, a mixed vegetable salad (again dressed with peanut sauce) was pleasantly refreshing, beef rendang could have benefited from a longer simmer, while the giant prawns steamed in banana leaf – though indeed gigantic and fresh – swam in a coconut milk-based curry sauce that was tasty but a tad watery. Still, the dishes are exotically alluring and they are prepared with pride. From the traditional Balinese handicrafts and artwork that adorn the room to the careful selection of dishes on offer, the restaurant – run by the children of a high-ranking Indonesian minister exiled in Paris from the mid-1960s – remains a welcoming showcase of the Spice Islands' fragrant cuisine.

KOREAN

Han Lim

6 rue Blainville, 5th (01.43.54.62.74). Mº Place Monge or Cardinal Lemoine. **Open** 7-10.30pm Mon, Tue; noon-2.30pm, 7-10.30pm Wed-Sun; Closed Aug. **Average** €30. **Lunch menu** €14. **Credit** MC, V. **Map** J8.
If home-style Korean cuisine is what you're after, this 20-year-old haunt is your place. Koreans and foreigners alike come here for their fix of comfort food and garlic. Bring an appetite because the portions are plentiful. We started with the deep-fried pork- and vegetable-filled gyoza, which were fresh and well-cooked. Vegetarians should sample the hefty but reliable classic Korean pancake with spring onion. The menu is brief but there is something for everyone. If you have a penchant for beef, try the traditional bulgogi – sweet and juicy marinated strips that you cook yourself, accompanied by an array of home-made side dishes such as hot and spicy daikon, fresh kimchi and the milder spinach with sesame – mind the garlic. Another speciality to consider sharing is the crispy fried chicken with garlic, big enough to fill you up for the day. We waddled out, doggy bag in hand.

Gin Go Gae ★

28 rue Lamartine, 9th (01.48.78.24.64). Mº Cadet. **Open** noon-2.30pm, 7-11pm Mon-Sat; 7-11pm Sun. **Average** €20. **Lunch menu** €9.50, €10. **Credit** MC, V. **Wheelchair access. Map** J3.
We had been coming here about once a week for the €9.50 lunch menu, surely one of the best bargains in Paris, but had always been intrigued by the à la carte offerings (after all, who could resist the order of 'non-spiced soup of cowhead meat'?). One day, in a desperate bid to shake off a vicious cold, we pointed at the kimchi soup, a broth spiked with the fermented spiced cabbage that is perhaps the essence of Korean cooking. Ever kind and discreet,

International

the owner looked at us as if to say, 'are you sure you know what you're doing?' before returning with a lidded bowl brimming with the sinus-clearing stuff. We can't swear that this concoction cured us, but it certainly cheered us up immensely, as does every meal at this modest yet comfortable spot. On an ordinary day, we usually settle for the juicy fried gyoza or crisp galettes de soja (a sort of vegetable croquette) to start, followed by the raw fish with rice or the bibimbap, a hearty bowl of beef, vegetables and rice tossed together with an invigorating sauce. Every meal comes with several small bowls of vegetables, such as marinated spinach, potatoes and mung beans. It's food for thought that elsewhere in this neighbourhood €9.50 barely buys you a sandwich and a drink.

Restaurant Euro

65 rue du Fbg-Montmartre, 9th (01.53.21.07.89). Mº Notre-Dame-de-Lorette. **Open** noon-3pm, 7-11pm daily. **Average** €28. **Lunch menu** €8-€15. **Prix fixe** €19-€25. **Credit** DC, MC, V. **Wheelchair access. Map** J3.

Traditional food, as cooked by Madame Oh at Restaurant Euro, rests on a foundation of garlic, ginger, soy sauce, rice vinegar and sesame oil, always accompanied by medium-grained white rice, in a steel bowl to match the metal chopsticks. Begin with a tasty binn dae teok, a type of fried bean pancake, or a kimchi version called kim tchi jeon. The vermicelli noodle starter, chapchae, is fried with tender carrots, mushrooms and pork. Dol sot bibimbap, or the veggie oh saek bibimbap, combines lettuce with seaweed, egg, beansprouts, carrots and spinach, and if you look clueless enough your server will mush it all up for you in true local style. The most pleasing part may be discovering the panchan, various ceramic dishes filled with pickled ferns, dried fish, seasoned beansprouts, cucumber salad, or any of the various kimchis (cabbage, but also radish or aubergine), automatically appearing with most dishes. The at-your-table charcoal barbecues are on the pricey side, but budget diners can fry their own gas wok versions of beef, chicken or seafood, especially excellent value when part of the €15 dinner menu (the cheapest lunch menu, served on a TV dinner-style tray, costs just €8). Diners should know that dishes can be laced with spicy changs or jangs, femented soybean and chilli pastes, which add a distinctive zing.

Korean Barbecue

22 rue Delambre, 14th (01.43.35.44.32). Mº Vavin. **Open** noon-2pm, 7-11pm daily. **Average** €25. **Prix fixe** €19-€27. **Lunch menu** €10.50, €15. **Credit** MC, V. **Wheelchair access. Map** G9.

This stalwart trio of Left Bank Koreans doesn't seem as exotic as it did the first time we visited 15 years ago. In fact, it's a tough call to decide if their food is delicately seasoned or bland, especially when other outposts of Korean cooking make the point that the fire in this cuisine doesn't come uniquely from the gas burners, but from the kimchi (cabbage

Djakarta Bali. *See p179.*

fermented with chilli peppers). Still, you'll get a good feed with one of the set menus. The €19 menu leads off with grilled gyoza (delicate dumplings stuffed with vegetables and beef), while the €27 prix fixe debuts with five little appetisers, including deep-fried squid, gyoza and cucumber salad. The meal continues with a bowl of hot broth, pleasantly lashed with sesame oil, and the waiter fires up your gas grill when a big plate of thinly sliced beef arrives. From here on, you'll be so busy grilling that conversation will likely stall, and this is surely another reason that these places are so popular – the DIY relieves everyone of the need for too much social effort. No reservations are taken on Friday and Saturday nights, when the restaurant is busiest.

Other locations: 1 rue du Dragon, 6th (01.42.22.26.63); 39 rue du Montparnasse, 14th (01.43.27.69.53).

Odori

18 rue Letellier, 15th (01.45.77.88.12). Mº La Motte-Picquet or Emile Zola. **Open** noon-2.30pm, 7-10.30pm Tue-Sun. **Average** €30. **Credit** MC, V. **Map** C8.

It's out of the way, hidden down an obscure street, yet it's perpetually packed with Korean diners – an encouraging sign of delicious, authentic food, confirmed at the first piquant bite. You might balk at the thought of steak tartare in an unfamiliar environment, but this sublime starter is worth the gamble. Not that there is one: the ice-cold meat, scented with sesame oil and textured with slivers of Fuji apple, raw garlic and a raw egg, is always fresh and cleanly prepared. Follow this mild dish with a

comforting beef and leek soup, a Korean staple that is just hot and spicy enough to be warming rather than blazing. Pork and tofu sautéed with spicy sauce is equally balanced in flavour, although not in ingredients. The tender slices of pork were all too few. The classic Korean barbecue comes with the usual side dishes of kimchi and various root vegetables, marinated in vinegar or tossed in the same lively chilli paste. Korean beef arrives sizzling on a hot plate surrounded by a moat of sweet but mild stock. Those who prefer to cook over a real charcoal (not gas) grill should choose the Korean short ribs instead. Service is friendly but harried – not surprising given the noise from the cigarette-puffing, Shoju-swilling diners and the pungent smoke from the sizzling, open grills.

MALAYSIAN

Chez Foong

32 rue de Frémicourt, 15th (01.45.67.36.99). M° La Motte-Picquet-Grenelle or Cambronne. **Open** noon-2.30pm, 7-11pm Mon-Sat. Closed 21 July-26 Aug. **Average** €15. **Prix fixe** €14.50, €15 (Mon-Thur, Sat lunch). **Lunch menu** €9.90 (Mon-Fri). **Credit** MC, V. **Non-smoking room. Map** D8.

There aren't many Malaysian restaurants in Paris and this one is well worth the trek. There is a bewildering array of choices on the main menu, but the best bet is to go for the great-value prix fixe. We started off with the potage chinois, a spicy chicken soup with slivers of tasty black Chinese mushrooms.

This contrasted nicely with the beignets de légumes, crisply fried vegetables with the magical addition of a peanut sauce. The main courses spanned a variety of seafood, meat and poultry dishes; we enjoyed the chicken cooked in soy sauce and lemongrass, served with sugary caramelised onions. Lamb, beef and chicken brochettes were accompanied by a rich satay sauce made with shallots, garlic, tamarind, lemongrass and ground peanuts. Small, cigar-shaped pancakes filled with coconut and drizzled with a honey sauce, and a crisp, amazingly light pineapple fritter rounded off the meal.

THAI AND LAOTIAN

Silk & Spice ★

8 rue Mandar, 2nd (01.44.88.21.91). M° Etienne Marcel or Sentier. **Open** noon-3.30pm, 7.30pm-midnight daily. **Average** €40. **Prix fixe** €45 (dinner only). **Lunch menu** €19-€32. **Credit** AmEx, MC, V. **Non-smoking room. Map** J5.

The name might sound like a hackneyed slogan from a travel brochure, but don't be cynical. This stylish Thai restaurant genuinely delivers a treat for both the eye and the palate. Chocolate-coloured silk placemats and silk-bound chairs give textural warmth to the two rooms, painted glossy black and discreetly lit by dramatic, gold-leaf lanterns. A spray of orchids completes the lacquered box motif. At first the menu appears fashionably contrived, with items such as squid macaroons on the list of starters. We discovered, however, that it's just a fancy way

Barbecue time at perenially packed Korean favourite **Odori**. *See p180.*

of saying squid cakes. All this style comes with just as much substance: the cuisine is as close to authentic as you'll find in Paris. The larb nua on was listed as a minced beef salad, but came instead with long, tender slices of meat tossed with chilli, mint and other Thai herbs, in a piquant vinaigrette. The pomelo salad maintained our expectations of being refreshing, sweet, spicy and sour, but the star of the show was a main course of duck in red curry with lychee and pineapple. The coconut milk sauce was so rich, creamy and flavoursome, we could not help but finish it off with our spoons. Dishes come with a one, two or three pepper rating, all of which can be individually adjusted. Faithful to Thailand's reputation for hospitality, the service was prompt and friendly, and the welcome was warm.

Mai Thai

24 bis rue St-Gilles, 3rd (01.42.72.18.77).
M° Chemin-Vert. **Open** noon-2.30pm, 7-11.30pm
Mon-Fri; 7-11.30pm Sat, Sun. **Average** €50. **Lunch
menu** €12.50. **Credit** MC, V. **Map** L6.
If you like the idea of Thai food but can't handle the heat, Mai Thai may not be a bad option. Chilliphobes can train their palates on the unusually mild Thai dishes on offer. A typically piquant tom yum prawn soup was distilled down to a watery, tangy broth filled with tender prawns, baby corn and button, not Thai, mushrooms. Classic green papaya salad was slightly more animated, although very basic: shredded papaya and carrots tossed with only a tart, nam pla vinaigrette. Larb, a classic minced meat starter normally served with lettuce wrappers, was made here without a single fleck of chilli, resulting in a dish that had little flavour and no kick. It was also served without lettuce, as though the neophyte diner wouldn't notice. Duck curry with lychee and pineapple was appropriately creamy, its

coconut milk sauce alive with flavour. Too bad the duck was overcooked. It was also exceptionally mild despite its two-chilli rating. Fish steamed in banana leaf was unexpectedly dense and heavy as the fish is mashed with coconut milk rather than steamed whole or as a fillet. The cosily small restaurant, tastefully decorated with thick ivory curtains and slate green walls, was filled to capacity with mainly French customers.

Blue Elephant

*43 rue de la Roquette, 11th (01.47.00.42.00/
www.blueelephant.com). M° Bastille.* **Open** noon-
2.30pm, 7pm-midnight Mon-Fri, Sun; 7pm-midnight
Sat. **Average** €45. **Prix fixe** €29 (Sun brunch),
€44. **Lunch menu** €19.50. **Credit** AmEx, DC, MC,
V. **Wheelchair access**. **Non-smoking room**.
Map M6.
At this Paris outpost of an international chain with a very good reputation you have to wander through a forest of tropical trees and tinkling fountains to find your table. The menu has lots of seductive choices, some of which have been framed into 'chef's suggestion' boxes, and elephant symbols denote the degree of spiciness. We were impressed by the seafood platter borne to our neighbour's table but plumped instead for the marché flottant for two (€23), a Thai-style bouillabaisse served in its own copper ring kept warm by candles. Having ladled the last morsels of this fantastic soup with its tasty chunks of black cod, prawns and mussels floating in a broth liberally flavoured with lemongrass and coriander, we could happily have left then and there, but we had already ordered a beef salad flavoured with mint, lemon and chillies, and pla neung mana (a steamed sea bass dish from north-east Thailand) for mains. Both were impressive and huge – the two-elephant salad is extremely hot, and the whole fish,

deliciously seasoned with lime and served on a banana leaf, was only slightly over-cooked. We finished with passion fruit and lemon sorbets – shiveringly zingy and citrusy.

Khun Akorn

8 av de Taillebourg, 11th (01.43.56.20.03).
M° Nation. **Open** noon-2pm, 7.30-11pm Tue-Sun.
Average €35. **Credit** AmEx, MC, V. **Non-smoking room. Map** Q7.
We had made a reservation but we were still relegated to the smaller upstairs room, filled with cigarette smokers. The much more salubrious main dining room, divided into intimate spaces by carved wood columns and railings, was already noisily packed. This is a popular place and it's understandable why. The warm decor – terracotta walls, dark hand-carved furniture and Thai objets d'art – is easy on the eye, while the menu, though limited in variety, is easy on the palate. The best dishes are devoted to diners with 'soft tongues'. As we didn't fit into that category, the cooks ably complied with our request to fire up the starters. A perfectly grilled squid salad tossed with tomatoes, scallions and shallots was appropriately tart and piquant, thanks to the bird's eye chillies thrown in for our masochistic pleasure. The beef salad turned out to be a replica of this dish, with tender slices of pink beef taking the place of the squid. We should have reminded the waitress of our penchant for pain, because the roast duck curry with lychee arrived lacking the requisite kick. The sauce, while fragrant, was also too watery. Efforts to tame the curry's fire, it seems, can go a little too far.

Rouammit & Huong Lan ★

103 av d'Ivry, 13th (01.53.60.00.34). M° Corvisart.
Open noon-3pm, 7-11pm Tue-Sun. **Average** €20.
No credit cards.
Fans of south-east Asian food eventually learn to seek out Laotian holes-in-the-wall in Paris rather than splurge on flashier Thai restaurants. A perfect example is this plainly decorated Chinatown joint (bare tables, strips of carved wood here and there), easy to spot thanks to the queue out the door. Show up early or be prepared to wait: the food here is cheap and delicious and the service super-efficient and friendly. To sample the full range of flavours – hot, sour, aromatic, sweet – it's best to go in a group. Nine of us initially ordered nine dishes, only to order several of them again: among the repeats were the lap neua (often spelled laab), a tongue-tickling, chilli-spiked salad made with slivers of beef and tripe; the lacquered duck in curry sauce; the khao nom kroc, Laotian ravioli filled with shrimp; and the sweet, juicy prawns stir-fried with Thai basil. Even the sticky rice was exceptional. The Asians in our group stuck to Chinese Tsingtao beer rather than the Thai Singha version, which is slightly sweeter, while the French shared a bottle of Tavel rosé (€16.50). If you're in the mood for dessert, try the assortment of gelatins, whose worm-like shapes and fluorescent colours appeal only to the adventurous.

Banyan ★

24 pl Etienne-Pernet, 15th (01.40.60.09.31/
www.lebanyan.fr). M° Felix-Faure. **Open** noon-3pm,
7-11.30pm Mon-Sat. **Average** €35. **Prix fixe** €30 (dinner only). **Lunch menu** €18, €23. **Credit** AmEx, MC, V. **Wheelchair access. Map** C9.
This compact dining room is one of the best Thai restaurants to open in Paris for a long time. Run by Oth Sombath, a former chef at the Blue Elephant, the kitchen achieves a freshness and authenticity that will delight anyone who really knows south-east Asian cuisine. Beautiful flower arrangements and soft lighting transform an otherwise plain space in a sleepy neighbourhood into a pleasant dining room that's become an instant hit with the locals. Start with the mixed starters, including an excellent raw beef salad, nems and grilled prawns, and then opt for the sublime green curry chicken or maybe the sea bass cooked in a banana leaf. Desserts, unusually for a Paris Thai restaurant, are excellent here, including a superb lychee panna cotta and chocolate nems. Good tropical cocktails, a nice wine list and very friendly service.

Lao Siam

49 rue de Belleville, 19th (01.40.40.09.68). M°
Belleville. **Open** noon-3pm, 7-11.30pm daily. **Average** €18. **Credit** MC, V. **Non-smoking room. Map** N3.
Lao Siam can be hellish on a weekend evening: on a noisy and crowded Saturday night, the service was harassed and erratic. On a rainy Monday evening, however, the staff were efficient – if not exactly enthusiastic or informative – and we all received our food at the same time. Spring rolls, coconut milk-laced soups, Peking duck and other familiar specialities are perfectly acceptable here, but it's worth straying off the beaten track. The bœuf séché, strips of tender but chewy lemongrass-scented dried beef, makes a great starter and goes down well with a glass of Asian beer. The comforting banana shoot and papaya salad was only slightly beleaguered by the inclusion of two insipid peeled shrimps, one of which remained uneaten. We used balls of sticky rice to greedily mop up the tangy dressing of the salade de couenne de porc (crunchy grilled pork rind), and the juices of the pork spare ribs on a bed of garlic, and washed it down with a pot of jasmine tea, which the waiters replenished willingly if unsmilingly.

TIBETAN

Pema Thang

13 rue de la Montagne Ste-Geneviève, 5th
(01.43.54.34.34). M° Maubert-Mutualité. **Open** 7-10.30pm Mon; noon-2.30pm, 7-10.30pm Tue-Sat.
Average €20. **Prix fixe** €13-€17. **Credit** MC, V.
Wheelchair access. Non-smoking room. Map J8.
The Dalai Lama smiles benignly down through his spectacles from a portrait on the wall. There's a little light chanting on the hi-fi. The woman who takes your order is as calm and beautiful as the hills and the food she brings is a good introduction to the

International

little-known cooking of Tibet. First-time visitors are well advised to try the set menu that lets you sample the specialities of the three regions of Tibet. These are shadré (mild lamb curry), dingrul (beef stew) and langsha shemok (steamed beef ravioli served with a coriander sauce). We found them all delicately flavoured and original. Desserts were good too – grilled barley cake with home-made yoghurt and rice pudding with dried fruit. As for the tricky question of what to drink with Tibetan food, we recommend beer. Tibetan tea is probably just what you need after a long morning herding yak but, the rest of the time, tea with butter and salt tastes pretty much what it sounds like: disgusting. Our waitress did warn us it was 'spécial', which is what French people often say when they mean 'really bad'. We should have believed her.

VIETNAMESE

Restaurant Pho

3 rue Volta, 3rd (01.42.78.31.70). M° Arts et Métiers. **Open** 10am-4pm Mon-Sat. Closed Aug. **Average** €10. **No credit cards. Map** K4.
Beef pho, Vietnam's fragrant, herb-infused noodle soup seasoned with chillies, basil, beansprouts and lemon, is the star of the show. Here, what you see is what you get, an austere decor and fresh, piping hot soup at reasonable prices. Eating elbow-to-elbow in this tight space is an adventure. It takes a friendly Asian soup house to bring urbanites this close together. The staff's French is limited but their smiles are frequent and charming. The menu is straightforward: the choices are beef soup with meatballs or roast pork, or bo bun (which includes vermicelli noodles, sliced beef and chopped nem (spring rolls), and on Mondays you can also try banh canh, the chicken soup alternative. Portions are generous; all soups are replete with meat, noodles, broth and sprouts. Half the fun is spicing it up – the tables are loaded with hot and exotic sauces. You could go for a body-cleansing touch of black vinegar or fire it up straight with red chilli. Eat in or take away, this is one serious soup-slurping, spoon-scraping, cold-fighting canteen.

Thuy Long

111 rue de Vaugirard, 6th (01.45.49.26.01). M° Montparnasse or St-Placide. **Open** 11.30am-9.30pm Tue-Sat. Closed Aug. **Average** €15. **Prix fixe** (dinner only) €12.90, €14.90. **Lunch menu** €10.90, €12.90. **Non-smoking room. Credit** MC, V. **Map** G8.
It isn't big, it isn't glamorous, but once you've found this Vietnamese canteen crammed into a former crêperie, you'll make a point of avoiding the big Asian restaurants on the boulevard to sneak around the corner and get your noodle fix here. With a welcoming north Vietnamese owner and a cheerful south Vietnamese cook, the menu has an impressive range of dishes, especially considering that everything is lovingly prepared in a tiny kitchenette (unfortunately, a microwave is used to heat up

certain dishes). Take-out is popular, but many regulars pop by to chat and eat on the spot. Try a traditional pho (soup), or order a bo bun, which features your choice of meat (the five-spice pork is particularly tasty) on top of thin rice noodles, salad, slivers of carrot and lemongrass. The menu includes a choice of dumplings or nem (both are excellent) and gives you a small dessert. The price is hard to beat, but what really makes people come back is the warm welcome and reliable food.

Le Lotus Blanc

45 rue de Bourgogne, 7th (01.45.55.18.89). M° Varenne. **Open** noon-2.30pm, 7-10.30pm Mon-Sat. Closed 10-25 Aug. **Average** €30. **Lunch menu** €15-€29.80. **Credit** MC, V. **Non-smoking room. Map** F6.
Despite the gentrification of Vietnamese restaurants in recent years, there remain places where nothing seems to have changed for decades. This minuscule restaurant, opened in 1975, retains the shabby charm of that era: crimson velveteen banquettes and chairs, faded photos and Vietnamese knick-knacks gathering dust on the exposed stone wall. The owner, who immigrated to France in 1964, also possesses an old-world geniality. Trust his recommendations when ordering off the long menu, which covers all the classics. As we discovered, they were by far the best dishes. Lamb wrapped in mulberry leaf was tender and tasty, moistened with a rich, flavourful sauce. Giant prawns stir-fried in salt, pepper and five-spice with onions and scallions was equally excellent – piquant and perfectly cooked. Beef with basil, chicken with lemon balm, and pork spare ribs were also well done, but not extraordinary. Then again, they were not the recommendations of the house. Neither was the hors d'oeuvres platter, which unfortunately contained a medley of chewy dumplings. If you ask him, the owner will happily sit down and regale you with tales of growing up in pre-war Saigon. It will help you appreciate the unfussy cuisine here for what it really is: an authentic home-cooked meal.

Dong Huong ★

14 rue Louis-Bonnet, 11th (01.43.57.18.88). M° Belleville. **Open** noon-11pm Mon, Wed-Sun. Closed two weeks in Aug. **Average** €15. **Credit** MC, V. **Non-smoking room. Map** M4.
If you're puzzled about where to find great Asian food in Belleville, go with a map to locate this hidden treasure, which is no secret to the city's Vietnamese immigrants. Once you've tasted the crunchy nems and steaming pho, you'll find yourself drawn back again and again. On our most recent weekday visit, the dining room – which attracts up to 2,000 customers a day – was as busy as ever. Make it known if you're non-smokers – the front room is blessedly smoke-free. You might start with bành cuôn, steamed Vietnamese ravioli stuffed with minced meat, mushrooms, beansprouts, spring onions and deep-fried onion, or bite into freshly fried nems, wrapped in lettuce leaves with sprigs of mint. The pho, however, is easily a meal in itself – our

favourite is the peanutty, spiced-up satay version, despite it being one of the messiest soups we have ever eaten. Grilled meats such as the com ga lui (chicken with lemongrass) are popular with Asian diners, but we haven't ever got that far. If you're in the mood to forgo wine or beer, try one of the alarming-looking sweet Asian drinks or an iced Vietnamese coffee.

La Tonkinoise

20 rue Philibert Locut, 13th (01.45.85.98.98). Mº Maison Blanche or Porte de Choisy. **Open** noon-3.15pm, 7-10.30pm. Closed Tue-Sun in Aug. **Average** €20. **Lunch menu** €9.60. **No credit cards.**
Though the overlit Formica setting doesn't offer much to trill over, the food at this deservedly popular Vietnamese on a charmingly quiet and mostly Asian side street in the 13th is excellent. Come with friends so that you can share, and start with some of the best nems in Paris, lotus root salad (water lily stems garnished with fried onions, prawns, herbs and peanuts), rare beef salad in lemon (a ceviche-like dish, in which thin strips of beef are marinated in herbs and lemon juice), and wonderful Vietnamese ravioli. The main course not to miss is the catfish caramelised in palm sugar in a marmite (earthenware casserole); otherwise, try the skewered pork with shallots and minced prawns on sugar cane sticks. Note, too, that you won't need extra vermicelli noodles or rice – all dishes come appropriately endowed. After a trial run with the sour house rosé, the chilled Côtes du Rhône turned out to be the right quaff.

Kim Anh

49 av Emile Zola, 15th (01.45.79.40.96). Mº Charles Michels. **Open** 7.30-11pm Tue-Sun. Closed two weeks in Aug. **Average** €45. **Prix fixe** €34. **Credit** AmEx, MC, V. **Wheelchair access. Non-smoking room. Map** B8.
We had been told that the refined, traditional fare was worth the steep prices at this upmarket Vietnamese. But, on a recent visit, the quality of the dishes ranged from the sublime to the sub-standard. Imperial rolls stuffed with crab and shrimp were cooked to light, crispy perfection and served in a basket full of fresh lettuce, coriander and mint. The cold beef salad was a celebration of flavours and textures that included thinly sliced beef, fresh basil, cashew nuts, vermicelli and bamboo shoots. By contrast, the steamed ravioli stuffed with mushroom and pork was mushy and bland. The star of our mains was the steamed caramelised bong lau fish, imported from Vietnam. The thick white fish arrived bubbling hot in its clay bowl and slightly sweet, sticky sauce. Sliced duck in a tangy orange sauce was a close second. Unfortunately, barbecued pork ribs were tough and under-spiced and the braised chicken our waitress had recommended didn't taste fresh. (Our complaint was met with an apologetic shrug.) For dessert, we enjoyed the exotic fruit cup and soupy corn and coconut milk, the only two choices on the prix fixe menu. Despite the hit-and-miss food, the dining room was nearly full and the fortysomethings sipping Champagne and chilled Chinon seemed pretty content.

International

Le Lotus Blanc.
See p184.

Indian

If too many cream sauces have left you craving curry, it's best to keep your expectations in check. Paris has nothing like the standard of Indian cooking you might find in Britain: most restaurants cater to timid French tastebuds with dumbed-down curries and set menus that offer no culinary surprises. However one little-known neighbourhood, La Chapelle (in the 10th arrondissement, near Gare du Nord), has some hidden gems – it's the next best thing to hopping on a plane to southern India or Sri Lanka. For kosher Indian food, see the **Jewish** chapter (*pp201-202*).

International

Gandhi-Opéra ★

66 rue Ste-Anne, 2nd (01.47.03.41.00/www. restaurant-gandhi.com). M° Quatre-Septembre. **Open** noon-2.30pm, 7-11.30pm Mon-Sat; 7-11.30pm Sun. **Average** €35. **Prix fixe** €23, €27.50 (dinner only). **Lunch menu** €11, €14, €19. **Credit** AmEx, DC, MC, V. **Wheelchair access**. **Map** H4.

So frequently had we been disappointed by Indian meals in Paris that we had almost given up when Gandhi-Opéra came to the rescue. The clientele is largely French, but instead of pandering to the Gallic fear of spices the chef has taken one of the plusses of the French respect for tradition – excellent quality meat – and used it in authentic-tasting dishes. The menu is wide-ranging but a speciality is the tandoori grill. We were thrilled by our hot, minty chicken starter of Gandhi mixt murg pudina, plus not one but two tandoori quails. Then followed a delicious, sizzling Bombay-style chicken dish with spaghetti-thin strips of onion and wonderful spices. The lamb vindaloo, requested 'very hot', was nowhere near, but such were the quality and flavour that we weren't disappointed. The highlight, though, was definitely the vegetable side dish of saag paneer (spinach in a creamy cheese sauce) – a chef's speciality. We were glad we plumped for desserts too. The kulfi was crunchy and tasted home-made, and the rose sorbet took us to heaven.
Other locations: Gandhi, 54 av Edouard Vaillant, 92100 Boulogne (01.47.61.05.04).

Yugaraj

14 rue Dauphine, 6th (01.43.26.44.91). M° Odéon or Pont-Neuf. **Open** noon-2pm, 7-10pm Tue-Sun. **Average** €50. **Prix fixe** €32.80, €44.80. **Credit** AmEx, DC, MC, V. **Map** H6.

With its wonderful collection of Hindu statuettes and colonial teak furniture dating from as early as the 18th century, this luxurious restaurant clearly echoes the antique shops that cram the area. It took some time to wade through the small-print encyclopaedic explanations of each dish but we finally settled on the sampler starter with various spiced (and unspiced) titbits: fried fish cubes, chicken kebabs and bhajias served with a selection

of colourful sauces and chutneys. Our tandoori-baked cheese naan was delicious but the plain one was, well, rather plain. The highlight of the meal was two delectably plump, free-range Vosges quails, the legs fried and medium-spiced and the wings bathed in a creamy sauce of spice, herbs and raisins. We mopped up every last morsel. Our other main, the gosht rada, featured chunks of lean lamb prepared in a fragrant mixture of fenugreek, ginger and garlic. The chocolate and spice bouquet of a lush Rosé des Riceys from Morel provided the perfect foil.

Kastoori

4 pl Gustave Toudouze, 9th (01.44.53.06.10). M° St-Georges. **Open** 6.30-11.30pm Mon; 11.30am-2.30pm, 6.30-11.30pm Tue-Sun. **Average** €16. **Prix fixe** €13. **Lunch menu** €8, €10 (Mon-Fri). **Credit** MC, V. **Map** H2.

It's no surprise that Kastoori's terrace, on this delightful 19th-century square, is often full: this friendly, family-run Indian restaurant remains one of the few good-value eateries in the area. We're not talking ubiquitous mass-produced buffets: Kastoori has excellent value set menus at lunch and dinner, each dish prepared with care and home-mixed spices. Amid lanterns, Indian fabrics and incense inside, or under the hot lamps outside, start by ordering some popadoms to taste the home-made chutneys served in an ornate metal boat, and choose from tangy raita and kaleji (coriander-sprinkled curried lamb liver) for starters, followed by a choice of tandoori chicken, chicken curry, saag paneer or the dish of the day, which revolves from the à la carte menu. Each northern Indian dish is delectably different from the others, and is accompanied by a choice of cheese naan or saffron rice. You can bring your own wine with no corkage fee, but don't miss out on the delicious lassis and kulfis.

Bharath Cafe ★

67 rue Louis Blanc, 10th (01.58.20.06.20) M° La Chapelle. **Open** 9am-midnight daily. **Average** €10. **Credit** MC, V. **Map** L2.

For the most authentic south Indian/Sri Lankan food in town, venture out to La Chapelle. Of all its gems, the best we have found is this Sri Lankan eaterie.

Don't be deterred by the basic decor, brusque service or the throngs of men loitering in and around the café. These Tamil immigrants are fussy about their food. We started with meat rolls – compact deep-fried pancakes stuffed with mutton, potatoes and spices. Tempting as they are, don't take more than two or you will have no room for the tantalising main dishes. One of our favourites is the lamb kotta roti (shredded thick chapatis mixed with tender meat, eggs, green chillies and onions), big enough for two. Another house speciality is masala dosai (crêpes filled with yellow curry, potatoes and mustard seed), originally a breakfast dish but equally filling for dinner. Braver souls should try the stronger dishes, including the spicy chicken curry with rice and a small helping of lentil curry. You will be mopping your brow while begging for more. From the array of colourful desserts, we finally opted for the red dodhal (a firm, very sweet jelly with nuts) – a bit of an acquired taste.

Ganesha Corner

16 rue Perdonnet, 10th (01.46.07.35.32). M° La Chapelle. **Open** 9am-11pm daily. **Average** €10. **Lunch menu** €8. **Credit** MC, V. **Map** L2.

This corner institution in the Sri Lankan and south Indian neighbourhood attracts probably four times as many customers as its nearby rivals. Why? It's cheap, fast and delicious. Ganesha Corner serves as the café, pub and meeting place for dozens of locals – mostly men plus the occasional family – who constantly stream out of the tiny yellow and pink dining room, or clog the entryway ordering breads and sweets from the take-away counter. The waiters may be hard to track down, but they are inevitably kind and laid-back (not blinking an eye when we knocked a glass of water on to a pile of menus) and happy to explain some of the more mysterious dishes. Begin with a fried vadai (made from lentils, chickpeas and vegetables) or a patis (potato and fish dumpling) as you sip a lassi, but be careful to save room for the main dishes. Mounds of fried noodles, biryani or any of the dosai, such as masala dosai, are unfinishably huge. For the more adventurous there's a deep brown, strong and spicy fish curry. Idli is another southern favourite: saucer-like steamed rice and lentil cakes served with an assortment of cabbage and aubergine-based stews plus a fiery coconut, lime and chilli paste. A little rice pancake and sweet coconut sauce sandwich (appam) was perfect with masala tea made so fresh that green cardamom pods floated on the surface.

New Pondichery

189 rue du Fbg-St-Denis, 10th (01.40.34.30.70). M° Gare du Nord or La Chapelle. **Open** 11.30am-11pm daily. **Average** €10. **Prix fixe** €7.50, €9. **Credit** MC, V. **Map** K2.

We were hungry, but clearly had not fasted enough for New Pondichery's scrumptious spread. Enticed by nearly every south Indian dish on the menu (and tempted, too, by the rock-bottom prices), we went overboard, ordering several starters, breads and

North Indian delights at **Kastoori**. *See p186.*

mains. The pleasant but non-intrusive waiters first brought over cardamom-flavoured lassi, which we sipped while nibbling a bonda (mustard seed-flecked fried potato dumpling) and an order of idli (steamed rice cakes) – tasty with a sambar stew and coconut pastes for dipping. Then came the breads: a huge, veggie-packed naan, and surely Paris's chewiest, flakiest pan-fried paratha with a dark and spicy onion sauce. A deep breath before the main event: massive crêpe-like brahmane dosai with curried fresh cabbage and potato, and a pea-and-carrot mix, tender chicken korma (a refreshingly lighter version of the standard cashew/cream treatment), and a cheesy spinach palak paneer, which we may not have ordered but happily demolished. Our bellies bursting, we tried to avoid dessert, but a slice of semolina-based barfi arrived nonetheless, all washed down with the house chai. The modest dining room eschews Indian clichés with peach and beige walls and minimalist carved wood trim. But who cares about the no-frills atmosphere when the feast is this irresistibly filling?

Aux Comptoirs des Indes

50 rue de la Fontaine au Roi, 11th (01.48.05.45.76). M° Goncourt or Couronnes. **Open** noon-2.45pm, 7-11.30pm Mon-Sat. **Prix fixe** €11. **Credit** AmEx, DC, MC, V. **Map** M4.

Silk curtains, hanging lanterns and Hindi pop music create a welcoming, low-key ambience at this unassuming yet ambitious restaurant. The kind owner hails from Pondichery in the south, but his

menu's signature dishes stretch from India's tip to tail. We began with the evening's only sour note: a house lemon-lime drink called nimbu pani that tasted oddly artificial. Otherwise, we had nothing but praise for the expertly cooked fare. The assortment of pakoras and crisp samosas arrived piping hot and seasoned with chopped herbs, and the naan contained pieces of fresh garlic. Chicken korma proved exceptionally chunky and nutty, while jinga prawns in a tomato-coconut sauce had been prepared with whole curry leaves. With a topping of cardamom pods, cloves and fried onions, even the basmati rice demonstrated an uncommon level of care. The frozen kulfi dessert came with colourful candy sprinkles. All in all, Aux Comptoirs des Indes displays a rare attention to detail.

Arti

*173 rue Lecourbe, 15th (01.48.28.66.68). M°
Vaugirard.* **Open** 6.30-11.30pm daily. **Average** €25.
Prix fixe €20 (lunch and dinner). **Lunch menu** €9,
€11.50. **Credit** MC, V. **Wheelchair access**. **Map** D9.
Ducking into this long-time neighbourhood fixture on a cold, rainy Monday night, we were pleased to find it half full with locals. Cheered by the appetising aromas, complimentary kir and crimson-coloured interior hung with Indian jewellery, we settled on the €20 prix fixe, which offers all the house specialities. Large, juicy chunks of tandoori chicken and aubergine and potato pakoras were generous starters, served with soft cheese naan or buttery paratha. Mains arrived in attractive copper pots, each set over a low flame to keep the food warm. We fell in love with the richly spiced chicken biryani, which was packed with bite-size morsels of chicken and studded with black cardamom pods. Our thick chicken curry was spicy, as requested. As dahl addicts, we couldn't resist an order from the à la carte menu and Arti's version provided a comforting fix. For dessert, the home-made kulfi (Indian ice-cream) flavoured with green cardamom and ground pistachio sent us straight to nirvana.

Kirane's

*85 av des Ternes, 17th (01.45.74.40.21). M° Porte
Maillot.* **Open** noon-2.30pm, 7.30-11.30pm Mon-Sat.
Average €35. **Prix fixe** €29.50, €33.50 (dinner
only). **Lunch menu** €15.50. **Credit** AmEx, DC, MC,
V. **Map** B2.
Would the €29.50 menu pay off with better quality and bigger portions than the €15.50 menu? We decided to find out during a weekday lunch at this popular northern Indian. From the lower-priced menu we chose chilled shrimp salad, a comforting concoction of small shrimp in a fresh green coriander sauce with chopped cucumber. The plat du jour – chicken breast in tomato sauce with green peppers – exceeded expectations, as did the accompanying basmati saffron rice with soft golden raisins. When we complained that the dish of rice was too small, the friendly waiter quickly brought us an additional serving at no charge. We wished he could have been so generous with the bread. Plain naan was included,

but the cheese naan we had ordered instead came with a €2 supplement. The €29.50 menu played by the same rules, but offered a wider selection. Our highlight was an excellent palak paneer (creamy spinach with soft chunks of white cheese). Medium-sized prawns in a bland masala curry sauce was a disappointing main course. For dessert, grated carrot flavoured with cardamom and sliced almonds was refreshing, but we grumbled at having to shell out another €4 for a cup of tea. Conclusion: stick with the €15.50 menu unless nothing appeals to you.

Les Jardins de Shalamar ★

*174 rue Ordener, 18th (01.46.27.85.38). M° Guy
Môquet.* **Open** noon-2.30pm, 7-11pm daily. **Average**
€20. **Prix fixe** €16.50, €20. **Lunch menu** €9,
€12. **Credit** AmEx, MC, V. **Wheelchair access**.
On the dark side of Montmartre lies this little gem of an Indo-Pakistani eaterie. The menu at first glance seems ordinary, divided into appetisers, tandoori, meat, seafood, poultry, biryani and the like, but even the humble pakoras and samosas are exquisite. Our appetisers arrived on a platter festooned with a hedgehog-like carrot stick centrepiece. We were continually impressed by the freshness and vivid colours of every ingredient in our yoghurt raita, chewy garlic naan bread, cinnamony dahl, tangy green aubergine bagan bartha, and tender chicken jalfrezi stewed with tomatoes, green peppers and coriander. Puddings impressed us too – gujrela (a rich slab of carrot and pistachio), badam halwa (a mild, bright-orange semolina cake), and the frozen cardamom kulfi were all delicious. Shalamar tea, creamy and steeped with cardamom, wrapped up an ideal evening.

Le Gange

65 rue Manin, 19th (01.42.00.00.80). M° Laumière.
Open noon-2.30pm, 7-11.30pm daily. **Average** €30.
Prix fixe €15. **Credit** AmEx, DC, MC, V.
Wheelchair access. **Map** N2.
Indian restaurants are in hot competition around Buttes Chaumont and Le Gange wears its plaudits loud and clear. Could it live up to its PR? We were not initially impressed by a single lukewarm popadom, but the decor of carved wood screens, attractive lighting and gentle Indian music soon warmed things up. Our waiter from Chandigarh was enthusiastic with his recommendations and we were soon tucking into spicy, succulent tandoori quails, and deep-fried aubergines which could have been crisper but tasted divine with the sweet liquid relish that was one of three pickles. Cheese and garlic naans sprinkled with pepper and garlic were a delicious accompaniment. Of our main courses the lamb biryani was the star, wonderfully moist rice with delicate spices, the tenderest lamb, almond flakes and sultanas. The tangy karahi prawn was slightly overpowered by onion. We then tasted a delectable mango sorbet and one of the best kulfis we'd ever had, and were offered a digestif on the house. Better still the milky chai with cardamom, served generously in a pot, is the perfect finish.

International

Italian

The current Parisian love affair with Italian food is no guarantee of quality in the pizzerias and trattorias that are cashing in on the infatuation all over town. For perfect pasta, crisp-crusted pizza and distinguished meat dishes, you'll have to do a bit of sleuthing. Prices for the best Italian food can be stunningly high and regional cooking is still almost unknown, but a few stand out from the crowd.

Il Cortile

Sofitel Demeure Hôtel Castille, 33 rue Cambon, 1st (01.44.58.45.67/www.alain-ducasse.com).
M° Madeleine. **Open** noon-2.30pm, 7.30-10.30pm Mon-Fri. **Average** €50. **Prix fixe** €85. **Lunch menu** €45. **Credit** AmEx, DC, MC, V. **Wheelchair access. Non-smoking room. Map** G4.

With a pattering fountain creating a refreshing backdrop in the small forest of white canvas umbrellas that fill this trompe l'œil-painted courtyard, Il Cortile is one of the more discreet fashion restaurants in Paris, popular not only with folks from Chanel next door but big-hitters from Dior, Lacroix and other houses. Chef Tjaco Van Eyken, a Dutchman, has not only learned the masters' (Alain Ducasse and Nicolas Vernier) lessons well, but has created a brilliant Parisian riff on Italian cuisine that updates traditional recipes while always respecting their inherent logic. Curiously, the only false note in an otherwise exceptional meal was the amuse-bouche, a vivid green lettuce soup that was bland and over-salted. No matter, several different focaccie were delicious, as is all the bread here, and a starter of vitello tonnato, fine slices of rare roast veal with creamy tuna sauce and long-stemmed capers from Lipari, was sensual and satisfying, as was the asparagus risotto that followed. It was the main courses that were outstanding, though. A superb sea bass fillet came with a silken citrus-accented beurre blanc and a powdered condiment of dried fish skin, salt and dried citrus peel, while perfectly cooked spit-roasted lamb fillet was wrapped in bacon and a savoury coating of Perugina sausage. Wines, served by a charming and very talented young female sommelier, were a huge treat, including a delicious

L'Osteria attracts a stellar Marais crowd for its heavenly pasta. *See p191.*

bone-dry Soave with the vitello tonnato and a velvety dolcetto d'Alba for a very reasonable €27. Another nice surprise: the first-rate Italian cheese course. A great place for a romantic night out.

Vincent et Vincent

60 rue Jean-Jacques Rousseau, 1st (01.40.26.47.63). M° Les Halles. **Open** noon-2.30pm, 7.30-11pm Mon-Thur, noon-2pm, 7-11.30pm Fri; 7.30-11.30pm Sat. **Average** €25. **Lunch menu** €12.50, €15. **Credit** MC, V. **Map** J5.

It's easy to see why a happy young fashion-and-design crowd has quickly adopted this Italian on the northern fringe of Les Halles. Aside from that catastrophic French propensity to put cream in absolutely everything, the pasta here is DeCecco, one of the better Italian brands, it's not over-cooked and it's offered in a variety of different shapes and sauces. Start, though, with the excellent mixed antipasti plate. It's an all-vegetarian affair that includes borlotti beans, broad beans, braised baby onions, grilled peppers, fried aubergine and courgettes dressed with generous shavings of parmesan. To help those who are not completely pasta-literate, there's a blackboard with pasta shapes displayed next to their names, but you can't really go wrong here. The penne with gamberetti (shrimps) in a light tomato sauce, and cassarecia in a boscaiola (mixed mushroom) sauce were both very good. The Italian wines are pricey, but the Côte du Ventoux at €9 is a good bet.

La Bocca

59-61 rue Montmartre, 2nd (01.42.36.71.88). M° Sentier or Etienne Marcel. **Open** noon-2.30pm, 8-11pm daily. Closed 25 Dec, 1 Jan. **Average** €32. **Credit** MC, V. **Map** J5.

This two-floor Italian bistro is totally enchanting and in the evening it's one of the most romantic addresses you could choose for dinner, with its mirrors, candles, Murano glass chandeliers and cosy Napoleon III armchairs. Even the waiter, sporting tight black sweater and two diamond studs, was beautiful. The blackboard menu features various starters followed by one meat, one fish and four pasta dishes, two of which were vegetarian. It's the vegetables that star here, with a melanzana parmigiano consisting of thin layers of succulent aubergine interspersed with mozzarella, parmesan, tomato purée and fresh basil. The squid and green bean starter was deliciously fresh too, seasoned with flat-leaf parsley on a bed of mesclun, and both were so generous that we thought we'd ordered mains by mistake. The farfalle with courgettes, tomato and basil was perfectly al dente, but the one false note was the costata with sautéed potatoes – a fatty veal escalope entirely swamped by a bland cream sauce that bore little trace of the promised thyme. Italian wines tend to be expensive in France; we were not terribly impressed by our Il Falcone Reserva 1999 at €36.50, though it was a good match for the food. Stick with the pasta, and finish with the peppermint panna cotta with kiwi fruit coulis and almonds.

Al Filo delle Stagioni

8 rue de Beauce, 3rd (01.48.04.52.24). M° Temple or République. **Open** 11.30am-3pm, 7.30pm-midnight Mon-Sat. **Average** €25. **Prix fixe** €25, €30. **Lunch menu** €20, €25. **Credit** MC, V. **Map** L5.

A young and rather ambitious team with Auvergnat-Italian origins is behind this fashionable new northern Marais restaurant (they previously ran a French restaurant, Au Fil des Saisons, whose name they clearly liked). The dressed-up, stone-walled dining room buzzes even at lunch. On the autumn day we visited, the owner was dashing from table to table with a truffle (black, not the priceless white Alba variety), which he shaved over everything – not a touch you would normally expect from such an affordable menu, which for €25 includes three courses plus a glass of wine and coffee. We reluctantly bypassed one speciality, the foie gras and artichoke terrine, to try the more Italian breaded and fried mozzarella – a generous plate of high-quality, crunchy-crusted fried cheese made colourful with rocket and cherry tomatoes. Pigeon roasted with pine nuts was a juicy choice, served perhaps inauthentically with a plate of pasta on the side – but who's complaining when it's topped with fresh truffle? A carpaccio of high-quality beef fillet arrived too cold to be fully appreciated – next time we'll try the delicious-looking risottos, such as the gorgonzola with walnut. The mille-feuille de tiramisu was a bold variation on a classic, layering still-crisp ladyfingers and coffee-infused cream and served with a matching ice-cream. We don't know what a feng shui expert would make of the triangular tables, but we left happy and not much poorer.

Gli Angeli

5 rue St-Gilles, 3rd (01.42.71.05.80). M° Chemin-Vert. **Open** noon-2.30pm, 8-11pm daily. Closed Aug. **Average** €35. **Credit** MC, V. **Wheelchair access.** **Map** L6.

It might not be the most authentic Italian in town, but in this location, a few steps from the Place des Vosges, it's miraculous to find any restaurant this friendly and good. The greeting is as warm and Italian-accented as you could hope for, and the bistro setting with stone walls and wood tables feels inviting and spacious. Coming in midwinter, we couldn't resist ordering the most festive dish: delicate fresh pasta tossed with truffle cream and topped with paper-thin slices of melt-in-the-mouth parma ham. Other tempting options included Sicilian-style pasta with tuna fish, mussels with garlic and tomato sauce, and steak with balsamic vinegar. If you're tired of tiramisu, try the home-made semifreddo with candied fruit – and don't forget to finish with a satisfying shot of espresso before rejoining the tourist throngs.

L'Osteria

10 rue de Sévigné, 4th (01.42.71.37.08). M° St-Paul. **Open** 8-10.30pm Mon; noon-2.30pm, 8-10.30pm Tue-Fri. Closed Aug, 25 Dec, 1 Jan, Easter Monday. **Average** €80. **Credit** MC, V. **Map** L6.

International

This railroad car-like dining room in the Marais is a maddening place for a meal. The food is delicious, but it's run like a private club. Risotto, a dish for which L'Osteria is famed, is not listed on the menu, and since they're keen to turn tables you'll be warned off it unless you're a regular. It's also so crowded and smoky that it's hard to relax, and the atmosphere is decidedly self-conscious. This doesn't seem to stop a stellar crowd from eating here, though – Claudia Cardinale looked pretty pleased with her tagliolini al ragu the night we came in, and there were a host of *m'as tu vu*-type television and movie people as well. This is just about as close to real Italian cooking as you'll find in Paris without going somewhere absurdly expensive. Starters of mozzarella in carrozza (fried in a light egg batter) and octopus, both bedded on peppery rocket, were delicious, as were amazingly delicate tortelloni stuffed with beef and spinach, and a perfectly cooked tagliolini in cinammon-spiked veal ragu. There are some nice wines, too, including a Barbera Maracini for €26.

Alfredo Positano

9 rue Guisarde, 6th (01.43.26.90.52). M° Mabillon. **Open** noon-2.30pm, 7-11.30pm Tue-Sat. Closed Aug. **Average** €40. **Credit** MC, V. **Wheelchair access**. **Map** H7.

Alfredo Positano has long been one of the liveliest and most reliable of the Italian joints around the Marché St-Germain, but prices seem to have shot up since our last visit for a mundane array of pasta dishes (several over €20). The antipasti assortment was good and easy enough to share between three, including tasty caramelised onions, roast aubergine slices, stewed aubergine and tomato, marinated peppers and white beans, though the slices of cold boiled carrot tasted watery and bland. A pizza quattro stagione skimped on mushrooms but came with a generous chunk of aubergine and large, tangy capers, while pasta alla siciliana – with aubergine, tomato and mozzarella – was decidedly gloopy, with too much stringy cheese. A firm but satisfying tiramisu raised our spirits, as did a pleasant if rather heavy Tuscan Montepulciano vino nobile – from a short and expensive list.

Chez Bartolo

7 rue des Canettes, 6th (01.43.26.27.08). M° St-Germain-des-Prés or St-Sulpice. **Open** noon-2.30pm, 7-11.30pm Tue-Sat; noon-3pm Sun. **Average** €35. **No credit cards**. **Map** H7.

Accept the fact that your bill will be high and the service inexplicably sullen (these are supposed to be sunny Neapolitans), and you might just enjoy eating here because the food is reliable. That's the reason, as opposed to the kitsch decor of Vesuvius in all her erupting glory, that it's always packed. Stick with starters such as chicory filled with warm gorgonzola and pistachio sauce, and forget the marinated peppers which weren't worth their €10 price tag. The pizzas and pasta are decent – try the classic spaghetti alle vongole (clams) – whereas our wood-fired prawns arrived severely charred with a minuscule side of bruised young spinach leaves posing as a 'salad'.

Il Gattopardo ★

29 rue Dauphine, 6th (01.46.33.75.92). M° Odéon. **Open** 12.30-2.30pm, 8-11pm Mon-Fri; 8-11pm Sat. **Average** €35. **Credit** MC, V. **Map** H6.

Angelo Procopio, founding chef of Il Vicolo (*see below*), knows what Parisians want from Italian food. Having left Il Vicolo, he has opened this intimate restaurant, most of which is up a steep flight of stairs on the first floor of an old Left Bank house. The cheerful, slightly corny service sets a laidback, happy mood for some decent eating. Procopio, one of the best pasta cooks in town, offers a short but tempting menu which tantalises with the likes of tagliolini with white truffle shavings, fettucine with a superb home-made tomato sauce, ravioli and tortellini. Tagliata, another of his signature dishes, consists of thinly sliced steak in a delicious herby, garlicky green sauce, and there's also a changing assortment of fish. Desserts aren't terribly interesting, but the wine list has some good buys, especially the Sardinian and Sicilian bottles. A great little hole in the wall for dinner with friends, but be sure to book as it has become very popular.

Il Vicolo

34 rue Mazarine, 6th (01.43.25.01.11). M° Mabillon or Odéon. **Open** 12.30-2.30pm, 8-11pm Mon-Sat. **Average** €40. **Lunch menu** €21. **Credit** AmEx, MC, V. **Map** H6-7.

Il Vicolo's attractive dining room is Milanese bold, with fibre optic lights in the parquet and an orange-piped brown banquette running the length of one wall. The room feels a bit clubby, but service is prompt and polite. The menu offers light modern eating from all over the boot. The carpaccio of bresaolo (air-dried beef) and rocket salad was enlivened by a dab of delicious citrus peel-spiked ricotta. Home-made spaghetti with pesto sauce, green beans and potato slivers, a Genoan classic, was delicious, as was the tuna steak cooked in balsamic vinegar. All the pastas are freshly made and perfectly sauced, and the wine list offers a fine selection of Italian bottles. Skip the dull desserts for cheese, or head directly to the good coffee and a grappa.

Café Minotti ★

33 rue de Verneuil, 7th (01.42.60.04.04) M° Rue du Bac. **Open** noon-3pm, 7.30-10.30pm Tue-Sat. **Average** €50. **Prix fixe** €26, €32. **Credit** AmEx, MC, V. **Non-smoking room**. **Wheelchair access**. **Map** G6.

Nicolas Vernier, who formerly cooked at the Ducasse-run restaurant Il Cortile, has gone out on his own with this pricey but wonderful new restaurant on the Left Bank. Gorgeous tomato-red Murano chandeliers create a dramatic atmosphere, and Vernier is at the top of his game with a brilliant produce-driven menu that stars superb Tuscan charcuterie and a perfect tempura of langoustines to

International

start, followed by wonderfully inventive pasta. Squid-ink spaghetti came dressed in a discreet vinaigrette and was generously garnished with vongole (tiny clams), baby squid and octopus, while boned guinea hen in a rich reduction sat atop maltagliati (home-made spinach noodles), which were then doused with a foamy chestnut cream at the table to make a splendid winter dish. A trio of panna cotta flavoured with vanilla, mandarin orange and liquorice was a perfect dessert for sharing. Already popular with the local publishing crowd, this place is starting to pull celebrities, indigenous and visiting, in the evening. Food is also served in the more relaxed low-ceilinged bar area.

Le Perron

6 rue Perronet, 7th (01.45.44.71.51). M° St-Germain-des-Prés. **Open** noon-2.30pm, 7.30-11pm Mon-Sat. **Average** €40. **Credit** AmEx, MC, V. **Map** G6.
If Italian restaurants were judged on looks alone, then you probably wouldn't choose this one: dark wood beams and a mish-mash of half-levels make it look more like an old-fashioned St-Germain tavern. But the warm welcome is genuinely Italian and the cuisine, with its range of antipasti, risottos, pasta and veal dishes, is closer to a true Italian trattoria than many of Paris's flashier places. Enticing first courses include vongole in umido (a dish of lightly sautéed clams), salsicce abruzzese alla griglia (sausages marinated in wild fennel), and antipasto del Perron (sun-dried tomatoes, courgettes, aubergines, mushrooms and chicory baked to melting point in olive oil). Whatever was meant to go with the morels on the plat du jour had run out, so they paired them up with a tender veal escalope instead, and also concocted a simple ragoût for a child. Pièce de résistance, though, was the excellent zabaglione: hot, highly alcoholic and frothy, and overflowing down the sides of the glass.

Le Bistrot Napolitain ★

18 av Franklin D Roosevelt, 8th (01.45.62.08.37). M° St-Philippe-du-Roule. **Open** noon-2.30pm, 7-10.30pm Mon-Fri; noon-2.30pm Sat. Closed Aug. **Average** €35. **Credit** AmEx, MC, V. **Map** E4.
This rather chic Italian off the Champs-Elysées is as far from a tourist joint as it is possible to be. On weekday lunchtimes (it doesn't even bother to open on Saturday night or Sunday) it is packed with suave Italian-looking businessmen in modish pinstripes and St-Tropez types with silicone lips. The decor is plain, the tablecloths starched white, and the kitchen open with the pizzaiolo shoving pillowy pizzas in and out of the oven while orders are shouted over the heads of diners. Generosity was our overwhelming feeling about the food – not just big plates but lashings of the ingredients that others skimp on, such as the slices of tangy parmesan piled high over rocket on the fresh and tender beef carpaccio we shared for a starter. The pizzas are as good as they say they are. The Enzo came with milky, almost raw mozzarella and really tasty tomatoes. For pasta you can choose between dried

or fresh with some interesting variations: the fresh saffron tagliatelle was rich and creamy, enhanced by the flavour and colour of this delicate spice. Helpings are so big that you really have to be Italian to stomach a meat or fish course after this. We couldn't even face a tiramisu and finished with delicious ice-cream instead.

I Golosi ★

6 rue de la Grange-Batelière, 9th (01.48.24.18.63). M° Grands Boulevards or Richelieu-Drouot. **Open** noon-2.30pm, 7.30pm-midnight Mon-Fri; noon-2.30pm Sat. Closed two weeks in Aug, one week at Christmas. **Average** €30. **Credit** MC, V. **Map** J3.
Not far from *Le Figaro* and a couple of big-hitting French news magazines, this original and fresh Italian is effervescent with French journalistic talent. Sipping a crisp prosecco, we noted the presence of one recently released reporter-hostage and another notable *grand reporter*. Their sources were good on this occasion as the cooking here is original, high-quality and reasonably priced. Drawn by the racy meat-and-fish-in-the-same-plate idea we went for a shared starter of vitello tonnato, wafers of veal in a tuna and caper sauce – tangy and interesting. We then stuck into suckling pig baked with turnips and artichokes, and a bracing tartare of (raw) veal. We had some excellent panna cotta with the last of our rosso di Montalcino Fornacino. Fabulous food with efficient and good-looking service.

Pizza Marzano

30 bd des Italiens, 9th (01.47.70.33.33/www.pizza marzano.com). M° Opéra. **Open** 11.30am-midnight daily. **Average** €17. **Prix fixe** €16.90. **Credit** AmEx, MC, V. **Wheelchair access**. **Map** H4.
The modern look of this restaurant, part of the Pizza Express chain, seems designed to attract the well-heeled: purple tulips in blue glass vases, marble tables, minimalist seating and pulsing pop music. We enjoyed the little bread discs served warm with our salads – a decent Caesar and a tomato-mozzarella whose sun-dried tomatoes offset the otherwise anaemic winter ones – but the pizza itself struck us as disturbingly pre-fab. Sure, we could see the guy across the dining room making each pie, but the dough had that processed texture and was rather raw in the middle. At least the Cajun pizza had colourful red onions and red peppers, and a spicy tabasco kick to counter the cocktail shrimp. Desserts include ice-cream bombes or tiramisu.
Other locations: 2 pl St-Michel, 6th (01.44.07.32.27); 10 bis pl de Clichy, 9th (01.40.16.52.30).

Da Mimmo

39 bd de Magenta, 10th (01.42.06.44.47/www.cityvox. com). M° Jacques-Bonsergent. **Open** noon-2.30pm, 7-30-11.30pm Tue-Sat. Closed Aug. **Average** €35. **Lunch menu** €26. **Credit** MC, V. **Map** L4.
Superficially Da Mimmo appeared to be just another pizza joint on this noisy boulevard. The first hint that this touch of Naples might be a cut above average was the big table of antipasti, which looked

unusually fresh and tempting. The menu of pizzas and pasta also seemed mundane, but then our eye caught the list of specials, which included pasta with truffles, funghi porcini, scampi and other original dishes. Warming to our task, we settled down with a bottle of Chianti and a platter of antipasti, served with some wonderful pizza bread. For mains, linguine con scampi was the real thing, perfectly cooked al dente pasta with just a hint of chilli and garlic tossed with a few crustaceans – a genuine Neapolitan taste. What was not Neapolitan was the price of €34 per head which, even allowing for the seafood, might shock Mimmo's mamma.

La Madonnina ★

10 rue Marie et Louise, 10th (01.42.01.25.26).
M° République. **Open** 12.30-2.30pm, 8-11pm Mon-Thur; 12.30-2.30pm, 8-11.30pm Fri, Sat. Closed Aug.
Average €25. **Lunch menu** €11. **Credit** MC, V.
No-smoking room. Map L4.
La Madonnina is a labour of love for Gianni, the personable host who will pull up a chair to explain the entire (if small) menu, take your order and recommend a wine. If you ask, he'll even show you pictures of the renovations that transformed the former space into this little Italian outpost. But no red-checked, romantic spaghetti clichés here: you're enveloped in a home-grown decor, complete with blinking lights and Virgin Mary shrines. Thankfully, they worship food here too: luscious salads and roasted veggies are displayed on a kind of antipasti altar, next to the waiter station where reggae and funk CDs help spin the night away. Every dish was a revelation of fresh, simple ingredients – starters of tender marinated calamari amid potatoes and rocket and a scrumptious aubergine parmigiano, served with a generous heap of rocket; mains such as the exquisite pesto-truffle-mushroom ravioli; red pesto, linguini and shrimp; and bucatini (a long, hollow pasta) with tangy pork sausage and sautéed rocket. The portions were so generous we could only squeeze in a shared dessert, a silken coconut panna cotta tinged with lemon zest.

Les Amis de Messina

204 rue du Fbg-St-Antoine, 12th (01.43.67.96.01).
M° Faidherbe-Chaligny. **Open** noon-2.30pm, 7.45-11pm Mon-Fri; 7.45-11.30pm Sat. **Average** €35.
Prix fixe €25 (dinner only). **Credit** AmEx, DC, MC, V. **Non-smoking room. Map** N7.
Sicilian cuisine is one of the finest in Italy and this airy restaurant with its open kitchen features a number of island specialities such as pasta alla Norma – the composer Bellini was born in Catania. Our starters included a classic melanzane alla parmigiana and a more interesting plate of perfectly fried vegetables. Not remarkably original dishes, but prepared with unusual care and precision. Pasta with funghi porcini topped with a dome of parma ham was a delicious mixture of the cooked and the raw, and the spaghetti alle vongole had a generous serving of clams and just the right balance of olive oil, garlic and parsley. Puddings included a first-rate

tiramisu and that great Sicilian speciality, canoli (sweet tubular cakes), as good as any you'll taste in Paris. The whole meal was served by a friendly team who recommended an excellent Sicilian red, reasonably priced at €24.50, and a couple of limoncellos to see us on our way.

Sardegna a Tavola ★

1 rue de Cotte, 12th (01.44.75.03.28). M° Ledru-Rollin. **Open** 7.30-11.30pm Mon; noon-2.30pm, 7.30-11.30pm Tue-Sat. Closed Aug, 25 Dec, 1 Jan.
Average €35. **Credit** AmEx, MC, V. **Wheelchair access. Map** N8.
Success has allowed the Sardinian couple who run this sunny restaurant to dress up the formerly sparse decor, making it more authentically Sardinian. Even with these efforts, though, Sardegna a Tavola would be worth a considerable detour for its beautifully prepared island specialities and hard-to-find wines. A meal might start with thinly sliced charcuterie and chunky vegetables – fat beans, aubergines cooked with wine, roasted peppers, courgette and cauliflower – unless you're feeling up to horsemeat carpaccio. Then choose from perfectly prepared pastas such as hearty ravioli stuffed with ricotta and mushrooms in a thick, tomato-mushroom sauce; farfalle pasta with a typically Sardinian combination of mint, crushed almonds, fresh (though mild) chilli pepper and plenty of olive oil; or linguine with a refreshing sauce of langoustines and orange. The house wine, served by the carafe, is delicious; the sweet Sardinian wines are also worth sipping with almond cakes for dessert.

Sale e Pepe

30 rue Ramey, 18th (01.46.06.08.01). M° Château Rouge or Jules Joffrin. **Open** noon-2.30pm, 8-11.30pm Mon-Sat. **Prix fixe** €20. **Credit** MC, V. **Non-smoking. Wheelchair access. Map** J1.
Though it's sensible to be wary of a restaurant review that suggests you accept average quality in favour of a good time, this little Italian in Montmartre really is worth relaxing your scruples for. The small, marble-walled room is run by a generous, friendly Italian and his young chef, and it's packed to the rafters with a happy mix of arty locals who love the relatively inexpensive and well-chosen Italian wines and all-in formula – you get an antipasto, pizza, pasta and dessert for just €20. Everyone eats the same thing, but the menu changes daily and rarely includes anything off-putting. A recent dinner began with rolled aubergine stuffed with cheese and garnished with parmesan shavings and a few leaves of rocket, and continued with a ham and mushroom pizza, salmon penne and a choice of tiramisu or panna cotta. If the pizza was tasty enough, the salmon penne was undercooked rather than al dente, with a rather meagre sauce. Desserts were fine, though, and the coffee and complimentary grappa ended a meal that was enjoyable more due to high spirits (and lots of them) than the cooking. On other occasions, however, the pasta has been much better, so we'll definitely be back.

La Madonnina. *See p194.*

Japanese

French and Japanese cuisine have many qualities in common, including a love of seasonality and often exquisite presentation, so it's not surprising that Japanese restaurants are thriving in Paris. Pre-made sushi aside, it's possible to eat astonishing food in restaurants that serve anything from showy teppanyaki dishes to kaiseki, the sensual Japanese take on haute cuisine – often at jawdropping prices. Rue Ste-Anne and rue St-Honoré are the heart of all things Japanese in Paris, though there are outposts to be found around St-Germain and in the 17th arrondissement.

International

Kinugawa ★

9 rue du Mont-Thabor, 1st (01.42.60.65.07).
M° Tuileries. **Open** noon-2.30pm, 7-10pm Mon-Sat.
Average €100. **Prix fixe** (dinner only) €86-€108.
Lunch menu €30-€54. **Non-smoking room.**
Credit AmEx, DC, MC, V. **Map** G5.

Speak softly and carry a big wallet. Kinugawa is a hushed, plush temple to Japanese haute cuisine – exquisite and expensive. Aptly situated on an unassuming street near the posh shops of rue St-Honoré, this two-storey restaurant is something of an institution, having served countless well-heeled Japanese and Parisians for more than 20 years. Service is discreet and solicitous, tempting you to almost whisper your order. Not a problem if you forgo the long list of à la carte items in favour of the set meals or kaiseki, the most refined and rarefied form of Japanese cuisine. Essentially a succession of finely prepared dishes elaborately crafted from the freshest, most seasonal ingredients, kaiseki is much more than a meal; it is an experience. The first course – designed to whet the appetite – included jewel-like portions of compressed fish cake, herring roe, grilled slivers of cuttlefish painted with egg, a rouleau of smoked salmon rolled in wafer-thin tamago, and a cold poached fig in sesame sauce. The next succession of dishes included a very fresh turbot sashimi; a purifying 'teapot' consommé of shrimp and field mushrooms that was clean and clear, yet opaque with flavour; chunks of marinated raw beef grilled at the table over a smouldering charcoal broiler; braised daikon in a glutinous broth, subtly enhanced by button mushrooms, shrimp, lime and scallion; a refreshing, cold salad of wakame, abalone and sea cucumber; and steamed fish in a scallop broth. The impressive culinary parade ended with a whimper, however, in an uninspired plate of sushi that lacked taste and presentation. Dessert, too, was the standard green tea ice-cream with red bean – tasty if somewhat unoriginal. At Kinugawa, you might not get the full impact of Japan's mind-blowing kaiseki, but you will get a very good introduction indeed.
Other locations: 4 rue St-Philippe du Roule, 8th (01.45.63.08.07).

Laï Laï Ken

7 rue Ste-Anne, 1st (01.40.15.96.90). M° Pyramides.
Open noon-2.45pm, 8-10pm daily. **Average** €15.
Prix fixe (dinner only) €13.50, €21. **Credit** AmEx, MC, V. **Map** H5.

Just off the north-east end of rue de Rivoli, Laï Laï Ken is a canteen-style operation catering to the comfort-food cravings of a thriving Japanese clientele of students (mostly male) and chain-smoking, power-dressed execs (mostly female). Forget Zen and the art of persuading slivers of raw fish into pale pink rose-bud formations on exquisite lacquered platelets: this place dishes up the oriental equivalent of shepherd's pie and steamed jam sponge with custard. Western diners were few on our visit, as the regulars wolfed down steaming noodle soups and authentic, well-made stir-fries. Though the room was packed to capacity on a freezing weekday lunchtime, the courteous, efficient staff kept the buzz below a frenzy – lone diners were never invited to double up, and no one was rushed. Belly pork strips in a rich, flavoursome broth were suitably satisfying – complete with large pieces of uncompromisingly slippery tofu – while a dessert of steamed sweet red bean dumplings was disappointingly dry, but helped down by frequent refills of jasmine tea or sizeable cans of Asahi beer.

Nodaiwa

272 rue St-Honoré, 1st (01.42.86.03.42/www.
nodaiwa.com). M° Tuileries or Pyramides. **Open** noon-2.30pm, 7-10pm Mon-Sat. Closed 15 Aug-1 Sept.
Average €30. **Prix fixe** €44-€55. **Lunch menu** €15-€23. **Credit** AmEx, DC, MC, V. **Map** G5.

This elegant modern branch of one of Tokyo's oldest and best 'unagi' restaurants is for eel lovers only. The grilled Japanese delicacy, prepared from a generations-old recipe, is without doubt the star attraction: the brief menu offers portions à la carte according to weight or as part of the reasonably priced set meals. The lunch menu served up a sublime slab of chopstick-tender eel in a large bowl of Japanese sticky rice, as well as a lightly seasoned crisp green salad and chawanmushi – a slippery, savoury custard steamed with flecks of eel, daikon

Japanese

radish and shiitake mushrooms. The side dishes in the 'matsu' menu included generous cuts of fresh tuna sashimi, miso soup and a tiny bowl of pickled vegetables. For dessert, green tea bavarois, a subtle gelatine-based terrine, slipped down as easily as the melt-in-the-mouth grilled eel had.

Takara ★

14 rue Molière, 1st (01.42.96.08.38). M° Palais Royal. **Open** 12.30-2.30pm, 7-10.30pm Tue-Fri; 7-10.30pm Sat, Sun. Closed Aug. **Average** €30 (lunch), €50 (dinner). **Prix fixe** €29-€60. **Lunch menu** €23-€27. **Credit** AmEx, DC, MC, V. **Map** H5.
It would be tempting to utter a string of superlatives to describe the dazzling cooking here. But it would probably be more effective to state that this is simply the best Japanese food you'll find anywhere in Paris. An exaggeration, you say? Erase your doubts by starting the meal with four plump raw oysters, served out of the shell and in a light vinegar sauce topped with shredded green onions and a pinch of peppery, grated radish. Succumb to the aphrodisiac powers of this seasonal starter then satiate your desire with a quivering morsel of fresh scallop sushi. Follow it with the monkfish liver sushi, an unusual and delightful mélange of cubed, creamy monkfish liver and rice wrapped in crispy nori. Then move on to the fresh turbot sashimi: roll up each translucent sliver with a sprig of chives, a sprinkle of chopped green onion and a dab of grated radish. Dip it into the vinaigrette and chew it slowly. When you open your eyes, rouse yourself back to reality with some bolder flavours: the maguro tuna with blanched leeks in miso paste provides just the right kick. Grilled eel maki with cucumber is melt-in-the-mouth tender; chawanmushi – a seafood and vegetable custard – slips seductively down the throat. Think it's perfect so far? Try the astonishing agedashi tofu: deep-fried cubes of the silkiest tofu coated in a light, subtly elastic batter, delicately softened by a warm mirin-based broth. Beyond perfect, it is ingenious. Takara also specialises in sukiyaki and shabu shabu – a kind of self-serve Japanese hotpot. Amazed by what we had already eaten, we did not dare to ruin the moment by cooking anything for ourselves.

Aki

2 bis rue Daunou, 2nd (01.42.61.48.38). M° Opéra. **Open** noon-2.30pm , 7-11pm Mon-Fri; 7-11pm Sat. Closed Aug. **Average** €30 (lunch), €50 (dinner). **Prix fixe** €29, €43, €60. **Lunch menu** €23. **Credit** AmEx, DC, MC, V. **Map** G4.
The two-level Aki is more moody than minimalist with its cushy red velvet chairs, gold walls, soft lighting and chunky dark wood tables. Chef Kazunari Kono's menu is equally modern – you'll find sushi, sashimi and a lunchtime bento box (popular with the Japanese business set), but the cooked dishes are where his creativity shows. Ignoring the prix fixes, which in Parisian Japanese restaurants rarely go out on any kind of limb, we started with the confit aubergine – chunks of aubergine, prawns and gelatinous igname in a

succulent peanut sauce. Next, the wafu beef fillet may not have been Kobe beef, but the thinly sliced rare meat couldn't have been more tender, with miso and soy-lemon sauces for dipping. We couldn't resist a sashimi platter, and were rewarded with something akin to Zen bouquet – there was fuchsia, lavender, artful twigs and fish sculpted into a rose with black roe in the centre. The salmon, tuna and sea bream were squeaky fresh; the octopus, however, defeated our jaws. We skipped dessert and relaxed over cups of smoked rice tea.

Bizan

56 rue Ste-Anne, 2nd (01.42.96.67.76). M° Pyramides. **Open** noon-2pm, 7-10pm Tue-Fri; 7-10pm Sat. Closed three weeks in Aug. **Average** €80. **Prix fixe** €40, €60. **Lunch menu** €19-€30. **Credit** AmEx, MC, V. **Map** H4.
After a long period of renovation, popular sushi bar Isse has reopened under a new name, though it hopes to ride on the stellar reputation of its former incarnation: its business cards come with a reminder, 'in the style of Isse'. Certainly, on the absolute freshness of the fish, Bizan has held to tradition. Seductively displayed inside individual wooden boxes arranged on top of the tiny sushi bar, the restaurant's ever-changing selection of raw fish is available in a choice of beautiful guises – simply sliced and served as sashimi or sushi, or more unusually or elaborately prepared, as in the delightful sesame-crusted, seared tuna tataki that was offered as a starter on the tasting menu. Available at lunch or dinner, the menu dégustation Bizan offered a generous series of meticulously prepared dishes that tickled the palate with a variety of taste sensations. A main dish of tempura soft shell crab with sweet mustard mayonnaise was a wonderful surprise, not least because of the rarity of this crustacean in Parisian restaurants. A smoke-scented consommé of wild Japanese mushrooms put shame to the miso soup that normally comes with such meals, while the sashimi offering of tuna and yellowtail was predictably fresh. There is also a lunch menu, which, though more moderately priced, offers considerably less. Still, the Bizan spécial does have its merits, mainly in the moist tonkatsu – breaded pork fillet served with a rich sweet-and-sour dipping sauce. The minuscule restaurant itself is not unlike the bento box some of the food is served in: blonde wood, clean lines and compartmentalised into three floors seating only a handful of people each.

Isami

4 quai d'Orléans, 4th (01.40.46.06.97). M° Pont Marie. **Open** noon-2pm, 7-10pm Tue-Sat; 7-10pm Sun. Closed three weeks in Aug. **Average** €45. **Credit** MC, V. **Map** K7.
Unobtrusively located down a quiet street on the edge of the Ile St-Louis, this box of a sushi bar feels miles away from the tourist hordes that descend regularly on the island. In fact, once inside the brightly lit room – with its compact sushi counter and handful of tables – it's not difficult to feel miles

International

away from Paris altogether, especially as you may well be rushed through your meal to accommodate diners queuing for the second sitting. This is the place to go for a quick bite of very fresh, no-frills sushi and sashimi. Not unlike the food you would find in any nondescript neighbourhood sushi bar scattered throughout Japan, dishes here are slapped together hastily, but tastily. A starter of fresh tuna and natto – a glutinous, fermented soybean – was satisfyingly well balanced in texture and flavour; another starter of cuttlefish with spicy cod roe was equally appetising. The assorted sashimi platter included typical fare such as scallop, salmon, tuna, mackerel, snapper, sweet prawn and sea bream. The ingredients were faultless in freshness, but again could have benefited from more thoughtful presentation, and slightly more generous portions. We filled up on two orders of makimono: the grilled eel was very good despite the rather paltry portion of eel rolled within the rice and seaweed; the fatty tuna roll with green onions came without much tuna and without any green onions, probably forgotten by the slapdash sushi chef. Still, in an unpretentious eaterie where efficient service and fresh fish are the order of the day, such shortcomings are easy to digest, particularly if washed down with the ice-cold Asahi beer on offer.

Abazu ★

3 rue André-Mazet, 6th (01.46.33.72.05). M° Odéon.
Open noon-2pm, 7.30-10.30pm Tue-Sat; 7.30-10.30pm Sun. **Average** €35 (lunch), €50 (dinner). **Prix fixe** €33, €39. **Lunch menu** €15.50-€18.50. **Credit** AmEx, MC, V. **Non-smoking room**. **Map** H7.
Westerners gather on the main floor and Japanese downstairs at Abazu, but it's by choice. In the compact main room you can watch the teppanyaki chef at work, which is a thrill for those who rarely witness such a performance. This being our first visit, we decided to sit at the counter for a prime view of the confident and unflappable chef. Pre-cooked ingredients are poised around him in pretty Japanese bowls, ready to be thrown on to the grill, sliced or chopped, tossed with other ingredients and drizzled with sweet, gingery sauces. Settling on the €39 menu Abazu, which started with an amuse-bouche of puréed squash and a delicate scallop flan, we chose our starters and main courses, some of which come with price supplements. The aubergine miso, prepared in the small kitchen at the back, was the silkiest half-aubergine we have ever tasted, cut into small cubes to be scooped out with a little wooden spoon. Equally juicy were four squares of tofu, topped with minced chicken in a delicious sweet sauce. Razor clams cooked with ginger before our eyes were a rare autumn treat, while scallops, also with a touch of ginger, were fat and beautifully seared – both of these came with a glistening selection of vegetables, pearly rice and a bowl of soup. Saké seems a must here and we tried the bubbly Tsukino Katsura from Kyoto. Next time we'll have it with the seared foie gras in honey sauce.

Abazu.

Japotori

41 rue Monsieur-le-Prince, 6th (01.43.29.00.54).
Mº Odéon. **Open** noon-3pm, 6-11.45pm daily. Closed
24, 25 Dec. **Average** €10. **Prix fixe** €5.49-€14.48.
Credit MC, V. **Map** H7.
Low prices draw a young, lively crowd to this
popular joint specialising in yakitori (Japanese-style
kebabs), and at weekends it gets completely packed.
Don't be surprised to see people queuing up outside;
be prepared to do the same. The menus feature
yakitori in varying styles and number – the top price
brings eight. All menus include rice and soup with
thin slices of onion and mushroom. The yakitori are
delivered in batches of two or three – duck, chicken,
molten cheese wrapped in a thin slice of beef, whole
grilled mushrooms, meatballs and pork. A tiny cup
of saké tops it all off at the end. Fun, filling and just
about unbeatable value.

Yen

*22 rue St-Benoît, 6th (01.45.44.11.18). Mº St-
Germain-des-Prés.* **Open** noon-2pm, 7.30-10.30pm
Mon-Sat; 7.30-10.30pm Sun. Closed two weeks in Aug,
two weeks at Christmas and one week at Easter.
Average €45. **Prix fixe** €55 (dinner only). **Lunch
menu** €30.50. **Credit** AmEx, DC, MC, V. **Map** H7.
Like the minimalist, blonde decor of this two-storey
space, the cooking here is clean, stylishly muted and
faultlessly presented. Serving mainly soba – a
slender Japanese buckwheat noodle – and tempura,
Zen-like Yen is the perfect stop for a satisfying,
healthy lunch. The deluxe lunch special arrived in a
two-tiered wood bento box, the delicate morsels of
each tiny course encased in its own compartment. A
cake of compressed rice with taro root; marinated
spinach; avocado and fresh tuna in sesame sauce;
fried cubes of salmon fillet with marinated
cucumber; squishy wedges of flavourful tofu; and a
terrine of compressed braised chicken breast acted
as light, appetite-enhancing accompaniments to the
main fare of perfectly fried mixed tempura. The
excellent, home-made soba – served hot or cold
according to preference – came with shredded green
onions, a thimble of wasabi and a bowl of mirin-
based dipping sauce. We had just enough room to
try the dessert, provided by pâtissier Sadaharu Aoki:
ginger and white sesame ice-cream topped with
black sesame and green tea macaroons.

Jipangue

*96 rue La Boétie, 8th (01.45.63.77.00). Mº St-
Philippe-du-Roule.* **Open** noon-2pm, 7-11pm Mon-Fri,
7-11pm Sat. **Average** €30. **Prix fixe** €18.30-€37.
Lunch menu €12.70-€14.50. **Credit** AmEx, MC, V.
Map E4.
This unatmospheric eaterie labels itself a Japanese
restaurant, yet most customers seem to come for the
Korean barbecue on the second floor. At dinner, the
sushi bar downstairs was practically empty, but not
so upstairs, where multilingual chatter mingled with
the sizzle of grilling meat. We decided to give both
house specialities a try, starting with the 'superior'
sashimi selection. The plate (not even a platter)

dished up a paltry selection of salmon, scallops, tuna
belly and snapper – although, happily, each cut was
divinely fresh. To fill up, we ordered the California
maki, stuffed with generous chunks of creamy
avocado and cooked prawns (rather than the usual
fake crabsticks) then rolled in toasted sesame. Barely
sated, we moved on to the grilled meats, which again
were offered in small portions. Delicately thin raw
beef fillet, marinated in sesame oil, melted in the
mouth after a quick swirl on the grill. The beef
cutlets, which required longer cooking, were thick
with flavour, reminiscent of prime rib steak. On the
side, we opted for the spicy cucumbers stuffed with
shredded kimchi, a distinctly Korean staple.

Momoka

5 rue Jean-Baptiste-Pigalle, 9th (01.40.16.19.09).
Mº Trinité. **Open** 8.30-10.30pm Tue-Sat. **Prix fixe**
€39, €55. **Credit** MC, V. **Non-smoking. Map** G3.
In this adorable little restaurant, Masayo, a
charming and talented cook, offers no à la carte, only
prix fixe menus working on a sort of all-you-can-eat
basis. There are only 14 seats, so a meal here is a
gentle, relaxed, intimate experience, with a menu
that changes daily according to the market. This is
not a typical Parisian Japanese either – instead of
sushi, sashimi and yakitori, you might begin with
salmon and tuna tatakis (the fish being lightly
grilled so that it's still raw in the middle), stewed
baby squid, tuna marinated with ginger before being
fried, salads, and occasionally sushi. First-rate
quality and a winsome atmosphere make this a place
well worth discovering – though only those who
have reserved will be admitted.

Kifuné

44 rue St-Ferdinand, 17th (01.45.72.11.19).
Mº Argentine. **Open** 7-10pm Mon; noon-2pm,
7-10pm Tue-Sat. Closed bank holidays, two weeks
in Aug, two weeks in winter. **Average** €50. **Lunch
menu** €25. **Credit** MC, V. **Map** C3.
This gem of a neighbourhood sushi bar is
particularly prize-worthy for its authentic izakaya
atmosphere, complete with chain-smoking Japanese
businessmen, and surprisingly generous cuts of
fresh sushi and sashimi, albeit at Tokyo prices: a
small carafe of hot saké, astronomically priced at
€10, sets the tone. Sashimi of tuna, tuna belly and
salmon arrive like pliant marble slabs, opulently
cold and thick – the tuna belly or toro so unctuously
dense its flesh was opaque and pearly. Scallop sushi,
again, was first-rate in freshness and heft, its ivory
flesh drooping off the edges of a finely vinegared
finger of pressed rice. A starter of slivered raw
cuttlefish with sea urchin was appropriately
sublime, although the paltry spoonful of uni seemed
more like a creamy sauce than the main attraction.
We noticed, however, that the same starter delivered
to a Japanese man next to us was plumped up with
much more of the delicacy. A special order? Or
preferential treatment to a regular customer? With
Japanese clients filling most of the tiny, smoke-filled
room, it could well be either or both.

Jewish

The first wave of Jewish cooking reached Paris as Ashkenazi (Eastern European) Jews drifted into the capital during the 19th century. Tumult in Eastern Europe and Russia greatly increased Paris's Jewish population at the beginning of the 20th century, and independence movements from French North African colonies brought an influx of Sephardic and North African Jews in the early 1960s and '70s. Head for Belleville to sample Algerian and Tunisian Jewish specialities, and the Marais for Central European and Middle Eastern eats – pastrami, chopped liver, chicken soup and falafel. There is also a significant Jewish community in the 17th arrondissement, which now has its own kosher Indian restaurant.

Spice it up at **Maison Benisti**. *See p202.*

L'As du Fallafel

34 rue des Rosiers, 4th (01.48.87.63.60). Mº St-Paul. **Open** 11am-midnight Mon-Thur, Sun; 11am-mid-evening Fri. **Average** €12. **Credit** MC, V. **Wheelchair access. Map** L6.

Once you have tried the falafel here you will understand why this place is so popular. It can get noisy and crowded, but there is a positive energy in the air which makes the overall experience rather fun. We received a warm welcome on a rainy day from the rushed, but never rude waiters. Our umbrellas were taken for us before we were ushered over to a corner table, squeezing past the densely packed diners on our way. Though the mouth-watering aroma of the sizzling chawarmas was very tempting, we tried the falafel spécial, which comes with fried aubergine, Turkish salad and houmous, and we were not disappointed. We also made short work of the deliciously spicy chilli sauce, provided on every table, as an accompaniment to our plate of chips. Just as we were thinking of ordering a second beer, our bill arrived – judging from the throng of people milling around outside the door, our table was hot property. L'As du Fallafel is certainly not a place to relax and unwind, but if you want exceptionally well-prepared food at cheap prices and come with an eat-and-run attitude, you will leave here happy and full, vowing to return.

Chez Marianne

2 rue des Hospitalières-St-Gervais, 4th (01.42.72.18.86). Mº St-Paul. **Open** 11am-midnight daily. **Average** €20. **Credit** MC, V. **Map** K6.

With its homespun philosophical statements painted on the windows, Chez Marianne is a popular Marais institution, with Jewish North African dishes combined with Eastern European stalwarts. On a Monday lunchtime, both rooms of the restaurant were bursting with a crowd for the most part familiar with the menu, which allows you to put together your own platter from the various zakouski (snacks). Outstanding items on our six-element version (€17.50) included first-rate chopped liver, a crispy beef-stuffed brik, excellent houmous and some of the best falafel in Paris, which can also be enjoyed in a sensational takeaway sandwich. Choose your items carefully to avoid doubling up on flavours and textures. Our veteran neighbour was rich in anecdotes of his mother's meatballs, apparently moister than Marianne's rather dry version, and his recipe has been noted for future home use. He also gently chastised us for eating too fast and drinking the excellent Fleurie too rapidly, not leaving enough to wash down a substantial mixed fruit strudel and a generous plate of sweet halva. The jolly but haphazard service in part explains the popularity of the place, which is no longer a bargain.

Jo Goldenberg

7 rue des Rosiers, 4th (01.48.87.20.16/www. restaurantgoldenberg.com). M° St-Paul. **Open** 8.30am-11pm daily. **Average** €28. **Credit** AmEx, DC, MC, V. **Non-smoking room. Map** L6.

A Tuesday evening may not have been the best time to visit this legendary Jewish delicatessen/ restaurant as the emptiness gave us more time to dwell on the decor. A mixture of grim, gaudy and kitsch, the cluttered walls are a meeting place for strange paintings and tired black-and-white photographs. The tasty starter of aubergine caviar was easily the most successful dish of the evening. Potato cakes, while a little on the stodgy side, were by no means greasy and just needed a touch more seasoning to cheer them up. A main-course platter of smoked beef pastrami was generous but not particularly noteworthy, while the long-awaited stuffed pepper (which arrived half an hour after the rest of our meal) truly deserves a mention as a dish to avoid at all costs. Served with lumpy mashed potato and rice, the poor thing came swimming in a watery orange sauce. Puffy hot apple strudel was a vast improvement, but beware of the cream squirted 'fresh' from the can.

Pitchi Poï

7 rue Carron, 9 pl du Marché Ste-Catherine, 4th (01.42.77.46.15/www.pitchipoi.com). M° St-Paul. **Open** 10.30am-3pm, 6-11pm daily. **Average** €28. **Credit** AmEx, DC, MC, V. **Wheelchair access. Non-smoking room. Map** L6.

The all-you-can-eat Sunday brunch buffet is justly famous, but Pitchi Poï deserves a look-in at any time for its hearty Eastern European specialities: beef goulash, tchoulent (duck confit with slow-baked potatoes, Polish giant beans and barley) or klops with mamaliga (veal loaf with polenta). Vegetarians needn't despair as there's also datcha (smoked salmon with baked potatoes, soured cream and herbs) or vegetable strudel with salad. Lighter options include zakouski platters of chopped liver, gefilte fish and real taramasalata (creamy-smooth and almost white), with frequently replenished bread baskets of matzoh, pumpernickel and rye. The decor shows the same careful attention to quality and detail – low on shtetl nostalgia, high on eastern Mediterranean charm (jewel-coloured scatter cushions, hand-decorated stained-glass tea lights). And all on a cobbled, leafy, traffic-free square in the Marais. At lunch on a winter bank holiday the dining room and terrace gradually filled with multi-generational Jewish families and arties, while we devoured osso bucco with fresh pasta (expertly twirled for our kids, fork-and-spoon style, by the owner), followed by fabulously thick, cinnamon-scented fromage blanc with a compote of baked

preserved fruits. Wines include Hungarian tokay and Israeli cabernet sauvignon, but you'd be mad not to sample at least one of the range of vodkas on offer. An iced goldwasser with our coffee completed a perfect meal – frosty on the outside, warm and honeyed on the inside, and twinkling with tiny slivers of gold.

Margoa

7 rue Waldeck Rousseau, 17th (01.45.72.39.41). M° Porte Maillot. **Open** noon-2.30pm, 7-11.30pm Mon-Thur, Sun; noon-2.30pm Fri; 7-11.30pm Sat. **Average** €50. **Prix fixe** €18.33. **Lunch menu** €18. **Non-smoking room. Credit** AmEx, MC, V.

Blink and you'll miss Paris's one and only kosher Indian restaurant, which is tucked away in a tiny side street near Porte Maillot. The fusion of kosher methods with Indian recipes results in divine, surprisingly light Indian food. Each starter is accompanied by a rack of various sauces and a waiter explains the taste of each one. To warm up your taste buds, try the aubergine fondue, with its enticing smell of spices and melting texture. The meat samosas were almost as good, though a little too salty. The menu boasts a wide range of chicken, fish and beef dishes, making it virtually impossible to choose. After much deliberation, we finally opted for the chicken tikka saag and the fish jalfrezi, both of them juicy and well-spiced. Also deserving of a special mention are the naans. The texture was perfect – neither too crisp nor too soggy. We were too stuffed for dessert, but the gasps of our neighbours were enough to vouch for their excellent quality. Although it's expensive, Margoa is definitely a cut above what you're likely to find down your local Indian.

Maison Benisti

108 bd de Belleville, 20th (no phone). M° Belleville. **Open** 9am-10pm daily. **Average** €15. **No credit cards. Map** N4.

Looking like a launderette that's had its machines ripped out and replaced with serving counters and plastic chairs, Benisti is all you could ever wish for in a Jewish eaterie. A man kneads couscous with his bare hands, another grins from behind his sandwich counter, while in the dining room behind him whole families are tucking into steaming bowls of soup and men sit huddled in their cloth caps and anoraks (wrap up in winter as there doesn't seem to be any heating). If you eat in, the best idea is to go to the counters and point to what you want. Couscous comes with delicious, coriander-flavoured meatballs and tender beef floating in its broth; or there are whole pike-perch and tuna steaks baked in an oily tomato sauce. A load of little plates of salads also appeared at our table. But what sets this Tunisian restaurant apart from other North Africans in Paris is the spicing, which has extra chutzpah. Benisti is first and foremost a pâtisserie so don't miss out on the fabulous sticky cakes which come dripping with honey.

North African

In a country where many international cuisines have been watered down to satisfy suspicious tastebuds, North African food tastes refreshingly authentic. This can be partly explained by immigration – there are enough Algerians, Tunisians and Moroccans in Paris to support good restaurants – but it's also because this cuisine is simply so easy to like, with its warm spices, hearty grilled meats, sweet tagines and honey-drenched cakes. Parisians, usually so wary of anything 'hot', have even embraced the fiery chilli paste harissa, which is stirred into the couscous broth. Another reason for the popularity of North African restaurants is their festive atmosphere. See the **Trendy** chapter (*pp98-103*) for the most fashion-conscious addresses in the capital.

Chez Omar

47 rue de Bretagne, 3rd (01.42.72.36.26). M° Temple or Arts et Métiers. **Open** noon-2.30pm, 7-11.30pm Mon-Sat; 7-11.30pm Sun. **Average** €30. **No credit cards. Map** L5.

Gone are the days when dinner at Omar's meant that you'd be rubbing shoulders with the likes of Naomi Campbell and Herb Ritts, and that means you now stand a slightly better chance of snagging a table. Omar doesn't take any reservations and by 9pm the queue stretches the length of the long zinc bar and out the door. Everyone is waiting for the same thing: couscous. Prices range from €11 (vegetarian) to €24 (royale); there are no tagines or other traditional Maghreb mains, so those who don't like couscous have to make do with a selection of French classics (duck, fish, steak). If it's your first visit keep your eye on neighbouring tables as the affable, overstretched waiters magically slip through the crowds with mounds of semolina, steaming vats of vegetable-laden broth, and steel platters heaving with meat and more meat. You won't be disappointed by the grilled slabs of lamb méchoui, but what keeps us coming back is the merguez. These spicy lamb sausages are tangily top-notch with each bite surprisingly fresh. Really big appetites might manage to find room for a starter but more alluring is the giant platter of Algerian pastries the waiter leaves at your table. Mint tea is de rigueur. Diners looking for oriental atmosphere should set their sights elsewhere (the converted bistro looks as French as it did 25 years ago when Omar moved into the place), but the hospitality is 100 per cent genuine: even on packed nights an offer of seconds – completely gratis of course – will encourage you to stay on a little longer. Non-smokers need to beware: the proximity of your neighbours means that you'll share more than just their conversation.
Other locations: Café Moderne, 19 rue Keller, 11th (01.47.00.53.62).

404 ★

69 rue des Gravilliers, 3rd (01.42.74.57.81). M° Arts et Métiers. **Open** noon-2.30pm, 8pm-midnight Mon-Fri; noon-4pm (brunch), 8pm-midnight Sat, Sun. **Average** €23. **Lunch menu** €17, €21 (brunch) **Credit** AmEx, DC, MC, V. **Wheelchair access. Map** K5.

Algerian-born Momo has a secret formula: however much others try to copy, they can't replicate the unique atmosphere of his Paris and London restaurants. It might be the fact that the exquisite lamps are real antiques, there's real tadelakt in the bathroom, or that celeb friends like Ozwald Boateng might drop in; most likely it's because the staff in their tastefully decorated T-shirts just can't wait for the party to kick off. Book for the late sitting if you like to dance on the tables: before you've finished your mint cocktails the waiters will already be gyrating on the bar. Through the haze of alcohol, after repeated bottles of a quaffable gris de Guerrouane, we can nevertheless say that the food was richly satisfying. Starters include some more unusual additions to the traditional briks, such as the salade méchouia (a refreshing combination of diced tomato, red peppers and garlic), zalouk (aubergine and garlic) or stuffed sardines. Of the mouthwatering tagines the chicken with pear is a winner, but the real revelation of our meal was the fish tagine absolutely bursting with flavour. We also liked the moist pastilla (sugar-dusted brik pastry with a pigeon filling), although by the end it left us digging into others' leftovers to kill the sugar overload. The fruit salads and pistachio pastries were more of an afterthought as the soundtrack brought everyone to their feet.

L'Atlas

12 bd St-Germain, 5th (01.44.07.23.66). M° Maubert-Mutualité. **Open** 7.30-11pm Tue; noon-2.30pm, 7.30-11.30pm Wed-Sun. **Average** €33. **Credit** AmEx, DC, MC, V. **Non-smoking room. Map** K7.

Park your camel at **Wally le Saharien** for some seriously good couscous. *See p205.*

If there is such a restaurant genre as 'Parisian Moroccan', Atlas exemplifies it: there is a certain dressed-up quality to the decor, service and food that is very much in keeping with its older, Left Bank clientele (Jussieu and Institut du Monde Arabe academics are often to be found eating here). There's a glassed-in terrace filled with chain-smokers in close proximity so, looking through to the richly decorated non-smoking bit, we asked to be moved. Despite a profusion of empty tables, we were seated right next to the kitchen door, which was constantly swinging open as waiters burst forth bearing tagines. The starters were impressive – 'cigars' of crisp filo pasty stuffed with spinach and a 'mosaic' of marinated vegetables with smoked palomette mushrooms arrived delicately seasoned and beautifully presented on the plate – but further elements of perfunctory service marred our meal. When the quail and pumpkin plat du jour we had ordered was unavailable, a sugary pigeon with dates was substituted without warning. The tagine aux trois poissons safranés, one of an imaginative selection of tagines, was more successful. Desserts are expensive, but the assiette gourmande – sorbets surrounded by masses of fresh fruit and little cakes – is copious enough to share. We can't help thinking, however, that l'Atlas is resting on its laurels: if you want to pay this much, go to classy Ziryab instead.

Le Ziryab

L'Institut du Monde Arabe, 1 rue des Fossés St-Bernard, 5th (01.53.10.10.16/www.yaer-prestige. com). M° Jussieu. **Open** noon-2pm, 3-6pm (tea room), 7.30-11pm Tue-Sat; noon-2pm, 3-6pm Sun. **Average** €50. **Prix fixe** €26, €34. **Credit** AmEx, DC, MC, V. **Wheelchair access**. **Map** K7.

Having passed through airport-style security and zoomed to the top floor of the Institut du Monde Arabe in a glass lift, you can't help but feel a little privileged. With a change of chef, Ziryab has returned to doing a superior take on traditional Morrocan cuisine, and after the ubiquitous lanterns and ornate plasterwork of so many North African restaurants, it comes as a refreshing change to enjoy couscous and tagines in a setting where crisp tablecloths, minimalist red lamps and an amazing view, lit up periodically by the passing bateaux-mouches, form the only decor. We settled on a mixed meze to share as a starter. Smoky puréed aubergine, smooth houmous, tabouleh and a selection of hot, stuffed brik pastries were served in individual dishes and accompanied by piping hot pitta bread – each one was sublime. There are quite a few fruity variations on the tagine – we chose the chicken with pineapple, whose cinammony aroma was announced with aplomb when the waiter whisked off its terracotta cone in the manner of a silver dome.

The couscous méchoui did not disappoint either, with its broth full of tasty vegetables, a hunk of lamb that fell off the bone and the welcome addition of fresh mint. Desserts of crème brûlée delicately flavoured with liquorice and a fruit salad in a minty nage with green tea ice-cream showed finesse. Our sole regret was taking the waiter's recommendation of the Coteaux du Mascara red, which made a rather heavy accompaniment to this food. It all feels a bit like being in a swanky hotel and the attentive staff did not make us feel in the least bit rushed when we were the last people there.

Le Méchoui du Prince
34-36 rue Monsieur-le-Prince, 6th (01.43.25.09.71). Mº Odéon or St-Michel. **Open** noon-2.30pm, 6.30pm-midnight Mon-Sat. **Average** €24. **Lunch menu** €11.90. **Brunch** (Sat only) €21. **Credit** DC, MC, V. **Wheelchair access. Map** H7.
If you love North African food and want a festive night out, this is a fine destination for a little exoticism and some really good eating. Though it's quickly found its way on to the celebrity circuit – don't be surprised to see recognisable faces in the crowd – service is warm, relaxed and almost disarmingly humble. The comfortable dining room is a Marrakech-lavish sort of setting, all golds and reds. The menu will tantalise anyone who knows Maghreb cooking well, including some superb dishes rarely seen elsewhere in Paris – notably a lamb tagine with dates and walnuts. Otherwise start with the assorted hors d'oeuvres, including salads and briks (crunchy pastry turnovers filled with cheese, meat or spinach), then order the couscous royale, a massive amount of food that includes spicy merguez sausages, lamb chops and kebabs; the lighter chicken couscous; or maybe chicken pastilla, a recipe brought to Morocco by Spanish Jews in the 15th century. Here it's a flaky, savoury concoction of filo pastry layered with stewed poultry, raisins and pine nuts, and spiked with a judicious sprinkling of sugar. A rather grand wine list is available, but one of the sturdy North African wines makes the perfect accompaniment.

Wally le Saharien
36 rue Rodier, 9th (01.42.85.51.90). Mº Notre-Dame-de-Lorette or Anvers. **Open** noon-2pm, 7.30-10.30pm Tue-Sat. **Average** €25 (lunch only). **Prix fixe** €40.40 (dinner only). **Credit** MC, V. **Wheelchair access. Map** J2.
At dinner don't ask for the menu – they hit you with everything they've got. Expect to start with a seriously spicy tomato soup, hints of coriander and mint sometimes overpowered by the pervasive peppers. That is followed by a mini-pastilla, a magnificent sugar-dusted pastry stuffed with pigeon, nuts, raisins and cinnamon. What comes next depends on availability. Wally's famous stuffed sardines had the night off when we visited, but were ably replaced by a lightly spiced ratatouille served with nutty brown bread. Then things get serious. On a bed of dream-light couscous, Wally serves

tender roast lamb and succulent merguez, both first-class. Forget the vegetable broth: when the grains are this good, you don't need it. We sampled a red wine, an undistinguished 1992 Coteaux de Zaccar – poor value at €28. Dessert is a platter of Berber pastries, light and unsticky, washed down with as much mint tea as you and your camel could store. The service is friendly, informed and well-paced. The only problem is the price. If Wally was prepared for some souk-style haggling over the bill, he'd have a queue around the block.

L'Homme Bleu
55 bis rue Jean-Pierre Timbaud, 11th (01.48.07.05.63). Mº Parmentier. **Open** 7pm-1am Mon-Sat. Closed Aug. **Average** €30. **Credit** MC, V. **Wheelchair access. Map** M5.
Go with a group to L'Homme Bleu to best tackle its tempting array of Maghreb specialities, not to mention big portions. Just be sure to arrive by 8pm to secure a table, as the popular restaurant does not take reservations. Our group of five ordered four starters and four mains to share with the express purpose of saving room for the platter of jewel-like Algerian pastries brought to the table at the end of the feast. The friendly Algerian and Moroccan waiters were happy to oblige and it wasn't long before hot appetisers were circling our table in the cosy stone cellar. Lmhajeb, a flaky pancake filled with sautéed tomato, onions and green peppers; burek, a brik casing oozing mild white cheese; brik s'tmellalt, an envelope of thin pastry stuffed with tuna, egg and coriander; and pastilla, a sugar- and-cinnamon-dusted pastry filled with chicken, toasted almonds, onions, egg and orange flower water, all disappeared quickly. Next came the tagines and couscous. Our favorites were tagine s'laxrif, a sizzling stew of lamb, dates, figs, raisins, almonds and cinnamon, and the couscous merguez, featuring a pile of the long, spicy sausages. The bottle of Medea rouge from northern Algeria was very drinkable at €13.75, though a tiny glass of lemonade was not worth €3.96. Sweet mint tea was the perfect accompaniment to our delicious pastries.

Le Mansouria
11 rue Faidherbe, 11th (01.43.71.00.16/www.mansouria.com). Mº Faidherbe-Chaligny. **Open** 7.30-11pm Mon, Tue; noon-2pm, 7.30-11pm Wed-Sat. **Average** €45. **Prix fixe** €29, €44. **Credit** MC, V. **Non-smoking room. Wheelchair access. Map** N7.
The jury is still out on whether Fatema Hal's chic and fairly expensive restaurant is substantially better than our far less elaborate neighbourhood couscous joint. There is no question about the look of the place: the subtle Moroccan decor is relaxingly elegant and on our last visit the restaurant was pleasantly full with a fashionable crowd. The starters lived up to the classy culinary reputation too: a plate of briouates all had distinctly different fillings, the cheese version being particularly delicious. These were accompanied by generous

salads, including a seriously good aubergine purée. The harira, a hearty Moroccan soup that can be heavy going, was here delicately spiced and bursting with flavour. By comparison the main courses were banal; lamb tagine with almonds and prunes was pleasant, but the disintegrating meat had not fully absorbed the flavours of the sauce. A note to short-sighted diners with expensive dentists: telling the difference between a prune stone and an almond takes practice. The other tagine featured wonderful walnut-stuffed figs, but the chicken was distinctly dry. Both dishes were accompanied by couscous, and the sweetest of waitresses allowed us to deviate from the usual wheat couscous and have our favourite barley version with a nuttier flavour instead. We finished our meal with glasses of mint tea, sticky dates and the last drops of an excellent Moroccan rosé.

Restaurant des Quatre Frères

127 bd de Ménilmontant, 11th (01.43.55.40.91). Mº Ménilmontant. **Open** noon-4pm, 6-11pm Mon-Thur, Sat; 3-11pm Fri. **Average** €10. **Credit** MC, V. **Map** N5.

Have you ever wondered what 'family dining' might be like in Algiers? For less than €10 the four brothers who run this unassuming local hot-spot (paper cloths on Formica tables and help-yourself soft drinks) will give you a good introduction. A tiny blackboard menu lists the essentials but regulars know to ask for the extras (like bottles of olive oil for dousing the chickpea soup). For starters try the mhadjeb (a thickish crêpe stuffed with lightly spiced red peppers) or tangy chorba soup. Couscous, the most expensive main, boasts some of the lightest, fluffiest semolina in Paris, but the daily special is worth the adventure. On our visit it was a chicken chakchoukha: a thick crêpe covered in a saucy portion of potatoes and chickpeas and topped with a succulent, pan-grilled quarter chicken. The pot of harissa on the table lets you adjust the zing accordingly. What pulls in the locals, though, is the dazzling array of skewered meat (beef, lamb, turkey, liver, a liver-heart combo plus, of course, merguez), cutlets, chops and herb-filled patties, all laid out buffet-style. The waiter will whisk them off to the open grill (fanned inventively with a hairdryer) and before you know it you'll be chomping away like everyone else at an Algerian barbecue.

Le Souk ★

1 rue Keller, 11th (01.49.29.05.08). Mº Ledru-Rollin or Bastille. **Open** 7.30pm-midnight Tue-Fri; noon-2.30pm, 7.30pm-midnight Sat; noon-2.30pm, 7.30-11pm Sun. *Tea room* 2-7pm Tue-Sun. **Average** €25. **Prix fixe** €31, €35 (for groups of 8 or more only). **Credit** MC, V. **Map** N7.

Potted olive trees mark an unassuming entrance where savvy diners push past the battered kilim covering the doorway into a lively den of Moroccan cuisine. The swirl of animated conversation, aromas of incense and cumin and harem-like decor provide a heady introduction to an authentic dining experience. We started with pastilla, a savoury pastry stuffed with duck, raisins and nuts, flavoured with orange blossom water and sprinkled with cinnamon and powdered sugar. It made instant converts of our two uninitiated dining companions, who were also seduced by the creamy aubergine scooped up with hunks of fluffy Moroccan bread, baked on the premises. Don't fill up on starters, though, as the enormous tagines and couscous are first rate. Our favourite was tagine canette, duckling stewed with honey, onions, apricots, figs and cinnamon then showered with toasted almonds. The luscious combination of tender meat, sweet plump fruits and crunchy nuts was also irresistible in the tagine de palmeraie, made with chicken, dates, onions and almonds. Couscous bidaoui arrived in handsome earthenware – a bowl of the semolina atop an urn of rich broth containing carrots, turnips and cabbage. A hefty shank of lamb was served on the side as were little bowls of chickpeas, harissa and golden raisins. Cold beer went down very well with the meal, but we also would have been happy with a bottle of Algerian or Moroccan red wine, reasonably priced at €17. For dessert try the excellent mille-feuille with fresh figs and the crème brûlée with honey, spices and pistachios. Sweet mint tea poured in a long stream by a djellaba-clad waiter was the perfect ending to a terrific meal. Book in advance.

Au P'tit Cahoua ★

39 bd St-Marcel, 13th (01.47.07.24.42). Mº St-Marcel. **Open** noon-2pm, 7.30-11pm daily. Closed 25 Dec. **Average** €27. **Lunch menu** €12.50. **Credit** AmEx, MC, V. **Map** K9.

The tented interior packed with North African earthenware tagines, bowls and lamps gives Au P'tit Cahoua an intimate souk feel, the word 'cahoua' being slang for café. On a miserable bad-weather day, we were instantly transported to warmer climes. This couscous haunt has always been one of the best in town, an impression confirmed by our crispy courgette fritters and triangular briouates, even if the fillings seemed to have shrunk somewhat in the frying process. The pigeon pastilla is a difficult dish to prepare well; here it was a total success, the sweet sugar topping contrasting intriguingly with the savoury pigeon filling. Méchoui was served on a hot cast-iron plate, a huge melting joint of lamb, served with a spicy ratatouille of fresh vegetables. The fluffy grains of the couscous were highly praised by our office-partying neighbours, a group of stiffly polite ladies who were resolutely not on Christian name terms, even after a plate of sticky Moroccan cakes and several bottles of Moroccan gris. Service was extremely friendly, but one waiter was insufficient for a full restaurant. Miraculously, though, he still managed to pour out glasses of deliciously fragrant mint tea from a gravity-defying height.

Other locations: 24 rue des Taillandiers, 11th (01.47.00.20.42).

International

Spanish

Tapas has made its mark on the haute cuisine world, with chefs such as Pierre Gagnaire, Joël Robuchon, Hélène Darroze and Alain Dutournier embracing the 'small plate'. But if it's pearly paella, succulent jamón and sangria-fuelled atmosphere you're looking for, head to this handful of Iberian haunts.

International

Caves Saint Gilles ★
4 rue St-Gilles, 3rd (01.48.87.22.62). M° Chemin Vert. **Open** noon-3pm, 8pm-midnight daily. **Average** €23. **Credit** DC, MC, V. **Map** L6.
You've got to love this place, if only for the staff with their gorgeous Spanish-accented French (and sometimes English) and their enthusiastic welcome. You can't book so if it's packed (as it usually is) sidle up to the bar, grab some olives and a beer and watch the restaurant frenzy. Prices might be higher than you'd pay in Spain but that doesn't bother the Spanish ex-pats and with-it Parisians, of all ages, who troop in for the trad tapas and the lively atmosphere. And who can blame them? Tortilla, patatas bravas (spicy fried potatoes), chipirones (small squid) straight from the grill, and gambas pil pil (big prawns grilled and doused in garlic and chilli) are first-rate. Also good are the jamón pata negra – other ham seems pedestrian after this one – and red peppers stuffed with salt cod. Forget the ice-creams and go straight for the crema catalana, the wonderful Spanish take on crème brûlée. Wines are pricey but the red Rioja Paternina is well worth it.

Fogón Saint-Julien
10 rue St-Julien-le-Pauvre, 5th (01.43.54.31.33). M° St-Michel or Maubert-Mutualité. **Open** 7pm-midnight Tue-Fri; noon-2.30pm, 7pm-midnight Sat, Sun. Closed last week in Aug, first week in Sept and first two weeks in Jan. **Average** €35. **Prix fixe** €35. **Credit** MC, V. **Map** J7.
It was a mistake to turn up at this elegant Spanish restaurant with a toddler, even one with gourmet tastes. 'That pushchair won't fit in here,' was the waitress's frosty greeting. We probably should have taken the hint and left, but instead produced a child seat and were pointed to the worst table in the empty dining room. This uncomfortable start aside, Fogón Saint-Julien is a wonderful (and idyllically located) place for lovers of Spanish cuisine and culture. Though tempted by the all-tapas menu – both savoury and sweet – we couldn't resist sampling the speciality of paella, which must be ordered by at least two people. Our meal started with a tongue-teaser of chilled Jerusalem artichoke 'gazpacho', before seasonal tapas including tangy salt cod paste with caviar, crunchy croquettes, shrimp salad and anchovies with olive paste on toast. Next came the paella valenciana – Spanish Calasparra rice pungent with high-quality saffron and loaded with chunks of rabbit, chicken and vegetables. The youngest member of our party, though delighted with the food, horrified the waitress further by rubbing saffron rice into the pristine white tablecloth. Mortified, we skipped dessert and strolled over to the Ile St-Louis for ice-cream instead.

La Catalogne
4-8 cour du Commerce St-André, 6th (01.55.42.16.19/ www.catalogne.infotourisme.com). M° Odéon. **Open** noon-3pm, 7-11pm Tue-Fri; noon-3pm, 7-11pm Sat. Closed Aug. **Average** €25. **Prix fixe** €14, €18. **Lunch menu** €11. **Credit** AmEx, DC, MC, V. **Map** H7.
Huge fans of Catalonian cooking, from simple arroz nero to the dizzying heights of Ferran Adria's avant-garde cooking in Rosas, we were thoroughly disappointed by this tourist-office restaurant in St Germain. The dining room is overlit and under-decorated, and this off-centre setting was the cue to the meal that followed. A selection of Catalonian charcuterie was barely acceptable – fatty, flavourless and tossed on a bed of wilted greens – while tapas selections of chorizo with mashed potatoes and red peppers, and aubergines sautéed with garlic brought ambitious airline food to mind. A couple from Valencia were outraged by the version of fideu (vermicelli noodles cooked in fish stock with shellfish and served with lashings of garlic mayonnaise), so we snagged our friendly waitress and asked if we should change our order. She reassured us, but the dish that arrived was sad indeed, under-seasoned and flecked with tough, overcooked shellfish. Our other main, chicken breast with crayfish and potatoes, was a disappointment as well, and in the end the only thing we liked about this place was the Raimat Temparillo wine.

Bellota-Bellota
18 rue Jean-Nicot, 7th (01.53.59.96.96). M° Pont de l'Alma, La Tour Maubourg or Invalides. **Open** 10am-3pm, 6-11pm Tue-Fri; 10am-11pm Sat. **Average** €45. **Credit** AmEx, MC, V. **Non-smoking room. Map** E6.
Attractively done up with blue-and-white Spanish tiles, wooden tables, a bar and soft lighting, this is a very pleasant destination for a snack or light supper. Bellota ('acorn' in Spanish) is a reference to the preferred food of the black, free-grazing Iberico race of pig, which produces this ham. The restaurant

serves five different Bellota-Bellota hams from four different geographical regions of southern and western Spain, and each one is purported to have a slightly different flavour and consistency. The ham is served with manchego ewe's milk cheese from La Mancha province, anchovies, olives, pickled garlic and pimentos, and tuna, as part of various tasting platters, accompanied by excellent bread. A first-rate assortment of Spanish wines, by the bottle or glass, friendly service and reasonable prices make this a very attractive address.

La Paella

50 rue des Vinaigriers, 10th (01.46.07.28.89).
M° République, Jacques Bonsergent or Gare de l'Est.
Open noon-2.30pm, 7-11pm Mon-Thur; noon-2.30pm, 7pm-midnight Fri; noon-2.30pm, 7pm-12.30am Sat.
Average €35. **Prix fixe** €27. **Credit** AmEx, DC, MC, V. **Map** L3.

Anyone looking for a breather from the relentless trendiness of the Canal St-Martin should make tracks to this homely Spanish spot that has just re-opened after a top-to-bottom makeover which has left it looking like a neighbourhood paella place in Valencia – that is, slightly spare and rather over-lit. Paella is the name of the game here, as it's cooked to order and served in vast portions, a fact that makes this place popular with Paris's resident Spanish community. Depending on how hungry you are, you can nibble your way through an assortment of tapas while waiting the requisite half-hour for paella, or, knowing that the Iberian rice dish is to arrive in an imminent avalanche, you might want to share a platter of really excellent Spanish charcuterie – chorizo, lomo, etc – and bide your time. This place really gets jumping on Saturday nights, when it pulls an intriguingly varied crowd, so be sure to book. Very friendly service and a nice wine list.

La Plancha ★

34 rue Keller, 11th (01.48.05.20.30). M° Bastille or Ledru-Rollin. **Open** 6.30pm-1.30am Tue-Sat. Closed Aug and one week for Christmas. **Average** €30.
No credit cards. Map M6.

What with the Basque flags, pelota scoops, bullfighting posters, a photo of a rugby scrum and

a couple of Lufthansa life jackets hanging from the ceiling like jamón, you can just about squeeze into this tiny and lively bodega. Though the owner assumes everyone with an accent can't speak French, we warmed to his patter once a jug of spicy sangria arrived. 'Take your time, we're open until 2am,' he assures everyone. Don't bother trying to scrutinise the menu pinned to the wall – just say whether you prefer meat, fish or vegetables and leave it to the kitchen. Our trio of tapas comprised generous portions of marinated red peppers, the freshest deep-fried squid and chorizo with a smattering of patatas bravas. Our meat-loving neighbours got small snails in tomato sauce. After a pause we enjoyed seared tuna steaks and gambas from the plancha (grill) with a crusting of sel de Guérande – so fresh that we started to wonder whether we were in Donostia. Crème brûlée and gâteau Basque straight from the oven were of the same standard. Aside from the great food, the atmosphere here is killer – the crammed seating and the wine loosen tongues and by the end of the night it feels like a great summer party south of the border.

Casa Eusebio

*68 av Félix Faure, 15th (01.45.54.11.88). M°
Boucicaut.* **Open** noon-2.30pm, 8-10.30pm Tue-Sat. Closed Aug and one week at Christmas.
Average €25. **Lunch menu** €12.50. **Credit** MC,
V. **Map** B9.

This tiny bistro is like many in Spain – simple and straightforward – despite the full-on French interior of a former café: huge mirrors and ceramic tiles depicting 18th-century court scenes at Versailles are somewhat at odds with the basic, unpretentious food. The tapas is limited to chorizo, cheese (manchego), fish or meat empañadas, anchovies, tortilla, and both jabugo (pata negra) and serrano ham. All perfectly fine. Mains include a generous serving of paella topped with a langoustine and some prawns and tender small calamari swimming in a bowl of their own black ink. It's a small, family-run place (the owner is also the waiter) and it's always busy. If you find yourself in the nether regions of the 15th and feel like a Spanish fix, this will sate, but it's not really something you need to cross town for.

Casa Eusebio.

Other International

For an insight into Paris's smaller international communities, visit the restaurants in this chapter, which serve not just as ambassadors for their country's cooking but also as meeting places for the homesick.

AFGHAN

Koutchi
40 rue du Cardinal Lemoine, 5th (01.44.07.20.56). M° Cardinal Lemoine. **Open** noon-3pm, 7pm-midnight Mon-Sat. **Average** €20. **Prix fixe** €15.50 (dinner only). **Lunch menu** €9.20, €12.50. **Credit** MC, V. **Map** K8.

There can be few better places to broaden your food horizons in Paris than at this cheerful little blue-painted restaurant in the Latin Quarter, named after the Afghan word for 'nomad'. The wood-panelled and carpet-draped dining room feels especially hospitable on a blustery day, when you can warm up with the gently spiced stews typical of Afghan cooking. Ordering from the two set lunch menus, we started with a well-made Afghan salad (finely diced tomato and cucumber topped with shredded lettuce) and lightly spiced stewed aubergines topped with tangy fresh cheese. Main course dahl with chunks of veal proved subtler than its Indian counterpart yet intriguingly aromatic, while the pilawa was a winning mix of savoury and sweet, with a spiced meat sauce for ladling over a plate piled with rice, raisins, almonds and shredded carrot. Dogh, a yoghurt and mint drink, seemed the necessary accompaniment, but there is also a simple wine list. Our bargain menus included a pistachio and rosewater flan – nothing earth-shattering but, like the rest of this meal, unusual and agreeable. Though Koutchi has been around for some time, the owner's enthusiasm was evident – another reason for this restaurant's loyal following.

GERMAN

Le Stübli
11 rue Poncelet, 17th (01.42.27.81.86/www. stubli.com). M° Ternes. **Open** 9am-7.30pm Tue-Sat; 9am-1pm Sun. **Lunch served** noon-3pm; tea room until 6.30pm. Closed three weeks in Aug. **Average** €25. **Prix fixe** €14.50. **Credit** MC, V. **Map** C2.

It may be rare to hear anyone extolling the gastronomic charms of Germany – one rather expects the wurst – but the quiet fact is that one can eat extremely well there, and few countries in the world offer charcuterie of such quality. All of this explains why this cheerful delicatessen with a small dining area has such a fiercely loyal following among sausage-lovers, with connoisseurs going into a frenzy over the bratwurst and real frankfurters, tangy sauerkraut and Black Forest ham. They also serve first-rate herring, potato salad, and salmon koulibiac, and the desserts are superb; try the poppyseed strudel or the Black Forest cake. There is a good selection of German beers and wines, too. This is a place worth bearing in mind if you want to rustle up a hearty wintry feed for friends without doing a lot of work in the kitchen.

HUNGARIAN

Le Paprika
28 av Trudaine, 9th (01.44.63.02.91/www.le-paprika.com). M° Anvers or Pigalle. **Open** noon-midnight daily. Closed 25 Dec, 1 Jan. **Average** €30. **Prix fixe** (Mon-Sat dinner only) €19, €22. **Lunch menu** (Mon-Sat) €13.50, €16.50. **Credit** MC, V. **Wheelchair access. Map** J2.

This genteel Hungarian bastion is a charming hybrid of 1950s Mitteleuropa – a home from home for elderly Eastern Europeans, with its interior of glass lamps, cream damask tablecloths and gypsy musicians in the evenings – and a brasserie where younger locals come for a drink and plat du jour by the bar or on the heated terrace. Be prepared for the orange spark of paprika and such prodigious amounts of cream as to make Normandy cuisine look frugal: this food is not for the faint of heart or thin of mind. From the no-choice €18.50 daily Hungarian lunch menu, we had a starter of hortobágyi palacsinta, a crêpe stuffed with a thick, minced veal ragoût in a paprika and cream sauce; and a bowl of székely gulyás, a mildly spicy, deep-red paprika-stained goulash of tender stewed veal, with a big dollop of sour cream and Transylvanian-style cabbage (sauerkraut in cream). We also tried csàky bélszin, thick beef fillet with a slab of fried foie gras on top (a reminder that Hungary is a major producer of foie gras) in a cream and morel sauce with a dish of little spaetzle-style noodles, before sharing the menu's apple strudel with nicely crisp filo pastry and plenty of cinnamon. The wine list includes both French and Hungarian wines, from famous sweet white Tokaj to inexpensive but easily drinkable red Egri Bikaver by the carafe. The rich, filling, timeless Hungarian cuisine is surely close to what our Hungarian great-grandmother would have eaten, and certainly rather better than what we ate on holiday in Budapest a few years ago.

POLISH

Mazurka

3 rue André-del-Sarte, 18th (01.42.23.36.45).
Mº Anvers or Château Rouge. **Open** 7-11.30pm
Mon, Tue, Thur-Sun. **Average** €25. **Prix fixe**
(dinner only) €18, €23. **Credit** AmEx, MC, V.
Wheelchair access. Non-smoking room.
Map J1.

It would be difficult to find a restaurant with more
depressing decor than the Mazurka. The walls are
hung with various abandoned musical instruments
and moth-eaten national dresses, crowned by, on
this occasion, a collection of grotesque oil paintings
of would-be endearing peasantry (thankfully just
a temporary exhibition). The jazz pianist had a

repertoire which ranged from very sad to fairly sad,
and an adjacent table had apparently not been
cleared since lunchtime. This is a pity as our meal
was excellent, good value and caringly served. We
began with a plate of smoky Polish charcuterie,
accompanied by white horseradish and an excellent
beetroot version. Some first-rate blinis were served
with salmon roe on a bowl of crushed ice, all
accompanied by a small carafe of pepper vodka,
which was the ideal drink for this hearty cuisine.
Bigos was a long-cooked version of choucroute, an
unappetising caramel-coloured dish but bursting
with authentic flavour, while pierogi were a rib-
sticking take on ravioli. Polish puddings are limited
to a home-made poppyseed cake or cheesecake, but
we were offered a glass of juniper vodka to send us

O Por do Sol. *See p212.*

on our way. By the time we left the restaurant had filled up and was almost jolly. With an overhaul of the decoration we would all be dancing mazurkas right to the top of Montmartre.

PORTUGUESE

O Por do Sol

18 rue de la Fontaine-du-But, 18th (01.42.23.90.26). M° Lamarck-Caulaincourt. **Open** noon-2pm, 7-10.15pm Mon, Tue, Thur, Fri, Sun; 7-10.15pm Sat. Closed Aug. **Average** €30. **Prix fixe** €21. **Credit** MC, V. **Map** H1.

Bacalhau, or salted cod, has been a staple of the Portuguese diet since the 16th century; they call it 'fiel amigo' (faithful friend), and in José and Elesia's tiny dining room you'll find out why. We started by sharing a plate of beignets de morue – fluffy cod fritters that left us fighting for the last bite – followed by two cod mains. Grilled cod, brushed with olive oil and pepper, was thick, moist and the perfect choice for those who like tasty, simple fish. But we were hard pressed to imagine anything better than the morue du chef, layered with roasted onion, pepper, tomato and potato in a heaving casserole. Portugal's favourite pasteis de nata, delicious custard tarts, finished the meal and left us swapping memories of remote villages with our convivial hosts. About the wine: vinho verde (young, green wine that has a distinctive fizz) is a perfect, refreshing match for the hearty cuisine. You'll find the white on the menu, but the red is kept secret: chilled, it is an excellent authentic accompaniment for the cod. Don't hesitate to ask Elesia to break open a bottle and give your tastebuds an adventure.

ROMANIAN

Doïna

149 rue St-Dominique, 7th (01.45.50.49.57). M° Ecole-Militaire or RER Pont de L'Alma. **Open** noon-3pm, 6pm-midnight Tue-Sun. **Average** €25. **Prix fixe** €12. **Credit** AmEx, MC, V. **Map** D6.

Practically under the skirts of the Eiffel Tower, this Romanian restaurant attracts an expat crowd eager for home cooking. The host makes a point of greeting each table personally, and candles, scenes of Bucharest and blaring Romanian folk music add to the mood. Bowls of pickled cauliflower and peppers go well with the local Murfatlar wine, a sweet and fruity pinot noir. We passed on tripe salad to sample comforting corn polenta sprinkled with a tangy cheese, then dived into our mains. A moussaka made with aubergine and plenty of minced beef proved rib-stickingly satisfying. Fried sandre (pike-perch) came with capers and boiled potatoes but we found the batter greasy. Watch your head on the way down to the loo or you'll knock yourself out before you can sample the torte Bucharest, which ended the meal with a chocolate-and-Chantilly flourish.

Athanor

4 rue Crozatier, 12th (01.43.44.49.15). M° Reuilly-Diderot. **Open** noon-2pm, 7-10.30pm Tue-Sat. **Average** €29. **Prix fixe** €23. **Lunch menu** €12. **Credit** AmEx, MC, V. **Wheelchair access. Map** N8.

Initially Athanor's distressed decor might seem like a sophisticated design concept but, once settled in, you realise that the collection of bric-a-brac – ranging from old carpets to a copy of a Mondrian painting – is just part of the homely atmosphere which extends from the motherly welcome to the delicious Romanian cuisine. We began with a couple of shots of vodka: a sweet Amande céleste and a drier, appetite-inducing number. On paper the mix of cheese terrine, tarama, and herring pâté looked mundane, but they were all tasty and home-made, accompanied by one of the many Romanian wines on offer – our Fetească Albá was an outstandingly supple golden white. A melting, long-cooked pork dish with figs was served on a bed of tasty savoury rice, while the perch (the restaurant specialises in freshwater fish) with creamy dill sauce and triangles of polenta was equally delicious. The puddings, a nut cake and a cherry cake, were unsophisticated but comforting and needed just a suitable digestif to finish off a delightful lunch. The patronne recommended the 60° Slivovitz pascale, which left us in a childish haze of happiness for the rest of the afternoon.

RUSSIAN

Dominique

19 rue Bréa, 6th (01.43.27.08.80). M° Vavin. **Open** 7.30pm-midnight (bar/boutique noon-midnight) Tue-Sat. **Average** €50. **Prix fixe** (dinner only) €40. **Credit** AmEx, DC, MC, V. **Map** G9.

Of all the Russian restaurants in Paris, this is the one that has best preserved the ambience of the old emigré haunt. Though it's expensive, it is possible to escape without your wallet getting a KGB-type seeing-to from men in long leather coats. The best option is to sit yourself down on one of the stools in the splendid and atmospheric bar with its red walls, long wooden counter and marble tables. Here you can down glasses of vodka chilled to the consistency of engine oil and snack on zakouski (the herring plate is particularly fine) or a bowl of borscht with pirojki (beef-stuffed pastries). Finish up with a slice of their delicious vatrouchka (cheesecake). A tip when it comes to the vodka: order by the glass, even if there are several of you, to sample some of the more wonderful creations from Russia, Poland, Scandinavia and, er, France. As for the restaurant, it has a warmer tapestries-and-samovar feel and songs from Brezhnev-era protest singer Vladimir Vissotski. A few silver spoons of caviar, a bottle of Cristall and the 'Prince Potemkin-style' salmon koulibiaka (wrapped in light pastry) in a cep mushroom sauce and you could soon be feeling (and spending) like an oligarch on a big night out.

On the Town

Cafés

For better or worse, the scruffy neighbourhood caff is becoming a thing of the past – modern light fixtures, shiny new parquet and re-upholstered banquettes are de rigueur, and prices have climbed accordingly. Add to that the apparition of several Starbucks and the beloved Paris café scene looks to be in danger. Yet some things remain reassuringly familiar: cafés are still havens for smokers (as some restaurants actually enforce non-smoking policies); the waiters remain true pros, even if they take a while to warm up to strangers; wine is often cheaper than (mineral) water; and no one seems in a rush. For people who must make do with tiny, often kitchen-less living spaces, cafés still serve as a home away from home. So if you think of your 2 coffee as a kind of rent on the table you'll be occupying for the next hour or three, it starts to look more reasonable. A word about coffee: the French expresso, or express, is not to be confused with the more sophisticated Italian espresso. Ask for it serré if you prefer it more concentrated and allongé if you're craving an American-style coffee. A crème is made with milk but good, frothy cappuccino is rare. If you want a little frothy milk in your express, ask for a 'noisette'. Milk on the side will be provided on request – at a price – for either coffee or tea. Be warned, however, that tea in a café usually consists of water in a burning-hot metal pot with a tea bag on the side. It's worth remembering that prices can vary in cafés – it's usually cheapest to stand at the bar, and most expensive to sit on the terrace. Most places do light meals as well as more substantial lunches.

1ST ARRONDISSEMENT

Bar de l'Entr'acte
47 rue Montpensier, 1st (01.42.97.57.76). M° Palais Royal. **Open** 10am-2am Mon-Fri; noon-midnight Sat, Sun. **Food served** noon-3pm, 7-11pm daily. **Plat du jour** €10. **Credit** MC, V. **Map** H5.
Aside from stalking French actors, there is no real reason to be hanging around the back of the Palais Royal theatre – unless, that is, you know about this atmospheric little haunt. Its tiny terrace and scruffy bar give way to a shabby room downstairs whose velvet drapes, fresco-clad walls and mosaic-topped tables could easily be part of a forgotten film set. Food is basic but generous with anything from sandwiches to their special pasta dishes. Even when the kitchen is closed a 'mini-carte' is available with meats and cheeses.

Le Café des Initiés
3 pl des Deux-Ecus, 1st (01.42.33.78.29). M° Louvre-Rivoli or Les Halles. **Open** 7.30am-1am Mon-Sat. **Food served** noon-5pm, 6.30-11pm. **Plat du jour** €14. **Credit** AmEx, MC, V. **Wheelchair access. Map** H5.
Upon entering Le Café des Initiés, you can't help but be taken with the sleek and beautiful, yet calming decor. Regulars congregate at the bar for a few drinks while diners enjoy very reasonably priced food chosen from the blackboard. The succulent duck breast was accompanied by dauphinoise potatoes done to perfection, while hearty tuna steak was also a good choice. The lights are subtly dimmed as the night progresses (highlighting the strategically placed tea-candles dotted around the interior), making this an ideal spot for a first date or an intimate catch-up with an old friend.

Café Marly ★
93 rue de Rivoli, cour Napoléon du Louvre, 1st (01.49.26.06.60). M° Palais Royal. **Open** 8am-2am daily. **Food served** 11am-1am. **Plat du jour** €22.50. **Credit** AmEx, DC, MC, V. **Non-smoking room. Map** H5.
Don't be intimidated by the impossibly beautiful and well-dressed staff – stride in as if you own the place, sit back and soak up the lifestyles-of-the-rich-and-famous atmosphere that awaits within Café Marly. This Costes brothers' classic oozes old-world sophistication and elegance. In summer, the stunning terrace overlooking the Louvre's glass pyramid is the place to be, while the plush interior is perfect for a cosy winter's afternoon. Come for a coffee, a glass of wine (€5-€8), nibble on smoked salmon or the club sandwich and you'll enjoy yourself so much that the bill will seem irrelevant (provided that you didn't order the €90 caviar). Oh, and don't forget to keep your eyes peeled for celebrities.

Café Ruc

159 rue St-Honoré, 1st (01.42.60.97.54). M° Palais Royal. **Open** 8am-1am daily. **Food served** noon-midnight. **Plat du jour** €25. **Credit** AmEx, DC, MC, V. **Non-smoking room. Wheelchair access. Map** H5.

Going to this Costes brothers café near the Louvre became a political act in recent months when its nine Sri Lankan cooks picketed outside the door for better work conditions and (eek!) hygiene (after 31 days they obtained what they wanted). Should you venture inside, expect seductive red velvet banquettes, a flurry of cocktails and café snacks, jazz tinged background muzak and (of course) waiters who are better dressed than anyone else in the room.

La Coquille

30 rue Coquillière, 1st (01.40.26.55.36). M° Les Halles. **Open** 6am-midnight Mon-Sat. **Food served** 11.30am-3.30pm, 7-10pm. **Plat du jour** €7.80. **Credit** MC, V. **Map** J5.

Mix with the growly-voiced locals in this dated (1950s vintage), small and smoky café. If you are tired of pretentious Parisian chic, or if you refuse to pay €14 for a toasted sandwich, then come and try the croque Coquille (a delicious toasted ham, cheese and tomato sandwich with a perfectly fried egg on top) served with a side salad for the bargain price of €5. Beer and wine (by the carafe) are also ludicrously cheap and the waiter was nothing other than a perfect gentleman throughout.

Taverne Henri IV ★

13 pl du Pont-Neuf, 1st (01.43.54.27.90). M° Pont-Neuf. **Open** 11.30am-9.30pm Mon-Fri, noon-5pm Sat. **Food served** all day. Closed Aug. **Plat du jour** €9. **Credit** MC, V. **Wheelchair access. Map** H6.

Blink and you'll miss it: the Taverne Henri IV, under new ownership, is a delightful little place, smack bang on the tip of the Ile de la Cité. The emphasis here is on simple French fare washed down with a good glass of wine – all at very reasonable prices. The eggs baked with blue cheese and ham were delectable and a glass of white Beaujolais (€4) even better. If you are having trouble deciding which wine to pick, the hilarious and chatty barman will be happy to make a few suggestions. For the decor, think 'legal profession' – dark wooden bar, certificates on the wall, wine bottles on display, and a few dusty books thrown in for good measure.

2ND ARRONDISSEMENT

Le Café

62 rue Tiquetonne, 2nd (01.40.39.08.00). M° Etienne-Marcel. **Open** 10am-2am Mon-Sat. **Food served** noon-10pm Mon-Sat. **Plat du jour** €11.50. **Credit** MC, V. **Wheelchair access. Map** J5.

Navigate this Marco Polo's attic of travel knick-knacks to a table beneath a tribal print ceiling. The kitchen serves up huge portions of hearty traditional cooking such as duck stew, smoked salmon salad and a variety of tarts. With such a cosy interior, you'll feel at home despite the clattering plates and brusque service. Come early on weekend nights – popular with a young, hip crowd, the place will be packed by 8pm. The rhythmic music may entice you to dance, particularly after a few beers from the bar.

Le Dénicheur

4 rue Tiquetonne, 2nd (01.42.21.31.01). M° Etienne-Marcel. **Open** noon-3pm, 7pm-1am daily. **Food served** noon-2.30pm, 7.30-11.30pm daily, Sun brunch 12.30-4pm. **Plat du jour** €7. Closed 25 Dec. **No credit cards. Map** J5.

Café Marly. See p214.

Groove to house music that throbs in this bohemian joint. Walls are splashed with bright colours and the tiled floor catches light reflecting from spinning disco balls, while little gnomes guard kitsch wax candles on each table. You can't argue with the price of the three-course €8.50 lunch menu or the €15.50 dinner menu, but you get what you pay for. Salads are small and the kitchen's valiant attempts at fusion result in unbalanced fare, like overly sweet grilled pork on jasmine rice. Yet Le Dénicheur redeems itself with scrumptious home-made desserts, such as hot apple crumble with a dollop of cream.

Lézard Café

32 Etienne Marcel, 2nd (01.42.33.22.73).
M° Etienne-Marcel. **Open** 9am-midnight Mon-Sat. **Food served** noon-4pm. **Plat du jour** €13. Closed 25 Dec, 1 Jan. **Credit** AmEx, MC, V. **Map** J5.
Bright overhead lights, wooden tables and brick walls are reminiscent of a sports bar, with the smoke and music, but without the dartboard. This gay-friendly joint offers a relaxed atmosphere for a nearly all-male clientele to unwind over beers and cigarettes. Chat with the bartender while he expertly mixes you a special cocktail. The jeans-clad waiters are welcoming and friendly. Catch lunch at one of two small outdoor tables, or bring your laptop to surf the internet.

La Tourelle ★

43 rue Croix des Petits Champs, 2nd
(01.42.61.35.41). M° Bourse or Palais Royal. **Open** 7am-10pm Mon-Fri. **Food served** noon-3pm. Closed first two weeks in Aug. **Plat du jour** €8. **Credit** MC, V. **Non-smoking room.** **Map** H5.
Sunlight floods this corner establishment on a pleasant day. A copper-topped bar with beer taps and an espresso machine dominates the simple front room – enjoy prime people-watching from ample windows or an outdoor table. Service is prompt and friendly, while the food is excellent: €7.50 will buy a delicious open-faced sandwich topped with smoked duck, grilled red peppers and tapenade. For €9, try a generous gourmet salad such as La Tourelle with manchego, cured ham, artichokes and sun-dried tomatoes. Once a month, a jeans-wearing crowd gathers for a €13 pot au feu Thursday dinner.

Au Vide Gousset

1 rue Vide-Gousset, 2nd (01.42.60.02.78).
M° Bourse. **Open** 7.30am-8.30pm Mon-Fri; 9am-7.30pm Sat. **Food served** 11am-5pm. Closed first three weeks in Aug. **Plat du jour** €8.50. **Credit** MC, V. **Map** H5.
A stone's throw from the elegant place des Victoires, this café-tabac is the archetypal smoke-filled Parisian café, complete with battered tables, shiny crimson banquettes and hideous 1970s lights. Nonetheless, it attracts a diverse clientele of expensively perfumed professional shoppers, stockbrokers, caffeine addicts and Gitane-smoking barflies. Simple but pricey food is served at lunch.

3RD ARRONDISSEMENT

L'Apparemment Café ★

18 rue des Coutures-St-Gervais, 3rd
(01.48.87.12.22). M° Filles du Calvaire or St-Paul. **Open** noon-2am Mon-Fri; 4pm-2am Sat; 12.30pm-midnight Sun. **Food served** 12.30-3pm, 7pm-midnight Mon-Fri; 7pm-midnight Sat; 12.30-4pm, 6-11.30pm Sun. **Plat du jour** €12. **Credit** MC, V. **Wheelchair access.** **Map** L5.
Light wood panelling, smooth jazz tunes, velvet lounge chairs and soft lighting make this an irresistible setting for a rendez-vous. The atmosphere is casual yet romantic, the waiters young and helpful. The menu has a do-it-yourself attitude: for €7.60-€10, choose the ingredients for a made-to-order salad. Brunch includes seafood, meat and cheese dishes, with choices of drinks and accompaniments. Options might appear confusing at first, but offer you ultimate control. Visitors to the nearby Picasso Museum will find this a convenient place to refuel at.

Le Café. See p215.

Better latte than never

Herein lies the appeal, and yes, although tourists still make up a fairly solid proportion of customers and the French are still reluctant to drink coffee in the streets, it's catching on.

Columbus paved the way for other American and American-style cafés, including Starbucks and the excellent Coffee et Friends. Basic coffees in each of the three tend to be good, particularly at Coffee et Friends, although the American influence is found in each in the predictably awful flavoured beverages. The food is similarly hit and miss. The muffins at Columbus are divine (try the double chocolate or poire-vanille), but elsewhere the offerings are reminiscent of English coffee chains with food resting on the ever-growing French love of le sandwich anglais.

The 2004 arrival of Starbucks in Paris led to much ruminating on the state of the Parisian café scene. Sentimentalists bemoaned the replacement of porcelain with cardboard cups, the loss of the chocolate on the side, and the hours whiled away without a bill in sight.

But the serious business of coffee is no place for sentimentalism. And, if we're being honest, porcelain cups are disappearing just as fast as Lavazza can make inroads, your average Parisian café is too stingy to serve anything on the side, and as for the waiting not everyone can afford to spend 25 minutes trying to get the waiter's attention.

Preceding Starbucks was Columbus Café, not an American chain but a French one based on the American model created by the enterprising Monsieur Philippe Bloch, who wondered why it was not possible in France to receive good coffee to go at a reasonable price. And with Bloch's super-friendly (and super good-looking) staff, you know you're never going to be scowled at for having no change.

Comfy sofas and the general novelty, however, are still drawing people in, suggesting that the arrival of the new, American-style cafés in Paris is not only timely, but is going to shake the city till the coffee beans rattle. If these places can force their longer-established competitors, with unreliable coffee and grouchy service, to make an effort to treat their customers like customers, this can only be good. And if not, as the French director of Starbucks pointed out, they make up only a few cafés in a city of several thousand.

Coffee et Friends
23 bd Beaumarchais, 4th (01.42.71.07.77).

Columbus Café
25 rue Vieille du Temple, 4th (01.42.72.20.25) and 14 other branches in Paris.

Starbucks
26 av de l'Opéra, 1st (01.40.20.08.37) and several other branches in Paris.

On the Town

Les Arts et Métiers

51 rue de Turbigo, 3rd (01.48.87.83.25). M° Arts-et-Métiers. **Open** 6.30am-1am Mon-Sat; 7am-2am Sun. **Food served** 11am-midnight daily. **Plat du jour** €17.50. **Credit** MC, V. **Non-smoking room.** **Wheelchair access.** **Map** K5.

A pleasant spot to soak up the city (with the requisite dose of exhaust fumes), the ample terrace of this corner café is the best in the neighbourhood. Groups of friends gather for drinks, and visitors rest their feet after a visit to the adjacent museum of the same name. The interior has dark curtains, an art deco motif, moody lighting and a hardwood floor. The menu is pricey for mains such as fillet of beef with roquefort (€22). However, the hot sandwiches (€8.70-€12) and fried mussels (€12) are popular. A well-stocked bar offers a good range of beers on tap.

4TH ARRONDISSEMENT

Baz'Art Café

36 bd Henri IV, 4th (01.42.78.62.23/www.bazart cafe.com). M° Sully Morland or Bastille. **Open** 7.30am-2am daily. **Food served** noon-12.30am. **Plat du jour** €28. **Credit** AmEx, DC, MC, V. **Non-smoking room.** **Map** L7.

A calm refuge from the tourist-laden islands, Baz'Art's gothic-like chandeliers combine with red velvet banquettes to create an arty atmosphere that's perfect for whiling away a rainy afternoon. Steer away from the coffee and choose instead from the list of more than 20 cocktails, ranging from the aptly named 'virgin chichis' (non-alcoholic) to the highly drinkable house-made punch or sangria. Food leans towards French traditional and there is a range of snacks to accompany the two-for-one drinks deals at happy hour (6-8pm).

Café BHV

11 rue des Archives, 4th (01.49.96.38.91) M° Hôtel de Ville. **Open** 9.30am-9pm Mon-Thur; 9.30am-10pm Fri, Sat; 11am-7pm Sun. **Food served** all day. **Plat du jour** €8. **Credit** AmEx, DC, MC, V. **Wheelchair access.** **Map** K6.

This novel addition to the BHV department store stable combines a florist and café specialising in 'cuisine anglaise de qualité [sic]'. Cute furniture, flowers on each table, and puzzles for entertainment make this cafeteria cheerier than many across the Channel but dreary soups and dried-out cheese-and-chutney sandwiches may remind you all too much of home. Happily, everything else on offer, including quiches, gratins and tartines, bears the French touch. With most items costing €3-€7, and unlimited help-yourself bread, this is almost certainly one of the cheapest places to eat in the Marais.

Café Beaubourg

43 rue St-Merri, 4th (01.48.87.63.96). M° Hôtel de Ville or RER Châtelet-Les Halles. **Open** 8am-1am Mon-Wed, Sun; 8am-2am Thur-Sat. **Food served** all day. **Plat du jour** €15. **Credit** AmEx, DC, MC, V. **Non-smoking room.** **Map** K6.

Christian de Portzamparc's design for this beacon of fashionable Parisian café culture opposite the Centre Pompidou dates back to 1985 and it's starting to show its age. The red velvet curtains over the entrance seem wearily heavy, while the minimalist sheen of the walls is broken up by cracks in the peeling paint. Yet somehow this absent-minded grubbiness only enhances its charm, providing the ideal setting for rich kids in ripped denim to sip on expensive cocktails while poring over their laptops.

Café des Phares

7 pl de la Bastille, 4th (01.42.72.04.70). M° Bastille. **Open** 7am-3am Mon-Thur, Sun; 7am-4am Fri, Sat. **Food served** all day. **Plat du jour** €8.50. **Credit** MC, V. **Map** M7.

Café des Phares likes to push its status as Paris's 'first' bistro to offer philosophical debates, a tradition started by late Sorbonne lecturer Marc Sautet and continued each Sunday morning at 11am. Unfortunately, the menu is less enlightened, with a stock range of omelettes, hot dogs and burgers. Cocktails, including a reasonable Mojito, are slightly better, and will no doubt aid the expansion of the mind. Watch out for the occasional geopolitical debates on Thursday evenings.

L'Escale ★

1 rue des Deux-Ponts, 4th (01.43.54.94.23). M° Pont-Marie. **Open** 7.30am-10pm Tue-Sun. **Food served** noon-3pm. **Credit** MC, V. **Map** K7.

On a freezing winter's day, this old-fashioned brasserie/wine bar offered a retreat from the windy corridors of the Ile St-Louis and comfort food in the form of chou farci, a divine leek quiche and, that Parisian café rarity, the goldenest, crispiest pile of home-made chips imaginable, complete with fluffy interior. Quality wines are reasonably priced, and desserts, including a deliciously eggy clafoutis, are all (thankfully) homemade. Its crowd of regulars range from scruffy locals to business types discussing 'le marketing': all are on friendly terms with waiter Colette and as ready to offer you their newspaper as to scrap over the last serving of monkfish.

L'Etoile Manquante ★

34 rue Vieille du Temple, 4th (01.42.72.48.34/www.cafeine.com). M° Hôtel de Ville or St-Paul. **Open** 8.45am-1am daily. **Food served** noon-1.30pm. **Plat du jour** €12. **Credit** MC, V. **Map** K6.

L'Etoile Manquante forms part of a small coterie of venues on Vieille-du-Temple owned by Xavier Denamur and is definitely the hippest of the bunch. The cocktails are punchy, the trad tipples just as good, but it's the design and buzz that are the big draws here. The decor is trendy and comfortable with wonderful lighting and interesting art works on the walls. As ever with Denamur's places, no visit is complete without a trip to the loo. An electric train runs between cubicles, starlight beams down from the ceiling and a hidden camera films you washing your hands. Don't worry, the images aren't bound for TF1 – just the screen on the wall behind you.

Le Flore en l'Isle

42 quai d'Orléans, 4th (01.43.29.88.27). M° Hôtel de Ville or Pont Marie. **Open** 8am-2am daily. **Food served** 11am-midnight daily. Closed 24 Dec. **Plat du jour** €17.50. **Credit** MC, V. **Map** K7.

Although the terrace here attracts the summer hordes in search of Berthillon ice-cream, sitting at a window table overlooking the Seine and Notre Dame with a coffee and its accompanying plate of chocolate truffles is a favourite Île-St-Louis pastime. Egg- and seafood-based brunch dishes are popular as are the house desserts, including a truly scrumptious gratin aux poires, but avoid the rest of the menu which is oddly organised, expensive and often inexcusably bad. Don't be fobbed off into the usually empty tea room next door.

Grizzli Café ★

7 rue St-Martin, 4th (01.48.87.77.56). M° Châtelet. **Open** 9am-2am daily. **Food served** noon-11pm. Closed 1 Jan, 1 May, 25 Dec. **Plat du jour** €13. **Credit** AmEx, MC, V. **Map** K6.

According to legend, this café was home to a dancing bear, whose memory is preserved in a framed sketch opposite the bar. With a welcoming terrace, a main floor with white moulded ceilings, and an upstairs of modern black wood, this outstanding café-restaurant offers a symphony of atmospheres and great service. Half-pitchers of good house wine (€6) accompany excellent cuisine with interesting twists. Try the delicate shrimp ravioli or the seared tuna with Asian mushrooms. Convenient to Les Halles and Beaubourg, this place gets its share of tourists, but remains popular with locals, always a good sign.

L'Imprévu Café

9 rue Quincampoix, 4th (01.42.78.23.50). M° Hôtel de Ville or Châtelet. **Open** noon-2am daily. **Credit** MC, V. **Wheelchair access. Map** J6.

Behind the red door of L'Imprévu lies an eclectic interior that aims somewhere between alter-mondialiste and a teenage boy's bedroom. The front room draws a crowd of tisane-sipping bobos (bohemian bourgeois); the back room, complete with card-players, is more down-to-earth. Cocktails range from 'les chérubins' to 'les machos', and although ours seemed overly sweet we may just not have ventured far enough down the list. The staff seemed tense and somewhat hostile on our visit, but it's still worth a visit for the house hot chocolat.

Le Petit Fer à Cheval

30 rue Vieille du Temple, 4th (01 42 72 47 47/ www.cafeine.com). M° St-Paul. **Open** 9am-2am daily. **Food served** noon-1am daily. **Plat du jour** €11. **Credit** MC, V. **Map** K6.

If Glasgow's Horseshoe boasts the UK's longest bar counter, its Parisian counterpart contains one of the smallest across the Channel. Certainly by Parisian standards it's tiny, and far too charming by half, a marble ring surrounded by old film and promotional posters and headed by an old clock and an ornate mirror backdrop. It's all done by mirrors, in fact,

Baz'Art Café. *See p218.*

because behind the glassy façade hides a friendly dining room lined with old Métro benches, offering space, but not the scenery of the handful of tables out front looking out on to the Vieille-du-Temple bustle. In business since 1903.

Le Petit Marcel

65 rue Rambuteau, 4th (01.48.87.10.20). M° Rambuteau. **Open** 7am-midnight Mon-Thur; noon-midnight Fri, Sat. **Food served** all day. Closed first three weeks in Aug. **Plat du jour** €18. **No credit cards. Map** K5.

Everything about this 'micro-bistro' is quaint, from the wooden chests and painted windows to its caricature of a French chef in the tiny corner kitchen. Tartines (made on pain Poilâne of course), commendable house frites and a stand-out plat du jour enliven the menu of standard bistro food. The coffee is good and the waiters friendly, making this an especially good stop off after the Centre Pompidou. The only downside to its micro-ness is your proximity to neighbouring tables – bad news for those who don't like to ingest smoke with their food. One customer's objection to the no-credit-cards policy required a visit from the gendarmes, but the professional staff retained their calm throughout.

Les Philosophes

28 rue Vieille du Temple, 4th (01.48.87.49.64/ www.cafeine.com). M° Hôtel de Ville. **Open** 9am-2am daily. **Food served** noon-1am. **Plat du jour** €17. **Credit** MC, V. **Map** K6.

Smack in the centre of the Marais, Les Philosophes does a booming business morning, noon and night. It's part bistro (turning out succulent honey-pepper confit de canard and heaving slices of the deepest amber tarte Tatin, though the salads can be uneven) and part philosophical pretension. Each of the two all-steel loos has a one-way window (at least we hoped it was one-way) looking on to a bookshelf filled with posey titles, while judiciously placed inspirational slogans encourage you to linger longer.

On the Town

Le Comptoir du Panthéon

5TH ARRONDISSEMENT

Café Delmas

2-4 pl de la Contrescarpe, 5th (01.43.26.51.26).
M° Place Monge. **Open** 8am-2am Mon-Thur, Sun;
8am-4am Fri, Sat. **Food served** 11.30am-11.30pm
daily. **Plat du jour** €13. **Credit** DC, MC, V. **Non-smoking room. Map** J8.

Place de la Contrescarpe was one of Hemingway's
numerous stomping grounds and it still retains
an alcoholic theme with two prominent cafés
dominating either side of the square. One, Café
Delmas, has gone decidedly upmarket, and is now
shoulder-to-shoulder perma-tanned style gurus and
Gucci-clad fashionistas. When darkness descends,
things become a little less civilised as students and
tourists stumble out of nearby kebab joints.

Le Comptoir du Panthéon ★

5 rue Soufflot, 5th (01.43.54.75.36/www.comptoir
dupantheon.com). **Open** 7am-1am
Mon-Sat; 9am-7pm Sun. **Food served** 11.30am-1am
daily. **Plat du jour** €10. **Credit** MC, V. **Non-smoking room. Map** J8.

You can't go wrong with this terrace view of the
majestic Panthéon. Take a seat and contemplate the
monumental buildings along the wide avenue. There
is no prix-fixe menu, but à la carte fare is attractively
priced. The kitchen gets creative with tandoori
Caesar salad and wok chicken. Delicious escargots
are buttery and well-seasoned, while onion soup
comes with a browned crust of melted gruyère.
At night, a diverse crowd gathers in an interior
highlighted by dark purple curtains.

La Contrescarpe

57 rue Lacépède, 5th (01 43 36 82 88). **M° Cardinal**
Lemoine. **Open** 7am-2am daily. **Food served** all
day. **Plat du jour** €12. **Credit** MC. **Non-smoking**
room. Wheelchair access. Map J8.

Chocolate lovers will adore this place. A €7.50 drink
and dessert menu from 3-6pm allows you to tuck
into such indulgent choices as chocolat viennois and
fondant au chocolat. Enjoy your confections on the
comfortable terrace on pedestrian place de la
Contrescarpe (or the hidden interior courtyard), or
settle into an upholstered chair for indoor reading.
Shelves of books, lamps, and low coffee-house tables
invite you to stay for hours. Should you require
sustenance, order a two-course menu for €14, or a
plat du jour, such as salmon fillet or baked chicken
with mushrooms. Students take advantage of the
6-8pm happy hour.

Les Pipos

2 rue de l'Ecole-Polytechnique, 5th (01.43.54.11.40).
M° Maubert-Mutualité. **Open** 8am-2am Mon-Sat.
Food served 11.45am-11pm. **Plat du jour** €12.
No credit cards. Map J8.

It's impossible not to like this ancient, cramped café
with its cracked-tile floor, wooden tables and
polished zinc bar – no decorator has come near here
in decades, if not centuries, and that's as it should
be. So endearing is the setting that we were even able
to forgive the waiter for ignoring us as we waved
our arms in a desperate attempt to attract his
attention – when a regular pointed us out, he calmly
replied, 'yes, I've seen them' – then serving us bone-dry Poilâne bread with our (albeit generous) plate of
saucisson. The drinkable Beaujolais Nouveau lifted
our spirits, as did a glass of Menetou-Salon. Come
for the atmosphere, not the service.

Le Reflet

6 rue Champollion, 5th (01.43.29.97.27). **M° Cluny-**
La Sorbonne. **Open** 11am-2am daily. **Food served**
11am-11pm. **Plat du jour** €6. **Credit** AmEx, DC,
MC, V. **Map** J7.

Black walls, stage lighting and prints from classic
Italian flicks reflect this café's location opposite the
excellent Reflet Médicis cinema. Sip your beer or hot
chocolate (avoid the badly made coffee) under the
eye of a young Orson Welles, along with elderly
couples waiting to see their favourite Jean Gabin film
and brooding loners at the bar doing their best to
look cinematic as they add to the pile of cigarette ash
at their feet. On our visit the window table drew a
series of kissing couples seemingly inspired by
cinematic romance; those who want to try the
sandwiches or confit de canard might prefer the
back section. Bad music played loudly ruined the
atmosphere; if only they'd stick to film soundtracks.

Tabac de la Sorbonne

7 pl de la Sorbonne, 5th (01.43.54.52.04). **M° Cluny-**
La Sorbonne or RER Luxembourg. **Open** 6.30am-
2am daily Apr-Oct; 6.30am-10pm daily Nov-Mar.
Food served all day. **Plat du jour** €8.40. **No**
credit cards. Wheelchair access. Map H7.

This reassuringly unfashionable café is positively
Melville-esque, from the orange banquettes and
movie-set telephone cabin to the moustachioed
waiter with a long white apron and, not surprisingly,

On the Town

a smoker's cough. The outside terrace draws the populace in summer while the glassed-in winter terrace doubles as a fumoir for smokers too serious to direct their ash to the ashtray. The inside tabac satisfies the cravings of the local student crowd and the adjoining bar serves up a range of standard cocktails, wines and sensibly priced hot food, including croques, salads, meat-frites combinations and house desserts. Good coffee too.

Le Verre à Pied

118 bis rue Mouffetard, 5th (01.43.31.15.72). *M° Censier-Daubenton.* **Open** 9am-8.30pm Tue-Sat; 9am-3pm Sun. **Food served** noon-2.30pm. Closed two weeks in Aug. **Plat du jour** €9. **No credit cards. Map** J9.

When Amélie Poulain retreated here for a steadying Cognac she brought new fame to this slice of old working-class Paris. Le Verre, literally at the pied (foot) of the rue Mouffetard, is easy to miss amid the bustle of the market, and perhaps the owners prefer it that way. The tobacconist, narrow bar area and tiny lunch room at the back draw in market workers during the week and, on Sundays, the after-church crowd from St-Médard. Assiettes and sandwiches are inexpensive, the plat du jour is written on a serviette stuck on the mirror behind the bar and a small pichet of merlot goes for €2.80.

6TH ARRONDISSEMENT

Bar du Marché

75 rue de Seine, 6th (01.43.26.55.15). M° Odéon. **Open** 7.30am-2am daily. **Food served** 7.30am-6pm. **Plat du jour** €10. **Credit** AmEx, DC, MC, V. **Wheelchair access. Map** H7.

Locals prefer the sunny terrace here, but the cheery inside is equally fun with its increased potential for watching the tartan-capped, slightly offbeat staff. Our waiter, something of a performer, yelled 'J'arrive' at least five times before doing so, and regularly told customers to shut up, reducing two girls nearby to singing for their coffee. An expertly cooked omelette and generous assiette végétarienne were to standard and reasonably priced, although food here could in general do with some of the waiter's flair. Wines were less than inspiring, so if your drinks order is refused it's not the end of the world.

Café de Flore

172 bd St-Germain, 6th (01.45.48.55.26/www.cafe-de-flore.com). M° St-Germain-des-Prés. **Open** 7.30am-1.30am daily. **Food served** all day. **Plat du jour** €18. **Credit** AmEx, MC, V. **Map** H7.

Bourgeois locals crowd the terrace tables at lunch, eating club sandwiches with knives and forks, while anxious waiters frown upon couples with pushchairs or single diners occupying tables for four. This historic café, once the HQ of the Lost Generation intelligentsia, also attracts plenty of tourists who eye passers-by hopefully. And, yes, celebs have been known to alight here from time to time (recent sighting: Jude Law). But a café crème is

€4.60, a Perrier will set you back €5, and the omelettes and croque monsieurs are shockingly poor (the better dishes on the menu range from €15-€25). Play readings are held every Monday night and philosophy discussions on the first Wednesday of the month, both at 8pm, upstairs, in English.

Café de la Mairie

8 pl St-Sulpice, 6th (01.43.26.67.82). M° St-Sulpice. **Open** 7am-2am Mon-Fri; 8am-10pm Sat; 9am-9pm Sun. **Food served** all day. **Plat du jour** €15. **No credit cards. Non-smoking room. Map** G7.

This Left Bank institution is good for people-watching and, as such, was the base for part one of Georges Perec's *Tentative d'Épuisement d'un Lieu Parisien* (1975). The interior is now a bit grimy, and although it's still packed on chilly weekends, it's best to wait until the weather is warm enough for the terrace where you can sit under the watchful eye of Fenelon and Bossuet carved into the monstrous fountain. Coffee is good and served in old-fashioned floral china, while a range of assiettes provide a perfect accompaniment to the beer.

Les Deux Magots

6 pl St-Germain-des-Prés, 6th (01.45.48.55.25/www.lesdeuxmagots.com). M° St-Germain-des-Prés. **Open** 7.30am-1am daily. **Food served** all day. Closed one week in Jan. **Plat du jour** €20. **Credit** AmEx, DC, MC, V. **Wheelchair access. Map** H7.

Stand outside Les Deux Magots too long and be prepared to photograph visitors wanting proof of their encounter with 'French philosophy'. This former haunt of Sartre, de Beauvoir et al now draws a less pensive crowd that can be all too 'm'as-tu vu', particularly on weekends when staff pack the Anglo and Anglophile hordes into the terrace. The hot chocolate is still good (and seemingly the only item served in generous portions), but like everything else, it's overpriced. Best to visit on a weekday afternoon when the editors return, manuscripts in hand, to the inside tables, leaving enough elbow room to engage in some serious discussion.

Les Editeurs

4 carrefour de l'Odéon, 6th (01.43.26.67.76/ www.lesediteurs.fr). M° Odéon. **Open** 8am-2am daily. **Food served** noon-2am. **Plat du jour** €30. **Credit** AmEx, MC, V. **Non-smoking room. Map** H7.

Of the three café terraces on the carrefour, Les Editeurs is the most chic, attracting low-key celebs such as chansonnier Benjamin Biolay to sip an aperitif and watch the world go by. You don't need to be feeling sociable; the shelves are stacked with books from nearby publishers. Should hunger strike, order some choucroute or lighter dishes such as a club sandwich or roast cod.

Le Nemrod ★

51 rue du Cherche-Midi, 6th (01.45.48.17.05). M° Sèvres-Babylone. **Open** 6am-11pm Mon-Sat. **Food served** noon-3pm, 7-11pm Mon-Fri; noon-4pm, 7-11pm Sat. Closed two weeks in Aug. **Plat du jour** €14. **Credit** MC, V. **Map** G7.

With a big sunny terrace, saucy waiters, and a bargain prix-fixe at dinner, this café-bistro is one of the most popular places on the Left Bank, so come early to snag a table. The owner is rightly proud of his excellent wines, including a delicious Morgon Vieilles Vignes, and the salads are fresh, gargantuan and generously garnished. Our favourite is the Auvergnat, with country ham, cheese, tomatoes and walnuts, but they do a variety of other versions, all of which are good.

La Palette

43 rue de Seine, 6th (01.43.26.68.15). M° St-Germain-des-Prés. **Open** 9am-2am Mon-Sat. **Food served** noon-3.30pm Mon-Sat. Closed Aug. **Plat du jour** €12. **Credit** MC, V. **Non-smoking room**. **Map** H7.

Located behind the Ecole des Beaux-Arts and on a street lined with private galleries, La Palette unsurprisingly numbers quite a few gallery owners or frequenters among its clientele. The atmosphere on the large, popular terrace is slightly reserved during the day. At night, however, things can get downright wild. Service can be occasionally surly.

Au Petit Suisse

16 rue de Vaugirard, 6th (01.43.26.03.81). M° Odéon. **Open** 7am-midnight Mon-Sat; 7am-10.30pm Sun. **Food served** noon-midnight Mon-Sat; noon-10.30pm Sun. Closed Aug. **Plat du jour** €11. **Credit** DC, MC, V. **Map** H7.

Named after Marie de Médicis' Swiss guards, the compact Au Petit Suisse has an enviable location next to the Jardins du Luxembourg and so pulls in a range of posh locals, au pairs escaping from their charges and garret-room, and Gauloise-puffing Sorbonne students. The formal waiters excel in French snottiness, but it makes this place all the more authentic and tourist-free. Brave the haughty stares for one of the few tables, order a kir with a side of sneer and lap up a genuine 6th-district café experience.

Le Rostand ★

6 pl Edmond-Rostand, 6th (01.43.54.61.58). RER Luxembourg. **Open** 8am-2am daily. **Food served** noon-3pm daily. **Plat du jour** €13. **Credit** MC, V. **Non-smoking room**. **Map** H6.

Le Rostand has a truly wonderful view of the Jardins du Luxembourg from its classy interior, decked out with oriental paintings, a long mahogany bar and wall-length mirrors. It's a terribly well-behaved place and you should definitely consider arriving in fur or designer sunglasses if you want to fit in with the well-heeled regulars. The drinks list is lined with whiskies and cocktails, pricey but not as steep as the brasserie menu. Still, with a heated terrace in winter, it's perfect for a civilised drink after a quick spin round the gardens.

Le Select

99 bd de Montparnasse, 6th (01.42.22.65.27). M° Vavin. **Open** 7am-2am Mon-Thur, Sun; 7am-4.30am Fri, Sat. **Food served** noon-1am. **Plat du jour** €16. **Credit** MC, V. **Map** G9.

For a decade between the wars, the junction of boulevards Raspail and Montparnasse was the centre of the known universe. Man Ray, Cocteau and Lost Generation Americans hung out at its vast glass-fronted cafés (Le Dôme, La Coupole), socialising, snubbing and snogging. Eighty years on, Le Select is the best of these inevitable tourist traps. Sure, its overpriced menu is big on historical detail, short on authenticity ('cockney brunch' of eggs, bacon and jam at €15), but generally Le Select holds on to its Man Ray heyday with dignity. Intello locals hang out at the bar, spreading out the highbrow cultural section while Mickey the house cat wanders over the newsprint. Happy hour from 7pm makes history affordable, the cocktail and whisky list is extensive, and Mickey is honoured with a prominent framed portrait.

Au Vieux Colombier

65 rue de Rennes, 6th (01.45.48.53.81). M° St-Sulpice. **Open** 8am-11pm Mon-Sat; 11am-5pm Sun. **Food served** noon-10.30pm Mon-Sat; noon-5pm Sun. **Plat du jour** €10. **Credit** MC, V. **Map** G7.

Nostalgic souls yearning for a taste of St-Germain before it became a glorified high street will be charmed by the faded elegance of this art nouveau-style café. Basking in the soft glow of the diamond-shaped chandeliers, we whiled away a lazy Saturday morning nursing a petit crème and watching an entertaining mix of locals buzz in and out. Behind the authentic curved zinc bar was a waiter who should be up for sainthood, as he didn't even bat an eyelid when the little boy and puppy we had in tow got up to some unholy rough-housing. A miracle by Paris standards.

7TH ARRONDISSEMENT

Bar Basile ★

34 rue de Grenelle, 7th (01.42.22.59.46). M° Rue du Bac or Sèvres-Babylone. **Open** 7am-9pm Mon-Sat. **Food served** noon-3.30pm. Closed two weeks in Aug. **Plat du jour** €10. **Credit** MC, V. **Map** G7.

Bar Basile has just undergone a lengthy renovation, but it's a case of 'plus ça change, plus c'est la même

La Frégate. *See p223.*

Granterroirs. See p225.

chose'. Retro '70s-style decor of bold colours and Formica tables is the backdrop for serious-looking political science students from neighbouring Sciences-Po to engage in erudite repartee or peruse the house copies of *Le Monde Diplomatique*, while nonchalant waiters float around the café, dispensing to the student populace words of wisdom hewn from the université of life. Things get more hectic at lunchtime as students and their professors sit at banquettes and tables to refuel on salads, club sandwiches, and more substantial plats du jour.

Café Le Dôme

149 rue St Dominique, 7th (01.45.51.45.41). RER Pont de l'Alma. **Open** 7am-2am daily. **Food served** all day. **Plat du jour** €11. **Credit** MC, V. **Map** D6.
With its terrace-side view of the Eiffel Tower, silly illustrated multilingual menus, postcards and overpriced drinks (€4.90 for a tiny bottle of water? You must be joking!), Le Dôme is definitely a tourist trap, but a rather benign one. The decor has a nice feel and the food is straightforward. Juicy burgers, big salads and fluffy crêpes for afters are right on the money for famished sightseers. Le Dôme is also great for kiddies: the children's menu is so generous it verges on the obscene, and the tykes can run riot without fear of being told off by the super-chirpy staff (must be something in that pricey water).

Café des Lettres

53 rue de Verneuil, 7th (01.42.22.52.17/www. cafedeslettres.com). M° Rue du Bac. **Open** 9am-midnight Mon-Sat; noon-4pm Sun. **Food served** noon-4pm, 7-10pm Mon-Sat; brunch noon-4pm Sun. Closed two weeks at Christmas. **Plat du jour** €14. **Credit** MC, V. **Map** G6.
Café des Lettres has a moody feel, with dark furniture, deep turquoise- and maroon-coloured walls, deeply meaningful abstract art and a heavy Gauloise-pervaded atmosphere. There may even be the odd brooding intellectual as the salon is used

by the neighbouring Maison des Ecrivains for literary discussions and novel-reading sessions. Contrastingly airy, the courtyard is a good place to drop in on for an expresso on a summer's afternoon. Food can be of disappointing quality for the price, which reflects the swish location.

Le Café du Marché

38 rue Cler, 7th (01.47.05.51.27). M° Ecole-Militaire. **Open** 7am-midnight Mon-Sat; 7am-5pm Sun. **Food served** 11.30am-11pm Mon-Sat; 11.30am-3.30pm Sun. **Plat du jour** €10. **Credit** MC, V. **Map** D6.
For an in-the-action location amid the 7th's most lively market street, you can't do much better than Le Café du Marché, which serves as a hub of neighbourhood activity but is equally comfortable welcoming tourists and the curious. Dozens of tables are spread among interior dining rooms, a canopy and plastic-covered area plus an open-air terrace, so you have your choice of seating depending on the sun-cloud-rain continuum. Big salads at €9.50 and classic French main dishes at €10 (confit de canard, poulet rôti, entrecôte) are bargains, though quality varies depending on the dish (a fish special was fine, but pasta with a mix of both red and green pesto sauces was uneventful). Service had been friendly in the past, but was indifferent on our latest visit.

La Frégate

1 rue du Bac, 7th (01.42.61.23.77). M° Rue du Bac. **Open** 7am-midnight Mon-Fri; 8am-midnight Sat, Sun. **Food served** 11.30am-11pm daily. **Plat du jour** €14.50. **Credit** AmEx, MC, V. **Map** G6.
Slotted between the Musée d'Orsay and the Louvre, this is an ideal pit stop for Paris visitors with a fondness for kitsch. Frégate is the French for a frigate, and here the nautical theme is played to the hilt: the dining room is straight out of the movie *Titanic*, tiny anchors are engraved on the metallic tables and fish dominates the menu. And there's no denying that La Frégate's owner runs a very

Le Réveil du 10ème.
See p227.

tight ship as the waiters are lightning-quick (despite being near geriatrics). Unfortunately, rather than overlooking the big blue sea, the terrace gives on to a very noisy embankment.

Le Roussillon

186 rue de Grenelle, 7th (01.45.51.47.53). M° La Tour-Maubourg. **Open** 6.30am-2am Mon-Sat. 6.30am-4pm Sun. Closed 25 Dec, 1 Jan. **Plat du jour** €10.50. **Credit** MC, V. **Wheelchair access**. **Map** D6.

This schizo little café is nestled beside the rue Cler market. In the morning it's the favoured haunt of grey-suited politicians hashing out their day over brekkie (€7-€8.50). Come noon they give way to a more colourful fauna – botoxed ladies who lunch, feverishly trading gossip as they tuck into opulent salads. The nights belong to the trustafarians from the nearby American University of Paris, who come in to have a little boogie and study the cocktail list more assiduously than they do for their finals. The potent potions are served up by bartenders as pretty as they are rude – and boy are they ever pretty.

Le Tourville

1 pl de L' Ecole Militaire, 7th (01.44.18.05.08). M° Ecole Militaire. **Open** 7am-2am daily. **Food served** all day. **Plat du jour** €12. **Credit** MC, V. **Non-smoking room**. **Map** D6.

This is the snoozerific 7th arrondissement's latest stab at a swank venue. With its spacious terrace, intimate but dramatic decor, super-swift service and extensive menu offering everything from an old-fashioned Brown Bomber cocktail to a lip-smackingly good Oreo milkshake, Le Tourville does its best to impress. Yet, instead of being the bustling hub of trendiness, the bar stands half empty even on a Saturday night. Its clientele is primarily made up of rich boys in velour jackets, posing for an invisible audience. The Tourville experience appears to prove that the 7th remains impervious to even the most valiant attempts to loosen it up a little.

Le Varenne ★

36 rue de Varenne, 7th (01.45.48.62.72). M° Rue du Bac. **Open** 7am-8pm Mon-Wed, Sat, Sun; 7am-11pm Thur. **Food served** noon-3pm daily. Closed two weeks in Feb and Aug. **Plat du jour** €15. **Credit** MC, V. **Map** G6.

The trek down rue de Varenne could be dubbed the 'walk of death', as the endless parade of grey, identical government buildings could sap the will to live in even the sunniest soul. Coming across a place as welcoming as Le Varenne on this bleak stretch is akin to finding an oasis in the Sahara. The couple behind this miracle are Caroline and Francis Tafanel, sticklers for first-rate ingredients from the best local suppliers. So just sit back and watch the be-suited civil servants come alive in the warm surroundings as they dig into the scrumptious offerings from the daily-changing blackboard menu.

8TH ARRONDISSEMENT

Atelier Renault ★

53 av des Champs-Elysées, 8th (01.49.53.70.00/ www.atelier-renault.com). M° Franklin D Roosevelt. **Open** 10.30am-2am daily. **Food served** noon-12.30am. **Plat du jour** €18.50. **Credit** AmEx, DC, MC, V. **Credit** MC, V. **Map** E4.

A futuristic and funky mix of aluminium, wood and glass awaits upstairs at the Atelier Renault. There's a bar on the mezzanine with stools thoughtfully curved in the shape of your bottom, or better yet, see if you can nab a table on one of the five walkways with a view of the showroom or the Champs-Elysées below. Even late on a Sunday evening, this place was buzzing with a diverse mix of people, all checking each other out over a cocktail (€8) or a coffee. If you're hungry there's a good range of contemporary cuisine such as wok-sautéed pasta or Caesar-style chicken breast salad, or you might just like to go for one of their delectable ice-cream sundaes.

Bar des Théâtres

6 av Montaigne, 8th (01.47.23.34.63). M° Alma-Marceau. **Open** 6am-2am daily. **Food served** all day. **Plat du jour** €15. **Credit** AmEx, MC, V. **Map** D5.

Nestling between Valentino and Emanuel Ungaro, bang opposite the Théâtre des Champs-Elysées, this popular bar/café is always buzzing in the evenings after the curtain falls, and attracts a steady daytime stream of trendy fashionistas. Yet Bar des Théâtres couldn't be less pretentious. Its cosy, informal atmosphere and service are reflected in the simple, though pricey, brasserie-style fare served in the café area or the slightly more formal restaurant section.

Granterroirs ★

30 rue de Miromesnil, 8th (01.47.42.18.18/www.granterroirs.com). M° Miromesnil. **Open** 9am-8pm Mon-Fri. **Food served** noon-3pm. Closed three weeks in Aug. **Plat du jour** €16.50. **Credit** MC, V. **Wheelchair access. Non-smoking room. Map** F3.

A little bit of countryside in the heart of Paris, this gourmet delicatessen dedicated to French regional produce doubles up as a café, serving lunch only to a mostly business crowd who return time and time again for food, wine and service of the highest quality. The whole place exudes rustic charm from the stacks of bottles, jars and tins of mouthwatering goodies for sale lining the walls to the fabulous centrepiece of the back dining area – a giant picnic table. We tried the 'assiette italienne', a magnificent feast of cured ham, sundried tomatoes, marinated artichoke, aubergine, mushrooms, parmesan shavings and a generous side salad. Our dessert, a pear tarte Tatin, was equally impressive.

Le Petit Bergson

10 pl Henri-Bergson, 8th (01.45.22.63.25). M° St-Augustin or St-Lazare. **Open** 11am-3pm Mon-Fri. **Food served** all day. Closed two weeks in Aug. **Plat du jour** €11. **Credit** MC, V. **Map** F3.

Le Petit Bergson's main selling point is its fabulous location – on the corner of one of the prettiest squares in Paris, with a view over a small park and the back of the St-Augustin church. At lunch the terrace is packed with local office workers enjoying a selection of set-price menus, which start at €11. A free fruit juice or kir might be offered if you have to wait for a table, and the service is friendly. The food is mainly salads, quiches and pies, plus a few hot dishes. The jovial owner bustles in and out but your bill might not arrive promptly because he keeps stopping to have a drink with his mates at the bar.

9TH ARRONDISSEMENT

Café Gallery

78 rue de Provence, 9th (01.48.74.55.63). M° Chaussée d'Antin. **Open** 9.30am-9pm Mon-Sat (daily in Dec). **Food served** all day. **Plat du jour** €11. **Credit** MC, V. **Non-smoking room. Map** G3.

If you are looking for peace and tranquillity after a busy morning of shopping, you may be disappointed as lunchtime in the Café Gallery (a stone's throw from Galeries Lafayette) is a smoky, hectic affair with waiters barely able to stand still for one minute while you place your order (warning: any hesitation in the ordering process will result in your waiter leaving you in mid-sentence only to return after hurriedly delivering someone else's lunch). That said, the snazzy brown-and-cream decor (featuring some rather eye-catching lamps) and the bustling mix of locals and tourists do make this a better alternative to the numerous sandwich and fast-food vendors in the area, especially once the lunch crowd has thinned.

Café de la Paix ★

12 bd des Capucines, 9th (01.40.07.36.36). M° Opéra. **Open** 7.30am-12.30am daily. **Food served** 7.30am-11am (terrace only), noon-3pm, 6pm-midnight. **Plat du jour** €39. **Credit** AmEx, DC, MC, V. **Wheelchair access. Non-smoking room. Map** G4.

Reopened after a 15-month restoration to resurrect its Napoleon III past, this café has a clientele list that reads like a veritable who's who – everyone from Maupassant to Zola, Oscar Wilde to Caruso, Josephine Baker to John Travolta. If you're on the way to or from the glittering Palais Garnier, treat yourself right and stop for a kir (or why not Champagne) on the glassed-in terrace abutting the opulent celestial-ceiling dining room. You can dress up, or you can wander in from your Saturday shopping spree on boulevard Haussmann and rejuvenate with an incredible ice-cream sundae, such as the house 'coupe' made with vanilla, hazelnuts, coconut, chocolate mousse, meringue and whipped cream. There's a separate bar scattered with red velvet couches under a huge glass atrium. Touristy and expensive, but fun.

P'tit Creux du Faubourg

66 rue du Fbg-Montmartre, 9th (01.48.78.20.57). M° Notre-Dame-de-Lorette. **Open** 8am-8pm Mon-Sat. **Food served** all day. Closed mid-July to mid-Aug. **Plat du jour** €9. **Credit** MC, V. **Map** H3.

This modest little café is a great place to drop by if you're in the area and fancy a good-value, good-quality lunch. When we last visited our salade composée was just right – a hearty mix of crunchy fresh lettuce, waxy new potatoes, eggs, emmental and tender ham all sprinkled with a delicious mustardy dressing. Ravioli stuffed with salmon and spinach and served in a rich creamy sauce was nothing short of a revelation – the meaty pink fish flesh bursting out of the large pasta squares. With a jovial, croaky-throated patron to match its homely setting, this café is an unbeatable pit stop for locals and passers-by alike.

Rose Bakery ★

46 rue des Martyrs, 9th (01.42.82.12.80). M° Notre-Dame-de-Lorette. **Open** 9am-7pm Tue-Sat, 10am-5pm Sun. **Food served** all day. Closed two weeks in Aug. **Plat du jour** €13. **Credit** MC, V. **Wheelchair access. No smoking. Map** H3.

Rose Bakery has a knack for making even the humble grated-carrot salad look incredibly appetising. This English-themed café run by a Franco-British couple stands out for the quality of its ingredients – organic or from small producers – and too-good-to-be-true puddings, such as carrot cake, sticky toffee pudding, and in winter an enormous chocolate-chestnut tart. The compose-your-own salad plate is crunchily satisfying, but the thin-crusted pizzettes, daily soups and occasional risottos are equally good choices – don't expect much beyond scones, though, in the morning. Popular with health-conscious locals (smoking is strongly discouraged) and expats who can't believe their luck, the dining room – which looks as if it might have once been a garage – is minimalist but welcoming. Service is friendly enough.

The World Bar

Level 5, Printemps de l'Homme, 64 bd Haussmann, 9th (01.42.82.78.02). M° Havre-Caumartin. **Open** 11.30am-10pm Mon-Wed, Sat, Sun; 9.30am-10pm Thur. **Food served** noon-3pm. **Plat du jour** €15. **Credit** AmEx, DC, MC, V. **Map** G3.

This Paul Smith-designed café provides a suitable setting for fashion-conscious shoppers to take stock of their latest acquisitions. Breezeblock walls are plastered with yellowing newspapers dating from Paul Smith's birth and a velvet Union Jack hangs decadently above the bar as house music pulses around the room. Food, provided by the ubiquitous Flo Group, is a continental version of modern pub grub that mixes French standards such as confit de canard with favourites from abroad that include spring rolls and nachos.

10TH ARRONDISSEMENT

Balbuzard Café

54 rue René-Boulanger, 10th (01.42.08.60.20). M° République. **Open** 10am-midnight Mon-Thur; 10am-2am Fri-Sun. **Food served** 11.30am-3pm, 7pm-midnight. **Plat du jour** €8. **Credit** MC, V. **Non-smoking room. Map** K4.

Popular with ambitious young things working in television production, publishing or music, this happening café is a bona fide neighbourhood hangout – as opposed to the bogus spots that have popped up to cash in on the 10th's growing cool – where a laidback vibe prevails. It's easy to while away an evening here over great Corsican wine and charcuterie with friends. Sometimes on the weekends there's more action, when a changing crew of DJs spin house to create a club mood.

Chez Prune ★

71 quai de Valmy, 10th (01.42.41.30.47). M° République. **Open** 8am-2am Mon-Sat; 10am-2am Sun. **Food served** noon-3pm; snacks 7-11pm. Closed one week at Christmas. **Plat du jour** €11. **Credit** MC, V. **Map** L4.

A gem of a café situated on the Canal St-Martin, this is the sort of place you come to for a quick coffee and

then accidentally end up staying for five hours. The slightly battered-looking interior of this oh-so-laid-back neighbourhood haunt plays host to all of the cool, young things living in the area, their comings and goings providing non-stop entertainment. For something to nibble on, try one of the assiettes such as the 'trois couleurs', a plate of houmous, olive tapenade, taramasalata and a selection of bread, or the crudités with cream cheese.

Chez Sésame

51 quai de Valmy, 10th (01.42.49.03.21). M° République. **Open** 11am-7pm Mon-Fri; 10am-8pm Sat, Sun. **Food served** all day. **Plat du jour** €10. **Credit** MC, V. **Non-smoking room. Map** L4.

We tried to like Sésame. Really we did. With its banquettes, huge windows overlooking the Canal St-Martin, and heavenly fruit smoothies it should have been the ideal location for Sunday brunch. Only the presence of not one, but two French film stars seemed to have turned the waiter's head. Lesser mortals had to wait…and wait…and wait…before finally receiving some very rude service followed by some very mediocre food in the form of a sub-standard panino and miserly tartines. The huge mugs of tea and tall lattes looked good; too bad we were never granted the chance to try them.

La Chope des Artistes

48 rue du Fbg-St-Martin, 10th (01.42.02.86.76). M° Château d'Eau. **Open** 6pm-4am Tue-Sat. **Food served** 7.30pm-midnight. **Plat du jour** €15. **Credit** MC, V. **Map** K3.

Arriving inside this candlelit café at 10.30pm we were disappointed that the only other customer was a dishevelled-looking gent nursing a solitary glass of red wine. Fifteen minutes later however, we were squeezing up to make space for the lively crowd flocking in from the neighbouring Théâtre Splendid. Discussion of the evening's performance buzzed around both the mirror-lined walls of the front bar and the cosy back dining room. But the biggest round of applause was saved for the much-maligned 'gent' who sprang into life at 11.30pm, knocking out a succession of big show numbers on the bar's upright piano.

Le Jemmapes

82 quai de Jemmapes, 10th (01.40.40.02.35). M° Jacques Bonsergent or République. **Open** 11am-1.30am daily. **Food served** noon-3pm, 8-11pm daily. **No credit cards. Map** L4.

This destination canalside café provides as good a reason as any for many to join the lazy throng along the St-Martin embankment. In fine weather, this leads to a bottleneck of contented couples mini-picnicking on the waterfront, others brunching on the narrow bar terrace, where weekend tables are at a premium. Inside is small and arty, but not so much it puts you off, not with Chimay Bleue and Duval available anyway. Flavoured vodkas are another speciality – there's a slight Polish touch to the extensive lunchtime menu – but location is the

---

deciding factor here. Come in the week for a more boho crowd than the somewhat self-satisfied contingent of bric-a-brac browsers.

Le Petit Château d'Eau
34 rue du Château d'Eau, 10th (01.42.08.72.81). M° Château-d'Eau or Jacques Bonsergent. **Open** 9am-11pm Mon-Fri. **Food served** noon-3pm. Closed Aug. **Plat du jour** €10.50. **Credit** MC, V. **Map** L4.
A gem of a café on a grim street, this place oozes relaxed, classy charm. The high-ceilinged main room is stacked with flowers and dominated by a large circular bar around which regulars perch to knock back cheap glasses of Beaujolais and Bordeaux. It's the perfect spot for a lunchtime omelette or an early-evening demi, and a good place for meeting friendly locals.

Le Réveil du 10ème ★
35 rue du Château-d'Eau, 10th (01.42.41.77.59). M° Château-d'Eau or Jacques Bonsergent. **Open** 7am-8.30pm Mon-Sat. **Food served** noon-3pm Mon-Wed, Fri, Sat; noon-3pm, 7.30-9.30pm Thur. **Plat du jour** €11.50. **Credit** MC, V. **Map** K4.
The perfect old-fashioned Parisian lunch? This snug corner café-cum-bistro à vins decorated with faded photos chronicling the place's history has tables packed with regulars, including the couple in the corner who've been coming once a week for the past 50 years. Mouthwatering portions of meaty food (chunky saucisse d'Auvergne, juicy rib steak, crispy confit de canard) are quickly delivered by the attentive staff and cheese and dessert boards are irresistible. It's all washed down with an extensive wine list that specialises in thirst-quenching Beaujolais. Yes, in a word, perfect.

Le Sporting
3 rue des Récollets, 10th (01.46.07.02.00). M° Gare de l'Est. **Open** noon-1am daily. **Food served** noon-2.30pm, 7-10.30pm daily. Closed 24, 25 Dec, 1 Jan. **Plat du jour** €15.50. **Credit** MC, V. **Map** L3.

Le Sporting is a little bit more grown-up than most of the cafés along the Canal St-Martin: the dining room carries its elegant trimmings of chandeliers, colonial-style plants and chocolate banquettes with real style. The best time to come here is Sunday afternoon, when lunch and brunch are served until 4pm and diners can boozily stretch out the length of their meals. Quality ingredients and cooking produce dishes such as a delicious melon and coppa salad, fried king prawns with Thai basil, and mushroom and scorpion fish risotto. Brunch looks tempting, too.

11TH ARRONDISSEMENT

Ba'ta'clan Café
50 bd Voltaire, 11th (01.49.23.96.33/www.bataclan cafe.com). M° Oberkampf. **Open** 7am-2am daily. **Food served** 9am-1am. Closed 24 Dec. **Plat du jour** €13. **Credit** MC, V. **Wheelchair access**. **Map** M5.
Being annexed to the concert venue of the same name, this café often gets late consignments of excitable music fans cooling off after a gig. For the rest of the time, it looks and feels like a drowsy colonial hideout. Dominated by a gorgeous circular bar and pagoda-style columns (part of an old theatre), this is a good place for a chat among friends, settled on dog eared leather sofas or wicker chairs. Food options are limited mainly to pasta and croques but it's useful as a late-night hunger option. Mystic evenings are held on Mondays, salsa nights on Sundays and the Sunday brunch with classical music is popular. The prices seem in proportion with the very high ceiling, and be warned there are ticket touts outside trying to rip you off.

Le Bistrot du Peintre ★
116 av Ledru-Rollin, 11th (01.47.00.34.39). M° Ledru-Rollin. **Open** 7am-2am Mon-Sat; 10am-2am Sun. **Food served** noon-midnight daily. Closed 24, 25 Dec. **Plat du jour** €12. **Credit** MC, V. **Map** N7.

Le Bistrot du Peintre.

The Pause Café across the street gets more hype, but if you love cafés Le Bistrot du Peintre is the real classic in this area. Not only is the 1907 art nouveau interior a gem, but the food is unusually good for a café, if a little inconsistent (the plats du jour and meatier dishes such as confit de canard are usually reliable bets, and the salads are good too). The upstairs dining room, though less historic, is appealing in its own way with a more spacious feel (that's relative here) and view of the plane trees outside. The noisy terrace doesn't get much sun, but wherever you sit this café has undeniable romance.

Café de l'Industrie

16/17 rue St-Sabin, 11th (01.47.00.13.53).
M° Bastille. **Open** 10am-2am daily. **Food served** noon-1am. **Plat du jour** €10. **Credit** DC, MC, V. **Non-smoking room**. **Map** M6.
This popular hang-out of the turtleneck and thick-rimmed eyeglasses crowd has engulfed a former Moroccan restaurant across the street, bringing its total seating capacity to 350 and adding frequent jazz concerts. But the flea-market-chic decor remains the same in both locales, an exceptionally pleasing combination of vintage furniture and eclectic paintings. Food is reasonably priced (most mains €10-€12) and fast, but the quality is hit or miss: a salmon tartare with tagliatelli was tenderly divine, but a plate of dull and gloopy gorgonzola pasta disappointed. We love the industrial-themed steel saucers and holders for the clear glass coffee cups. Quiet in the off-hours between meals, at lunch and late nights the place is positively buzzing.

Extra Old Café

307 rue du Fbg-St-Antoine, 11th (01.43.71.73.45).
M° Nation. **Open** 7am-2am Mon-Sat; 7am-midnight Sun. **Food served** noon-3pm, 7-11pm. **Plat du jour** €12. **Credit** MC, V. **Map** P7.
Service can be extra slow on busy weekend nights, but this gives extra time for exploring the fantastic wine menu. Food is generally fresh and inventive and although the house cheeseburger, bizarrely made on an undercooked English muffin, was uninspired, everything else was superb, including a starter of fresh goat's cheese whipped with herbs and sun-dried tomatoes, and a courgette, roasted pepper and pine nut crumble. Our friendly, Amélie-like waitress added to the congenial atmosphere on the heated terrace where locals kept dropping in for drinks until the early hours of the morning.

Pause Café

41 rue de Charonne, 11th (01.48.06.80.33).
M° Ledru-Rollin. **Open** 7.30am-2am Mon-Sat; 9am-8pm Sun. **Food served** noon-midnight Mon-Sat; noon-5pm Sun. Closed 25 Dec. **Plat du jour** €10. **Credit** AmEx, MC, V. **Map** M7.
We've suspected for some time now that the Pause Café has been resting on its *Chacun cherche son chat*-induced cinematic fame. Our last visit proved it. Our red wine arrived already decanted, fresh from the fridge. Vegetable lasagne was flavourless and dried

out. The steak proved even worse: despite a request for saignant, it arrived bien cuit and didn't taste fresh. Frustratingly blunt knives and a forgotten request for water hardened our hearts further, as did the floor which on this occasion was filthy. The terrace is still popular; the local trendies who frequent it should know better.

Polichinelle Café ★

64-66 rue de Charonne, 11th (01.58.30.63.52).
M° Ledru-Rollin. **Open** 10am-1am daily. **Food served** noon-3.30pm, 7.30-11.30pm daily. **Plat du jour** €12.50. **Credit** MC, V. **Map** N7.
This colourful café not far from the Bastille has many moods, from morning coffee at the bar to louche summer lunches on the terrace to cosy winter dinners on the banquettes inside. After a long absence we returned, to be greeted as always by motherly Hélène. Happily, little had changed: the place was packed out on a Friday night with noisy groups of friends and while we ate in the inner dining room locals sat up at the bar chatting over live jazz. Our substantial starters of mozzarella nems and bruschetta were both accompanied by leafy, well-dressed salads – mesclun for the bruschetta and crunchy Chinese cabbage and apple for the nems. Then it was back to old favourites for the main courses: juicy magret de canard with pain d'épices sauce accompanied by the superlative, olive oil-laced mashed potato topped with a single cherry tomato, and daily special filet mignon de porc, piled on top of a mound of potato and cabbage. The moelleux au

Au Roi du Café.
See p231.

On the Town

Francis Labutte. *See p232.*

chocolat with orange sauce was so meltingly delicious that we were hard pushed to restrain ourselves from licking the plates clean.

12TH ARRONDISSEMENT

L'Arrosoir

75 av Daumesnil, 12th (01.43.43.64.58).
M° Montgallet. **Open** 8am-1am daily. **Plat du jour** €15. **Credit** MC, V. **Map** N8.
Seriously good food, soaring ceilings and an elegantly rustic fit-out belie the casual moniker of this sophisticated space (literally 'the watering can'), set amid pricey antique shops in an arrondissement better known for its eclectic ethnicity. Waiters in denim and black T-shirts beat a staccato rhythm on exposed timber floorboards as they rush to serve an upmarket clientele: businessmen order côte de boeuf (at €40 for two) and first-class roast veal, while sophisticated ladies with gravity-defying hairstyles opt for smoked salmon salad with an eye to their régimes. Expect nothing less than Berthillon ice-cream and Mariage Frères teas, best enjoyed in the heated, enclosed terrace. The ideal spot for a very grown-up tête-à-tête.

Chez Gudule

58 bd de Picpus, 12th (01.43.40.08.28). M° Picpus. **Open** 8am-2am Mon-Sat; 3.30pm-midnight Sun. **Food served** noon-3pm Mon-Sat. Closed in Aug. **Plat du jour** €11.50. **Credit** MC, V. **Map** Q8.
This far-flung branch of Chez Prune offers full meal service at lunch as well as snacks all day, and the food quality lives up to the smart digs and chatty staff. A select group of young and middle-aged locals fills the quasi-industrial interior decorated with bicycles and upside-down tables hanging from the ceiling. Music ranges from Brazilian to old soul and funk. Earth Wind and Fire with your consommé de ravioli, anyone?

T pour 2 Café

23 cour St-Emilion, 12th (01.40.19.02.09). M° Cour St-Emilion. **Open** 11am-2am daily. **Food served** 11.45am-2pm, 6.45-11.30pm daily. **Plat du jour** €12. **Credit** AmEx, DC, MC, V. **Non-smoking room.** **Wheelchair access. Map** P10.
This fashionable modern café, restaurant and bar in the renovated Bercy wine district offers a vast selection of teas and coffees ranging from the traditional (lapsang souchong) to the exotic (Guadeloupe bonifieur) and the just plain amusing (grand jasmin monkey king). The atmosphere is relaxed – big comfy chairs, mugs of coffee and Fashion TV and M6 playing. There is a selection of light foods including desserts, sandwiches and salads.

Viaduc Café

43 av Daumesnil, 12th (01.44.74.70.70). M° Ledru-Rollin or Gare de Lyon. **Open** 9am-2am daily. **Food served** noon-3pm, 7pm-midnight. **Plat du jour** €11. **Credit** MC, V. **Non-smoking room. Map** M8.
Built into great stone arches, the ambitious Viaduc serves up contemporary cuisine with mixed results. The imaginative potato accompaniments, including such combinations as potato and chestnut mash, are wonderful; unfortunately they show up everything else. Our red wine was served already poured and icy cold. Barely-warm cheese ravioli in lobster sauce proved an odd combination and pork cutlets were dried out, though we've had much better luck on previous visits. Desserts looked promising, but due to the slow service we had to skip them to catch the last Métro. The Sunday jazz brunch, although expensive, is perhaps a better option – or, if you live nearby, drop in for a late drink at the stylish bar.

13TH ARRONDISSEMENT

Café Banal ★

39 bd de Port-Royal, 13th (01.43.31.27.39). M° Glacière or RER Port Royal. **Open** 11am-midnight Mon-Fri. **Food served** 11am-10pm. Closed last two weeks of Dec and three weeks in Aug. **Plat du jour** €7. **No credit cards.**
'Sortez de l'ordinaire' is the slogan of the Café Banal and little choice do you have in a cafe where every drink and every dish except the plat du jour costs just €1.50. Banal here refers to its older meaning of 'communal', which this place – run by a former bank robber with a conscience – certainly is. Pensioners and students pack the Formica-topped tables, and a piano is wedged in against one wall. While the plat du jour goes for €6.50-€7.50, the standard menu offers the possibility of compiling exactly what you feel like eating, such as poulet fermier and real home-made frites (€3 in all) or tarte à l'oignon and green salad followed by a delicious crème caramel.

Chez Lili et Marcel

1 quai d'Austerlitz, 13th (01.45.85.00.08). M° Quai de la Gare. **Open** noon-11.30pm Mon-Sat; noon-6pm Sun. **Plat du jour** €11. **Credit** MC, V. **Wheelchair access. Map** M9.

On the Town

Le Rendez-vous des Quais. *See p232.*

This large revamped bar-resto guards the entrance to the north-east corner of the equally revamped 13th, its yellow awnings pointing towards the river and Bercy opposite as you step down from Quai de la Gare Métro station high above. Done out like an old grocery, with packets of post-war Omo and the like on display, L&M's offers genuine cuisine de famille along with pâtisserie to boot. The sunlit terrace is as lovely as you'll find along this stretch of the Seine, and all in all this is the nicest of the options before catching a film at the MK2 cinema round the corner.

Le Village de la Butte

23 rue de la Butte aux Cailles, 13th (01.45.80.36.82). M° Place d'Italie. **Open** 9am-2am Mon-Sat; 9am-midnight Sun. **Plat du jour** €7. **Credit** MC, V.

An oasis of authenticity on this quickly gentrifying street, Le Village de la Butte has a genuine village feel. Regulars idle at the front and chitchat with the barman, a no-nonsense lady sells lotto tickets at the cash register, and the chef, when things are slow, flips the pages of the most recent issue of L'Auvergnat. The reliable €10.50 menu keeps the back dining room buzzing with people who work in the neighbourhood. One does wonder how framed photos of naked French soccer stars made it into the decor but, other than that, there's no reason to ask too many questions about this place. Just be glad some things never change.

14TH ARRONDISSEMENT

Café de la Place

23 rue d'Odessa, 14th (01.42.18.01.55). M° Edgar-Quinet. **Open** 7.30am-2am Mon-Sat; noon-11pm Sun. **Food served** noon-1am Mon-Sat; noon-10pm Sun. **Plat du jour** €15. **Credit** MC, V. **Map** G9.

At Café de la Place, you can choose between the homely, dark wood-panelled interior, the glassed-in terrace or, during warmer weather, the pavement under a canopy of green trees. We went for the giant Poilâne-bread croques: the vegetarian tomato and cheese version was served atop a huge pile of salad. At the edge of the famous cemetery, you'll feel miles away from Montparnasse mania.

La Chope Daguerre

17 rue Daguerre, 14th (01.43.22.76.59). M° Denfert-Rochereau. **Open** 7am-8pm Mon, Sun; 7am-midnight Tue-Sat. **Food served** noon-3pm Mon; noon-3pm, 6.30-11pm Tue-Sat. **Plat du jour** €10. **Credit** MC, V. **Map** G10.

Of the many cafés along this market street, La Chope leads the way. The dark interior with red lampshades is great for evening, but by day the locals prefer the cosy terrace overlooking the street. Huge salads are the draw here, but the waiters will also recommend their favourites from the blackboard menu. A tender brochette of lamb and the goat's cheese salad hit the spot, although the accompanying piles of greenery could have been fresher. Save room for the dessert: tempting fruit tarts can be found atop the bar.

Le Plomb du Cantal ★

3 rue de la Gaîté, 14th (01.43.35.16.92). M° Gaîté or Edgar Quinet. **Open** noon-midnight daily. **Food served** noon-3pm, 6-11.30pm. **Plat du jour** €18. **Credit** MC, V. **Map** G9.

This lively homage to the Auvergne, bravely holding its own between the sex shops of the rue de la Gaîté, may suffer from its 1980s decor, but with food like this, who cares? Aligot and truffade come by the plateful, the house-made shoestring fries arrive by the saucepan-load, and the omelettes are made with three eggs, 300g of potatoes, and if you're really hungry, a supplement of tomme cheese. The roast chestnut-based salade corrézienne is delicious and, like all salads here, too enormous to finish. Wines are generally good, and speedy service and low prices mean that Le Plomb is always packed. Definitely the pick of the street for a post-theatre – or strip show – late-night meal.

Les Tontons

38 rue de Raymond Losserand, 14th (01.43.21.69.45).
M° Pernety. **Open** 7.30am-1.30am daily. **Food**
served noon-2.30pm, 7.45-11pm. **Plat du jour** €12.
Credit MC, V. **Map** F10.

Taking its name from a 1960s gangster comedy,
newcomer Les Tontons has kept the old zinc bar,
mosaic interior and habitués of its former
incarnation Le Cadran, but is rapidly becoming
popular for dinner with friends or a late-night drink.
Inspired by the south-west, the offerings include a
rich duck in foie gras sauce with mushrooms, or, for
the serious meat-lover, ten different types of tartare.
Giant salads, amply decorated with physillis (a
house signature) help to balance things out, although
vegetarians are fobbed off with the usual bizarre
concoctions. Wines are excellent but can be pricey,
so choose with care. Be sure to try the crème brûlée,
flavoured with pistachio, pear or vanilla.

15TH ARRONDISSEMENT

Au Dernier Métro ★

70 bd de Grenelle, 15th (01.45.75.01.23/www.au
derniermetro.com). M° Dupleix. **Open** 6am-2am daily.
Food served noon-1am daily. Closed 25 Dec, 1 Jan.
Plat du jour €12. **Credit** AmEx, MC, V. **Map** C7.

This adorable café makes you feel at home. The
walls are covered with colourful memorabilia and a
football game plays on the small TV behind the bar.
Lots of the Basque-influenced dishes tempt – we
tried the juicy fish brochettes served with saffron
rice and one of the big salads, both made with care.
There's a bit of pavement seating and the big
windows open right up. Beer is a bargain for the
neighbourhood. Service could not have been
friendlier or more attentive – where else might the
waiter address two diners as 'my angels'?

Au Roi du Café

59 rue Lecourbe, 15th (01.47.34.48.50). M° Sèvres-
Lecourbe. **Open** 7am-midnight daily. **Food served**
noon-11.30pm. **Plat du jour** €11.50. **Credit** MC, V.
Map D8.

If you happen to be in this corner of the 15th, this
scruffy art deco gem makes a pleasant stop for a
cheap carafe of wine or an unusually good coffee;
it's one of the only bits of retro Paris on an
architecturally challenged street. You'll find the
basics – croque monsieur and madame on Poilâne
bread, typical café salads, omelettes and soupe à
l'oignon. The decor is the real reason to spend an
hour or three here, soaking up a slice of Paris gone
by. Shame about the charmless service.

16TH ARRONDISSEMENT

Café Antoine

17 rue La Fontaine, 16th (01.40.50.14.30). RER
Kennedy-Radio France. **Open** 7.30am-11pm Mon-Sat.
Closed two weeks in Aug. **Food served** noon-3pm,
7-10.30pm. **Plat du jour** €14. **Credit** AmEx, DC,
MC. V. **Map** A7.

On a cold autumn day the prettily tarnished interior
of Café Antoine warms like an artfully tied Parisian
scarf. Intimately spaced tables are devoid of menu
cards – for this you must look to the child-size
blackboards hung haphazardly on dust pink walls
between atmospheric paintings and charming
trinkets. Food is bistro-classic but a little hit and
miss: a strangely gelatinous sauce marred a plate of
tender veal stew. Next time we'll make a play for
razor-thin slices of beef carpaccio drizzled in olive
oil enjoyed by a lone Frenchman and his hound, or
golden pommes de terre savoyardes (potatoes baked
with milk and cheese). The mille-feuille and first-
class coffee are a must. A wonderful spot to idle.

Le Village d'Auteuil ★

48 rue d'Auteuil, 16th (01.42.88.00.18). M° Michel-
Ange Auteuil. **Open** 9am-11pm daily. **Food served**
noon-11pm. **Plat du jour** €12. **Credit** MC, V.

Le Village is just a local caff, but this is Auteuil, so
it's permanently stocked with gilded youth, little old
ladies with small dogs, women of a certain age with
Chanel shades hiding recent eye-jobs and dapper
chaps reading *Le Figaro*. This is a quintessential
posh Parisian café: all-heated terrace, brushed zinc
bar (complete with huge Champagne bucket – no one
drinks demis here), moustachioed waiters, strong
coffee, decent wine and excellent food. A planche
nordique comes complete with good smoked salmon,
potato salad thankfully not drowned in mayonnaise,
chopped eggs, cod roe and Poilâne toast, while
anything served with their amazing aligot is comfort
food heaven and their charcuterie platters are a
carnivore's most hardcore fantasy. Surprisingly for
such a posh place, the staff are fantastically friendly.

17TH ARRONDISSEMENT

Le Dada

12 av des Ternes, 17th (01.43.80.60.12). M° Ternes.
Open 6am-2am Mon-Sat; 6am-midnight Sun. **Food**
served noon-11pm. **Plat du jour** €11. **Credit**
AmEx, MC, V. **Map** C3.

One café, three incarnations: variety is the spice of
life at Le Dada, the deliberately eclectic two-floor
café just around the corner from rue Poncelet's
colourful food market. Do early morning coffee and
croissants among the bistro tables and mosaic-tiled
floor downstairs and save the terrace for a long
lunch, where choice ranges from a litany of croques
to standard brasserie salads and decent expresso.
The café's womb-like upper room – complete with
red quilted ceiling and made-to-linger seating – is a
cosy respite and the perfect spot to indulge in classic
steak-frites.

18TH ARRONDISSEMENT

Le Chinon ★

49 rue des Abbesses, 18th (01.42.62.07.17). M°
Abbesses. **Open** 7am-2am daily. **Food served** 7am-
1am. **Plat du jour** €12. **No credit cards. Map** H1.

Many of the bars and restaurants in Montmartre are filled entirely with tourists, but in this stretch of the road the atmosphere is more Parisian. With trendy tables and chairs worthy of a collector, this café can almost be forgiven for serving watery-tasting wine, such as our Vieilles Vignes Chinon. As long as you stick to coffee or beer, like the mostly French clientele, you should be fine.

Other locations: Le Troisième Chinon, 56 rue des Archives, 4th (01.48.87.94.68).

L'Eté en Pente Douce
23 rue Muller, 18th (01.42.64.02.67). M° Château Rouge. **Open** noon-midnight daily. **Food served** all day. **Plat du jour** €10. **Credit** AmEx, MC, V. **Map** J1.
Long-time locals regard this haunt as something of a secret – albeit one poorly kept if the overflowing tables are any indication. The buzz here is lively and purely Parisian (not a tourist to be heard), with the Sacré-Coeur as a film-set backdrop to outdoor tables strewn haphazardly on a cobblestone courtyard. The interior pays homage to Montmartre's bohemian image: Chinese lanterns cast a rosy glow over a dimly-lit interior where hip twentysomethings consume good house red alongside fork-tender veal stew, meaty rôti de porc and a delicate fillet of perch. Vegetarians have their own menu – tofu lasagne, anyone? The coffee is outstanding.

Francis Labutte
122 rue Caulaincourt, 18th (01.42.23.58.26). M° Lamarck-Caulaincourt. **Open** 8.30am-2am daily. **Food served** noon-3pm, 7.30-10.30pm. Closed 25 Dec. **Credit** MC, V. **Map** H1.
In striking distance of the Sacré-Coeur, yet tucked away from the main drag of tourist traps up the hill, is this chilled-out drinkerie. The tasteful faux-antique decor hinting at rustic pretensions is somewhat undermined by the main road, but that said, it's worth planting yourself in the cosy nook of the heated terrace. The wine selection may be small, but this can hardly be said for the platters of cheese and charcuterie, well-chosen and moreish.

Chez Ginette de la Côte d'Azur
101 rue Caulaincourt, 18th (01.46.06.01.49). M° Lamarck-Caulaincourt. **Open** 9am-2am daily. **Food served** noon-midnight. Closed 25 Dec, 31 Dec. **Plat du jour** €15.50. **Credit** AmEx, MC, V. **Map** H1.
Round the back end of the Sacré-Coeur, in a neighbourhood visited only by the more intrepid tourists, Ginette de la Côte d'Azur creates a holiday mood with its curvy wooden chairs, whimsical painted ceiling and inviting terrace. The menu occasionally touches on the Provençal theme with dishes such as seared tuna on ratatouille (for a whopping €18.90), though there was nothing southern about the decent hamburger with fat frites, also shockingly priced at €15.90. Unless you're feeling flush to the point of recklessness, come here just for a coffee and the warm atmosphere.

19TH ARRONDISSEMENT
La Kaskad'
2 pl Armand-Carrel, 19th (01.40.40.08.10). M° Laumière. **Open** 9am-1am daily. **Food served** noon-midnight. Closed 25 Dec. **Plat du jour** €15. **Credit** MC, V. **Wheelchair access**. **Map** N2.
Named after the manmade waterfall in the Buttes-Chaumont park opposite, La Kaskad' has been a real hit with the local glitz. Pose on the terrace and watch the limos roll up for wedding pictures in the park, or sit in the stylish taupe and mahogany interior and sip a cocktail to nu-jazz sounds. The food, while not cheap, is delicious, including mains such as luscious pork cheeks and steaks, and huge salads for €10.40; if you're feeling flush there are some serious wines on the list.

Le Rendez-vous des Quais
MK2 sur Seine, 10-14 quai de la Seine, 19th (01.40.37.02.81/www.mk2.com). M° Stalingrad or Jaurès. **Open** 10am-1am daily. **Food served** noon-1am. **Plat du jour** €13. **Credit** AmEx, DC, MC, V. **Wheelchair access**. **Map** M2.
You can easily while away hours watching the barges and tour boats from your table at this relaxed café on the esplanade of the Bassin de la Villette. Food-loving film buffs can't miss with the menu ciné, which includes a ticket to the adjoining MK2 cinema. The food is a cut above café fare, and desserts tend towards the rich and gooey.

20TH ARRONDISSEMENT
Entrepot's ★
2 rue Sorbier, 20th (01.43.49.59.17). M° Ménilmontant. **Open** 8am-midnight daily. **Food served** noon-3pm, Mon-Sat. **Plat du jour** €8.50. **Credit** MC, V. **Map** P5.
On the high reaches of Ménilmontant, off the tourist trail but near a little enclave of restaurants by pretty parc Sorbier, this is a locals' café that always offers a welcoming smile; sometimes even a hug and kiss if the Algerian owners are feeling jovial. There's a zinc bar, paintings, posters and bric-a-brac, good coffee and a great-value two-course prix fixe for €11. You can depend on the entrecôte to be juicy, the frites to be fat, and the desserts to be fresh. Works of art are discussed here and at least one book has been written in the café itself; but it's never pretentious. In the evenings candlelight softens the atmosphere and the same cast gets merry over pots of red wine.

Le Soleil
136 bd de Ménilmontant, 20th (01.46.36.47.44). M° Ménilmontant. **Open** 9am-2am daily. **No credit cards**. **Map** N5.
Aptly named, as the terrace catches most of the afternoon sun, this brightly lit café is a standby for local artists, musicians and hipsters and always an interesting place to strike up a conversation. It's totally unexceptional inside, but you want to be outside anyway. No food, but plenty of beer.

Bars & Pubs

More than in most other European cities, bars in Paris are defined by their neighbourhoods. The 5th and 6th arrondissements are the haunts of students and Anglo expats, while the 13th, particularly the villagey Butte-aux-Cailles, attracts thrifty yet dedicated drinkers from the nearby Cité Universitaire. The Marais is more style-conscious, with a strong gay contingent (see *pp276-277* **Gay & Lesbian**), boisterous rue de Lappe near the Bastille is beloved of the banlieusards, and Oberkampf attracts bourgeois youth from across town who think they are roughing it. Models, wannabes and Eurotrash congregate around the Champs-Elysées, which promises glitz but doesn't always deliver. No longer up-and-coming, the Canal St-Martin is bobo (bohemian bougeois) territory – for more cutting-edge drinking holes, head to the 18th, 19th or 20th arrondissements. Most bars have happy hours, but drinks are otherwise generally pricey. Don't be surprised to see tables laid for dinner early in the evening – many bars double as restaurants and turn into drinking dens only later (arriving early for a meal can be the best way of snagging a table at the most popular spots).

1ST ARRONDISSEMENT

Le Comptoir

37 rue Berger, 1st (01.40.26.26.66). M° Les Halles or Louvre-Rivoli. **Open** noon-2am daily. **Food served** noon-3pm, 7-11.30pm. Closed 24, 25 Dec. **Happy hour** 5-8pm. **Credit** MC, V. **Map** J5.

Amid the urban monstrosity that is Les Halles, there is Le Comptoir: an oasis of calm overlooking the gardens beside St-Eustache. The decor is Moroccan to the last detail: deep-red rugs, coloured-glass chandeliers, low-slung leather stools and banquettes piled high with cushions. A young, international crowd lounges around drinking mint tea – served as it should be with pine nuts bobbing on top. The service is friendly and the cocktails lethal.

Le Fumoir

6 rue de l'Amiral-de-Coligny, 1st (01.42.92.00.24/ www.lefumoir.com). M° Louvre-Rivoli. **Open** 11am-2am daily. **Food served** noon-3pm, 7.30-11.30pm. Closed two weeks in Aug. **Happy hour** 6-8pm. **Credit** AmEx, MC, V. **Wheelchair access.** **Map** H6.

This elegant bar opposite the Louvre has become a bit of a Parisian institution: neo-colonial fans whirr lazily, oil paintings adorn the walls and even the bar staff seem to have been included in the interior decorator's sketches. A sleek crowd sipping martinis or browsing the papers at the mahogany bar (originally from a Chicago speakeasy) gives way to young professionals and pretty young things in the library. It can feel a little try-hard and well-behaved, but some expertly mixed cocktails and a little friendly flirting with the PRs on the prowl are guaranteed to take the edge off the evening.

Hemingway Bar at the Ritz ★

Hôtel Ritz, 15 pl Vendôme, 1st (01.43.16.30.31/ www.ritzparis.com). M° Madeleine or Concorde. **Open** 6.30pm-2am Mon-Sat. **Tapas served** 6.30pm-2am. Closed first two weeks in Jan and Aug. **Credit** AmEx, DC, MC, V. **Wheelchair access.** **Map** F5.

This much-lauded bar has become a cocktailers' cliché, but that's because it's simply one of the loveliest places in Paris to do drinkies. The dark wood, muffled laughter, black-and-white photos of the Old Man and the old-school charm of Colin the head barman and lovely Ludo his second make the bar a cocoon from the horrors of the outside world. Leather seating and five-star service (a glass of berry-scented water appears upon 30 seconds of arrival) preface cocktails as near to alcoholic nirvana as possible – not least the divine raspberry martini. Pulling in its fair share of characters, honeymooners and expense-account nerds, it's also a wonderful place to see what the human race does in its spare time. Opened across the corridor is the Cambon Bar: the original Ritz bar, done up as it was back in its '20s heyday.

Jip's

41 rue St-Denis, 1st (01.42.21.33.93). M° Châtelet or Les Halles. **Open** 9am-2am Mon-Sat; noon-2am Sun. **Food served** noon-3pm, 7-11.30pm. **Credit** MC, V. **Map** J5.

In a desert of commercial dross and chain restaurants, little Jip's bright yellow awning brings life and light to the street. During winter, goblets of spicy vin chaud recharge numbed shoppers while in summer the outside terrace becomes a festival of

On the Town

Seriously fashionable **Andy Wahloo** – a beautiful bar for beautiful people. *See p237.*

On the Town

colours and action. Jip's has an unkempt charm; there are myriad tribal sculptures and grass skirts adorning the walls but the bar, with its colourful jolly of rum bottles, fairy lights and punch bowls of sangria, remains the focal point of the place. This is a cheery spot for a Latino-inspired drink and nibble, the unfussy atmosphere and good choice of (often live) music attracting a multi-ethnic, multi-generational crowd.

Kong ★

1 rue du Pont-Neuf, 1st (01.40.39.09.00/www.kong.fr). M° Pont Neuf. **Open** noon-2am Mon-Sat. **Food served** noon-midnight. **Happy hour** 6-8pm. **Credit** AmEx, MC, V. **Map** J6.

Philippe Starck's latest addition to the Paris scene is, predictably, one of the city's hottest places to do cocktails, ideally located on the top two floors of the Kenzo building overlooking the Pont Neuf. The bright mishmash interior is manga-inspired with lots of neon, Hello Kitty knick-knacks, comfy grey leather sofas and rocking chairs at the main dining tables. The best bet is to perch at the long bar, flirt with the too-beautiful-to-bartend staff and order an excellent vodkatini or three. After dark you can make a music suggestion with each order – at weekends they somehow carve out a tiny dancing space for the trendy crowd to strut their stuff on. Wear plenty of designer labels and try your best to keep looking cool while half-cut.

2ND ARRONDISSEMENT
Café Noir

65 rue Montmartre, 2nd (01.40.39.07.36). M° Sentier. **Open** 8am-2am Mon-Sat. **Food served** noon-2.30pm Mon-Sat. **Credit** AmEx, DC, MC, V. **Map** J5.

During the day you'll have to squeeze past the cluster of expresso-drinking journalists from *Le Figaro* to get to one of the small tables at which you can enjoy a cheap and well-prepared lunch. After the sun goes down, the music (usually jazz during the day; at night all bets are off) gets even louder and the large photo of Gainsbourg by the door sets the tone: raucous conversation, strong drinks, and an open-spiritedness that can accommodate the branché and bohemian clientele together. Look out for the mobiles, a jamboree of multi-cultural papier-mâché dolls, perhaps banished from their theme-park home for serious drug problems.

Le Coeur Fou

55 rue Montmartre, 2nd (01.42.33.91.33). M° Sentier. **Open** 4pm-2am Mon-Sat. **No credit cards**. **Map** J4.

Once you have discovered the address (self-promotion is, after all, very uncool) you'll find a chic study in whitewash perennially packed with the hipsters and chancers of the Montorgueil in-crowd. Or perhaps that should be 'get-them-in' crowd, as the vibe is not as poised as the muted spot-lit decor or amount of texturising hair product on display may suggest. Le Coeur Fou is a flirty, noisy place to clink Caipirinhas and have a darned good night. Space is pretty limited, but at the back there is a little raised sofa section to rest your distressed-denim clad derrière (although beware the surcharge on drinks).

Footsie

10-12 rue Daunou, 2nd (01.42.60.07.20). Mº Opéra. **Open** noon-2.30pm, 6pm-2am Mon-Thur; noon-2.30pm, 6pm-4am Fri, Sat. **Food served** noon-2.30pm, 7-11pm. **Credit** AmEx, MC, V. **Map** G4.

The Footsie is based on an elementary play on words, and a principle so sound it should be floated on the stock market itself. Bar prices modelled on shares which rise and fall every four minutes depending on how many people buy them. Popular brews and anything remotely stylish go up, cocktails you wouldn't touch with a rusty bargepole stay cheap. Footsie goads you into mixing your drinks and playing City whizz-kids till dawn. A whisky can fluctuate between €5.80 and €10.50 in seconds. A number of drinkers look up at the screens, scanning for bargains; most don't, waiting for the occasional crash and windfall booze-up.

The Frog & Rosbif

116 rue St Denis, 2nd (01.42.36.34.73/www. frogpubs.com). Mº Etienne Marcel. **Open** noon-2am daily. **Food served** noon-11pm. Closed 24, 25 Dec. **Happy hour** 6-8pm. **Credit** MC, V. **Map** J5.

Paul Chantler and Thor Gudmundsson must be delighted with the success of their chain of English pubs that started with this one. Their ads call it 'a quintessential English pub', and it is, with thick wooden pews, autographed rugby shirts, traditional pub grub and five screens to broadcast the UK's top sporting events. The Frogpubs serve their own beers – bitters, lagers and stouts – all brewed on the premises and available on tap. We particularly enjoyed the strong bitter Parislytic and the full-bodied stout Dark de Triomphe. Staff are well marshalled, the atmosphere friendly and there's even a good blend of testosterone and oestrogen. **Branches**: The Frog & British Library, 114 av de France, 13th (01.45.84.34.26); The Frog & Princess, 9 rue Princess, 6th (01.40.51.77.38); The Frog at Bercy, 25 cour St-Emilion, 12th (01.43.40.70.71).

Harry's New York Bar

5 rue Daunou, 2nd (01.42.61.71.14/www.harrys-bar.fr). Mº Opéra. **Open** 10.30am-4am daily. **Food served** 11am-3pm Mon-Fri. Closed 24, 25 Dec. **Credit** AmEx, DC, MC, V. **Map** G4.

Paris's quintessential American bar is still the smoky, pennant-bedecked institution beloved of expats, visitors and hard-drinking Parisians. The white-coated bartenders mix some of the finest and most lethal cocktails in town, from the trademark bloody Mary (invented here, so they say) to the well-named pétrifiant, a paralysing elixir of half a dozen spirits splashed into a beer mug. They can also whip

up a personalised creation: we remember (patchily) a string of delicious vodka concoctions that had us swooning in the downstairs piano bar and outrageously overtipping the artiste.

La Jungle

56 rue d'Argout, 2nd (01.40.41.03.45). Mº Sentier. **Open** 10am-2am Mon-Fri; 4pm-2am Sat, Sun. **Food served** noon-2pm, 7pm-midnight Mon-Fri, 7pm-midnight Sat, Sun. **Credit** AmEx, DC, MC, V. **Map** J5.

Contending for the smallest bar in Paris prize, La Jungle packs quite an intoxicating punch. The cocktail list alone could make your eyes water with drinks named Gorilla Bone and Agony 4, featherweights should perhaps stick to a fruit mix or a tonsil-tickling Bushman (Champagne and ginger). With live Afro-jazz bands every Wednesday and Friday, La Jungle rocks with easy sociability and is an oasis of unaffected fun in this trendy district. Decor is all tribal masks and shabby animal skin but the impeccably dressed patron, Georges from Cameroon, sets standards for behaviour: winking at the ladies, dancing and cajoling himself into an impromptu bongo set.

Somo

168 rue Montmartre, 2nd (01.40.13.08.80/www.hip bars.com). Mº Sentier. **Open** noon-2am Mon-Fri; 6pm-4am Sat. **Food served** noon-3pm Mon-Fri; 7-11pm Sat. **Happy hour** 5-8pm Mon-Fri; 6-8pm Sat. **Credit** AmEx, DC, MC, V. **Map** J4.

The thoroughbred in the expat-owned Hip Bars stable, Somo is a sleeker, more grown-up offering than the Lizard Lounge, Stolly's and the Bottle Shop. Popular with suits from the nearby Bourse after work, it chills out later on in the evening and at weekends when bright young things arrive to party amid the fairy lights, aided and abetted by well-mixed €9 Absolut-based cocktails. Full menu, too; the €13.90 dinner a snip, the €9 bar snacks not so. Weekend DJ spots are a fixture on the Saturday-night circuit.

Le Tambour ★

41 rue Montmartre, 2nd (01.42.33.06.90). Mº Sentier. **Open** noon-6.30am daily. **Food served** noon-3.30am. Closed 25 Dec. **Credit** MC, V. **Map** J5.

This classic nighthawks bar is decked out with vintage transport chic, its slatted wooden banquettes and bus-stop-sign bar stools occupied by chatty regulars who give the 24-hour clock its best shot. Neither tatty nor threatening, Le Tambour comprises a small counter area of friendly banter twixt staff and souses, a busy conservatory and a long dining room memorable for its retro Métro map from station Stalingrad and iconic image of Neil Armstrong. Pride of place is given to a philosophical quotation about this being the perfect match of urban and bucolic. Bang on, Tambour, bang on.

Le Truskel

10 rue Feydeau, 2nd (01.40.26.59.97/www.truskel. com). Mº Bourse. **Open** 8pm-2am Tue, Wed; 8pm-5.30am Thur-Sat. Closed Aug. **Credit** MC, V. **Map** H4.

On the Town

bubar

a special wine bar
loved by:
vogue, cosmopolitan, elle,
time out, paris dernière...

open every day from 7pm
3 rue des tournelles
paris 4°   métro bastille

+ tv's, football, rugby & darts...

Lush Bar 16 rue des Dames,
Paris 17 métro: Place Clichy

+ pool table, big screens, lunch...

Rush Bar 32 rue St Sebastien
Paris 11 métro: St Sebastien

Oirish meets indie at this pub-cum-disco a stone's throw from the stock exchange. The formula is simple: an excellent selection of beers, fruity Belgian and quality Czech included, attends to your throat while a complete repertoire of Britpop assaults your ears and, if you're sitting in the dark dog-leg bar area, forces you to watch the video too. The back area is for dancing, think school disco. Malcontent expats love it, but not as much as French boys who cannot hold their Murphy's, and for whom a shoulder-hug and a communal wail of *Live Forever* somehow allows access to a secret club. To add to the pretence, a bar-bell rings for no reason whatsoever, causing first-time UK visitors to down their drinks in one and rush to the bar, heh heh.

3RD ARRONDISSEMENT

Andy Wahloo ★
69 rue des Gravilliers, 3rd (01.42.71.20.38). M° Arts et Métiers. **Open** 4pm-2am Mon-Sat. **Tapas served** 4pm-midnight. **Happy hour** 5-8pm. **Credit** AmEx, DC, MC, V. **Map** K5.
Proving that size really doesn't matter (this place brings new meaning to the word 'bijou'), a formidably fashionable set crowd in here and fight for a coveted place on an upturned paint can (who needs a divan when you've got Dulux?). Andy Wahloo – created by the people behind its neighbour 404 and London's Momo and Sketch – is Arabic for 'I have nothing'. From head to toe, it's a beautifully designed venue crammed with Moroccan artefacts, and enough colours to fill a Picasso. Quiet early, there's a surge around 9pm and the atmosphere heats up later on.

Le Connétable
55 rue des Archives, 3rd (01.42.77.41.40). M° Hôtel de Ville or Rambuteau. **Open** 11am-3pm, 6pm-midnight Mon-Sat. **Food served** noon-3pm, 7pm-midnight Mon-Sat. Closed Aug. **Credit** AmEx, DC, MC, V. **Map** K6.
Look no further for the ultra-Parisian Piaf-and-pastis bar that you always hope you'll stumble on. Le Connétable is one of those wonderfully rare spots where you can find the much vaunted joie de vivre and bonhomie the French are supposed to be famous for and is normally in rather short supply. Expect old geezers getting hammered on rough red, faded divas holding court in the corner, young couples getting fruity on a stuffing-free sofa and up-for-it locals chatting to anything with a pulse and the ability to slur. Best seen after midnight.

4TH ARRONDISSEMENT

Bubar
3 rue des Tournelles, 4th (01.40.29.97.72). M° Bastille. **Open** 7pm-2am daily. Closed 24, 25, 31 Dec, 13 Feb, 14 July. **Credit** MC, V. **Map** L7.
Only steps from the busy Bastille, you'll be stunned to find such a relaxed and local atmosphere… if you can find it at all. Nearly unmarked, this tiny bar is

all red, like the wine to which it is dedicated. It's a special pleasure to sample so many good non-French labels, including reds and whites from Chile, Argentina, Italy, Spain and South Africa, for less than €5 a glass. Little tapas including carrots, tomatoes and nuts await you at the bar, making you feel like you're having an apéro at a friend's.

Chez Richard
37 rue Vieille-du-Temple, 4th (01.42.74.31.65). M° St-Paul. **Open** 6pm-2am daily. **Food served** 6pm-midnight Tue-Sat. Closed Aug. **Happy hour** 6-8pm. **Credit** AmEx, DC, MC, V. **Map** K6.
A compromise between the style-conscious L'Etoile Manquante across the street and the grunge chic of Les Etages next door, Chez Richard pulls in couples, after-work drinkers and clubbers who are equally comfortable sipping chilled Champagne, a well-dosed cocktail, or simply a beer. The upstairs restaurant serves decent no-nonsense food at reasonable prices. It's a pleasure to be ensconced at the bar with its padded elbow rest. Elegant and unpretentious.

Les Chimères
133 rue St-Antoine, 4th (01.42.72.71.97). M° St-Paul. **Open** 24 hours daily. **Food served** noon-3pm, 5pm-midnight. Closed 25 Dec. **Happy hour** 6-8pm. **Credit** MC, V. **Map** L6.
With a prime view of St-Paul Métro – a popular meeting point in the Marais – this neighbourhood café with a few tables on the pavement is one of the few in this part of town to be open around the clock. Visit at 8am on a Sunday and you'll have your café crème with diehards who have been here since 8pm the night before. It's this clash of night and day that makes an otherwise unremarkable café such an amusing place.

Les Etages
35 rue Vieille-du-Temple, 4th (01.42.78.72.00). M° Hôtel de Ville or St-Paul. **Open** 3.30pm-2am daily. **Happy hour** 3.30-9pm. **Credit** AmEx, DC, MC, V. **Map** K6.
Take Les Etages at its word. Below decks, the street-level bar is so cramped that economy-class syndrome is inevitable. Two lines of low chairs and metal stool tables link drinkers into a conspiracy of Chinese whispers – privacy is at a premium. Space, forget it. Backsides contort to shape the needs of someone's idea of fashionable furniture, hands grasp cocktails (€7-€8.50) presented in clunky Coke glasses, fingers pick from a bowl of sickly-sweet nuts. All it needs is for a net of red ants to drop from the ceiling and it would be perfect torture TV. In the relatively airy upstairs, though, these same seats serve as a sounding board for squatting intellectuals with more calf muscle than brain cell by the end of the evening. Pseudo as hell, so lapped up by locals.

The Lizard Lounge ★
18 rue du Bourg-Tibourg, 4th (01.42.72.81.34/ www.hip-bars.com). M° Hôtel de Ville. **Open** noon-2am daily. **Food served** noon-3pm, 7-10.30pm. **Happy hour** 5-10pm. **Credit** MC, V. **Map** K6.

The only thing red-brick about the Lizard Lounge are the walls – all the rest is sheer, expat-style funk. People-watchers crowd the metal mezzanine (with its great view over the bar and strange but handy metal toilet that makes nipping off to the loo like a trip into a space capsule), while Anglophone socialites and disco divas fight for space on the ground floor and downstairs cellar where barmen, disguised as DJs, splice more than just the screaming orgasms. Their Sunday brunch is an institution with its legendary eggs Benedict, cheap bloody Marys, syrupy pancakes and an all-you-can-eat cereal bar.

Le Pick-Clops

16 rue Vieille-du-Temple, 4th (01.40.29.02.18). *Mº Hôtel de Ville or St-Paul.* **Open** 7am-2am Mon-Sat; 8am-3am Sun. **Food served** noon-midnight. Closed 25 Dec. **Credit** MC, V. **Map** K6.

This bright and vividly coloured café is ideally placed at one of the Marais' southern gateways. Inside, this may be as close as Paris gets to a '50s diner. The intricately tiled floor, mismatched vinyl chairs, primary colour Formica, mirrors, giant peanut bin and stainless steel fixtures set the stage for a retro-ish hangout that welcomes both grimy construction workers and leather-jacketed locals. The calm morning coffee and tartine scene becomes a packed beer-drinking zone by day's end.

Stolly's

16 rue Cloche-Perce, 4th (01.42.76.06.76/www.hipbars.com). *Mº Hôtel de Ville or St-Paul.* **Open** 4.30pm-2am daily. Closed 24, 25 Dec. **Happy hour** 4.30-8pm. **Credit** MC, V. **Wheelchair access.** **Map** K6.

This seen-it-all drinking den has been in action since 1991, serving a mainly expat crowd with vodka tonics and old Velvets tunes for nights immemorial. The staff make the place, helping you feel like part of what passes for furniture, and smoothing an easy passage from arriving sober to sinking them until you're stotious. A terrace eases libation, as do long happy hours, but don't expect to faff about with food.

Le Trésor

7 rue du Trésor, 4th (01.42.71.35.17). *Mº St-Paul.* **Open** 9am-2am daily. **Food served** noon-3pm, 7pm-midnight Mon-Sat; noon-4pm, 7pm-midnight Sun. **Happy hour** 5-8pm Mon-Sat. **Credit** AmEx, MC, V. **Map** K6.

Le Trésor's facelift of eye-catching pink, green, white and grey, and fairground concave mirrors may be a little garish but it hasn't deterred the mixed crowd of hotties. The food and wine have a distinct Franco-Italian twist, and the loos are definitely worth a gander, with live goldfish swimming in the cisterns. Don't worry, you can't flush them away.

5TH ARRONDISSEMENT

The Bombardier

2 pl du Panthéon, 5th (01.43.54.79.22). *Mº Maubert-Mutualité/RER Luxembourg.* **Open** noon-2am daily. **Food served** noon-4pm. Closed 24-26 Dec.

The 5th Bar – oasis of kitsch. *See p241.*

Happy hour 4-9pm. **Wheelchair access.** **Credit** MC, V. **Map** J8.

Snuck into a niche opposite the Panthéon, the Bombardier is a convincing recreation of a Home Counties pub (minus the retired colonels), with Bombardier beer on tap from Bedford brewery (and proprietor) Charles Wells. Despite the swirly glass and olde worlde tapestry, it's a lot less hardcore Anglo than most English pubs in Paris, managing to pull in healthy measures of pretty young French things. Great for a pint over the Sunday papers, the weekend footie or a raucous rugby session.

Café Léa ★

5 rue Claude Bernard, 5th (01.43.31.46.30). *Mº Censier-Daubenton.* **Open** 8.30am-2am Mon-Fri; 9am-2am Sat; 10am-2am Sun. **Food served** noon-3.30pm. Closed 31 Dec, 1 Jan. **Credit** MC, V. **Map** J9.

A splash of colour and a dash of youth is what this part of the 5th needed, and market shoppers next door at rue Mouffetard would do well to step over and sip at the wellspring of it here. Earthen tones with a touch of ethnic chic dominate the bright one-room space, surrounded by windows, with a thin terrace space for those sunnier days. Simple dishes during the day and a reasonably priced brunch (€17 buys you orange juice, coffee, toast, pancakes and a dish such as chicken-mushroom pie or cured ham with melon) make it a favourite, but it's just drinks and snacks, no dinner, after dusk.

Le Crocodile

6 rue Royer-Collard, 5th (01.43.54.32.37). RER Luxembourg. **Open** 10.30pm-6am Mon-Sat (closing varies). Closed Aug. **Happy hour** 10.30pm-12.30am Mon-Thur. **Credit** MC, V. **Map** J8.

It's worth ignoring the apparently boarded-up windows for a cocktail at Le Crocodile. Young, friendly regulars line the sides of this small, narrow bar and try to decide on a drink – we were assured that there are 267 choices, most of them marginally less potent than meths. Pen and paper are provided to note your decision; the pen comes in handy for point-and-choose decisions when everything gets hazy. We think we can recommend an accroche-coeur, a supremely '70s mix of Champagne and Goldschläger, served with extra gold leaf.

The 5th Bar

62 rue Mouffetard, 5th (01.43.37.09.09). M° Place Monge. **Open** 4pm-2am Mon-Thur, Sun; 4pm-3am Fri, Sat. **Happy hour** 4-10pm. **Credit** MC, V. **Map** J8.

If you'd heard anything about this spot before, it would probably be linked to generous happy hours (on originally pricey drinks) and the friendly English-speaking bar staff. Yet there are several other major factors behind the success. One is the carefully assembled kitsch, which includes a leopardskin curtain, plastic fish and a Stars and Stripes flag. And the other is the impossible number of giggling American girls just dying for a chat. Nostalgic tunes and true Uncle Sam-style cocktails ensure the bar area is almost always packed. If it is, there's a downstairs chill-out lounge at the back.

Finnegan's Wake

9 rue des Boulangers, 5th (01.46.34.23.65). M° Jussieu. **Open** 11am-2am Mon-Fri; 6pm-2am Sat. **Sandwiches served** noon-3pm Mon-Fri. **Happy hour** 6-8pm. Closed two weeks in Aug. **No credit cards.** **Map** K8.

Beams, bonhomie and beer are all on offer at Finnegan's Wake, which steers clear of the piss-up-and-pulling atmosphere of many faux-Irish pubs. As it's popular with French students from nearby Jussieu, you're more likely to come across black clad thinkers discussing their dissertations than twinkly-eyed charmers with firsts in sweet-talk. Exactly the kind of place you always thought you'd find in the Latin Quarter. Bone up on your Yeats and ponder all things philosophical over a pint.

La Gueuze

19 rue Soufflot, 5th (01.43.54.63.00). RER Luxembourg. **Open** 11am-2am daily. **Food served** 11.30am-12.45am. **Happy hour** 4-7pm. **Credit** MC, V. **Non-smoking room.**

This Belgian boozer is heaven for those who could murder a pint, and hell for aesthetes. Indeed La Gueuze's fabulously tacky mock-abbey decor would drive anyone to drink – thankfully there are more than a dozen draft beers on tap as well as a variety of about 150 international beers, including your basic

Bud. Those wanting to live more dangerously can sample more out-there brews like Mort Subite, or a tangy raspberry Gueuze Bécasse. To chase down all those bubbles, tuck into a steaming plateful of moules-frites or choucroute, and have a post-guzzle stumble around the nearby Jardin du Luxembourg.

The Hideout

11 rue du Pot-de-Fer, 5th (01.45.35.13.17). M° Place Monge. **Open** 4pm-2am Mon-Thur, Sun; 4pm-5am Fri, Sat. Closed 25 Dec. **Happy hour** 4-10pm. **Credit** AmEx, MC, V. **Map** J8.

The end of many a big night out and the beginning of many morning after nightmares, the Hideout remains a top spot on any serious pub crawl. Dingy, dark and frequently rather damp (it gets very hot in here), it's definitely not a place to arrive at sober. Friendly staff, massive measures, cheap beer and music so loud that body language is the easiest means of communication all add to the fun. Full of language students, Americans on their grand tour, Brits on the piss and stag parties on the lookout.

Le Pantalon ★

7 rue Royer-Collard, 5th (no phone). RER Luxembourg. **Open** 11am-2am Mon-Sat. **Happy hour** 5.30-7.30pm. **No credit cards.** **Map** J8.

Mad as a bag of frogs, Le Pantalon is a local café that seems at once deeply familiar and utterly surreal. It features the standard fixtures and fittings you find at your corner caff, including the old piss-artist propping up the bar – plus a strange vacuum-cleaner sculpture, disco-light loos and the world's most prosaic proposal of marriage. But aside from the offbeat decor, it's the regulars and staff who tip the balance firmly into eccentricity. Friendly and very funny French grown-ups and international students chat away in a mish-mash of accents and languages. Happy hours are fantastic, but drinks here are always cheap enough to get happily tipsy without worrying about a cash hangover.

Le Piano Vache

8 rue Laplace, 5th (01.46.33.75.03). M° Maubert-Mutualité. **Open** noon-2am daily. **Food served** noon-2.30pm. **Happy hour** noon-9pm. **Credit** MC, V. **Map** J8.

A Left Bank drinking haunt for many a decade, this has all the hallmarks of what any beer-stained smoke hovel should be: dark, cramped, filled with a hardcore drinker/student clientele, the walls covered four times over with posters and indeterminate pub grime, and the greatest hits of alternative '80s synth-pop on the stereo. Note that weekday opening hours switch to evenings only out of term time.

Rhubarb ★

18 rue Laplace, 5th (01.43.25.35.03). M° Maubert Mutualité. **Open** 5pm-2am daily. **Happy hour** 5-10pm. **Credit** MC, V. **Map** J8.

A wonderful little spot near Mouffetard, Rhubarb is the latest offering from the crew that put the Fu Bar on the map. As you'd expect, the cocktails are

On the Town

excellent and while Sean's famous apple martini is still sublime, we think we might plump for his watermelon concoction or chocolate martini in future. A relaxed vibe abounds and a mixed crowd mingle happily at the bar. The cellar is all crumbling pale stone and high ceilings, and while a quiet corner is ideal seduction territory the space works equally well for gaggles of mates on a big night out.

Aux Trois Mailletz

56 rue Galande, 5th (01.43.25.96.86/www.lestrois mailletz.fr). M° St-Michel. **Open** 6.30pm-4am daily. **Food served** 7.30pm-3am. **Credit** AmEx, MC, V. **Map** J7.

Upstairs in this St-Michel legend you can have a sedate drink to the accompaniment of live piano or songs and innocuous food. Downstairs is where the action is: the arched medieval cave with long wooden tables hosts a talent show-like soirée of Star Academy proportions. Expect youthful crooners doing Tina Turner and Roberta Flack covers. The female tourists from Texas and Connecticut seem to be enjoying themselves as much as the single middle-aged Frenchmen. Perfect for a tongue-in-cheek night out; the show goes on until the wee hours.

Le Violon Dingue

46 rue de la Montagne-Ste-Geneviève, 5th (01.43.25.79.93). M° Maubert-Mutualité. **Open** 8pm-4.30am Tue-Sat. **Happy hour** 8-10pm. **Credit** MC, V. **Map** J8.

The haunt of many a dodgy dragueur, this stalwart of the American collegian run is perhaps the best bar to go to alone, if you intend to leave accompanied. Alcoholic slush puppies, lethal Long Island iced teas and a generous happy hour help to move things along. If you spend more than half an hour without a chat-up line, it's definitely a very slow night. It's buzziest at the back of the bar; only the very bravest (or most desperate) should venture downstairs.

6TH ARRONDISSEMENT

La Mezzanine de l'Alcazar ★

Alcazar, 62 rue Mazarine, 6th (01.53.10.19.99/ www.alcazar.fr). M° Odéon. **Open** 7pm-2am daily. **Food served** 7-10.30pm. **Credit** AmEx, DC, MC, V. **Wheelchair access. Map** H7.

It would be fair to assume that the Mezzanine would be over by now: hip bars tend to fade once their first flush of youth is gone. But the Mezzanine still somehow pulls it off. The sleek velvet banquettes, polished aluminium bar and the vantage point over the restaurant and into the private dining room all help of course, but really this place is worth paying for because it's posh without being poncey and the drinks are great. The Monday night easy-listening sessions are a must.

Le Bar ★

27 rue de Condé, 6th (01.43.29.06.61). M° Odéon. **Open** 10pm-3am Mon-Sat. Closed two weeks in Aug. **Credit** MC, V. **Map** H7.

Le Bar is one of those strange little places that you only ever visit when it's very, very late and you're very, very drunk. It's almost pitch black, has a shrine-type affair at the back of the bar, gravel on the floor, everyone seems to talk in whispers and they serve very strong drinks. A few words of warning about this place: once you've been here, you'll find yourself strangely drawn back at inappropriate times when you really should go home to bed, and at least one member of the party always falls asleep on the comfy black leather banquettes. Finally, there's a strange echo effect in the corridor down to the toilet, so if Le Bar is your last-ditch attempt to pull before the sun comes up, don't discuss your strategy too loudly.

Le Bar Dix

10 rue de l'Odéon, 6th (01 43 26 66 83). M° Odéon. **Open** 6pm-2am daily. **Happy hour** 6-8pm. **No credit cards. Map** H7.

The decor of this popular and long-running hang dates back to the previous owners, a Spanish couple who sold up in 1986, but who left a tradition of sangria behind. If hearing the name of this fruit-filled Spanish punch makes you wince, you've never tried theirs, which hasn't made anyone blind during the course of almost 20 years of assiduous over-indulgence by a global pack of punters. As almost every other café in St-Germain turns into a tacky version of a lounge bar, it's nice to find a funky place with a bit of character – the jukebox plays Piaf and Brassens, and the same Toulouse Lautrec prints have been on the walls for going on half a century.

Le Comptoir des Canettes

11 rue des Canettes, 6th (01.43.26.79.15). M° Mabillon. **Open** noon-2am Tue-Sat. Closed Aug, 25 Dec-2 Jan. **Credit** MC, V. **Map** H7.

Le Comptoir des Canettes (aka Chez Georges) provides an appropriate mix of young and old in the heart of St-Germain. The upstairs fills with locals sipping a beer or a glass of wine; the basement plays host to a talkative young beer-drinking crowd hoping to catch an occasional live band. On warm summer nights, both young and old spill out the front door, turning the street into one big party.

Coolin

15 rue Clément, 6th (01.44.07.00.92). M° Mabillon. **Open** 10.30am-2am Mon-Sat; 1pm-2am Sun. **Food served** noon-3pm, 7.30-10.30pm Mon-Sat; 1-3pm, 7.30-10.30pm Sun. **Happy hour** 5-8pm. **Credit** MC, V. **Wheelchair access. Map** H7.

It's so tempting to slate the Coolin for being some corny hotchpotch of Oirishness. Yes it does look straight out of one of those cheesy Guiness adverts. And yes there is a bit of potato overkill on the menu. But despite this the Coolin remains a likeable oasis of liveliness, in the middle of the stultifyingly dead Marché St-Germain. So go on and sup on a cold one or dig into a lusty slice of Bailey's cheesecake, as you take in the match on the big telly, and trade some cheeky banter with the cuties manning the bar. Mighty cushty as they say in ole Dub.

Oberkampf bar crawl

Despite its nickname, the 'Oberkampf strip' bears only a passing resemblance to Las Vegas – an illusion created by the neon tabac and kebab signs as you look up from Métro Parmentier. It would, however, be completely possible to replicate Nicolas Cage's cirrhosis odyssey in *Leaving Las Vegas* in this little part of the 11th because Oberkampf is alcohol nirvana. This is the only part of town where you see French people falling off their chairs and scoffing kebabs on the street. With its cheap happy hours it's a great place for a bar crawl and you can, if you wish, go on almost till dawn, although most bars close at 2am. One word of warning: get cash before you set off as the sole ATM always has a queue.

It all started with **Café Charbon** (109 rue Oberkampf, 01.43.57.55.13), a former belle époque dancehall that became a hip hangout in the mid-1990s. But while Charbon's decor makes it an atmospheric café during the day, and it's still very buzzy in the evenings, you can end up crushed uncomfortably at the bar. A better place to start is newcomer **L'Abreuvoir** at no.103 (01.43.38.87.01), where Carole, a passionate mixologiste, runs a bar in what feels like a minuscule '70s living room. Her speciality is beer cocktails; not for beer purists, but we lapped up the Colombo – blonde beer with tequila and strawberry liqueur – yum! The White Russian was just as it should be too, and for 3.50 at happy hour you can't go

wrong. The music was funky and, as the place filled up with a gang of young happy things, it really started to rock.

On the other side of the street, **La Mercerie** (no. 98, 01.43.38.81.30) captures the original spirit of Oberkampf, grungy and pub-like with a snug room that's a bit like a squat where you can lounge on a carpet in a niche. Our favourite remains **Boteco** (no.131, 01.43.57.15.47), a fabulous little Brazilian bar with a great vibe, wonderful Mojitos and a crowd who take little provocation to get up on the benches and dance. Next door, **Gecko Café** (no.133, 01.43.57.81.44), with heat lamps in winter, also harbours a lively crowd.

The Oberkampf scene spread out long ago to neighbouring rue Jean-Pierre Timbaud, where **Café Cannibale** (no.93, 01.49.29.95.59) started the trend. The general feel is more intellectual, although it was on this street that we witnessed the chair-falling incident, in the trendy and still groovy **Troie Tôtards** (no.16, 01.43.14.27.37). Pravda has closed, but you can still take your pick along this street. There's the **Chat Noir** (no.76, 01.48.06.98.22) with live jazz, **Vestiaire Sports Café** (no.64, 01.43.55.42.50) with salsa on Fridays (but at 7 for a Vittel they must be joking), dark-red **Bakara Lounge** (no.61, 01.48.07.17.04) and **Au Petit Garage** (no.63, 01.48.07.08.12), where most nights you can sit in near darkness listening to Sonic Youth and The Ramones.

We plumped for **Café Bleu** (no.83, 01.58.30.81.79), with its piano and stacked bookcase, run by the improbably named Jacky Longjohn. We didn't have the best Mojitos we'd ever had, but we certainly met an eclectic group of punters ranging from two Caribbean lads on the pull to what seemed like a librarians' congress. When we tried to leave, Jacky decided to take the whole bar with us, locked us in, closed up and said: 'So where are we going?' After crashing a private party in **Les Couleurs** (117 rue St-Maur, 01.43.57.95.61), we headed to **Au Plein Soleil** (open till 5am Fri, Sat, 90 av Parmentier, 01.48.05.41.06), a sunny café by day which turns into a free DJ bar by night. With drunken couples swaying to happy house, there was certainly some mileage yet, but the hangover we woke up with the next morning left us happy we had crawled home when we did.

On the Town

Fu Bar

5 rue St-Sulpice, 6th (01.40.51.82.00). M° Odéon.
Open 5pm-2am daily. **Happy hour** 5-9pm. **Credit**
MC, V. **Map** H7.

As Right Bank nightlife streaks ahead in the trendy
stakes, so Left Bank bars become far more relaxed
places to quaff. Case in point: this homey cocktail
joint which shakes up tasty mixes for late-
twentysomethings content to wind down after work
in the kind of orange and purple decor that was hip
when they were at college. Anglo staff are lovely and
there is a healthy amount of banter above the pop
soundtrack. Scrumptious melon martinis are served
in an appropriately wide glass: be careful not to tip
it down your blouse. Extra seating upstairs.

The Highlander ★

*8 rue de Nevers, 6th (01.43.26.54.20/www.the-
highlander.fr). M° Pont-Neuf.* **Open** 5pm-5am Mon-
Fri; 1pm-5am Sat, Sun. **Happy hour** 5-8pm. **Credit**
MC, V. **Map** H6.

The Highlander always feels a bit like a house party
and if you don't already know everyone in there, you
will by the end of your pint. A truly great local, this
place has a fiercely loyal crowd of regulars, probably
because once you've spent a night getting hammered
at the long wooden bar you'll definitely come back
and do it again. It's quiet and cosy early evening
with people nursing pints and setting the world to
rights, and degenerates into a pissed-up pulling spot
after 9pm. Barman Jimmy serves up generous
measures and banter in equal parts. The cellar bar,
used for anything from poetry readings to private
do's, is open till 5am at weekends and resembles the
type of school disco you know you really shouldn't
want to go to anymore, but secretly still do.

Hôtel Lutétia

*45 bd Raspail, 6th (01.49.54.46.46/www.lutetia.com).
M° Sèvres-Babylone.* **Open** 9am-1am daily. **Credit**
AmEx, DC, MC, V. **Map** G7.

The decor is a colourblind interior designer's folly,
the over-dressed waiters are uptight, and fatigued
cigar-smoking businessmen are perhaps not the
funkiest company, but the Lutétia's trio of bars is as
popular as ever, thanks to its range of potent
cocktails. The main attraction is the fabulous low-
lit and louche Ernest bar, where ladies-who-shop
become ladies-who-down-vodkas.

La Marine

*59 bd du Montparnasse, 6th (01.45.48.27.70).
M° Montparnasse-Bienvenue.* **Open** 6am-3am
Mon-Thur, Fri; 6am-5am Sat; 6am-2am Sun. **Food
served** all day. Closed 24 Dec. **Happy hour** 5.30-
7.30pm Mon-Fri. **Credit** MC, V. **Map** F8.

Looking every bit the standard northern French
tavern and with all the requisite moules-frites on the
menu, La Marine distinguishes itself with a liver-
threatening selection of quality beers. Fifteen brews
on tap (including the excellent Kwak in its bulb-
bottomed glass in a wooden holder) are supplemented
by some 250 bottles from around the world.

Le Mazet

*61 rue St-André-des-Arts, 6th (01.43.25.57.50).
M° St-Michel or Odéon.* **Open** 4pm-2am Mon-Wed,
Sun; 5pm-5am Thur-Sat. Closed 24, 25 Dec. **Credit**
AmEx, MC, V. **Map** J7.

Regulars line the bar of Le Mazet while visitors sip
pints outside watching this lively quartier. This pub
is reminiscent of student union days – especially at
night when it's heaving with bodies. This is no
doubt due to the crowd-pulling themed nights.
Wednesday is sports night when all major football
matches are shown on two screens, live DJs spin the
latest tunes late into Saturday night and, on certain
evenings, ladies are privileged with cocktails at
€5 all night. The completely bilingual staff are
amiable and the service is good. The only thing
missing is munchies.

The Moose

*16 rue des Quatre-Vents, 6th (01.46.33.77.00/www.
mooseheadparis.com). M° Odéon.* **Open** 4pm-2am
Mon-Fri; 11.30am-2am Sat, Sun. **Food served**
4-11pm Mon-Sat, 11.30am-3.30pm, 4-11pm Sun.
Happy hour 4-9pm. Closed 24, 25 Dec. **Credit** MC,
V. **Map** H7.

This is not so much a Canadian bar as a bar full of
stuff from Canada, including snowshoes, hockey
sticks and a wooden Mountie. Hockey-craving expats
crowd in to watch playoff games with a cold Labatt's
or Moosehead, though we didn't see any Canucks
crazy or homesick enough to try the maple-syrup
cocktail. The menu includes burgers and steaks as
well as some gastronomy dear to the Great White
North, such as poutine (French fries, cheese and
gravy) and smoked-meat sandwiches (what, no
beaver tails?). A generous brunch is served on
Sundays. Leafs fans be warned: the Moosehead is a
partisan supporter of the Montreal Canadiens.
Other locations: The Beaver, 19 rue des Deux-
Ponts, 4th (01.43.26.92.15).

Le Purgatoire

*14 rue Hautefeuille, 6th (01.43.54.41.36/www.
lepurgatoire.com). M° St-Michel.* **Open** 6pm-2am
Tue-Thur; 6pm-5am Fri-Sat. **Happy hour** 6-8pm.
Credit MC, V. **Map** J7.

You probably wouldn't find your way into this
happy little den unless someone had told you about
it, since the heavy wooden front door is rather off-
putting. Once inside, though, you'll find yourself in
one of the rare bar-clubs in one of the world's most
touristy neighbourhoods that's actually frequented
by locals. Upstairs is devoted to drinking, while
downstairs in the ancient vaulted stone basement
it's all about dancing from Thursday through
Saturday when a DJ spins a mix of the puzzling rock
pop that only the French could really enjoy.

La Taverne de Nesle ★

32 rue Dauphine, 6th (01.43.26.38.36). M° Odéon.
Open 6pm-4am Mon-Thur, Sun; 6pm-6am Fri, Sat.
Food served non-stop. Closed 1 May. **Happy hour**
6-11pm. **Credit** MC, V. **Map** H6.

On the Town

La Taverne, a late-night staple for people who just can't go home before daylight, has four distinct drinking areas: a zinc bar at the front; a sort of Napoleonic campaign tent in the middle; a trendily lit ambient area at the back, and a dreadful 1980s disco downstairs where girls in pearls do their best to look sexy. The separate spaces correspond to stages of drunkenness and encourage a gradual progression to the horizontal state. Among the hundred or so brews you'll find the best of Belgium, but it's the choice of French ones that sets it apart. Don't miss the house special L'Epi, brewed in three different versions: Blond (100% barley); Blanc (oats) and Noir (buckwheat) – or Corsican Pietra on tap.

7TH ARRONDISSEMENT

Café Thoumieux

4 rue de la Comète, 7th (01.45.51.50.40/www. *thoumieux.com). M° La Tour-Maubourg.* **Open** noon-2am Mon-Fri; 5pm-2am Sat. **Snacks served** all day. Closed 24 Dec-2 Jan, Aug. **Happy hour** 5-9pm. **Credit** AmEx, MC, V. **Map** E6.
A Spanish flavoured café/bar for the gilded youth of the 7th, the Thoumieux – a more recent annex of the vintage bistro around the corner – can be a cosy place to meet and have some tapas in the early evening, or a late-night purveyor of that last vanilla vodka you don't need. On our last visit the animated barman was sharpening his impersonation of Tom Cruise in *Cocktail*, tossing liquor bottles high into the air and flipping them over his shoulder to catch them behind his back, or missing them as they fell to the floor. Quite a cost. Perhaps this explains why the happy 'hour' was surreptitiously truncated?

8TH ARRONDISSEMENT

The Bowler

13 rue d'Artois, 8th (01.45.61.16.60). M° St- *Philippe-du-Roule or Franklin D Roosevelt.* **Open** 5pm-2am Mon-Fri; 1pm-2am Sat, Sun. **Food served** 7-10.15pm. Closed 25 Dec, 1 Jan. **Happy hour** 5-11pm. **Credit** AmEx, DC, MC, V. **Map** E3.
This is the local away from home for many Brits. On weeknights it's favoured by men in suits, but generally it's the scene for expats to have a good ol' banter. This pub by no means reflects its affluent locality. It's bright, airy and has more of a country feel. The bar staff act like they have known you forever, drinks are reasonably priced and they have a wide range of whiskies and alcopops. Their Sunday night quiz is supposedly the best in town.

Le V ★

Hotel Four Seasons George V, 31 av George V, *8th (01.49.52.70.00). M° George V.* **Open** 10.30am-2am daily. **Food served** 11am-midnight. **Credit** AmEx, DC, MC, V. **Wheelchair access**. **Map** D4.
The swanky V bar (read 'cinq') is the place to indulge any oil magnate fantasies. Dark wood, a roaring fire, amazing floral displays and utterly loaded punters

combine to make it a must for bling-bling beverages, although we weren't quite brave enough to go for the mysterious 'monkey's gland'. The martini list is superb, the purple being the best. A barman appears at your table to make like Tom Cruise and shake it just for you, the parma-violet-flavoured drink is then poured into a stemless crystal triangle, resting in a bowl of crushed ice, all lovingly cocooned on a posh silver tray. Looks and tastes divine but more than two and the stem-less glass becomes tricky.

Freedom

8 rue de Berri, 8th (01.53.75.25.50). M° George V. **Open** 5pm-2am Mon-Thur, Sun; 1pm-4am Fri, Sat. **Food served** 7-11pm. **Credit** AmEx, DC, MC, V. **Map** D4.
As we approached the bar, a buxom, puppy-faced American was twiddling her straw as a pin-striped nine-to-fiver listed over her drink – that's the sort of place Freedom is. Despite the excessive number of English pubs in Paris, even this unremarkable tavern has little trouble pulling in the punters. Most come for a few pints and a chance to exorcise the demons of the day; others are unashamedly on the pull. The barmen are dog-friendly, a bit dizzy but always keen to cheer on the good-time bands and DJs.

Hôtel Plaza Athénée ★

25 av Montaigne, 8th (01.53.67.66.65/www.plaza- *athenee.paris.com). M° Franklin D Roosevelt.* **Open** 6pm-2am daily. **Snacks served** non-stop. **Credit** AmEx, DC, MC, V. **Wheelchair access**. **Map** D5.
Its international hotel location hasn't stopped this posh bar from becoming probably the coolest in town, with a very dashing crowd. Whether you perch on a stool at the ice-blue bar or sink into one of the sofas, you'll feel at the centre of it all, especially after a rose royale – Champagne and raspberry coulis – or three. Beware the lethally alcoholic jellies that parade around looking like children's sweets.

Impala Lounge

2 rue de Berri, 8th (01.43.59.12.66). M° George V. **Open** 9am-2.30am Mon, Tue; 9am-3am Wed-Thur; 9.30am-5am Fri, Sat. **Food served** noon-midnight. **Credit** AmEx, DC, MC, V. **Map** D4.
Dubbed the 'African Bar' by regulars, this wannabe hip spot hams up the colonial with zebra skins, tribal masks and a throne hewn out of a tree trunk. Beer, wine and tea can all be found here, but the best beverages are the cocktails, one of which claims to boost a waning libido with its mystery mix of herbs and spices. It's not quite as cool as it thinks it is, but at least it doesn't try too hard either. DJs rock Sunday afternoon away.

Latina Café

114 av des Champs-Elysées, 8th (01.42.89.98.89/ *www.latina.fr). M° George V.* **Open** 9am-5am daily. **Food served** noon-1am. **Happy hour** 5-8pm. **Credit** MC, V. **Map** D4.
The Champs-Elysées entrance makes you feel like a Hollywood star as you glide down its red carpet. But once you enter, all illusions come to an abrupt end.

The dark and dismal interior is more sordid than seductive as couples huddle over tables or shy away in corners. Lonely older men sit at the bar waiting for easy prey. The service is horrendous. We waited 20 minutes for our order to be taken and a further 20 minutes to be served. The cocktail list is limited and you're strongly advised against ordering away from it. We wish we could tell you what their tapas were like, but they never came. Huge disappointment.

Nirvana

3 av Matignon, 8th (01.53.89.18.91). M° Franklin D Roosevelt. **Open** 10am-5am Tue-Sat. **Food served** noon-3pm, 7-11.30pm. **Credit** AmEx, DC, MC, V. **Map** E4.

This bar screams Bollywood glitz and glamour. The clashing fuchsia, orange and purple decor is almost blinding, but surprisingly it works. The scattered shrines to Hindu deities are more interesting than kitsch. The scene is incredibly seductive with low tables and cushioned chairs shaped like little flames. However, we half expected coy girls to jump out of the wings bursting into song and dance. Expect to mingle with Paris's rich and beautiful. Even the waiters are probably models by day. The cocktails are divine, but the prices are steep. Great place to people-watch.

Pershing Lounge

Pershing Hall Hotel, 49 rue Pierre Charron, 8th (01.58.36.58.00/www.pershinghall.com). M° George V. **Open** 6pm-2am daily. **Food served** 8pm-midnight. **Happy hour** 6-8pm. **Wheelchair access**. **Credit** AmEx, DC, MC, V.

Design guru Andrée Putmann has conjured up the perfect HQ for monied Americans wanting a taste of elegant Parisian nightlife. The showstopper is the vertical garden in the inner courtyard overflowing with hundreds of exotic plants and flowers. Overlooking it you feel light years away from the urban chaos of the French capital. Drinks prices are similarly out of this world – if only they packed more of a punch for their buck, so they could help loosen up the stiff clientele who take the notion of see-and-be-seen to a ridiculous extreme. Even the staff are too busy posing to give you the time of day.

9TH ARRONDISSEMENT

Le Général Lafayette

52 rue Lafayette, 9th (01.47.70.59.08). M° Le Peletier. **Open** 10am-4am daily. **Food served** all day. Closed 24 Dec. **Credit** AmEx, DC, MC, V. **Map** J3.

The neighbourhood is a little bleak, but there's nothing terribly wrong with this old belle époque bar/café, whose recently redone interior manages to attract lost tourists and others wandering up from Galeries Lafayette and the Opéra Garnier. Waiters have that no-nonsense, old-school demeanour. Expect frankfurters and frites, cheese platters, Poilâne bread and plenty of beers on tap from this sober, businesslike establishment that speaks of old Paris, not the new wave of designer watering holes.

Pershing Lounge.

10TH ARRONDISSEMENT

L'Atmosphère ★

49 rue Lucien-Sampaix, 10th (01.40.38.09.21).
M° Gare de l'Est or Jacques Bonsergent. **Open** 5pm-
midnight Mon; 10am-2am Tue-Sat; noon-9pm Sun.
Food served 10am-2am Tue-Fri; noon-2am Sat;
noon-9pm Sun. **No credit cards. Map** L3.

L'Atmosphère remains at the centre of the Canal St-
Martin renaissance and sums up the spirit of the area.
Parisians of all kinds chat, read and gaze from the
waterside terrace, while within the simple, tasteful
interior, animated conversation and cheapish drinks
provide entertainment enough. It's always packed,
but brave the crowds on Sundays for the early-
evening world and experimental music slots.

Bar Le Panier

32 pl Ste-Marthe, 10th (01.42.01.38.18).
M° Belleville. **Open** 10am-2am Tue-Sat. **Food**
served noon-2am Tue-Sat. Closed two weeks in Dec.
No credit cards. Map M3.

Place Ste-Marthe feels refreshingly down to earth,
just a quiet cobbled square bordered by three cafés.
Bar Le Panier is especially homely, with candles
flickering against the orange walls. We were settled
in minutes and lingering over a mint tea, then wine,
nibbles of popcorn sprinkled with cumin, and
toasted baguette with anchovy paste.

De La Ville Café ★

34 bd Bonne-Nouvelle, 10th (01.48.24.48.09).
M° Bonne Nouvelle. **Open** 11am-2am daily. **Food**
served noon-midnight. **Credit** MC, V. **Map** J4.

One of the largest café terraces in Paris has
everything you need for a summer night of tippling
under the stars: moderate prices, a very mixed crowd
that's sniffing around for a good time, lounge music
and a decent look. On the weekends a DJ spins, and
what really surprises is that the mixes work for
everyone from the thirtysomething bobo types
who've just bought flats nearby to suburban kids
who know they're not taking the last train home.
Staff, though, seem to have landed here by accident
– the last thing they want to do is wait tables.

L'Ile Enchantée

65 bd de la Villette, 10th (01.42.01.67.99).
M° Colonel Fabien. **Open** 8am-2am Mon-Fri; 5pm-
2am Sat, Sun. **Food served** noon-3pm, 8-11.30pm.
Credit MC, V. **Map** M3.

This café-bar-restaurant near the headquarters of
the French Communist party has gueule, or
character. On the ground floor, arty twenty- to
thirtysomethings fill the café with pale blue smoke,
while the upstairs room is a former apartment with
red-painted stucco mouldings. Beyond the sassy
soft-techno played by the DJ, what's made this place
popular is the mix of events here – one night, a guest
DJ from Berlin spinning German underground
sounds, another a debate animated by Daniel Cohn-
Bendit. If many make a night of it here, it's also an
ideal place to hang out before heading to a club.

La Patache

60 rue de Lancry, 10th (01.42.08.14.35). *M° Jacques
Bonsergent.* **Open** 6pm-2am daily. **Cold food**
served non-stop. **No credit cards. Wheelchair**
access. **Map** L4.

Abdel, flirting and bickering with that week's
barmaid less than half his age, presided over this
dilapidated diamond long before the nearby Canal
St-Martin became des res. The iconic Hôtel du Nord
poster is no pose, but a reference to the real pre-war
venue just over the bridge, whose starring role in
Marcel Carné's 1938 film classic would have been
enjoyed by the bar regulars of the day. They're still
here, in spirit, their present-day counterparts still
arguing, cursing, smoking, drinking, falling in and
out of love. Abdel provides scraps of paper at each
table should they no longer be speaking to each
other. Otis no longer wails from the long-dead
jukebox, more's the pity, but it's a small price to pay
for living history.

Le Sainte Marthe

32 rue Ste-Marthe, 10th (01.44.84.36.96).
M° Goncourt or Belleville. **Open** 7pm-2am Mon-Sat.
Closed 25 Dec. **Food served** 8-11.30pm. **Happy
hour** 7-10pm. **No credit cards. Map** M3.

Away from cars, crowds, tourists and tucked-down
stiffs in suits, this cosy square hides one of the city's
best terraces, dropped squarely in the middle of a
ragged working-class neighbourhood. The place Ste-
Marthe itself could be a petting zoo of bobos – young
and middling hipsters mingle en masse at its three
bars and restaurants and spill out over the
cobblestones in summer. Le Sainte Marthe is
certainly the most culinary, with some tasty light
dishes, even though on some hot August nights its
waiters run short on smiles, and even on red wine.

La Soupière ★

12 rue Marie-et-Louise, 10th (01.42.08.10.41).
M° Jacques Bonsergent. **Open** noon-2am Tue-Sun.
Credit MC, V. **Map** L4.

Part of the semi-underground scene in the
burgeoning 10th of the mid-1990s, by the end of the
decade La Soupière had breathed its last. Now
blessed with dynamic new management, this boho
classic near the Canal St-Martin has reopened to
provide a crowd-free alternative to the quayside
snobbery nearby. Resolutely arty – poetry readings,
the odd DJ at weekends – La Soup' features a jazzy
interior of Chinese lanterns, vulgar oil paintings and
cacti, and a scattering of streetside tables which
catch the last of the afternoon's rays. The prices are
friendly – Maes and rare draught Jenlain at under
€2.50 a pop – and the clientele cool. Recommended.

Le Zorba

137 rue du Fbg-du-Temple, 10th (01.42.39.68.68).
M° Belleville. **Open** 5am-2am daily. **No credit
cards. Map** M4.

Perhaps the three-hour interval during which this
place is closed daily is a kindness, since it offers a
decent chance at coming to your senses after a long

session at this drinker's institution and local classic just off Belleville's equivalent of Piccadilly Circus. Definitely not for anyone after poncey cocktails and a high design setting, but a treat for those who like a walk on the wild side, since this place pulls all thirsty comers, from PMU gamblers to beer-swigging North Africans, with a good measure of arty odd bods thrown in. It's cheap and working-class, so don't be surprised by red strip lighting, squat toilets or tobacco-stained walls. A much better measure of Paris today than anything you'll find in the 8th arrondissement or St- Germain-des-Prés.

11TH ARRONDISSEMENT

L'Armagnac
104 rue de Charonne, 11th (01.43.71.49.43).
M° Charonne. **Open** 7am-2am Mon-Fri; 10.30am-2am Sat; 10.30am-midnight Sun. **Food served** noon-3.30pm, 7-11pm. **Credit** MC, V. **Map** P6.
Beginning its evenings as a traditional bistro and finishing them as a thumping bar, L'Armagnac is many different things to many different people. There's even a magic show every Wednesday around 9pm. Reserve if you want a table, as the traditional bistro nosh here, though not particularly good, is very popular. (If you're sitting close to the kitchen, watch for the chef's fanatical devotion to the blowtorch: there's hardly a dish on the menu that escapes it!) The service is overworked but very friendly, having to turn people away at the door for lack of space, yet never rushing customers, even when they are savouring a third after-dinner cigarette.

L'Ave Maria ★
1 rue Jacquard, 11th (01.47.00.61.73). M° Parmentier.
Open 7pm-2am daily. **Food served** 8pm-midnight. Closed 24, 25 Dec, 1 Jan. **No credit cards**. **Map** M5.
Caribbean steam cabin or Brazilian beach hut? It's a bonhomie-fusion thang here, the kind of place that likes to imagine there's a permanent but indistinct tropical rainstorm outside. A fuggy, orangey glow lights a cosy bar, dolled up with kitsch knick-knacks, making a Mojito obligatory. There's more restaurant space at the back, where the world food comes courtesy of Favela Chic's former chef, who shoots from the hip to tasty effect with meat, fruit and spicy vegetables. Packed by mid-evening.

Bar des Ferrailleurs
18 rue de Lappe, 11th (01.48.07.89.12). M° Bastille.
Open 5pm-2am Mon-Fri; 3pm-2am Sat, Sun. **Happy hour** 5-10pm. **Credit** MC, V. **Map** M7.
The name alludes either to swashbucklers or scrap (metal) dealers. As the walls are festooned with broken surfboards, old skis and golf clubs, one is tempted to assume it's the latter. This is one of the least overtly trendy bars on the rue de Lappe, and, thus, one of the cheapest. Its extended happy-hour rum cocktails seem to be a particular favourite of the young regulars, who down them in quick succession in an atmosphere of fairy lights and techno.

Mojitos all round at **L'Ave Maria**.

La Bonne Franquette
151 rue de la Roquette, 11th (01.43.48.85.88).
M° Voltaire or Père Lachaise. **Open** 10am-midnight daily (mid Apr-Sept); 10am-midnight Mon-Sat (Oct-mid Apr). **Food served** noon-2.30pm, 7.30-10.30pm. **Credit** MC, V. **Map** P6.
This fantastic family-run expo-bar is the antithesis of its name ('bonne franquette' means rough-and-ready food), serving delicious couscous dishes and oriental pastries to hungry crowds of bohemians, TV types and faithful locals. On a sunny day the giant terrace is a godsend, but when it's full, and in winter, the interior holds its own delights with its cool urban-chic decor and North-African influenced detail (check out the handmade rugs on the benches). Monthly art exhibitions also cover the walls and the waiters won't hesitate to talk to you about the paintings. Possibly the friendliest bar in Paris.

Le Fanfaron
6 rue de la Main-d'Or, 11th (01.49.23.41.14).
M° Ledru-Rollin. **Open** 6pm-2am Tue-Sat. **Happy hour** 6-8pm. Closed two weeks in Aug. **Credit** MC, V. **Map** N7.
Le Fanfaron (named after Dino Risi's cult 1962 movie) is a brand-new haunt for musically inclined retro-dudes. Envious buffs come from far and wide to listen to owner Xavier's personal collection of rare film soundtracks. The decor is an ode to kitsch-cool with Rolling Stones and Iggy Pop memorabilia, second-hand furniture, 1960s film posters and Lucy

the legless mannequin who reveals all on one side of the bar. At weekends MR Raw whacks on LPs way into the wee hours and if the inexpensive booze gets the stomach acids rising, try Xavier's chèvre à ma façon (goat's cheese my way) or an entire saucisson for a measly hunger-waning €4.

Favela Chic ★

18 rue du Fbg-du-Temple, 11th (01.40.21.38.14/ www.favelachic.com). M° République or Goncourt. **Open** 7.30pm-2am Tue-Thur; 8pm-5am Fri, Sat. **Food served** 8pm-midnight. **Credit** MC, V. **Map** L4.
A hot and immensely popular Latin cocktail joint which makes the easy switch from eaterie to bar/club at some point afore midnight. The dancefloor gets so crowded you can feel the air dripping sweat (this is a good thing, we assure you), and the cocktails err on the side of potent. DJs occasionally veer from South America and don't be surprised if you end up in a drum 'n' bass night – or, for that matter, listening to anything from Britpop to Viennese waltzes.

F.B.I. Paris (Freestyle Bar)

45 rue de la Folie-Méricourt, 11th (01.43.14.26.36/ www.fbiparis.com). M° St-Ambroise. **Open** 7pm-2am Mon-Sat. Closed Aug. **Happy hour** 7-10pm. **Credit** MC, V. **Map** M5.
Wander into this cringingly named but entertaining bar for a cocktail before heading to Oberkampf. The bartender will serve you a beer, but he'd rather juggle his bottles and mix up a concoction worthy of a legendary American bar. Why not experiment with the Japanese slipper (Midori, Cointreau and lime juice cordial) or stick to the tried and true gimlet (gin with lime), served in a bathtub-sized glass.

Le Lèche-Vin

13 rue Daval, 11th (01.43.55.98.91). M° Bastille. **Open** 7pm-2am Mon-Sat; 7pm-midnight Sun. **Credit** MC, V. **Map** M5.
An old Bastille stand-by, best known for its kitsch religious figures and pornographic pictures decking out the toilet, tee hee. Yet the iconic imagery and papier-mâché creations – eg the witch with archery targets for nipples dangling over the bar – should not distract from the fact that this is a damn good bar even without the blasphemy. Quality Belgian beers on tap and in bottles pass across the zinc counter with regularity, to a bohemian clientele of all ages and hairstyles, who prefer to avoid the suburbanites and tourists strolling down bar-starred but past-it rue de Lappe nearby. Generous happy hours till 10pm usher in a €3.50 price tag on cocktails, and ensure lively banter till the early hours.

Planète Mars

21 rue Keller, 11th (01.43.14.24.44). M° Ledru-Rollin. **Open** 6.30pm-2am Mon-Sat. **Happy hour** 7-10pm. Closed two weeks in Aug. **Credit** MC, V. **Map** M6.
From the dour grey of a Bastille backstreet, enter a world of colour. Shimmery disco balls and bright red walls tell you straight off that, yes, you are in retro heaven. Kitsch objects line the walls, a space-age bar

is buttressed by impatient queue jumpers, funky cocktails abound (top Mojitos), and drink prices defy inflation so much you'd half suspect them to still be using old francs. Add to this DJs in a little corner spinning everything from funk to Northern Soul to 1980s disco and back again, and what have you got? A red planet full of fun, that's what.

Pop In ★

105 rue Amelot, 11th (01.48.05.56.11). M° St-Sébastien-Froissart. **Open** 6.30pm-1.30am Tue-Sun. Closed two weeks in Dec and Aug. **Happy hour** 6.30-9pm. **Credit** MC, V. **Wheelchair access**. **Map** L5.
The Pop In seems to be a contradiction in terms, or at the very least an exercise in postmodern irony. A bar so uncool that it is in fact cutting edge, a place that is so hip it seems tragic. Since it hosted a Christian Dior after-show party and was subsequently colonised by fashion hangers-on, the Pop In has won a reputation as a place that doesn't care, doesn't try, but manages to be cool anyway. It's scruffy, cheap and the staff are genuinely nice. Add in a cellar bar that alternates between an open-mike night and a club for DJs and you have a recipe for a top night out.

Le Zéro Zéro

89 rue Amelot, 11th (01.49.23.51.00). M° St-Sébastien Froissart. **Open** 5pm-2am daily. Closed two weeks in Dec. **Happy hour** 6.30-8.30pm. **Credit** MC, V. **Map** L5.
Revolutionary when it opened in 1999, the ZZ still has a chip on its shoulder. It's as wee as a wardrobe, it drinks like a fish and its music kicks like a mule, so there. And many – menfolk, invariably – rally to the cause. They gather round the miniscule L-shaped bar and utter musings, so profound at the time, so pitiful when chalked up in bare white-and-black over the counter. Attention should be drawn, though, to the cocktail blackboard, which is extensive and potent, incorporating a Zéro Zéro of dark rum, ginger and lime. And even the ZZ has had to succumb to happy hour discounts (6.30-8.30pm) despite a more than reasonable pricing structure. Oh, and the decorators haven't touched it since the day it opened.

12TH ARRONDISSEMENT

Barrio Latino

46-48 rue du Fbg-St-Antoine, 12th (01.55.78.84.75). M° Bastille. **Open** 11.30am-2am daily. **Food served** noon-3pm, 7.30pm-midnight. Closed 25 Dec, 1 Jan. **Credit** AmEx, DC, MC, V. **Wheelchair access**. **Map** M7.
Like a Baz Luhrmann set kicking up 'ay caramba', Barrio Latino shudders with flamboyant excess in a blood-red rendition of a fantasy Havana hotel. Beware the after-8pm €8 entry fee. Young things come early to scan the talent before Rio-types dance manically on the tables and stairs, like a bunch of over-keen extras shaking their way to fame in a Christina Aguilera video. Effective antidepressant – take with Mojito and weekend salsa classes.

On the Town

China Club ★

*50 rue de Charenton, 12th (01.43.43.82.02/www.
chinaclub.cc). M° Bastille or Ledru-Rollin.* **Open** 7pm-
2am Mon-Thur, Sun; 7pm-3am Fri, Sat. **Food
served** 7pm-12.30am. Closed Aug. **Happy hour**
7-9pm. **Credit** AmEx, MC, V. **Map** M7.

The deep leather Chesterfields and 14-metre-long
mahogany bar are key parts of the theme: a Hong
Kong gentlemen's club of the 1930s (think Tintin in
The Blue Lotus). An audacious conceit in a working-
class neighbourhood, but it's pulled off brilliantly.
A lovely and relaxing bar in which to pontificate on
the dryness of one's martini over a background of
Callas or Caruso, the China Club also offers good dim
sum and other Cantonese stalwarts. Thirty different
digestifs are on offer, as well as a selection of single-
malt whiskies. There is often free live music on
Fridays and Saturdays (check website for details).

La Liberté

*196 rue du Fbg-St-Antoine, 12th (01.43.72.11.18).
M° Faidherbe-Chaligny.* **Open** 9am-2am Mon-Fri;
11am-2am Sat, Sun. **Food served** noon-3pm. **Credit**
MC, V. **Map** N7.

By day La Lib is a relaxed spot to muse over a plat
du jour. The decor is a little primitive, to be sure, and
rubbing elbows is inevitable, but convivial is the
word you're looking for. Good food too, a notch above
the average bar grub and a notch cheaper. By night,
though, it's ripped to the tits and still thirsty with it.
If you're bored with twee bobonia elsewhere in Paris
and are in need of a little edge, La Lib will provide.
Attracting drunks of every stripe, La Lib comprises
a small terrace and a narrow bar area dangling with
knick-knacks and invariably choc-a-block. The back
room is used for groups who actually want to talk to
each other. The rest guzzle (house punch or decent
Belgian brews by the bottle), guffaw and cop off, and
at some point everyone gets a turn to dance like a
maniac on the bar counter. The music is always right.
African beats, Burning Spear or Little Richard
howling Lucille, it's just there. Reliably raucous.

13TH ARRONDISSEMENT

Le Couvent

*69 rue Broca, 13th (01.43.31.28.28). M° Les
Gobelins.* **Open** 9am-2am Mon-Fri; 6pm-2am Sat.
Food served noon-2pm, 7-10pm. **Happy hour**
6-8pm. **Credit** MC, V. **Map** J10.

For an address in the middle of nowhere, this heavily
beamed bar creates a delightful hideaway. It first
appeared in Pierre Gripari's novel *Contes de la rue
Broca*, but has come a long way since those dingy
days. Nowadays it's the chouchou of students and
thirtysomething couples, especially at concert time
when live chords get feet tapping.

La Folie en Tête

*33 rue de la Butte aux Cailles, 13th (01.45.80.65.99).
M° Place d'Italie or Corvisart.* **Open** 5pm-2am
Mon-Sat. Closed 25 Dec-2 Jan. **Happy hour** 6-8pm.
Credit MC, V

The happy-hour apéros for only €1.50 are a bargain
even among the deflated pricing of the bucolic Butte-
aux-Cailles. There's a laid-back feel in the evening as
couples and friends gather around the low tables,
sitting on little wooden footstools which, though
convivial, can numb the bum rather quickly. This is
less of a problem as the night progresses, as live music
or a DJ get people on their feet. The walls are covered
with bruised violins, horns, and organs that look as
if they've been retired after long careers of Métro
busking. Very down-to-earth and friendly.

14TH ARRONDISSEMENT

L'Entrepôt

*7-9 rue Francis-de-Pressensé, 14th (01.45.40.60.70/
www.lentrepot.fr). M° Pernety.* **Open** 8am-1am daily.
Food served noon-2.30pm, 7-10pm. **Credit** MC,
V. **Non-smoking room**. **Wheelchair access**.
Map F10.

This converted paper warehouse has something for
every taste: a bar, a restaurant with leafy outdoor
courtyard and an independent, three-screen arts
cinema. Chill out and listen to music (jazz on
Thursday, world music on Friday and Saturday) for
a mere €5 or just drop in and see what's going down.

Le Rosebud

*11 bis rue Delambre, 14th (01.43.20.44.13). M°
Vavin or Edgar-Quinet.* **Open** 7pm-2am daily. **Food
served** 7-11pm. Closed Aug. **Credit** MC, V. **Map** G9.
Designed to satisfy the alcoholic needs of
Montparnasse's mass of intellectuals, the Rosebud
has been a social hub since 1962. Today, it pulls in
a more varied clientele: cocktail lovers, the odd
tourist and eccentrics. The interior is classic aristo-
chic but the real stars are the white-jacketed barmen.
Down a daiquiri or a vodka and orange and enjoy
the ethereal jazz before your senses are blurred.

Le Tournesol

*9 rue de la Gaîté, 14th (01.43.27.65.72). M° Edgar-
Quinet.* **Open** 8.30am-2am Mon-Sat; 5.30pm-1am
Sun. **Food served** noon-2.30pm, 6.30-11pm Mon-Fri;
noon-11pm Sat, Sun. **Credit** MC, V. **Map** G9.

With theatres and sex shops for neighbours, this
sibling of La Fourmi was always going to draw an
unstuffy crowd – it's just a shame the staff don't
have the same attitude. Apart from the eponymous
sunflowers behind the bar, it's industrial chic all the
way, with rope-wrapped ducts and raw concrete
walls. Food runs to brasserie standards, salads and
tartines. Cocktails are well-made classics, though the
large drinking area is packed at most times, so
chances are you'll be nursing that gin fizz at the bar.

15TH ARRONDISSEMENT

Le Bréguet ★

72 rue Falguière, 15th (01.42.79.97.00). M° Pasteur.
Open 5pm-4am Mon-Sat. **Food served** 7pm-
midnight. **Happy hour** 5-8pm. **Credit** MC, V.
Map E9.

OK, so it's in the middle of nowhere and the decor is nondescript, so why bother? Well, aside from the fact that it's rare to find somewhere with this much atmosphere in the fun-free 15th, it's worth the Métro journey for the eclectic drinks list. As well as the usual beers on tap, there is Strongbow cider, commendably smooth Guinness, vodkas and exotic quaffs like Limoncello. Work your way down the list, you know you want to.

16TH ARRONDISSEMENT

Bar Panoramique

Hôtel Concorde La Fayette, 3 pl du Général-Koenig, 17th (01.40.68.51.31/www.concorde-lafayette.com). M° Porte Maillot. **Open** 5pm-3am daily. **Credit** AmEx, DC, MC, V. **Map** B3.

Perfect for lovers or the alone and pensive, Bar Panoramique comes up tops with visual therapy, gazing from the 33rd floor over the Eiffel Tower, Arc de Triomphe and La Défense. At night, the mirrored '70s interior and city skyline create a soft-lens glamour, enjoyed by American business travellers, cupped in tiers of leather banquettes. Beware the 9.30pm watershed, when the piano bar hikes all drinks up to €20.50, from Champagne to coffee.

Petit Défi de Passy ★

18 av du Président-Kennedy, 16th (01.42.15.06.76/ www.defidepassy.com). M° Passy. **Open** 10am-midnight Mon, Tue; 10am-2am Wed-Sat; 4pm-midnight Sun. **Food served** noon-2pm, 7.30-10pm Mon-Sat; 7.30-10pm Sun. **Happy hour** 5-8pm Mon-Fri. **Credit** AmEx, MC, V. **Non-smoking room**. **Map** B6.

In permanent rebellion against its posh postcode, this refreshingly no-fuss bar-restaurant challenges the local chi-chi rule, jollying along friendly students and English teachers through happy hour in a distinct whiff of late adolescence. It's positively bursting with toff totty (albeit rather on the young side) and the best bit is, it's exceedingly cheap. Impress the fillies by buying a bottle of Absolut for around €60 and keeping it behind the bar with your name on: not only might you gain entry into gilded youth, at the very least you can stake a claim in the 16th.

Tsé

78 rue d'Auteuil, 16th (01.40.71.11.90). M° Porte d'Auteuil. **Open** 10.30am-2am Mon, Sun; 10.30am-3am Tue-Thur; 10.30am-4am Fri, Sat. **Food served** noon-2.30pm, 7-11.30pm Mon-Sat; noon-4pm, 7-11.30pm Sun. **Credit** AmEx, MC, V. **Wheelchair access**.

The Asian fusion formula has even crept out as far as villagey Auteuil, a hotbed of snooty old people and thirtysomething hipsters in desperate need of a hotspot to call their own. Now they have it in the form of Tsé, a stylish squeezed into the old railway station. A Franco-Sino-Japanese bar-restaurant-club, it peddles kudos and alcoholic regeneration, at a price, to a vogueish clientele bearing sharp specs and media manners and talking into their dinky mobile phone ear-pieces rather than

Tsé – Asian fusion reaches Auteuil.

to their drinking partners. The enticing dark-red and gilt interior is rampant with oriental lanterns, tassels and carved wood, while the drinks menu lapses into poncey Zen babble. Although it's a bit far up its own concept, this is a relaxing and opulent neighbourhood spot, with attentive pretty-boy staff, live jazz and funk DJs, sushi nibbles, simply fantastic Asian-styled cocktails and an utterly glorious sun-trap roof terrace.

17TH ARRONDISSEMENT

Le Cyrano

3 rue Biot, 17th (01.45.22.53.34). M° Place de Clichy. **Open** 9am-2am Mon-Fri; 5pm-2am Sat. **Food served** noon-2.30pm Mon-Fri. Closed 24 Dec, 1 Jan. **No credit cards**. **Map** G2.

Once the finest football bar in all France, the Cyrano has not lost its communal touch after a recent change of management. The missing scarves, flags and pennants – hopefully dutifully mounted elsewhere – now give way to a series of bar scenes intricately created in papier-mâché, and allow the colourful tiling and tubas of the retro decor to shine through. A busy interior in which thesps from the nearby L'Européen theatre mingle with mechanics, students and assorted layabouts reflects the multi-communal mix of the vicinity. A spot outside allows a grandstand view of the pedestrian flow along rue Biot to and from its place de Clichy estuary.

Lush ★

16 rue des Dames, 17th (01.43.87.49.46/www.lushbars.com). M° Place de Clichy. **Open** 5pm-2am daily. Closed 25-28 Dec. **Happy hour** 6-8pm Mon-Fri. **Credit** MC, V. **Map** G1.

At a prime address in Batignolles, Lush is a sleek lair for chilled-out drinking. Soft grape purples and comfy banquettes provide a suitable setting for inexpensive pints, well-chosen New World wines and delicious cocktails. Premiership football and rugby on big-screen TV, and half-decent live music, drag punters from across the city.

3 Pièces Cuisine

25 rue de Chéroy/101 rue des Dames, 17th (01.44.90.85.10). M° Rome or Villiers. **Open** 8am-2am Mon-Fri; 9.30am-2am Sat, Sun. **Food served** noon-11pm. Closed 25 Dec, 1 Jan. **Credit** MC, V. **Wheelchair access. Map** G1.

This bar looks like a scruffy old neighbourhood caff that's been taken in hand by a young *Elle Déco* reader. Red flock wallpaper and green study lamps create an intimate parlour at the back, with a few salvaged cinema seats thrown in for boho credibility. Staff are cheery, but the clientele keep their voices pretty low – you get the impression that talk is more Serge Gainsbourg than Johnny Hallyday. Try the chocolate milkshake – it has far more ice-cream in it than your mum would ever have allowed.

18TH ARRONDISSEMENT

La Divette de Montmartre

136 rue Marcadet, 18th (01.46.06.19.64). M° Lamarck Caulaincourt. **Open** 3pm-1am Mon-Fri; 5pm-1am Sat, Sun. **Credit** MC, V.

Serge, the barrel-bellied barman, is responsible for this cavern of colourful nostalgia. Slightly tucked away in Montmartre's hilly backstreets but worth the trek for all that, this is Serge's *Recherche du Temps Perdu*, in LP cover, poster and table-football form. Beatles' albums lined up over the bar, Stones ones under it and an Elvis clock in between. The old red phone box in the corner reinforces Serge's cross-Channel affinities. On tap, Wieckse Witte, Afflighem and Pelforth, and bar-room gossip of the days when Manu Chao were regulars.

Doudingue

24 rue Durantin, 18th (01.42.54.88.08). M° Abbesses. **Open** 6pm-2am Mon-Sat. **Food served** 7.30pm-1am. Closed two weeks in Aug. **Credit** AmEx, DC, MC, V. **Map** H1.

This bar is just how one might imagine Anthony and Cleopatra's pad to have looked had things worked out, with lots of indulgent, palatial details (big plumplicious cushions, cherubs on the ceiling and dainty chandeliers). The food, such as tuna steak with wild rice, is generally delicious. And the atmosphere and music swing to the right side of the wannabe meridian. Would Tony and Cleo have waited an hour for their drinks to arrive, as we did? Not likely, but mere mortals could do a lot worse.

La Fourmi ★

74 rue des Martyrs, 18th (01.42.64.70.35). M° Pigalle. **Open** 8am-2am Mon-Thur; 8am-4am Fri, Sat; 10am-2am Sun. **Food served** noon-3.30pm, 7-11pm Mon-Fri; noon-11pm Sat, Sun. Closed noon 24 Dec-noon 25 Dec. **Credit** MC, V. **Map** H2.

Flavour of the month in many quarters, and rightly so. Set on the cusp of the 9th and 18th, a short (steep) walk from lively Abbesses and busy boulevard stroll to place Pigalle, La Fourmi is retro-industrial at its best. An old bistro has been converted for today's tastes – picture windows giving natural light and visual bustle to the spacious, roughshod sand-coloured main interior, the prime seats on the podiums at the back. The classic zinc bar is crowned by industrial lights, the ornately carved back bar features the ant in question. A sound music policy and hip clientele seal the recommendation.

Le Sancerre

35 rue des Abbesses, 18th (01.42.58.47.05). M° Abbesses. **Open** 7am-2am Mon-Thur; 7am-4am Fri, Sat; 9am-2am Sun. **Food served** 9am-midnight. **Credit** MC, V. **Map** H1.

Of the many choices along rue des Abbesses, this is probably the most popular, its terrace invariably full, its large dark-wood interior an attractive mix of cool and cosy. Impressive draughts of Paulaner, Grimbergen and Record line up alongside Belgian bottled beauties such as Kriek and Mort Subite; the standard cocktails, all €5.50 on Mondays, are made with the same care as the tastefully presented food. Where's the catch? Well, the service is teeth-grindingly slow; this is particularly galling on the evenings when a well-meaning duo will be murdering your favourite Roy O number. Loudly. That heinous crime apart, pull up a chair.

19TH ARRONDISSEMENT

AbracadaBar

123 av Jean-Jaurès, 19th (01.42.03.18.04/www.abracadabar.fr). M° Laumière. **Open** 6pm-2am Mon-Wed, Sun; 6pm-5am Thur-Sat. Closed Aug. **Happy hour** 6-7.30pm. **Credit** MC, V. **Map** M2.

Scruffy and camp, AbracadaBar ain't your normal Paris corner bar. Apart from the late licence, there's a huge concrete fountain in front of the bar. Then there's the shrine to trolls, menus on springs and, the night we went, a band thumping out cracking funk to a delighted twentysomething crowd. Our Mojitos resembled an overgrown garden, but at twice the usual size, we weren't complaining.

Bar Ourcq ★

68 quai de la Loire, 19th (01.42.40.12.26). M° Laumière. **Open** 3pm-midnight Mon-Wed, Sun; 3pm-2am Fri, Sat. **Food served** noon-2pm Mon-Fri. **No credit cards. Map** N1.

Overlooking the Bassin de la Villette, this laid-back café-bar with a decor of globe lanterns hanging over a corner furnished with low tables and plump cushions is an uber cool place to lounge and entertain cheap thoughts over cheap drinks. It pulls an arty young crowd from the neighbourhood, although after many Parisians 'discovered' this refreshing body of water during the 2003 heat wave, the fauna is less local than it used to be. A DJ spins on Sunday afternoons, and there's always some kind of music happening here. A great address when you're up for a night out but don't feel like clubbing.

Café Chéri(e)

44 bd de la Villette, 19th (01.42.02.02.05).
M° Belleville. **Open** 8am-2am daily. **Food served** noon-2am. **Credit** MC, V. **Map** M3.
Partly responsible for the revival of the boulevard that separates upper Belleville from the rest of Paris, this bar is like the neighbourhood itself writ small – a dingy ethnic bar revamped as a hip DJ-styled lounge and youthful corner, where good feelings flow with bad wine and decent beer. We were greeted everywhere with a smile, a multilingual babble of upbeat chatting between strangers. If you feel a strange nostalgic twinge for cafeteria food, you can order at all hours from a vending machine containing freshly made dishes. Each night brings a different DJ's beat, but the same bon enfant spirit.

Café Parisien

2 pl Rhin-et-Danube, 19th (01.42.06.02.75).
M° Danube. **Open** 7am-10pm Mon-Sat. Closed Aug.
No credit cards.
Emerge from Danube, an obscure stop on a one-way offshoot of line seven in the far 19th, and you'll find a pretty square lapped by this oasis of nostalgic calm. At lunchtime, salads are served on the modest terrace bathed in sunlight – or around the small, tiled counter and its half-dozen tables. After dusk, this cosy interior becomes an honest-to-goodness locals' bar, cigarette smoke wafted away by an enormous fan, showing the gaudy colours of the vintage film posters in their true glory. The French titles bring a smile and, coupled with friendly service and near-provincial prices, should see you docking at the Danube again before too long.

20TH ARRONDISSEMENT

Aux Folies Belleville

8 rue de Belleville, 20th (01.46.36.65.98). M° Belleville.
Open 6.30am-2am daily. **No credit cards. Map** N4.
Zazou meets Zizou in this lively open-fronted café, its roots in the classic Hot Club days of waifs and wide boys, its current regulars and barstaff Kabyle expats originally from Algeria. Touches of art deco, a little neon and old slices of vinyl on tabletops can be discerned during convivial daytime opening, but once the surrounding chairs and long zinc counter start filling, you'll see nothing but exaggerated hand gestures, elegant puffing of cigarette smoke and the occasional flash of a clean-shaven waiter in tie and apron. Mojito punch for €4 is promised, as well as a boast of 75-year-old origins, but really this place is as timeless as it is unashamedly trendless.

La Fontaine d'Henri IV

42 bis rue des Cascades, 20th (no phone).
M° Jourdain. **Open** 6pm-2am daily. **No credit cards. Map** P4.
The poster outside says it all: 'Specialités: 1664 et Ricard'. La Fontaine d'Henri IV is possibly the city's oddest bar and its owner Zoubair one of the most affable. Just when you want to leave he locks you in, when it's a lovely day he's closed, and when you're not hungry he's laying on a free barbecue. Payback comes when you are sitting outside, polishing off your third glass with the sun sinking over Paris.

Lou Pascalou ★

14 rue des Panoyaux, 20th (01.46.36.78.10).
M° Ménilmontant. **Open** 9am-2am daily. **Food served** non-stop. **No credit cards. Map** N4.
Dress down for the scruffy but lovable Lou Pascalou, on a charmed square which has changed little with the decades. The bar, too, is much as it has been for years – blue with smoke, local and loose in the day, bohemian by night, and always cheap. It boasts an amazing array of hard alcohols, but when we actually asked for whiskies and bourbons there were only a few available. So much for variety – but you don't come here for the refined cocktail, only for a game of chess, an outdoor chat, a pression drawn straight up, no fuss.

Les Lucioles

102 bd de Ménilmontant, 20th (01.40.33.10.24).
M° Ménilmontant. **Open** 8am-2am Mon-Fri; 10am-2am Sat, Sun. **Food served** noon-3pm, 8pm-midnight. Closed 1 May. **Credit** AmEx, MC, V. **Map** N5.
If you've got an interesting scarf and want to show it off, this is the place. You'll be competing for attention with dangling birdcages and old apothecary jars. It's boho a go-go as animated chatter reaches ant-nest feverishness on slam poetry nights (Tue 10.30pm). The mike is open to all and sundry, allowing Paris's lowest-profile poets to declaim their latest and greatest, with a free drink proffered in return. There are also concerts on Sunday, occasional experimental cinema nights, and some nice-looking food.

Le Piston Pélican

15 rue de Bagnolet, 20th (01.43.70.35.00).
M° Alexandre Dumas. **Open** 8am-2am Mon-Fri; 10am-2am Sat, Sun. **Food served** noon-3pm, 7-11.30pm. **Credit** AmEx, MC, V. **Map** Q6.
Since its change from a discarded old hostelry into a gleaming, semi-retro music bar-café, the PP has attracted younger regulars to this slightly obscure part of the 20th. There's a large, raised dining area at the back, done out like a station waiting room, and a small, neat bar area out front. Attention is drawn to the long line of beer taps (Leffe, Pelforth, Guinness) before the eye discerns, amid the unwise maroon and mustard stucco of the decor, a shorter line of big old vats. House white, cider and… sweet mother of Abraham Lincoln, look at that, they've got snakebite on keg!

On the Town

Tea Rooms

This might be the city of le petit noir (black coffee), but Parisians take their tea seriously – particularly in the many Asian salons where tea-brewing becomes an art. Whether you want to sample rare leaves or simply sink back into silk cushions with a silver teapot, you'll find the perfect place to whet your thirst. (Keep in mind that tea is almost always a disappointment in cafés, where a pot of barely hot water comes with a tea bag on the side and costs a fortune.)

Angelina's

226 rue de Rivoli, 1st (01.42.60.82.00). M° Tuileries. **Open** 9.30am-6.45pm Mon-Fri; 9am-7pm Sat, Sun. **Tea** €5.75-€6. **Pâtisseries** €4.80-€6. **Credit** AmEx, MC, V. **Map** G5.

Stepping into Angelina's is like travelling back to the turn of the 20th century, and the new owners (who also own Brasserie Lipp) have promised the gentlest of facelifts. With its leather armchairs, green marble tables and bright murals, this classic tea salon has been serving its world-famous African hot chocolate (€6.40) to tourists and locals alike for decades. We had a decent raspberry tart, but the house speciality has always been the Mont Blanc – a chewy meringue topped with whipped cream and piped chestnut cream. Our visit was marred by two unpleasant waitresses who plonked our order on the table, but the hot chocolate was almost good enough to make us forgive them.

Jean-Paul Hévin

231 rue St-Honoré, 1st (01.55.35.35.96). M° Tuileries. **Open** noon-6.30pm Mon-Sat. Closed Aug. **Tea** €4.90-€6.40. **Pâtisseries** €3.90-€5.80. **Credit** AmEx, DC, MC, V. **Map** G5.

Master chocolatier Jean-Paul Hévin seeks to maximise your chocolate consumption by displaying his chocolates and cakes in the shop downstairs like museum treasures. We were so mesmerised by the gleaming golden tarte Tatin that we ordered a slice before looking at the rest of the menu. With its wood floors and chrome staircase, the minimalist setting might lead one to expect cold service, but our waiter was warm and extremely helpful while we looked at the pictorial menu, showing each gooey, chocolatey cake in all its glory. From the tea menu we chose the Marco Polo, described as Tibetan fruits and flowers, and the thé à l'opéra, green tea with red fruit. Both were aromatic and unique. While the tarte Tatin did not disappoint, the bittersweet chocolat framboise was of an entirely different confectionery class.

A Priori Thé

35-37 galerie Vivienne, 2nd (01.42.97.48.75). M° Bourse. **Open** *tea* 3-6pm Mon-Fri; 4-6.30pm Sat-Sun; *brunch* noon-4pm Sat-Sun. **Tea** €4.50. **Pâtisseries** €6-€7. **Credit** MC, V. **Non-smoking room. Map** H4.

American Peggy Ancock knew exactly what the capital's creatures of comfort were lacking when she opened A Priori Thé in 1980. The tea room inhabits one of Paris's glitziest covered passages, but its charm comes from its frumpy insouciance towards the gilded surroundings – and its comfort food. Alongside 25 staple brews such as orange pekoe and Darjeeling, Ancock serves up a blissfully fluffy cheesecake with raspberry coulis, intense chocolate brownies and deep-dish fruit crumbles, all in colossal portions. Though the tables under the arcade afford ample people-watching, regulars always fill up the wicker, cushioned chairs in the dining room first.

La Charlotte en l'Ile

24 rue St-Louis-en-Ile, 4th (01.43.54.25.83). M° Pont Marie. **Open** noon-8pm Thur-Sun. Wed tea and puppet show by reservation only; Fri 6-8pm piano tea. Closed July and Aug. **Tea** €4. **Pâtisseries** €2.50-€4.50. **Credit** MC, V. **Map** K7.

This tiny tea shop is full of the stuff of fairy tales – pictures of witches on broomsticks, lanterns, carnival masks. The only thing lacking is gingerbread. Quirky poetess and chocolatier par excellence Sylvie Langlet has been spinning her sweet fantasies here for more than 25 years. In the minuscule front room she sells her superb dark chocolate and candied fruit sticks, while at six tightly packed round tables she offers 36 teas of a quality that would put some five-star hotels to shame. Our choices of violet and apricot were served in simple blue and yellow bowls from dinky cast-iron teapots; their aroma alone perked us up. The desserts are magic, the hot chocolate probably the most potent in town.

Le Loir dans la Théière ★

3 rue des Rosiers, 4th (01.42.72.90.61). M° St-Paul. **Open** 11.30am-7pm Mon-Fri; 10am-7pm Sat, Sun. **Tea** €4. **Pâtisseries** €6. **Credit** MC, V. **Non-smoking room. Map** L6.

Named after Alice in Wonderland's dormouse in the teapot and decorated with Alice murals, Le Loir has a warm and welcoming feel that is far from the stereotyped stuffiness of some Parisian salons de thé. Shabby, mismatched furniture and kind and patient staff help to make even a first-timer feel like one of Alice's best friends. There are roughly 15 teas ranging from the traditional Earl Grey and green mint to the more exotic jasmine or lotus. Desserts such as lemon meringue pie and apple cinnamon nut cake are served in slices big enough for three, although the menu can be hit and miss in terms of quality. Le Loir must be one of the top spots for a chat with your best friend – if you glance around, you'll notice almost everyone is doing just that.

Café Maure de la Mosquée de Paris

39 rue Geoffroy St-Hilaire, 5th (01.43.31.38.20). Mº Place Monge. **Open** 9am-midnight daily. **Tea** €2. **Pâtisseries** €2. **Credit** AmEx, MC, V. **Wheelchair access**. **Map** K8.

Blue tiles, brass tables and a stunning coffered ceiling inside, with a terrace shaded by fig trees outdoors, transport you to a much more exotic location than this quiet street facing the Jardin des Plantes. No need for a menu; you order pastries from the counter on the way in and the sweet mint tea in tiny glasses from the quick-footed waiters. The honey-fig and pistachio-almond cakes provide a sugar rush which is only enhanced by the tea. The Mosquée also houses a steam room and massage parlour, although be sure to check ahead to see if it's a men's or a women's day in the hammam. A pleasant change from the stresses of life in a fast-paced city.

La Fourmi Ailée

8 rue du Fouarre, 5th (01.43.29.40.99). Mº Maubert-Mutualité or St-Michel. **Open** *tea* 3-7pm daily; July-Aug 5-7pm daily. **Tea** €3.50-€4.50. **Pâtisseries** €5.50-€6.50. **Credit** MC, V. **Non-smoking room**. **Map** J7.

The funky decor here can't really be called vintage, but it definitely aspires to an aged look, with its mustard-yellow vinyl banquettes, forest-green faux-marble tabletops, woven-straw laminated wallpaper and a quirky collection of books, Christmas garlands and framed butterflies draping the high-rising walls. La Fourmi Ailée is the quintessential Latin Quarter tea room – cultivating a stay-all-day ambience and lengthy intello head-bangs over its immense glass ashtrays. (Light-loving creatures should camp out in the bright, airy annexe upstairs.) Among a tea selection of Chinese, Ceylon, Assam and interesting flavour blends such as caramel-orange, we have a soft spot for the green tea with jasmine and always pair it with the bourdaloue pear-walnut tart.

L'Artisan de Saveurs ★

72 rue du Cherche-Midi, 6th (01.42.22.46.64). Mº St-Placide. **Open** *tea* 3-6.30pm Mon, Tue, Thur-Sun; *brunch* noon-3pm Sat, Sun. **Tea** €5.60-€6.60. **Pâtisseries** €6.50-€7.90. **Credit** MC, V. **No smoking**. **Map** F8.

You can't blame L'Artisan for banning smoking in its butter-yellow tea room, as the slightest speck of ash would stain the delightful provincial flavour here. Linen tablecloths, tasteful paper napkins and ivory-coloured tea sets stoke up country-home elegance. The selection of teas and pastries, meanwhile, surpasses urban sophistication. L'Artisan's menu eloquently explains 40 teas – from the standard Darjeeling to the more exotic Marco Polo varieties – while a long list of innovative pastries, prepared to order, defies description. On a recent winter visit, we warmed up with a frothy pineapple gratin spiked with kumbawa, a succulent fruit reminiscent of lime.

Forêt Noire

9 rue de l'Eperon, 6th (01.44.41.00.09). Mº Odéon or St-Michel. **Open** *tea* noon-7pm Mon-Sat; 3-7pm Sat, Sun; *brunch* noon-3pm Sun. **Tea** €4-€6. **Pâtisseries** €6. **Credit** DC, MC, V. **Non-smoking room**. **Map** H7.

The real adventure in the wilderness in the Forêt Noire is trying to decipher its odd (and strictly enforced) opening hours. After being turned away from a half-empty dining room midweek for tea, we returned over the weekend to greater success. Comfy red plaid chairs and exposed stone walls add to the country ambience. From the diverse tea list, we had the forêt noire, a mélange of dark berries and a nice complement to their moist lemon tart. The Black Forest cake is not to be missed, oozing with fresh cream and jam.

Mariage Frères

13 rue des Grands-Augustins, 6th (01.40.51.82.50) Mº Odéon or St Michel. **Open** *tea* noon-7pm daily. Closed 1 May, one week at Christmas. **Tea** €7-€10. **Pâtisseries** €7.50-€10. **Credit** AmEx, MC, V. **Non-smoking room**. **Map** H7.

Mariage Frères

This tea room on a quiet St-Germain street is the 149-year-old chain's most peaceful. After taking the stairs to the elevated seating area – a colonial backdrop with high-backed wooden chairs, hardwood floors, billowing flora and silver tea service – let white-tailed waiters guide you through the labyrinthine menu cataloguing 500 teas from across the globe. Choosing a pastry requires only one eye on the dessert tray, the work of Philippe Langlois. Many selections, such as his Indes galantes, a saffron-flavoured sponge atop an Assam-tinged mousse decorated with poached pears and a pear coulis, use tea as an ingredient. A simple 'fantaisie' brew, such as cardamom, pairs nicely with the elaborate pastries. On a warm day, opt for the mousse de jade – cold milk beaten with matcha (green tea).
Other locations: 30-32 rue du Bourg-Tibourg, 4th (01.42.72.28.11); 260 rue du Fbg-St-Honoré, 8th (01.46.22.18.54).

Pâtisserie Viennoise

8 rue de l'Ecole de Médecine, 6th (01.43.26.60.48). M° Odéon. **Open** 9am-7pm Mon-Fri. **Tea** €2.60-€3.70. **Pâtisseries** €3. **No credit cards. Non-smoking room. Map** H7.
If you're in need of a strudel fix, then look no further than Pâtisserie Viennoise with five to seven different strudels available depending on the whims of the baker. The decor is sparse, but the three tiny rooms of this hole in the wall are filled with the delicious smell of warm apples and cinnamon. Naturally one should drink either the coffee or viennoise hot chocolate topped with sweet whipped cream. For our snack, we chose the traditional apple strudel and the flanni, an apple and mashed poppyseed layered pastry. Surprisingly, we found the apple strudel dry and were salivating over our neighbour's cheese strudel. In the future, we'll make our pastry choice by looking in the window instead of at the menu.

Les Deux Abeilles

189 rue de l'Université, 7th (01.45.55.64.04). M° Pont de l'Alma or Ecole Militaire. **Open** 9am-7pm Mon-Sat. **Tea** €4.50. **Pâtisseries** €6. **Credit** MC, V. **Map** E5.
The capital's fashionistas still swan here in droves for some very chic tea and sympathy. Helmed by a slightly eccentric mother-and-daughter duo, this is an enticing cross between grandma's cosy front room and an elegant colonial era gazebo. Nostalgia is also literally on the menu – the olde style cakes, scones and brioches are so gorgeous that you'll feel guilty about actually tucking in. But remember, looks aren't everything – discovering that your ever-so-dainty pear tart has been brutally nuked within an inch of its life is definitely enough to break the spell of being momentarily whisked back to a more genteel space in time.

Le Bristol

112 rue du Fbg-St-Honoré, 8th (01.53.43.43.00). M° Miromesnil. **Open** 3-6.30pm daily. **Tea** €8. **Pâtisseries** €5-€11. **Credit** AmEx, DC, MC, V. **Wheelchair access. Map** E4.

Cross the apricot marble foyer and trip down the steps to the right to a vast lounge complete with marble columns, magnificent bouquets and a view across the lawns. The hotel's teas appear to have been picked by a connoisseur, as confirmed by our choice of the excellent grand Foochow fumé pointes blanches and Assam doomou. The accompanying little sandwiches of tuna, smoked salmon and cheese were deliciously buttery, although the absence of cucumber was a tad disappointing.

Hôtel Plaza Athénée ★

25 av Montaigne, 8th (01.53.67.66.65). M° Alma-Marceau. **Open** 8am-8pm daily. **Tea** €8. **Pâtisseries** €12. **Credit** AmEx, DC, MC, V. **Wheelchair access. Map** D5.
In the 18th century-style Galerie des Gobelins, you can watch the wealthy mingle. On our visit, the Iranian royal family had gathered for tea, next to them a famous opera singer and further down an eminent statesman. People-gazing, however, is a very minor pleasure compared to the Plaza's superb teas and dessert trolley. Try the fraisier, a strawberry and pistachio cream cake that is close to perfection. As for the teas, don't miss the mélange Plaza, a masterly blend of fig, hazelnut, quince and grape. Listening to the harpist and pouring another cup from the armoury of silverware, we felt part of it all. Even the head waiter played the game, slipping us some juicy celebrity gossip.

Ladurée

16 rue Royale, 8th (01.42.60.21.79/www.laduree.fr). M° Madeleine or Concorde. **Open** 8.30am-7pm Mon-Sat; 10am-7pm Sun. **Tea** €6-€7. **Pâtisseries** €4-€15. **Credit** AmEx, DC, MC, V. **Non-smoking room. Map** F4.
A Paris landmark, Ladurée serves a wide range of teas, pastries and its trademark macaroons in a down-to-earth setting (compared to the glitzy Champs-Elysées branch). We had the rose tea and the yin hao jasmine; both pots arrived filled with fragrant fresh tea leaves. Our chocolate macaroon was excellent and we regretted not trying all of the flavours (including coffee, rose, pistachio, coconut and mint). The St-Honoré à la rose, a rose and raspberry cream confection, was positively divine. Unfortunately, Ladurée has squeezed roughly twice as many seats as would be comfortable into an already cosy room. Expect minimal attention from whoever decides to lower himself to wait on you.
Other locations: 21 rue Bonaparte, 6th (01.44.07.64.87); 75 av des Champs-Elysées, 8th (01.40.75.08.75).

Les Cakes de Bertrand

7 rue Bourdaloue, 9th (01.40.16.16.28). M° Notre-Dame-de-Lorette. **Open** 9.30am-7.30pm daily. **Tea** €4. **Tea with mini-cakes** €7. **Pâtisseries** €4-€4.50. **Credit** MC, V. **No smoking. Map** H3.
With its baby-blue cabinetry, tapestry-covered chairs and crystal chandeliers, Les Cakes de Bertrand feels like a collector's-item doll's house.

On the Town

The art of tea

The French still consume a lot less tea than the British – 200g versus 3.15kg per person per year, to be exact – but it's quality, not quantity that counts this side of the Channel. The city's range of Far East-influenced tea rooms is impressive and diverse, from the simple setting at **T,cha** (6 rue du Pont de Lodi, 6th, 01.43.29.61.31) – a Chinese tea room with tasty but no-frills sweets such as apple loaf and ginger cookies – to the elaborate spread at **Toraya** (10 rue St-Florentin, 1st, 01.42.60.13.48), a Japanese tea room with a groovy decor and modern, artistic revisions of classic Japanese desserts.

Paris is also strong on tea-related learning experiences. At **La Maison de la Culture du Japon**, two weekly tea ceremonies are constantly booked. The ritual, fundamental to Japanese notions of hospitality, takes place in a teahouse replica perched in a fifth-floor, glass-enclosed space overlooking the Seine. After a detailed demonstration, visitors sample a bowl of matcha, an intense, foamy green tea.

For an introduction to Chinese tea, **La Maison des Trois Thés** (33 rue Gracieuse, 5th, 01.43.36.93.84) is the place to begin. With one of the largest tea cellars in the world, boasting more than 1,000 blends, the tea house is decorated with some 700 canisters of tea, suspended on the main wall of the unique brick-and-iron interior. Two menus list the likes of vintage (dating to 1890) and more humble brews, but a peek at the second-tier menu must be pre-approved by Madame Tseng. A soft-spoken waiter presents the menu before bringing boiling water to the chunky, high-rising tables carved from old Chinese doors, and then meticulously explains the infusion process. Before the sipping, of course, comes the sniffing. Our blue-green si ji chun seduced with notes of coconut and acacia, and tasted subtly of honeysuckle. It's best to book in advance, especially on weekends.

L'Empire des Thés (101 av d'Ivry, 13th, 01.45.85.66.33), another upmarket Chinese establishment, has drawn a predominantly French crowd to the heart of Chinatown since its opening two years ago. The shop serves 160 teas at four miniature tables in its earthy but elegant,

butter-beige sitting area. You can also play chess while munching on a pastry provided by the Japanese pâtissier Sadaharu Aoki. His sesame macaroons and cool, green-tea éclairs with perfect choux pastry complement any of the multi-coloured brews. Green teas sell best, along with grand jasmin Impérial – rolled tea-leaves resembling miniature pearls. Though L'Empire has little trouble selling rare white teas at ¤60 for 100g to connoisseurs, the shop also caters to beginners with tea initiations on the final Sunday of every month.

Neophytes also frequent **La Maison de la Chine**'s teahouse (76 rue Bonaparte, 6th, 01.40.51.95.00). The regularly changing menu includes some intriguing names for the house-created blends: felicity, prosperity and serenity, for instance. Our 'pledge of love', a semi-green with peony petals which is often shared by a couple on the verge of marriage, came with a tiny, dried rosebud floating in the teacup.

Nowhere is tea's newfound popularity more evident than at **Mademoiselle Li** in the Jardin d'Acclimatation, which attracts BCBG pilgrims. Nine different blends are served in frumpy crockery alongside bowls of sunflower, pumpkin and watermelon seeds. Try to grab the cushions at the low-lying tables near the entrance.

For something completely different... nestled among the Japanese noodle shops of the neighbourhood between Bourse and Opéra is **Zenzoo** (13 rue Chabanais, 2nd, 01.42.96.27.28), a Taiwanese tea room that will change the way you look at this simple or sophisticated drink. Here, it's not a question of sniffing, swirling and slurping, as in some elegant Asian tea rooms – the speciality is zenzoo, a 'liberal transcription' of zhenzhu naicha, meaning pearl in Chinese. Bobbing within the cold and hot teas are big, amber-coloured tapioca pearls, which you slurp up with the giant straw provided. They have a weird and rather wonderful texture, a bit like jujubes. You can order your zenzoo to go, or you can sit in the sleek and cosy tea room and enjoy the French or Asian lunch special of the day. Zenzoo has already become extremely popular with Asians, who pack the place out in the afternoon.

On the Town

Dainty porcelain tea sets and fairytale placemats heighten the tea-taking experience here. Alongside cheesecake, fondant au chocolat and fromage blanc with a fruit coulis, Bertrand's famous cakes – fruit and nut loaves, or one version with green tea – make a lighter complement for a South African red or Assam tea. With chai, a robust Indian blend spiked with cardamom, we enjoyed a plate of mini-cakes in a variety of flavours – pine-nut, chocolate, raisin, orange confit, walnut and almond. The tea room seats 18, who are served, at tea time, by just one.

Antoine et Lili, La Cantine

95 quai de Valmy, 10th (01.40.37.34.86/www. antoineetlili.com). M° Jacques Bonsergent. **Open** noon-7pm daily. Closed 19 Dec-7 Jan. **Tea** €2-€4. **Pâtisseries** €3-€5. **Credit** AmEx, DC, MC, V (€15 minimum). **Wheelchair access. Non-smoking room. Map** L4.

Welcome to the temple of kitsch, cooked up by the women's fashion and home-decor designers Antoine and Lili. This whimsical duo won over Paris's deep-pocketed, bobo-chic hearts with faux-vintage, Eastern-inspired prints and patterns, and now it has tickled everyone pink by hosting a zanily dressed tea loft near its flagship on the Canal St-Martin. Self-service is the principle here. Take your tray – with a white-chocolate tart with raspberries, and almond green tea – to a plastic-clothed table in the antique-red and pink-Technicolor smoking and non-smoking rooms. There is great seating for groups both on leopard-print stools and parrot-print benches. Our only gripe is the throwaway tableware.

L'Oisive Thé

1 rue Jean-Marie Jego, 13th (01.53.80.31.33). M° Place d'Italie. **Open** noon-7pm Tue-Thur; noon-8pm Fri-Sun. Brunch noon-6pm Tue-Sun. Closed in Aug. **Tea** €4.40-€5. **Pâtisseries** €3-€5. **Credit** MC, V.

L'Oisive Thé maintains a French country-Zen feel in a friendly and intimate setting with plenty of natural light. While bright yellow walls, Japanese tea sets and straw floor mats create the distinctive ambience, the fresh feel in the room probably comes from the air purifiers quietly ridding the room of the smoke that pervades other Parisian establishments. From their extensive tea menu (with more than 50 to choose from), we chose the aromatic fleur de geisha, a green tea with cherry blossoms, and the corromondel, a not-too-sweet blend of caramel and vanilla, and were disappointed by neither. Rather than order off the menu, we stuck with the daily specials – a mediocre crème caramel and one of the best chocolate cakes we had ever tasted.

Cold comfort

Spoiled by too many spectacular pastries, Parisians don't give frozen desserts their due. Yet, using the finest ingredients, a select group of glaciers churn out what must surely be some of the world's most intense ice-creams and sorbets.

Leading the way is **Berthillon** (31 rue St-Louis-en-l'Ile, 4th, 01.43.54.31.61), whose recent renovation and expansion has left the tea room looking like a purple hotel lobby. Take-away cones are scooped indoors, with flavours changing according to the seasons. Frustratingly, Berthillon closes all summer, but several cafés on the island continue to dish up its glaces.

Just as strategically located is **Le Bac à Glaces** (109 rue du Bac, 7th, 01.45.48.87.65), up the street from the Bon Marché department store. In its cramped, café-like setting, you can treat yourself to a selection of home-made ice-cream served in something like a giant escargot dish, or have an adult float of sorbet in a glass of Perrier. Flavours range from the classic (bourbon vanilla) to the wacky (mango with Sichuan pepper).

Intense French ice-creams are facing stiff competition from ambitious Italian-style upstarts such as **Amorino** (47 rue St-Louis-en-l'Ile, 4th, 01.44.07.48.08 and several other Paris addresses) and **Gelati d'Alberto** (45 rue Mouffetard, 5th, 01.43.37.88.07). The former looks set to conquer Paris with its fluffy, fresh-tasting gelati in flavours such as limone or marron glacé, while Alberto is more of an iconoclast with his lovingly sculpted gelato roses (shame about the grumpy staff).

La Butte Glacée (14 rue Norvins, 18th, 01.42.23.91.58) is an unpretentious gelateria near the Sacré-Coeur. After the long climb up reward yourself with stracciatella and banana yoghurt sorbet or a jaw-crunching crocante.

Further off the beaten track, **Raimo** (61 bd de Reuilly, 12th, 01.43.43.70.17) has been in the business since 1947. Though the white-shirted waiters are not overly attentive, the ice-cream more than makes up for it. The fleur de lait is heavenly, as is the woody Vermont maple. Cheaper scoops are available at out-of-the-way **La Tropicale** (180 bd Vincent-Auriol, 13th, 01.42.16.87.27), which offers jazz music, friendly service, and fabulous curaçao and mango sorbets. At the equally remote **Glacier Calabrese** (15 rue d'Odessa, 15th, 01.43.20.31.63), a '70s-style glacier, Luigi Calabrese serves up ginger, liquorice and a brilliant basil sorbet.

Wine Bars

If you find Paris wine lists baffling with their endless lists of mysterious appellations, wine bars are just the place to brush up on your terminology. Welcoming and unpretentious, they often serve food to rival top-quality bistros (or you can usually nibble on a plate of cheese or charcuterie). With a few exceptions (Juvénile's and the Italian wine bars), you'll find nothing but French wines on their lists, but there is plenty of territory to explore and you can cover a lot of ground if you order by the glass. Don't necessarily expect to be given the appropriate glass for each wine – it's an everyday drink in France, and thus is often served with little ceremony.

Juvénile's

47 rue de Richelieu, 1st (01.42.97.46.49). M° Palais Royal or Pyramides. **Open** 6-11pm Mon, noon-11pm Tue-Sat. Food served 6-11pm Mon; noon-11pm Tue-Sat. **Glass** €3-€10. **Bottle** €14-€400. **Credit** AmEx, MC, V. **Map** H4.

Tim Johnston, the quirky Scot who owns this tiny slice of wine bar, is a kid at heart, albeit one with pretty grown-up tastes. He knows what he likes (screw caps) and what he doesn't (George Bush), and he won't hesitate to tell you. Red is 'real wine'; 'real cheese' is English; and the weekly 'grunts' (cheap, cheerful, but thoughtfully selected) are always a good bet. The combination is a winner; and not just among expats in search of steaming plates of haggis. The baby-faced sommelier from the oh-so-posh George V came here to celebrate his big-league wine-tasting victory the day we visited and there's a staunch local following of informed tipplers and serious buyers. Johnston has none of the French phobia for new world wines, so if it's an Argentinian you're after, don't hesitate to ask. Excellent Basque charcuterie or plates of mâche and magret fumé, highlights from a small yet surprisingly varied menu, will help keep you sober.

Le Père Fouettard

9 rue Pierre Lescot, 1st (01.42.33.74.17). M° Etienne Marcel or RER Châtelet-Les Halles. **Open** 8am-2am daily. Closed 24, 25 Dec. Food served noon-1am. **Glass** €2-€4.50. **Bottle** €14-€507. **Credit** MC, V. **Map** J5.

This is a useful address in the heart of Les Halles, decorated in traditional style with the obligatory shiny zinc bar, a small dining room and a large terrace. The pumping soundtrack is slightly at odds with the junky decor, but it wasn't discouraging a steady flow of youngish customers on a freezing night. The selection of wines by the glass threw up a Rasteau 2000 from Trapidis; a good flinty Sancerre, Domaine Cherrier 1998; and a delicious, rich Vin de Pays des Bouches du Rhône 2001 from Château Roquefort. A Brouilly 2000 from Descombes was disappointingly dusty, but swiftly

replaced by the accommodating barman with a more interesting Morgon from Flache. We didn't have dinner, preferring just to nibble a little platter of saucisson sec served with cornichons, but reassuring signs such as Duval charcuterie and Berthillon ice-cream suggest there was no reason not to. Meaty mains – steaks, duck confit, etc – were on offer at around €15, plus a welcome 'coin végétarien' for herbivores.

La Robe et le Palais

13 rue des Lavandières-Ste-Opportune, 1st (01.45.08.07.41). M° Châtelet. **Open** noon-2pm, 7.30-11pm Mon-Sat. Food served noon-2pm, 7.30-11pm. **Glass** €3.50-€5. **Bottle** €14-€60. **Credit** MC, V. **Map** J6.

With its penchant for punny humour, we should have guessed this Seine-side spot would have attitude. Although our waiter was a little snide about our shared starter of marinated girolles (which indeed hardly sustained us as we waited an hour for our mains) and was slow to fill our water pitcher, he came up trumps when asked to pick a wine: an off-the-list 2003 white Faugères (from Ollier Taillefer) made our fish dishes taste better than they were and hung in long enough to wash down the spiced-apple rice pudding a treat. By the end of a long evening, the more jovial kitchen staff had moved behind the bar to do their own tasting from open bottles and the cheese platter; next time we'll do the same.

Au Sans Souci

183 rue St-Denis, 2nd (01.42.36.09.39). M° Réaumur-Sébastopol. **Open** 7.30am-9pm Mon-Fri (Sat opening for major sports events). Food served noon-3pm. Closed Aug. **Glass** €3-€4. **Bottle** €15-€20. **Credit** MC, V. **Map** K5.

Michel Godon, the charming, sparkly-eyed owner, has been holding the fort amid the quartier's sex shops for 29 years, though it was only in 1998 that he revamped this former café and concentrated on the wine. Slightly incongruous for your average wine bar are the pinball, TV and a fantastic jukebox full of French hits from the 1970s. One lone regular

Say cheese

For anyone wanting an introduction to French cheese, for anyone ever intimidated by the choice in fromageries or for cheese freaks in general, the answer is now here. Cheese bars, 'invented' by Lionel Mougne of Androuët, are the new way to try a variety of cheeses without having to sit through an entire meal to get there. To date, there are only a few, but the trend has caught on in such a big way with the Parisian lunch crowd that others are sure to follow.

Androuët's **Sur le Pouce** (49 rue St Roch, 1st, 01.42.97.57.39), with an actual (cow-themed) bar from which cheese is served, leads the way, providing very stylish platters of cheese in denominations of five, eight, 11 or, for the brave, 15. Tartines and assiettes, each matched with the perfect wine, provide alternatives to be followed by dairy-based desserts such as cheesecake.

Across town, sun-filled **Fil'O'Fromage** (12 rue Neuve Tolbiac, 13th, 01.53.79.13.35), near the Bibliothèque François Mitterrand, takes a similar approach, with assiettes froides (three cheeses, three cold meats and salad) and tempting cheese-based 'poêlons'. Friendly staff provide a torrent of advice in order to help you achieve the ultimate 'alchemic explosion', showing that here both food and customers are taken seriously. Don't miss the Fontainebleau or the expertly made coffee.

Recently established cheese shop **Fromagerie 31** (64 rue de Seine, 6th, 01.43.26.50.31) has its own modern cheese and wine bar behind a glass partition and a small terrace in summer. You can order plates of five, seven or nine cheeses, arranged from mildest to strongest, or opt for cheese-themed salads in summer or warm cheese tarts in winter, followed by cheesecake or fromage blanc.

was so moved he drained his glass, took out his air guitar and really went for it. Not so frivolous was the careful selection of the wines by the glass, with everything served in 7cl tasters at mad student prices (nothing over €2). We were suitably impressed by a very respectable gewurztraminer, crisp white Sancerre from Philip Raimbault, sound Vire Clesse and others. Then we were blown away by the superb raspberry fruit of a St-Chinian, Marquise des Mûres. You can have tartines and charcuterie at the bar, and lunch is served upstairs.

Les Enfants Rouges

9 rue de Beauce, 3rd (01.48.87.80.61). M° Temple. **Open** noon-3pm Tue-Sat; 7pm-2am Thur, Fri. Food served noon-2.30pm, 7pm-midnight. Closed three weeks in Aug and one week at Christmas. **Glass** €3-€4. **Bottle** €16-€90. **Credit** MC, V. **Map** L5. This lively wine bar next to the Marché des Enfants Rouges does very brisk business, lunch and dinner. Many of its patrons seem to know the owner, Dany Bertin-Denis, and her husband from their previous venture, Le Moulin à Vins, which served as an after-

hours hangout for Paris's sommeliers. The new place, with its cheerful dining room and tiny attached bar, seems to be suiting everyone just fine. The couple offer a popular lunch menu, as well as a blackboard of meaty bistro basics including lapin à la moutarde and an entrecôte with some very fine house-made frites. What keeps this place packed, however, is its authoritative and exciting wine list, which draws proficiently from every region in France, particularly the Loire and Rhône valleys and the south-east. The list notes each wine's producer, as well, and the patronne seems to know them all personally. The wines of the week are available by the glass, but otherwise one must commit to a full bottle, hardly a problem when they all come from France's finest winemakers.

L'Estaminet

Marché des Enfants Rouges, 39 rue de Bretagne, 3rd (01.42.72.34.85/www.aromes-et-cepages.com). M° Temple. **Open** 9am-8pm Tue-Sat; 9am-4pm Sun. Food served from noon Tue-Sun. **Glass** €2.50-€4. **Bottle** €5-€25. **Credit** DC, MC, V. **Wheelchair access**. **Non-smoking room**. **Map** L5.

This bright and airy wine bar with wooden tables and a modern zinc bar has become the soul of the revamped Enfants Rouges market. We started with two Gaillac wines, one a light and delicate still, the other sparkling. Brunch is served on Sundays but we were tempted by the seafood platter, which was traipsed in by the market's fishmonger in his wellies, coat and apron. We accompanied this breath of sea air with an interesting Touraine white, made from old vines of the obscure grape variety fie gris from producer Jacky Prey. Bliss.

La Belle Hortense

*31 rue Vieille-du-Temple, 4th (01.48.04.71.60).
M° St Paul or Hôtel de Ville.* **Open** 5pm-2am Mon-Fri. **Glass** €3-€7. **Bottle** €15-€35. **Credit** MC, V.
Non-smoking room. Map L6.
Bookshop, literary salon, wine bar and off-licence meet at this unusual Marais spot. Good wines by the glass include a strong contingent from the Rhône by Guigal. It's standing room only at the bar, but the non-smoking reading room at the back is sure to enhance your intellectual credibility.

L'Enoteca

25 rue Charles V, 4th (01.42.78.91.44). M° St-Paul or Bastille. **Open** noon-2.30pm, 7.30-11.30pm daily.
Closed one week in Aug. **Glass** €3-€8. **Bottle** €18-€300. **Credit** MC, V. **Map** L7.
If you like Italian wine, then this classy Marais trattoria is a must. The list is astounding, with plenty of hard-to-find wines from all the best producers: Gaja, Aldo Conterno, Vajra, Felsina Berardenga and a stack of vintages. And what a pleasure to taste by the glass – we tried Moscato d'Asti and Barbera from Piedmont, and Sant'Agata dei Goti from Campania (the selection changes weekly). The food is delicious too, with antipasti such as porchetta alla romana, generous portions of pappardelle al ragu di salsiccie, plus a few reliable meat and fish mains. Booking is advised.

Le Rouge Gorge

8 rue St-Paul, 4th (01.48.04.75.89). M° St-Paul or Sully Morland. **Open** noon-3.30pm, 6pm-2am Mon-Sat. Food served noon-3pm, 7-11pm. Closed last two weeks in Aug. **Glass** €3-€5. **Bottle** €19-€35. **Credit** AmEx, MC, V. **Wheelchair access. Map** L7.
The charming façade is as much an incitement to a visit as the enticing but slightly pricey wine list. At the heart of the old antique dealers' quarter, this small wine bar, all wooden beams and exposed stone, exudes Parisian charm. François Briclot makes each and every client feel like part of the family as he lines up sample bottles on your table. Wine themes change every three weeks; on our last visit we tried a succession of succulent Corsican whites and reds, something of a speciality here as Briclot has close links with many winemakers on the 'Ile de Beauté'. The female Moroccan chef, Elhamraoui Touria, logically offers a fine, fragrant couscous rendered even more colourful than usual

with the addition of pumpkin, but the Jura speciality of chicken with morels was slightly too dry. Wines are also available for take-away.

Les Papilles

30 rue Gay-Lussac, 5th (01.43.25.20.79/www.les papilles.fr). M° Cluny-La Sorbonne or RER Luxembourg. **Open** 9am-midnight Mon-Sat.
Food served noon-2pm, 7-11.30pm. **Glass** €3-€6.
Bottle €7-€200. **Credit** MC, V. **Wheelchair access. Map** J8.
Walking into this hybrid épicerie and wine bar steps away from the Jardins du Luxembourg will, indeed, set your papilles (taste buds) to work. The long space glows with the warm colours of southern France, its walls lined with bottles of wine, jars of conserves and pots of confit. The two couples that run this enterprise have an enviable existence: Gérard Katz and Pierre Martin trawl the French countryside for exciting new wines, while their wives, Brigitte and Julie, run the kitchen. The short provençal menu runs to quality charcuterie and salads taken from the refrigerated case at the front of the shop, some simple pastas, and a plat du jour that changes with the seasons. The focus here, however, is the wine. A substantial selection from all over France is available by the glass, including a vin du mois selected by the propriétaires. We sampled, among others, a formidable 1999 Faugères from the Domaine Leon Barral (€3.20 a glass). The owners are happy to open any of the bottles they have on sale for you, in addition to those listed on their blackboard. The place feels a bit sombre at night, so opt for a light lunch here and take the time to study this fine oenological collection.

Caves Miard

*9 rue des Quatre-Vents, 6th (01.43.54.99.30).
M° Odéon.* **Open** 10am-10pm Tue-Sat. Food served noon-3pm; cold plates until 8pm. Closed 25 July-25 Aug. **Glass** €2-€6. **Bottle** €4-€1,000. **Credit** MC, V.
No smoking. Map H7.
The proprietors of this tiny vintage crèmerie have restocked its once cheese-laden marble shelves and cupboards with a fine collection of organic wines from all over France. You can stop in just to pick up a bottle and benefit from their enthusiastic suggestions, or, better yet, you can seat yourself at one of the six tables and sample some of their very interesting wines that really taste of the grapes from which they were made. At lunch, they turn out some surprisingly good hot food. The rest of the day, beautiful little plates – fresh goat's cheese from the famous Quatrehomme shop served with a circle of fresh pesto and tiny organic tomatoes or wedges of aged parmesan with a jammy mostarda – show their reverence for quality and tradition. Presenting our board of excellent Italian charcuterie, the waiter concluded with real excitement, 'and here you have the best coppa in the world'. Perched at our little table and cosseted by the chatter of a 1940s film running over the restaurant's speakers, we didn't doubt him for a minute.

On the Town

Fish

*69 rue de Seine, 6th (01.43.54.34.69). M° Odéon or
Mabillon.* **Open** noon-2pm, 7-10.45pm Tue-Sun. Food
served noon-2pm, 7-10.45pm. Closed first two weeks
in Aug and two weeks at Christmas. **Glass** €4-€10.
Bottle €15-€200. **Credit** MC, V. **Wheelchair
access. Map** H6.

The title suggests a fish bistro, but it is actually
named for us wine lovers who 'drink like fish'.
Friendly service from an all English-speaking crew,
precision-cooked dishes and a copious, interesting
wine list that favours the Languedoc are what keep
the French and international clientele happy. Co-
owned by a New-Zealander and an American, who
also preside over the truly excellent La Dernière
Goutte wine shop around the corner, Fish proposes
such elusive treasures as an Egly-Ourlet
Champagne, tasty bottles from Charles Hours,
several vintages of Domaine Les Aurelles and
Faillard's Côte de Puy Morgon. By-the-glass
offerings are chalked up on the board. We feasted
on the great-value €29.50 menu, highlights being sea
bream roasted whole with garlic and fennel, breast
of guinea fowl stuffed with foie gras in orange and
coriander sauce and, for dessert, the creamy basil-
flavoured panna cotta with a berry fruit coulis.

L'Evasion

*7 pl St-Augustin, 8th (01.45.22.66.20/www.
levasion.net). M° St-Augustin.* **Open** 8am-1am Mon-
Fri. Food served noon-2.30pm, 7.30-11pm Mon-Wed.
Glass €3.60-€20. **Bottle** €17-€1,000. **Credit** AmEx,
DC, MC, V. **Wheelchair access. Map** F3.

Take one corner café, give it a lick of yellow paint
and cover the walls with little blackboards listing
the food and wines on offer. This seems all that was
deemed necessary at L'Evasion, in terms of
decoration, to turn the place around. The real
changes are in your glass and on your plate.
Consequently the clientele seems to be neatly
divided between serious wine geeks and guys
drinking beer at the bar and looking puzzled. For the
wines we are talking natural, bio-dynamic growers:
Crozes Hermitage from Dard et Ribo, Morgon from
Jean Foillard, Domaine Gramenon in Côtes du
Rhône. By the glass, a Costières de Nîmes from
Domaine de la Perillière was full of fruit, while
Chablis from Laurent Tribut was crisp and good. To
eat: top saucisson sec or thinly shaved Parma ham
for incurable nibblers. More substantial appetites
could choose from pan-fried guinea fowl, flank steak
with marrow, cod, or veal kidneys, finishing with
cheeses or ice-cream from Berthillon.

Le Coin de Verre

*38 rue de Sambre-et Meuse, 10th (01.42.45.31.82).
M° Belleville.* **Open** 8pm-midnight Mon-Sat. Food
served 8pm-midnight. **Glass** €2.50-€3. **Bottle** €10-
€15. **No credit cards. Map** M3.

A very special, rather secret destination, Le Coin de
Verre is identifiable only by a single strip light over
the door. It's cloak-and-dagger stuff – reservations
are imperative and you ring the doorbell to be
admitted. So we rang, then we rang again, and then
we called by mobile phone to explain we were
outside. Following this eccentric rigmarole we were
greeted with extraordinary warmth by Michel, who
led us past boxes and cases of wine, through to the
rustic back room where a log fire was roaring. Here,
Hugues set about us with paternal cordiality at a
beautifully leisurely pace. The blackboard (all
seriously cheap, nothing over €11.50) offered simple

Caves Miard. *See p263.*

On the Town

charcuterie and cheese plates; we were advised to go for the daily specials (simple blanquette de veau or grilled andouillette) before they ran out. From a small selection of carefully chosen producers' wines with nothing over €15, he selected a Coteaux du Languedoc, Domaine de la Perrière 2000 which was fruity and smooth. Hugues smiled almost ruefully when challenged about their current success with a steady stream of bohemian insiders – not exactly what they'd set out for, but inevitable.

Le Verre Volé

67 rue de Lancry, 10th (01.48.03.17.34).
M° République or Jacques Bonsergent. **Open** 10am-11pm Mon-Sat. Food served 12.30-2.30pm, 7.30-10pm Mon-Sat. Closed Aug. **Glass** €3.30-€4.50. **Bottle** €10-€100 (plus €5 per table). **Credit** MC, V. **Map** L4.
A popular favourite of this newly cool quartier near Canal St-Martin, Le Verre Volé specialises in food and drink from the Ardèche region of France. Unsulphured, unfiltered wines join hearty black puddings, andouillette and pâté in a cheery atmosphere. Opened in 2000, it is run by two friends who clearly love their job and make every effort to ensure their customers have a good time. It's tiny, little more than a few very basic tables in a shop, but it's always full to bursting in the evening.

Le Clown Bar

114 rue Amelot, 11th (01.43.55.87.35). M° Filles du Calvaire. **Open** noon-3.30pm, 7pm-1am Mon-Sat; 7pm-midnight Sun. Food served noon-2.30pm, 7pm-midnight Mon-Sat; 7pm-midnight Sun. **Glass** €3.50-€5. **Bottle** €15-€75. **No credit cards**. **Map** L5.
Come to this wine bar nestled next to the Cirque d'Hiver on a Sunday night, and you will find its tables filled with locals happy to have this dependable restaurant on their doorstep. Here, they can dig into a satisfying bowl of creamy brandade or an onglet au poivre under the watchful eye of proprietor Joe Vitte, whose attention to detail shows from his loving maintenance of the listed interior with its turn-of-the-century clown-covered tiles and unusual painted glass ceiling, to the new jewel-toned plates on which he serves his food. The menu offers standards such as goose rillettes and oeuf en meurette, but is reaching a little further, with daily specials such as pork cheeks with lemongrass or a chicken pastilla. The very reasonably priced wine list ranges all over France, only slightly favouring the Côtes du Rhône, from which we sampled a very good 2002 Crozes Hermitage from producer Alain Graillot.

Jacques Mélac

42 rue Léon Frot, 11th (01.43.70.59.27).
M° Charonne. **Open** 9am-midnight Mon-Sat. Food served noon-3pm, 7.30-10.30pm. **Glass** €2.80-€3.66. **Bottle** €15-€32. **Credit** MC, V. **Non-smoking room**. **Map** P6.
The welcome at this long-established wine bar is as warm and broad as the proprietor's handlebar moustache. Just don't try ordering water – which, a

sign posted above the bar cautions, is reserved for cooking potatoes. Instead, start with a pelou, a kind of Auvergnat kir made with chestnut liqueur, before diving into a generous plate of first-rate charcuterie; or, if you're feeling up to it, one of the meaty and satisfying plats du jour. One of the well-seasoned servers will gladly help you choose from among their selection of hardy, young wines from the south-west. If you ask nicely, Jacques will bring out his Barbary organ (a beautiful contraption, like an accordion-sized music box) and regale you with classic French songs, to which all the locals in the room will inevitably join in.

Le Melting Potes

16 rue des Trois Bornes, 11th (01.43.38.61.75).
M° Parmentier. **Open** 11am-2am Mon-Sat. Food served noon-10.30pm. Closed 24 Dec and public holidays. **Glass** €2.20-€7.10. **Bottle** €10.90-39.50. **Credit** AmEx, DC, MC, V. **Map** M4.
The longer you spend in the Melting Potes, and the more of their wine you drink, the more meanings you can see in their name. With a zinc bar and quirky decor including a barber's chair (try to avoid sitting on it unless you want to look ridiculous), this is a Corsican wine bar with other facets thrown into the mix. An interesting wine list includes Corsican discoveries, wines from the Languedoc, St-Chinian, Côte Roannaise and Chile among others, and these are accompanied by wonderful tartines Poîlane, huge salads (the Folledingue features foie gras, three types of duck and pine kernels), and Corsican specialities such as the delicious figatelli (spicy sausage that tastes like a mixture of chorizo and black pudding, served on tomato-topped Poîlane bread with a pot of white beans cooked in the Corsican style with tomato sauce). They also do top-quality Mojitos, enhanced with a touch of Angostura bitters, and have a collection of flavoured rums, although we weren't keen on the melon and kiwi one we tasted. Perhaps best of all, you can order any bottle of wine and they just bill you for what you drink. Ask for suggestions and there will always be a surprise hidden away that's not on the menu, such as the fabulous Mont Ventoux red (€20) that we had to seriously restrain ourselves from finishing.

La Muse Vin

101 rue de Charonne, 11th (01.40.09.93.05).
M° Charonne. **Open** 10.30am-2am Mon-Sat; noon-10pm Sun. Food served noon-11pm Mon-Sat; noon-9.30pm Sun. **Glass** €2-€8. **Bottle** €15-€105. **Credit** MC, V. **Map** N7.
Though this tremendously popular new wine bar teeters on the brink of being a bit too groovy for its own good, to say nothing of a tiny bit impressed by its own success, you can't argue with its basic fabulousness. Not only does it pull a fascinatingly arty and trendy young crowd, but as long as you've had the sense to book well in advance, an evening here feels like being included in a very friendly, free-wheeling party. Decorated with contemporary art and fluorescent colors, it's surprisingly professional

Les Enfants Rouges. *See p262.*

Le Petit Chavignol. *See p269.*

when it comes to its wines, too, including really nice offbeat bottles from all over France. The two young proprietors are justly proud of their food, too – cheese and cold meat plates, plus a couple of hot dishes. You know that you're going to eat well when a whole baguette is brought to the table, along with a bowl of sea snails with garlic mayonnaise.

Le Vin de Zinc
25 rue Oberkampf, 11th (01.48.06.28.23).
M° Oberkampf or Filles du Calvaire. **Open** noon-2pm, 8-11pm Tue-Sat. Food served noon-2pm, 8-11pm. Closed three weeks in Aug & one week at Christmas. **Glass** €4-€6. **Bottle** €20-€56. **Credit** MC, V. **Map** M5.

This spacious bar is a welcome newcomer to the boho Oberkampf area, with simple red Formica tables and blackboards listing the day's specials. Winning starters – lovely, clean-tasting piquillo peppers stuffed with goat's cheese; little, fat snail ravioli with minced vegetables – were followed by less successful mains. A dryish tuna steak was cheered up by a herb salad and grilled veg, while creamy veal kidneys came with a delicate celery flan. The wine is all very new-school: lots of unsulphured and naturally produced bottles. A glass of Vire Clesse 1999 from Vergé had a delicate taste of star anise. The Morgon Côte de Py from Foillard was gorgeous and concentrated. An Anjou Villages from René Mossé was slightly on the woody side and a Vin de Bugey was a bit spritzy. The only real disappointment of Vin de Zinc is the frostiness of the grim patronne.

Le Baron Bouge
1 rue Théophile-Roussel, 12th (01.43.43.14.32).
M° Ledru-Rollin. **Open** 10am-2pm, 5-10pm Tue-Thur; 10am-10pm Fri, Sat; 10am-2pm Sun. Cold food served all day. **Glass** €1.30-€3.50. **Bottle** €14-€22. **Credit** MC, V. **Map** N7.

Le Baron Bouge, next to the boisterous place d'Aligre market, may appear rather rough and ready, but the wines – including varied Loire selections, small châteaux from Bordeaux or Condrieu from the Rhône – are chosen with an eye for quality. There's a bit of bar food – charcuterie and some good goat's cheese – but few tables, so stand at one of the casks and try to act as insouciant as the habitués.

Les Cailloux
58 rue des Cinq-Diamants, 13th (01.45.80.15.08).
M° Corvisart or Place d'Italie. **Open** 12.30-2.30pm, 7.30-11pm Tue-Sat. Closed Aug, 25 Dec-3 Jan. **Glass** €2-€3. **Bottle** €17-€65. **Credit** MC, V. **Wheelchair access**.

Les Cailloux offers more than 40 wines. Only six or so are by the glass, and half the list is Italian, reflecting the first language of the staff and cooks. You can't really hang out by the bar, but expect a fine Italian meal with superb service and atmosphere. Mozzarella salad and grilled vegetables with gorgonzola, pastas such as linguine with crab or girolle mushrooms, and panna cotta, a wobbly baked cream, are some of the carefully prepared, satisfying dishes. With lights hanging over each table and plenty of distractions for the taste buds, we could happily while away many a winter's evening here.

Couleurs de Vigne

2 rue Marmontel, 15th (01.45.33.32.96).
M° Vaugirard or Convention. **Open** noon-2pm,
8-11pm Mon-Fri. **Glass** €2-€3.50. **Bottle** €6-€40.
Credit MC, V. **Wheelchair access. Map** D9.
This new wine bar has become tremendously
popular for the warm welcome of owner Alain
Touchard and the excellent bottles he has selected
from all over France. It's a wonderfully idiosyncratic
viniferous offer, which makes it fun to come here on
a regular basis, since Touchard is always
suggesting something new, making this a great
place to deepen a knowledge of wine without having
it feel like some scholarly chore. The decor is
appealing as well, with olive green walls, cork-
coloured floors and open bins stocked with bottles
to take away, and the food is simple and appealing.
The meat and cheese plate – generous enough to
feed two – is a real winner with good Auvergnat
products, including cantal and bleu des causses,
cured sausage and ham from the Laguiole region,
plus country terrine.

Le Vin dans les Voiles

8 rue Chapu, 16th (01.46.47.83.98). M° Exelmans.
Open noon-2.15pm Mon; noon-2.15pm, 8-10.15pm
Tue-Fri; 7.30-10.30pm Sat. **Glass** €3.50-€4. **Bottle**
€6-€40. **Credit** MC, V. **Wheelchair access. Non-
smoking room.**
Occupying a vestpocket space, this engaging new
bistro à vins quickly won a neighbourhood
following for its warm welcome, easy-going
atmosphere, great cooking and nice selection of
wines. Sporting a generous moustache and usually
wearing a red apron, the jovial proprietor obviously
enjoys reciting the brief menu, while encouraging
you to discover the unusual bottles he has come
across. The menu changes often, but our pressée of
rabbit with tarragon, provençal-style squid in
tomato sauce, risotto with peas and asparagus, and
strawberry-rhubarb crumble were all delicious. You
can also pop by for a quick sip with a plate of cheeses
or charcuterie, and here again the quality is
impressive. One way or another, this is a charming
hideaway for a tête-à-tête or a good-value lunch
(€24). Just be advised that it's a bit of trek from
central Paris.

Caves Pétrissans

30 bis av Niel, 17th (01.42.27.52.03). M° Pereire.
Open 10am-10.30pm Mon-Fri. Food served noon-
2.30pm, 8-10.30pm. **Glass** €4-€12. **Bottle** €16-€3,000.
Credit MC, V. **Non-smoking room. Map** C2.
A unique address, Caves Pétrissans is so
authentically French as to be unmissable. A classic
turn-of-the-20th-century wine merchant-cum-
restaurant, coyly shielded by dingy net curtains
from the avenue Niel, it's split in three: the main
dining room, slightly overlit but rich with cornicing,
zinc bar and mosaic tiles; another smaller room
which serves as the shop; and a tiny, booth-like
corner room. Happily we were seated in the main
room where we could best observe the bourgeois

crowd of epicurean locals getting down to some
serious eating and drinking. Tables are so tightly
packed that conversation with the neighbours was
inevitable, and enthusiastically taken up by the
patronne. A three-course menu of robust classics
was available at €31, but we chose à la carte. We
shared a generous slab of foie gras to start, which
permitted a rich oeuf en meurette to pass as a main.
Steamed chicken with a creamy tarragon sauce came
with perfect basmati rice. Weekly-changing wines
by the glass were irreproachable: interesting Arbois
chardonnay from Tissot; zingy Quincy 2001 from
Jerôme de la Chaise; supple Côtes de Brouilly 2001
from Domaine Pavillon; nicely concentrated
Bourgueil (Gauthier 2000). You can also choose from
hundreds of bottles at shop price plus a hefty €16
corkage charge.

Le Petit Chavignol

78 rue de Tocqueville, 17th (01.42.27.95.97).
M° Malesherbes or Villiers. **Open** 8am-1am Mon-Sat.
Food served noon-3.30pm, 7-11.45pm. **Glass** €2.50-
€7.50. **Bottle** €12-€100. **Credit** MC, V. **Map** E2.
There's a rustic feel to this popular little bistro with
its copper bar and warm welcome from the woman
behind it. We were soon chomping delicious
saucisson sec from the Maison Conquet with a glass
of rather banal Sancerre which had seemed the
obvious aperitif in a bar of this name. It was all go:
the bearded boss in his leather waistcoat was taking
orders from a swelling crowd of locals, including a
wonderful greying Jean-Paul Belmondo lookalike
with a fluffy lapdog. The lure is simple: a good
selection of artisanal charcuterie and hearty,
generous hot dishes. We felt obliged to try the crottin
de chavignol, which was suitably crumbly and
served warm with salad. A handwritten wine list
covering most regions included some lesser-known
small producers.

Le Baratin

3 rue Jouye-Rouve, 20th (01.43.49.39.70).
M° Pyrénées or Belleville. **Open** noon-2am Tue-Fri;
8pm-2am Sat. Closed three weeks in Aug . Food
served noon-2.30pm, 8-11pm. **Glass** €3-€5. **Bottle**
€18-€100. **Wheelchair access. Credit** MC, V.
Map N3.
A faint frostiness over the telephone quicky melted
on arrival in this packed little bistro up in the
farthest reaches of the 20th. We were offered little
glasses of an unusual sweet Corsican wine from
Antoine Arena as we waited at the bar for a table.
The menu was a refreshing read. Mackerel and
beetroot tartare enhanced with a little lemongrass
was astonishingly good, while a generous hunk of
cod was fresh, perfectly cooked and crowned with
poached baby leeks. The wines are all from small
artisan producers and prices stay under €30 or so.
We drank famous Morgan Côtes de Py from Jean
Foillard, reassuringly good at €26. Rammed with a
lively bunch of thirtysomething locals and
professional wine geeks, this is hardly the best-kept
secret in the East, but it's well worth the hike.

On the Town

Kris Gautier

Discover the Show of the Most Famous Cabaret in the World !
Dinner & Show at 7pm from €140 • Show at 9pm : €97, at 11pm : €87

Montmartre - 82, boulevard de Clichy - 75018 Paris
Reservations : 01 53 09 82 82 - www.moulin-rouge.com

Eating with Entertainment

When the chips are down and the steaks are low, 'ave a gamble and put some oomph back into dinner with cruises, jazz clubs, guinguettes and café-théâtres.

BAWDY SONGS

Chez Michou

80 rue des Martyrs, 18th (01.46.06.16.04/ www.michou.fr). M° Pigalle. **Dinner** 8.30pm daily. **Show** 11pm daily. **Admission** with dinner €95; show & drink €35. **Credit** MC, V. **Map** H2.

Well-presented food (along the lines of smoked salmon, lamb cutlets and chocolate gâteau), lashings of Champagne and wall-to-wall mirrors combine to produce a mirthful *Cage aux Folles* atmosphere, where the false eyelashes have been defying gravity for over 40 years. Each night drag queens romp through a whirlwind of Charles Aznavour, Tina Turner and Brigitte Bardot impersonations. Book ahead if you want to dine and look out for Michou himself who will only ever be seen wearing blue.

BOATS

La Balle au Bond

(01.40.46.85.12/www.laballeaubond.fr). Oct-Mar: facing 55 quai de la Tournelle, 5th. M° Maubert-Mutualité. Apr-Sept: quai Malaquais, 6th. M° Pont-Neuf. **Bar** 11am-2am Mon-Sat; 6-10pm Sun. **Restaurant** May-Oct only. Prix fixe hot/cold buffets €38; dinner €49. **Concerts** 9pm. **Admission** €5-€6. **Credit** AmEx, MC, V. **Map** K7.

From its prime mooring position, this concert-hall barge provides a good spot from which to soak up sunnier days on the Seine. Depending on when you visit, you will also be able to enjoy a range of concerts, plays and food. Ideal for a hot evening when you feel like sipping an exotic cocktail and watching the river go by.

Bateaux Parisiens

Port de La Bourdonnais, 7th (01.44.11.33.44/meal reservations 01.44.11.33.55/www.bateauxparisiens. com). M° Bir-Hakeim or RER Champ de Mars. **Departs** lunch cruise 12.15pm daily; dinner cruise 7.45pm daily. **Lunch** €50-€70. **Dinner** €92-€135. **Credit** AmEx, DC, MC, V. **No smoking. Map** C6.

With about two million visitors per year, the Bateaux Parisiens cater solely for the tourist market. Expect to be herded in with the multitudes to a vast and overcrowded dining area by waiters who have their small talk (in English of course) down to a T.

The food itself is pleasant enough with well-presented dishes such as an open sandwich with mozzarella and tomato chutney for starters, followed by roasted salmon or pan-fried duck breast. As you cruise down the Seine, the huge glass windows offer stunning scenery by day and night; however, the onboard musical entertainment and running commentary can be intrusive to put it mildly.

Bateaux Mouches

Pont de L'Alma, rive droite, 8th (01.42.25.96.10/ recorded information 01.40.76.99.99/www.bateaux-mouches.fr). M° Alma-Marceau. **Departs** lunch cruise 1pm daily; dinner cruise 8.30pm daily. **Lunch** €50. **Dinner** €85, €125. **Credit** AmEx, DC, MC, V. **Map** D5.

A dinner cruise with Bateaux Mouches allows you to dine in peace while taking in the floodlit sights along the Seine. The set menu was hit or miss (desserts were disastrous) but covered all of the stereotypical 'French' dishes such as foie gras, frogs' legs and snails for starters, then lobster, roast quail and rack of lamb. English-speaking waiters were friendly and efficient, but remember you only have a set amount of time to get through your meal. Dress smartly (jacket and tie required for men).

CAFE-THEATRE

Au Bec Fin

6 rue Thérèse, 1st (01.42.96.29.35). M° Pyramides. **Shows** 7pm, 8.30pm, 10pm daily; matinées for children 2.30pm, 4pm during school holidays. Closed Aug. **Tickets** €14; €12 students, €9 children; €36 dinner & show. **Credit** MC, V. **Map** H5.

This tiny café-theatre claims a 300-year-old pedigree and provides wholesome entertainment for the whole family. Dine downstairs on traditional French cuisine such as frogs' legs and snails (watch out for the strong garlic butter), before heading up the rickety staircase to see anything from Oscar Wilde in French to a modern-day *Cindarella* for the kids.

L'Ane Rouge

3 rue Laugier, 17th (01.47.64.45.77). M° Ternes. **Shows** 8pm-2am daily. **Admission** show & one drink €30; dinner & show €50-€85. **Credit** MC, V. **Map** C2.

On the Town

La Balle au Bond. *See p271.*

Each evening true comic cabaret combines with a great atmosphere in this glittery café-théâtre. Dine on interesting regional dishes (including roasted donkey), then sit back and listen to comedians new and old let rip with all the mirth they can muster.

Le Restaurant Lectures Gourmandes

28-30 rue de la Goutte d'Or, 18th (01.42.64.61.17). M° Barbès-Rochechouart. **Open** noon-2.30pm Mon-Thur; noon-2.30pm, 7.30-11pm Fri (shows also on some Thur eves, ring to check). **Dinner & show** €21-€25. **Credit** MC, V. **Map** K1.

As the new neighbourhood favourite, this 'restaurant artistique' doubles up as a café-théâtre and an art gallery, bringing a fresh cultural edge to the grotty Goute d'Or district. Run by the charity 'Aurore', an association giving social aid to the unemployed and those overcoming illness, this quaint, Provençal-style restaurant stages shows from singers, musicians, actors and poets every Friday night.

CLASSICAL

Bel Canto

72 quai de l'Hôtel de Ville, 4th (01.42.78.30.18/ www.lebelcanto.com). M° Hôtel de Ville. **Dinner** from 8pm daily. **Prix fixe** €60. **Credit** AmEx, V. **No smoking. Map** K6.

A novel idea that works brilliantly, the quartet of waiting staff at this Italian restaurant double up as the evening's entertainment by singing opera at your table. As the first note on the piano is played, the waitress, who only two minutes before was serving your crab tagliatelle, starts to sing a favourite aria from great operas by Verdi, Mozart, Puccini or Rossini. The compulsory set menu is a little on the pricey side (as is the wine list) but seems irrelevant as you're shouting 'bravo!'.

Casse-Croûte à l'Opéra

Studio Bastille, Opéra National de Paris, 120 rue de Lyon, 12th (01.40.10.17.89/www.opera-de-paris.fr). M° Bastille. **Free concert** 1-2pm most Thur (ring or consult website to check what's on). **Food served** 12.30-2.30pm. **Snack** €7. **Credit** MC, V. **Map** M7.

Thursday lunchtimes need never be boring again thanks to the French National Opera's latest attempt to democratise classical music. Free chamber music concerts (performed by the Opéra National de Paris) and a series of lectures and documentaries are put on most Thursdays, and are served up with basic snacks (mostly sandwiches) for €7.

GLITZY CABARET

While several glitzy cabarets provide food and feathers in equal proportions, these two biggies still balance top nosh with boobies and sequins more reliably than anywhere else in town.

Le Lido

116 bis av des Champs-Elysées, 8th (01.40.76.56.10/ www.lido.fr). M° Georges V. **Dinner** with show 7pm daily. **Show** with Champagne 9.30pm, 11pm daily. **Admission** with dinner €140, €170, €200; kids' menu (7pm show) €30; 9.30pm, 11pm show €80-€100. **Credit** AmEx, DC, MC, V. **No smoking. Wheelchair access. Map** D4.

The Lido's current revue, Bonheur, is supposedly based around the theme of a woman's quest for happiness. The pre-show atmosphere is undeniably buzzy as diners, stuffed full of overpriced foie gras, smoked salmon, duck and crème brûlée, start looking expectantly towards the stage. The show itself is aptly named as long as your definition of 'happiness' involves impressively choreographed song and dance numbers executed by a whole host of near-naked, dancing, prancing girls and boys.

Le Moulin Rouge

82 bd de Clichy, 18th (01.53.09.82.82/www.moulin-rouge.com). M° Blanche. **Dinner** 7pm daily. **Show** 9pm, 11pm daily. **Admission** with dinner €135-€165; show €95 (9pm), €85 (11pm). **Credit**

AmEx, DC, MC, V. **No smoking. Wheelchair access. Map** G2.

The Moulin Rouge, with its revue 'Féerie', is the most traditional glamour revue and the only place with French can-can. Glittery lampposts and fake trees lend a tacky charm to the hall, while the dancers cover the stage with faultless synchronisation. Costumes are flamboyant, the entr'actes acts funny (look out for the talking dog) and the sets strikingly solid: one number takes place inside a giant tank of underwater boa constrictors. The dinner option will fill you up with posh nosh such as foie gras, goose and caviar.

GUINGUETTE & DANCING

Chez Raymonde

119 av Parmentier, 11th (01.43.55.26.27). M° Parmentier or Goncourt. **Open** 7pm-1am Tue-Fri; 8pm-1am Sat. **Average** €22. **Prix fixe** €19 Tue-Fri; €38 Sat. **Credit** AmEx, DC, MC, V. **Map** M4.

Beware, ladies: the chef may ask you to tango (though only on Saturdays). Halfway through the dîner-dansant meal here – solidly French and scrumptious – the lights dim to rosy reds, the host sprinkles some magic dust on the tiny dancefloor, introduces a piano/accordion duo and invites the chef out of the kitchen and into his arms to inaugurate an evening of waltz, swing and other fancy steps. The meal is satisfying enough on its own at Chez Raymonde; add in the dance, and the soirée delivers pure enchantment.

Chez Gégène

162 bis quai de Polangis, allée des Guinguettes, 94340 Joinville-le-Pont (01.48.83.29.43/www.chez-gegene.fr). RER Joinville-le-Pont. **Open** noon-2.30pm, 7-10.30pm Tue-Sun. Closed Jan-Mar. **Average** €25. **Admission** with dinner €38 (Fri, Sat); with drink €13.72, €15.24 (Fri, Sat); Sun lunch €45. **Credit** MC, V. **Wheelchair access.**

Typically French and thoroughly un-Parisian, Chez Gégène attracts dance addicts, grannies and urban hipsters. The band (Friday, Saturday nights, Sunday afternoons) sprinkles tango, foxtrot and musette with disco hits, so those less sure of foot don't feel left out. Between dances, feast on steaks, moules-frites and wine.

Olé Bodéga

Ile de Monsieur, 2 rte de St-Cloud, quai de Sèvres, Sèvres (01.53.02.90.85/www.olebodega.com). M° Pont de Sèvres. **Shows** from 8pm Wed-Sat. **Tickets** €16 disco only (including two drinks); **Dinner & show** €29-€45. **Credit** MC, V.

Olé Bodéga may be a tacky circus chain with four big top venues in France alone, but the Paris version is a fun alternative to a cheesy dinner-dance somewhere in the city centre. Dine on Basque specialities and tapas while jamborees of acrobats wow the crowds with astonishing displays overhead. At the end of the show, space is cleared for everyone to have a late-night boogie to nostalgic Euro-pop tunes.

On the Town

What Londoners take when they go out.

LONDON'S WEEKLY LISTINGS BIBLE

IN ENGLISH

Le Caveau des Oubliettes ★

52 rue Galande, 5th (01.46.34.23.09). M° Maubert-Mutualité. **Open** 5pm-2am Mon-Thur, Sun; 5pm-5am Fri, Sat. **Happy hour** 5-9pm. **Credit** MC, V. **Map** J7.

Considered primarily as a music venue, this historically themed brick bar of Irish character attracts a good Franco-Euro mix of punters to its street-level pub before people venture down the stone staircase to the clammy cellar with its small stage and separate bar counter. Upstairs is best known for its tatty turf floor, scuffed by the soles of too many Doc Martens and spotted with too much Beamish, and its genuine guillotine from 1793. Atmosphere is provided by the sense of drinking in the heart of the Latin Quarter, in one of the oldest streets in all Paris. Sports TV, too.

The Bowler Pub

13 rue d'Artois, 8th (01.45.61.16.60). M° St-Philippe-du-Roule. **Shows** 9pm, days vary. **Tickets** €10 (including one pint of beer). **Dinner** €10. **Credit** AmEx, MC, V. **Map** E3.

If French is not your forte and you need some homegrown grub, the Bowler Pub is a top scorer. Chips, pints and belly laughs are doled out in large portions in this British beer temple, where on-the-up comedians hop off the Eurostar to test their new-fangled wares on homesick ex-pats. Once you know who's on stage, check out their comedy credentials at www.comedycv.co.uk.

JAZZ

Le Franc Pinot

1 quai de Bourbon, 4th (01.46.33.60.64). M° Pont Marie. **Open** 7pm-midnight Tue-Sat. Closed Aug. **Admission** €10-€15 (free on Tuesdays). **Concerts** 9pm. **Prix fixe** €35-€55. **Credit** MC, V. **Map** K7.

Housed in the centuries-old cellars of Ile Saint-Louis, this intimate jazz den serves up a warming mix of rhythm and food. Loved-up couples, old friends and jazz enthusiasts rub shoulders in the shadows. The menu offers popular comfort food (lobster bisque, steak and chips, chocolate cake, crème anglaise) that can be enjoyed without taking too much attention away from the music.

Le Bilboquet

13 rue St-Benoît, 6th (01.45.48.81.84). M° St-Germain-des-Prés. **Open** 8pm-2am Tue-Sun. **Admission** free. **Drinks** €18. **Concerts** 9pm-1am Tue, Wed, Sun; 9.30pm-1am Thur-Sat. **Dinner** €50. **Credit** AmEx, MC, V. **Map** H7.

With its carpeted red walls and funky jazz-themed paintings, this famous St-Germain venue has lost none of its edge since it first opened in 1947. Today it attracts an older, mellower crowd than during its post-war days, but that hasn't stopped wealthy American tourists or big names such as David Bowie and ZZ Top from homing in on the pricey fun. The jazz here is of the highest calibre, and the excellent, traditional food is served in the mezzanine overlooking the stage. Smart dress is preferable.

Autour de Midi-Minuit

11 rue Lepic, 18th (01.55.79.16.48). M° Blanche. **Open** noon-2.30pm, 7pm-2am (no food after 11pm) Tue-Sun. Closed Aug. **Admission** €10 (free on Tuesdays), €5 when eating. **Concerts** 10pm Fri-Sat. **Jam session** 9.30pm Tue. **Dinner** €22-€35. **Credit** AmEx, DC, MC, V. **Map** H2.

This Montmartre institution is perhaps the best-value jazz venue in the city thanks to its top acts and copious French cuisine. Almost every day the chef finds a different way to make his guests' bellies swell, and on concert nights everyone heads down to the jazz lair where names big and small bop and swing into the wee hours. Drinks are reasonably priced, the crowds are mixed and the waiters are pleasant.

Le Moulin Rouge. *See p273.*

On the Town

Gay & Lesbian

GAY BARS & CAFÉS

Banana Café
*13 rue de la Ferronnerie, 1st (01.42.33.35.31/www.
bananacafeparis.com). Mº Châtelet.* **Open** 5.30pm-
7am daily. **Credit** AmEx, DC, MC, V. **Map** J5.
One of Paris's only open-all-night gay bars – which
guarantees a steady throng of cruisers craning to
watch the go-go boys gyrating on the counter.

Le Duplex
*25 rue Michel-le-Comte, 3rd (01.42.72.80.86).
Mº Rambuteau.* **Open** 8pm-2am daily. **Credit** MC,
V. **Map** K5.
Despite all the trappings of a philo-café – art on the
walls (changed every month), an educated crowd of
students, professors and saloon politicos, the near
permanent smoky fug – this small split-level bar
doubles up as a championship cruising ground. Pull
up a stool and get, er, philosophical.

Amnesia Café
*42 rue Vieille-du-Temple, 4th (01.42.72.16.94).
Mº Hôtel de Ville or St-Paul.* **Open** 10am-2am daily.
Credit MC, V. **Map** K6.
This bar is the height of cosiness. Stools at the bar
for a drink *tout seul*, mirrored walls, nice leather
armchairs in secluded corners for relaxing with
mates – comfort is a given. In the sweaty basement,
camp French classics get the crowd roaring.

Le Central
*33 rue Vieille-du-Temple, 4th (01.48.87.99.33).
Mº Hôtel de Ville or St-Paul.* **Open** 4pm-2am Mon-
Fri; 2pm-2am Sat, Sun. **Credit** MC, V. **Map** K6.
One of the oldest gay bars in Paris, and feeling her
age (30-plus), Le Central has seen the bright young
things move on to sprucer joints. Handy for a quick
beer in the Marais – but on a slow night you'll rattle
around in it, the silence only punctuated by the
scrape of bar stools.

Le Coffee-Shop
*3 rue Ste-Croix-de-la-Bretonnerie, 4th
(01.42.74.24.21). Mº Hôtel de Ville or St-Paul.*
Open 10am-2am daily. **No credit cards**. **Map** K6.
Mini-landmark snack bar that's been keeping the
Marais boys in café au lait and gossip for more than
two decades, morning, noon and night.

Le Cox
*15 rue des Archives, 4th (01.42.72.08.00). Mº Hôtel
de Ville.* **Open** 12.30pm-2am Mon-Thur; 1pm-2am
Fri-Sun. **No credit cards**. **Map** K6.
This is one of the hottest outposts of the Marais, a
gay zoo that sure packs them in. Afternoons are
sedate, but after dark out come the nighthawks. In
summer, they're spilling out on the street by 8pm.

Okawa
*40 rue Vieille-du-Temple, 4th (01.48.04.30.69).
Mº Hôtel de Ville or St-Paul.* **Open** 10am-2am daily.
Credit MC, V. **Map** L6.
It's impossible to miss this low-lit corner café-bar
done out in lumberjack chic. It's an undressy,
straight-friendly place with a decent 50/50 gay-
lesbian split, and there are always a few high-backed
stools and soft pouffes free, except during fortune-
telling sessions.

Open Café
*17 rue des Archives, 4th (01.42.72.26.18). Mº Hôtel
de Ville.* **Open** 11am-2am Mon-Thur, Sun; 11am-4am
Fri, Sat. **Credit** MC, V. **Map** K6.
A magnetic corner bar where gay boys meet up
before a night out. The spectacular, gender-free WCs
are a talking point. The same management runs the
Raidd (23 rue du Temple, 4th, 01.42.77.04.88), one of
the ritziest, sexiest bars in the Marais, with bright
lights, go-go dancers and plasma screens.

Quetzal
*10 rue de la Verrerie, 4th (01.48.87.99.07/www.
quetzalbar.com). Mº Hôtel de Ville.* **Open** 5pm-5am
daily. **Credit** MC, V. **Map** K6.
The cruisiest bar in the Marais, with a posey front
bar popular with bear boys, and a dancier back area
full of muscle men. It has just had a makeover and
the terrace, at a strategic crossroads, is a vantage
point for gay men of a certain age.

Le Thermik
*7 rue de la Verrerie, 4th (01.44.78.08.18).
Mº Hôtel de Ville.* **Open** 5pm-2am daily. **Credit**
MC, V. **Map** K6.
Technicolor signage belies the fact that this is a spit-
and-sawdust kind of place. Downstairs at weekends
it has a village-disco-meets-rugby-club feel, the DJ
spinning CDs worthy of the finest wedding do.

GAY RESTAURANTS

Pig'z
*5 rue Marie-Stuart, 2nd (01.42.33.05.89/www.pigz.
fr) Mº Etienne Marcel.* **Open** 8pm-midnight Tue-
Sun. **Credit** AmEx, DC, MC, V. **Map** J5.
Where gay gourmets pig out on classic fusion food
such as Scottish salmon with lemon vinaigrette,
oriental-influenced chicken, and ravioli stuffed with
button mushrooms.

Aux Trois Petits Cochons
*31 rue Tiquetonne, 2nd (01.42.33.39.69/www.aux
troispetitscochons.com). Mº Etienne Marcel.* **Open**
8-11.30pm daily. Closed Aug. **Credit** AmEx, DC,
MC, V. **Map** J5.

On the Town

Three Little Pigs eschews international boystown cuisine in favour of a tasty, daily-changing menu. High quality, so reservation only.

Le Curieux

14 rue St-Merri, 4th (01.42.72.75.97). M° Hôtel de Ville. **Open** 11.30am-midnight daily. **Credit** MC, V. **Map** K6.
This brash new kid on the block is brightly lit by bar chandeliers which draw in crowds like moths. The menu is stripped down, the atmosphere hot Latin.

Au Tibourg

29 rue du Bourg-Tibourg, 4th (01.42.74.45.25). M° Hôtel de Ville. **Open** noon-2pm, 7pm-midnight Tue-Sun. **Credit** MC, V. **Map** K6.
A beamed roof, glazed terracotta jugs and framed paintings – classic hallmarks of many a timewarped French restaurant. In this one, in a Marais side street facing a gay sauna, there are gay and lesbian couples at every table. Besides the meaty dishes of the day and à la carte options, there's a vegetarian menu for €15.

GAY CLUBS

Le Transfert

3 rue de La Sourdière, 1st (01.42.60.48.42/www. letransfert.com). M° Tuileries or Pyramides. **Open** midnight-7am Mon-Fri; 4-10pm, midnight-7am Sat, Sun. Also 6-10pm first & third Thursday of month. **Credit** AmEx, MC, V. **Map** G5.
Small leather and S&M bar used by regulars, though trainers fetishists also get their kicks at a special Sunday nighter. At other times, it gets going late.

Le Dépôt

10 rue aux Ours, 3rd (01.44.54.96.96/www.ledepot. com). M° Rambuteau. **Open** 2pm-7am daily. **Admission** €6-€12 (includes one drink). **Credit** AmEx, MC, V. **Map** K5.
Your basic sex disco, cutely positioned next to a police station. The decor is jungle netting and exposed air ducts, the dancefloor surrounded by video screens for idle cruising.

Full Metal

40 rue des Blancs-Manteaux, 4th (01.42.72.30.05/ www.fullmetal.fr). M° Rambuteau. **Open** 5pm-4am Mon-Thur, Sun; 5pm-6am Fri, Sat. **Credit** MC, V. **Map** K6.
At this basement drinking den, against a backdrop of brickwork decorated with netting and handcuffs, the cute staff wear black armbands and open-ended chaps. Home to regular theme events, including Paris's only night for skins. Older, hardcore crowd.

QG

12 rue Simon-le-Franc, 4th (01.48.87.74.18/ www.qgbar.com). M° Rambuteau. **Open** 4pm-8am daily. **Credit** MC, V. **Map** K6.
There's no entrance fee but one of the strictest dress codes in town: only the hardest set (doormen favour military gear) get in.

LESBIAN BARS & CLUBS

La Champmeslé

4 rue Chabanais, 2nd (01.42.96.85.20). M° Bourse or Pyramides. **Open** 3pm-dawn Mon-Sat. **Credit** MC, V. **Map** H4.
The oldest girl bar in town – it opened in 1979. There are imported beers on draught, regular cabaret (the Fetish Fantasm night is a highlight) and art shows. It's also an unofficial part of the Lady Di tour – her driver Henri Paul was allegedly drinking here before he chauffered her car.

Pulp

25 bd Poissonnière, 2nd (01.40.26.01.93/www.pulp-paris.com). M° Grands Boulevards. **Open** midnight-5am Wed-Sat. **Admission** free-€9. **Drinks** €5-€9. **Credit** MC, V. **Map** J4.
The leading lesbian disco in Paris – and certainly the grooviest – Pulp has also opened its doors to a mixed midweek crowd. The gay girls come out on top with DJs such as UK French Chloe. Check out the website for groovy animated flyers.

Le Boobsbourg

26 rue de Montmorency, 3rd (01.42.74.04.82). M° Rambuteau or Arts et Métiers. **Open** 5.30pm-2am Tue-Sat. **Credit** V. **Map** K5.
Named by expat ex-pop star Tanita Tikaram, who noticed how US tourists mispronouce Beaubourg, this scuffed, slightly off-scene and old-fashioned neighbourhood dyke bar has Marais prices – €3.80 a vin rouge. There's a kitchen serving assiettes of cheese and charcuterie – go on, treat your girlfriend – and an upstairs dancefloor used for monthly films.

Unity Bar

176-178 rue St-Martin, 3rd (01.42.72.70.59). M° Rambuteau. **Open** 4pm-2am daily. **No credit cards. Map** K5.
This raucous pool bar near the Centre Pompidou (look for the subtle spray-painted graffiti sign and huge windows), attracts a cruisy female crowd, hard-drinking, militant but non-threatening. Chalk up a cue, or try cards and board games on Sundays.

Bliss Kfé

30 rue du Roi-de-Sicile, 4th (01.42.78.49.36). M° St-Paul. **Open** 5pm-2am daily. **Credit** MC, V. **Map** K6.
This laidback lesbian lounge is the perfect spot for cocktails, aperitifs and weekend discothequing, too. Male friends of this lively crowd are also bar fixtures.

Le Mixer

23 rue Ste-Croix-de-la-Bretonnerie, 4th (01.48.87.55.44). M° Hôtel de Ville or St-Paul. **Open** 5pm-2am daily. **Credit** MC, V. **Map** K6.
In this clubbiest of the main Marais bars, music is taken most seriously. In this mixed crowd lesbians can hang easy. It's happy hour from 6pm to 8pm; open decks events pull in notable bedroom DJs.

On the Town

Shops & Markets

Though charcutiers and quirky little places are increasingly rare, Paris still has plenty to offer the food-obsessed. It would be easy to spend an entire holiday (if not a lifetime) exploring the enormous variety of breads, pastries, cheeses and chocolate, and open-air markets continue to beckon with their displays of fresh, seasonal goods (*see p284* **Market forces**). The chain concept is catching on: there seems to be a Paul bakery on every corner and even renowned fromageries such as Quatrehomme have been popping up in different neighbourhoods. The good news is that overall quality remains impressive – and you need only look around to realise that cream-filled pastries won't make you fat.

BAKERIES

Le Boulanger de Monge
123 rue Monge, 5th (01.43.37.54.20). M° Censier Daubenton. **Open** 7am-8.30pm Tue-Sun. **Credit** MC, V. **Map** K9.
Dominique Saibron uses spices to give inimitable flavour to his organic sourdough boule. About 2,000 bread-lovers a day visit his boutique, which also produces one of the city's best baguettes.

Kayser
8 & 14 rue Monge, 5th (01.44.07.01.42/ 01.44.07.17.81). M° Maubert-Mutualité. **Open** 6.45am-8.30pm Mon-Fri; 6.30am-8.30pm Sat, Sun. **Credit** MC, V. **Map** J7.
In a few years Eric Kayser has established himself as one of the city's star bakers. The bakery at 14 rue Monge is devoted to organic loaves.
Other locations: 5 rue Basse des Carmes, 5th (01.44.07.31.61).

Poilâne
8 rue du Cherche Midi, 6th (01.45.48.42.59/www. poilane.com). M° Sèvres-Babylone or St-Sulpice. **Open** 7.15am-8.15pm Mon-Sat. **No credit cards. Map** G7.
Apollonia runs Poilâne after her father's demise. Nothing has changed in the tiny shop, where locals queue for freshly baked country miches, flaky-crusted apple tarts and buttery shortbread biscuits. See website for other locations.

Arnaud Delmontel
39 rue des Martyrs, 9th (01.48.78.29.33). M° St-Georges. **Open** 7am-8.30pm Mon, Wed-Sun. **No credit cards. Map** H2.
With its crisp crust and chewy dough scattered with irregular holes, Delmontel's Renaissance baguette is easily one of the finest in Paris. He puts the same skill and perfectionism into his pastries.

L'Autre Boulange
43 rue de Montreuil, 11th (01.43.72.86.04). M° Nation or Faidherbe Chaligny. **Open** 7.30am-

1.30pm, 4-7.30pm Mon-Fri; 7.30am-12.30pm Sat. Closed Aug. **No credit cards. Map** P7.
Michel Cousin rustles up 23 kinds of organic loaf in his wood-fired oven, such as the flutiot (rye bread with raisins, walnuts and hazelnuts), the sarment de Bourgogne (sourdough and a little rye) and a spiced cornmeal bread ideal for foie gras. Great croissants and chaussons for superior snacking.

Moisan
5 pl d'Aligre, 12th (01.43.45.46.60). M° Ledru-Rollin. **Open** 7am-1.30pm, 3-8pm Tue-Sat; 7am-2pm Sun. **No credit cards. Map** N7.
Moisan's bakeries are spreading around Paris, and the quality of his organic bread, viennoiseries and rustic tarts remains outstanding. At this branch, near the place d'Aligre market, the queue snakes out the door.
Other locations: throughout the city.

Le Moulin de la Vierge
166 av de Suffren, 15th (01.47.83.45.55). M° Sèvres-Lecourbe. **Open** 7am-8pm Mon-Sat. **No credit cards. Map** E8.
Basile Kamir learned bread-making after falling in love with an old abandoned bakery. Each of his branches has an irresistible fragrance, matched by the quality of his sourdough breads.
Other locations: 82 rue Daguerre, 14th (01.43.22.50.55); 105 rue Vercingétorix, 14th (01.45.43.09.84).

CHEESE
The sign 'maître fromager affineur' denotes merchants who buy young cheeses from farms and age them on their premises; 'fromage fermier' and 'fromage au lait cru' signify farm-produced and raw milk cheeses respectively.

Fromagerie Quatrehomme
62 rue de Sèvres, 7th (01.47.34.33.45). M° Vaneau. **Open** 8.45am-1pm, 2-7.45pm Tue-Sat. **Credit** MC, V. **Map** F8.

On the Town

The award-winning Marie Quatrehomme is behind this inviting fromagerie. Justly famous for classics such as comté fruité, beaufort and the squishy st-marcellin, it sells more unusual specialities such as goat's cheese with pesto and truffle-flavoured brie.

Marie-Anne Cantin
12 rue du Champ-de-Mars, 7th (01.45.50.43.94/ www.cantin.fr). M° École Militaire. **Open** 8.30am-7.30pm Mon-Sat. **Credit** MC, V. **Map** D6.
Cantin, a vigorous defender of unpasteurised cheese and supplier to many posh Paris restaurants, is justifiably proud of her dreamily creamy st-marcellins, aged chèvres and roquefort réserve.

Alléosse
13 rue Poncelet, 17th (01.46.22.50.45). M° Ternes. **Open** 9am-1pm, 4-7pm Tue-Thur; 9am-7pm Fri, Sat; 9am-1pm Sun. **Credit** MC, V. **Map** C2.
People cross town for these cheeses – wonderful farmhouse camemberts, delicate st-marcellins, a choice of chèvres and several rarities.

Fromagerie Dubois et Fils
80 rue de Tocqueville, 17th (01.42.27.11.38). M° Malesherbes or Villiers. **Open** 9am-1pm, 4-8pm Tue-Fri; 8.30am-8pm Sat; 9am-1pm Sun. Closed three weeks in Aug. **Credit** MC, V. **Map** E2.
Superchef darling Dubois stocks 80 types of goat's cheese plus prized, aged st-marcellin and st-félicien. **Other locations:** 79 rue de Courcelles, 17th (01.43.80.36.42).

CHOCOLATE

Cacao et Chocolat
29 rue de Buci, 6th (01.46.33.77.63). M° Mabillon. **Open** 10.30am-7.30pm daily. **Credit** AmEx, DC, MC, V. **Map** H7.
This shop recalls chocolate's ancient Aztec origins with spicy fillings (honey and chilli, nutmeg, clove and citrus), chocolate masks and pyramids. **Other locations:** 63 rue St-Louis-en-l'Ile, 4th (01.46.33.33.33).

Christian Constant
37 rue d'Assas, 6th (01.53.63.15.15). M° St-Placide. **Open** 8.30am-9pm Mon-Fri; 8.30am-8.30pm Sat; 8.30am-7pm Sun. **Credit** MC, V. **Map** G8.
Master chocolatier and traiteur Constant is revered by all. Trained in the arts of pâtisserie and chocolate, he scours the globe for new ideas. Ganaches are flavoured with verbena, jasmine or cardamom.

Jean-Paul Hévin
3 rue Vavin, 6th (01.43.54.09.85/www.jphevin.com). M° Vavin. **Open** 10am-7pm Mon-Sat. Closed Aug. **Credit** AmEx, MC, V. **Map** G8.
Jean-Paul Hévin dares to fill his chocolates with potent cheeses, served with wine as an aperitif. Even more risqué are his aphrodisiac chocolates. **Other locations:** 231 rue St-Honoré, 1st (01.55.35.35.96); 16 av de La Motte-Picquet, 7th (01.45.51.77.48).

Pierre Marcolini
89 rue de Seine, 6th (01.44.07.39.07/www.pierre marcolini.com). M° Mabillon. **Open** 10.30am-7pm Tue-Sat. **Credit** AmEx, MC, V. **Map** H7.
This Belgian newcomer to Paris is known among chocoholics worldwide for his 44 ganache flavours, including ginger, jasmine and tea with lemon.

Debauve & Gallais
30 rue des Sts-Pères, 7th (01.45.48.54.67/www. debauve-et-gallais.com). M° St-Germain-des-Prés. **Open** 9am-7pm Mon-Sat. **Credit** MC, V. **Map** G7.
This former pharmacy, its façade dating from 1800, sold chocolate for medicinal purposes. Its intense tea, honey or praline flavours still heal the soul. **Other locations:** 33 rue Vivienne, 2nd (01.40.39.05.50).

Richart
258 bd St-Germain, 7th (01.45.55.66.00/www. richart.com). M° Solférino. **Open** 10am-7pm Mon-Sat. **Credit** AmEx, MC, V. **Map** F6.
Each chocolate ganache has an intricate design, packages look like jewel boxes and each purchase comes with a tract on how best to savour chocolate.

La Maison du Chocolat
89 av Raymond-Poincaré, 16th (01.40.67.77.83/www. lamaisonduchocolat.com). M° Victor Hugo. **Open** 10am-7pm Mon-Sat. **Credit** AmEx, MC, V. **Map** B4.
Robert Linxe opened his first Paris shop in 1977 and has been inventing new chocolates ever since. See website for branch details.

GLOBAL

Kioko
46 rue des Petits-Champs, 2nd (01.42.61.33.65). M° Pyramides. **Open** 10am-8pm Tue-Sat; 11am-7pm Sun. **Credit** MC, V. **Map** H4.
This supermarket has everything fans of Japanese cooking might crave – including ready-made sushi.

Izraël
30 rue François-Miron, 4th (01.42.72.66.23). M° Hôtel de Ville. **Open** 9.30am-1pm, 2.30-7pm Tue-Fri; 9.30am-7pm Sat. Closed Aug. **Credit** MC, V. **Map** K6.
A Marais fixture, this narrow shop stocks spices and other delights from Mexico, Turkey and India.

Pasta Linea
9 rue de Turenne, 4th (01.42.77.62.54). M° St-Paul. **Open** 11am-9pm Tue-Fri; noon-8pm Sat, Sun. **Credit** AmEx, DC, MC, V. **Map** L6.
Artichoke ravioli with truffle cream sauce or fresh linguine with tomato and rocket are among the heavenly hot pastas you might find here, plus quality dried pastas and prepared sauces to eat at home.

Mexi & Co
10 rue Dante, 5th (01.46.34.14.12). M° Cluny La Sorbonne. **Open** noon-midnight daily. **No credit cards. Map** J7.
All you need for a fiesta: marinades for fajitas, dried chillies, Latin American beers, cachaça and tequilas.

Allicante. *See p283.*

Petrossian
18 bd de la Tour-Maubourg, 7th (01.44.11.32.32/ www.petrossian.fr). M° Invalides. **Open** 9.20am-8pm Mon-Sat. **Credit** AmEx, DC, MC, V. **Map** E6.
Russian-themed delicatessen offering silky smoked salmon, Iranian caviar and gift boxes with little drawers to impress even the most jaded of the jet set.

Jabugo Ibérico & Co
11 rue Clément-Marot, 8th (01.47.20.03.13). M° Alma Marceau or Franklin D Roosevelt. **Open** 10am-8pm Mon-Sat. **Credit** MC, V. **Map** D4.
This shop specialises in Spanish hams with the Bellota-Bellota label, meaning the pigs have feasted on acorns.

Sarl Velan Stores
87 passage Brady, 10th (01.42.46.06.06). M° Château d'Eau. **Open** 10am-8.30pm Mon-Sat. **Credit** AmEx, DC, MC, V. **Map** K4.
In a crumbling arcade lined with Indian restaurants, this is a prime source of spices and Indian produce.

Tang Frères
48 av d'Ivry, 13th (01.45.70.80.00). M° Porte d'Ivry. **Open** 9am-7.30pm Tue-Sun. **Credit** MC, V.

Leading supplier to local restaurants in Chinatown, this is the best one-stop shop for a Chinese or South-east Asian stir-fry.

Les Délices d'Orient
52 av Emile-Zola, 15th (01.45.79.10.00). M° Charles Michels. **Open** 7.30am-9pm Tue-Sun. **Credit** MC, V. **Map** B8.
Shelves here brim with Lebanese bread, falafel, olives and all manner of Middle Eastern delicacies. **Other locations**: 14 rue des Quatre-Frères-Peignot, 15th (01.45.77.82.93).

Merry Monk
87 rue de la Convention, 15th (01.40.60.79.54). M° Boucicaut. **Open** 10am-7pm Mon-Sat. **Credit** MC, V. **Map** B9.
Expat essentials such as ginger biscuits and loose tea, with a section dedicated to South Africa.

PATISSERIES
Finkelsztajn
27 rue des Rosiers, 4th (01.42.72.78.91). M° St-Paul. **Open** 11am-7pm Mon; 10am-7pm Wed-Sun. Closed 15 July-15 Aug. **No credit cards. Map** L6.

This motherly shop stocks dense Jewish cakes filled with poppy seeds, apples or cream cheese.

Pascal Pinaud

70 rue Monge, 5th (01.43.31.40.66). M° Place Monge. **Open** 8am-8pm Tue-Sat; 8am-7pm Sun. **Credit** MC, V. **Map** K8.

A former pastry instructor at the Paris Cordon Bleu, Pascal Pinaud now shows how it's done in this oustanding neighbourhood pastry shop with creations such as the tartelette orange-praliné, brut de chocolat, éclat de framboises and an exceptional Mont Blanc with Chantilly and chestnut cream.

Gérard Mulot

76 rue de Seine, 6th (01.43.26.85.77). M° Odéon. **Open** 6.45am-8pm Mon, Tue, Thur-Sun. Closed Aug. **No credit cards. Map** H7.

Mulot rustles up some truly stunning pastries. Typical is the mabillon – caramel mousse with apricot marmalada.

Pierre Hermé

72 rue Bonaparte, 6th (01.43.54.47.77). M° St-Sulpice. **Open** 10am-7pm Tue-Sun. **Credit** DC, MC, V. **Map** G7.

Pastry superstar Hermé attracts the connoisseurs of St-Germain with his seasonal collections. **Other locations**: 185 rue de Vaugirard, 15th (01.47.83.29.72).

Sadaharu Aoki

35 rue de Vaugirard, 6th (01.45.44.48.90). M° St-Placide. **Open** 11am-7pm Mon-Sat. **Credit** AmEx, DC, MC, V. **Map** G8.

This Japanese pastry chef combines French techniques to produce original (and pristine) pastries.

Arnaud Lahrer

53 rue Caulaincourt, 18th (01.42.57.68.08). M° Lamarck Caulaincourt. **Open** 10am-7.30pm Tue-Sun. **Credit** MC, V. **Map** H1.

Look out for the strawberry- and lychee-flavoured bonheur and the chocolate-and-thyme récif.

TREATS & TRAITEURS

Torréfacteur Verlet

256 rue St-Honoré, 1st (01.42.60.67.39). M° Palais Royal. **Open** *Shop* 9.30am-6.30pm Mon-Sat. *Tea shop* 9.30am-6.30pm daily. **Credit** MC, V. **Map** G5.

The freshly roasted coffee here smells as heavenly as the priciest perfume. Eric Duchaussoy roasts rare beans to perfection – sip a p'tit noir at a wooden table, or take home the city's finest coffee.

Goumanyat

3 rue Dupuis, 3rd (01.44.78.96.74/www.goumanyat. com). M° Temple. **Open** 11am-7pm Tue-Fri. **Credit** AmEx, DC, MC, V. **Map** L5.
Jean-Marie Thiercelin's family has been in spice since 1809, and his spacious, rather secretive shop (buzzer entry) is a treasure trove of super-fresh flavourings. Star chefs come here for Indonesian cubebe pepper, gleaming fresh nutmeg, long pepper (an Indian variety), and Spanish and Iranian saffron.

L'Epicerie

51 rue St-Louis-en-l'Ile, 4th (01.43.25.20.14). M° Pont Marie. **Open** 11am-8pm daily. **Credit** MC, V. **Map** K7.
This perfect gift shop is crammed with nice bottles of blackcurrant vinegar, five-spice mustard, tiny pots of jam, orange sauce, honey with figs and indulgent boxes of chocolate snails.

Jean-Paul Gardil

44 rue St-Louis en l'Ile, 4th (01.43.54.97.15). M° Pont Marie. **Open** 9am-12.45pm, 4-7.45pm Tue-Sat; 8.30am-12.30pm Sun. **Credit** MC, V. **Map** K7.
Rarely has meat looked so beautiful – geese hang in the window and a multitude of plaques confirm the butcher's skill in selecting the finest meats, such as milk-fed veal and lamb, coucou de Rennes chickens, Barbary ducklings, and Bresse poulard and geese.

Da Rosa

62 rue de Seine, 6th (01.40.51.00.09/www.darosa.fr). M° Odéon. **Open** 10am-10pm daily. **Credit** AmEx, MC, V. **Map** H7.
José Da Rosa sought ingredients for top Paris restaurants before opening his own shop, designed by Jacques Garcia: Spanish hams, spices from Breton chef Olivier Roellinger, truffles from the Luberon.

Huilerie Artisanale Leblanc

6 rue Jacob, 6th (01.46.34.61.55). M° St-Germain-des-Prés. **Open** 2.30-7pm Mon; 11am-7pm Tue-Sat. Closed two weeks in Aug. **No credit cards.** **Map** H6.
The Leblanc family started out making walnut oil from its family tree in Burgundy before branching out to press pure oils from hazelnuts, almonds, pine nuts, grilled peanuts, pistachios and olives.

Fauchon

26-30 pl de la Madeleine, 8th (01.47.42.60.11/ www.fauchon.com). M° Madeleine. **Open** 9.30am-8pm Mon-Sat. **Credit** AmEx, DC, MC, V. **Map** F4.
It may be the city's most famous food shop, but glitzy Fauchon seems to lack soul after a series of revamps.

Hédiard

21 pl de la Madeleine, 8th (01.43.12.88.88/www. hediard.fr). M° Madeleine. **Open** 8.30am-9pm Mon-Sat. **Credit** AmEx, DC, MC, V. **Map** F4.

The first establishment to introduce exotic foods to Paris, Hédiard specialises in rare teas and coffees, spices, jams and candied fruits. The original shop, dating from 1880, has a posh tea room upstairs. See the website for other addresses.

Terre de Truffes

21 rue Vignon, 8th (01.53.43.80.44). M° Madeleine. **Open** 10am-9.30pm Mon-Sat. **Credit** AmEx, MC, V. **Map** G4.
Famous for his truffle-based cuisine, Provençal chef Clément Bruno recently opened this truffle boutique and bistro where the truffle aroma hits your nostrils as you enter. Indulge in a fresh truffle for your cooking or more accessible truffle products, such as an almond truffle cream.

Allicante

26 bd Beaumarchais, 11th (01.43.55.13.02/ www.allicante.com). M° Bastille. **Open** 10am-7.30pm Mon-Sat. **Credit** AmEx, DC, MC, V. **Map** M6.
A trove of oily delights, including rare olive oils from Liguria, Sicily and Greece; fragrant pine nut, pistachio and almond varieties; oils extracted from apricot, peach and avocado pits; even pricey argania oil, pounded by hand by Berber women in Morocco.

Poissonnerie du Dôme

4 rue Delambre, 14th (01.43.35.23.95). M° Vavin. **Open** 8am-1pm, 4-7pm Tue-Sat; 8am-1pm Sun. **Credit** MC, V. **Map** G9.
The fish here are individually selected, many coming straight from small boats off the Breton coast. Each one is bright of eye and sound of gill. Try the drool-inducing (but bank-breaking) turbot, the giant crabs or the scallops, when in season.

Beau et Bon

81 rue Lecourbe, 15th (01.43.06.06.53/www. beauetbon.com). M° Volontaires. **Open** 10.30am-2pm, 3-7.30pm Tue-Sat. **Credit** MC, V. **Map** D8.
The aptly named Valérie Gentil has transformed her passion for rare condiments into a treasure trove of an épicerie. Come here for dried fruit chutneys from Brittany, cardamom jelly, saffron vinegar, puzzle-shaped cake trays and fantasy decorations for kids' birthday cakes.

WINE, BEER & SPIRITS

Legrand Filles et Fils

1 rue de la Banque, 2nd (01.42.60.07.12). M° Bourse. **Open** 11am-7pm Mon-Fri; 10am-7pm Sat. **Credit** AmEx, DC, MC, V. **Map** H4.
This old-fashioned shop offering fine wines and brandies, teas and bonbons has a showroom for its tasting glasses and gadgets, housed within galerie Vivienne. Wine tastings on Thursdays.

Julien, Caviste

50 rue Charlot, 3rd (01.42.72.00.94). M° Filles du Calvaire. **Open** 9.30am-1.30pm, 3.30-8.30pm Tue-Fri; 9.30am-8.30pm Sat; 10am-1.30pm Sun. **Credit** MC, V. **Map** L5.

The tireless Julien overflows with enthusiasm for the small producers he has discovered, and often holds free wine tastings on Saturdays.

Ryst Dupeyron
79 rue du Bac, 7th (01.45.48.80.93/www.ryst-dupeyron.com). M° Rue du Bac. **Open** 12.30-7.30pm Mon; 10.30am-7.30pm Tue-Sat. Closed one week in Aug. **Credit** AmEx, DC, MC, V. **Map** F7.
The Dupeyron family has sold Armagnac for four generations, and has bottles dating from 1868. Treasures include some 200 fine Bordeaux.

Les Caves Augé
116 bd Haussmann, 8th (01.45.22.16.97). M° St-Augustin. **Open** 1-7.30pm Mon; 9am-7.30pm Tue-Sat. Closed Mon in Aug. **Credit** AmEx, MC, V. **Map** E3.
The oldest wine shop in Paris – Marcel Proust was a regular customer – is serious and professional.

Les Caves Taillevent
199 rue du Fbg-St-Honoré, 8th (01.45.61.14.09/www.taillevent.com). M° Charles de Gaulle Etoile or Ternes. **Open** 2-7.30pm Mon; 9am-7.30pm Tue-Sat. Closed three weeks in Aug. **Credit** AmEx, DC, MC, V. **Map** D3.
Half a million bottles make up the Taillevent cellar.

La Maison du Whisky
20 rue d'Anjou, 8th (01.42.65.03.16/www.whisky.fr). M° Madeleine. **Open** 9.30am-7pm Mon; 9.30am-8pm Tue-Fri; 9.30am-7.30pm Sat. **Credit** AmEx, MC, V. **Map** F4.
Jean-Marc Bellier explains which whisky matches which food, and also hosts a whisky club.

Bières Spéciales
77 rue St-Maur, 11th (01.48.07.18.71). M° Rue St-Maur. **Open** 10.30am-1pm, 4-9pm Tue-Sat. **Credit** AmEx, DC, MC, V. **Map** N5.
Belgian brews dominate but you'll also find Polish, Scottish, Corsican, Portuguese and Chinese types.

Les Domaines qui Montent
136 bd Voltaire, 11th (01.43.56.89.15). M° Voltaire. **Open** 10am-8pm Tue-Sat. **Credit** MC, V. **Map** N6.
A shop and café, where wines cost the same as they would at the producer's. Saturday tastings, too.

Market forces

When pressed, Parisians will shop at the supermarché, but they are far happier queuing (jostling, as often as not) at their local open-air market. Markets have eternal appeal, their products perceived as a more 'natural' alternative to supermarket fare. The city council has made them more accessible to working people by extending opening hours and creating late-afternoon markets in previously overlooked areas. Even if quality can be variable, there is no better place in Paris to soak up some neighbourhood atmosphere while tracking down a pungent goat's cheese, a dozen fresh Cancale oysters, a bunch of ruby chard or a jar of sunflower-yellow honey.

The 66 roving markets in Paris have retained their atmosphere and variety, although street and covered markets can be a bit of a letdown, with clothing stores and chains replacing traditional food shops. Here is a selection of the best roving markets, open from 8am to 2pm unless otherwise specified:

Marché Monge (place Monge, 5th, Wed, Fri, Sun), though compact, is pretty and set on a leafy square. It has an unusually high proportion of producers and is much less touristy than nearby rue Mouffetard, a long-established street market. Be prepared to queue for the best quality.

Saxe-Breteuil (av de Saxe, 7th, Thur, Sat) has an unrivalled setting facing the Eiffel Tower, as well as the city's most chic

produce. Look for farmer's goat's cheese, rare apple varieties, Armenian specialities, abundant oysters and a handful of dedicated small producers.

Marché Square d'Anvers (9th, 3-8pm Fri) is a new afternoon market, adding to the village atmosphere of a peaceful quartier down the hill from Montmartre. Among its highlights are untreated vegetables, hams from the Auvergne, cheeses and award-winning honey.

Marché Bastille (bd Richard-Lenoir, 11th, Thur, Sun) is one of the biggest and most boisterous in Paris. A favourite of political campaigners, it's also a great source of local cheeses, farmer's chicken and excellent affordable fish.

Marché d'Aligre (rue d'Aligre, 12th, Tue-Sun), next to a covered market, is proudly working-class. Stallholders out-shout each other while price-conscious shoppers don't compromise on quality.

Marché Président-Wilson (av Président-Wilson, 16th, Wed, Sat) is a classy market attracting the city's top chefs, who snap up ancient vegetable varieties. Genuine Breton crêpes and buckwheat galettes are available as you shop.

Marché Batignolles (bd des Batignolles, 17th, Sat) is more down-to-earth than the Raspail organic market, with a quirky selection of stallholders, many of whom produce what they sell. Prices are higher than at ordinary markets, but worth it.

Learning & Tasting

COOKERY COURSES

Ritz Escoffier Ecole de Gastronomie Française

38 rue Cambon, 1st (01.43.16.30.50/www.ritz.paris).
M° Opéra. **Courses** start each Mon; demonstrations
3-5.30pm Mon,Thur; 9am-3pm Sat. **Fees**
demonstration €47; half-day hands-on from €125.
Professional training available. **Enrolment** in
advance. **Credit** AmEx, DC, MC, V. **Map** G4.

The Ritz cooking school, founded in 1988, offers a
number of quality hands-on and demonstration
classes for enthusiasts of all levels. Across from the
world-famous kitchen and deep in the hotel's bowels,
students work with state-of-the-art equipment and
experienced chefs who are willing to answer any
question. A four-hour shellfish and crustacean
seasonal workshop (in French only) began with a
lobstercide – the barehanded dismembering of live
lobsters – and ended with a perfectly simmered
bisque, a genuine summer treat. Other short-term
courses and demonstrations might focus on
chocolate or jams, foie gras or wine-and-food matches
(often with English translations) and there are a
number of half-day options for kids (from €85), with
titles such as My First Terrine and Happy Mother's
Day. For the more ambitious student, diploma
courses are offered and could lead to an internship
in the Ritz's kitchen. Book in advance, as the most
intriguing offerings fill up quickly.

Françoise Meunier

7 rue Paul-Lelong, 2nd (01.40.26.14.00/
www.fmeunier.com). M° Bourse or Les Halles.
Classes 10.30am-1.30pm Wed-Fri. **Fees** €90 per
class; five classes €400; classes and exam/diploma
€1,500. **Credit** MC, V. **Map** J4.

Greeting her students warmly with a cup of coffee
and an apron, Françoise Meunier plays host to a calm
and convivial cooking school in her spacious kitchen.
A well-travelled Ecole Hôtelière graduate, she covers
everything from seasoning to silverware as a mix of
international students prepares a balanced three-
course meal. The highlight of our class was a juicy,
perfectly cooked rôti de porc à la dijonnaise, although
menus can be designed according to students'
preferences. The course provides lots of hands-on
learning and easy-to-follow printed recipes. Schedule
in advance as popular classes are limited to ten.
English translations available with advance notice.

L'Ecole du Thé

Le Palais des Thés, 64 rue Vieille-du-Temple, 3rd
(01.43.56.96.38/www.palaisdesthes.fr). M° Hôtel
de Ville. **Classes** daily. **Fees** connaissances
and découvertes €16; évasions €32. **Credit** AmEx,
MC, V. **Map** L6.

L'Ecole du Thé offers a variety of interesting and
well-organised courses (in French only) to increase
your appreciation of the humble cuppa. The 45-
minute 'découvertes' allow you to sample five or six
different teas based around a specific theme, while
the 90-minute 'connaissances' combine a presentation
and tasting session on general subjects such as 'the
origins of tea' or 'the art of tasting'. For serious tea
connoisseurs, or those who need professional
grounding, the 'Initiation à la dégustation' course
consists of four modules (changed quarterly) and
covers more weighty subjects such as tea cultivation,
brewing techniques and the sensory perception and
isolation of flavours and aromas. The school also
organises off-site 'évasions', where an expert
imparts wisdom on such subjects as the medical
benefits of green tea, the ins and outs of the Japanese
tea ceremony, or how to use tea in cooking.

Promenades Gourmandes

187 rue du Temple, 3rd (01.48.04.56.84/www.
promenadesgourmandes.com). M° Temple.
Classes 9am-3pm/6pm Tue-Fri. Closed Aug.
Fees €100-€300. **Enrolment** preferably at least
two weeks in advance. **Credit** AmEx, MC, V (by
internet). **Map** L5.

A cultural experience as well as a culinary one, Paule
Caillat's classes begin at the market, where she will
show you how to select the finest seasonal
ingredients, such as line-caught fish and vegetables
from small producers, before tackling a three-course
menu at her custom-designed Marais apartment.
'All the necessary steps and no unnecessary ones' is
the philosophy that has made her classes so popular
with visiting Americans, Brits and Australians (the
lively Paule is bilingual and teaches in English).
Once you have mastered a few techniques –
particularly her break-all-the-rules pastry – Paule's
hearty French recipes are truly foolproof, perfect for
impressing friends back home. The full-day offering
includes an afternoon stroll to various places of
culinary interest, such as Poilâne bakery, at which
Paule and her guests benefit from a VIP welcome.

Astuces et Tours de Mains

29 rue Censier, 5th (01.45.87.11.37/www.astuces
ettoursdemains.com). M° Censier-Daubenton.
Classes 1-4pm Mon, Thur, Fri; 10am-2pm Sat.
Fees €100, Sat €115; €440 for five (weekdays only).
Enrolment up to six months in advance. **No credit
cards. Map** K9.

Laurence Guarneri's lovely little school is located in
her custom-built kitchen in a renovated tannery with
lots of natural light. Seated on comfortable stools at
the counter, students can take notes on Laurence's
tips while having a good view of the day's creation.
The style is modern French, with recipes inspired

Learn from the masters at the **Cordon Bleu** cookery school. *See p289*.

by chefs such as Alain Ducasse, and workshops might include 'Italian vegetarian'. Most courses are booked up well in advance. The atmosphere is both professional and convivial as many of the students are regulars – an opportunity to meet people with similar interests and pick up valuable skills. Excellent, if your French is up to it or if you can convince a bilingual, food-loving friend to translate.

Ecoles Grégoire Ferrandi

28 rue de l'Abbé-Grégoire, 6th (01.49.54.28.03/ www.egf.ccip.fr). M° St-Placide or Rennes. **Classes** cooking, pâtisserie and wine tasting courses 6.30-10.30pm Thur. **Fee** €70 per class. Professional training available. **Enrolment** three weeks in advance. **No credit cards. Map** G8.

This state-run cooking school offers evening cooking or pastry classes (maximum 12 people) for the general public. There are different seasonal themes to choose from – autumn's cassoulet or summer's 'festive dishes'. This is also a good place to learn classic desserts – crêpes, fondant au chocolat, and more. For the student committed to full-time professional training, Ferrandi also offers long diploma programmes – a good deal at half the price of the Ritz or the Cordon Bleu. In January 2005 it launched a course with none other than the 'Picasso of pastry', Pierre Hermé, for pastry professionals only (in French).

L'Atelier des Chefs

10 rue de Penthièvre, 8th (01.53.30.05.82/www. atelierdeschefs.com). M° Miromesnil or St-Philippe-du-Roule. **Classes** Mon-Sat (hours vary). **Fees** €15-€130. **Enrolment** two weeks in advance advised. **Credit** MC, V. **Map** F3.

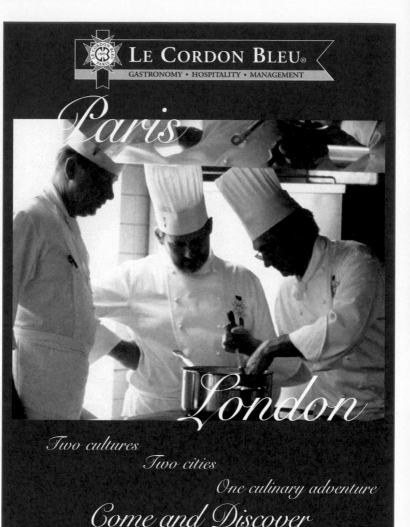

LE CORDON BLEU®

GASTRONOMY • HOSPITALITY • MANAGEMENT

Paris

London

Two cultures
Two cities
One culinary adventure

Come and Discover
the world of Le Cordon Bleu

www.cordonbleu.edu

Le Cordon Bleu Paris
8 rue Léon Delhomme
75015 Paris
T : +33 (0)1 53 68 22 50
F: +33 (0)1 48 56 03 96
paris@cordonbleu.edu

Le Cordon Bleu London
114, Marylebone Lane
London, W1U 2HH, U.K.
T : +44 20 7935 3503
F: +44 20 7935 7621
london@cordonbleu.edu

PARIS   LONDON   OTTAWA   JAPAN   U.S.A.   AUSTRALIA   PERU   KOREA   LIBAN   MEXICO

Considering the chic location, it's surprising to learn that classes are so democratically priced at this innovative and well-organised new cooking school: from €15 for a half-hour class followed by a meal (with extras, such as dessert or wine, costing €2 or €3 each). After reserving on the internet, we received a text message reminder on the day of the class with Jean-Sébastien Bompoil, who formerly worked at the Ritz. Arriving a little early, we drooled over the cookbooks and high-tech kitchen tools on display before donning a plastic apron and entering the airy kitchen, with space for 20 people. The half-hour class (in French) – wok-fried pork with diced pumpkin and mace on this occasion – takes place at breakneck speed, but the chef is full of useful tips and the atmosphere is friendly, particularly when it's time to enjoy the results around a long table. More involved workshops on French or foreign cuisines take place in the mornings and afternoons, some of them in English. Not surprisingly classes fill up well in advance.

Ecole Lenôtre

Pavillon Elysée, 10 av des Champs-Elysées, 8th (01.42.65.97.60/www.lenotre.fr). M° Champs-Elysées Clemenceau. **Classes** 9am-1pm, 2-6pm Mon-Sat; 7-10pm Thur; 2-3.30pm, 4.30-6.30pm Wed (children's classes). Closed Aug, 20 Dec 10 Jan. **Fees** demonstrations €46; half-day workshops €100-€105; one-day €185-€275; children €33. **Enrolment** three weeks in advance. **Credit** AmEx, DC, MC, V. **Map** F4.

A warm welcome awaits at the Ecole Lenôtre where you are invited to discover the culinary secrets of master chefs in a relaxed and friendly environment. The school offers a wide variety of themed cooking and pâtisserie workshops, demonstrations and programmes for children (all held in French). With a maximum of eight students per class, the chef encourages you to join in as little or as much as you like. You can get your hands dirty pulling the heads off some langoustines in preparation for the perfect seafood risotto, or if you prefer, just sit back and take notes for future reference. Disappointingly, we were not able to scoff our creations there and then, rather each student was given a generous portion to take home and sample. All well and good, although our perfect risotto had predictably turned into a container full of glug by the time we got home to try it. However, after an overnight stint in the fridge, our rum and raison riz au lait with orange zest was nothing short of spectacular.

L'Atelier des Sens

40 rue Sedaine, 11th (01.40.21.08.50/www.atelier-des-sens.com). M° Voltaire. **Classes** Tue-Sun (hours vary). **Fees** €34-€85 (one to three hours). Subscriptions available. **Enrolment** one week in advance. **Credit** MC, V. **Map** M6.

Nestling romantically at the end of a Parisian courtyard, the Atelier des Sens has nothing of an intimidating cooking school. The atmosphere created by director Natacha Burtinovic in the smart demonstration kitchen is relaxed and informal. Covering all aspects of French and international cuisine (in French), courses normally last two or three hours. There is also the attractive option of a one-hour course at lunchtime or suppertime, where a main course is prepared and then eaten in the atelier or packed up as a take-away. On a recent visit Moroccan chef Mohamed showed us all about making a designer tagine, in which he treated his own printed recipe with endearing flexibility, making for lots of eager note taking from the amusingly diverse group of seven or eight people. We played with chicken breasts, stuffing them and then rolling them in clingfilm. Anything involving film and stuffing always breaks the ice at a class, and we were soon comparing our work before Mohamed did magical plating, giving our efforts a genuine professional touch, which was impressive in just an hour.

Le Cordon Bleu

8 rue Léon Delhomme, 15th (01.53.68.22.50/www.cordonbleu.edu). M° Vaugirard. **Classes** 8.30am-7pm Mon-Fri; 8.30am-3.30pm Sat. **Fees** demonstrations €29-€39; one-day workshops from €139; four-day workshops €879. Professional training available. **Enrolment** three months in advance for long courses, two weeks for one-day courses. **Credit** MC, V. **Map** D9.

Founded in Paris in 1885, Le Cordon Bleu has now spread to 15 different countries and hosts more than 18,000 students worldwide. Running alongside the more serious nine-month diploma programme, they offer numerous demonstrations and workshops (some with English translations) for anyone wishing to improve their culinary skills. The daily demonstrations, designed for the long-term students attending the school, can be somewhat rushed and impersonal, but are a good way of observing the techniques involved in a specific area ranging from anything such as French pastry-making, to cooking with red meat. For a more leisurely approach, you can watch an experienced chef prepare two dishes in the 'chef's secrets' demonstration which are later sampled with a glass of wine, or try a 'market tour', which includes a market visit with a master chef, lunch at the school and a demonstration. If you are not content to merely observe the masters at work, the 'cooking with friends' and other gourmet workshops start with a demonstration and are followed by a practical session in one of their well-equipped kitchens.

WINE COURSES

Le Jardin des Vignes

91 rue de Turenne, 3rd (01.42.77.05.00). M° St-Sébastien-Froissart. **Courses** on request, usually 8-10pm Tue, Wed or Thur. **Fees** evening session €85, three-session introductory course €250. **No credit cards.** **Map** L5.

Caviste Jean Radford is passionate about helping people understand the art of dégustation. His four starter classes at the Jardin des Vignes cover the history of winemaking, different grapes and regions and the basics of tasting.

Grains Nobles

5 rue Laplace, 5th (01.43.54.93.54/www.grains nobles.fr). Mº Cardinal-Lemoine. **Courses** introductory courses begin mid-Sept, details of evening courses on website. **Fees** Soirées from €65; single class from €85; courses from €250. **Enrolment** by post with cheque. **No credit cards.** **Map** J8.

Established in 1991, André Bessou's wine school offers courses and soirées to satisfy the most sophisticated tastebuds. More concerned with tasting than theory, Bessou cracks open some of France's most precious vintages during his regional étude du terroir and soirées prestige (wine lists a surprise), which are followed by a meal. The initation/perfectionnement session consists of three courses, each three hours long, and dissects 21 quality wines. Other regional soirées take to the revamped cellar to study the work of one particular château. A prior knowledge of wines is helpful and, if you don't speak French, tant pis.

Centre de Dégustation Jacques Vivet

48 rue de Vaugirard, 6th (01.43.25.96.30/ www.ecoleduvin.net). RER Luxembourg. **Classes** Mon, Tue, Thur evening (times vary). **Fees** four introductory classes €185; four advanced classes €200-€300. **Enrolment** a few weeks in advance. **No credit cards. Map** H7.

When Jacques Vivet opened his tasting centre more than 20 years ago, most of his clients were foreigners – French people apparently believing innate knowledge of wine to be a national birthright. However, the French have now wised up and humbly come to his introductory and perfectionnement courses. The introductory course covers the theoretical side of wine – the elements that make up its flavour – as well as lots of dedicated tasting practice. The perfectionnement course brings in more developed vocabulary and some very special wines. After his courses, Vivet hopes that 'you'll no longer just drink the wine, as you did before, instead you'll taste it'.

Ecoles Grégoire Ferrandi

28 rue de l'Abbé-Grégoire, 6th (01.49.54.28.03). Mº St-Placide or Rennes. **Classes** 7-10pm four Wed or Thur evenings. **Fee** €260. **No credit cards.** **Map** G8.

Known mostly for its state-run cooking school (*see p287*), Ecoles Grégoire Ferrandi dabbles in wine as well. The initiation course covers all aspects of wine, beginning with soil and climate before moving towards tasting techniques, wine vocabulary and the significance of the grandes appellations. A session is dedicated to Champagne, and the last session is held over dinner, at which various wines are tasted with the dishes to which they are best suited.

Les Vins du Terroir

34 av Duquesne, 7th (01.40.61.91.87). Mº St-François-Xavier. **Classes** 8.30-10pm Tue, Thur. **Fees** €60 per class. **Enrolment** one week in advance. **Credit** MC, V. **Map** E7.

Alexandre Gerbe opened this wine shop in 1998 and runs an evening class about once a month, each time tasting seven wines from a particular region. Classes run throughout the year except during the summer holidays, and accept a maximum of 12 people.

L'Ecole du Vin Ylan Schwartz

17 passage Foubert, 13th (01.45.89.77.39). Mº Tolbiac. **Fees** €340-€600. **Enrolment** phone in advance. **No credit cards.**

Oenologist Ylan Schwartz brings an original approach to learning about wine. An advocate of 'the harmony between wine and music', Schwartz works with a Baroque ensemble and musicians from the Orchestre Philharmonique de Radio France in evenings (prices vary) that combine dinner, wine tasting and the music to suit it, matching a specific château to a particular piece or even movement of music. Other classes deal with matching wine and cheese, regional tastings, grands crus to go with grand food, and vineyard tours. Some classes are available in English or Spanish.

Institut du Vin du Savour Club

11-13 rue Gros, 16th (01.42.30.94.18/www.le savourclub.fr). RER Kennedy-Radio France. **Classes** Tue certain dates. **Fees** three classes €150. **Enrolment** at least one month in advance. **Credit** AmEx, DC, MC, V. **Map** A7.

Georges Lepré, former Ritz and Grand Véfour sommelier, heads these courses, taught in French, which focus on how to match wine to dishes. Courses on offer include 'an approach to wine' and 'a passion for wine'. The first involves three sessions, each covering six wines. Courses teach the basics of tasting, how best to stock a wine cellar and how to match wine with food. Classes are also available on specific subjects, such as dessert wines. Horizontal and vertical tastings and special wine-making processes are part of a second set of three classes.

Le Musée du Vin

rue des Eaux, 16th (01.45.25.63.26/www.musee duvinparis.com). Mº Passy. **Courses** for information contact Monique Josse on 01.64.09.44.80. **Open** museum 10-6pm Tue-Sun; courses 10am-noon Sat Sept-June. **Fees** €42 per session; students €37. **Enrolment** at least two weeks in advance. **No credit cards. Map** B6.

This small museum is housed in 14th-century vaulted cellars that were once part of the Abbaye de Passy, which produced a wine enjoyed by Louis XIII himself. Discover the history and processes of wine-making (labels in French only) through displays of vats, corkscrews and cut-outs of medieval peasants, followed by a short dégustation. Classes cover many different French regions, grape varieties and sensory analysis of wines.

Index & Maps

A-Z Index

Index

Index

Index

Index

Index

Arrondissement Index

Index

Index

Index

Index

Index

Le Square
Trousseau p59
1 rue Antoine-
Vollon, 12th
(01.43.43.06.00)

Brasseries

Le Train Bleu p94
Gare de Lyon, pl Louis-
Armand, 12th
(01.43.43.09.06/
www.le-train-bleu.
com)

Budget

L'Encrier p146
55 rue Traversière, 12th
(01 44 68 08 16)

**Le Pays de
Vannes** p147
34 bis rue de
Wattignies, 12th
(01.43.07.87.42)

Cafés

Chez Gudule p229
58 bd de Picpus, 12th
(01.43.40.08.28)

T pour 2 Café p229
23 cour St-Emilion, 12th
(01.40.19.02.09)

Viaduc Café p229
43 av Daumesnil, 12th
(01.44.74.70.70)

Classics

Au Pressoir p108
257 av Daumesnil, 12th
(01.43.44.38.21)

L'Oulette p107
15 pl Lachambeaudie,
12th (01.40.02.02.12/
www.l-oulette.com)

Le Traversière p108
40 rue Traversière, 12th
(01.43.44.02.10)

Eating with Entertainment

**Casse-Croûte à
l'Opéra** p273
Studio Bastille, Opéra
National de Paris, 120
rue de Lyon, 12th
(01.40.10.17.89/
www.opera-de-paris.fr)

Far Eastern

La Coloniale p174
161 rue de Picpus, 12th
(01.43.43.69.10)

Italian

**Sardegna a
Tavola** p194
1 rue de Cotte, 12th
(01.44.75.03.28)

**Les Amis de
Messina** p194
204 rue du Fbg-
St-Antoine, 12th
(01.43.67.96.01)

Other International

Athanor p212
4 rue Crozatier, 12th
(01.43.44.49.15)

Regional

Au Trou Gascon p129
40 rue Taine, 12th
(01.43.44.34.26)

Pataquès p127
40-42 bd de Bercy,
12th (01.43.07.37.75)

Wine Bars

**Le Baron
Bouge** p268
1 rue Théophile-
Roussel, 12th
(01.43.43.14.32)

13th Arrondissement

African & Indian Ocean

Entoto p160
143-145 rue Léon-
Maurice-Nordmann, 13th
(01.45.87.08.51)

Bars & Pubs

**La Folie en
Tête** p252
33 rue de la Butte
aux Cailles, 13th
(01.45.80.65.99)

Bistros

Anacréon p60
53 bd St-Marcel, 13th
(01.43.31.71.18)

**Au Petit
Marguery** p61
9 bd du Port-Royal, 13th
(01.43.31.58.59/
www.petitmarguery.fr)

L'Avant-Goût p60
26 rue Bobillot, 13th
(01.53.80.24.00)

Bioart p61
1 quai Francois-
Mauriac, 13th
(01.45.85.66.88)

Chez Paul p61
22 rue de la Butte-
aux-Cailles, 13th
(01.45.89.22.11)

L'Ourcine p61
92 rue Broca, 13th
(01.47.07.13.65)

Le Terroir p62
11 bd Arago, 13th
(01.47.07.36.99)

Budget

**Le Temps des
Cerises** p147
18 rue de la Butte-
aux-Cailles, 13th
(01.45.89.69.48)

Cafés

**Chez Lili et
Marcel** p229
1 quai d'Austerlitz, 13th
(01.45.85.00.08)

**Le Village de la
Butte** p230
23 rue de la Butte
aux Cailles, 13th
(01.45.80.36.82)

Far Eastern

**Rouammit &
Huong Lan** p183
103 av d'Ivry, 13th
(01.53.60.00.34)

La Tonkinoise p185
20 rue Philibert
Locut, 13th
(01.45.85.98.98)

Tricotin p176
15 av de Choisy, 13th
(01.45.84.74.44)

North African

Au P'tit Cahoua p206
39 bd St-Marcel, 13th
(01.47.07.24.42)

Regional

**L'Auberge
Etchegorry** p129
41 rue de
Croulebarbe, 13th
(01.44.08.83.51)

Tea Rooms

L'Oisive Thé p260
1 rue Jean-Marie
Jego, 13th
(01.53.80.31.33)

Wine Bars

Les Cailloux p268
58 rue des Cinq-
Diamants, 13th
(01.45.80.15.08)

14th Arrondissement

Bars & Pubs

Le Rosebud p252
11 bis rue
Delambre, 14th
(01.43.20.44.13)

Le Tournesol p252
9 rue de la Gaîté, 14th
(01.43.27.65.72)

Bistros

L'O à la Bouche p63
124 bd du
Montparnasse, 14th
(01.56.54.01.55)

Contre-Allée p62
83 av Denfert-
Rochereau, 14th
(01.43.54.99.86/
www.contreallee.com)

**Les Petites
Sorcières** p63
12 rue Liancourt, 14th
(01.43.21.95.68)

Natacha p63
17 bis rue Campagne-
Première, 14th
(01.43.20.79.27)

La Régalade p64
49 av Jean-Moulin, 14th
(01.45.45.68.58)

Brasseries

La Coupole p94
102 bd du Montparnasse,
14th (01.43.20.14.20/
www.coupoleparis.com)

Cafés

**La Chope
Daguerre** p230
17 rue Daguerre, 14th
(01.43.22.76.59)

Les Tontons p231
38 rue de Raymond
Losserand, 14th
(01.43.21.69.45)

**Le Plomb du
Cantal** p230
3 rue de la Gaîté, 14th
(01.43.35.16.92)

Caribbean

La Créole p169
122 bd du
Montparnasse, 14th
(01.43.20.62.12)

Le Flamboyant p169
11 rue Boyer-
Barret, 14th
(01.45.41.00.22)

Classics

**Le Pavillon
Montsouris** p108
20 rue Gazan, 14th
(01.43.13.29.00/
www.pavillon-
montsouris.fr)

Contemporary

Montparnasse 25 p117
Le Méridien Montparnasse,
19 rue du Commandant
René Mouchotte, 14th
(01.44.36.44.25)

Far Eastern

Korean Barbecue p180
22 rue Delambre, 14th
(01.43.35.44.32)

Fish & Seafood

Le Bar à Huîtres p132
112 bd du Montparnasse,
14th (01.43.20.71.01)

Bistrot du Dôme p133
1 rue Delambre, 14th
(01.43.35.32.00)

La Cagouille p133
10-12 pl Constantin
Brancusi, 14th
(01.43.22.09.01/
www.lacagouille.fr)

Le Dôme p134
108 bd du Montparnasse,
14th (01.43.35.25.81)

Regional

L'Opportun p125
64 bd Edgar
Quinet, 14th
(01.43.20.26.29)

Trendy

Apollo p102
3 pl Denfert-
Rochereau, 14th
(01.45.38.76.77)

Vegetarian

Aquarius p156
40 rue de Gergovie, 14th
(01.45.41.36.88)

Index

Index

Index

Lexicon

Food

a

A point medium-rare (meat).
Abats offal.
Accra salt-cod fritter.
Agneau lamb.
Aiglefin haddock.
Aiguillettes thin slices.
Ail garlic.
Aile wing.
Aïoli ground garlic sauce.
Airelle cranberry.
Algues seaweed.
Aligot mashed potatoes with cheese and garlic.
Aloyau beef loin.
Amande almond; – **de mer** small clam.
Amer/amère bitter.
Ananas pineapple.
Anchoïade anchovy paste.
Anchois anchovy.
Andouille pig's offal sausage, served cold.
Andouillette grilled chitterling (offal) sausage.
Aneth dill.
Anguille eel.
Anis aniseed.
Araignée de mer spider crab.
Artichaut artichoke.
Asperge asparagus.
Assiette plate.
Aubergine aubergine (GB), eggplant (US).
Avocat avocado.

b

Baies roses pink peppercorns.
Ballotine stuffed, rolled-up piece of boned fish or meat.
Bar sea bass.
Barbue brill.
Basilic basil.
Bavarois moulded cream dessert.
Bavette beef flank steak.
Béarnaise hollandaise sauce with tarragon and shallots.
Belon flat, round oyster.
Betterave beetroot.

Beurre butter; – **blanc** butter sauce with white wine and shallots; – **noir** browned butter.
Beignet fritter or doughnut.
Biche deer, venison.
Bien cuit well done (for meat).
Bifteck steak.
Bigorneau periwinkle.
Biologique organic.
Blanc white; – **de poulet** chicken breast.
Blanquette a 'white' stew (with eggs and cream).
Blette Swiss chard.
Boeuf beef; – **bourguignon** beef stew with red wine; – **du charolais** charolais beef (a breed); – **gros sel** boiled beef with vegetables; – **miroton** sliced boiled beef in onion sauce; – **de salers** salers beef (a breed).
Bordelaise sauce with red wine, shallots and marrow.
Boudin blanc white veal, chicken or pork sausage.
Boudin noir black (blood) pudding.
Bouillabaisse Mediterranean fish and shellfish soup.
Bouillon stock.
Bourride fish stew.
Brandade de morue salt cod puréed with olive oil.
Brebis sheep's milk cheese.
Brik North African filo pastry package.
Brochet pike.
Brochette kebab.
Brouillé(s) scrambled (egg).
Brûlé(e) literally, burned, usually caramelised.
Bulot whelk.

c

Cabillaud fresh cod.
Cabri young goat.
Caille quail.
Calamar squid.
Campagne/campagnard country-style.
Canard duck.

Canette duckling.
Cannelle cinnamon.
Carbonnade beef stew with onions and beer.
Carré d'agneau rack or loin of lamb.
Carrelet plaice.
Cassis blackcurrants, also blackcurrant liqueur in kir.
Cassoulet stew of haricot beans, sausage and preserved duck.
Céleri celery.
Céleri rave celeriac.
Céleri rémoulade grated celeriac in mustard mayonnaise.
Cèpe cep or porcini mushroom.
Cerfeuil chervil.
Cerise cherry.
Cervelas garlicky Alsatian pork sausage.
Cervelle brains.
Champignon mushroom; – **de Paris** cultivated button mushroom.
Chantilly whipped cream.
Chapon capon.
Charcuterie cured meat, such as saucisson or pâté.
Charlotte moulded cream dessert with a biscuit edge.
Chasseur sauce with white wine, mushrooms, shallots and tomato.
Châtaigne chestnut.
Chateaubriand fillet steak.
Chaud(e) hot.
Chaud-froid glazing sauce with gelatine or aspic.
Chausson pastry turnover.
Cheval horse.
A cheval with egg on top.
Chèvre goat's cheese.
Chevreuil young roe deer.
Chicorée frisée, or curly endive (GB), chicory (US).
Chiffonade shredded herbs and vegetables.
Chipiron squid.
Choron béarnaise sauce with tomato purée.
Chou cabbage; – **de Bruxelles** Brussels sprout; – **frisé**

kale; – **rouge** red cabbage;
– **fleur** cauliflower.
Choucroute sauerkraut
(garnie if topped with cured
ham and sausages).
Ciboulette chive.
Citron lemon.
Citron vert lime.
Citronelle lemongrass.
Citrouille pumpkin.
Civet game stew in blood-
thickened sauce.
Clafoutis thick batter baked
with fruit
Cochon pig; – **de lait**
suckling pig.
Cochonnailles cured pig parts
(ears, snout, cheeks...).
Coeur heart.
Coing quince.
Colin hake.
Concombre cucumber.
Confiture jam.
Congre conger eel.
Contre-filet sirloin.
Coq rooster.
à la Coque in its shell.
Coquelet baby rooster.
Coquillages shellfish.
Coquille shell; – **St-Jacques**
scallop.
Cornichon pickled gherkin.
Côte/côtelette rib or chop.
Côte de boeuf beef rib.
Cotriade Breton fish stew.
Coulis thick sauce or purée.
Courge vegetable marrow
(GB), squash (US).
Courgette courgette (GB),
zucchini (US).
Crème anglaise custard.
Crème brûlée caramelised
custard dessert.
Crème fraîche thick, slightly
soured cream.
Crêpe pancake.
Crépinette small, flattish
sausage, often grilled.
Cresson watercress.
Creuse oyster with long,
crinkly shell.
Crevette prawn (GB), shrimp
(US); – **grise** grey shrimp.
Croque-madame croque-
monsieur topped with
an egg.
Croque-monsieur toasted
cheese and ham sandwich.
Crottin small, round goat's
cheese (literally, turd).

Croustade bread or pastry
case, deep-fried.
en Croûte in a pastry case.
Crudités raw vegetables.
Crustacé shellfish.
Cuisse leg (poultry).
Curcuma turmeric.

d

Darne fish steak.
Datte date.
Daube meat braised slowly in
red wine.
Daurade/dorade sea bream.
Demi-glace meat glaze.
Demi-sel slightly salted
Désossé(e) boned.
Diable demi-glace with
cayenne and white wine.
Dinde turkey.
Duxelles chopped, sautéed
mushrooms with shallots.

e

Echalote shallot.
Ecrémé skimmed (milk).
Ecrevisse crayfish.
Eminçé fine slice.
Encornet squid.
Endive chicory (GB), Belgian
endive (US).
Entrecôte beef rib steak.
Entremets cream or milk-
based dessert.
Eperlan smelt; whitebait.
Epicé(e) spicy.
Epices spices.
Epinards spinach.
Escabèche fish fried,
marinated and served cold.
Escalope cutlet.
Escarole slightly bitter,
slightly curly salad leaves.
Espadon swordfish.
Espelette small, hot
Basque pepper.
Estouffade meat stew.
Estragon tarragon.
Etrille small crab.

f

Faisan pheasant.
Farci(e) stuffed.
Faux-filet sirloin steak.
Fenouil fennel.
Feuille de chêne oak leaf
lettuce.
Feuilleté puff pastry.
Fève broad bean.

Figue fig.
Filet mignon tenderloin.
Financier small rectangular
cake.
Fines de claire crinkle-shelled
oysters.
Fines herbes mixed herbs.
Flambé(e) sprinkled with
alcohol, then set alight.
Flet flounder.
Flétan halibut.
Florentine with spinach.
Foie liver.
Foie gras fattened liver of
goose or duck; – **cru** raw
foie gras; – **entier** whole
foie gras; – **mi-cuit** barely
cooked (also called frais or
nature); **pâté de** – liver pâté
with a foie gras base.
Fondu(e) melted.
Fondue savoyarde bread
dipped into melted cheese.
Fondue bourguignonne beef
dipped in heated oil.
Forestière with mushrooms.
au four oven-baked.
Fourre(e) filled or stuffed.
Frais/fraîche fresh.
Fraise strawberry; – **des bois**
wild strawberry; – **de veau**
part of the calf's intestine.
Framboise raspberry.
Frappé(e) iced or chilled.
Fricadelle meatball.
Frisée curly endive (GB),
chicory (US).
Frit(e) fried.
Frites chips (UK), French
fries (US).
Friture tiny fried fish.
Froid(e) cold.
Fromage cheese; – **blanc**
smooth cream cheese.
Fruits secs dried fruit
and nuts.
Fruits de mer seafood,
especially shellfish.
Fumé(e) smoked.
Fumet fish stock.

g

Galantine pressed meat or
fish, usually stuffed.
Galette flat cake of savoury
pastry, potato pancake or
buckwheat crêpe.
Garbure thick vegetable and
meat soup.
Garni(e) garnished.

Index & Maps

Gelée jelly or aspic.
Genièvre juniper berry.
Gésiers gizzards.
Gibier game.
Gigot d'agneau leg of lamb.
Gigue haunch of game, usually venison or boar.
Gingembre ginger.
Girofle clove.
Girolle wild mushroom.
Gîte shin of beef.
Gîte à la noix topside or silverside of beef.
Glace ice, also ice-cream.
Glacé(e) frozen; ice-cold; iced (as in cake).
Glaçon ice cube.
Gombo okra.
Gougère choux pastry and cheese mixture in a ring.
Goujon breaded, fried strip of fish; also a small catfish.
Goût taste.
Goûter to taste, or snack.
Graisse fat, grease.
Granité water-ice.
Gras(se) fatty.
Gratin dauphinois sliced potatoes baked with milk, cheese and garlic.
Gratiné(e) browned with breadcrumbs or cheese.
Grattons pork crackling.
à la Grecque served cold in olive oil and lemon juice.
Grenade pomegranate.
Grenadier delicate, white-fleshed sea fish.
Grenoblois sauce with cream, capers and lemon.
Grenouille frog.
Gribiche sauce of vinegar, capers, gherkins and egg.
Grillade grilled food, often mixed grill.
Grillé(e) grilled.
Griotte morello cherry.
Gros(se) large.
Groseille redcurrant.
Groseille à maquereau gooseberry.
Gros sel rock salt.

h

Haché(e) chopped, minced (GB), ground (US).
Hachis minced meat (hash); – **Parmentier** minced meat with mashed potato topping.

Haddock smoked haddock.
Hareng herring.
Haricot bean.
Herbe herb; grass.
Hollandaise sauce of egg, butter, vinegar, and lemon.
Homard lobster.
Huile oil.
Huître oyster.
Hure cold sausage made from boar's or pig's head.

i

Ile flottante poached, whipped-egg white 'island' in vanilla custard.

j

Jambon ham; – **de Paris** cooked ham; – **cru** raw, cured ham; – **fumé** smoked ham; – **de pays** cured country ham.
Jambonneau ham hock; – **de canard** stuffed duck drumstick.
Jardinière with vegetables.
Jarret shin or knuckle.
Joue cheek or jowl.
Julienne finely cut vegetables; also ling (fish).
Jus juice.

l

Lait milk; **(agneau/cochon) de lait** milk-fed lamb/suckling pig.
Laitue lettuce.
Lamproie lamprey eel.
Landaise in goose fat with garlic, onion and ham.
Langue tongue.
Langouste spiny lobster or crawfish.
Langoustine Dublin Bay prawns or scampi.
Lapereau young rabbit.
Lapin rabbit.
Lard bacon.
Lardon cubed bacon bit.
Légume vegetable.
Lentille lentil.
Levraut young hare.
Lièvre hare.
Liégoise coffee or chocolate ice-cream sundae.
Lieu jaune pollack.
Limande lemon sole.
Lisette small mackerel.

Litchi lychee.
Lotte monkfish.
Loup sea bass.
Lyonnais served with onions or sautéed potatoes.

m

Mâche lamb's lettuce.
Madère Madeira.
Magret de canard duck breast.
Maïs maize, corn.
Maison home-made, or house special.
Mangue mango.
Maquereau mackerel.
Marcassin young wild boar.
Mariné(e) marinated.
Marjolaine marjoram.
Marmite small cooking pot, or a stew served in one; – **dieppoise** Normandy fish stew.
Marquise mousse-like cake.
Marron chestnut.
Matelote freshwater fish stew cooked in wine.
Mélange mixture.
Ménagère home-style.
Menthe mint.
Merguez spicy lamb or lamb and beef sausage.
Merlan whiting.
Mesclun mixed young salad leaves.
Meunière fish with browned butter and lemon.
Meurette red wine and stock used for poaching.
Mi-cuit(e) half/semi-cooked.
Miel honey.
Mignon small meat fillet.
Mille-feuille puff pastry with many layers.
Minute fried quickly.
Mirabelle tiny yellow plum.
Mirepoix chopped carrots, onion and celery.
Moelle bone marrow.
Morille morel mushroom.
Mornay béchamel sauce with cheese.
Morue cod, usually salt cod.
Mou lights (lungs).
Moules mussels; – **marinières** cooked in white wine with shallots.
Moulu(e) ground, milled.
Mousseline hollandaise sauce with whipped cream.

Saved by a phrase

Get out of sticky situations in Paris restaurants...

Is there any raw shellfish in this dish?
Y-a-t'il des fruits de mer crus dans ce plat?

I'm allergic to... peanuts/seafood.
Je suis allergique aux... arachides/ fruits de mer.

I can't eat anything that contains... milk/wheat/fat.
Je ne peux rien manger qui contient... du lait/du blé/de la graisse.

I'm a vegetarian – no white or red meat, no fish.
Je suis végétarien – je ne mange ni viande blanche, ni viande rouge, ni poisson.

Will you ask the chef not to put too much salt in it, please?
Pourriez-vous demander au chef de mettre très peu de sel, s'il vous plaît?

I'm on a diet, what do you recommend?
Je suis au régime. Pourriez-vous me conseiller un plat diététique?

Does the special include any pork/offal?
Est-ce que le plat du jour contient du porc/des abats?

What can you recommend for children?
Que pouvez-vous conseiller pour les enfants?

Do you have any less fragrant cheeses?
Avez-vous des fromages moins forts?

Which of the desserts is the lightest?
Quel est le plus léger des desserts?

Do you have any sandwiches without mayonnaise?
Avez-vous des sandwichs sans mayonnaise?

I liked it very much, but I have a small appetite.
C'était très bon, mais j'ai un petit appétit.

I'd love to eat something really spicy.
J'aimerais manger quelque chose de tres épicé.

Mousseron type of wild mushroom.
Moutarde mustard.
Mouton mutton.
Mulet grey mullet.
Mûre blackberry.
Muscade nutmeg.
Myrtille bilberry/blueberry.

n

Nage poaching liquid.
Nantua crayfish sauce.
Nature plain, ungarnished.
Navarin lamb stew.
Navet turnip.
Nid nest.
Noisette hazelnut, or small, round piece of meat, or coffee with a little milk.
Noix walnut.
Nouilles noodles.

o

Oeuf egg; – **à la coque** soft-boiled; – **cocotte** baked with cream; – **dur** hard-boiled; – **en meurette** poached in red wine; – **à la neige** see île flottante.
Oie goose.
Oignon onion.

Onglet similar to bavette.
Oreille ear, usually pig's.
Orge barley.
Ortie nettle, used in soup.
Os bone.
Oseille sorrel.
Oursin sea urchin.

p

Pain bread; – **d'épices** honey gingerbread; – **grillé** toast; – **perdu** French toast.
Palombe wood pigeon.
Palourde a type of clam.
Pamplemousse grapefruit.
en Papillote steamed in foil or paper packet.
Panaché mixture.
Panais parsnip.
Pané(e) breaded.
Parfait sweet or savoury mousse-like mixture.
Parmentier with potato.
Pastèque watermelon.
Pâte pastry.
Pâté meat or fish pâté; – **en croûte** in a pastry case (similar to pork pie).
Pâtes pasta or noodles.
Paupiette meat or fish rolled

up and tied, usually stuffed.
Pavé thick, square steak.
Pêcheur based on fish.
Perdreau young partridge.
Perdrix partridge.
Persil parsley.
Petit gris small snail.
Petit pois pea.
Petit salé salt pork.
Pétoncle queen scallop.
Pets de nonne ('nun's farts') light puffy fritters.
Pied foot (or trotter).
Pigeonneau young pigeon.
Pignon pine kernel.
Piment pepper or chilli.
Pimenté(e) spicy.
Pince claw.
Pintade/pintadeau guinea fowl.
Pipérade Basque egg, pepper, tomato, onion and ham mixture.
Pissaladière anchovy, tomato and onion tart.
Pistache pistachio nut.
Pistou Provençal basil and garlic pesto, without pine nuts.
Plat dish; main course.
Plate flat-shelled oyster.

Index & Maps

Pleurotte oyster mushroom.
Poché(e) poached.
Pochetot skate.
Poêlé(e) pan-fried.
Poire pear.
Poireau leek.
Poisson fish.
Poitrine breast cut.
Poivrade peppery brown
  sauce served with meat.
Poivre pepper.
Poivron red or green pepper.
Pomme apple.
Pomme de terre potato (often
  referred to as pomme); –
  à l'huile cold, boiled
  potatoes in oil; – **au four**
  baked potato; – **dauphines**
  deep-fried croquettes of
  puréed potato; – **lyonnaises**
  sliced potatoes fried with
  onions; – **parisiennes**
  potatoes fried and tossed
  in a meat glaze; – **soufflées**
  puffed-up, deep-fried potato
  skins; – **voisin** grated
  potato cake with cheese.
Porc pork.
Porcelet suckling pig.
Potage thick soup.
Pot-au-feu boiled beef with
  vegetables.
Potée meat and vegetable
  stew.
Potiron pumpkin.
Poudre powder or granules.
Poularde chicken or hen.
Poule hen; – **au pot** stewed
  with vegetables and broth.
Poulet chicken.
Poulpe octopus.
Poussin small chicken.
Praire small clam.
Pressé(e) squeezed.
Primeur early or young, of
  fruit, vegetables or wine.
Printanière springtime;
  served with vegetables.
Profiterole ice-cream filled
  pastry puff, served with
  melted chocolate.
Provençal(e) with garlic and
  tomatoes, and often
  onions, anchovies or olives.
Prune plum.
Pruneau prune.

q

Quenelle poached dumplings,
  usually pike.

Quetsch damson plum.
Queue tail.
Queue de boeuf oxtail.

r

Râble saddle.
Racine root.
Raclette melted cheese
  served with boiled potatoes.
Radis radish.
Ragoût meat stew.
Raie skate.
Raifort horseradish.
Raisin grape.
Râpé(e) grated.
Rascasse scorpion fish.
Ratte small, firm potato.
Ravigote thick vinaigrette.
Ravioles de Royans tiny
  cheese ravioli.
Recette recipe.
Récolte harvest.
Régime diet.
Réglisse liquorice.
à la Reine with chicken.
Reine-claude greengage
  (plum).
Reinette dessert apple.
Rémoulade mayonnaise with
  mustard, chopped herbs,
  capers and gherkins.
Rillettes potted meat, usually
  pork and/or goose.
Rillons crispy chunks of
  pork belly.
Ris sweetbreads.
Riz rice; – **sauvage** wild rice.
Rognon kidney.
Romarin rosemary.
Roquette rocket.
Rosbif roast beef.
Rosette dry, salami-like pork
  sausage from Lyon.
Rôti roast.
Rouget red mullet.
Roulade rolled-up portion.
Rouille red, cayenne-
  seasoned mayonnaise.
Roussette rock salmon
  (dogfish).
Roux flour- and butter-based
  sauce.
Rumsteck rump steak.

s

Sabayon frothy sauce made
  with wine and egg yolks,
  sometimes a dessert.
Sablé shortbread biscuit.

Saignant rare (for meat).
Safran saffron.
St-Pierre John Dory.
Saisonnier seasonal.
Salé(e) salted.
Salmis game or poultry stew.
Sandre pike-perch.
Sang blood.
Sanglier wild boar.
Sarrasin buckwheat.
Sarriette savoury (herb).
Saucisse fresh sausage.
Saucisson small sausage.
Saucisson sec dried
  sausage, eaten cold.
Sauge sage.
Saumon salmon.
Saumonette sea eel.
Sauvage wild.
gratin Savoyard potatoes
  baked in stock with cheese.
Scarole see escarole.
Sec/sèche dry.
Seiche squid.
Sel salt.
Selle saddle or back.
Sirop syrup.
Soisson white bean.
Soja soya.
Soubise béchamel sauce with
  rice and cream.
Souper supper.
Souris d'agneau lamb
  knuckle.
Speck Italian smoked ham.
Sucre sugar.
Sucré(e) sweet.
Supion small cuttlefish.
Suprême breast; – **de volaille**
  fowl in a white roux with
  cream and meat juice.
crêpe Suzette pancake
  flambéed in orange liqueur.

t

Tapenade Provençal black
  olive and caper paste,
  usually with anchovies.
Tartare raw minced steak
  (also tuna or salmon).
Tarte Tatin caramelised
  upside-down apple tart.
Tartine buttered baguette or
  open sandwich.
Tendron de veau veal rib.
Tête head.
Thon tuna.
Thym thyme.
Tian Provençal gratin cooked
  in an earthenware dish.

Tiède tepid or warm.
Timbale rounded mould, or food cooked in one.
Tisane herbal tea.
Tomate tomato; – **de mer** sea anemone.
Topinambour Jerusalem artichoke.
Toulouse large sausage.
Tournedos thick slices taken from a fillet of beef.
Tournesol sunflower.
Tourte covered tart or pie, usually savoury.
Tourteau large crab.
Tranche slice.
Travers de porc spare ribs.
Trénels lamb's tripe.
Tripes tripe.
Tripoux Auvergnat dish of sheep's tripe and feet.
Trompette de la mort horn of plenty mushroom.
Truffade fried potato cake or mashed potato with cheese.
Truffe truffle, the ultimate fungus, **blanche** (white) or **noire** (black); chocolate truffle.
Truffé(e) stuffed or garnished with truffles.
Truite trout; – **de mer/saumonée** salmon trout.

V

Vacherin a meringue, fruit and ice cream cake; or soft, cow's milk cheese.
Vapeur steam.
Veau veal; – **élevé sous la mère** milk-fed veal.
Velouté sauce made with white roux and bouillon; creamy soup.
Ventre belly, breast or stomach.
Vénus American clam.
Verdurette vinaigrette with herbs and egg.
Viande meat.
Vichyssoise cold leek and potato soup.
Volaille poultry.

Y

Yaourt yoghurt.

Z

Zeste zest or peel.

Drink

Appellation d'Origine Contrôlée (AOC) wine (or food) conforming to specific strict quality rules.
Bière beer.
Bock 12cl of beer.
Boire to drink.
Boisson a drink.
Blanche pale wheat beer.
Blonde lager (GB), beer (US).
Brune dark beer.
Café small espresso coffee; – **allongé** 'lengthened' (twice the water); – **au lait** milky coffee; – **crème** coffee with steamed milk; – **serré** strong espresso (half the water); **grand** – double espresso.
Calvados apple brandy.
Cardinal kir with red wine.
Chope tankard.
Citron pressé freshly squeezed lemon juice.
Chocolat (chaud) (hot) chocolate
Décaféiné/déca decaffeinated coffee.
Demi (demi-pression) 25cl of draught beer; – **ordinaire** 25cl of the least-expensive lager.
Demi-litre half a litre (50cl).
Express espresso; **double** – double espresso.
Gazeuse fizzy/carbonated.
Grand cru top-quality wine.
Infusion herbal or fruit tea.
Jus de fruits fruit juice.
Kir crème de cassis and dry white wine – **royal** crème de cassis and Champagne.
Lait milk.
Marc clear brandy made from grape residues.
Mauresque pastis with almond syrup.
Mirabelle plum brandy.
Noisette espresso with a drop of milk.
Orange pressée freshly squeezed orange juice.
Panaché beer and lemonade shandy.
Pastis anise apéritif.
Perroquet pastis with mint syrup.
Pichet jug or carafe.

Plat(e) still, non-carbonated.
Poire Williams pear brandy.
Porto port.
Pot lyonnais 46cl carafe.
Pression draught lager.
Quart quarter litre (25cl).
Rousse red, bitter-like beer.
Thé tea.
Tilleul linden flower tea.
Tisane herbal tea.
Tomate pastis with grenadine syrup.
Verveine verbena tea.
Vieille Prune plum brandy.
Xerès sherry.

Savoir faire

Addition bill.
Amuse-gueule (or amuse-bouche) appetiser or hors d'oeuvre.
Assiette plate.
A la carte ordered separately (ie not on the fixed-price menu or formule).
Carte des vins wine list.
Cendrier ashtray.
Commande order.
Commander to order.
Compris(e) included.
Comptoir counter.
Couvert cutlery, also used to express the number of diners.
Couteau knife.
Cuillère spoon.
Dégustation tasting.
Eau du robinet tap water.
Entrée starter.
Espace non-fumeur non-smoking area.
Formule set-price menu.
Fourchette fork.
Majoration price increase.
Menu set-price selection, also called a formule or prix fixe.
Menu dégustation tasting menu, sampling several different dishes.
Monnaie change.
Plat main course.
Pourboire tip.
Serveur/serveuse waiter/waitress.
Rince-doigts finger bowl.
Verre glass.
Zinc bar counter.

Index & Maps

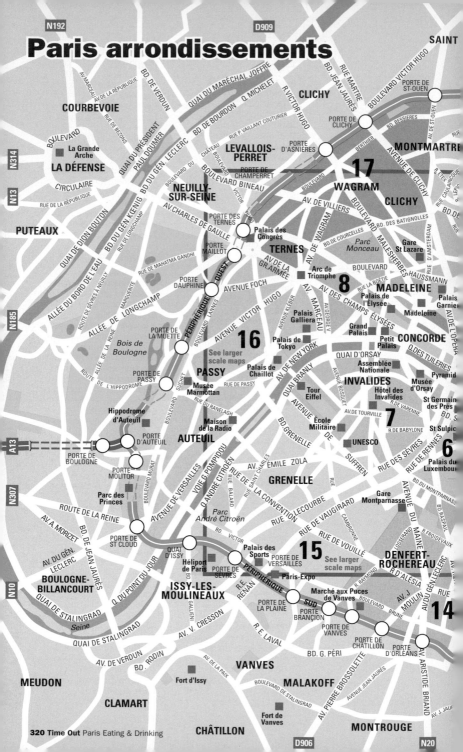

Paris arrondissements

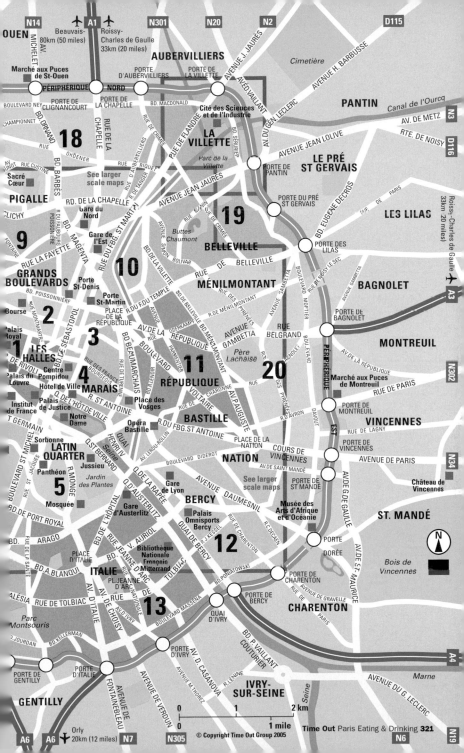

5

AV. GEORGES Trocadéro Ⓜ
MANDEL
Cimetière TROCADERO ET
de Passy DU 11 NOVEMBRE
PL. DU

Palais de
Chaillot

NATIONS UNIES

AV. ALBERT DE MUN RUE FRESNEL

AVENUE DE NEW YORK

AV. ALBERT DE MUN

Pont de
l'Alma Ⓡ

QUAI

QUAI

R. COGNACQ

BOULEVARD ÉMILE AUGIER

RUE RICHARD

RUE DE SIAM

RUE DE LA POMPE

RUE CORTAMBERT

RUE SCHEFFER

RUE L. DAVID

RUEL SCHEFFER

VINEUSE

FRANKLIN

R. L. LE TASSE

AVENUE PAUL DOUMER

RUE DE LA TOUR

RUE E. MANUEL

RUE NICOLO

RUE DE LA TOUR

PONT D'IÉNA

PONT D'IÉNA

Tour
Eiffel

QUAI BRANLY

RUE DE L'UNIVERSITÉ

AV. DE SUFFREN

AV. DE MONTTESSUY

AV. RAPP

R. ED. VALENTIN

AVENUE BOSQUET

RUE LANDRIEU

PGE DE L'EXPOSITION

6

RUE DE PASSY

RUE DE PASSY

RUE Boulainvilliers

RUE SINGER

RUE Duban

PL. DE
COSTA
RICA

Passy Ⓡ

RUE DE L'ANNONCIATION

RUE DE PASSY

RUE RAYNOUARD

AV M. PROUST

CHERNOVIZ

ALBONI

AV. DU PRÉSIDENT KENNEDY

Seine

BD.
DELESSERT

CHARDONNET

AV DES

Champ de Mars
Tour Eiffel Ⓜ

AVENUE

AV. OCTAVE GREARD

Parc du

Champ

de Mars

AV. GUSTAVE EIFFEL

AV. JOSEPH BOUVARD

AV. CHARLES FLOQUET

AVENUE CHARLES RISLE

AV. ÉMILE DESCHANEL

AV. ELISÉE RECLUS

S. DOMINIQUE

AVENUE DE LA BOURDONNAIS

AVENUE DE

LA

BOURDONNAIS

7

RUE RAYNOUARD

AVENUE DE LAMBALLE

RUE DE L'ANKARA

R. D'ANKARA

Kennedy-
Radio France

Maison de
la Radio Ⓡ

RUE DE L'ASSOMPTION

RUE DU
RANELAGH

RUE DE
RANELAGH

AVENUE DU
RANELAGH

RUE DES
MARRONNIERS

RUE DES
VIGNES

RUE DES
BAUCHES

BOULEVARD BEAUSÉJOUR

RUE
DESGRAIS

RUE DE VERSAILLES

AVENUE DE VERSAILLES

AV. LOUIS-BLÉRIOT

BOULEVARD

BOULAINVILLIERS

RUE DE LA FONTAINE

AVENUE THÉOPHILE GAUTIER

RUE GROS

QUAI P. MIRABEAU

AV. DU PONT DE GRENELLE

Bir Hakeim Ⓜ

QUAI DE GRENELLE

RUE NELATON

RUE SAINT-SAËNS

RUE DESAIX

BOULEVARD DE GRENELLE

RUE DU DOCTEUR FINLAY

RUE VIALA

RUE VIALA

AVENUE DE SUFFREN

AVENUE DE LA MOTTE

AVENUE DE

AV. CHARLES

RUE JEAN REY

AVENUE DE SUFFREN

RUE DE PRESLES

RUE DE PRESLES

RUE DUPLEIX

RUE ALASSEUR

PLACE DUPLEIX

RUE DE PONDICHERY

D. STERN

HUMBLOT

Dupleix Ⓜ

BOULEVARD DE GRENELLE

La Motte-Picquet
Grenelle Ⓜ

AVENUE

RUE JUGE

RUE TIPHAINE

RUE FRÉMICOURT

Cambronne Ⓜ

8

QUAI ANDRÉ CITROËN

RUE DE L'INGÉNIEUR R. KELLER

RUE LINOIS

RUE DE

Javel Ⓡ

AVENUE ÉMILE ZOLA

RUE SAINT CHARLES

RUE GINOUX

RUE DU THÉATRE

RUE LOURMEL

RUE EMERIAU

RUE DU THÉATRE

RUE ROUELLE

AVENUE ÉMILE ZOLA

Avenue
Émile Zola Ⓜ

RUE FONDARY

RUE DU THÉATRE

RUE VIOLET

R. LETELLIER

RUE FALLEMPIN

AVENUE DE LA MOTTE-PICQUET

Charles
Michels Ⓜ

RUE DES ENTREPRENEURS

RUE DE LOURMEL

RUE DE L'ÉGLISE

PLACE DU
COMMERCE

RUE DU COMMERCE

RUE GRAMME

RUE DU THÉATRE

LAKANAL

RUE DE LA CROIX

Commerce Ⓜ

RUE MADEMOISELLE

RUE VIOLET

QUINAULT

VILLA DRE

RUE DE L'AMIRAL ROUSSIN

RUE MADEMOISELLE

VILLA DE LA CROIX

RUE CAMBRONNE

RUE MIO

RUE DE VAUGIRARD

9

RUE ANDRÉ CITROËN

RUE BALARD

QUAI ANDRÉ CITROËN

RUE CAUCHY

RUE DUCRUT

RUE VITU

RUE DE LOURMEL

RUE DE GUTENBERG

RUE DE JAVEL

RUE SÉBASTIEN MERCIER

RUE DES CÉVENNES

RUE GUTENBERG

RUE DE LA CONVENTION

RUE SAINT CHARLES

RUE DE LOURMEL

RUE DE L'ÉGLISE

RUE DE JAVEL

RUE OSCAR ROTY

Félix
Faure Ⓜ

AVENUE FÉLIX FAURE

RUE FRÈRES MORANE

RUE DE LA CROIX NIVERT

Boucicaut Ⓜ

Hôpital
Boucicaut

RUE DE PLELO

RUE DUBANTON

RUE DE LA CONVENTION

RUE JAVEL

RUE DE LA CROIX NIVERT

RUE CH. LECOCQ

RUE DE L'ABBÉ

R. T. RENAUDOT

RUE JEAN FORMIGE

RUE LECOURBE

RUE LÉON LHERMITTE

RUE BLOMET

RUE DE L'ABBÉ GROULT

R. F. FABRE

RUE A. CHARTIER

RUE PÉTEL

RUE BLOMET

RUE MAUBLANC

Vaugirard Ⓜ

RUE LECOURBE

RUE D'ALLERAY

RUE DE L'ABBÉ

Parc
André Citroën

RUE LEBLANC

RUE LEBLANC

RUE BALARD

VILLA THORETON

AVENUE FÉLIX FAURE

Lourmel Ⓜ

AVENUE JEAN MARIDOR

RUE DE VASCO

RUE DE GAMA

RUE SAINT LAMBERT

RUE DECK

RUE MIL CLOS

RUE FEUILLERAIES

RUE DESNOUETTES

RUE SAINT CHARLES

RUE LEBLANC

RUE DESNOUETTES

RUE R. GIBEZ

RUE LANGEAC

RUE DOMBASLE

RUE LEFRICHE

Convention Ⓜ

RUE RE. GIBEZ

RUE DE VOU

10

Héliport
de
Paris

BOULEVARD GAL MARTIAL VALIN

Marine
Nationale

RUE DU GÉNÉRAL LUCOTTE

AV. DE LA PORTE DE SÈVRES

PORTE DE
SÈVRES

Balard Ⓜ

RUE DE LA
PORTE D'ISSY

Palais des
Sports

Paris-
Expo

BOULEVARD VICTOR

Porte de
Versailles Ⓜ

BOULEVARD LEFEBVRE

RUE LACRETELLE

RUE FIRMIN GILLOT

RUE DE LA CROIX NIVERT

RUE DU HAMEAU

RUE DE VAUGIRARD

RUE OLIVIER DE SERRES

RUE VAUGELAS

RUE DE LA SAIDA

RUE DES MORILLONS

Fourrière
Municipale

RUE DANTZIG

RUE DE CRONSTADT

RUE BRANCION

RUE DANTZIG

Parc
Georges
Brassens

MORILL

A   **B**   **C**   **D**

ABCDEFGHJKLMNPQ
1
2
3
4
5   La Villette
6   Inset
7
8   p 322-3   p 324-5
9
10   p 326-7   p 328-9

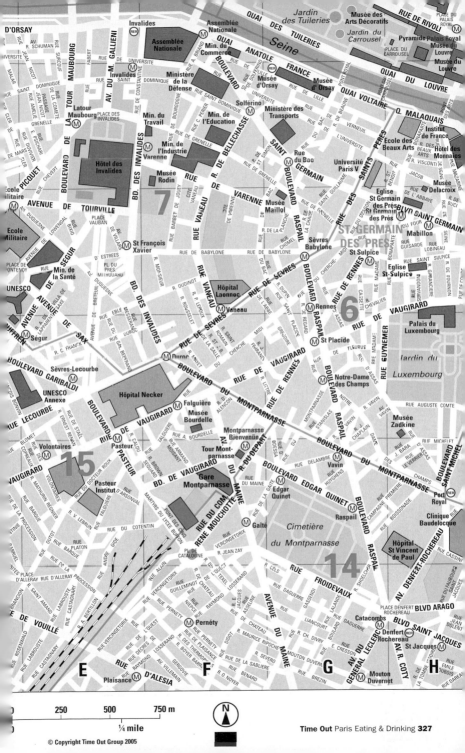

250   500   750 m

¼ mile

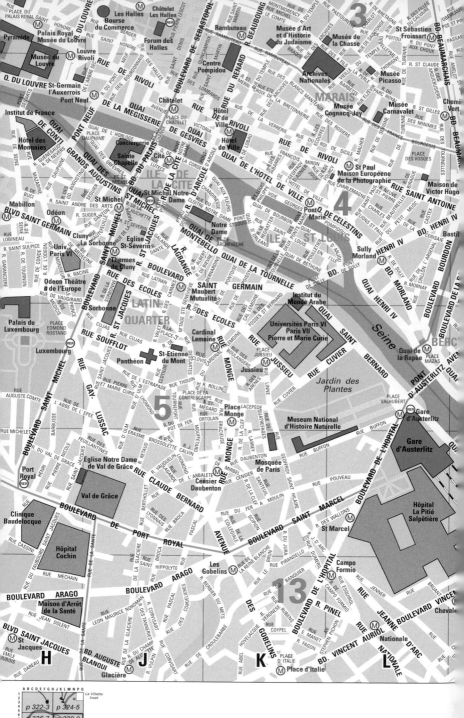

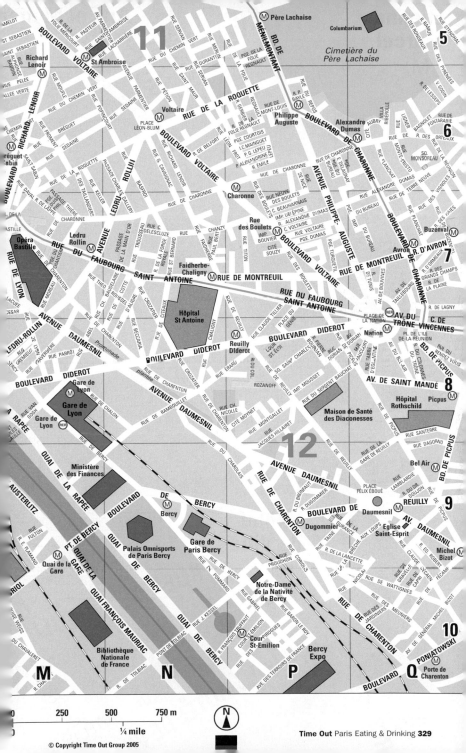

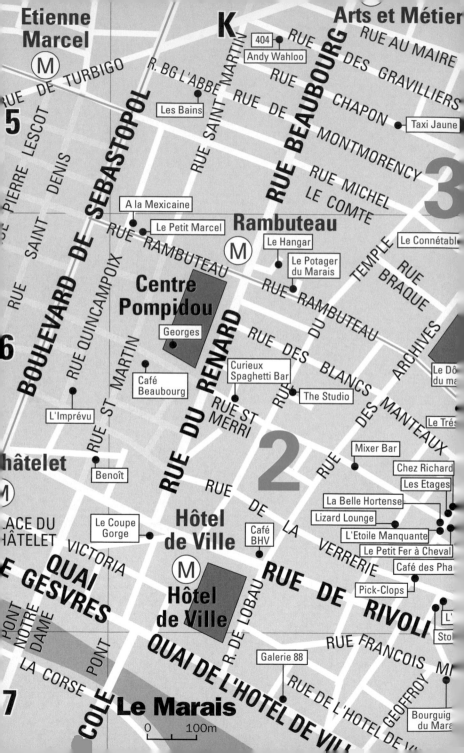

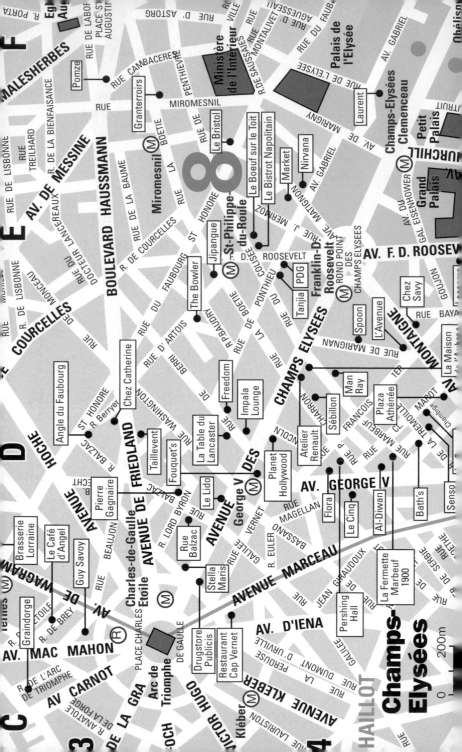

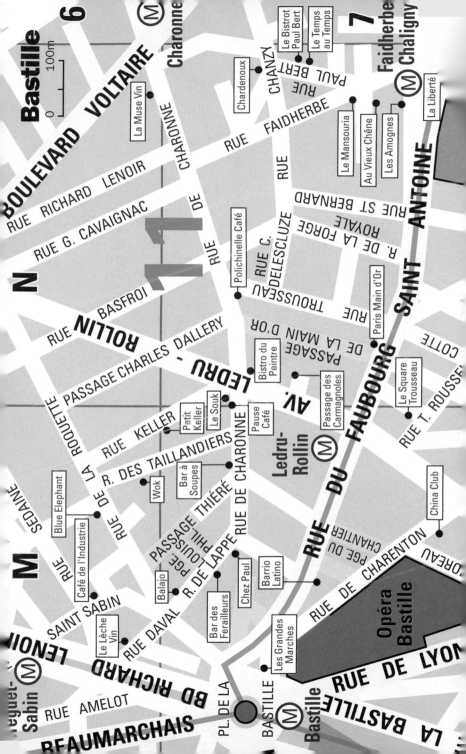

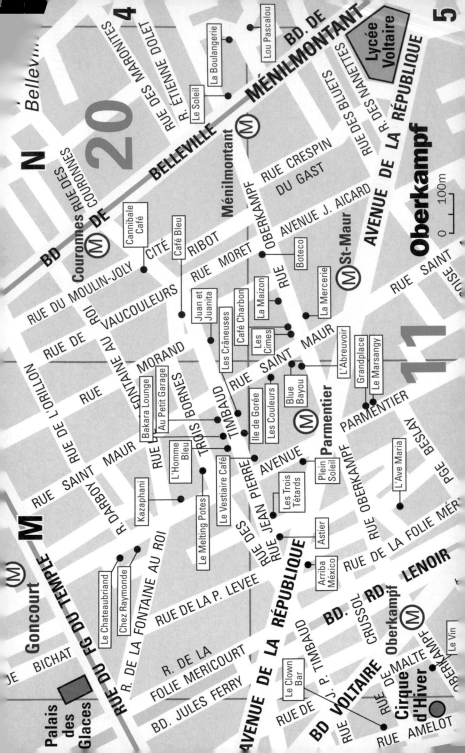

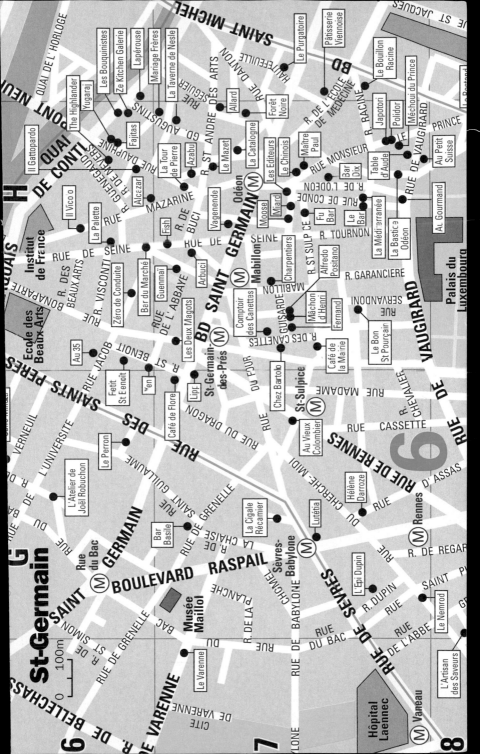

Paris Métro

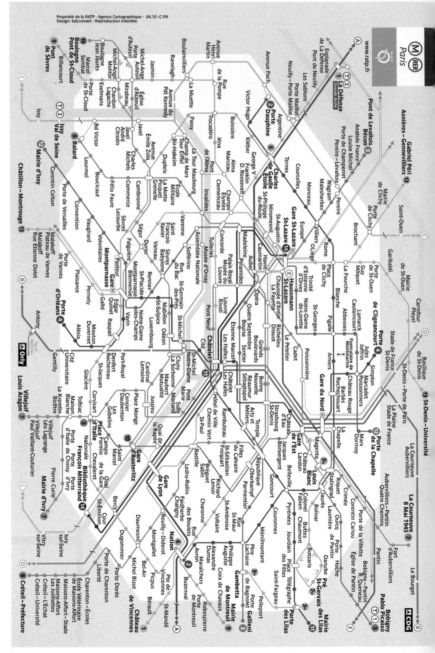

Propriété de la RATP - Agence Cartographique - 04.10 - C.PR
Design: bdcconseil - Reproduction interdite